The Don Juan Papers

QVOVSQVE TANDEM
ABVTERE CASTANEDA
PATIENTIA NOSTRA

The Don Juan Papers

●

Further Castaneda Controversies

Edited by
Richard de Mille

ROSS-ERIKSON PUBLISHERS
Santa Barbara   1980

Cover/jacket executed by Fran Smith, Don French Graphic Design. Interior graphics by Schlesinger, Linda Trujillo, Neil Erickson, Erin Matson, and Julie Durrell. Interior design by Graham Mackintosh.

Type set by Mackintosh and Young. Printing and binding by The Book Press.

 First published in 1980 by Ross-Erikson Publishers
629 State Street, Santa Barbara CA 93101

Library of Congress Cataloging in Publication Data

Main entry under title:

The Don Juan papers.

Bibliography: p.
Includes index.
1. Castaneda, Carlos—Addresses, essays, lectures. 2. Juan, Don, 1891-   —Addresses, essays, lectures. 3. Anthropologists—United States—Biography—Addresses, essays, lectures. 4. Yaqui Indians—Addresses,   essays,   lectures.   I.   De   Mille,   Richard,   1922-
F1221.Y3C375   306'.092'4 [B]   80-10158
ISBN 0-915520-25-7   ISBN 0-915520-24-9 pbk.

Alternative Cataloging in Publication Data

De Mille, Richard, 1922-   editor.
    The Don Juan papers: further Castaneda controversies. Santa Barbara, Ross-Erikson Publishers, copyright 1980.
    Forty-three essays and conversations, by the editor, Mary Douglas, Hans Sebald, Robert L. Carneiro, Agehananda Bharati, Kenneth Minogue, Paul Riesman, Carl A. P. Ruck, Barbara G. Myerhoff, and twenty others.
    PARTIAL CONTENTS: Validity is not authenticity.-Ethnomethodallegory.-Cataloging Castaneda.-Publishing the factoids.-Sonoragate.-Castaneda and parapsychology.-Learning by not-doing.-Chicanos in the web of Spider-Trickster.-Epistemallegory.-A portrait of the allegorist.
    APPENDICES: Alleglossary.-Notes.-References.-Index.

    1. Castaneda, Carlos, 1925?-   —Criticism and interpretation. 2. Juan, Don, 1891?-   3. Fraud in anthropology. 4. Fraud in publishing. 5. Gullibility—Case studies. 6. University of California—Los Angeles. Dept. of Anthropology. 7. Hoaxes—Case studies. 8. Paranormal phenomena. 9. Mysticism. 10. Witchcraft. I. Title. II. Title:Further Castaneda controversies. III. Title:Castaneda controversies.

    BF 1571   133.4

Alternative Cataloging in Publication Data is directed by Sanford Berman, Head Cataloger, Hennepin County Library, Edina MN 55435

CONTENTS

V. Understanding Castaneda

VI. Appendices

ILLUSTRATIONS

Al hombre común le importa que las cosas sean
verdaderas o falsas; al guerrero no. Si se dice
que las cosas son verdaderas, actúa por *hacer.*
Si que son falsas, actúa de todos modos
por *no-hacer.* ¿Ves lo que quiero decir?
(The average man wants things to be either true
or false, but the warrior doesn't care. If things
are said to be true, he acts for the sake of
doing. If they are said to be false, he still
acts, for the sake of *not-doing.* See what I mean?)

——DON JUAN

. . . truthfulness and lie are of the most far-
reaching significance for relations among men.
. . . Our modern life is based to a much
larger extent than is usually realized
upon the faith in the honesty of the other.
[An example is] our science, in which most
scholars must use innumerable results
of other scientists which they cannot examine.

——GEORG SIMMEL

The Art of Stalking Castaneda

The scene is the American Booksellers' Association convention in Los Angeles. The time, Memorial Day 1979. Beside a towering stack of Harold Garfinkel's *Agnes Redux: Confessions from the Ivory Closet,* Robert Crichton, author of *The Great Impostor,* is talking with Stringfellow Bean, president of Columbia University Press—and a short man in a tan leisure suit. As I walk by, Crichton seizes my arm.

"Richard! Here's somebody I want you to meet. Carlos, this is Richard de Mille."

The man in the tan leisure suit smiles roguishly. "How do you do?"

"*Fine!*" I pump his hand. "I'm very glad to meet you after all this time. Five years writing about you, and we've never met."

Carlos looks puzzled. "You've been writing about *me?*"

"Good Lord, man!" says Bean. "Haven't you read *Castaneda's Journey?*"

"I read very little," says Carlos, "but it sounds like something I ought to look at. Why don't you send me a copy?"

"I sent you three letters," I remind him. "You didn't answer."

Carlos looks pained. "Where did you send them?"

"In care of your agent."

"I'll have to talk to Ned about that," he says. "When you get so much mail, it's hard to keep track of everything. Last week I got a Christmas card from Mexico. Did you know Mexican airmail stamps have a picture of a bicycle on them?" Bean and Crichton burst out laughing.

"It's true!" Carlos insists.

"What are you writing about now?" I ask.

Carlos looks down at a notebook he is holding in his hand. He looks up. "It's, um, it's a story about a literary hoaxer."

"*Really?*"

"Yes." He nods. "It has to do with a Mexican Indian who writes—in his native language, of course, which is Toltec—about a tribe of Indians that never existed. When the anthropologists go looking for the tribe, the hoaxer says they've gone to the other world."

"That's intriguing," I say. "Where does don Juan fit in?"

Carlos smiles. "I asked don Juan if I should write such a book, and he said, 'Go ahead! It's the only thing you know how to do.' And he laughed. But I told him, maybe it's a waste of time to write a book about a hoaxer, and don Juan said, 'It doesn't make any difference whether he's a hoaxer or not. What matters is whether he's *impeccable*.' He said the word *impeccable* with a particular emphasis. 'If he's an *impeccable* hoaxer,' don Juan said, 'he's worth writing about.' "

"Sounds like don Juan all right."

"That's what he told me." Carlos grins. "And he said I have a lot in *common* with the man I'm writing about——"

"He said *that*?"

"Yes, but I told him, I don't have the *mechanics* to be a hoaxer. I could never get away with it."

"You'd tip your hand."

"Oh yes," Carlos shakes his head. "One thing I'm no good at is lying. If I tell just the smallest, most innocent lie—maybe even to make a friend feel better—I get a horrendous headache, and I have guilty feelings for hours."

"That's remarkable."

"Yes, you see, my father always accused me of lying, even when I was telling the truth. As a matter of fact, that's why I stopped writing to him, because he doesn't believe the letters. He thinks I can't be trusted, and there's no power on earth that can make him change his mind about me."

"That's too bad," I say.

"It's my curse," says Carlos. At this point Udo Strutynski, of the University of California Press, hauls Carlos away to meet novelist Jerzy Kosinski. Bean says:

"Imagine that! Carlos is so wrapped up in his writing he doesn't realize you wrote a book calling him a hoaxer."

"So it would seem."

"What do you suppose he'd say if he knew?"

"He'd say he's writing a book about a hoaxer."

Like Carlos's fabulous first meeting with don Juan at the border between the ordinary and nonordinary worlds, the foregoing encounter is strictly a figment of a writer's imagination—which is why I call the central character "Carlos" instead of "Castaneda," a name reserved here for the actual person I have been stalking since 1975. *The Don Juan Papers* may look like a collection of essays, but it is really the story of a five-year mission to go where no social scientist has gone before: into the mind of one of the world's great hoaxers, round the comical traps he set for readers and reviewers, pundits and professors, hippies and self-transcenders, across the no man's land of social conflict and misunderstanding he embodies. Among the kaleidoscopic surprises of this voyage, the greatest wonder to me is that the mission was ever completed, for it could have been shot down in flames or grounded at some frigid way station almost any time by Castaneda's academic patrons at the University of California, Los Angeles. Book-publishing ventures need multiple drives, and one of the main thrusts of this enterprise was to answer the question: What happened at UCLA? A frank and simple admission of error by Castaneda's patrons would have brought the project to a grinding halt. The mission was saved by the fateful fact that some people just can't admit making a mistake, even a relatively harmless one that will be instantly forgiven once admitted. By refusing to give an inch since 1975, those Castaneda cling-ons who mistook a champion hoaxer for a doctoral candidate "just like every other . . . except he was a hell of a lot better writer" provided perfect maintenance and unlimited fuel for the engines of investigative reporting and social criticism while paying a heavy price in public embarrassment and professional disdain. If anyone ever writes a book to explain this self-destructive behavior, I'll be eager to read it. In the meantime, we have all we can do to understand Castaneda.

The don Juan hoax has been a test of judgment in several fields: anthropology, of course, but also sociology, psychology, philosophy, religious studies, parapsychology, psychoanalysis, psychotherapy, counseling, literature, publishing, book reviewing, library science, biographical reference, and journalism. More people have passed the test than failed it, but the failures tell us such fascinating things about what can go wrong with human judgment and how irrational rational discourse can become that they will be treated at length in the next 42 chapters.

Along the way additional topics will come up: the unsimplicity of truth, the different worlds habitually perceived by skeptics and subscribers, the attempt to turn science into religion or religion into science, the confidence with which people say preposterous things, the certitude with which they propose that a particular way of looking at something is the only possible way to look at it, or the only way that matters, the complacency, elitism, snobbery, and self-serving double-talk of the ivory tower, and the sad, mysterious spectacle of a talented man substituting a preoccupation with power for a desire to give and receive love.

Conflicts of purpose and value illuminate social processes, and Castaneda has furnished plenty of things for people to argue about. His admirers and disadmirers are well represented in this book, which is more a construction than a collection, 37 of its chapters having been assigned by the editor to persons qualified in some particular way to practice or enhance the art of stalking Castaneda. During two years of preparation, countless letters were exchanged; tenured professors were dragooned; virgin authors were nurtured; fat sheaves shrank to three pages; paragraphs exploded into dissertations; antagonists were transformed into collaborators; correspondents became contributors; strangers turned into friends.

After reading *Castaneda's Journey* (the first volume of this study) an editor at the University of California Press opined it was an enjoyable tour de force but not an effective critique, because of its "self-indulgent style and parodistic hypotheses"—by which I suppose he meant its literary versatility and penetrating analysis of misconduct by editors at the University of California Press. "The 'real' work on Castaneda," he concluded, "remains yet to be written." I am grateful for his challenge, which helped determine that a second book was needed. *The Don Juan Papers* is meant to complete "the 'real' work on Castaneda." Though more straightforward and serious in tone that *Castaneda's Journey*, it offers many passages written in popular styles and several chapters that will entertain the reader while informing him. Scholarly apparatus has been banished to the back of the book, where it will not offend or intimidate non-scholars but where scholars will find it as solid and thorough as before, though spiced with occasional levity. Try as I may, I can't write without humor. This is no doubt a serious flaw, but there is nothing to be done about it.

From hundreds of hours in libraries emerged a curious fact: many an article about Castaneda is missing from the stacks. Though previous users could easily carry it to the xerox machine, someone preferred to rip the article out of the bound volume. I take this to be a sign of religious fervor. The ripper wanted not only the commentary on don Juan's gospel but the parchment on which it was printed. All of us are driven by unstatable purposes, sometimes deep into the woods or over a cliff. I believe Castaneda succeeded so well with professors, friends, and readers chiefly because he is a shifting, shimmering, uncertain social object on which people project images of desires they can hardly name. Professors recognized in him the incarnation of social theories they wished to validate; friends saw a suffering visionary they wanted to help; readers found a guide to the world of their dreams.

Castaneda preserved his social ambiguity by practicing what he called "the art of stalking." So doing, said Robert de Ropp, he was "following a way that involved becoming invisible. It was not a new idea. Gurdjieff had often said that those in the Work should know how to become invisible. The secret lay in not engaging the attention of those around one. One should be able to move through a crowd without being noticed, without making any impression on anyone." "In dress," said *Time*, "Castaneda is conservative to the point of anonymity." "The art of sorcerers," said one of don Juan's witches, "is to be outside of everything and be unnoticeable." "To weasel in and out of different worlds," Castaneda said, "you have to remain inconspicuous. The more you are known and identified, the more your freedom is curtailed." When don Juan talked about hunting, he was talking about disguises. "A man who really knows how to stalk appears to the deer as a deer, to the coyote as a coyote," mused Michael Korda, Editor-in-Chief at Simon and Schuster. Asked about Castaneda's next book, Korda said: "All I know for certain is that the title will be *The Art of Stalking*."

To complement Castaneda's art of invisible stalking, contributors to this book will practice the visible art of stalking Castaneda. Is that fair? I think it is not only fair but right and necessary. Though it would be unkind as well as fruitless to drag some mystical recluse out of his Happy Cave in the Upper Nyang Valley, the equivocal Castaneda has made a million dollars manipulating the trust of gullible scholars and exploiting his various unreliable images. Whatever credit one may wish to give him for accomplishments as writer or trickster-teacher, it is clear he does not qualify as a holy hermit exempt from examination and criticism.

The power of Castaneda and his works is to catch some people at the borders of their world and fix them there, to hold them at the boundary between what they think they know and what they would like to believe, to take them on a voyage into mystery without requiring them to leave familiar territory. It has been a remarkable performance, but the time has come to sort it out and make sense of it. I signed on for the trek because I was not content to merely appreciate Carlos Castaneda; I wanted to understand him. If you feel the same way, beam aboard, and report to Chapter Two.

I.

Seduction
of the Sophisticates

Carlos Castaneda in 1965

The Shaman of Academe

Carlos Castaneda said he was born in Brazil in 1935. His immigration record said he was born in Peru in 1925. He said his father was a professor of literature. *Time* said his father was a goldsmith. He said he had no interest in mysticism. His former wife said mysticism was all they ever talked about.

In 1973 Castaneda received a Ph.D. in anthropology for interviewing a mystical old Mexican Indian named don Juan Matus on many occasions from 1960 to 1971, and for documenting the interviews at great length in three volumes of field reports, the third of which was accepted as his dissertation at the University of California, Los Angeles. In all of that, there is nothing particularly unusual.

The three volumes of field reports sold millions of copies coast to coast and around the world. That's unusual.

Don Juan, the mystical old Mexican Indian, was an imaginary person. That's extraordinary.

"Is it possible that these books are non-fiction?" exclaimed Joyce Carol Oates. Novelists Oates and William Kennedy and science fiction writer Theodore Sturgeon were quick to recognize Castaneda as a fellow story teller.

Carlos (as I call the young anthropologist in the story told by Castaneda) goes to Arizona to learn how the Indians use peyote but to his utter amazement is chosen by the imperious don Juan, whom he has accidentally met in a Greyhound bus station, to become "a man of knowledge," which means he will after long and arduous training enter "a separate reality" and *see* the essence of the world as mystics do. Published during the psychedelic years, *The Teachings of Don Juan* and *A Separate Reality* recount 22 wondrous drug trips through which don Juan guides Carlos, but as new-age consciousness gained favor in the media *Journey to Ixtlan* suddenly discovered a wealth of neglected drugless techniques in some piles of old fieldnotes Carlos had stupidly set aside. *Tales of Power* and *The Second Ring of Power* reflected later popular trends toward occultism and feminism.

If the trendy Castaneda could write at least five best sellers in a row, why did he bother with the anthropology hoax? An obvious economic reason is that competition was too steep in the fiction market. Defective style, weak dramatic structure, poverty of detail, cardboard characters that do not develop (but are suitable for allegory), stereotyped emotions, and absence of ordinary human relationships make his books unsalable except as fact. Readers love a true adventure even if badly told.

A more important, psychological reason is that anyone who would keep up such a difficult and complicated pretense for eight years before getting any material reward is a person who habitually refuses to follow the rules of society and insists on winning the game of life by playing tricks. As with Castaneda, this lifelong pattern often includes personal charm, high intelligence, and some genuine accomplishments along with the con job.

Professors do get conned, admitted Clement Meighan, a member of Castaneda's doctoral committee, "but someone's going to have to prove this." The proof comes in three forms. First, the so-called field reports contradict each other. Carlos meets a certain witch name La Catalina for the first time in 1962 and *again* for the first time in 1965. Though he learns a lot about *seeing* in 1962, unaccountably he has never heard of it in 1968. *The Teachings* tells a gothic tale full of fear and wonder, barren of joy and amusement. Throughout its five narrative years, 1960–1965, don Juan is a hard master, a brooding presence who seldom cracks a joke. When, in narrative-1968, Carlos takes up the second part of his apprenticeship, recounted in Castaneda's second book, *A Separate Reality*, he finds "the total mood of don Juan's teaching ... more relaxed. He laughed and also made me laugh a great deal. There seemed to be a deliberate attempt to minimize seriousness in general. He clowned during the truly crucial moments of the second cycle."

The text bears out this description, and when we get to the third book, *Journey to Ixtlan*, don Juan is a regular cut-up, a walking koan, a Zen buffoon, notwithstanding the incongruous fact that *Ixtlan* is set back in the early period, of the cheerless *Teachings*. So we are asked to believe "the total mood of don Juan's teachings" changed from day to day during narrative 1961–1962, from bright to sombre, in perfect concordance with our reading of either the first or the third book. Don Juan, of course, shows many flashes of precognition, but I do not believe the most gifted psychic could infallibly assume the proper mood each day to fit the tone of one of two books in which his mood would be contradictorily described seven and eleven years later. Nor can I think of any writerly excuse for the contradiction. If don Juan's chronicler could not distinguish smiling from frowning or gloomy silence from roaring laughter throughout two years, or if he didn't care which way he reported them, why should we credit his report?

A second kind of proof arises from absence of convincing detail and presence of implausible detail. During nine years of collecting plants and hunting animals with don Juan, Carlos learns not one Indian name for any plant or animal, and precious few Spanish or English names. No specimen of don Juan's hallucinogenic mushroom was brought back for verification, though Gordon Wasson had challenged its identification in 1968. Don Juan's desert is vaguely described, his habitations are all but featureless. Incessantly sauntering across the sands in seasons when (Hans Sebald will tell us) harsh conditions keep prudent persons away, Carlos and don Juan go quite unmolested by pests that normally torment desert hikers. Carlos climbs unclimbable trees and stalks unstalkable animals. With prodigious speed and skill he writes down "everything" don Juan says to him under the most unlikely conditions. No one but Carlos has seen don Juan.

Since it has recently come to light that Castaneda met serious early resistance from skeptics in the UCLA faculty, we must believe any supporting evidence he had at his disposal — Indian vocabulary, plant specimens, photographs of places, tape recordings he says were made, or Carlos's "voluminous field notes" — would have been promptly presented to counter that resistance. No such presentation occurred, which leads to the reasonable inference that no such evidence existed and that the fieldwork that would have furnished it did not exist either, except in Castaneda's highly developed imagination.

A third kind of proof is found in don Juan's teachings, which sample American Indian folklore, oriental mysticism, and European philosophy. Indignantly dismissing such a proof, don Juan's followers declare that enlightened minds think alike in all times and places, but there is more to the proof than similar ideas; there are similar words. When don Juan opens his mouth, the words of particular writers come out. An example will show what I mean. Though I have condensed lines and added italics, I have not changed any words:

> The Human Aura is seen by the psychic observer as a *luminous cloud*, *egg*-shaped, streaked by fine lines like stiff *bristles* standing *out in all directions*.
>
> A man looks like an *egg* of circulating fibers. And his arms and legs are like *luminous bristles* bursting *out in all directions*.

Of these two passages, the first comes from a book published in 1903, the second from *A Separate Reality*, a direct quote from don Juan. What I find piquant about this seventy-year echo is the contention that don Juan spoke only Spanish to Carlos. Somehow, in the course of translating don Juan's Spanish, Castaneda managed to resurrect the English phrases of Yogi Ramacharaka, a pseudonymous American hack writer of fake mysticism whose works are still available in occult bookstores.

Could such correspondence be accidental? Despite the close matching of words and ideas, one would have to allow the possibility if this were the only example, but it is not. Of the two following passages, the first is condensed from the *Psychedelic Review*, the second from *The Teachings of Don Juan*. Again I have added italics but no words:

> *My eyes* were closed, and a large *black* pool started to open up *in front of* them. I was able to see a *red spot*. I was aware of a most unusual *odor*, and of different parts of my body getting extremely *warm*, which felt extremely good.

> What was very outstanding was the pungent *odor* of the water. It smelled like cockroaches. I got very *warm*, and blood rushed to my ears. I saw *a red spot in front of my eyes*. 'What would have happened if I had not seen red?' 'You would have seen *black*.' 'What happens to those who see red?' 'An effect of pleasure.'

This goes beyond accidental correspondence. These two passages, each of which is drawn from less than a page of original text, have in common at least five specific word combinations as well as seven ideas: drug hallucination, seeing black, seeing red, unusual odor, parts of the body, getting very warm, and pleasure.

How many stylistic echoes would be needed to prove that don Juan's teachings and Carlos's adventures originated not in the Sonoran desert but in the library at UCLA? The Alleglossary, at the back of this volume, lists some 200 exhibits many of which clearly demonstrate and all of which suggest literary influence of earlier publications on Castaneda's supposed field reports. The list convinces me, but it may never convince another contributor to this volume, who said the don Juan books are "beneficially viewed as a sacred text," which prepares us "to witness, to accept without really understanding." Could that be the voice of Baba Ram Dass addressing the Clearlight Conference? No, it is Professor Stan Wilk writing in the leading official journal of the American Anthropological Association. Do most anthropologists feel that way about Castaneda? No again. Such views are held by a small but devout minority, who see Castaneda as an emissary to an ideal world of anthropological discovery, now returned to teach his colleagues perfect fieldwork. In that other world, which so far only Carlos has been privileged to visit, the fieldworker completely shares the worldview of his informant, unobstructed by language barriers, culture conflict, grant limitations, departmental demands, fashions in theory, or modernist conceptions of reality. This monumental achievement required many years and would have been impossible without the tutelage of don Juan, a unique and persistent teacher, now departed, but some comfort can nevertheless be derived from certain knowledge that one indomitable pioneer has scaled the heights. Though Carlos's admirerers could not accompany him into those Elysian fields, they can at least still lose themselves in reports of the fieldwork written by Castaneda.

Thousands of years before there were any priests or holy books or churches, human dealings with transcendental agencies were conducted by spiritual technicians who traveled between this and other worlds, convoying the dead to safety, retrieving souls lost by the living, finding cures for the sick, and bringing back power to control the elements and knowledge of hidden realms. To make those perilous passages easier they often ate, smoked, or rubbed their bodies with visionary plants that helped them fly into the sky. Anthropologists call such special men (and sometimes women) *shamans*, which is what they were called by the Tungus tribe of Siberia. *Shaman* means "one who knows." In his singular way, Carlos Castaneda is the shaman of the academy, the special person who goes to another world to bring back indispensable knowledge only he can obtain.

Proofs like those I have just offered do not impress the loyal clients of Castaneda-Shaman. Contradictions, they say, don't matter, because Castaneda was not writing a factual account; he was trying to convey a subjective experience. If, then, his reports are nowhere tied to ordinary fact, how shall we distinguish them from ordinary fiction?

Castaneda, say his defenders, was right to waste no time describing the Sonoran desert, because we already knew what the desert was like. Against this, one must point out that the few details he does give contradict what is known about the Sonoran desert.

Castaneda's partisans have not yet faced up to don Juan's surprising habit of quoting in Spanish from English-language texts, by Alexandra David-Neel, Suzanne Langer, Edward Sapir, Ludwig Wittgenstein, Gordon Wasson, Lama Govinda, Gilbert Ryle, or D. T. Suzuki. I have no doubt their faith will find an explanation. True belief survives all tests. As one of Castaneda's academic champions confided to me: "The whole don Juan business may somehow reflect a UFO encounter."

Castaneda is "really a shaman," said his friend, anthropologist Michael Harner. One thing a shaman routinely does is trick his clients. This does not mean he takes advantage of them. It means he deceives them for their own good. Even in societies where shamanism is traditional, ordinary people are not fully attuned to the invisible realms and so cannot readily see everything a shaman sees. Conjuring tricks furnish evidence visible to everyone of events seen only by the shaman. When, for example, a curing shaman is about to suck a deadly magical dart from the belly of a suffering victim of sorcery, he first hides a solid dart in his mouth. As the magical dart is sucked into his mouth, it is immediately absorbed by the solid dart, which the shaman noisily spits out and triumphantly shows to patient and family. "He is not really lying," Harner explains, for without visible proof his clients would not know the operation had succeeded, and would not pay him. Surely they have a right to know, and he has a right to be paid. From this, it can be seen that shamanism is a subtle profession involving secret maneuvers easily mistaken for fakery and exploitation if one is not properly informed.

As with other shamans, Castaneda's conjuring can be condemned or condoned. Since 1976 I have vigorously personified the skeptical scientist exposing tricks and deceptions, which more thoughtful persons were ignoring or discounting. "It is unfortunate," Harner wrote—about me—"that the persons chosen to review Castaneda's books are not really experts on shamanism." Well, Harner is certainly an expert on shamanism, so let's listen to him.

"I think Castaneda's work is 110 per cent valid," he said. "He conveys a deep truth, though his specific details can often be justifiably questioned." The don Juan books are especially valuable, Harner believes, because they were written like novels. "Most of what anthropologists write is dry as dust," he said.

This dispute appears to turn on the difference between science and story-telling. Science requires facts; story-telling can take them or leave them. Scientific reports in which "specific details can often be justifiably questioned" are likely to be discredited, because specific details are often crucial in science; the fabric of observation and reporting can display only so many holes before being tossed into the trashcan. As science, the don Juan books are a farce. As fiction, they form an ingenious allegory wherein experts like Harner can recognize much anthropological truth. What Harner neglects to add is that you have to *be* an expert to know which parts are true and which are false. Though don Juan makes quite a fuss over smoking mushrooms, for example, nobody had actually tried to smoke them until Castaneda's books were published, and then it didn't work.

Like countless wizards before him, Castaneda prospers as the shaman of academe by admitting nothing. Despite repeated ironical hinting, too subtle for his more adoring colleagues, he has not once stepped out of character in all the nineteen years since Carlos met don Juan but has played the role of Carlos-Fieldworker in every situation. Not one journalist, teacher, colleague, employer, friend, or relative has heard a frank admission of pretense or fictioneering. Such triumphant coggery outdoes even the brilliant but fitful impostures of Ferdinand Demara, who was always being unmasked and having to flee the scene. Like that great impostor, Castaneda deceived people for their own good; unlike him, Castaneda has not broken the law and has acquired a permanent clientele. Native talent, relentless hard work, strict specialization, and faultless role-playing have brought him both fame and financial independence.

No matter how many professors have been conned or hippies have gone looking for don Juan, few of Castaneda's critics condemn him as an antisocial character. Most gladly or grudgingly allow he has made the world a more interesting place without doing it much harm; those he has made fools of had only themselves to blame. So perceived, Castaneda becomes Coyote, the original Amerindian shaman, a trickster who abuses people's trust while teaching them valuable lessons.

One thing Trickster could teach us is not to go on forever being fooled. Though Castaneda's fee for this service has been fairly low, some have found the lesson too hard to learn. The mortal yearning for Paradise is very strong indeed, and anyone who promises to lead us there is trusted. For the born-again the promised land is Beulah, for Marxists a classless society, for futurists like Timothy Leary a homey mechanical doughnut in the sky. For a handful of professors and thousands of pseudo-anthropology fans, Paradise is a balmy purple desert where one can have endless private metaphysical conversations with a mystical old Indian named don Juan.

RdeM

Outstanding among Castaneda's scholarly commenders is Mary Douglas, whose "Authenticity of Castaneda" (first published in 1973) treats only the initial don Juan trilogy. Highly respected in her profession, Douglas is the author of such well known books as *Purity and Danger, Natural Symbols,* and *Implicit Meanings.* Since 1970 she has been Professor of Social Anthropology at University College, London. Recently she has been Research Scholar and Director for Research on Culture at the Russell Sage Foundation, in New York. Taking the legendary Carlos to be not a character in a story but more or less the same person as author Castaneda, Douglas does not distinguish between them as I have done and as most contributors to this book will do.

The Authenticity of Castaneda

If ever there was a writer tuned to his age or work likely to attract success, it must be Carlos Castaneda and his account of his apprentice years with a Mexican Indian sorcerer. There can be few who have never dreamed of such an adventure. Here is a young college student, who makes friends with a magician, no less, and persuades him to reveal his secrets.

The style is the adventure story of *Boy's Own* of eighty years ago. The hero's blood runs cold, his heart pounds, his throat parches, his pulse races, temperature soars or drops, his lungs burst, he faints, he recovers and is sick, he falls or faints again. He weeps with remorse or happiness. He can hardly ever believe his eyes, nor his ears. The pains he endures are excruciating, the hungers and long marches nigh impossible.

His Indian mentors are Olympic athletes, and disarmingly light-hearted. The training is long. He interrupts it frequently, sometimes because of university requirements, sometimes from sheer terror. After ten years he is told that the apprenticeship is over, he is fully trained, the rest is up to him.

Much has been said as to whether this is real anthropology or whether the pseudonym, don Juan, hides any one real person, or where precisely the elements of fiction and truth are found. The purpose of this article is to consider whether the latest campus cult deserves serious attention from anthropologists. The answer is obviously, Yes.

In itself the philosophy of ascetic mysticism, so gradually pieced together, is enough evidence of truth in the tale. It would be flippant to dismiss it. But to take it seriously is to challenge most of what anthropologists tend to assume about the subject. The adage about primitive religions being this-worldly and world religions other-worldly can never again carry the same conviction.

The order of publication needs to be related to the order of events. The first book, *The Teachings of Don Juan* published in 1968, describes how an anthropology student from the University of California at Los Angeles, seeks an Indian to help him with his thesis on ethno-botany. He wants to classify and study the hallucinogenic plants, particularly peyote. In this book don Juan introduces him to three such plants and their use: peyote (*Lophophora williamsii*), Jimson weed (*Datura inoxia syn. D. meteloides*) and a mushroom (possibly *Psilocybe mexicana*).

Under supervision he experiences extraordinary visions. But it is clear from the start that the controlled use of drugs is only the tip of the iceberg, much more importance is attached to learning how to interpret their effects.

Our vicarious apprentice, Mr Everyman, is as obtuse as we would be; he pesters don Juan to tell him about the plants and feels he is being put off when instead of a lecture he is treated to a show or involved in a dramatic experience. Part of the extraordinary skill of the writing is the way that the reader is led to identify both with the student, doggedly asking questions and with the enigmatic teacher the meaning of whose riddling answers are clearer to us, thanks to the writer's hindsight, than they were to the student at the time of asking.

The first book brings the story to September 1965, with Castaneda terrified nearly to death, his mind rocking, vowing never again to ingest the hallucinogenic plants. The appendix gives a so-called structural scheme, written in a totally different style. Let us hope his university teachers were satisfied with what they must be presumed to have drafted: a careful précis of the teachings to date and a distinction between three kinds of reality.

The first, ordinary reality, achieved by everyday consensus; the second, a non-ordinary reality achieved by special consensus; and the third, special states of ordinary reality through cueing. The ethnomethodologists' programme is laid out in classic simplicity in this appendix.

One of the intriguing aspects of the series for the anthropologist is to read it as a struggle between two sets of teachers. UCLA versus the old Indian sorcerers. In this first book, the anthropologists have won. Their cut-and-dried analysis prevails over the sorcerers' insistence that the world is more marvellous than anything that human reason can comprehend.

The second book, *A Separate Reality*, takes up the story from 1968 when the writer returns with his note pad and certain questions he has formulated about how the special consensus or non-ordinary reality is achieved. He has a theory that at every peyote meeting there is a *de facto* leader who lays the interpretative cues for the others.

No sooner does he state his tidy little question than the battle is on again. Don Juan launches fairly and honestly into the problem of how consensus is achieved by taking it at its most general level. This book is about what he calls *seeing*, the faculty of initiates to discern a realm of being which other men miss by applying too ploddingly the criteria from their ordinary life.

Just as we would in his place, the student is slow to realize that his question is being answered and slow to realize that *seeing* is not a matter of vision, but also of hearing and feeling in a special way. It involves a commitment to hold in suspense the judgments from the ordinary world, to switch off one set of responses and to be entirely open to anything that the senses may suggest.

But not entirely open, it soon becomes clear, for the apprentices are pushed to interpret their hallucinations in a stable way. They cannot report that they *see* until they recognize each man as a luminous egg from whose abdominal region powerful threads of light flicker out, sustaining and informing him.

Very delicate is the line which appears between the alleged freedom of each apprentice to interpret a world for himself and the actual monitoring of their efforts which results in a consensus over certain broad principles of the common universe in which their experiences unfold. Ultimately the only reality taught for sure is that men are luminous beings who will one day die. The rest of their learning is about the arbitrary, factitious character of all knowledge.

This book is incomplete without the third, since the latter contains the conversations about death and reality which were verbal background to the astonishing conjuring tricks, hypnotic or trance-induced effects which again drive the student to the edge of reason and send him away in despair in 1970.

At this stage one might judge the contest between UCLA anthropology and the teachings of don Juan to have resulted in a draw. The Indian tutor shows he knows the questions and delivers his answers with dazzling virtuosity. But the pupil cannot understand nor relay the message back home. He is beset with anxiety about his attempt to live in two worlds of reality, a problem whose validity is utterly denied by don Juan.

The third book, *Journey to Ixtlan*, goes over all the ground again from the beginning in 1961. All the conversations with don Juan which the university requirements for a doctoral dissertation had previously screened out as irrelevant are put back into context. The whole experience takes on a very different tone as the full moral stature of don Juan is revealed.

Now we discover that from their first encounters he has squarely established that the project of knowledge is a project in asceticism and non-attachment. He has quickly punctured the pupil's pretensions and exposed his personal weakness and vanity. To seek knowledge for the sake of a thesis is to be a pimp. The only valid seeking is for one's own life project. Knowledge is not to be divorced from living. To learn, the pupil must change his life, accept the thought of his own death, control all his own thought and action within that perspective.

When these pressures are revealed one can understand how the apprenticeship goes more quickly for some Indian boys and how they can learn to *see* and move in the other world with creative confidence. Our representative, trying desperately to satisfy two schools, cannot give his heartfelt allegiance to his teacher's discipline. He is literally torn between two worlds of reality. To his effort to control his vision in both, we owe this report.

The dialogue with don Juan was originally conducted in Spanish. The translation reeks with clichés of spiritual writing in all the traditions which have flowed into our language. To be impeccable is only slightly different from 'Be ye perfect'. Change your life, leave your friends, drop your personal history, stop the world, learn the techniques of not-doing, the injunctions have familiar echoes. No wonder the books have sometimes been dismissed as imaginative fiction.

When the third book is added to the first two, however, it is necessary to accept them as a serious challenge. The naiveties of expression can be taken as evidence of authenticity. The philosophy thus revealed is startlingly contemporary. Admittedly, the conscious concern with processes of validation, which preoccupies both phenomenologists and Yaqui Indian shamans, can make the suspicious-minded reviewer smell more fiction. But take the lessons, go along with the teachings, and quite a lot appears that is totally unexpected, new and provocative.

First for the common ground, whether set there by the writer wittingly or unwittingly: since he cannot escape the structures of his own cognitive tradition and nor can we, it is worth enumerating how much philosophical overlap his material was made to bear.

The other world of non-ordinary reality was known to a number of other so-called sorcerers who were on their way to becoming men of knowledge. They each had their own way of achieving extraordinary effects, by hypnosis, sleight-of-hand and any of a hard-to-catalogue range of stage-setting, clueing procedures.

They seemed to hold each other in high esteem, even fear. Each was reckoned to be a master, in his own way, of dangerous powers in the universe. One was a master of equilibrium, he could vanish, cross a waterfall, appear ten miles away, before and behind, and create impressions of thunderous noise. Another's predilection was dancing, another was a herbalist. Don Juan was aiming to become a man of knowledge.

There were four enemies to be overcome by anyone who took his path. The seeker could first be stopped by fear. That overcome, he risked being seduced by his own clarity of mind. That temptation subdued, he could be seduced by the power he could now exert. After that the only enemy was old age which would sap his will to know.

The first book ends when the apprentice admits he has been defeated by fear; the second when he decides to protect the threatened clarity of his mind. The third ends ambiguously. He is tempted by power, but not yet past the hurdles of clarity or fear.

Throughout the trilogy tricks and horseplay interweave with themes of spirituality. The former recall the miracles of the early Judaeo-Christian tradition: the widow's curse; St Dorcas out-smarting the devil; St Jerome cherished by wild beasts; St Gregory by birds. The usual anthropological treatment of such stories is the full myth analysis. But perhaps we should now reverse the procedure and ask whether the tales of our own early religion do not bear witness to an ancient corpus of shamanistic skills. For these old men are just as witty in their pranks and as effective in controlling the winds or vanishing in smoke as any of our ancient saints.

We can ask whether the sorcerers' cosmology is more dominated by fear or love. All the apprentices when they meet, and most of the sorcerers, show touching affection for each other. One exception is an evil witch who takes the form of a blackbird and is allegedly out to kill don Juan and his apprentice. Since fear is explicitly one of the techniques of training, the question of whether don Juan really believes in her malice is left uncertain.

He certainly believes the world to be full of dangers and inimical powers. But once he has confessed that his pupil cannot learn for lack of sufficient motive and that the fear of a worthy opponent is necessary to force him to use his new found faculties, we cannot be sure how much the sorcerer's universe is dominated really by fear.

After the first book there is less said about joy and love. But a synoptic reading shows that the place of Mescalito needs to be restored to the later narratives. He is the being in the first book who guides and protects and who induces ecstatic joy in his elect. Once they have learnt to meet him in a peyote session, his reappearance can be triggered by various means, producing intense ecstasy and ruthless self-examination in his devotees.

The other world of reality seems to belong specially to Mescalito, so

the accounts which exclude him are likely to be misleading. With Mescalito reinstalled at the centre, the attitude of the sorcerers to each other
becomes very much like that recorded of mystics and wonderworkers in
our history: self-deprecating and insisting on the spiritual heights
reached by their fellows. Teresa of Avila speaking of John of the Cross
might have exclaimed something equivalent to Vicente.

> 'You may say that I am only a man of lyric knowledge', he said.
> 'I'm not like Juan, my Indian brother.' Don Vicente was silent
> again for another moment. His eyes were glassy and were star-
> ing at the floor by my left side. Then he turned to me and said
> almost in a whisper, 'Oh, how high soars my Indian brother!'

Don Juan, on hearing of this tribute, gruffly rebuts it—'lyric knowledge, my eye! Vicente is a brujo.' So much for the crude divisions between religion and sorcery used in anthropological typologies.

It may be difficult to judge the spirituality of the religion revealed in
this series because of the deafening clichés in which it is perforce ren
dered. But it would be more difficult to defend formally the view that
their echoing of contemporary philosophical concerns is proof of their
bogus character. For they are consistently knitted into an attitude towards life and death and human rationality whose very coherence is alien
to our own contemporary thought.

In the Hegelian aftermath, when Cowper Powys gave a character in
Maiden Castle a remark about Being and Non-Being, it was a wry and
fanciful aside; when Kierkegaard or Husserl contrasted thought and existence, they conveyed a yearning sense of problem and insoluble dilemma; when don Juan teaches the difference between doing and not-
doing he is entirely matter of fact.

But in one context after another he demonstrates that focusing
thought or intention or appetite or sensory responses creates one kind of
intelligibility. Unfocusing is a technique for ridding the mind of its preconceptions of the everyday world and opening it to the inexplicable
mysteries unleashed in hallucinations.

He teaches his novice to stare at foliage, focusing on the dark space
between the leaves; he must stare at a bank of cloud until his eyes see it
as a dazzling pattern of light; then he must deliberately undo that pattern
by focusing on the dark holes between the lines of light until the pattern
reverses. He must do the same with hearing until he can shut out the
sounds he normally selects and listen to silence. Harder still, he must

learn to control his dreams; the most not-doing of all not-doing is to control sleeping experience, but abandon the will to impose any pattern on waking experience.

Somehow, this balance between strict control and strict readiness to take on any vision that is offered and sustain it as long as possible is the condition of *seeing*.

The last book ends with two old sorcerer-saints recalling their lives. They have been splitting their sides with laughter at elaborate jokes at the expense of their pupil. Then, replying to his questions, they look back on a long tale of withdrawal from worldly delights and sadness overwhelms them. One by one they have rejected the comforts of friendship for the sake of holding to their hard-won knowledge. They know that all doings are unreal: 'to hinge yourself to either one is a waste of time, because the only thing that is real is the being in you that is going to die. To arrive at that being is the *not-doing* of the self.'

Somewhere between the words of surrealists, phenomenologists and ethnomethodologists, somewhere between secular modern Zen and John Cage's not-music and saying nothing, this philosophy makes a split-level version of what everyone is currently hearing. The young apprentice may have imposed more than he realized of our own culture upon the non-doing of *seeing*. But, even so, this remarkable document throws a big spanner in the works of anthropologists who have put much more doing than he has into the recording of primitive religions.

The temporary discomfiture of a few professionals is not the important issue. Much more interesting are the suggestions about how different forms of visual experience are induced, by squinting, focusing and unfocusing and rapid sideway scanning. Most interesting of all are the ways in which a spatial metaphor is used for pegging the otherworldly experiences, rather in the style of the Renaissance memory theatre.

From these ideas we are likely to get advances in anthropology.

RdeM

From eloquent subscription we turn first to amused dissent, then to resolute repudiation. A professor of archaelogy at the University of Calgary, Jane Holden Kelley has written two books about the Yaqui Indians. *The Tall Candle* (co-authored by Rosalio Moisés and William Curry Holden, and now retitled *A Yaqui Life*) tells the story of a man whose candle, as he believed, was lit in heaven at his birth in 1896; a tall candle, it didn't burn down till 1969. Better informed about Yaqui ways than his more famous but less substantial counterpart, Rosalio Moisés was sure don Juan had picked up all those odd, unYaqui ideas from the Mexicans; he could hardly guess don Juan's literary ally had been reading the *Psychedelic Review*. There is, however, one idea I think don Juan did learn from a Yaqui—Rosalio's own preoccupation with signs and portents, which appeared in print just as Castaneda was writing *Journey to Ixtlan*, where it is saucily imitated by don Juan's jet roar, falling rock, and perking coffeepot.

Kelley's second book recounts the lives of four women surviving as Yaquis through deportation, virtual slavery, revolutionary soldiering, sanctuary in Arizona, and rebuilding in Sonora. The anecdote here titled "A Yaqui Way of Kidding" is taken from that book, *Yaqui Women*. Pascua Nueva, mentioned in the story, is a Yaqui settlement near Tucson, Arizona.

Kelley's savory tidbit can only whet your appetite for Hans Sebald's rare roast of Castaneda. A professor of sociology at Arizona State University, Sebald writes this time as an informed layman. While his most colorful qualification for grilling a flying sorcerer is that his grandmother was a prominent witch—benign, he hastens to add—still his most pertinent preparation was to arrive in the Sonoran desert just two years after Carlos and live there ever since. In his book *Witchcraft*, Sebald said he would disagree with Castaneda on almost every point of environmental description. Reading that, I invited him to make his argument here.

A Yaqui Way of Kidding

As everyone knows, Carlos Castañeda's books have had a tremendous impact on a wide audience, and Castañeda's don Juan is a Yaqui. I would assume that every anthropologist who has worked with the Yaquis has been bombarded with inquiries about Yaqui drug use, sorcery, and what have you. I have received letters from people wanting an introduction to a Yaqui *brujo* (witch or sorcerer), and the subject of my Yaqui research is never mentioned without someone asking me if there really is a don Juan. Do I know him or people like him? Or are all Yaquis like don Juan? To such inquiries, I can only say that I have not encountered don Juan or anyone like him, an admission guaranteed to lower my social value on the spot.

The Yaquis themselves are now approached by outsiders in search of don Juan. A Pascua Nueva Yaqui leader related that no few Volkswagen buses, usually with California license plates, find their way to Pascua Nueva. The inhabitants of the VW buses are described as "long-haired hippies," for the word *hippie* has deeply penetrated Yaqui consciousness with strong negative connotations. The Pascua Nueva leader explained with some delight his tactics for dealing with these unwelcome intrusions. When inquiries begin, he says he has never heard of don Juan. Slowly he shifts to admitting cautiously that there is a don Juan but he must be protected. Finally he weakens and tells the inquirers where don Juan lives. There actually is an old man named don Juan who lives in Pascua Nueva, one said to have considerable ingenuity in spinning tales. Everyone is vastly amused and the hippies are usually good for a little money, cigarettes, beer, and other things before they realize they have been had.

Roasting Rabbits in Tularemia
or The Lion, the Witch,
and the Horned Toad

My critique aims at Carlos Castaneda's claim that his psychic experiences took place in a particular down-to-earth environment: the Sonoran desert. Because of this claim, a good part of his credibility must depend on his plausibly describing the natural setting. The critique would be ill advised were Castaneda to allow that his adventures took place while he was ensconced in an armchair in southern California, savoring Acapulco Gold or Owsley's Acid, collecting hallucinations for belletristic tales. Castaneda makes no such admission, but offers his stories, especially the first three volumes, as field reports. We are therefore obliged to look at his "field."

Relying here mainly on personal experience, I speak as an outdoorsman who has been turned on to the southwestern desert for the past 17 years. Literally from my backdoor I have spied on bobcats, quail, rattlesnakes, hawks, rodents, and coyotes—though none of the latter have spoken to me. Trudging along under heavy backpacks or lighter daypacks, I have crisscrossed some of the wildest territory in Arizona, particularly the Superstition Mountains Wilderness. The last ten years have given me ample opportunity to compare Castaneda's version of the Sonoran desert with the version that begins where my backyard ends.

Though some despise Castaneda's writings because they portray magical happenings, others retort that magic seems absurd only to "straights" or spiritual midgets. I shall avoid this dispute by concentrating on absurdities that cannot be excused on grounds of magic but are part of the *unmagical setting* of the reported magical events. While skepticism about don Juan's magic could be condemned as insensitivity to the Zeitgeist, skepticism about the supposed natural setting cannot be so easily dismissed. If I tell you that my favorite baseball team just won the World Series by kicking a field goal, you need not renounce your belief in baseball to suspect that I did not actually go to the game. When Castaneda describes a desert quite unlike the Sonoran in flora, fauna, and climate, one need not give up any belief in shamans or psychic powers to suspect that both Castaneda's desert and the interviews conducted there are literary inventions. This review, then, resolutely ignores supernatural or nonordinary events, like flying with crows or chatting with coyotes, to focus on Castaneda's claims about the natural setting.

Most suspect among those claims are the descriptions of hiking in the desert during the months of June, July, August, and September. When on numerous occasions don Juan and Carlos wander through the desert for hours, even days, Castaneda overlooks the fact that temperatures soar well above 100 degrees in the shade and stay there (often throughout the night) during these summer months. It is not uncommon for the temperature to exceed 110 degrees and fluctuate little for weeks on end. At the same time, the humidity usually stays below ten percent. In the hot season the toughest hikers refuse to enter the desert. Only utterly inexperienced and foolhardy persons set out across the summer sands, and then not for long, because death soon taps them on the left shoulder. The land blisters with heat, the rocks feel incandescent, and the body dehydrates so fast that exhaustion and collapse must follow in a matter of hours. Nearly every summer, viewers of Arizona telecasting see helicopter rescue teams retrieving the bodies of persons as uninformed as Castaneda from the scorched desert. I myself have administered first aid to a man who had lost his way in the desert near my house and had been without water for a little more than a day—in May, when the temperature was only in the 90s. Yet Carlos and don Juan nonchalantly saunter into the desert morning, night, or noon to spend whole days climbing indefatigably in and out of canyons, catching quail and rabbits, and roasting rattlesnakes. June is usually the hottest month. On the 29th of June, Carlos hunted quail all day, so absorbed in don Juan's instructions that "a whole day went by and I had not noticed the passage of time. I even forgot to eat lunch." Not content with omitting all reference to heat, Castaneda describes the evening wind as "cold."

On July 24th, "around mid-afternoon, after we had roamed for hours in the desert," don Juan sat down in the shade and talked about the metaphysics of hunting. A more appropriate theme would have been the metaphysics of roasting to death. "Around noon" on August 19th, Carlos and his sorcerer hike into a canyon and then climb to the top of a hill "to rest in the open unshaded area" until dusk. If indeed attempted, such a rest stop would probably bring delirium and coma.

Castaneda's fatuous conception of the Sonoran summer is matched by his foolish description of the Sonoran winter. One December evening, as Carlos huddles against what seems to be a rock, "lukewarm" rain soaks his legs but does not keep him from falling asleep. Actual desert hikers

know that winter rains are cold, often falling as snow at the higher eleva-
tions. Desert nights get very cold, often below freezing, and chill one to
the bone. An unprotected sleeper soaked by rain would suffer severe
exposure and might die. Carlos, in contrast, wakes in the morning feeling fine, despite having been described as a city dweller without any
unusual stamina or endurance in the out-of-doors.

Castaneda's animal lore is equally untrustworthy. Hunters know it is
very difficult to capture quail alive, but that is how don Juan prefers to do
it. Disdaining the more plausible snare, don Juan teaches Carlos to throw
together "a most ingenious trap," presumably just like the one don Juan
later assembles "with astounding speed and skill." Though a practical
cage trap requires hours of expert collecting, preparing, and assembling
of materials, Carlos's hasty pile of sticks catches not just one quail but
five, of which don Juan roasts two and lets three go. Not since Noah's ark
have animals been so cooperative.

Perhaps the first to question don Juan's tale of the lion was Gordon
Wasson, who said zoologists would yawn when they read that an unpro-
voked puma "began to charge" don Juan. I second Wasson's yawning and
go on to point out that no area of the Sonoran desert, whether Mexican
or Arizonan, "is crawling with mountain lions, " as don Juan avers. Not
only have the animals been nearly exterminated but such a concentration
contradicts their territorial instinct. Pumas are solitary hunters laying
claim to large preserves in which they will not tolerate other pumas.

A puma that would mosey right under a tree in which an "extremely
nervous" intellectual is hiding would be a real loser. Feline eyes would
penetrate the night, sensitive ears would detect quaking and gasping
among the branches, and a discriminating nose would readily sort out
Carlos's odor-masking willow leaves, bathless hikes, and nervousness.
No self-respecting puma would come anywhere near those sweating
metaphysicians.

Though mountain lions shun people and normally don't think of attacking them, don Juan goes on at length about the danger of being
attacked. Juanists may argue that the sorcerer is only fooling his apprentice, but surely the fooling would not continue forever; eight years later
we find Carlos still trying to climb up a tree to escape possible lions,
which was a pretty silly maneuver in the first place, since mountain lions
climb trees better than people do. Don Juan should have known more
about lions than that.

And Castaneda should have known more about trees. The Sonoran
desert holds few big trees that are not palo verde, ironwood, or mesquite,

and these three are nearly impossible to climb. Branches tangle into a thorny thicket and six feet up are too weak to support a man. If Castaneda had actually climbed such a tree, wouldn't he have told us how difficult it was?

Don Juan used "squealing rodents" to lure the lion. Confined in a cage that did not maim, the rodents were unharmed. What kind of rodent squeals without being hurt? Rabbits sometimes scream, but these non-rabbits were described as "chubby squirrel-like rodents." Such mysterious creatures should have been brought back and donated to the Arizona-Sonora Desert Museum.

Though Carlos meets creatures that don't exist, he fails to meet creatures that do--in great and menacing numbers. The desert does not crawl with lions, but it certainly crawls with scorpions. Despite countless bivouacs in the bush, frequent rock turning, and don Juan's elfin habit of rolling on the ground when something strikes him funny, not one scorpion crawls into his collar or the story.

Equally odd is Castaneda's failure to mention the saguaro fruit fly, which swarms every May in the vicinity of tall blooming cacti. Going for eyes, ears, and nostrils like so many tiny demons, these sticky tormentors make life miserable for human beings. Oblivious to the hazard, Carlos strolls the sands untroubled or tranquilly scribbles his notes in front of don Juan's desert house--all in the month of May, when saguaro flies are swarming.

Don Juan's fat squirrel-like rodent, or "water rat," first outruns predators, then stands on its hind legs on top of a rock to look around and groom itself. In the ordinary world, rabbits outrun predators but other rodents hide in burrows and under rocks. Except in pet shops, where Castaneda may have observed them, rodents rarely groom themselves before the eyes of carnivores, preferring to do it in safe seclusion.

While still a desert novice, Carlos easily catches a rabbit with his bare hands. "I was very calm and moved carefully," he says, "and I had no trouble at all in catching a male rabbit." This claim betrays monumental ignorance. The swiftest coyote works hard to catch a rabbit. Castaneda does not distinguish cottontails from jackrabbits, but even a cottontail can go from a dead stop to 30 miles an hour in seconds and makes a tricky target for a shotgun. Only a sick rabbit could be nabbed with no trouble at all by a visiting phenomenologist.

Which brings up another point. Desert hunters know that during the hot season sluggish rabbits are likely to have tularemia, or rabbit fever, whose microbes can penetrate uninjured human skin and cause a fever lasting several weeks. Carlos not only grabs a presumably sluggish rabbit in July but then is told by don Juan to skin, roast, and eat it. The old sorcerer must have been pretty fed up with his apprentice on that particular summer day.

When don Juan tells him to kill the rabbit, Carlos stomps on the cage, pulls the rabbit out, and holds it limp in his hand. Somehow the beast is instantly dead. Anyone who has killed a rabbit knows that a rabbit's death throes are ferocious. Even shot through the brains it will flop about for several seconds, a fact I am quite sure of, having lived on a farm that raised rabbits. Castaneda's rabbits run like ducks and die like decoys.

Carlos himself runs terrified through the desert by day and by night untouched by the hooks and spines of its bloodthirsty cacti. He picks cholla needles for his lizard-sewing kit without once stabbing his fingers. Don Juan's repeated warnings against hostile spirits and entities of the night are not matched by warnings against barrel cactus and prickly pears. Carlos spends eight years worrying about lions but never worries or even hears about the javelina, a wild desert pig that can be more dangerous than a lion. And where, one may ask, are the nine-inch centipedes, the tarantulas big as saucers? Where are the king snakes, scarlet racers, chuckawallas, horned toads, gila monsters, kit foxes, kangaroo rats, squirrels, and skunks? Where are the owls and the road-runners? In *nagual's* name, where are the deer?

Castaneda's errors of omission and commission have not been fully catalogued, but these examples should make the point. While almost any one of these environmental anomalies could arise from poor observation or unusual circumstances, the accumulation of many such incongruities conclusively disauthenticates the setting of Castaneda's purported fieldwork. If the setting is imaginary, why should one credit the magical feats, or the magician who performs them, or the interviews between magician and apprentice? If the field is a fake, how can the fieldwork be genuine?

Validity is not Authenticity:
Distinguishing Two Components of Truth

$Time's$ 1973 cover story raised serious questions about Castaneda's truthfulness. Where had he really been born and when? How solid a being was don Juan? Were the books fact or fiction? Rebuking $Time$ for setting its "hired leeches" on Castaneda's works and person, a reader declared the don Juan story "no less true or honest" if wholly invented. Should don Juan prove imaginary, wrote Peter Matthiessen in $The Snow Leopard$, "then spurious ethnology becomes a great work of the imagination; whether borrowed or not, the teaching rings true." "The most vividly convincing documents I have read," Carl Rogers told fellow psychologists, "come from one man, Carlos Castaneda." "He may be lying," hedged $New Age$, "but what he says is true." Truth, apparently, is not a simple matter.

When a $Los Angeles Times$ book reviewer said $Castaneda's Journey$ had offered evidence "strong enough to sow seeds of doubt in the firmest bedrocks of belief," an exasperated reader charged him and me and skeptics in general with missing the point, which was that Castaneda had provided a system of thinking meant precisely to break readers out of the bonds of having to ask whether metaphysical books are based on fact. "If the system is valid," our correspondent said, "its source is rather irrelevant." I answered that philosophy is not the only game in town; some people wish instead to play anthropology, where sources are not only relevant but sometimes crucial.

"Either Castaneda is recording an encounter with a master . . . or else he is himself that master," wrote Joseph Margolis a professional player of the philosophy game; "in this sense, it makes no difference whether the books are a record of an actual encounter or whether Castaneda is the author of a clever fiction." I gladly grant Margolis his point if strictly confined to the teaching of metaphysics, but in the game of science it makes a big difference whether or not a field report is based on actual trips to the field.

Psychoanalist Elsa First distinguished naïve skeptics who reject the don Juan books simply because they report anomalous or apparently supernatural events from more knowledgeable skeptics who find Carlos's desert novitiate simply too good to be true--don Juan too much the oriental guru, his teachings too close to Sufism, Tantric Buddhism, or the Hindu chakra system. "This could well be explained," First countered, "by the fact that the 'natural mind' everywhere perceives similarly." The point was well made, and the explanation in terms of worldwide mysticism must be seriously considered, but in the end, after further conceptual analysis and an examination of particular evidence, it will definitely be rejected.

When poet Robert Bly wrote in the *New York Times* that Castaneda "ransacks the work of genuine researchers like Michael Harner" to prepare his "spiritual goulash" and that his "thefts" are convincingly documented in *Castaneda's Journey*, Harner emphatically protested what he said was the mistake "of assuming that similarities between Castaneda's material and that published by others on shamanism is due to plagiarism by Castaneda"; "apparently," he continued, Bly and de Mille "are unaware that remarkable parallels exist in shamanic belief and practice throughout the primitive world."

In keeping with Harner's wish that those who write about Castaneda should be better informed, I have by this time read several books beyond Harner's own outstanding works on the Jivaro—books by such authorities as Bean and Saubel, Furst, the Leightons, Myerhoff, Opler, Petrullo, Sharon, Steward, and Underhill—and I think I have now grasped the general outlines of shamanic belief and practice. While I was writing *Castaneda's Journey* I had barely dipped into Eliade, who tells us, for example, that "the shamans lay the novice on the ground and cover him with leaves and branches." Don Juan did the same to Carlos, of course, covering him first with branches, then with leaves, and then with earth. Such a parallel Harner no doubt had in mind to illustrate his conception of Castaneda as a source of valid ethnographic ideas, and there is certainly nothing in the example to raise anyone's suspicions, but other parallels are more richly textured.

In her 1968 dissertation, Barbara Myerhoff described the ritual peyote hunt in the sacred land of the Huichol ancestors. After the baskets had been filled, the shaman told his party of hunters they must all leave as quickly as possible, for it was dangerous to remain there. "We were puzzled," Myerhoff wrote, "but fell into our places at the end of the line and found ourselves barely able to keep up, for the group was nearly running."

In his 1973 dissertation, also known as *Journey to Ixtlan*, Castaneda described a night spent in the hills practicing the "gait of power." Having frightened Carlos sufficiently with ghost stories and bird calls, don Juan announced he was ready to leave. "Let's get out of here," he said and began to run. Carlos wanted to stay in the hills until dawn, but don Juan retorted "in a very dramatic tone" that to stay there would be suicidal. "I followed him," wrote Castaneda, "but . . . I could not keep up with him, and he soon disappeared in the darkness ahead of me."

Harner would surely have no trouble with this example. Fear of holy places, he might say, is universal. When people are afraid, they run. The less fleet have a hard time keeping up with the more fleet. It's really quite simple, if you're not blinded by a passion for turning honest reporters into clever hoaxers.

Very well, then, the example is not evidential. But what about don Juan's "gait of power"? Where did that come from? In *Magic and Mystery in Tibet* (published in 1932, re-issued in 1971) Alexandra David-Neel described the *lung-gom-pa* trance-walker: "The man proceeded at an unusual gait and, especially, with an extraordinary swiftness." In *Journey to Ixtlan* (published in 1972) Castaneda averred: "He then proceeded to demonstrate a special way of walking in the darkness, a way which he called 'the gait of power.' "

"Sunset and clear nights," David-Neel wrote, "were favorable conditions for the walker." "The gait of power is for running at night," don Juan whispered in Carlos's ear.

Commenting on David-Neel's account in *his* 1971 book, *The Way of the White Clouds*, Lama Govinda added: "The feet seem to be endowed with an instinct of their own, avoiding invisible obstacles and finding footholds, which only a clairvoyant consciousness could have detected in the speed of such a movement and in the darkness of the night." Castaneda went on to say (in 1972): "My body seemed to be cognizant of things without thinking about them. For example, I could not really see the jagged rocks in my way, but my body always managed to step on the edges and never in the crevices, except for a few mishaps when I lost my balance because I became distracted."

"There is no greater danger," Govinda concluded, "than the sudden awakening to normal consciousness. It is for this reason that the *lung-gom-pa* must avoid speaking or looking about, because the slightest distraction would result in breaking his trance." "The degree of concentration needed to keep scanning the area directly in front had to be total," concluded Castaneda; "as don Juan had warned me, any slight glance to the side or too far ahead altered the flow."

Those of us who judge the don Juan books a hoax will see obvious literary influence working in these passages, but those for whom don Juan remains authentic will see instead the workings of the universal mystic mind. Psychologist Michael Gorman, for one, found it fascinating that "a Polish count, an Indian philosopher, and a Yaqui sorcerer" all took the central human error to be confusing one's own way of looking at the world with the way the world actually is. Don Juan, you may recall, said one's view of the world arises from "a description, which is given to us from the moment of our birth." What I find more fascinating here than don Juan's sharing of an abstract idea with Korzybski and Krishnamurti is his sharing of concrete language with Edward Sapir, who said that one's view of personal conduct arises from "arbitrary modes of interpretation that social tradition is constantly suggesting to us from the very moment of our birth."

Apparently deaf to such verbal resonances, numerous writers have marveled at don Juan's traditional mysticism or psychodelic lore. "Interestingly enough," comments Marlene Dobkin de Rios, "many of the insights Casteñeda gleans from his teacher seem to have widespread application in other societies where plant hallucinogens are used. This is perhaps due to the limiting parameters of the drug itself, insofar as they effect man's central nervous system in a patterned way." A plausible hypotheses, if one has confidence in the authenticity of Castaneda's reports. Lacking such confidence, one suspects the common psychodelic themes arose not from characteristics of drugs administered by don Juan but from contents of books read by Castaneda. Does this suspicion make any difference to the validity of don Juan's teachings? Does it matter whether they came directly from don Juan to Castaneda or directly from a book to Castaneda? Unfortunately it does make a difference. An observer who cannot be trusted to tell us where and how he got his information cannot be trusted to preserve the integrity of that information either. Don Juan may not only be imaginary, he may also be handing us a line. An expert on plant hallucinogens will no doubt recognize some valid elements in don Juan's psychodelics, but an expert who trusts don Juan's authenticity may go beyond expertise to accept invalid elements invented by Castaneda, such as the famous smoking of the mushroom.

If anthropologists can be misled, what will happen to non-anthropologists? Elmer Green, psychophysiologist of yoga practices at the Menninger Foundation, found it "interesting" that don Juan's teachings paralleled those of Sufist Jacques Ramano, who taught that truth is to be lived, not merely talked about. He thought it "entertaining" that Eastern metaphysics had been succinctly expressed in the independent teachings of Amerindian don Juan. He was intrigued by don Juan's idea of "the double" and thought his calling the true self "a cluster" was "remarkably similar" to Gordon Allport's idea of "functional autonomy." I agree that if an actual *curandero* came up with a series of ideas also found in books by Robert Ornstein, Otto Rank, D.T. Suzuki, and Gordon Allport, his sources would be worth looking into. The correspondence, noticed by Green, between the solar-plexus chakra and don Genaro's tentacles would surely make scientists sit up and take notice, if they believed don Genaro existed. When one believes the two dons to be imaginary, however, what one finds interesting and entertaining is Castaneda's remarkable success in pulling the wool over otherwise sharp professional eyes. At one point Green ponders the similarity between don Juan's "path with heart," the Tibetan heart chakra, and Jesus' comment that a man is as he thinketh in his heart. Suddenly one wishes for don Juan's own reflections on such reverence.

"Don Juan," I whispered, "did you know that according to Jesus a man *is* as he thinks in his heart?"

Don Juan forgot about stalking the rabbit and stared at me in amazement.

"You must be kidding!" he said.

"I'm not kidding, don Juan."

Sadly he shook his head. "It's very clear to me," he said, "that Jesus didn't *see*. Otherwise he would have known that a luminous being doesn't think in his *heart*. He thinks in his *tonal*." He looked at me suspiciously. "Have you been going to mass again?"

I laughed. "You know better than that, don Juan. It's something I read in Elmer Green's book."

"God damn it!" Don Juan threw his hat to the ground and stomped on it. "I knew it! If you'd stop reading those books and listen to *me*, nobody could say you were stealing ideas. Don't you see that?"

"I see it, don Juan," I said apologetically, "but many things in the books I read agree with things you say."

"Is that so." He squinted through the bushes looking for the rabbit, which had dragged itself away while we were talking.

"For example, " I persisted, "Green says the Sufis teach that truth is to be lived, not merely talked about."

Don Juan nodded. "They're right about that. Talk is cheap."

I reached for my notebook. "Is that a sorcerer's saying?" I asked.

"Is what a sorcerer's saying?"

"Talk is cheap."

Don Juan chuckled. "You heard a sorcerer say it, so it must be a sorcerer's saying."

I wrote it in my notebook.

"You want another one to go with it?" he said.

"Sure," I said.

"Actions speak louder than words," he said.

To me, the most surprising support for Castaneda has come from Mary Douglas, whose "Authenticity of Castaneda" (Chapter Three in this volume) exemplifies a widespread failure to distinguish two components of truth: authenticity and validity.

Validity, in this discussion, refers to the correspondence between the content of a scientific report and some established background of theory and recorded observation. A report is judged valid when it agrees with what we think we know. When people thought the world was flat, reports that the hull of a departing ship would disappear before its sail had to be ignored, denied, or explained away. When people thought the world was round, such reports would be accepted and cited to prove its roundness. The actual shape of the world, round or flat or cubical, does not come into the definition; only the correspondence between the report and the established theoretical and empirical knowledge about its shape.

Authenticity, in this discussion, refers to the provenance of the report. Did it arise from the persons, places, and procedures it describes?

Though these definitions are quite conventional in science, some scientists apparently do not keep them clearly in mind. An example may be useful. If (hypothetically) some anthropologists have reported, and most believe, that Ojibway shamans use *Amanita muscaria* mushrooms in curing rites, then my report that I have participated in such a rite on MinissKitigan (Garden Island) in the Michi-Tchigamig (Lake Michigan) may easily be accepted as a true report, and any details I add to the current description of the rite may also be accepted and become part of the anthropological literature on shamanism. If, after a few months, it is alleged that the closest I have been to Garden Island was when I picked up my new Hudson Hornet in Detroit in 1953, a shadow of doubt will fall across my report, and my added details may be questioned. If I then write a letter to the *American Anthropologist*, admitting that I have never set foot on MinissKitigan but citing specific pages of the forthcoming *Puhpohwee for the People* for my added details, my original report will be judged *wholly inauthentic*, but my added ethnographic details may be judged *wholly valid*, on the authority of Keewaydinoquay, a well-recommended Ojibway shaman, who is the author of the book I stole my ideas out of. Needless to say, any further reports I write will be treated with great skepticism.

Validity and authenticity, then, are substantially, though not completely, independent components of truth. Validity cannot be achieved without authentic observing and reporting, by someone, somewhere, some time, but when authentic-and-valid reports are available in a library, a clever pretender can put together a wholly inauthentic report (like *The Teachings of Don Juan*) containing many valid details (such as the idea that sorcerers try to steal each other's souls). Since most people, including anthropologists, care more about validity (which is theoretical and therefore interesting) than about authenticity (which is a rather boring practical condition for obtaining valid information), they tend to take authenticity for granted whenever they read a report whose content seems valid to them. I believe this is exactly the error Mary Douglas fell into.

Not the only error, however, for she reasons that anyone who writes as naïvely as Castaneda can hardly be fooling us. Could such a bumpkin have invented don Juan? Of course not! Her attempt to assess Castaneda's authenticity by analyzing his style, and through his style his character, fails because Castaneda's style does not simply or fully reflect his character. He is not in fact naïve but merely writes that way when describing the thoughts and comments of the fictive character I call Carlos-Naïf.

Ralph Beals made a similar error when he reasoned that don Juan must exist in some form or other because Castaneda had started talking about him way back in 1960. Could anyone keep up the charade year after year if there were no don Juan at all? Of course not! The inference failed because Beals did not guess the very wide difference between Castaneda's character and that of persons he was accustomed to dealing with in the university. As Castaneda has said: "My life is weird—more weird than it looks."

Such failures to read character may be expected. We normally assume other people are like ourselves. What I did not expect scholars to do was to infer don Juan's authentic existence or Castaneda's credibility from the validity of particular ethnographic contents scattered throughout the don Juan books. Douglas argues against judging the books bogus (inauthentic) on the ground that don Juan's attitude toward life and death is (she believes) alien to our own (and therefore like the attitude an anthropologist might expect to find in a pre-literate, Amerindian culture). This is clearly inferring authentic provenance from valid content: if don Juan says things we expect Indians to say, or things we expect non-Indians not to say, then don Juan must exist. It does not follow.

Don Juan's "philosophy of ascetic mysticism," Douglas says, "is enough evidence of truth in the tale." Manifestly she infers don Juan's existence from the quality of his teachings. Having accepted him as an authentic source of Indian lore, she invites her colleagues' attention to his techniques for inducing different kinds of visual experience: techniques of squinting, focusing and unfocusing, and rapid sideway scanning. "From these ideas," she says, "we are likely to get advances in anthropology."

At the very least, Douglas fails to say which aspect of truth she is talking about and leaves the false implication that don Juan's teachings came to Castaneda more or less as Castaneda said they did. It may be, as she says, that from ideas of squinting, scanning, or focusing, whatever their sources, one could get advances in self-development or spiritual training or even anthropology, but that is quite different from saying that these ideas arose in a particular Amerindian culture, perhaps a league of sorcerers, and that anthropologists should take them seriously as ethnographic findings.

Douglas dismisses "the temporary discomfiture of a few professionals" who get nervous when new approaches to fieldwork are proposed, but she overlooks a source of discomfiture more important to scientists than innovation, which is the well-grounded suspicion that one is reading fake field reports, which at least one respected colleague has called authentic.

Scholars for whom English is a second language are doubly unlikely to hear echoes of Opler and Petrullo, Suzuki and David-Neel in Castaneda's prose. Correspondences between don Juan's teachings and other people's writings "cannot simply be plagiarism," writes a German scholar, Dennis Timm, "because the worldwide correspondence of magical experiences is an ethnological banality." De Mille, Timm says, should have assessed his own deficient personal power before trying to write about the power of don Juan; de Mille is so preoccupied with proving Castaneda a thief "that he falls directly onto the open knife of his own argument."

I wrote to Timm that his disputatious knife cuts either me or him depending on whether one finds correspondences only of magical phenomena or correspondences also in the words describing the magical phenomena. I offered three examples. Timm replied that by trusting evidence of that kind Western scientists had trapped themselves in their own preconceptions. To support his position, he quoted Mary Douglas on the authenticity of Castaneda—which brings us full circle.

Don Juan's teachings, Timm said, are an esoteric matter, to which scientific generalizations have no access. "Scientific verification of the 'teachings' is impossible," he declared. "A confirmation of what Castaneda experienced can be established only by a 'special consensus,' which can be reached only by sorcerers."

I suspect Timm is quite right about the difficulty of confirming Carlos's experiences, but disconfirming Castaneda's field reports is well within the power and scope of science and is a worthy end in itself. I hope Timm will eventually grant that point, and then go on to a realization of greater import to him, which is that an esoteric document is more likely to reward the spiritual or magical seeker if it has arisen from the experiences it describes rather than from the imagination of a fiction writer, no matter how much magical literature that writer may have read. If there is no background of experience for the teachings of don Juan (Paul Heelas wrote), then we must judge don Juan (or, I would add, Castaneda) to be "a charlatan engaged in indoctrination."

Timm gives low marks not only to me but to Hans Peter Duerr, in whose much milder criticism of Castaneda he finds a betrayal of "alternative science." In the summer of 1963, anthropology student Duerr made a trip to the Southwest to explore the rock-caves at Puyé. While waiting for a Greyhound bus in the Albuquerque station, he fell into conversation with a Tewa *yerbatero*, an Indian who was very learned about plants. After some small talk, Duerr asked whether the Indian could help him find a family in one of the pueblos north of Santa Fé that would take him in for a few months, because he wanted to learn about the ritual dances in the subterranean kivas. The Indian lifted his head, looked Duerr squarely in the eyes—Duerr does not say, "with a stupendous look"--then smiled and told him the most suitable pueblo for his learning would be "el pueblo de Nuestra Señora la Reina de los Angeles," where the university libraries had plenty of information about kiva dances. Stung to the quick, Duerr hopped a bus going west and pursued his further studies of Indian lore "in the libraries of Los Angeles and other unfortunate places": fit preparation for a critic of Castaneda.

Unlike Mary Douglas, Duerr did not take Castaneda's arch naiveties for a sign of authenticity. "Even an American college student cannot be so foolish," he told himself. The many passages portraying Carlos Naïf, Skeptic, Etic, Western-Rationalist he found "stylized for didactic reasons." The talking animals belonged in fairy tales. Don Juan was too much the noble savage, Eastern guru, or grandfatherly superego. Once he had penetrated Castaneda's style to glimpse the trickster-teacher beneath, Duerr went on to link validity and authenticity in a sounder way than Douglas had done.

Though he gave Castaneda the benefit of many doubts, Duerr found his magic half-baked at best. Having himself flown on the wings of the Datura plant, Duerr did not recognize Carlos's affair with the devil's weed. He challenged Carlos's invincible stupidity in not ever being able to distinguish hallucinations from ordinary reality. He was suspicious of don Juan's mushroom smoking. He criticized Castaneda for distorting and exploiting the ineffable experience one has at the borders of reality. "Coyote always spoils everything"—he quoted a Paviotso shaman.

Finding *in*valid content in the books, Duerr inferred their *in*authenticity from that content. This is not a foolproof kind of inference but (for reasons I shall discuss) it is more likely to succeed than inferring authenticity from validity. The ploy was cutely capsulated in a letter I received from a poet who knew the books were fiction the minute she read don Juan's statement that a sorcerer can go to the moon but can't bring back a bag of rocks. "Don Juan would not have said *that*," she wrote. "He might have said a sorcerer *doesn't* bring back a bag of rocks. The difference is crucial, if we are to believe don Juan is impeccable." Here a poet's intuition of impeccability cannot tolerate certain discrepancies; so she concludes Castaneda is making up the story. Inauthenticity inferred from invalidity.

Since validity and authenticity are not wholly independent components of truth, we can try to predict one from the other but, as Mary Douglas has unintentionally shown, such prediction is hazardous. The figure Categories of Truthfulness represents the prediction problem by a four-fold table, in which I have classified eight well-known works as either valid-authentic $(++)$, valid-inauthentic $(+-)$, invalid-authentic $(-+)$, or invalid-inauthentic $(--)$. These assignments are not, of course, absolutely correct, since a work classified in one category may exhibit some characteristics of another category, but I think they are defensible.

Most anthropological works will be assigned by most judges to the valid-authentic category, which should not surprise us, since the profession of anthropology is dedicated to producing honest reports that are theoretically correct. Assigning the majority of works to any other category would be an admission of general failure in the field, and so would be rather unlikely. This does not mean that most anthropological works are theoretically faultless or perfectly honest but only that they satisfy some

	Authentic (+)	Inauthentic (−)
Valid (+)	(++) *An Apache Life-Way* 　—Opler 1941 *Peyote Hunt* 　—Myerhoff 1974 *Return to Laughter* 　—Bowen 1954	(+−) *The Teachings of Don Juan* *A Separate Reality* *Journey to Ixtlan* 　—Castaneda
Invalid (−)	*The Mountain People* 　—Turnbull 1972 (−+)	*Gold of the Gods* 　—von Däniken 1973 (−−)

CATEGORIES OF TRUTHFULNESS

explicit or implicit standard of theoretical correctness and reportorial honesty. They pass inspection on both counts. How severe the inspection should be is another question, which I shall not address.

The first two works I have chosen to illustrate the valid-authentic category are ethnographic reports. The third, *Return to Laughter*, is a work of anthropological fiction based on the author's professional experience in the field. All three are classified as valid, because their ethnographic content has been accepted as generally correct; all three, in other words, agree with what anthropologists think they know. All three are classified as authentic, because no one contends they did not arise from the persons, places, and procedures they describe. The first two claim to be ethnographic reports; the third claims to be a work of fiction, in which the persons and places are fictitious (though realistic) and the procedures combine field observation and fiction writing. All three have been used to teach anthropology. Students enjoy *Return to Laughter* because of its narrative appeal; professors do not hesitate to use it as a text, because they think it validly portrays experiences of fieldwork and validly describes features of a particular society.

Pseudo-anthropology is also a thriving field; so a great many books could be assigned to the invalid-inauthentic cell of the table. I have chosen one outstanding example, Erich von Däniken's *Gold of the Gods*, a tale of archaeological discovery in South America. "To me," writes von Däniken, "this is the most incredible, fantastic story of the century. It could easily have come straight from the realms of Science Fiction if I had not seen and photographed the incredible truth in person."

In 1972, von Däniken claims, explorer Juan Moricz personally conducted him on a tour of some tunnels 800 feet below ground, where he saw a hoard of golden artifacts, of which some samples had also been collected at Cuenca, Ecuador, by a priest named Crespi. Challenging the authenticity of von Däniken's story, Moricz himself later said he had never taken von Däniken through the tunnels but had only told him about them. Challenging its validity, archaeologist Pino Turolla said the eccentric Father Crespi's "priceless artefacts" were mere junk made by local Indian smiths out of materials such as the copper toilet bowl float Turolla spotted in the collection. Moricz's expedition to the caves had found stone carvings but none of the gold promised by a long-standing legend. If von Däniken did not visit the tunnels, his story is inauthentic; if there was no gold in the tunnels, his story is invalid as well (assuming a skeptical theory of El Dorado legends).

The ease with which one can assign many works to the like-signed

(++ and − −) cells of the table may give an impression of strong positive correlation between validity and authenticity, but I think the impression is wrong. Working against such a correlation is the general fallibility of theories and (to a lesser extent) of documented observations, both of which are frequently contradicted by accurate new observations they did not predict. More pertinent to an essay on Castaneda is the fact that any writer of an inauthentic report, whether he is a hoaxer or some less flamboyant cheater, does well to include as much valid material as he can, from whatever source, to make his report more plausible to such informed readers as professional colleagues or dissertation committee members. Conversely, an honest reporter is bound to make some mistakes and can easily make a lot of them. The weakness of theory, the existence of cheaters, and the ubiquity of error must reduce the correlation between authenticity and validity and may reduce it to the point where prediction of individual cases is at best a waste of time.

Honest errors in reports can arise from at least two sources: misperception of events, and unsound interpretation of events correctly perceived. Neither of these bear on authenticity; both bear on validity. I shall discuss them in order.

Misperception of events is no doubt less frequent than misinterpretation of events correctly perceived, but misperception raises questions more obviously relevant to the books of Castaneda, which offer tracts on social-science interpretation under the guise of stories about an apprentice's perceptions and quasi-perceptions of at least two kinds of non-social worlds, an ordinary (though not realistic) desert world and a nonordinary world of sorcery or magical vision. Since Castaneda substitutes visualizing for conceptualizing, thus turning Sapir's social world into don Juan's natural and visionary worlds, we are obliged here to consider the hazards of misperception in social science.

A paradigmatic illustration of seeing what is not there and not seeing what is there comes reportedly from a Viennese psychiatrist, Alexander Pilcz, who documented the East Indian rope trick by recording it with a motion picture camera. As the camera turned, Pilcz and several hundred other witnesses saw the following sequence of events. A fakir and a small boy walked into their midst, and the fakir tossed a coil of rope up into the air. The rope stood by itself. The boy climbed up the rope and disappeared at the top, whence his arms, legs, trunk, and head soon fell separately to the ground. The fakir collected these remains in a basket, climbed the rope carrying the basket, and disappeared at the top. After a decent interval, the fakir and the smiling, reassembled boy descended the rope. The rope fell like a pole and shattered. The broken pieces formed themselves into a rope again. The fakir and the boy took a bow.

Like the rest of the audience, the previously skeptical Pilcz was very impressed by this performance, but when the film was later projected, it showed the following sequence of events. The fakir tossed the coil of rope up into the air, whence it promptly fell down again in the normal way. For the rest of the time, the fakir and the boy stood beside the fallen rope doing nothing at all.

In Castaneda's terms, we have here two separate realities: a nonordinary reality experienced by Pilcz and the audience during the performance, and an ordinary reality experienced by Pilcz when the film was projected. We also have an opportunity to rank them or choose between them if we like. Players of the philosophy game may decline to choose, declaring their full satisfaction with the mere existence side by side of two kinds of reality. Occultists will no doubt say the fakir didn't want his trick recorded on film, and so projected an alternative sequence of images into the camera by thoughtography; if they are well-read occultists, they will mention the name of Ted Serios, a documented thoughtographer. Scientists, including anthropologists, will be inclined to take the film version as the correct one and the experience of the audience as an hallucination; if they like vacuous explanations, they may say the hallucination was caused by mass hypnosis. Anomalists, such as parapsychologists, will take the film version as a normal standard, but they may suspect what the audience saw had some substance to it all the same, of a kind not understood by them or anyone.

Well, what actually happened? Did the rope stand stiff or fall down? Did the boy climb up or remain on the ground? To answer such questions one needs a reality framework, and one needs to prefer that framework to any other. Though metaphysicians may declare they cannot answer such questions, practical people have no difficulty answering them. First, however, one must subscribe to the reality framework that is most familiar to everyone, Castaneda's ordinary reality, which philosophers William James and, later, Alfred Schutz called the "paramount reality." I have called it the "boss reality," because if you don't do what it wants you to do, it will knock you flat, and eventually it will knock you flat whether you do what it wants you to or not. Don Quixote's giants were Sancho Panza's windmills, but either way they unhorsed Quixote.

However much they may like to contemplate standing ropes, flailing giants, or heads turning into crows, scientists have to keep at least one eye on Pilcz's film, Panza's windmills, or the ordinary world of Carlos-Skeptic. The rules of science require them to ground any investigation in the ordinary, communicable reality, as Castaneda purported to do when he assigned calendar dates to the events in his imaginary fieldwork. Scientists are not forbidden to study or enter alternative realities but only required to tie their research at some points to the ordinary world. Apparent hallucinations like the rope trick and apparent anomalies or paranormal events like ESP and psychokinesis are quite acceptable objects for scientific study. Charles Tart even proposes that drugged or hypnotized experimenters might sometimes succeed where those in normal states of consciousness have failed. But whatever phenomena science approaches and whatever means it uses, its procedures and reports must to some extent be grounded in the ordinary reality. "The closed subuniverse of scientific reality," wrote Alfred Schutz, "although necessarily different from that of common sense, of everyday life is, also necessarily, tied to the process of empirical verification within the common-sense world in which we live and which we take for granted as our paramount reality." If a report is to have any authenticity, the narrator must have known in the ordinary way who conducted the experiment or observation, where it was conducted, and what means were used. To take an extreme example, a report of a dream must include the information that it was a dream; a dream reported as fieldwork is not authentic.

The fact that these points need to be discussed at all shows the recent influence of phenomenology, reintroducing the old idea that private thoughts are data for social science. Contemporary phenomenologists may object to this simple characterization of their methods, but I think some such conception has rendered certain social scientists incapable of distinguishing—or has helped them to avoid distinguishing—Castaneda's allegories from legitimate field reports. An erstwhile member of one of his graduate committees and still his stout defender, Theodore Graves said, "Castaneda's purpose was *not* to write factual ethnography but to convey the subjective experience of confronting a radical challenge to his notions of reality." Does this mean, I asked, that the don Juan story is creative writing having no necessary connection with an actual old Indian? No, he replied, though Castaneda organized, interpreted, and presented his facts creatively, he is a factual reporter. A few more factual reporters like that, and social science will be finished. In offering his cultural materialism as the paradigm for social science, Marvin Harris found Castaneda the perfect club with which to belabor phenomenologists. By doing fieldwork in his head for fourteen years,

Castaneda became the phenomenologist to end phenomenology.

Despite a renewed interest in what is real and how to recognize it, a more likely source of error and target of criticism is still the misinterpretation of ordinary events correctly perceived. Colin Turnbull's *The Mountain People* is a famous target, which I have assigned to the invalid-authentic cell of the table. Turnbull lived in Uganda with a starving tribe called the Ik, whose behavior he found utterly repulsive. The experience distressed him deeply, and he wrote a very successful book about it, which told the story of his distress and described the horrible life of the Ik.

The Mountain People is authentic because nobody has said Turnbull invented his observations. Fredrik Barth did accuse him of creating "a systematically false record" of his fieldwork, but Turnbull indignantly and successfully rebutted that charge, while Grant McCall wrote: "I do not wish . . . to imply . . . that I believe it to be a fiction. I am not . . . questioning the observations that he makes, or his competence to record them. Where I differ from Turnbull is in the interpretation of these data."

Turnbull admits he was baffled by the Ik. Their suffering laughter seemed bizarre to him. "I am simply not qualified to assess it," he wrote; "all I have done is to attempt to describe it." Having said, as an interpretation of the way he saw them living together, that the Ik had "no culture," Turnbull then granted that their gregariousness and laughter might have been signs of culture he had failed to grasp. "I . . . have been in other pretty trying circumstances," he said, "but have never quite lost my anthropological cool as I did with the Ik."

Though Turnbull's critics said his book painted an invalid portrait of the Ik, some of them praised him for giving a picture both authentic *and* valid of the trouble a fieldworker can get into and the emotional turmoil he may have to endure. More than that, some said all fieldwork is fraught with difficulties like Turnbull's, if usually less severe, and they admired his courageous exposure of trials and shortcomings common to all fieldworkers. A. K. Mark gave Turnbull and Castaneda similar credit for examining the fieldworker as closely as the informant; Carlos-Skeptic's perennial quandaries were likened to Turnbull's frank confessions. On a less positive note, Vincent Crapanzano dismissed Turnbull and Castaneda as shallow popularizers duped by idioms of the age, Turnbull by "facile politics," Castaneda by "the 'heavy' mysticism of the young drop-out." Beyond such similarities Mark and Crapanzano overlooked an important dissimilarity. Turnbull's fieldwork was conducted in the ordinary world, and a film of it by Professor Pilcz would have shown the Ik. Carlos's fieldwork was conducted in a world of fantasy, and a documentary film of Castaneda's life from 1960 to 1974 would not have shown don Juan. With the exception of those who will say don Juan could make himself invisible to Pilcz's camera, this brings us to the fourth cell of the table, where Castaneda's first three books are (perhaps too favorably, but necessarily for this discussion) classified as valid-inauthentic. I omit his fourth and fifth books, which are anthropologically less valid.

Castaneda's inauthenticity has been, I think, conclusively established in various ways by me and Hans Sebald. Contradictions within the supposed field reports, and between the reports and the desert environment they claim, convince most readers that the story did not arise from the persons, places, and procedures it describes. Additional evidence comes from many instances (listed in the Alleglossary) of obvious foraging in other people's published works. By now the more interesting question is how much and what kinds of validity the don Juan books have.

One has little difficulty finding valid ethnographic content in Castaneda's initial trilogy, some of which apparently derives from the very books by Opler and Myerhoff that occupy the valid-authentic cell of the table. Looking at the name Opler in the Alleglossary, we see ten items listed, of which those titled Campfire and Place demonstrate literary influence, while those titled Enemies, Gesture, Guardian, Power, and Rule contain ideas found in the trilogy, though they may fall short of proving imitation. Walter Goldschmidt was very impressed by don Juan's parable about the four enemies of a man of knowledge. While I think Goldschmidt should have felt more skepticism about don Juan's authenticity, or should have been more frank about the skepticism he felt, I recognize that the similarity between Opler's and don Juan's treatment of fear, clarity, power, and old age, which readily confirms the suspicions of a skeptic like me, can equally bolster the confidence of a believer (perhaps like Goldschmidt) when taken as signs not of imitation but of cultural diffusion or universal mind.

Turning to the name Myerhoff, we see 17 items listed, of which ten are common to Castaneda's trilogy and *Peyote Hunt*. None is particularly evidential, which helps to explain why Myerhoff, before reading *Castaneda's Journey*, found confirmations of her own work in the trilogy rather than imitations. When she read *Tales of Power*, however, Myerhoff was offended by what Castaneda had done with tonal and nagual, "two beautiful indigenous concepts" she thought he had utterly perverted. To Indians, tonal and nagual are fateful or metamorphic animals; to don Juan they are quasi-Buddhist notions of potentiality and actuality, or latency and manifestion. The nothing (nagual) that creates the something (tonal) is recognizably an East Indian idea. In Amerindian cultures, the world is explained as a product of transformation, not of creation *ex nihilo*; nature is fashioned out of dust by a superhuman potter, not manifested out of nothing by an indescribable principle. Encountering don Juan's oriental abstractions in *Tales of Power*, some formerly sympathetic anthropologists sadly concluded Castaneda had abandoned legitimate anthropology for phony mysticism, while at the same time mystically inclined readers were rejoicing over don Juan's finally getting down to business and giving them the true teachings. Whether a report is valid or not depends on the theory to which it is referred.

Much earlier, skeptical anthropologists had discovered invalid ethnographic contents in the trilogy as well. Most obvious was the so-called Yaqui way of knowledge spuriously offered by the subtitle of *The Teachings*. Despite authoritative declarations by Yaqui specialists Edward Spicer, Ralph Beals, and Jane Holden Kelley that the don Juan story had nothing to do with Yaqui culture, the Yaqui misnomer refused to die. Non-anthropologists and careless anthropologists went on and on referring to don Juan as "an old Yaqui sorcerer," and as late as 1977 the *American Anthropologist* complaisantly reproduced Simon and Schuster's full-page advertisement calling *The Teachings* and *A Separate Reality* studies of "religious practices of the Yaqui Indians," which they certainly are not. Castaneda's disingenuous disclaimers of any intent to suggest don Juan's way of knowledge was really a Yaqui way made the misnomer all the more inexcusable, both originally and in perpetuity.

Where did the misnomer come from? I should guess don Juan's vague connection with the Yaqui tribe was a device for superficially imitating genuine ethnography while getting round certain requirements such as travel to the field and burdensome cultural descriptions. The Yaquis were not so far away that an impoverished student might not claim to visit them in his automobile. When his first committee chairman, Ralph Beals, grew leery of thousand-mile weekend round trips, Castaneda simply abandoned him and went looking for a less critical chairman. As for cultural incongruities, the Yaquis had been exiled from their homeland for many years, so don Juan might have picked up all sorts of non-Yaqui knowledge during his travels in other parts of Mexico. Tolerance of the Yaqui misnomer by the University of California Press is harder to explain, but I shall try to make sense of it in a later chapter.

Next is don Juan's so-called sorcery. If the old wizard wants to call himself a *brujo* (sorcerer) or even a stockholder, that is his idiosyncratic privilege, but when Castaneda calls him a sorcerer, that is a scholarly or perhaps anti-scholarly error. As Beals made clear, don Juan is not a sorcerer in any accepted anthropological sense. Sorcerers are feared and hated by other members of their community because they employ evil spirits or magical projectiles to make people sick; don Juan is a hermit who has no enemies and employs his plant allies to discover other worlds and ontological essences. Far from being a sorcerer, he is a rather benign, mystical magician.

Other errors can be listed. Indians do not "sew" lizards with agave fiber and cholla thorn. Before *The Teachings*, they refrained from smoking mushrooms. Indians do not quote Lama Govinda on trance running and, so far as anyone knows, have not learned to levitate beside waterfalls by means of tractor beams projecting from the solar-plexus chakra. They don't bother to stalk rabbits bare handed, and they don't call peyote "mescal."

In view of such fallacies, the reader may think it unfair to classify Castaneda's trilogy as valid while Turnbull must languish among the invalids. I justify this merely illustrative classification in the following way: considering Turnbull's professional respectability and actual fieldwork, *The Mountain People* is surprisingly invalid; considering Castaneda's hoaxing and don Juan's insubstantiality, the trilogy is surprisingly valid, as a reading of the Alleglossary will show. The same cannot be said of *Tales of Power* or *Second Ring*, whose crude distortions of Amerindian culture belong with von Däniken's priceless toilet float. Whether *Tales* or *Ring* deserve any credit as valid mystical writing is another question; later in this volume Agehananda Bharati will sound a thundering *No*, while Philip Staniford croons a mellow *Yes*.

What are the hazards of prediction between authenticity and validity? Having no actuarial tables, I can offer only my common sense opinions. Within the constraints imposed by weakness of theory and ubiquity of error, a report accepted as authentic has a fair chance of being generally valid. Conversely, since hoaxers and other consistent cheaters who can produce convincing reports are greatly outnumbered by reasonably honest reporters, a report accepted as valid is likely to be authentic. This sounds reassuring, but it means that skillful hoaxers and cheaters will be accepted along with the honest reporters. Castaneda profited from this ambiguity.

A report judged inauthentic (from evidence bearing directly on authenticity) may be filled with garbage like *Gold of the Gods* or only larded with it like Castaneda's trilogy. An inauthentic report is not likely to be generally valid; reporters who misrepresent their sources will not hesitate, when it suits them, to distort their sources' information.

These three kinds of prediction, if made at all, have little utility. Maybe Indians smoke mushrooms, maybe they don't. Neither certain knowledge that Castaneda is a hoaxer nor firm belief that he is not can give us the answer. Conversely, Castaneda may be an honest reporter, but his correct assertion that sorcerers try to steal each other's souls does not prove him honest; he may have read about soul stealing in Michael Harner's "Jivaro Souls." The one prediction I put stock in is predicting inauthenticity from invalidity in those cases where many invalid observations (rather than interpretations) are found. Later in this volume, Robert Carneiro carries out this exercise while debunking a popular adventure tale called *Wizard of the Upper Amazon*. Carneiro succeeds because he has a lot of prior information that bears on validity and finds in the book many observations that contradict his prior information. He concludes the adventurer was a liar.

Owing to the general weakness of theory, even this fourth kind of prediction can lead one astray. Elsa First's naïve skeptics rejected the don Juan books because they reported paranormal events. If ESP and psychokinesis are self-evidently absurd, the books can be judged inauthentic (or perhaps merely invalid, where an honest observer may have been fooled) because of this absurd content. But if ESP and psychokinesis are not absurd, don Juan could be debunked for the wrong reason.

To help in such assessments, sociologist Marcello Truzzi systematically distinguishes narrators, narratives, and events. *Narrators* can be *credible* like Opler, Myerhoff, Bowen, and Turnbull or *noncredible* like Castaneda and von Däniken. *Narratives* can be *plausible* like (for the most part) *The Teachings of Don Juan* or *implausible* like *A Separate Reality* (which readers attuned to story-telling quickly recognized as fiction because of the manner in which the story was told). *Events* can be *ordinary* like Professor Pilcz's film of the rope falling down or *extraordinary* like his vision of the rope standing up. The three dimensions are formally independent.

Applying Truzzi's scheme to the don Juan books, one can say that in 1968 a credible Castaneda published a fairly plausible *Teachings* describing the ordinary existence of a rather unusual hermit. In 1977 a notoriously noncredible Castaneda published a somewhat implausible *Second Ring of Power* describing very extraordinary events, such as materializations, levitations, and out-of-body combat. During those ten years Castaneda grew less and less credible as more and more of his autobiographical anecdotes contradicted independent records and each other. His trilogy was widely reclassified as implausible when *Castaneda's Journey* analyzed its internal contradictions. His tales grew more and more extraordinary as he turned away from anthropology and toward occultism. It is instructive to note, however, that *Second Ring*, his most occult book, is implausible not because of its very extraordinary events but because of a few minor contradictions in the text. The trilogy, which contains many more contradictions than *Second Ring*, is therefore much less plausible, as an account. Application of Truzzi's scheme should reduce errors of naïve skepticism and naïve subscription alike.

Discussing validity and authenticity for months with various Juanists and Castanedists, I have met some typical objections, which I shall now list, along with my answers.

1. *Inventiveness is limited*. Much of what Castaneda claims must actually have happened to him, because no one could invent such outlandish adventures. *Answer*: The objector is obviously not a reader of fantasy or science fiction. Arthur C. Clarke has not been to the moon, but he did write *2001*; astronauts have been there but did not write it. *A Voyage to Arcturus* is far more outlandish than *Tales of Power* or *Second Ring*, yet no one believes David Lindsay went to Arcturus or had the visions he describes, except as a writer has visions. After reading the potsherd of Amenartas telling of the pillar of fire that brings eternal youth to the queen who stands in its flames, L. Horace Holley, fictive narrator of *She, A History of Adventure*, says: "My first idea [was] that my poor friend, when demented, had composed the whole tale, though it scarcely seemed likely that such a story could have been invented by anybody. It was too original." "The idea that I concocted a person like don Juan is inconceivable," Castaneda said. "He is hardly the kind of figure my European intellectual tradition would have led me to invent. The truth is much stranger. I didn't create anything. I am only a reporter." In the tradition of fantasy writing, Castaneda voices straight-faced doubts that anyone could invent the marvellous tale he has just invented.

2. *Castaneda is in good company*. Colin Turnbull writes imaginatively, but no one has accused him of making up his data. *Answer*: My point exactly: no one has accused Turnbull, many have accused Castaneda. While both have been praised as bringers of truth and condemned as purveyors of falsity, Turnbull has been praised for authenticity and condemned for invalidity, whereas Castaneda has been praised

for validity and condemned for inauthenticity. One is accused of honest mistakes, the other of slyly hiding his sources.

3. *Fact is fiction*. Since both informants and fieldworkers are rather unreliable, no ethnography is strictly factual. *Answer*: Error, misinterpretation, and fudging are not the same thing as gross fabrication. A tolerable degree of spuriosity can be distinguished from an intolerable degree. The don Juan books are accused not of being unstrictly factual but of being strictly unfactual.

4. *Castaneda's basic claims have not been disproved*. We have no conclusive evidence that Castaneda has not experienced odd events. *Answer*: Neither have we conclusive proof that the mysterious white man who two-thousand years ago walked from tribe to tribe throughout America healing the sick, raising the dead, and teaching Jesus' gospel in a thousand languages was not in fact Jesus. The objection puts the burden of proof not on Castaneda, where it belongs, but on the community of scholars, where it does not belong.

5. *In some form or other, don Juan could exist*. It doesn't matter if don Juan was not exactly as he appears in the books. Castaneda could have had one or more teachers whose essence he portrayed in the figure of don Juan. *Answer*: The vaguer don Juan becomes, the more likely his existence. If he was just an ordinary man Castaneda met, then certainly he exists. The don Juan books, however, are not at all vague. They are exact, and for purposes of science at least must be judged in their exactness. The only don Juan we know is the one Castaneda gave us. If he is really a combination of María Sabina, Suzuki, and Ramón Medina, one is better off reading *Mushrooms, Russia, and History*, *What is Zen?* and *Peyote Hunt*.

6. *No coin has only one side*. Insofar as the don Juan books are valid, they must have arisen from authentic observation and are, in that sense, authentic. Validity cannot be divorced from authenticity. *Answer*: Distinguishing wives from husbands is not divorcing them. Seed cannot be divorced from flower, yet anyone can sort seeds from flowers without error. To say, correctly, that authenticity and validity are not completely independent is not to say we cannot formally distinguish them as components of truthfulness and assess them by different tests. When information is sparse, we may not be able to test them, but that is not an excuse for discarding the categories or the tests. Error terms in mathematical predictions do not cause us to renounce predictions; on the contrary, they make us confident of predictions where error terms are small and cause us to look for more information where they are large.

Predictions and judgments do not have to be perfect to be worth making. Counterfeit coins have two sides, too. The don Juan books do not acquire any authenticity of their own by incorporating the valid contents of authentic books by other writers.

7. *All's fair in samadhi and satori*. Mystical experiences cannot be adequately described in factual reports. Castaneda was trying to communicate the ineffable, so he had to resort to novelistic interpretations. *Answer*: This objection confuses the ineffability of the mystical experience (which is a matter of validity, or how the experience is to be correctly described and understood) with the question whether the narrator himself actually had the experience (a matter of authenticity). However ineffable the experience, there is no intrinsic difficulty in saying whether one has had it. Saying one has had it when one has not had it is inauthentic reporting. Since so many of Castaneda's falsifiable claims have in fact been falsified (such as the claim that his chronology was authentic or the claim that his adventures occurred in the Sonoran desert), we are ill advised to gratuitously credit his unfalsifiable claims (such as claims of having mystical experiences).

8. *Fieldnotes are private*. Never in all my years as a graduate student did a member of the faculty ask to see my fieldnotes. Fieldnotes belong to the person who writes them. Castaneda had every right to keep his fieldnotes to himself. *Answer*: Fieldnotes are private in the sense that they are the literary property of the writer and are not to be published without the writer's consent. On the other hand, they are public in the sense that anyone who enters the scientific community to do research undertakes an obligation to preserve his data intact and unaltered, to submit them for examination when asked to do so by qualified colleagues with a legitimate scientific interest in them, and, if there is opportunity, to deposit them with a suitable common custodian, as in a museum or library, when he can no longer preserve them or no longer wants them. Fieldnotes are the primary data of anthropology. They are part of the scientific record. Refusal to submit them for examination violates the norms of scientific conduct and amounts to prima facie evidence of fraud. The fact that fieldnotes are sometimes (defensibly or indefensibly) taken for granted does not reduce the fieldworker's obligation to serve as their custodian in the interest of science. While your committee obviously trusted you, as most committees trust most candidates, Castaneda's first chairman grew suspicious. "I pressed him to show me some of his fieldnotes," Beals wrote, "but he became evasive and finally dropped from sight." Unlike some of his successors, Beals acted responsibly to

forestall scientific fraud. Competent, responsible examination of Castaneda's fieldnotes must have resulted in his disqualification from candidacy, or at least in the disqualification of *Journey to Ixtlan* as a dissertation reporting anthropological fieldwork, whether or not it might have been accepted on some other basis—say, as a literary work of interest to anthropologists. The committee members who did not ask to see the fieldnotes before signing what purported to be an account of fieldwork, or who examined them and found nothing wrong with them, were either negligent or, as Beals put it, naïve.

9. *Personal knowledge.* All this talk about Carlos's missing fieldnotes is asinine. I have seen them. They exist. Or did before they were destroyed when his basement flooded. I saw them in many notebooks and boxes during many wonderful hours in 1965 when Carlos and I were discussing both his apprenticeship to don Juan and my fieldwork among the Scotoma tribe, which Carlos always seemed to understand better than I did, though he said he had never visited the Scotoma. Wherever I had a blind spot, Carlos instantly helped me to see through it. I will always be grateful to him, and I resent these attempts by people who have never even met him to blacken the name of a sincere, studious, gifted man with accusations of fraud that must be motivated more by a desire to make a fast buck out of a bad book than to make any contribution to knowledge. *Answer*: By 1965 Castaneda had been working on his opus for five years. His habit was to write in notebooks, so by 1965 he had a pretty big collection of them. Since he was writing about imaginary fieldwork, his manuscript looked a lot like fieldnotes. As far as I have been able to discover, however, only 12 pages of those fieldnotes have ever been examined by a skeptic, the pages he sent to Gordon Wasson, which I shall examine again in Chapter 40. Here I need only say that those pages correspond with certain passages of *The Teachings* in just the way an early version of an invented story corresponds with a later version. No careful, informed examiner would have taken them for fieldnotes. You were inexperienced in those days and had no reason to doubt Castaneda's sincerity, but now you have an opportunity to realize that you have known one of the great hoaxers of the century.

10. *Subjectivity is science.* Some who are convinced that *Journey to Ixtlan* describes imaginary events accuse Castaneda of professional malpractice in offering the book as a dissertation, but they do not understand the latitude of science. It would be malpractice only if he did not *intend* to give an honest account of events *as he experienced them*. The entire text could be the product of a psychotic episode and still be an acceptable

phenomenological account. De Mille's proof that the events are imaginary is, in my opinion, a purely speculative web of inference, but even if Castaneda's committee had read the argument in 1972 and been convinced by it, they could not have proved an intent to deceive. Castaneda could still have believed he was telling the truth, and therefore, *would* have been telling the truth, about what he experienced. *Answer*: Phenomenological accounts may be useful in science, but their use does not abrogate the rule that a scientific report must somewhere be tied to ordinary reality. Though they may be of interest to scientists and may deserve academic recognition in some special category, subjective accounts that have no explicit objective framework at all are not scientific reports and should not be confused with or endorsed as scientific reports by doctoral committees. If Castaneda's committee suspected he was a gifted madman, they should not have treated what they thought were his ravings as though they were simply another sober report from a sane fieldworker. Nor was it their duty to prove him either psychotic or dishonest; the burden of proof was on him. The contradictions between *Teachings* and *Ixtlan* were sufficient grounds for disqualifying the dissertation as a scientific report.

11. *Fiction is truer than fact*. Fictionalized treatments add dimensions of truth that factual reports inevitably lack. *Answer*: This is a fashionable but tricky proposition. Rodney Needham urged fellow ethnographers to strive for the empathic penetration and literary discipline displayed in novels by George Eliot, Gorki, and Dostoyevsky. Thus, he said, their interpretations might partake of the humane significance imaginatively sought in art and metaphysics. Despite "professional misgivings on ethnographic grounds," Needham found in *The Teachings* "a remarkable example" of such striving, exhibiting "a gift that is peculiarly apt" to the interpretation of alien forms of experience. As the novelist needs to observe like an ethnographer, so the ethnographer needs to write like a novelist, if he is to capture the elusive, fragile, mythic cultural products of the archetypical unconscious mind. By seeming to fulfill such aspirations, Castaneda elicited praise from at least two outstanding anthropologists, first a rather reckless endorsement from Mary Douglas, later the circumspect appreciation of Rodney Needham. Though I will readily agree that Dostoyevsky is a more sensitive interpreter of human behavior than the typical scientific anthropologist, many fiction writers distort behavior as much as they portray it. Bowen and Castaneda both wrote fiction, but we have no reason to assume their fictions are equally true to life. Castaneda's cultural cargo is a collection of oddities whimsi-

Soul Catcher

cally adapted from several disparate traditions. His dramatic personages are broad caricatures synthesized "for didactic reasons." Don Juan embodies not only the animistic, concrete thinker I call "don Indian" but also the academic abstractionist I call "the Indian don." An allegorical struggle between direct knowledge and rational discourse is frozen solid for ten years, as Carlos-Apprentice and Carlos-Skeptic fail to merge into one person. While Castaneda offered this miracle play as a factual memoir, Laura Bohannan (writing as Elenore Bowen) turned her ethnography into fiction. If she had then published her novel as a factual report, she would have gained nothing in validity but lost everything in authenticity. Eventually her book would have wound up in a bin with many other novels masquerading as history. False true-stories are, of course, inauthentic by definition. Beyond that, as Clifford Irving, David Rorvik, and Jay Anson have amply shown, they are often also massively invalid: bad company for a good book like *Return to Laughter*.

While novels as well as ethnography can be both valid and authentic, novelistic ethnography raises questions about trustworthiness and utility. The reader is not sure what kind of information he is getting. If, for example, I toss off a few cocktail comments about babies playing with scorpions, your ears will prick up and you will immediately wish to be told whether I am novelistically evoking the fact that babies often engage in dangerous play, or trying to warn you without alarming the other guests that I can see your very own baby sitting this minute on the flagstones in the garden playing with something that looks to me very much as though it might be a scorpion. In the one case, you will sit back in your chair to hear the rest of my ruminations; in the other, you will leap to your feet and rush to save the baby. Such distinctions matter. If don Juan ever existed, some anthropologist besides Castaneda should look into his existence, or into the existence of similar novel sources of ancient wisdom. If don Juan is a device for our allegorical instruction, fieldtrips to find him can be left to hippies and other enthusiasts.

Scientists need to know whether they are dealing with credible or noncredible reporters. "Is this writer a liar?" is neither a trivial question nor one that should be evaded by appeals to the ineffability of mystical experience, the universality of phenomena, cultural diffusion, the truthfulness of novels, or the problem of subjectivity in the philosophy of science. It is a question scientists must sometimes ask if they don't wish to be led astray.

Castaneda is a fit object of such questioning, for though he collects valid ethnic elements, he likes to play around with them. For instance,

Bow Drum

his *spirit-catcher*, a loop of cord don Juan plucks to call out the spirit of the waterhole, combines the two devices shown here in illustrations: the *soul-catcher*, a loop of rope a shaman carries to collar wandering souls, and the *bow drum*, a musical bow and arrow with which Ramón Medina warned the invisible ancient ones that a party of *peyoteros* was approaching. Such literary invention may be art, but it is neither science nor valid ethnography. The fact that a handful of specialists can see through don Juan's spirit-catcher to the original elements beneath will not help a myriad of trusting undergraduates who learn from Castaneda's books about a supposed community of mystical magicians quaintly miscalling themselves sorcerers and wandering around an air-conditioned desert positing koans and twanging their loops.

As validity comes originally from authenticity, so invalidity springs often, if unpredictably, from inauthenticity. Coyote is a tricky teacher. "In parts, at least, of California," wrote Hartley Burr Alexander, "his deeds are represented as almost invariably beneficent in their outcomes; he is a true, if often unintentional culture hero." To keep the California faith, then, let me add that, intentionally or not, by forcing us to look anew into the subtle relationships between validity and authenticity, Castaneda has made a substantial contribution to social science. From these ideas, one might even say, we are likely to get advances in anthropology

Ethnomethodallegory:
Garfinkeling in the Wilderness

When Carlos got back from his first five years in don Juan's desert, Castaneda prepared a deadly dull academic explanation of what had happened there and tacked it onto the end of *The Teachings*. Not realizing it was part of the story, University Press editors begged him to get rid of it, but he refused to strike out a single boring, repetitive line. Reading this "Structural Analysis," Mary Douglas recognized "the ethnomethodologists' programme laid out in classical simplicity," having been drafted, she presumed, by Castaneda's university teachers. "As a piece of anthropological research," Douglass McFerran wrote of *The Teachings*, "it marks a significant effort to apply the phenomenologically oriented techniques of ethnomethodology . . . ."

Anthropologist C. Scott Littleton was led to believe his friend Castaneda's fifth book would "analyze don Juan's world view from an explicitly phenomenological and ethnomethodological standpoint." As it turned out, *The Second Ring of Power* said nothing academic, but digressed into Carlos's ascetic dalliance with the four weird sisters. If there was anything phenomenological or ethnomethodological in the book, it was strictly allegorical. Despite this incorrigible story-telling, Hans Peter Duerr referred to don Juan's chronicler as "the ethnomethodologist Castaneda." What, then, is an "ethnomethodologist," and why does Duerr think Castaneda is one?

Ethnomethodology was created by Harold Garfinkel, a sociology professor at UCLA from 1954 and one of five faculty members to sign Carlos Castaneda's dissertation. Beginning as a critique of sociological practice, Garfinkel's creation developed into something more or less independent of sociology, whether one would call it a discipline, a speciality, a sect, a cult, a rebellion, or a conspiracy to destroy social science from within. The central idea of ethnomethodology was that every kind of reality was a subjective, or at least "intersubjective," achievement of people talking about things. The fundamental practice was to question what usually went unquestioned, to make a problem of what had been unproblematical. The chief target of the questioning was sociology. Whereas sociologists asked how members of society went about their business, ethnomethodologists asked how sociologists went about their business.

Before completing his graduate work at Harvard, Garfinkel had visited the New School of Social Research to study with Alfred Schutz, who thereby became the conceptual grandfather of ethnomethodology. Schutz defined "intersubjective" reality as a "world of the We," a world not private though subjective, a world constituted in face-to-face exchanges between people who lived in the same physical and social environment. So situated, this shared subjective world could be constantly corrected by new readings of the environment, which kept it stable and dependable. Other realities were possible if the normal assumptions were suspended, worlds of special interest or make-believe, but most people returned to and depended on the normal world of the We, the commonsense reality of everyday life.

The virtues of the grandfathers are not necessarily bestowed upon the grandsons. Though Schutz had said the commonsense reality was paramount, some ethnomethodologists would not be so constrained. "My view of realities is different," wrote Hugh Mehan and Houston Wood. "I do not wish to call one or another reality paramount. It is my contention that every reality is equally real. No single reality contains more of the truth than any other." On this view, commonsense reality and scientific theorizing are not to be preferred to shared fantasies even by social scientists. All are constructed moment-to-moment by what people say to each other. What people say, in turn, depends on shared assumptions hidden in what they do not say but indicated by what they do say, if you follow me. Commonsense and scientific realities may seem stable and even objective (as though "out there" in front of us, like the physical and social environment we assume must also be out there to be subjectively read by us) but that is only because the assumptions on which they precariously rest are completely taken for granted. Call those assumptions into question, and you will quickly see how fragile are commonsense and scientific reality.

Garfinkel thought up some diabolical schemes for calling assumptions into question, techniques labelled "breaching" procedures because they tore holes in people's shared understandings and disrupted their social relations. Students were sent home on vacation with instructions to act like boarders. They were told to conduct conversations as though they suspected the other person were trying to trick or mislead them. They learned to talk with people whose noses their noses were almost touching. They were authorized to mistake people's social roles, like persis-

tently demanding a table in a full restaurant from a person who was only
another unseated customer. And, in a technique that was soon dubbed
"garfinkeling" on the UCLA campus, students were taught to pretend
they didn't know the meanings of ordinary words:

> "I think I just flunked an exam."
> "Flunked?"
> "Yeah. The midterm."
> "What do you mean, flunked?"
> "I flunked the damn midterm!"
> "Could you explain that?"
> "You know what flunking an exam is, don't you?"
> "I don't know what *you* mean by it."
> "I mean what everybody means by it."
> "What's that?"
> "What's eating you, anyway?"
> "How do you mean, eating?"
> "Why are you asking me these stupid questions?"
> "What do you mean, stupid?"
> "I mean *you*, stupid! See you around!"

Not all of the victims of breaching experiments got mad. "Bewilderment,
uncertainty, internal conflict, psycho-sexual isolation, acute and nameless anxiety along with various symptoms of acute depersonalization"
were the results Garfinkel expected and his students often achieved.
Families were thrown into chaos, youthful romances destroyed, delicate
mental balances tipped. This, however, was only a technique, whose
purpose was to teach the breachers that human interactions, particularly
conversations, depended on shared but unstatable assumptions. The procedure consisted largely of pressing people to state the unstatable in so
many words. The victims got upset, but the breachers learned their lesson.

Which was then applied to sociology. Ethnomethodologists said that in
going about their professional business sociologists depended on a lot of
assumptions they couldn't state in so many words. Hearing that, some
sociologists got mad and called ethnomethodology a new name for old
practices, an incoherent incompetency, a trivial sham, a meaningless
blur, a blot on science, another lunacy from the Golden State, an idiotic
perversion, a sadistic atrocity, and various less complimentary things.
After they cooled down a bit, they also said they could *so* state their

assumptions, and if they couldn't it didn't matter, because their assumptions were realistic and had always worked for them, enabling them to go about their business with no trouble at all, at least until the ethnomethodologists came along. The dispute is still simmering, but today ethnomethodology has grown in size and subtlety, adopted aliases, and seeped into the cracks of social science, so that it is no longer so obvious and irritating.

In the days when it was irritating indeed, Arnold Mandell, now a brain scientist and author of readable, self-revealing books, subjected himself to an academic apprenticeship under Harold Garfinkel of which he hated every minute. Some years later he conjectured that making up field reports might be one way to satisfy Garfinkel's insistence that the realities reported by social scientists are not discovered "out there" in the world but "achieved" as meaning is achieved by two people having a conversation. Mandell thought don Juan might be the perfect example of such achievement, a separate social-science reality manufactured out of imaginary conversations to fulfill Garfinkel's expectations. "Outgarfinkeling Garfinkel," he called it.

Such was Mandell's theory, and I subscribed to it at the time, but it left certain questions open. Did Garfinkel know he was being garfinkeled, or did he believe Castaneda's story because it fulfilled his expectations? Was he a dupe or a trickster? "Perhaps," wrote Stephen Murray, a contributor to this volume, "the whole cycle of don Juan books is a giant breaching experiment, showing how trust allows invention to be taken as ethnography." That was my view when I wrote Castaneda's Journey, but now I'm not so sure. In a dim light, expectations turn sleeping logs into dying monsters. Ethnomethodologists presumably suffer as many illusions as anyone else.

This came home to me from the pages of Mehan and Wood's Reality of Ethnomethodology, a quite readable first textbook on the subject, wherein a section called "The Permeability of Realities" proposes that a change of social conditions may cause a person to pass from an old reality to a new and different one, as through a permeable membrane. To illustrate this principle, the authors offer two examples from the literature, reports from the field that seem to support their hypothesis. It won't take a mystical magician to predict that one of those reports is the don Juan trilogy, and I was quite prepared for such a continuation of Garfinkel's breaching experiment, but then I encountered the other example, Tobias Schneebaum's Keep the River on Your Right.

Schneebaum, Mehan and Wood correctly state, is a painter who lives

periodically in New York; much of the time he travels the world pursuing his art. In 1955, they relate, he went to Peru, was irresistibly drawn
into the Amazon Jungle, and met the Akarama, a stone age tribe of
Indians "that had never seen a white man." I paused in my reading to
wonder at a New York painter who in the middle of the twentieth century finds a tribe that has never seen a white man. Then I began to
wonder how much checking Mehan and Wood had done on
Schneebaum's story. They do say he didn't write it until 13 years later,
but the delay seems not to worry them.

Schneebaum, they continue, learned to sleep in "bundles" with naked
tribesmen, all male, piled one on top of another to keep warm. He
learned to hunt and to speak the language. He learned to go without
clothing and to playfully touch the genitals of his companions. He went
on a cannibal raid and ate the heart of a murdered man. He watched as
one of his fellow cannibals sodomized another.

The account, say Mehan and Wood, "provides an example of a radical
shift in realities." As Schneebaum gradually adopted the Akarama reality, the moral facts changed for him, and he grew capable of things that
had been far beyond him before he entered the jungle: murder, cannibalism, homosexual display.

Deciding to check on Schneebaum's story myself, I looked for reviews
and found one by Napoleon Chagnon, known for his study of another
Amazonian tribe, the Yanomamo. Chagnon condemned Schneebaum's
book in no uncertain terms: "a highly fictionalized account, a gross and
inappropriate vilification of . . . South American Indians. . . . a macabre,
homosexual Walden." If Mehan and Wood had seen the review, they
must have disagreed with it sharply.

A few pages into *Keep the River on Your Right* I had to throw in with
Chagnon. Not only did the book exude fantasy, it seemed written literally from the first word by a man fully aware of his homosexuality and
intensely preoccupied by it. Though I did not suppose Schneebaum had
indulged in murder or cannibalism before going to Peru, it was a mystery to me how Mehan and Wood could believe going naked among
men, playfully touching their genitals, or witnessing homosexual displays had been foreign to his "reality" before he entered the jungle.

The Reality of Ethnomethodology is itself a breaching experiment, the
authors say, an attempt to introduce the reader to the possibility of
another reality. I determined to make a similar attempt. In March 1978 I
wrote a letter to Mehan citing published opinions that the works he had
adduced in support of his hypothesis were entirely or mostly fiction. I

asked whether he would currently judge them to be fact, and if not, whether he would be willing to say for the record that fictive illustrations could serve his didactic purpose as well as factual ones. My breaching experiment was not a complete success. Mehan replied in April that he would soon reply. In July I reminded him of his imminent reply, which arrived in August, saying he had to take the matter up with his co-author, in Hawaii. For all I know, they are still out there in the blue Pacific trying to figure out what to say about it.

In the meantime, I wrote to Schneebaum, telling him about Mehan and Wood and asking how long he had known he was homosexual. His answer, which follows this chapter, says homosexuality has been a part of his life since earliest childhood, overtly expressible several years before his trip to Peru. It has not, however, been the only thing on his mind. A recent memoir reveals that at the age of six or seven Schneebaum fell in love with the Wild Man of Borneo, seen in a sideshow. "That he might kill or cannibalize me did not occur to me; or if it did, it occurred as a hope, a suggestion that always underlay the strength and virilness that I expected from him." The men of Peru, Schneebaum confides, "committed the violence I had originally wished for: They killed men . . . ." Zulus, he writes, were "known to trap and mutilate all whites, tearing off their genitals and eating them to gain the white man's strength and magic. But I wanted it reversed; I wanted the wild man inside me, masticated, swallowed, absorbed." So in addition to homosexual display, it turns out murder and cannibalism were also part of Schneebaum's private reality long before he went to Peru, a fact Mehan and Wood should have suspected long before finishing his book. The uninhibited jungle pals Schneebaum describes fit perfectly into his fantasies of the previous 28 years. To illustrate a radical shift of realities Mehan and Wood needed a diary of life among the Akarama kept by someone who had *not* habitually daydreamed since childhood about homosexual display, murder, and cannibalism. Such a diary could be kept, of course, only if life among the Akarama was not itself just one more of Schneebaum's daydreams. Having conducted fieldwork since 1971 in the eight communities of the Amarakaeri (Schneebaum's "Akarama"), Thomas R. Moore presents the following evidence that Schneebaum's story is but slightly more factual than Mehan and Wood's alternative exhibit, the don Juan allegory:

> Tobias Schneebaum visited the Dominican mission, then at the juncture of the Pantiacolla and Alto Madre de Dios Rivers, in 1956, a time when some Amarakaeri were beginning to come to

the mission. During one of my visits, several Amarakaeri, as well as a Wachipaeri who had served as Schneebaum's interpreter, recalled his presence there and spoke of it to me. Identifiable Amarakaeri, Wachipaeri, and Machiguenga individuals appear in the text and photographs of *Keep the River on Your Right*, and the priest and medical missionary are recognizable historical figures. Many of the descriptive references are accurate, some with changes of name. Schneebaum provided the American Museum of Natural History with some Amarakaeri artifacts and generally accurate ethnographic notes.

On the other hand, *Keep the River on Your Right* is neither an ethnological study nor an accurate factual account, as Schneebaum himself makes clear. Though he says the story is "based on what I witnessed, heard, and lived through," he also says: "There will be no pretense of objectivity here. My memory is faulty, my mind continues as always to accept only the thoughts that pass through its narrow channel." Moreover, in the mass-market edition, Schneebaum added a further disclaimer: "This book is not an attempt at an anthropological account of a tribe, but a record of my own becoming."

There is no evidence for Amarakaeri cannibalism. Raids, frequent at the time of Schneebaum's visit, were to obtain women or garden produce; killing was rare and usually unintentional. The character Schneebaum calls "Manolo" and reports beheaded and probably cannibalized was living in Ayacucho in the early 1960s. The sleeping arrangements and homosexual practices Schneebaum describes are not part of the Amarakaeri tradition.

However accurate a picture it may be of Tobias Schneebaum's inner life, Mehan and Wood had plenty of opportunity to detect in *Keep the River on Your Right* a document most anthropologists and no doubt most sociologists would quickly reject as factually spurious or at best scientifically worthless. No matter how little they may have known about jungle tribesmen or urban homosexuals, or bothered about the opinions of Amazonian ethnographers, Mehan and Wood must have noticed Schneebaum's unrestrained rhapsodizing and conspicuous disclaimers. Their uncritical acceptance of his scenario cannot be explained on grounds of carelessness or dull-wittedness, for their own book is an impassioned and skillful treatment of difficult, abstruse ideas. The explanation must come from another quarter: the history and character of ethnomethodology.

"If all the reality of social science is manufactured," wrote Arnold Mandell, "why not fabricate it all?" If the process of "achieving reality" is so much more interesting than the product achieved, why not illustrate the process with examples that have no discoverable basis in fieldwork but achieve reality solely by fantastic writing and ethnomethodological reading? If the tail of sociology be thereby twisted, so much the better.

Swallowing Schneebaum and Castaneda whole fits this model well. Mehan's reluctance to answer questions from non-ethnomethodologists fits the model too. "My ethnomethodology," the co-authors declare, "is a form of life. It is not a body of theory nor of method. . . . It is a way of working [that] enables its practitioners to enter other realities (e.g., Castaneda, 1968, 1971, 1972)." Ethnomethodology, in other words, is a separate reality. If you haven't been there, you don't know what it's like, you can't understand a description of it, and there's no point in talking to you about it.

Perhaps you think Schutz's grandsons have intercepted Garfinkel's paternal pass and are running the wrong way with it. If so, let me tell you about Agnes, the Tobias of 1958. Agnes was a nineteen-year-old, unmarried, Caucasian typist referred to the UCLA Department of Psychiatry for clinical evaluation. Agnes had long blond hair, a pretty face, a pleasant alto voice, and a tight sweater modelling a 38-inch bust. Agnes wanted a sex-change operation.

From November 1958 to August 1959 Agnes was interviewed weekly by a team comprising a psychiatrist, a psychologist, and a sociologist. The sociologist was Harold Garfinkel, who recorded 35 hours of conversation with Agnes. In March 1959 the sex-change operation was performed, penis and testicles being removed and their skin used to construct the vagina and labia Agnes had lacked to complete her feminine identity.

Agnes had been born a boy, normal so far as anyone could tell. By the age of 17, however, he was having great difficulty managing his or her social role, and by the time she or he came to UCLA she was living as a woman. Analysis of body tissues and secretions led to a medical finding that Agnes was "a unique type of a most rare disorder: testicular feminization syndrome," a condition in which male gonads secrete female hormones in sufficient quantity to develop female genitalia and eventually breasts for a person who began life as a genetic male. The uniqueness of Agnes's case consisted in her possession of penis and testes along with ample breasts, beardlessness, soft skin, and feminized pelvis. Exploratory surgery found neither uterus nor ovaries, and further tests failed to provide evidence of any extraneous tinkering, such as taking synthetic hormones. The doctors concluded Agnes was indeed a rare bird.

This rarity furnished Garfinkel an opportunity to probe the ethnomethodological hypothesis that people take it for granted other people will play either the male or the female sex role, not something mixed or in between; conversely, the hypothesis continued, in order to get along with other people who take this for granted, people tend to play only one sex role.

Agnes's interviews revealed that unexpected anatomical changes at puberty had begun to turn an apparent boy into an apparent girl. During the period when she possessed outward characteristics of both sexes—penis, testicles, breasts—Agnes had worked hard to hide her masculine features and display her feminine features. For example, she had repeatedly refused to have intercourse with a young man who wished to marry her. Garfinkel explained this behavior as an attempt to get along with people by playing only one sex role. Though her body was still androgynous, not completely female, she had switched completely to the female role to avoid occupying an intersex status that would be socially unacceptable.

Preparing his *Studies in Ethnomethodology* Garfinkel devoted 70 pages to the case of Agnes, which resembles in several ways the later ethnomethodological case of Tobias, for which it furnishes an authoritative model. In both cases, a person presumed to have been playing one kind of sex role is rather quickly made to adopt a new role by unforseen conditions, in Tobias's case a stone-age homosexual environment, in Agnes's case a pair of testicles determined to act like ovaries and a social milieu that will not permit anyone to play an intermediate sex-role. A second similarity between the cases interests me for the light it throws on the consequences of hoaxes and on the obscure equivocations of academic sophisticates: both Tobias's and Agnes's reminiscences turned out to be unreliable.

Some eight years after the sex-change operation, in October 1966, Agnes confessed to Robert J. Stoller, the psychiatrist on the UCLA clinical team, two facts previously withheld: 1) there had been *no* unexpected anatomical changes at puberty, but since she had always wanted to grow up a woman, 2) Agnes began at age 12 stealing Stilbestrol from her mother and went on taking it in massive doses throughout adolescence. Not rogue testicles but stolen female hormones had developed her 38-inch bust. "My chagrin at learning this," said Stoller, "was matched by my amusement that she could have pulled off this coup with such skill."

Agnes had also pulled the biological rug out from under Garfinkel's one-sex-role hypothesis. If she had deliberately turned herself from an apparent male into an apparent female, then she had deliberately abandoned a recognizable, acceptable, unitary sex-role for a problematical, ambiguous, intersex role. Certainly her boyfriend could not understand the explanations he was given for why they could not go to bed together, and their quarrels got worse and worse—which is no way to get along with people. When Agnes finally revealed all to him, "the affair continued on this basis." Far from supporting the one-sex-role hypothesis, Agnes had sharply contradicted it.

For some reason not made perfectly clear, it was February before Garfinkel heard the boom of this October bombshell. "In February, 1967," he wrote, "after this volume was in press, I learned from my collaborator . . . that Agnes . . . was not a biologically defective male." Though cynics may suggest Garfinkel neglected to rewrite the case then and there because of the well known academic pressure to publish or perish, I doubt such pressure had much to do with it. Garfinkel was already a full professor, notorious as the promulgator of an offensive fad; his position and his reputation such as it was were both secure. A more plausible explanation is that Garfinkel just didn't think the case needed any rewriting. If, as Mehan and Wood's choice of examples testifies, ethnomethodological data can proceed as usefully from imagination as from the field, then any case at all can stand on its own two feet even if its feet are not standing in the field. By 1970 Garfinkel himself would be citing "Yaqui shamanism" as a legitimate empirical finding, though the finding would have been achieved only by Castaneda.

Documenting his psychiatric colleague's belated discovery in a four-page appendix, Garfinkel came to some remarkably unchagrined conclusions. "This news," he wrote, "turned the article [that is, the chapter of the book in press by February 1967] into a feature of the same circumstances it reported, i.e., into a situated report." One thing to be realized about the typical statement written by Garfinkel: it has to be translated before it can be understood; but, of course, it has to be understood before it can be translated. Ethnomethodologists call this kind of difficulty "reflexivity," which means one hand washes the other. Let me do what I can with the translation.

Garfinkel is saying, I think, that when an informant lies to you and you find out about the lying, the main thing that happens is that you acquire one more illustration of how reality is achieved in conversations where truthfulness is taken for granted but not always practiced. Your lack of chagrin when you find out about the lying is called "ethnomethodological indifference."

I'm not saying Garfinkel didn't know his hypothesis had been knocked into a cocked hat. Of course he knew it. But he was not primarily interested in hypotheses, which are, after all, merely products of theorizing. It's the process of achieving reality that counts, and those 70 pages of hard going for graduate students still illustrated the process. So why not publish them? The only concession Garfinkel made to conventional social science was to say that a subsequent study would be done, using 15 hours of interviews Stoller had conducted after the confession, reviewing the original tapes and records, and re-reading the article already in press. "To mark this prospect," he said, "the original article is called *Part 1*." It is now 12 years later, and *Part 2* has yet to appear. Perhaps someday it will wash up on the Malibu beach, having drifted from Hawaii in a bottle.

"Is all this true?" I asked don Juan.

He grinned. "I have to tell you very frankly, it doesn't matter a bit whether all this is true. That's where a warrior has an advantage over the average man."He poked the fire and the sparks flew up. "The average man cares to act on things he thinks are true, and he doesn't care to act on things he thinks are not true, but a warrior acts either way."

"As a warrior, then, how should Professor Garfinkel have acted when he found out Agnes had been lying for eight years?"

Don Juan picked up the cooking stick and inspected the pieces of rattlesnake meat. "In a case like that, one should practice controlled folly." He laid the stick back over the fire.

"What is controlled folly, don Juan?"

He turned the stick a half turn to brown the other side. "According to what you have said in the past about your friend Garfinkel, I think he would call it 'ethnomethodological indifference' [*indiferencia etnometodológica*]."

My thoughts went back to a day in 1967, at the annual meeting of the American Sociological Association, in San Francisco, where Garfinkel had said: "Ethnomethodological studies describe members' accounts while abstaining from all judgments about them. We call this policy 'ethnomethodological indifference.' "

"Controlled folly," don Juan went on, "is knowing that everything is equal and therefore unimportant. A warrior knows his acts are useless, yet he proceeds as though he didn't know it."

"Like publishing the case of Agnes knowing it was based on lies?"

"Sure!" Don Juan nodded vigorously. "Why not? A warrior isn't concerned with lies. A warrior acts."

"But Garfinkel said he was going to re-think the case and publish *Part 2*. It was never published. Is that acting?"

Don Juan shook his head. "You still don't get the point. How long have you been with me now?"

"Twelve years. Please explain it to me, don Juan."

He put his face close to mine so that our noses were almost touching and spoke very slowly and distinctly.

"If your friend was living like a warrior, then he didn't have to publish *Part 2*. He could still act, because a warrior has more choices in life than an average man. A warrior can choose *doing* or *not-doing*. He decides for himself which is best. He doesn't ask anybody else. Publishing *Part 2* would have been *doing*. Not publishing it was *not-doing*. Your friend chose *not-doing*, that's all."

"There was a lot of criticism," I said.

Don Juan turned the stick again. "A warrior follows the path he chooses wherever it may lead. He doesn't care where the path will take him or when he will reach the end of it. He doesn't care what people will say about it. He cares only about the journey. He can follow his path because he is free and he is free because he follows it. Do you understand now?"

"I think so, don Juan. Is it something like academic freedom?"

Don Juan lifted the stick off the fire and bit cautiously into one of the pieces. "This meat is done," he said. Then he added: "My benefactor used to say, freedom is where you find it."

He handed me a piece of the snake meat. It tasted a lot like chuckawalla.

Garfinkel had chided the anthropologists for not specifying how they collected their fieldnotes or turned them into professionally acceptable reports. Castaneda specified that Carlos had written down "everything that was said," whether he and don Juan were cooking snakes, climbing mountains, or escaping predatory pumas. He told how blocks of Carlos's notes had been condensed for readability and arranged in coherent sequences according to selected themes like drug use or drug non-use.

Garfinkel deplored the fact that anthropologists went into the field barely knowing the language of their informants and then reported what had been said in that language. Carlos stumbled on an informant whose language he already knew, having learned it thoroughly in Argentina before the age of 15. Backing Carlos up, Castaneda had learned the very same language as an infant in Peru.

Garfinkel said anthropologists could not say in so many words what the natives had been talking about but would nevertheless come back from the field and try to do just that. Castaneda tried to say in so many words what don Juan had been talking about in the first 140 pages of *The Teachings*. The result of this futile effort was the Structural Analysis, which Joyce Carol Oates quickly recognized as a parody. Two short excerpts prove her astuteness:

> The idea that an ally was tamable implied that as a power it had the potential of being used. Don Juan explained it as an ally's innate capacity of being utilizable.

> I have used the term "ingestion-absorption" because ingestion might have been aided by skin absorption in producing a state of nonordinary reality, or skin absorption might have been aided by ingestion.

Castaneda's pedantic insistence mildly parodies Garfinkel's crushing, obfuscating repetition:

> The definiteness of expressions resides in their consequences; definitions can be used to assure a definite collection of "considerations" without providing a boundary; the definiteness of a collection is assured by circumstantial possibilities of indefinite elaboration.

Definiteness, definitions, definite, definiteness, indefinite: anyone who writes like that doesn't need a parodist; the writing parodies itself. Castaneda took on a formidable task, and though he executed it admirably, he never dared equal the actual redundancy, impenetrability, and transcendental insufferability of Garfinkel's text. If he had matched the prose of the master, the University editors, eyeing the popular market, would have rejected his book outright. Tiresome as it is, the Structural Analysis can be read and understood by almost any patient reader; compared with Garfinkel, it is Mark Twain. When one knows it is a parody, it is even slightly funny. There is nothing funny about Garfinkel's original:

Alfred Schutz made available for sociological study the practices of commonsense knowledge of social structures of everyday activities, practical circumstances, practical activities, and practical sociological reasoning.

Practices of knowledge of structures of activities, circumstances, activities, and reasoning—*in saecula saeculorum, amen.* Anthony F. C. Wallace said Garfinkel's verbal compactions ought to be read as inspirational literature rather than technical prose, that they were "like a very bad interlinear translation of an obscure German philosopher. Serious graduate students," Wallace added, "may waste hours searching for the meaning of such seemingly oracular non-sentences."

The oddest thing about Garfinkel's style, however, is not its incomprehensible unreadability; many an obscure German philosopher can supply that. The oddest thing is that Garfinkel is quite capable of writing clear, straightforward sentences when he wants to. He just didn't want to most of the time.

Why didn't he want to? I should guess it was because however much a thinker and teacher he may have been he was more a guru or magus, a charismatic presence that inspired, mystified, enthralled, that initiated a few worthy disciples and drove the rest away. Inscrutable scriptures were the first barrier to stop unworthy postulants. Anyone smart enough, tireless enough, and obedient enough to slog through Garfinkel's semantic swamp deserved admittance to the separate social-science reality hidden at its center, where further, more exacting tests of devotion awaited, such as self-administered breaching procedures.

Having defected long before from the One True Church, Castaneda was not about to submit to any lesser authority. Donning his cap of naïvety and his cloak of mediocrity, he proceeded cleverly to construct a magic mirror that would reflect ethnomethodology back to its practitioners. Garfinkel's bad old sociologists and deplorable anthropologists appeared in the mirror as the Structural Analysis and as a thick-headed Carlos who could never understand what don Juan was talking about and kept begging him to say it all over again in so many words. Taking his own assumptions for granted, don Juan would retort that he *was* saying it in so many words and if Carlos weren't so stupid he would understand it.

Garfinkel's breaching experiments were portrayed in a hundred confusing conversations and meaningless tasks but most obviously and schematically in the horrendous confrontation at the end of *The Teach-*

ings, where Carlos suspected don Juan was pretending to be someone else, or someone else was pretending to be don Juan. Like many actual victims of breaching experiments, Carlos lost his sense of reality and suffered severe anxiety.

Schutz's world of the We turned into Castaneda's special consensus. Because this was allegory, the consensus had to be corrected by new readings not of the ordinary commonsense world but of a nonordinary psychodelic and eventually mystical world. Just as "a common sub-universe of discourse" was gradually established between Don Quixote and Sancho Panza, enabling them at last to agree on the existence of giants and magicians, so Carlos gradually accepted don Juan's view that cricket-persons and talking lizards were as real as notebooks and bus stations.

Garfinkel, one of his critics said, "conceives of the truly important part in the world as practically invisible, as so familiar that it is a world taken-for-granted and unnoticed." Carlos could not see the tentacles don Genaro took for granted in his levitations and had to continue as an apprentice for ten years before he *saw* the practically invisible "lines of the world."

People commonly accept phrases they disagree with or don't understand, hoping further conversation will bring agreement or understanding. Ethnomethodologists call this "bracketing." Don Juan's startling, cryptic comments about the ally forced Carlos to bracket the existence and nature of that mysterious entity for many chapters. "There is no way of saying exactly what an ally is," don Juan assured Carlos. "The way one understands the ally is a personal matter." Still, in that way, they managed to talk at great length about the ally. Speakers know what they are talking about *in that way*, Garfinkel had said.

"Meaning differently than he can say in so many words," Garfinkel explained, "is not so much 'differently than what he says' as that *whatever* he says provides the very materials to be used in *making out* what he says." "It became obvious to me," Castaneda wrote in *The Teachings*, "that don Juan's knowledge had to be examined in terms of how he himself understood it. . . . whenever he tried to explain his knowledge to me, he used concepts that would render it 'intelligible' to him. . . . my first task was to determine his order of conceptualization." "These steps," he added in *Ixtlan*, "can only be understood in terms of the description to which they belong. . . . I must then let his teachings be the only source of entrance into it. Thus, I have left don Juan's words to speak for themselves."

The Structural Analysis purported to be "an attempt to disclose the internal cohesion and the cogency of don Juan's teaching," but Garfinkel had said: "The task of describing a person's method of speaking . . . is not the same as showing that what he said accords with a rule for demonstrating consistency, compatibility, and coherence of meanings." Ethnomethodologically, then, the Structural Analysis was doomed from the start—and it was meant to be. Paul Riesman called it "a pathetic denial of the reality of experiences presented in the first part of the book"—and that was before he realized both parts of *The Teachings* were an invention. For Riesman's later view, see his chapter in this volume.

Many more parallels could be listed between the world of don Juan and the world according to Garfinkel. David Silverman has devoted a whole book to them, a version of which was offered as a lecture series in the UCLA sociology department in 1973. Though he had seen evidence *The Teachings* was not a factual work, Silverman said it did not in the least matter to him whether any of the 'events' reported by Castaneda ever 'took place' (his quotes). The question should be bracketed, he said; since, true or false, "Castaneda's accounts provide a fitting occasion to re-view the basis of the sociological enterprise"—which, of course, was how ethnomethodology got started in the first place.

Castaneda's study of anthropology strung out for 13 years, 1959-1972, most of which were spent allegorizing ethnomethodology, the peculiar preoccupation of a few sociologists. If he was going to be an anthropologist of sorts, why did he pursue the ethnomethodologists? Ralph Beals, his first graduate committee chairman in anthropology, asked to see fieldnotes and never saw Castaneda again. Chairman William Lessa thought Castaneda was a poor student who had been coddled by other faculty members. Chairman John Hitchcock advised him to take his quasi-Sonoran chronicles to a fiction publisher. Clement Meighan, first to encourage his interest in anthropology, served as chairman but only temporarily, perhaps because Meighan was an archaeologist and the only artifacts Castaneda wanted to dig up were buried in the library. Routine academic expectations were making things tough for a specialist in anthromantics.

One way to mitigate scholarly discipline in a modern university is to do an interdisciplinary study. A student who formally or informally attaches himself to advisers in two departments may be less rigorously supervised, since each side would be glad to let the other do the work. Castaneda could only improve his dwindling chances by seeking allies in the sociology department.

Kindred spirits make the best allies. "Carlos," said don Juan, "is a horse that doesn't like to be saddled." Castaneda was a secret rebel who hated to follow the rules. The ethnomethodologists were flagrant rebels in sociology. A specialty in which truth is whatever anybody says it is was made to order for a man who had already changed his name, age, country of birth, native language, and family history. Though justified by high-flown rationalizations, Garfinkel's breaching experiments were undeniably con jobs. A fellow who had sold broken watches in a Peruvian flea market to pick up a few sols must have found it pretty intriguing that someone could get to be a fellow in sociology by teaching students to be con men. Why not go this academic fellow one better?

By 1967 at least two ethnomethodologists had been lured out of the sacred swamp by Castaneda's marvellous magic mirror. Garfinkel had seen some of the manuscript as early as 1962 and had chatted with Castaneda and anthropologist Philip L. Newman about going down to Sonora to meet don Juan. In 1967 Robert B. Edgerton, who was both anthropologist and ethnomethodologist, found Castaneda's manuscript exciting and urged him to take it to the University Press. The ranking anthropologist on the University editorial committee at that time was Walter Goldschmidt, then chairman of the UCLA anthropology department, to whom *The Teachings* came with favorable recommendations from Edgerton, Meighan, and Garfinkel: two anthropologists and a sociologist—or, more to the point, two ethnomethodologists and an archaeologist. Some years later, only one additional anthropologist was needed to make up a viable doctoral committee: Philip Newman, who had been taken by Castaneda's writings in 1962 when, at the tender scholastic age of 30, he had been a first-year assistant professor. Since Garfinkel was a sociologist, Edgerton was attached to the medical school, and Meighan was an archaeologist, the chairmanship fell to Newman, the only committee member who was a cultural anthropologist actually in the department. The fifth member of the committee was UCLA historian of religion Kees Bolle. Out of three large departments, Castaneda had finally put together a small team that would, at least nominally, accept his fairy tale about fieldwork as a scientific report.

Though it bore the indelible brand of ethnomethodology, the fairy tale was ostensibly anthropology. To tie the two together Castaneda prepared a 500-word abstract in which he said three times that the story was an "emic account." The term is used in an anthropological specialty called ethnoscience, which has quite a bit in common with ethnomethodology.

The intent of ethnomethodology, John McKinney wrote, "is to discover how members of a system perceive, delineate, define, and classify, and how they actually perform these [just mentioned cognitive] activities. . . . The challenge is . . . to get inside the events to see what kind of perceptual equipment or theories the actors themselves are utilizing as they organize the phenomena in their daily lives." The two basic questions of ethnoscience, Stephen Murray says, are: "What phenomena are significant for the people of some culture?" and "How do *they* organize these phenomena?" The goal of ethnoscience, he adds, is to find how *natives* divide up their world.

Castaneda's personal link to ethnoscience seems to have been William Bright, a professor of linguistics and anthropology at UCLA and an intellectual descendent of the same Edward Sapir don Juan liked to quote when he talked about agreement, description, and order. Along with Meighan, Garfinkel, and Edgerton, Bright was one of six professors whose help and encouragement Castaneda acknowledged in *The Teachings*. Emic, Bright explained, "is intended to contrast with *etic*, which roughly speaking means 'classified in terms of universal physical distinctions,' while *emic* means 'classified in terms of the psychological distinctions made in a particular culture.' "

When Carlos wanted don Juan to distinguish bird flights from out-of-body trips, don Juan said flying was flying whether done by birds or by weed-eaters; he wouldn't accept Carlos's body-bound etic distinction. When Carlos laughed at a crow that flew overhead, don Juan said he shouldn't laugh because it was not a crow but an omen. Carlos said he had seen it and it was a crow. If he had accepted don Juan's statement, Carlos would have classified the event emically as an omen in addition to classifying it etically as a crow flying overhead.

William Bright may nor may not have "encouraged" Castaneda, but it is clear he did not persuade him to take emics seriously. Ethnoscience is mainly language analysis. As a dedicated emicist, Carlos would have pestered don Juan day and night about Indian terms for peyote, jimson weed, mushrooms, lizards, snakes, rabbits, coyotes, crows, allies, sorcerers, benefactors, *seeing*, *not-doing*, and so on. In a story titled "Carlitos and don Juan (*Karlosla into Achai Hoan*)" I showed how some of those terms might look in the Yaqui language. Since the dissertation (*Journey to Ixtlan*) contains *not one* Indian term for any concept in don Juan's system of thought, calling it "an emic account" was the height of effrontery, but served to give it a superficial pedigree in anthropology while disguising its ethnomethodological heredity.

Emic studies have been caricatured in anthropology as "getting inside the native's head." A rough ethnomethodological equivalent is "acquiring membership." "The notion of *member* is the heart of the matter," wrote Garfinkel. Acquiring membership meant mastering the language of a particular group and using it appropriately to define oneself and guide one's conduct. Transformed by Castaneda into a perceptual metaphor, Carlos's membership in don Juan's special consensus meant sharing "an endless flow of perceptual interpretations." The termination of Carlos's apprenticeship meant that he had "learned a new description of the world . . . and a new perception of the world, which matched its new description." Carlos "gained membership" when the luminous coyote talked to him and he *saw* the lines of the world.

Membership is the only technical term of ethnomethodology to escape allegorical transmutation in the don Juan books. Eight *memberships* and three *emics* in the first 12 pages of his dissertation were Castaneda's token tributes to social-science nomenclature; the rest was story-telling.

Castaneda's abstract deserves to be read, and I commend it to all who have access to *Dissertation Abstracts*, where it shines like fool's gold on scholarship's dull sand. Titled *Sorcery: A Description of the World*, the abstract gives no hint one is actually reading about *Journey to Ixtlan*, a popular book published the year before. The author begins by saying his dissertation is "an emic account of an apprenticeship of sorcery as it is practiced by the American Indians of Modern Mexico." Since an abstract is the means by which a dissertation is advertised to the community of scholars, this abstract as much as any other must arouse normal scholarly expectations. The sentence just quoted gives anthropologists to believe something rightly called "sorcery" is widely practiced in contemporary Mexican Indian communities. The implication is plausible enough unless one knows that after three volumes of anthromancing Castaneda's brand of sorcering is still limited to eleven imaginary Indians (don Juan, don Genaro, la Catalina, Sacateca, Pablito, Nestor, Eligio, and four nameless young men) and one imaginary Mestizo (don Vicente) not one of whom belongs to any identified community or claims his art is widely practiced. Moreover, don Juan's "sorcery" does not employ evil spirits or magical projectiles to make people sick, as anthropologists will assume, but eclectic yoga to manifest the essence of the world. A few pages later, when Castaneda blames this semantic perversion on don Juan, it is not to straighten out the confusion but merely to claim allegorical membership in don Juan's world of the We; anthropologists who are not members of that world have a right not to be misled by an unannounced misuse of the standard ethnological term *sorcery* in one of the chief retrieval systems for social-science information.

The second sentence declares that "after years of fieldwork" Castaneda has concluded that "sorcery does not have a cultural focus, but is, rather, a series of skills practiced, in one form or another, by all the American Indian societies of the New World." First "sorcery" is a specific neo-mystical concoction no one has ever heard of; then it has no particular form; then it is practiced in every Amerindian society, without exception, in no relation to culture. Don Juan must have advised the candidate that committee members who couldn't figure out what he was talking about wouldn't be able to pin him down with their thoughts during the doctoral oral.

While the body of *Sorcery/Ixtlan* relates happenings in Arizona and Mexico during narrative-1960-1962 and a few days in 1971, the second paragraph of the abstract professes that the data for the "present work" were collected "over a period of ten years of sporadic fieldwork in north-western Mexico." Anyone who has read *Ixtlan* must get the impression *Sorcery* is a different and more inclusive work.

The author regrets he "was not permitted to tape-record or photo-graph any event that took place" during that ten-year period. In contrast *A Separate Reality* reports tape-recordings made on 14 May and 4 September 1968, which could have helped conscientious committee members authenticate, or disauthenticate, the fieldwork. A prudent allegorist did well to banish those potentially troublesome tapes into a separate reality while preparing an abstract to be read by committee members in the opening pages of his dissertation.

The third paragraph translates Sapir's agreement-based social reality into don Juan's agreement-based non-social reality, and the fourth paragraph vivifies the metaphor by explaining that the world is not only subjectively transformed by ordinary perception but possibly also physically altered by a sorcerer's magical vision. This paranormal proposition is suggested with just enough ambiguity to arouse delight in magic without provoking censure of supernatural claims. The last two paragraphs of the abstract wave the banners of emicism and membership to signal ethnoscientists and ethnomethodologists that an ally is approaching.

Together with its academic alias, this tiny essay constitutes a highly misleading advertisement of a document that is in truth (as the committee members knew) no more than *Journey to Ixtlan*. Though Castaneda's abstract neatly capsulizes the themes of his allegory, it spuriously represents *Sorcery* as both a factual report and a work different from the don Juan books. Since the author has forbidden University Microfilms to distribute the complete document, consumer advocates of the commun-

ity of scholars must apply to the UCLA library if they wish to plumb the
depths of the deception.

Assuming for the moment Castaneda hoodwinked not only some
readers of *Dissertation Abstracts* but also some members of his committee, is such deception lying? Perhaps it isn't, since one view holds that a
playful or ironic statement is not an "assertion" and therefore not lying:
"for the speaker realizes that his audience is not justified in taking him
seriously." A few chapters into *A Separate Reality* I began to laugh,
suddenly knowing the author was kidding. Granted, I have a pretty active sense of humor. Castaneda, who has a very active sense of humor,
may have thought his professors were in on the joke when they weren't.
For two years now the notion has been nagging me that if there had been
even one live laugher on Castaneda's committee, somebody would have
called up Ralph Beals for what would have turned out to be a pretty
funny conversation, and Castaneda's doctorate would have been confer-
red in fiction-science rather than anthropology.

Though it is hard for us laughers to empathize with the solemn ones, I
am now almost ready to believe Clement Meighan, Philip Newman, and
Kees Bolle never saw the joke. Edgerton seems to be a sober fellow, and
perhaps he didn't get it either, despite being an ethnomethodologist. But
can one believe the inventor of the breaching experiment entertained
Castaneda for ten years without guessing what was going on? Maybe I'm
giving him too much credit. Agnes did fool him, of course, but Agnes
also fooled a psychiatrist, a psychologist, and a lustful boyfriend, and
Agnes didn't write three mutually contradictory volumes to prove she
was fooling. To me, the diagnostic sign in Garfinkel's reaction to Agnes
is not that he was fooled, which could have happened to anybody, but
that being fooled didn't bother him, which is a very unusual reaction.
Manifestly, a warrior, especially a warrior with tenure, has more choices
in life than an average academic. He doesn't need to worry about lies or
what people will say. He is free to follow the path he has chosen, however extravagant it may be.

As the incarnation of ethnomethodology, Garfinkel was the only implicated faculty member who had nothing to lose if Castaneda was kidding. Explicitly and repeatedly if not very lucidly he had said that reality
in social science is what you make it and that the process of making it is
more interesting than the product. Though his academic tribe was widely
despised, Garfinkel was acknowledged as its chief and, when Castaneda's
dissertation rolled round, had been a full professor for six years and was
not publishing any new work. What better time to carry out one last

breaching experiment? Though ethnomethodology was flourishing in numbers, Garfinkel may have recalled how his membership in the American Sociological Association had been challenged when he let it lapse in 1967 and wished to give a trickster's answer to that insult.

Besides, the way of the benefactor is hard. At about the same time, Mehan and Wood were lamenting "the hopelessness of attempting to alter science by reasonable persuasion." They planned to alter science by practicing ethnomethodology as a way of life. Autographing Castaneda's magic mirror may have been Garfinkel's way of living ethnomethodologically. Following the principle of reflexivity, the effect on science showed up in ethnomethodological writings. Whatever cunning one may suspect Garfinkel of, Mehan and Wood wrote more as disciples than as exploiters of don Juan.

"The world is the world because you know the *doing* involved in making it so," don Juan had told Carlos. "Any knowledge will produce the experience of a world that corresponds with that knowledge," responded Mehan and Wood.

"In order to be a hunter you must disrupt the routines of your life," don Juan had said. "Social scientists rarely risk disruption of their everyday routines" charged Mehan and Wood.

A warrior must leave everyone who knows him well, don Juan had said; must quickly leave the friends who have known him for a long time. The ethnomethodological program proposed by Mehan and Wood required: "disengagement from family, job, friends. . . . Few will be willing to give up their present lives so completely." Heady stuff. Who forsaketh not all he hath cannot be my disciple; who gazes into the magic mirror must live in don Juan's image.

Having gained membership in Garfinkel's rebellion by allegorizing its preconceptions, Castaneda wrote: "I have struggled to maintain myself as a truthful student. . . . I have defined truthfulness, in my role as a student of anthropology, as the effort to relate with fidelity everything that took place, neither inventing nor distorting anything. I did not go to the field to prove or disprove preconceived hypotheses."

"You always knew how to lie," don Juan had told Carlos. "The only thing that was missing was that you didn't know why to do it. Now you do."

"There may be better ways of being a man than trying to find the truth," conceded Mehan and Wood.

"Our modern life," Georg Simmel had written, "is based to a much larger extent than is usually realized upon the faith in the honesty of the other. [An example is] our science, in which most scholars must use innumerable results of other scientists which they cannot examine."

"It is through notions of truth and falsity that we live our lives together," added David Silverman. "We *can* assert that there is no difference between the two . . . but, in doing so, we would be proposing a non-existent society. For, to see no difference between truth and falsity is for us, on most occasions, to be recognizably crazy."

I take Silverman's statement to mean that even in ethnomethodology the question of don Juan's authenticity need not be bracketed forever. Perhaps this chapter will help unbracket it, thus providing a fitting occasion for re-viewing the ethnomethodological enterprise.

RdeM

Though the next two authors could hardly be more different, each in his own way convinces us that a book accepted by some as a factual account is best classified as a literary invention.

Tobias Schneebaum, whose book *Wild Man* was published in 1979, was described in the previous chapter as a New York painter who travels the world in pursuit of his art. Having unintentionally led the ethnomethodologists astray with his earlier book, *Keep the River on Your Right*, he now graciously assists my effort to disillusion them about the origins of his homosexual orientation and the reliability of his memoirs as factual reports. Since Schneebaum has never disguised or denied the rampant subjectivity of his writings, our purpose is well served by a brief sample of them titled, "Realities Loved and Unloved."

Instructors who list *The Teachings of Don Juan* as anthropology are likely also to offer their students *Wizard of the Upper Amazon*, a book respectfully reviewed in the *American Anthropologist* in 1972 and never until now challenged as fake ethnography. The challenger is Robert L. Carneiro, Curator of South American Ethnology at the American Museum of Natural History, in New York. *Wizard*, he says, was not debunked in 1972 because the only adequately prepared reviewer failed to do his scientific duty. In "Chimera of the Upper Amazon" Carneiro reveals the identity of the delinquent debunker.

Realities Loved and Unloved

An incident in *Wild Man* concerns my meeting two young Buddhist monks in Mandalay and inviting them to my hotel room:

> The friend sat cross-legged beside Aung San, in lotus position, with his flabby flesh flowing over his body in curves that gave him breasts and folds and bulges that were almost feminine. In that divine posture, he was smiling upon his friend, the pair of them halves of a whole, a yang and yin, the male recumbent, resting, the female upright, alert, and active. I watched the female half and saw in him a Bodhisattva, an androgynous incarnation looking out on me and on us all, the spirit of compassion surrounding him with an aura that could draw into itself all the ills of the world. He looked at me and his eyes threw into me the feeling that I was suddenly still, that my body and mind were at rest and that if I stayed that way for no more than a moment, I would come to the realization that I too am the world, that I am all its aspects, that I am free of all compulsion toward understanding. In the flash of an eye, this anonymous being had awakened in me an instant of repose.

The story goes on:

> At last they took up their robes and enveloped their bodies within them. They smiled back at me as they opened the door and left. Some minutes later, I got up and washed my face in a bowl of cold water. I put on my trousers and felt my pockets empty, my money gone. There hadn't been much—five dollars in kyats—but I had been rolled, rolled by two Buddhist monks, one of whom I had dreamed to be a Bodhisattva!

I quote this at length not to show that the stratagem of the monks exposed the pretentiousness of my vision but that after almost twenty years the intensity of my feelings for those men naked in front of me and the quality of the trance into which I put myself remain more real than the duplicity of the final act. The monk *was* a Bodhisattva when I saw him, and he is still one to me in spite of the theft.

In the same way, my extraordinary experience in the forest of Peru, living with a group of people who had never before seen outsiders, was so extreme in body and mind that whatever reality existed outside me was as much illusion as the reality of my interior. Through some process unknown to me I had willed true acts and emotions into a larger or different reality, which encompassed me and the men around me. *Keep the River on Your Right* recounts events that occurred both within and without. Whatever exaggeration appears was meant for me alone, having nothing to do with the eventual reader, not having been intended for him. I was writing only for myself. Napoleon Chagnon's speculation that the homosexuality I described was as I wished it may be valid, but there is no question that my moments of complete sexual joy with those men were real in every sense, and were manifold; they did not exist only in my mind.

I had thrown myself into the lives of the men of Peru, just as they had pulled, captured, and accepted me unto themselves. Our visions, impressions, and valuations of one another came from each of us individually, from dreams and fantasies that could never have coincided with any particular kind of reality—not mine, not the men's, not even Chagnon's. Those men, who were my friends, did not know me as I am or as I think I am, nor could I have known anything of them but what my eyes and emotions saw.

Keep the River on Your Right describes a circle of men whose leader touches his penis to the penises of the others. Though I did not witness this ritual in the context of hunting, as I wrote it, it had been demonstrated to me by the small group of men whose sleeping space I shared. Was it, then, an enactment of what they wished to be true? Of what *I* wished to be true? Were they enacting what they *thought* I wished to be true? Who, there, was breaching reality? External stimuli may alter customary traditions and manners. The men in their relationships with me appeared always open, attentive, responsive, and this may or may not have reflected the way they lived their lives before or after my stay with them.

An American anthropologist working in West New Guinea among people who had had almost no contact with whites, discovered that the ethnographic material he had collected was worthless to him. Every day his informants had sat with him telling stories and myths while smoking tobacco he offered in payment. After eight months of amassing material, he learned his informants had been inventing the stories to get the tobacco, to which they were addicted. So great were his anger and disappointment that he left the village for another, where he started work all over again. Too bad he did not see the stories were of equal value whether old or new, for invention could only have come from indigenous experience and conceptions. The deceivers could not have invented anything from outside their limited world. The anthropologist had only to mention this in his dissertation to secure its validity as folktale and myth. Likewise the men of Peru could have invented only out of themselves no matter what motives I might have provided.

Neither living in Peru nor later writing about the experience did I think or write like an anthropologist. I wrote from a need to describe to myself my thoughts, perceptions, and responses to what had happened around me. From earliest childhood homosexuality had been a part of my life, but had rarely been expressed overtly; nor had it been completely expressed until I went to Mexico in 1947 and lived there for three years. I had always been ashamed of my physical self, my unattractiveness, actively disliking the person I was. Not until I placed myself in an alien environment could I accept what I had always known about myself but had been too timid to declare or enter into. Foreign atmospheres made living easier for me. Though New Yorkers had usually rejected me, exotic, preliterate peoples always accepted me, whatever I was or however I may have appeared to them. The more alien they were, the easier was mutual acceptance.

The fact that I came from another world meant I would necessarily have strange attitudes, so nothing I did was ever upsetting or shocking. Rather my behavior was interesting and exciting. Alone with the forest people I learned to assert my feelings and desires without shame or loss of face, without reacting to frightening, humiliating rejection in a degree that provoked further rejection, which had always driven me into reclusiveness. In Mexico and Peru and elsewhere among foreign peoples any rejection I suffered was never a rejection of *me* but only of some act of mine, which was perhaps amusing, unsatisfying, or against tradition. The *idea* of the homosexual act rarely horrified or even displeased anyone. My foreignness made me attractive, offsetting whatever negative qualities my physical appearance may have presented. No one ever said I was ugly or even unhandsome.

Not that any group I entered was open to all suggestions, for no group was, but nearly every group I met admitted me and accepted my ways. This thrilled me and gave me a different sense of myself, enabling me to expand my relationships with people, to develop communication with others to the point where I became at last approachable and was able to approach other people with ease.

Chimera of the Upper Amazon

Man is never content with the truth. He always seeks to enlarge and embellish it. And in the process, he often succeeds in perverting it. Nowhere is this better exemplified than in the literature on South American Indians. Sixteenth-century chroniclers, half deluded by Indian legends of Amazon women and El Dorado, further elaborated these stories, and completely deluded their European audiences.

Nor has the twentieth century seen an end to such exaggeration. Books on South American Indians continue to appear that heavily embroider the fabric of reality. Among these we can cite Algot Lange's *In the Amazon Jungle* (1912), Leonard Clark's *The Rivers Ran East* (1953), Jane Dollinger's *The Jungle is a Woman* (1955), and Tobias Schneebaum's *Keep the River on Your Right* (1969). Commanding a high place in this genre is *Wizard of the Upper Amazon*, by the late Manuel Córdova-Rios and F. Bruce Lamb.

Though *Wizard* was published in 1971, the person who should have exposed it then (namely, the present writer) neglected to do so, thus permitting favorable reviews in both scientific and popular journals to stand unchallenged. The time has now come to lift the mask of respectability and reveal the imposture.

The history of this book goes back ten years before its publication, to the day in April 1961 when I first met its co-author, Bruce Lamb. The meeting occurred in Pucallpa, Peru, just after my return from several months of field work with the Amahuaca Indians. I don't recall now whether it was in Pucallpa or later in New York that Lamb first told me the story of Manuel Córdova. At any rate, during the course of his work as a forester for the U. S. Plywood Corporation, Lamb had met Córdova in the Peruvian Amazon city of Iquitos and heard his remarkable tale of being captured by the Amahuaca, living among them for some years, and finally becoming their chief. Knowing I had studied the Amahuaca, Lamb asked me if I thought the story could be true. I was guarded in my reply, but urged him to tape-record Córdova's narration in full and let me see the transcript.

Some months later, Lamb sent me a 30-page typescript of Córdova's story. After reading it carefully I told Lamb I thought it was an imaginative piece of jungle fiction, and gave him very specific reasons for my views. Lamb seemed disappointed, for he had already envisioned turning the narrative into a book of "true adventure." This meeting, which occurred in 1963, was the last time I saw Bruce Lamb.

As years went by, I assumed he had given up the idea of publishing Córdova's narrative, but one day Natural History Press asked me to review a manuscript, which turned out to be an expanded version of the one Lamb had sent me years before. Since the longer version was no truer than the shorter, I advised the Press to reject it, and they did. More years passed. Then in March of 1971, while reading *Time* magazine, I came upon a review of a book called *Wizard of the Upper Amazon*, by Córdova-Rios and Lamb, which had a most familiar ring. Lamb had finally found a publisher for his manuscript.

Córdova's story is essentially this. In 1907, at the age of 15, while a member of a team of Peruvian rubber gatherers, he was captured in the forest by a group of Indians. These Indians, who Córdova says were Amahuaca, took him back to their village. For the next six years he lived among them and was groomed by the old chief to succeed him. When the chief died, young Córdova took his place and remained head of the village for about a year until, tiring of his life with the tribe, he escaped down-river and returned to civilization.

While I cannot categorically state that Córdova's adventure never happened, I find it extremely difficult to believe. If Córdova was captured by any Indians, it was certainly not by Amahuaca. Many of the customs and practices Córdova attributes to the Indians he says he lived with are not Amahuaca traits at all. Rather, they are traits of tribes of the Northwest Amazon region, several hundred miles to the north, with whom Córdova actually had close associations. Why, then, did he pick the Amahuaca as a background for his fanciful adventures? Probably because they were so little known he thought he could say anything he wished about them and no one would ever be the wiser. But he guessed wrong.

To me, the most discordant part of his book is the portrayal of Xumu, purportedly chief of the Amahuaca. Time and again Córdova has Xumu exercising great authority over many aspects of the group's social life. Thus the chief is said to supervise puberty initiations, officiate at marriages, and adjudicate disputes over adultery. This portrayal contains a serious flaw. Not only does an Amahuaca chief lack these particular powers, he lacks all powers whatsoever because, in fact, the Amahuaca have no chiefs. An Amahuaca who attempted to direct anyone else's behavior would be ignored and disdained by his fellows. The only two Amahuaca "chiefs" I know of are creatures of *patrones* and missionaries, who find it convenient in dealing with the Indians to designate a certain man as leader, despite his lack of real authority.

Another dubious statement in Córdova's account is his claim that the Amahuaca village he was taken to had a population of 100. Strictly speaking, the Amahuaca have no villages. They live in small hamlets of 15 or 20 persons, the few houses in each community being so dispersed as often to be out of sight of one another. Moreover, the conical communal hut Córdova describes does not occur among the Amahuaca at all, nor in fact among any tribe in this part of Amazonia.

Córdova's manner of dressing the Amahuaca is also erroneous. He has the chief wearing a cotton *cushma* (resembling a nightshirt) when in fact no Amahuaca wears such a garment. The statement that Amahuaca men tied up their penises with a string is not exactly correct either. Some tribes of the Montaña do tie up the penis with a string, but what the Amahuaca do is insert the foreskin under a broad bark belt. And Amahuaca men do not cut their hair short as Córdova says but wear it long, halfway down the back. Moreover, could anyone live for years among the Amahuaca and fail to mention the bamboo crown, *paka máiti*, which is so distinctive of male attire? Yet Córdova fails to mention it.

Though Córdova knows a good deal about Amazonian hunting methods in general, he knows little or nothing about Amahuaca hunting methods in particular. Thus he describes the Amahuaca's use of lances, bird spears, hunting snares, and basketry traps, none of which they have. He talks about their "assigned" hunting territories, which they lack. And of the trophy skins from game animals that Córdova mentions several times I saw and heard nothing.

Córdova's characterization of Amahuaca ceremonial life does not ring true. The Amahuaca do not formally observe life crises, yet Córdova imputes to them a baptism ceremony, a wedding celebration, and an incorporation rite. He also alludes to their frequent use of fermented beverages, when in fact they almost never have them.

In his most revealing error, Córdova ascribes to the Amahuaca a tobacco-licking palaver during which the assembled men dip their fingers into a pot of tobacco juice and lick them as a sign of assent. Nothing remotely resembling this occurs among the Amahuaca. Indeed, the only tribes I know of in all of Amazonia that have this ritual are the Boro and Witoto of the Northwest Amazon, the area Córdova knows best and from whose tribes he draws most of the traits he falsely assigns to the Amahuaca.

What Córdova says regarding the Amahuaca method of disposing of the dead is a mixture of fact and fantasy. He correctly states that the Amahuaca practice cremation, but incorrectly says they do this only for victims of witchcraft. They do it for everyone. He also would have us believe the ashes of a cremated body are buried, when in fact they are mixed with banana drink and ingested by the close kin of the deceased. Needless to say, having no chiefs, the Amahuaca do not smoke and mummify a chief's body, as Xumu's body was supposedly smoked and mummified, nor do they treat anyone's body that way. Finally, having overlooked the verified Amahuaca practice of ingesting the ashes of kinsmen at funerals, Córdova falsely accuses the Amahuaca of eating members of other tribes.

A good part of the chapter titled "Legends" is devoted to recounting, in abbreviated form, what purport to be Amahuaca myths. These myths are like nothing I know of in Amahuaca mythology. Instead of giving, for example, the Amahuaca's classic myth about the origin of the moon, a variant of which is found widely in the Montaña, Córdova recounts a wholly different story of the moon's origin. Nor does he present, even in capsule form, any of the other major myths I recorded among the Amahuaca.

Though more ethnological objections could be raised, the foregoing should suffice to cast serious doubt on the veracity of Córdova's account. To be sure, a number of traits he attributes to the Amahuaca actually occur among them, such as tooth blackening, the use of pipes for smoking, the construction of hunting blinds in trees, and the use of ayahuasca to induce visions of spirits. But these traits are widely distributed in the Peruvian Montaña. Mentioning them does not prove any contact with or knowledge of the Amahuaca.

Nothing in *Wizard of the Upper Amazon* convinces or even suggests to me that Manuel Córdova was ever captured by the Amahuaca, that he ever lived among them, or that he was groomed to be their chief, let alone actually serving in that capacity. The story Córdova told Bruce Lamb consists of fragmentary ethnographic tidbits gleaned indiscriminately from many tribes and encased in a matrix of personal fantasy.

In submitting his manuscript to a publisher knowing there was a serious professional challenge to its authenticity, Lamb took a calculated risk. For nine years this risk has paid off. Lacking the background to evaluate the book, reviewers took fantasy for fact, while those with the knowledge to call Córdova's bluff have, until now, remained silent. Though we live in an age when falsehood, if engagingly told, often passes for a higher form of truth, perhaps this long-delayed critique will help prevent one such perpetration from finding a permanent place in the literature of South American ethnology.

On December 18, 1979, I received a letter from Carlos Alberto Seguin, Director of the Peruvian Institute of Social-Psychiatric Studies, who wrote as follows:

> I interviewed Manuel Córdoba when he came to Lima to be taken care of by a doctor. He was seriously ill and he died a few months later. Despite his illness, he appeared as a man much younger than his stated age. (It is my belief that he pretended to be older.) Completely lucid, he showed always that kind of supercilious irony typical of someone used to the admiration and credulity of everybody. He spoke about his life full of admirable events. He told us about his relationship with the Indians and how he was made a chief of them, etc, etc. We talked for more than two hours. He had always a half smile on his lips and a twinkle in his eyes that produced the impression that he was almost joking. When somebody showed awe, he said, smiling almost sardonically: *"No crean todo lo que les digo. Puede ser todo mentira."*

In translation, Córdova said to his listeners: "Don't believe everything I tell you. It could all be a lie."

Rdem

Though libraries throughout the land have routinely catalogued and shelved Castaneda's books with works of anthropology rather than of fiction, *Library Journal* said the fifth book, *Second Ring of Power*, raised the question whether these chronicles should be viewed as fiction, while *Booklist* bit the bullet and listed *Ring* under Fiction, calling it "a fictional coup in the creation of an otherworld."

As it became clear to more and more readers that all of the don Juan books were tales of imagination rather than field reports, library users began to ask whether the books would be moved to different shelves. Such a move cannot be made lightly, for the original cataloguing by the Library of Congress embodies great inertia.

In *Castaneda's Journey* I called the Library of Congress an innocent victim of Castaneda's tricks. Don Juan (I said—borrowing one of Castaneda's hyperboles) must have "roared, kicked, cried, coughed, and choked with laughter" when he saw the cataloguing data in *Tales of Power* giving no birthdate for Castaneda, who surely had one, but giving a birthdate for don Juan, who surely had none. "Despite a year's warning from me," I later prodded, "the Library of Congress goes right on classifying don Juan books as Yaqui history."

This playful banter fortunately fell under the serious, expert eye of Sanford Berman, an authority on cataloguing—which, like other librarians, he spells *cataloging*. He also calls the Library of Congress "LC." In "Cataloging Castaneda" Berman takes the "LC" to task for bibliosophic peccability and offers a warrior's way out of the taxonomic mess.

Cataloging Castaneda

Most libraries stock Castaneda's Canon. And by the way they've cataloged the don Juan titles, those libraries in effect declare: "These works are about Indians, specifically Yaqui Indians, and deal in particular with Yaqui religion, which involves the use of hallucinogenic drugs."

In May 1978, Richard de Mille wrote to Lucia J. Rather, Director for Cataloging at the Library of Congress, pointing out that don Juan's ethnic Yaquiness had been authoritatively rejected, his anthropological legitimacy denied, and his very existence seriously questioned. De Mille asked Ms. Rather to "state current policies and thinking on discovered hoaxes and present or prospective application of such policies and thinking to the don Juan hoax." He particularly wanted to know "whether Carlos Castaneda's works . . . will continue to be classified E99 Y3, and if so, what reasons are given for the continuation." In reply, Rather explained that "the Library is currently operating under two policies depending upon whether the misrepresentation is in the descriptive elements of a work or in the subject content." She continued:

> In descriptive cataloging a misrepresentation is corrected as soon as "the truth" becomes known. In certain situations (e.g., authorship ascription) supporting documentation would need to be fairly strong.
>
> In subject cataloging the general policy is to follow the statements of the author and publisher as long as the item has been issued as a legitimate work on the subject. Reclassification would not be undertaken without a statement from the author and/or publisher that a misrepresentation had occurred, although others may have determined that the work is one of the imagination. The basic goal in book classification is to bring similar works together on the shelves. Such an arrangement best serves the library user when browsing through the book stacks in search of material of interest. The cataloger fulfills his [sic!] role by identifying the topics of particular works and placing them with other works on the same topics. While some of these works may be outstanding contributions, others may be poor in quality,

based on inaccurate research, or even outright frauds. The cataloger does not and should not place value judgments on these works. For these reasons, Castaneda's works continue to be classified E99.Y3.

Now, what are the facts? The Library of Congress, upon which nearly all other libraries depend for cataloging data and guidance, has assigned both LC and Dewey Decimal numbers to every Castaneda opus. The consistently-applied LC-notation is "E99.Y3." That translates into "Yaqui Indians" (E99=Indians of North America; .Y3=Tribes: Yaqui). The Dewey-number given to all Castaneda tomes except *Journey to Ixtlan* is "299.7," which signifies "Religions of North American Indian origin." Each don Juan title has also received two or more subject headings, typically:

JUAN, DON, 1891–

HALLUCINOGENIC DRUGS AND RELIGIOUS EXPERIENCE

YAQUI INDIANS RELIGION AND MYTHOLOGY

That, in sum, is how Castaneda has been cataloged. And it is wholly possible to agree with Rather's tenets about "identifying the topics of particular works and placing them with other works on the same topics," as well as not making "value judgments" when cataloging, and *still* conclude that LC's treatment of Castaneda's donjuaniana is manifestly wrong.

Somewhat paraphrasing Rather's remarks, here are three basic principles of subject cataloging and classification:

Material should be classed where browsers would most likely *seek* it.

Similar materials should be found in the same or nearby shelf-ranges.

Materials should not be classed nor subject-cataloged in such a way that they seem to be something that they really aren't.

LC's Castaneda-handling violates every one of those principles: "don Juan," the alleged seer, is only nominally "Yaqui," and the "recorded" events or experiences are mainly paranormal in nature. Consequently, anyone desiring genuine, detailed information on *Yaqui* (or overall Native American) culture and religion would be disserved by finding Castaneda's materials on the shelf at E99 or 299.7, or in the catalog under YAQUI INDIANS. Where *do* they belong? Some, of course, would soberly and forcefully recommend the appropriate LC or Dewey numbers for "Fiction" or "Fantasy." But it would render no disservice to browsers, author, publisher, *or* critics if "133.4," the Dewey classmark actually assigned to one Castaneda title, *Journey to Ixtlan*, and its LC analogs, "BF 1563-1623," were uniformly assigned to *all* the don Juan titles. The numbers simply denote "Witchcraft" and "Magic." Don Juan performs magical feats that are, in Castaneda's account, either deceptive tricks or paranormal events, and these feats are consistently if unconformingly called "sorcery" by both don Juan and Castaneda. Moreover, Castaneda's publishers, though hardly admitting fraud or "misrepresentation," have often purveyed the message that the don Juan cycle fundamentally concerns magic, mysticism, witchcraft, and the occult, *not* Yaqui ethnography or religion. The jacket notes, as an example, for *Tales of Power* never mention "Yaqui" but describe that work as "the culmination of [Castaneda's] extraordinary initiation into the mysteries of sorcery." Indeed, terms like "sorcery," "sorcerer," "unknown," "mysterious," "secrets," and "tricks" appear more than ten times in the space of five short paragraphs.

The suggested "BF" or "133" notation doesn't necessarily imply that any so-classed work is either "scientific" or "fraudulent," but it does rightly signal that the topic (whatever its treatment, objective or fanciful) lies within the broad category of "Parapsychology and occultism," and not—in this case—within the sphere of either Religion or Social Science. Finally, as a complement to this classification reform, the subject tracing, YAQUI INDIANS—RELIGION AND MYTHOLOGY, deserves replacement by one or more of these exquisitely direct and non-contentious forms:

MYSTICISM. MAGIC (OCCULT SCIENCES). WITCHCRAFT.

Strangely, the very title correctly classed by LC in 133.4—that is, *Journey to Ixtlan*—bore only two subject tracings—JUAN, DON, 1891- and HALLUCINOGENIC DRUGS—which utterly failed to harmonize with the topic represented by the Dewey number 133.4. Worse, these tracings also failed to reflect the content of the book, which—according to de Mille—"is noted for its departure from the drug theme: *Ixtlan* is precisely the book in which the drug theme was abandoned in favor of drugless mystical methods."

To conclude: Rather's prototypical cataloger need not decide whether Castaneda perpetrated a hoax and need not place on the "Fiction" shelves books that no one—not author, publisher, critic, nor library user—would consider bona fide "novels." But it *is* incumbent on that cataloger—as a matter of professional duty and intellectual integrity alike—to decide where the don Juan volumes would prove most useful to browsers and what classification numbers and subject headings would most accurately express their apparent content. If Rather allowed that cataloger to try again, to start afresh with those three principles or objectives firmly in mind, the results might be very different. Thus far, LC's witless cataloging palpably misrepresents the material, limits its accessibility to potentially-interested readers, and embarrasses catalogers everywhere who take their craft seriously.

What LC has done could only satisfy someone with a highly-developed sense of mischief. A trickster. A prankster. An Eulenspiegel with a Ph.D. in Anthropology. A Carlos Castaneda.

Publishing the Factoids

In July of narrative-1973 a man identifying himself only as Max phoned science editor Richard Liebmann-Smith and asked if he had ever heard of Carlos Castinets. The answer was no. Castinets, Max explained, was a pedagogical impostor who had made a killing on a phoney bilingual primer, *I'm José, You're José*. The same thing could be done in biology. Liebmann-Smith was shocked. When Max offered a heavy advance for a nonfiction fantasy on the cloning of a baby, he laughed in Max's ear. Not in a million years, he said, would publishers fall for anything so far out.

The shockable skeptic was pretty dumb, for calendar-1978 brought David M. Rorvik's *In His Image: The Cloning of a Man*. When mouse-cloning experimenter Beatrice Mintz dubbed Rorvik "a fraud and a jackass," the publisher countered: "David Rorvik assures Lippincott [the story] is true." Though mouse-egg manipulator Clement Markert declared the claim "an absolute fraud," Lippincott said the book would be published "as nonfiction on the strength of Mr. Rorvik's credentials"— which included being a science-journalist who eight years earlier had said he was planning a pornographic science-fiction thriller titled *The Clone*.

To complicate the picture, Rorvik's former medical co-author, gynecologist and aspiring baby-cloner Landrum B. Shettles, praised Rorvik's sterling character and unimpeachable integrity. In contrast, the more cautious Simon and Schuster, already publishers of four famous but discredited volumes of donfiction, had rejected Rorvik's manuscript because he would not present or even promise any documentation— which seems a little unfair, for just as Castaneda had to protect the privacy of don Juan, Rorvik had to protect the baby clone, a mama hostess, and a mysterious millionaire daddy donor known to readers only as Max. Collectors of insignificant signs will wish to learn also that the jacket of Rorvik's book displayed the very same Escher drawing of hands drawing each other that had served as frontispiece for *The Reality of Ethnomethodology*.

At any rate, factoids were booming. The previous year had given us *The Amityville Horror: A True Story*, about which author Jay Anson later said: "I have no idea whether the book is true or not." Much of the blame or credit for the boom must go to Castaneda, who set a high and tempting standard for fiddlers in every field. "What a triumph," wrote

Robert de Ropp, "to be able—not once but five times—to hoist works onto the best seller list that are clearly fiction but solemnly labelled nonfiction by librarians, critics, and book reviewers!" What a triumph, that is, for Castaneda, and what a debacle for book evaluators. But did not some of those apparent victims help contrive their own misfortune?

Castaneda's greatest booster in the media was *The New York Times.* If it had been published as a novel, said reviewer Charles Simmons in August 1968, *The Teachings of Don Juan* would have been "destined for fame." The following month Dudley Young, in English at the University of Essex, found *The Teachings* to be a moving if incomplete memoir, a tantalizing confession that fell short both ethnologically and philosophically. The Structural Analysis he called "a sophomoric essay on the phenomenology of perception, about which the author clearly knows very little." Such qualified praise did not satisfy *The Times.* Hailing *The Teachings* in May 1971 as "an underground best seller" (the first recorded use of this famous conjuring phrase), reviewer Roger Jellinek said one could not exaggerate the significance of what Castaneda had done, for he was the first outsider to enter into a "pre-logical form that is no-one-knows how old," a shamanistic tradition he had described better than anyone else, including Eliade, the most prominent authority on shamanism. "Except for a dutifully appended 'structural analysis' that is almost a parody," he had wisely not imposed his own categories of meaning on the alien language he was trying to rescue from oblivion. In February 1972 author William Irwin Thompson applauded Castaneda's much needed attempt to integrate science with the occult.

One very sour note threatened to spoil the swelling chorus of acclaim. In the summer of 1972 a review copy of *A Separate Reality* went out to Peyotissimus Maximus Weston La Barre, who discordantly pronounced it "pseudo-profound, deeply vulgar pseudo-ethnography." With unbending editorial intent, *The Times* rejected La Barre's review. On October 17th, leaping into the breach, Roger Jellinek had to admit he didn't know what to make of *Ixtlan's* drugless visions, but October 22nd brought reassurance from Paul Riesman, a specialist in African cultures, that Castaneda's first three books were solid milestones on the road to better science. February 1973 saw *The New York Times Magazine* breaking ranks by publishing Donald Barthelme's raucous parody of *The Teachings,* but parody is only play, and *The Magazine* is only entertainment, after all. In October 1974 *The Times* resumed its journey on the path with heart, as psychoanalyst Elsa First credited Castaneda's "splendid" *Tales of Power* with outdoing Eliade, once more, by placing the reader "inside the shaman's consciousness."

Two years later *The Times* received a copy of *Castaneda's Journey*, containing many pages of documented evidence and coherent argument that *The Times's* favorite pre-logical traditionalist had been totally invented by *The Times's* front-running candidate to succeed Eliade. In an impeccable demonstration of *not-doing*, *The Times* did *not-review Castaneda's Journey*. Some one may have read it, though, for in December 1977 *Times* staffer John Leonard smartly changed the reviewing tune by calling *Second Ring of Power* a Zeitgeisty piece of anthropological fiction, its author "a Wizard of Oz for freaks. . . . not quite so funny as L. Ron Hubbard and not nearly so inventive as Frank Herbert." Three weeks later Robert Bly said it had been "obvious" since *A Separate Reality* that Castaneda was making up the conversations with don Juan. De Mille's documentation of the hoax, said Bly, "should satisfy anyone still in doubt."

Thus did *The Times* eat Castaneda's crow—or did it? Without an explicit admission of having been conned or self-deceived or self-indulgent, *The Times* looked rather like a person pretending to have said all along what he has just said for the first time and should have said much earlier. However obvious the hoax may have been to others in 1971, *The Times* sent La Barre's debunking review back to him in 1972 with a check and a cordial "no thanks." Do good grey institutions feel no embarrassment?

Perhaps we should ask the editors of *Saturday Review*, where a parallel course was followed (without, however, rejecting a knowledgeable review). In 1971 humanities professor Albert William Levi praised *Teachings* and *Separate Reality* for precision (La Barre's pseudo-ethnography) and sincerity (Bly's obvious hoax). In 1972 reviewer Joseph Kanon saluted the man he thought was the most remarkable of the few serious current experimenters in reality perception and psychic phenomena. Though intuitively and correctly describing Carlos and don Juan as "characters" in a "saga" interplaying like Watson and Holmes, Kanon could not bring to discursive expression an idea obvious to many: that Castaneda's account was as fictive as Conan Doyle's. Owing perhaps to this intrapsychic contradiction, *Saturday Review* fell mute for the next five years: neither *Tales of Power* nor *Castaneda's Journey* elicited comment. In 1978 *Second Ring* got short shrift from Thomas LeClair, who called it mind-mush, banality, and Mexican Gothic. LeClair said he had come to read Castaneda as fiction. It would be interesting to know just when and how the editors of *Saturday Review* came to read Castaneda as fiction, but all one got was a fast Bronx cheer for an author who had "finally run out of material." On the contrary, Castaneda's occultism promises to be inexhaustible. What finally ran out were the Juanist illusions of *Saturday Review* editors.

Am I being unfair? Is all this merely hindsight? Sad to say, it is not. In June 1969 *The New York Review of Books*—surely a publication not ignored by the editors of *The New York Times Book Review*—gave early warning caution was in order when anthropologist Edmund Leach said *Teachings* was "a work of art rather than of scholarship." Comparing it with T. Lobsang Rampa's pseudo-Tibetan mystical revelations, Leach said: "Castaneda's book is certainly not a complete spoof in this sense, but if it had been spoof, it might not have been very different. . . . It seems to me he has just fitted don Juan into a mold that is ready-made." The teachings, said Leach, were too much like Taoism, Yoga, Vedanta, and Zen to be true. As for the "Yaqui" way of knowledge: "If don Juan had been described as a man from Mars it would have made little difference." At best, Leach allowed, *The Teachings* might be a distorted literary account of some undisclosed actual experience. Faced with such authoritative dissent, a prudent *Times* reviewer would proceed warily. Indeed, both Simmons and Young recorded reservations, but they were superseded by more sanguine appreciators of pseudo-ethnography.

What excuse can be found for this headlong rush to approval? Should one grant editors can't read every book and must trust the judgment of their reviewers? Surely, but such editors do not then reject their most informed review. Perhaps La Barre's article was awkward or cranky? But if it had been defective, it could have been repaired by author or editor. In fact the article was fluent, competent, and readable, but quite uncompromising; its tone of outrage arose from a correct judgment that a scientific fraud was in progress. The *Times* sorely needed La Barre's review but promptly rejected it because it contradicted an already made-up editorial mind. In reviewing Castaneda, *The Times* preferred advocacy to criticism.

A better model was furnished by *Publishers Weekly*, where *Teachings* and *Separate Reality* drew high praise as enthralling accounts by an authentic pathfinder, respectfully interviewed in 1972. *Ixtlan's* slangy sorcerer and chronological retracings raised "some serious questions," but these were repressed in reviewing *Tales of Power*, and the four-book journey was called "consistent, luminous, profoundly exciting." When galley proofs of *Castaneda's Journey* arrived, there were handy excuses for passing them up: a small press on the West Coast, an unknown author. Responsible journalism, however, required *Publishers Weekly* to acknowledge a substantial challenge to its seven previous commendations of the don Juan books. In September 1976 a most complimentary review called *Castaneda's Journey* "a basic starting point for any serious discussion." The following year *Second Ring* was treated under nonfiction, but its authenticity was questioned.

To head off distracting sophistries and ad hominem rejoinders, it is necessary at this point to distinguish the aspirations of an author from the obligations of a reviewer. Ordinarily I should not expect a book by an unfamiliar author, coming from a small West Coast publisher, to be reviewed much of anywhere, let alone in the major reviewing periodicals, but this was not an ordinary case. *Castaneda's Journey* turned out to be quite reviewable: some 30 editors, not at *The Times*, accepted it for review. Two years later even *The Times* admitted its existence, but on the occasion when standards of good journalism required full and frank acknowledgement of a serious challenge *The Times* said nothing. If Castaneda had not then proceeded to write a book that offended practically everybody, I have no doubt the silence would have been permanent. That is hardly what one expects from a leading review periodical; grey it may be, good it is not.

The vogue of stone-age teachers caught on quickly. A year after don Juan surfaced in *The Times*, Grove Press published *Keep the River on Your Right*, whose search for exotic carnal knowledge was introduced by a prominent quotation from don Juan. Later, not meaning to suggest both were fictioneers, gay-journalist Jack Collins would write: "Schneebaum has portrayed male sexuality in the way Castaneda portrayed the visionary powers of the human mind." In 1971 Atheneum offered *Wizard of the Upper Amazon*, whose detailed acknowledgements neglected to mention Robert Carneiro's authoritative but private opinion that the book was jungle fiction.

Harper and Row joined the parade in 1972 with a lavishly illustrated volume promoted as "the first book about the ancient Ways of the Plains People to be written entirely by an Indian"—a claim called "patently untrue" by anthropologist John H. Moore, who listed four such books in the previous decade. Purporting to explain Cheyenne religion, *Seven Arrows* provoked widespread outrage in the tribe. The calmest comment Moore heard was: "complete B.S. from cover to cover." Author Hyemeyohsts Storm outdid Carlos's verbatim fieldnotes by producing long, abstract conversations that had supposedly taken place in sign language. Many details of the religion were wrong, and an earlier reviewer had called the book a desecration. Moore judged the philosophic framework to be primarily Buddhist. On the phone, the publishers admitted they had suspected *Seven Arrows* was inaccurate but had made no effort to verify the contents before presenting them to a naïve public as authentic Indian lore.

In 1976 Farrar, Straus and Giroux listed under "anthropology" a new translation of Antonin Artaud's poetic ravings about the Tarahumara Indians, inhabitants of the district Carlos and don Juan had visited to gather peyote and meet Mescalito. Artaud saw a shaman leap "with his army of bells, like an agglomeration of dazed bees caked together in a crackling and tempestuous disorder." He "saw that the rocks all had the shape of a woman's bosom with two perfectly delineated breasts." He "saw in the mountain a naked man leaning out of a large window. His head was nothing but a huge hole . . . in which the sun and moon appeared by turns." While few would mistake Artaud's mad metaphors for ethnography, publication of *The Peyote Dance* as anthropology paid obvious tribute to the popularity of Mescalito.

By spring 1977, according to Simon and Schuster, that popularity had sold nearly four-million don Juan books, every one in the name of nonfiction. S-&-S Vice President of Castanedics Michael Korda authored a book titled, *Power! How to Get It, How to Use It*, which appeared the year after *Tales of Power*. In this manual for mini-Machiavellis Korda gave lessons in manipulating fellow organization-persons, quoted reverently from the lessons of don Juan, and recounted a philosophical conversation he said had been held at the Central Park Zoo cafeteria with a tall, thin, New Yorker anthropologist friend of his, whose habits, character, interests, and vocabulary just happened to match Castaneda's point for point and term for term. Tom Bourne, a journalist to book sellers, interviewed Korda and quoted him as follows:

"I can't prove that don Juan exists. I don't have any photographs. But then, I can't prove that his critics exist, either—I take their word for it. Nobody could sustain the imaginative creation of don Juan the way Carlos has. Don Juan is terribly consistent. His character is not a variable inventive figure, as in works of fiction."

It may be Korda has never read Tolkien, whose name is dropped in his book, or any fiction writer except Castaneda, but I suspect he is just full of *buita* up to his *nakam*. A year after publishing *Second Ring* he called Castaneda "our most popular author." In fact, *Second Ring* showed up in remainder catalogues eleven months after publication, about the time Korda would have given the interview. In contrast, the trade edition of

Tales of Power had resisted remaindering for three-and-a-half years.

While factoids are still booming far and wide, don Juan seems to have peaked in *Journey to Ixtlan*. The "harrowing descent into the Stone Age mind" which "compelled" *Life* to "believe" in 1971 had become the "Gothic horror novel, stuffed full of infantile bogeymen" which repelled the *Sunday Times* of London in 1975. *Booklist* reviewed *Second Ring* under "fiction," and Castaneda's Mexican publisher had no plans to translate it into Spanish. Despite terminal puffery by power-powwower Michael Korda, the "most popular author" had been sharply demoted by reviewers and readers alike.

About the middle of Tuesday afternoon, 2 April 1979, Charley Trick and I were lunching at *Las Siete Flechas*, on the Paseo de la Reforma, with our guest, the prominent publisher Don Diógenes Lápiz-Saltillo y Quitacaretas, president of the Fondo de Cultura Etica, which had been publishing Charley's work in Spanish. Known to his fellow citizens as "Don D" (rhymes with *fawn grey* or *dawn* of *day*) the old gentleman has the odd but honored reputation of going about the city at noon with a flashlight in his hand—"because," he says, "of the darkness in the world"—asking passers-by to direct him to an honest man.

"*¿El hombre sincero—dónde está?*"—is what he used to say years ago, but now he just asks—"*¿Dónde?*"—and everyone knows what he means. Despite this eccentricity Don D has many wise things to say about the publishing game.

"I think it is not true," he rolled a long Chicharra cigar at his ear, "that Castañeda's only sorcery [*magia*] consisted of turning the University of California into an ass [*asno*]. He also made a monkey [*hizo un mono*] of *The New York Times.*"

Charley, who has a superb command of Spanish, burst out laughing, but Don D frowned.

"An honest man," he said, "ought to shed light in the world, not darkness." Drawing a small flashlight from his vest pocket, he shined it on the white tablecloth, saying, "This little spot of honest light [*luz honesta*] is worth more than the most imposing shadows of deception [*tinieblas del engaño*]."

Charley nodded solemnly, but I had to ask:

"Isn't each of us responsible for shedding his own light, Don D?"

The publisher put the flashlight exactly parallel with his cigar case. "Of course," he said.

"Well, then," I pressed my point, "isn't there a place for someone who makes 'night fall at noon,' if he also makes other people take out their own flashlights to find their way in the dark?"

Don D clipped his cigar with protracted finesse. Charley watched him warily. Finally Don D said:

"That would depend, I think, on why this man brings darkness. Does he suffer the darkness so that others may bring the light, or does he offer the light of others as an excuse for bringing his darkness? Which of the two does he love, the light or the darkness?"

"How can we know a thing like that?" I asked.

Don D raised the flashlight and played the beam across Charley's eyes. Charley smiled but said nothing.

"Perhaps even he doesn't know," said Don D.

As the world's champion anthromancer suffers defeat in the lists of best sellers, myriads of loyal cultists are gathering beneath a great opaque literary doom where they will welcome and keep him almost in the style to which a millionaire author grows accustomed, until he goes at last to join don Juan in the glimmering legend beyond. Did he love the light or did he love the darkness? Whatever one's answer, the cloning of a sorcerer by the Wizard of Westwood has been a tour de force the likes of which we shall not see for many a book season, if at all.

Uclanthropus Piltdunides Castanedae

"Don Juan may be the biggest hoax in anthropology since the Piltdown man," Marcello Truzzi wrote. The comparison is not superficial. Though Dawson's dawn man (*Eoanthropus dawsoni*) clung to the evolutionary tree 41 years (1912-1953) whereas Castaneda's UCLA-man trod quasi-Sonoran sands no more than eight (1968-1976), the episodes are alike in several ways.

Piltdown began with five pieces of a humanoid brain case and part of an ape-like lower jaw found by amateur geologist Charles Dawson in a gravel pit at the Piltdown prehistoric site, in Sussex. The fragments were assembled into a putative fossil skull by Dawson's friend Arthur Smith Woodward, of the British Museum. Though some doubted the validity of this reconstruction, Piltdown man was widely and confidently acclaimed as the missing link between simian and human beings, an evolutionary station now occupied by *Australopithecus*. Several hundred scientific articles were written about the discovery, nearly as many as about all other missing links put together, and only untimely death prevented the knighting of discoverer Dawson.

In 1953, when later finds had cast increasing doubt on Piltdown's theoretical status, his remains were critically re-examined. The bones turned out to have been chemically antiqued. The teeth bore tell-tale marks of artificial abrasion. The cranium had come from a modern man, the jawbone from an orang-utan, the latter judiciously broken off just at the point where its apehood would have become obvious, the teeth knowingly filed to simulate human wear.

Exposure of the forgery made it instantly clear Charles Dawson had been an unsavory character all along. For the next 19 years, billed as the Wizard of Sussex, he posthumously played the role of forger. In 1972 Ronald Millar argued that, whatever his technical accomplishments, Dawson had not been sufficiently grounded in evolutionary theory to prepare such a triumphant deceit and was very likely only a dupe of the real forger. Millar nominated Grafton Elliot Smith, a brilliant man of science, worried about his career and given to playing mordant jokes on his colleagues. Other writers would nominate Oxford's William J. Sollas and a man famous in quite another context, Teilhard de Chardin.

Science historian Ian Langham judges Grafton Elliot Smith to be the most promising candidate, with skull-assembler Woodward as possible accomplice. According to Smith, the brain had been the engine of human evolution. Reaching its human status before the features of the face, proto-man's enlarged brain endowed him with aesthetic propensities that made him an easy mark for a proto-pretty face. The small human jaw-bone had evolved through generations of his rejecting ugly, big-jawed proto-women and selecting prettier mates with smaller jaws. When found, the missing link should therefore have a humanoid brain case and an ape-like lower jaw. By fitting this prescription perfectly, Piltdown man proved Smith's theoretical acumen and revived his flagging career.

More important for science than the identity of the forger is the question asked by science historian Stephen Jay Gould: Why did anyone accept such an improbable creature as Piltdown man in the first place? Gould offers four kinds of reasons, which I list as: factional hopes, cultural biases, cognitive expectations, and taboo evidence. The factions were England and France. Though England had yet to come up with a single ancient ancestor, French paleoanthropologists could and did boast a superabundance of Neanderthals and Cro-Magnons. Piltdown furnished the English with an answer at last for the insufferable French. Cultural biases favored intelligence as the distinguishing human characteristic and the white race as the most advanced. Piltdown proved both the primacy of brain power and the primogeniture of Europeans. Cognitive expectations reduced the oddity of a human cranium attached to an ape's jaw by imaginatively perceiving human features in the ape jaw and ape features in the human cranium. The capacity of the cranium was underestimated; the teeth were said to be set in the jaw in a human fashion. Taboo evidence consisted of guarding the Piltdown specimens as holy relics too sacred to be handled. When Louis Leakey went to examine the Piltdown fossils in 1933, he was briefly shown the originals but allowed to work only with plaster replicas. Needless to say, signs of forgery could not be detected on the replicas.

One of the men who exposed the forgery offers a different version of the evidential taboo. Kenneth Oakley recalls three scientific visitors who were permitted to examine the Piltdown specimens at length, but when Carleton Coon thought he saw suspicious markings on the molars, he could not bring himself to mention them to anyone but his wife. The evidence was so small and uncertain, the implications so shocking and far-reaching that prudence dictated tactful silence. When zoologist Gerrit Miller concluded from long contemplation of plaster replicas that Piltdown was a fraud, colleagues persuaded him not to publish his conclusion, saying it was too serious an accusation to make without proof. Exposure had to wait another 23 years.

In light of the foregoing description, let me now list some similarities and differences between don Juan and Piltdown man:

Each was hailed by some as a giant step in science but was doubted from the beginning by others.

Each was the product of a clever deceiver who was very knowledgeable about the relevant scientific theory.

Each combined disparate elements—Piltdown bones of man and ape, don Juan pre-literate and modern conceptual systems.

Each provided superficially plausible support for a particular theoretical tendency—Piltdown for brain primacy, don Juan for ethnomethodology.

Each could have been exposed at once by a competent, skeptical inquiry—into the shape of Piltdown's teeth, into the existence of Carlos's voluminous Spanish fieldnotes, never offered for examination and now said to have been destroyed by flooding of Castaneda's basement.

Each wasted the time of or made fools of some trusting colleagues.

Each implicated possible but uncertain accomplices—Piltdown Teilhard de Chardin, William Sollas, and Arthur Smith Woodward; don Juan the professors who should have known they were dealing with an illusionist but apparently did not.

Each cast suspicion on an innocent party—Piltdown on Dawson, don Juan on Theodore Graves, who was said in the popular press to have been the "prime mover" of Castaneda's doctoral committee, though in fact he had left the country a year before Castaneda's dissertation was signed by five other professors.

Neither hoaxer confessed. Castaneda can still do so, of course, but frank confession would be quite out of character for him. His flagrant fourth and outlandish fifth books constitute a sort of implicit confession.

Each was supported by a faction—Piltdown by British paleoanthropologists, don Juan by anyone who thought publishing *The Teachings* or granting a doctorate to Castaneda would make merit for ethnomethodology or UCLA anthropology.

Each was rendered more congenial by cultural bias—Piltdown for favoring intelligence and white superiority, don Juan for demonstrating that an antirationalist noble savage could reflect 1960s idealism back to dissident but regular consumers of electricity and Kool-Aid as though from an ancient culture.

Each enjoyed the benefits of fallible cognition—as when Sir Arthur Keith thought he saw an orang's forehead on Piltdown's skull; as when academic readers consistently failed to notice how seriously the don Juan books contradicted each other.

Each was protected by taboo and tact—Piltdown must not be challenged by mere suspicions; Carlos's Spanish fieldnotes could not be demanded by scholars who deferred to colleagues on his committee, or by committee members to whom Castaneda seemed perennially on the verge of a nervous breakdown, psychologically too fragile to bear the normal burden of proof.

In other ways the episodes were quite different. The scientific cost of Piltdown was high, of don Juan low. Some forty years Sir Arthur Keith played dupe to Piltdown; much earth was moved in search of additional fragments; many lectures and articles expounded Piltdown's significance. Few anthropologists subscribed to don Juan; no scientific expeditions went out to find him; trifling research funds were diverted to him. The spate of Juanist writings has been literary, philosophical, and occult, seldom scientific.

Piltdown did more harm than good, his only contribution a warning against further frauds. Even in the realm of science don Juan may do more good than harm: exemplifying an inspiring if unattainable ideal of fieldwork, revealing a widespread confusion between authenticity and validity, and manifesting for laymen as well as professionals the rift between those anthropologists who, in Colin Turnbull's words, "regard anthropology primarily as a humanity and those who regard it primarily as a science."

The uses, costs, and benefits of lying have been treated by students of deception from Machiavelli to Sissela Bok. In his entertaining and instructive Hoaxes, Curtis D. MacDougall relates a number of schemes that furnished social benefits at apparently acceptable costs, whether by promoting worthy products, exposing misconduct, or testing public skepticism and finding it deficient. Violinist Fritz Kreisler often played unknown works of early masters discovered during his world tours. The pieces were, of course, well received and widely appreciated. After thirty years Kreisler confessed he had written them all himself. The editor of the Westchester News, while stealing a story from the Kennett Advertiser, failed to read backwards the names of Indian chief Yrotss Ihte Lotsi and his illustrious forebear, Ffutsse Lpoepre Htognil Aets, so spelled to catch him red handed. Journalist C. Louis Mortensen attributed many strange adventures to a certain Lester Green. One fall Lester flooded a meadow to insure a good ice crop for the summer. While cutting ice in February he found a setting of hen's eggs frozen in a block of ice. On thawing, the eggs hatched eight fur-covered chicks. When a Canadian farmer wrote asking to buy a pair of the furry chicks for arctic breeding, Mortensen declared they had all sweltered to death in the summer heat.

A less favorable cost-benefit ratio may be expected from scientific deceptions, which are not so rare as one might think. Newton made good use of fudge-factors in perfecting his quantifications. Cyril Burt's IQ distributions were systematically fabricated to fit the normal curve. Rodent ESP got a bogus boost at the Institute for Parapsychology. Skin grafts at the Sloan-Kettering Cancer Center turned out to be patches of paint.

The reasons for scientific fraud vary from pecuniary desire and professional ambition to an overwhelming impatience with data that stubbornly refuse direct passage to a blinding truth believed to exist just beyond them. Sometimes the belief is right and the fudger forgiven, sometimes it is wrong and the cheater chastised. Even in science, frauds that impose low costs and provide some visible benefits are likely to be called by the more friendly name of hoaxes. This is particularly true if their detection should have been easy in the first place. Don Juan is a good example.

One characteristic of the beneficial hoax is exposure by the perpetrator as soon as his object is accomplished. Since the didactic value of the don Juan books would be largely destroyed by admitting they are fictive, this course was not open to Castaneda, even after he had acquired a Ph.D. and become financially independent. On the other hand, after writing *The Teachings*, he did little to hide the fictive nature of his writings from the skeptical eye. Most laymen were tipped off by his second book. Requiring so much credulity from the reader and offering so much internal evidence of fabrication, the don Juan books hardly qualify as a serious, harmful fraud. I think it is reasonable to call them a remarkably successful, somewhat beneficial, self-revealing hoax.

One of don Juan's good deeds was to demonstrate that in a large academic department certain skeptical members would instantly recognize and reject an untrustworthy account, which other members would accept and persistently defend as legitimate, authentic work. In my judgment, this demonstration alone tips the scales of scientific costs and benefits in favor of the don Juan books.

A further revelation has been the reluctance of some uninvolved scientists to call the hoax by its right name, apparently because of a horror of frauds. Anthropologist Eugene N. Anderson Jr wrote:

de Mille exposed many inconsistencies that prove *either* that Castaneda was a brilliant fraud *or* that he was an incredibly careless and sloppy ethnographer in a disorganized department. If he was actually a brilliant faker, I think he would have covered his tracks better. Moreover, those of us who have met Castaneda and talked to him are, I am very sorry to say, more prone to believe the second alternative. The naive tone of his books is apparently not put on. . . . [Castaneda] could merely have been more clever a faker than von Däniken, but he could also have been what he says: a sorry ethnographer who mismanaged his field notes but got some real data.

I suspect Anderson's odd disjunction was born of a wish not to find scientific fraud so close to home. It is with difficulty that the same evidence will alternatively prove Castaneda a brilliant fraud and a careless, sloppy, mismanager of notes. Moreover, his writings are manifestly not careless, sloppy, and mismanaged but careful, neat, and coordinated. The "many inconsistencies" now recognized by Anderson were subtle enough to escape exposure for eight years. Having been taken in by Carlos-Naïf (the bumbler usually impersonated by the canny Castaneda) Anderson made the risky assumption no brilliant faker wants to be caught. But what fun is there in fooling people if they never find out they've been fooled and nobody sees how clever you are? After the success of his first book, Castaneda seeded his subsequent volumes with more and more clues that would lead us to our faker.

The attitude Anderson would like us to assume toward frauds in anthropology is suggested by his saying Castaneda may not have been an incompetent anthropologist but "merely more clever a faker than von Däniken," a statement that sharply depreciates faking as a scientific concern. To be more clever a faker than von Däniken is not much of an accomplishment, since von Däniken peddles blatant nonsense. Anderson's second strange implication is that brilliant hoaxing, unusual anywhere, is a "mere" alternative to something often seen in the academy: scholarly or technical incompetence.

The argument reflects a common tendency, when frauds or hoaxes are exposed, to say that no one, least of all the speaker, ever took them seriously. Historians, Langham observes, have tried to sweep the Piltdown episode under the rug, but to do so "is to ignore what was undoubtedly the mainstream of British physical anthropology for several decades." Likewise, some would dismiss the don Juan hoax as a money-making scheme or an administrative mixup having nothing to do with the mainstream of anthropology, but to do so is to forgo valuable lessons. By facing up to the implications of frauds and hoaxes, and of their acceptance in quarters where people should know better, and of attempts to dismiss them once exposed, we can learn much about the way science is conducted, about the nature of sophisticated beliefs, and about the surprising difficulty of achieving consensus through civil dialogue among well-disposed, intelligent, professional people who are at the same time passionately committed to particular theories of how the world is put together or to particular propositions about how to be a moral scientist doing proper science.

Sonoragate or Tales of Folly

In June 1969 *The Teachings of Don Juan* was reviewed in the *American Anthropologist* by an eminent ethnographer who said it was "an excellent piece of work" which "should attain a solid place in the literature of both hallucinogenic drugs and the field behavior of anthropologists." The reviewer found Castaneda's accounts better than Aldous Huxley's because apparently less distorted by literary reworking. As the leading authority on Yaqui culture, he rejected the subtitle, *A Yaqui Way of Knowledge*, but suspected it had been added by the publisher without the author's approval. Ten years later, *Second Ring of Power* was reviewed in the same journal by a non-anthropologist who labelled the don Juan books "spoofery" and "sham annals," which, he said:

> brilliantly melodramatize theoretical and methodological controversies that are troubling social science deeply. For all his trickery and playfulness, Castaneda knows as much about allegorizing ethnomethodology as actual field workers know about kinship charting or participant observing. His committee may have had good—if unusual—reasons for accepting *Ixtlan* under another name as a dissertation in anthropology. If so, they would have saved the rest of us a lot of confusion by announcing those reasons forthrightly.

The reviewer predicted *Second Ring* would be "the last Juan-book noticed by anthropologists."

Though don Juan spent ten years travelling this critical path from fact to fiction, his destination was posted from the start. In the same month when Edward Spicer preferred Castaneda's university-warranted factual accounts to Huxley's untrustworthy literary descriptions, another eminent ethnographer, Edmund Leach, said *Teachings* could surely not be "a complete spoof" like Lobsang Rampa's *Third Eye* but must still be "a work of art rather than of scholarship"; as such, he thought it was "very good indeed," though not up to the standard of *Moby Dick* or *The Ancient Mariner*. The conflicting courses thus calmly charted by these two disinterested senior anthropologists would collide nine years later in Los Angeles at a convocation of excited partisans. In the meantime scholars far and wide steered one course or the other.

Castaneda's most conspicuous patron was Walter Goldschmidt, whose laudatory Foreword commended *The Teachings* to scholars and laymen as an authentic report and a work of "ethnography." Spicer knew *Teachings* was not ethnography, since don Juan existed "in a cultural limbo," but he did take it to be an authentic report. Mary Douglas argued Castaneda's authenticity, and by October 1976 some 18 anthropologists had publicly accepted the don Juan books (or some of them) as factual accounts.

On the other side of the question, one of the early doubters was ethnobotanist Gordon Wasson, who "smelled a hoax" while reading *The Teachings*, judged *Separate Reality* "science fiction," and called *Ixtlan* "a romance." Spicer's colleague Keith Basso found don Juan "always slightly less than believable" and said the books "should not be mistaken for ethnography." Mexico's Jesús Ochoa told *Time* the books contained "a very high percentage of imagination," while Northwestern's Francis Hsu put them in a class with *Gulliver's Travels*. Weston La Barre, we know, called them "pseudo-ethnography."

Published in October 1976, *Castaneda's Journey* said the don Juan books were not only fiction but based in part on the very literary descriptions Spicer had preferred *The Teachings* to. Readers who had been suspicious of Castaneda liked *Castaneda's Journey* and said it proved the don Juan books a hoax. Readers who had taken don Juan at face value found much to criticize in *Castaneda's Journey* and said the case it made was weak or only circumstantial. What a strong or non-circumstantial case would have involved I'm not sure, but I suspect it would have required a confession from Castaneda, or maybe don Juan.

One reader to let his mind be changed was anthropologist Joseph K. Long, who had criticized Castaneda for scientific shortcomings but had himself gone pretty far out on a limb to meet don Juan. A specialist in the anthropology of psychic events, he was struck by Carlos's colorful divination of book-thieving and by don Juan's "extremely powerful telepathic abilities." He recognized don Juan's gait of power as Tibetan trance running. Both in a published essay and at his 1974 symposium on parapsychology and anthropology he credited Castaneda with forcing anthropologists to take the paranormal seriously. Taking the paranormal seriously was not the best way to advance one's career in anthropology, so Long was already at risk. When *Castaneda's Journey* convinced him the don Juan books were a hoax, he felt betrayed by Castaneda. The feeling was not assuaged by a review I wrote of his *Extrasensory Ecology*, in which I said its many respectful citations of Carlos's chimerical fieldwork provided comic relief. Long is a man of principle and determination, however, distractable only by sticks or stones.

"Unlike de Mille," Marcello Truzzi had written, "who seems somewhat amused by the whole episode, I earlier found myself aghast at the initial reactions of the social-scientific community to Castaneda's books and am outraged by the lack of serious reaction now that they are exposed as frauds." Truzzi's indignation was shared by Long, who presently felt compelled to launch a critical inquiry into Castaneda's works at the annual meeting of anthropologists. In February 1978 he began to draw up plans and write letters to the American Anthropological Association.

A frustrating series of exchanges soon made it plain that cooler heads at AAA were dragging their feet. The official position seemed to be that (an open) discussion of such a (delicate) matter would not be science and could therefore not be included in the main program, while at the same time the topic did have scientific implications and so did not qualify as a non-scientific special event. In desperation Long offered to bring the matter up from the floor of the business meeting. Weeks passed with no reaction from AAA. The champion of open inquiry began to worry that he had made enemies on high without getting anything here below. Walter Goldschmidt, recently President of AAA, drifted eschatonically through his nightmares, glumly shaking a patriarchal head. Then one day, without comment, the special session was approved.

During his maneuvering Long had submitted various proposals with different titles. The one that stuck was "Fraud and Publishing Ethics," which served to cover don Juan, Castaneda's faculty sponsors, and the University of California Press without naming any of them. Of course, everyone was invited. Duplicate letters went out to Castaneda at UCLA and in care of his literary agent in Beverly Hills. The members of his doctoral committee were invited. The University Press received an invitation—and was the only one to accept. Substitutes agreed to speak up for Castaneda, but apparently no one was willing to represent his doctoral committee.

Scheduled from 5:30 to 7:00 PM, Wednesday 15 November in the West Regency Ballroom of the Hyatt Regency Hotel, the session was described as a "panel discussion of books published as non-fiction but subsequently exposed as frauds and related ethical problems." Not really a grabber, but people would be standing at the back of the big room before the session was over. As I arrived, a pleasant looking young man was setting up professional tape-recording equipment. I asked him what would be done with the tapes, and he said each panelist would get a transcript. I was very glad to hear that because, unlike Carlos, I have difficulty writing down everything that is said in an animated conversation. I made a mental note to compliment Long on his thorough arrangements.

In his opening remarks Long said the panel had been precipitated by his own embarrassment at having accepted don Juan's authenticity for several years. He regretted the fact that most of the principal prospective speakers had not acknowledged their invitations and expressed a forlorn hope that some of them might still venture to the dais. In the meantime, he introduced me.

I spoke briefly and cautiously, my eye on the tape recorder. The University of California Press, I said, had published as a factual account and work of science *The Teachings of Don Juan*, whose authenticity had then been questioned in a review by a prominent anthropologist. Next, a doctoral committee at UCLA had accepted as a dissertation from the same author a book already popularly published under a different title and logically inconsistent with *The Teachings*. It was not possible, I said, that the book published by the University and the dissertation accepted by the University were both factual accounts. The still unexplained contradiction between them had raised questions of authenticity and propriety, which it had been my privilege to present in depth to the community of anthropological scholars. I concluded with the hope that this session would bring forth the answers for which so many had been waiting.

The next speaker was Agehananda Bharati, who read a version of his article reproduced in this volume. In sum, he said don Juan's mysticism was eclectic fakery, a patchwork of literary odds and ends. In passing he said Amerindian mysticism was third-rate when compared with Indo-Tibetan mysticism.

C. Scott Littleton, of Occidental College, retorted that Native American mystics were quite as adept as Indo-Tibetans. He said Castaneda had begun as a scientist but now felt himself a sorcerer, in which case it was perfectly all right for the teacher to be inside the pupil's head. Littleton's belief in the original authenticity of don Juan remained unshaken by de Mille's proof, which, he said, was not the "smoking gun" that would be needed to convict his old friend Carlos of perpetrating a fraud.

Joseph Long revealed that in keeping with the broad title of the session he had invited the publishers of *Tales of Power*, *The Amityville Horror: A True Story*, and *In His Image: The Cloning of a Man* to send representatives. The publishers had declined and one, displaying gallish wit, had threatened to sue if its book were mentioned. Long introduced the next speaker, and the audience sat a little straighter.

Philip Lilienthal, Associate Director of the University of California Press, said a manuscript had been received from Castaneda in 1967 and published in 1968. An academic press, he said, must rely on its professional consultants to judge the worth of any prospective publication. Concerning *The Teachings of Don Juan*, all of the recommendations had been favorable. I thought that was a dignified sort of statement, but I wondered why the Press had not sought the opinion of the man sitting next to Lilienthal at the table, who was not only an authority on the Yaqui Indians and a member of the UCLA faculty but also a former teacher of Castaneda's. It occurred to me that professional consultants can be selected so as to avoid recommendations uncongenial to sponsoring editors.

The man next to Lilienthal stood up, a tall, old man with a short, white beard, his voice gravelly but deep. He had come to admit a mistake. Ralph L. Beals had judged Carlos Castaneda to be academically unprepared for graduate study in anthropology but had been persuaded to sponsor him for admission into the program. When Castaneda said he had met a Yaqui shaman, Beals was surprised but thought shamanism might possibly have been overlooked among the secretive Yaqui. Presently, growing suspicious of Carlos's weekend field trips, he asked to see some fieldnotes and soon lost sight of Castaneda. The University Press had been careless, Beals thought, not to call on him or Spicer for an opinion of Castaneda's manuscript. "Some of my colleagues were naïve," he said, "in failing to insist on seeing his basic data before giving him a Ph.D." "Departments do make mistakes," he observed. "I remember complaining to a colleague about someone who had gotten a Ph.D., and he looked at me coldly and said: 'Would you have been willing to face the commotion that would have occurred if I had refused to give him a Ph.D.?' I agreed I wouldn't have faced it." It was not clear whether Beals was referring to Castaneda or some other candidate. "There was a mistake in my department," he concluded. "I'm sorry about it, and I'm apologizing for it."

Most of these comments reiterated things Beals had said in articles published during the preceding year, but saying them in a meeting of anthropologists, with his "naïve" or "careless" colleagues present at least in spirit, gave them a force that had not come from the printed page. Though I have talked several times with Beals and exchanged a few letters with him, I cannot say I know him very well. Nevertheless, I feel it must have hurt him to criticize men he had worked with for years, at least one of them a friend of early days. I think Beals felt he had to come to the meeting and say those things because others who should come would not. His attendance was an unpleasant duty resolutely done. Nor was I convinced that confronted with an unqualified doctoral candidate he would not have faced the commotion; I thought he would have faced it then as now.

Long proposed that anthropological dissertations discovered to be inauthentic should be reclassified as fiction by the committee that had granted the degree and that news of the reclassification should be disseminated to the community of scholars. He introduced Stan Wilk, who spoke along the lines of his contribution to this volume, commending Castaneda's works as a necessary complement to scientific anthropology, a mythic study of science to complete the scientific study of myth.

Long invited questions from the floor. One was whether anyone had seen evidence of Carlos's magical powers. I described an ESP study by UCLA anthropological psychologist Douglass Price-Williams, in which Castaneda had possibly influenced the dreams of other participants. I said this was no proof of his magical powers, since the paranormal agent could as well have been the experimenter as the sorcerer. Price-Williams, who was in the room, took this to be an insinuation of dishonest reporting, a misunderstanding that got cleared up the following day. Parapsychologist D. Scott Rogo rose to say that the most probable paranormal agents were the dreamers themselves, not the sorcerer or the experimenter.

Someone asked whether I had made a lot of money bad-mouthing a genius. I said, you better believe it, hundreds and hundreds of dollars. This question is asked by persons who resent criticism of their hero and know nothing about the comparative royalties paid to best-selling fiction writers and their scholarly or literary critics. Since the question is asked so often, I sat down afterwards and calculated hourly rates of compensation for my writing and Castaneda's. Ned Brown had said *Ixtlan's* paperback sales would make his client a millionaire. Setting an agent's exaggeration against the passage of subsequent years and Simon and Schuster's claim of four-million sales, we can reasonably assume Castaneda has received a million dollars for his writing. Ignoring the hours he put in on his academic requirements, and on driving a taxi or whatever he did to earn a living before the royalties started to roll in, we can call him a full-time writer and overestimate his writing time at 2000 hours a year for 20 years, or 40-thousand hours. On that basis we underestimate his hourly writing rate at $25. I worked at least two years, or 4000 hours, writing and promoting *Castaneda's Journey*, from which I have received ten-thousand dollars, so my hourly writing rate works out at $2.50. Readers who are not Juanist fanatics like my interrogator recognize that the full social value of Castaneda's work cannot be realized without adequate criticism and that whoever provides that criticism deserves to be compensated. If the necessary criticism is compensated at one-tenth Castaneda's rate and lower than the minimum wage, it is not exactly a parasite's free ride on the back of a great man, as one of Castaneda's committee members put it to me. I am satisfied with my compensation for the work, and I suppose Castaneda is satisfied with his. People whose main interest is making money don't go into writing of any kind unless they are misinformed about the prospects. Most freelance writers, good or bad, make very little money from writing. Castaneda belongs to the tiny fraction who get lucky. The rest do it for love alone. They do it because, like him, they are possessed by Calliope, Polymnia, Mescalito, or some other ally. Like Castaneda, they dream sometimes of being rich and famous, but they don't count on it. One thing most people, including most writers, don't know is that bad writers, commercial hacks, and literary prostitutes work just as hard and believe just as much in what they are doing as the best and most gifted writers. The proof is in the reading not the writing. Castaneda got where he is by focusing a modest writing talent on a trendy topic with unbending intent, the same way a lot of other writers have succeeded. If he had not been from the age of eight a habitual teller of tall tales, he could have become a successful professor of anthropology, in which case my interrogator would probably never have heard of him.

A woman rose to declare angrily that no one had ever asked to see *her* fieldnotes. (She can read my delayed answer as Point Eight in Chapter Six.) Stung by the implication that professors should never ask to see fieldnotes, Marcello Truzzi took the floor to deliver an impassioned plea for pulling anthropology's scientific socks up. From my notes, I reconstruct his remarks as follows:

> I'm concerned about what all this says not about Castaneda but about anthropology. What I've been hearing suggests an incredible scientific disarray. Anthropologists are quick to criticize exoheretics like von Däniken, but when it comes to endoheretics [deviant insiders] there's a great reluctance to talk. Most of the criticism has not come from anthropologists [Truzzi is a

sociologist], and when anthropologists do speak, they say something oblique. Our chairman, for example, calls Castaneda's books bad parapsychology. Bharati calls them lousy mysticism. What I want to know is, what kind of anthropology are they? Students find Castaneda in your introductory readers and think they are getting ethnography about a typical shaman. Do you really need a "smoking gun" before you can do something about this? Normally the burden of proof in science is on the claimant. If you shift that burden to the community of scholars, what will you do with all the subjective and fraudulent dissertations you will get—say they resonate beautifully, say they're symbolically true? What's happened to the canons of science? Where are organized skepticism, empirical falsifiability, and logical consistency in anthropology today? Or don't you know what anthropology is any more?

After some applause, Truzzi was answered by Wilk, who said shamans know as much as anthropologists do. If Truzzi had still held the floor, he would no doubt have replied that everybody knows as much as everybody else, but not about the same things. Shamans, real or imaginary, visit the other world, but they don't know how to do anthropology, which is what anthropologists are supposed to know.

A man asked me whether the best and bravest fieldworkers would be subjected to an inquisition like this every year from now on. I said I thought this would be the last time. Long, who had his wits about him, said it might be the last time but the important thing about it was that it was also the *first* time, having been overdue for some years. He asked if there were any further questions. A man stood up and said he had a statement to make. I didn't recognize him, but Long said: "By all means, Professor Goldschmidt. Please come up to the microphone"—or words to that effect. The room got very quiet. Goldschmidt strode rapidly to the dais, holding a prepared statement he had been saving throughout the session.

My thoughts went back to a day in 1975 when I had written a letter to Goldschmidt asking, on behalf of my readers, for "a sensible explanation of the most intriguing literary-academic puzzle of the decade." Though fair, the letter was far from ingratiating. It expressed my suspicion that Goldschmidt had endorsed *The Teachings* as an authentic account at a time when he had doubts whether Castaneda had actually carried out the fieldwork it described. Two things had raised this suspicion in my mind.

One was that Goldschmidt had reportedly told a common friend that he had this very doubt. The other was Goldschmidt's peculiar description of *The Teachings* as "both ethnography and allegory." I asked whether our friend had reported his comment accurately, and how a book could be both ethnography and allegory. I said his Foreword looked like a joke on his colleagues and the reader. I asked him to clarify the matter and point out any errors in my reasoning.

Goldschmidt didn't like the letter. More than that, he found it "totally unpleasant." Instead of answering it, however, he wrote to the Committee on Scientific and Professional Ethics and Conduct of the American Psychological Association, complaining that I was subjecting him to "intellectual blackmail" by telling him that if he did not answer my questions I would describe what had happened at UCLA in my own way, implying that his silence gave consent to that description. He was, of course, right in the sense that if he did not respond I should have to go ahead without him, and his silence would lead some people to infer that faculty members involved in the Castaneda episode could not think of a good answer to my speculations and might even recognize them as true. The normal thing to do in such a case would be to answer the challenge directly, not complain to some distant board of elders.

The Ethics Committee must not have met for quite a while, since three months went by before I got a letter from Goldschmidt telling me what he had done and relaying the Committee's judgment that I hadn't done anything unethical yet. He warned me, however, that he and the Committee thought I might possibly do something unethical if I treated his silence as consent. I replied that I had no intention of stating or implying that he endorsed my Castaneda theory, if he did not in fact endorse it, nor could I find anything in my previous letter that would suggest such a thing. "My intention," I said, "is only to give the first plausible explanation of a celebrated and perplexing academic anomaly." I pointed out that his decision to say nothing could not and should not deter me from my task of consumer advocacy in social science. Blackmail, I said, was hardly an appropriate term, since it meant I was threatening to reveal his private information if he did not cooperate, whereas his private information was precisely what I did not have any of even after receiving his much delayed letter. Perhaps, I said, he had meant extortion, which is a threat to do something unpleasant and unethical unless demands are met, but I said that model didn't fit either, because what I proposed to do, however unpleasant it might seem to him, was completely ethical and indeed obligatory, and I would do it whether he contributed his clarifying statement or not. Offering him an opportunity to have his say in my book was, I said, a courtesy, which ought to be appreciated rather than condemned.

That letter brought no response. Three months before Goldschmidt's unscheduled appearance at the microphone in the Hyatt Regency Ballroom, I wrote him in a conciliatory vein, reviewing our not exceptionally cordial previous correspondence, explaining the investigative reporter's tactical need to ruffle a few feathers, assuring him there was nothing personal in it, and proposing that we ascend to a higher plane of professional collaboration. I said I no longer suspected him of playing pranks but thought most likely he had simply misjudged *The Teachings*. I said, however, that no matter how charming the manuscript had been, someone had to be responsible for applying normal, routine skepticism and Goldschmidt, as both department chairman and ranking anthropologist on the Editorial Committee, had been the one most obviously in that position. I urged him to come to the meeting and candidly admit having made a mistake in commending the book as a factual account. I said such an admission would instantly elicit both gratitude and admiration from the profession and would put an end to rumors and accusations. Sitting only a few feet from Goldschmidt as he addressed the assembled supporters and detractors, I wondered what his answer would be.

Goldschmidt said he would speak neither for the University nor for the Anthropology Department but only for the particular members of the faculty who had been involved with Castaneda. As the statement developed, those turned out to be Goldschmidt and six faculty members who had served on Castaneda's graduate committees. It did not include all who had served but only those who had continued to look with favor on Castaneda's candidacy. For brevity, I shall call this group Castaneda's patrons.

The presentation began in a humorous spirit, recalling how Castaneda's fans had deluged the Department with demands for sorcering know-how and show-biz services, but soon Goldschmidt was deploring the fact that many potentially damaging statements had been made, along with suggestions of fraud and deceit. These charges, Goldschmidt said, had not been made in public, largely because they were libelous unless they could be proved. I was startled to hear that charges had been made in private and wondered who could have been making them, behind my back so to speak. Quite a number had been made in public during the preceding ten years, and a list of such charges serves below to organize the substance of the patrons' testimony, delivered by

Goldschmidt, most of which was a tedious recital of historical details emphasizing everything that was ordinary and blameless about Castaneda's graduate career. Across this academic boilerplate were studded a few riveting comments.

Ralph Beals had said Castaneda's undergraduate preparation was deficient, his coursework poor. The patrons responded that the candidate had been admitted to graduate study on the basis of examinations, had been required to take extra courses to make up his deficiencies, had done satisfactory course work, and had passed comprehensive predoctoral examinations. An effective answer, I thought.

Eugene Anderson had said: "Very few anthropology departments would have accepted *Journey to Ixtlan* as a thesis—I doubt if UCLA would today." He added, "in charity," that the problems of the UCLA anthropology department had been mostly cleared up "by better chairpeople." The patrons countered by saying Castaneda's dissertation had been unanimously accepted by his committee (which contained three anthropologists, two of whom were in the Department).

Spicer had said *The Teachings* lacked social context, Indian terms, and special terms for important Juanist concepts. I had asked where Carlos's fieldnotes, photographs, tapes, and plant specimens had been deposited. Goldschmidt disclosed that during the early fieldwork, when Castaneda was studying shamanism under archaeologist Clement Meighan, he had begun collecting basketry "of a type that had to be obtained directly from the Indians as they could not have been collected from commercial sources." These nondescript baskets supposedly linked Castaneda with Indians, and not with any middleman, but since there is nothing about baskets in the don Juan books, the link had no confirming implications. On the contrary, it was disconfirming, for a few irrelevant baskets of uncertain provenance are scant evidence for ten years of fieldwork. If the patrons had seen anything better, they would surely have mentioned it. If baskets was the best they had seen, why had they never concerned themselves about authentication? If a scrap of obviously inadequate evidence was worth mentioning, why was the complete absence of adequate evidence not worth mentioning? The patrons would have done better to leave the baskets out of it.

Goldschmidt said the Department had awarded Castaneda a small sum of money in 1962 to support his fieldwork with an Indian "curer." The statement caught my attention for two reasons. The less important was that Castaneda had told Bruce Cook: "Nobody helped me with the research. I had no grants." The more important was that don Juan is nowhere described as a curer, and no curer appears in the story. Apparently the patrons had a rather inaccurate idea of what their protégé was doing, or would later say he had been doing, with the aid of a small grant he would then deny having received.

Castaneda had told Sandra Burton of *Time* that Harold Garfinkel was his chief thesis adviser, and Arnold Mandell had drawn uncomplimentary inferences from that reported relationship, as had *Castaneda's Journey*. Mary Douglas believed Castaneda's professors had imposed an ethnomethodological analysis on *The Teachings*. Goldschmidt said Castaneda's research had involved several faculty members, most importantly Clement Meighan. It was hard for me to see how an archaeologist could have elicited from Castaneda an opus whose ethnomethodological significance took me a long chapter and David Silverman a whole book to expound, but perhaps Meighan has unsuspected phenomenologicogenic powers.

Two of Goldschmidt's departmental colleagues had published articles in the *American Anthropologist* listing the scientific deficiencies of Castaneda's field reports. Jacques Maquet charged Castaneda with "methodological neglect"; Ralph Beals said Castaneda had broken the rules of scientific reporting. Goldschmidt said Castaneda's work had the virtue of originality and was in the tradition of anomalistic phenomenology, where a person's own experience is appropriate for examination. I wondered whether he would also say the tradition of anomalistic phenomenology could accommodate wholly fabricated accounts. Clement Meighan had told Don Strachan: "A lot of people get distressed because [Castaneda] reports things like being a frog and jumping across a pond as if it's really going on." Perhaps they do, but what exercises Castaneda's scientific critics is that he reports things like meeting an old Indian in a bus station and doing ten years of fieldwork as if it's really going on. I wrote to Meighan asking whether a committee in scientific anthropology should accept an account of fieldwork that is *entirely* imaginary. In other words, is a daydream an informant? Is a fantasy a field report? Meighan did not reply.

Empirical falsifiability and logical consistency have been called generic cognitive norms of science. In plain language, one should test one's theory against observations and one's observations against further observations, and one's statements about theory and observations should hang together. Since field observations are very hard to duplicate, anthropology is systematically weak in empirical testing, which means that internal consistency is all the more important in judging field reports. The most effective scientific criticism of the don Juan books has been the analysis of their internal contradictions presented in *Castaneda's Journey*. By November 1978 this fact was known to many anthropologists, who had read about it in the *American Anthropologist*. It was not unknown to the patrons, some of whom had been complaining about it privately. Yet Goldschmidt said: "We possess no information whatever that would support the charges [of fraud and deceit] that have been made." Thus evidence and argument called by one anthropological reviewer "the strongest critique to date from a social scientist" was flatly rejected, not only as proof but even as supporting evidence. The patrons were not going to recognize that kind of evidence. It was not clear what kind of evidence they would recognize.

Had it not been for Goldschmidt's legitimizing Foreword to *The Teachings*, Joseph Long had written, Castaneda's writings might never have been considered more than psychedelic ramblings. Journalist Paul Preuss had interviewed Goldschmidt during the summer and reported that Goldschmidt had been "charmed" by Castaneda's manuscript, had presented it to the other members of the Editorial Committee, had read them the section about the four enemies of a man of knowledge, and had written the Foreword "at his own suggestion, in order to establish Castaneda's credentials as a UCLA graduate student." Goldschmidt reminded the audience in the Ballroom that four colleagues had written letters about *The Teachings*. "With these uniformly favorable reviews in hand," he said, "and having read the manuscript, I recommended publication, and the Editorial Committee approved, with the proviso that an appropriate foreword be prepared that would establish the credentials of the author as a graduate student in anthropology. I provided such a foreword to *The Teachings of Don Juan*. I am not going to say *mea culpa!*"

Which was clearly the answer to my letter. No mistake had been made in publishing *The Teachings* as a factual account, as a work of "ethnography," or as a study subtitled *A Yaqui Way of Knowledge*. Logical conflicts between *Teachings* and *Ixtlan* had no significance. Criticism from Maquet, Beals, and others was not worth acknowledging. Though Beals had apologized for the Department, the patrons would not apologize for themselves, would not admit making an error of any degree or kind, would not recognize the possibility that an error had been made, and would not entertain questions of validity or even authenticity.

"We do not consider it appropriate here," they said, "to evaluate the works of Carlos Castaneda."

"We cannot confirm or deny fraud."

Which was just what most of the audience had come to find out: Were Castaneda's works fraudulent or not? The patrons would not say they were, which surprised no one, and would not say they were not, which surprised nearly everyone. Goldschmidt returned to his seat.

Long came to the microphone, thanked the speaker, and said he was "satisfied" with the statement. How he could be satisfied I didn't know, since the patrons had refused to address the very questions that had convened the panel, but now I think his "satisfaction" was sudden relief that the speech had come to an end without the roof's caving in. Bharati rose to disagree with particular statements, whereupon Goldschmidt rushed back to the microphone to say he hoped Bharati didn't read as carelessly as he listened. From the audience, biophysicist Allen Ansevin deplored the lack of clarification in the patrons' statement and said the profession of anthropology had a duty to serve the public by answering the kinds of questions the patrons had deemed inappropriate.

One question that *had* been answered was whether *Ixtlan* had been published commercially before being accepted as a dissertation. Goldschmidt said it had not. Then he said it was his understanding that it had not. Then he said it was "a matter of total non-importance" whether it had or not. (For the record, *Ixtlan* was published 23 October 1972; Castaneda defended *Sorcery* in January 1973.) "It is my understanding," Goldschmidt said, "that the University has the privilege of awarding a doctorate for work already published." Most scholars would agree with that, but the question that occurred to me was: If you are going to award a doctorate "for work already published," why should its title be changed to one that will not be recognized as the same work?

The session began to break up. People were milling around. The young man with the recording equipment came up and asked me how to spell my name. Then he asked how to spell Castaneda, Goldschmidt, and various other names. He didn't take my address.

On the following day, the scientific program included a symposium titled: "Before Carlos C.: Experiential Anthropology and Altered States." Castaneda's name did not appear in any of the published abstracts, but most of the participants mentioned him. Joan Koss said his books had made it easier for anthropologists to report their own altered states of consciousness, which they may have been keeping secret to avoid embarrassment and loss of status in the profession. Lola Romanucci-Ross saw don Juan as a graduate-student exercise, a garfinkelling metaphor, not much of a guide on the path of knowledge whether discursive or visionary. Warren d'Azevedo recalled having endowed some of his early shamanic informants with unrealistic heroic traits like don Juan's while casting himself in a Carlosian role of humble seeker. Philip Staniford praised Carlos for bringing wisdom from other cultures. John Messenger confessed that a poltergeist had been pestering him for years but said he had little confidence in don Juan or Carlos. Lowell Bean told how he had washed eggs for the Indians and revealed that chickens are filthy beasts. He described his psychic experiences among the Cahuilla. He said our tendency to doubt Carlos Castaneda, "a fine, gentle, kindly young man," proceeded from envy of his abilities. "The problem," he said, "is not in Carlos Castaneda but in us." I felt that if there were one person who could convince me I was wrong about Castaneda it would be Lowell Bean, who seemed to share the amiability, dedication, and psychic powers of the legendary Carlos.

The next afternoon I addressed Joseph Long's symposium on anthropology and the paranormal, saying the don Juan hoax could help clarify three requirements of anomalistic anthropology: the need to distinguish anomalies (truly paranormal events) from superstitions (false beliefs about supernatural events); the fieldworker's obligation to examine his own attitudes toward the paranormal so as to avoid errors of either skepticism or subscription; and the need to distinguish validity from authenticity. Eugene Anderson had written: "There is really no way that a thesis committee can check on the claims of a student about his field work." I called the assertion a travesty of science and an insult to countless fieldworkers who have reported in good faith to the best of their ability. Abject submission to fraud, I concluded, is neither honorable nor necessary.

Anderson's assertion deduced too much from the fact that anthropologists rarely go into the field to replicate each other's work or test each other's claims. This familiar weakness of fieldwork does not mean there is *no* way ever to detect a fabricated account. Logically inconsistent reporting can be recognized and should be challenged. In some cases mismanaged records can be straightened out; in others fraud may be discovered. The members of Castaneda's committee were responsible for recognizing the inconsistency between *The Teachings* and *Sorcery/Ixtlan*. Having failed to recognize or to acknowledge it, they were all the more obliged to acknowledge it when it was recognized and pointed out to them by others.

The same day I had a pleasant conversation with James H. Clark, Director of the University of California Press, who had inherited the

Castaneda controversy from the previous director. A *Los Angeles Times* interview had quoted Clark saying he thanked God for marketable books like *Ishi* and *The Teachings*, which "allow us the luxury of having an editor spend a lot of time on an academic series that just won't sell." Both on the spot and in a letter I asked Clark whether he would put *Teachings* in the same class with *Ishi*, a book well received by scholars. Clark said he would not engage in the controversy over the scholarly merits of *The Teachings*; he had been talking about marketable books in general; *Ishi* and *Teachings* were just two examples of marketable books. I pointed out that while considering *Teachings* for publication the Press had consulted several anthropologists but had neglected to consult Spicer or Beals, both experts on the Yaqui, one of whom had advised Castaneda on his early plans for fieldwork, had been his teacher and his chairman, had objected to don Juan's being called a Yaqui, and was only a campus phone call away from the Los Angeles office of the Press. Clark answered that the Press had "exercised proper procedures in having the manuscript reviewed by three professional anthropologists who endorsed its publication based on their judgments at that time about the scholarly merit of the work. The Editorial Committee of the University of California Academic Senate reviewed these professors' evaluations and the recommendation of the committee member who read the manuscript, and they also recommended publication." A warrior grieves not for what is past.

Robert Zachary is an editor at the Los Angeles office of the University Press and one of the original "sponsoring editors" under the previous director. "Sponsoring editors," Zachary said, "are entrusted with a publishing program from start to finish. We find a manuscript, we evaluate it, we cost it, we're involved in design and printing, we advise on promotion, and we try to help the sales people." "We discovered Castaneda," Zachary said, "but we weren't sure what we had discovered. He sent us his manuscript in late 1967. . . . I thought it was quite novel. Two other editors read it and agreed. But would it pass muster with our Anthropology Department? When we showed it to them, they were all positive, and other anthropologists recommended it too."

"The University of California Press ballyhooed Castaneda's book for the pop trade, and edited it with this in mind," wrote Eugene Anderson. I don't know how Anderson found out what Zachary and his two co-editors had "in mind," but the advertisement the Press put on the back cover of the *American Anthropologist* of June 1968 called *Teachings* "nothing less than a revelation, [an] unprecedented . . . living document of the spirit," which sounds more like new-age religion than scholarship or fieldwork. Ten years later the Press was still hailing *The Teachings* as its winner for 1968, and the new director thanked God for books like that, but sponsoring editor Zachary seemed to have had second thoughts. "The University Press is not interested in best sellers," he told Herbert Mitgang. "Best sellers on a list tend to cheat all other books and distract from scholarly works." Mr Clark, meet Mr Zachary.

We are told that under its former director the Press "grew into a modern competitive publisher." Competing in the book world calls for popular books; university publishing requires scholarly books; occasionally the two go together, most of the time they don't. When they only seem to go together, enthusiastic editors and their sympathetic consulting scholars may allow themselves to be led astray. Called to account later, most will hide, a few will brazen it out, none will admit error. Those who are newly arrived on the scene will look on the bright side.

Academic departments also compete, for visibility in the world of scholars. They improve their standing by attracting able people and putting out superior work. Normally they don't seek popular fame, which would be resented by other scholars. Occasionally the prospect of a media coup may tempt their ambition. A book that promises to be an academic best-seller may be hard to resist. Some members of the UCLA faculty who thought *The Teachings of Don Juan* was respectable enough to publish may also have thought it would boost their institutional reputation. It didn't work out that way.

Though Robert Zachary recalled the departmental reaction to Castaneda's manuscript as "all positive," I can identify only four members who were so inclined. Against these can immediately be set two who were not. A departmental poll would surely have gone against publishing *The Teachings* as a field report, though the book might have squeaked through as an allegory. Beals has been distressed by all the flak his department has had to take from sharpshooters like me blazing away at the flying sorcerers. Now that the patrons have stood up to be counted, if not to relent, it's time to stop casting aspersions on the Department and UCLA. I'm not sure we can ever take Castaneda's asiniform curse off the University, but that's the power of a bon mot.

In *Castaneda's Journey* I said my guess about what had happened at UCLA was that Castaneda had seduced one or more faculty members into an early prank—publishing *The Teachings* as ethnography—which others had later covered up by accepting *Ixtlan* as a dissertation. Don Juan as a joke that got out of hand was both humorous and dramatic; professors making mistakes and refusing to admit them later was rather dismal. "There isn't a faculty member alive who's going to enter into a coverup for some other faculty member's dumb move," said Clement Meighan. "Okay," I said, "but what about faculty members covering up their own dumb moves?"

Early in 1977 Don Strachan was reviewing *Castaneda's Journey* for the *Los Angeles Times*. After requesting anonymity, a professor in the UCLA Anthropology Department told him *The Teachings* could not, of course, be accepted as a dissertation because it had already been published as a popular book; this, you will recall, was four years after *Ixtlan* had been accepted as a dissertation after being published as a popular book—which tells us how reliable this anonymous professor is going to be. The professor went on to say that Theodore Graves (who had left the country in December 1971 after serving two years on Castaneda's committee) had been the "prime mover" of Castaneda's doctorate (approved in January 1973). Graves "was aghast," the informant said, "that the Department had this guy running around under their noses and they didn't even know what they had. Graves shamed them, and got three or four people to back Castaneda, and they slapped a degree on him for *Ixtlan*."

Now, the point of this quotation is not that Graves would have rejected *Ixtlan/Sorcery* had he been present; he admired Castaneda and might conceivably have accepted it. The point is that the only professor named to Strachan had been ten-thousand miles away while the dissertation was being read, evaluated, and signed by five others, not named, who were still at UCLA while the informant was speaking. We have to ask ourselves what the informant hoped to accomplish by naming only a man who had been and still was ten-thousand miles away. The obvious inference is that he hoped to cover up the responsibility of the others and to separate the deed from the institution. Graves, it turned out, did not object to getting the extra credit, so the spokesman was not risking the scapegoat's wrath while sending the hounds of journalism down a false trail.

Something rather similar had happened a year earlier, but at a higher cost. Lewis Yablonsky, a criminologist and professor of sociology at California State University, Northridge, just over the Santa Monica Mountains from UCLA, was reviewing Daniel Noel's *Seeing Castaneda*, for the *Los Angeles Times*. Though he took Castaneda's "ethnographic research" at face value, Yablonsky recognized that many other social scientists did not. "The most important issue to be set straight in this review," he wrote, "is the controversy about the authenticity of Castaneda's work. I felt obliged to personally research this matter." Yablonsky was particularly concerned about *Time's* (correct) allegation, reproduced in Noel's book, that Castaneda's dissertation was (nothing more than) his popular *Journey to Ixtlan*. In Yablonsky's place I should have had to drive the half hour across the mountains to examine the dissertation in the UCLA library, or to request it through interlibrary loan, but Yablonsky had taught at UCLA and had more convenient resources. As a visiting professor in 1961-62 he had met Castaneda briefly and had become "closely acquainted with several of his anthropology professors." Checking "the facts at UCLA with several reliable sources," Yablonsky was reassured to hear that "contrary to the popular opinions of several critics in *Seeing Castaneda*, Castaneda's thesis was not *Journey to Ixtlan*. His thesis, accepted for the Ph.D. on March 23, 1973, was entitled: *Sorcery: A Description of the World*." "There is no question," Yablonsky continued, "that Carlos Castaneda is an able anthropologist who has performed at a unique level of excellence in his field."

About Castaneda's uniqueness I have no doubt, but what should one think of a group of "several" university professors who apparently deceive a former colleague about something they are responsible for which he is going to discuss in a published article? Believing Yablonsky must have either strong feelings about what had happened to him or some surprising explanation of it, I wrote to him on 5 March 1977 asking whether he did not think his colleagues at UCLA should have been considerate enough to tell him the truth. I mentioned the fact that he had been listed as a speaker in a one-day program on Castaneda at UCLA on 22 January 1977 but reportedly had not attended. I asked the reason for his absence. (Since my book had appeared shortly before the program, I thought he might have read in it that *Sorcery* was undeniably *Ixtlan* and decided to withdraw.) On 26 April 1978 I wrote again, reminding Yablonsky that he had not yet answered my letter of 5 March 1977. On 23 October 1978 he sent me the following handwritten note:

> Dear Mr de Mille: I meant to write you much sooner, but I had misplaced your letter. I have no intense interest in Castaneda. My main involvement was the review I was asked to do for the L. A. Times. I reviewed the book and its implications to the best of my ability. That's about all I know—or have to say on the subject. I hope this response is of some use to you. Best, Lew Yablonsky.

Here is a scholar who wrote that Castaneda had made "a major contribution to anthropology," on which he had scheduled a public lecture, who now has "no intense interest" in him; a scholar who was misled by several of his former colleagues but has nothing to say on the subject; a scholar who hopes his response is of some use to me: obviously a kindly man with great self-control. In his place I should have said some pungent things about my "several reliable sources"—which may be why I am in my place and he is in his. Best to you also, Lew Yablonsky, and better luck next time with your close academic acquaintances.

The anthropology meeting lasted through Saturday. From time to time chatter in the halls and around the luncheon table recognized and wondered at the Nixonian overtones of the patrons' statement, which had claimed responsibility while rejecting blame and avoiding explanation. No mention had been made of the three chairmen who had found fault with Castaneda's work and candidacy, though one of them was sitting nine feet to the right of the speaker and had just spoken about the faults that had been found. The most serious challenge to the authenticity of Castaneda's work had been flatly dismissed without being named, though its author was sitting six feet to the right of the speaker and had just spoken about the challenge. The numerous published requests for a forthright, sensible explanation of a puzzling situation had been sanctimoniously stigmatized as a campaign of libelous whispers. The fraudulence broached in the title of the session had deliberately been neither confirmed nor denied.

In the political arena such a performance would have been called defiant hypocrisy. What it should be called in the community of scholars I didn't know, but I was reminded of some wise words spoken by Walter Goldschmidt when he was president of the Association: "It is necessary to distinguish between the moralization expressed in words and the morality expressed in behavior." Some of us, no doubt naïvely, had hoped for a rather different kind of statement. As I had proposed to Goldschmidt, a frank, good-humored admission of even minor errors would have worked a sudden miracle of clarification and reconciliation. Suppose the patrons, having reviewed the routine, blameless details of Castaneda's academic career, had concluded with the following statement:

> We know, of course, that Castaneda's works are sufficiently different from the usual dissertation not to satisfy some of the routine and proper criteria for reporting fieldwork. We knew it

from the start. We knew it in the spring of 1962 when he began to show us a manuscript he hoped to submit as a master's thesis, a manuscript one of his chairmen advised him to submit somewhere as a novel. On the other hand, some of us felt that to boot him out of graduate school might be a worse mistake than trying to find a way he could be recognized for what he was, a very odd but remarkably talented young man who was dealing with concepts at the heart of social science in a way that might bring progress all anthropologists would some day thank him for, including those who have criticised him here tonight. Science, of course, is a common enterprise, which must not be ruled or perverted by idiosyncrasy, but at the same time science makes progress because of inspirations that come out of idiosyncrasy. We think it is better to risk publication of a nonconformist, inadequate, or even fraudulent report than to stifle a brilliant insight or interpretation that may redound to the benefit of science and society when it passes into the hands of less inspired but more disciplined practitioners.

Those of us who have been most intimately involved with Castaneda see him differently from those respected but more conservative faculty members who rejected him and his work. They did what they thought was right, and we commend them for it. We did what we thought was right, and we are sure they will commend us for that, now that they have heard our reasons. There is a lot of room in the academy for honest differences.

If we had known in 1962 or 1967 or 1973 some of the things that were later brought to light by Castaneda's critics, we should undoubtedly have proceeded differently, but we should still have sought a way to give Castaneda recognition for a unique and valuable contribution to anthropology. Hindsight is a wonderful thing. It tells us the University Press ought to have published *The Teachings of Don Juan* not as a report of fieldwork but as a model to be emulated by fieldworkers. It tells us the dissertation should have been handled differently. If Castaneda would not furnish supporting evidence, that did not inevitably mean his work was fraudulent, but it did mean we had to treat his work in a way that would not require anthropologists or laymen to assume it had a factual basis. A judgment of authenticity or inau-

thenticity need not have been made by us, though inescapably it
would have been made by others. It was apparently a mistake to
allow the candidate to rename *Journey to Ixtlan* when he submitted it as a dissertation, a mistake I believe was simply an
oversight. To anyone who has been inconvenienced by these
mistakes, we extend our apology.

We leave it to others to say whether the don Juan books are a
hoax, but we contend that if they are a hoax, they are a hoax
that has enriched both science and society, as some of Castaneda's sharpest critics have acknowledged. If we had it all to do
over again—and I'm very glad we don't! (LAUGHTER FROM
THE AUDIENCE)—if we had it to do over again, we should not
flunk Carlos Castaneda out of graduate school, but we should
certainly find a less controversial way to give him the recognition he deserves. I thank you.

*(Five-minute standing ovation, notebooks tossed into the air,
photographers flashing, Long impulsively embracing
Goldschmidt, Beals smiling benignly, Bharati shaking hands
with Littleton, Truzzi fraternizing with Wilk, de Mille furiously
taking notes.)*

During the summer of 1978 Paul Preuss conducted interviews with
several of Castaneda's patrons and elicited statements that were very
useful in filling out the skimpy public record of who had done what and
when and for which reasons. At the same time he offered his own defense of what had been done. Since his arguments were both specious
and appealing, they merit refutation here. Because the presentation was
informal and diffuse, I have restated Preuss's points as follows:

1. De Mille should not have suggested that Castaneda's patrons had
engaged in a hoax unless he was confident the charge could be proved.
Answer: Preuss mistakes the scientific norm of organized skepticism for
a criminal indictment. The patrons were not on trial, and the burden of
proof was not on some prosecutor. At first it was on Castaneda, who
made extraordinary claims but refused to furnish supporting evidence.
When this refusal went unchallenged by the patrons, they in turn were
suspected of being in on the hoax. De Mille's probing was intended to
elicit clarifying rejoinders from those who knew the inside story but had
been keeping it to themselves for years, namely the patrons. The tactic
worked slowly but achieved useful results. Considering the patrons' un-

responsiveness to politer inquiries by others, the tactic was proper and apparently indispensable. In a weightier case, Peter B. Medawar accused himself of lacking moral courage because he had not immediately said he thought William Summerlin's corneal-graft experiment was bogus. Frauds in cancer research are much more costly than hoaxes in anthropology, but that doesn't mean scholars should keep quiet when they suspect an anthropological hoax, or exempt particular persons from criticism. As Harriet Zuckerman has aptly said: Everyone in science is fair game for critical appraisal and all scientists are potential detectives.

2. De Mille read *Teachings* and *Ixtlan* virtually at a sitting; the patrons read them at a five-year interval. De Mille, then, had a much easier task of recognizing the contradictions between them. *Answer:* The contradictions were felt by many readers; de Mille just happened to be the first to list them in a table. "This ordering *should* have been done by Castaneda's Ph.D. committee," Stephen Murray wrote.

3. De Mille is a literary detective with a lot of free time on his hands; the patrons were professors burdened down by other duties; they didn't have time to solve puzzles. *Answer:* De Mille had more time than obligation, but the patrons had more obligation than de Mille. As an outsider, he had to make the best possible case. As official scientific gatekeepers, they needed only well grounded suspicions. The burden of proof was on Castaneda.

4. De Mille does not believe one can find a preliterate shaman who quotes Sapir and Wittgenstein; the patrons had no such bias. *Answer:* Why didn't they?

5. Nobody accused Charles Dawson's teachers of conniving in the Piltdown forgery. *Answer:* Dawson was self-taught, so the analogy fails. Moreover, the forger was more likely Grafton Elliot Smith, a respected scholar. One does not always get to the bottom of such a case by collaring the obvious culprit.

6. Bronowski says information can be exchanged among human beings only within an interplay of tolerance. *Answer:* Bronowski's tolerance is meant precisely for human beings, not for their errors and misdeeds. Before we can assist bumblers and forgive hoaxers, we must be able to recognize bumbles and hoaxes. If we don't want to go on tolerantly exchanging misinformation, we have to call things by their right names.

The persistent recalcitrance of the patrons was signalled by the first response I got, from Clement Meighan in 1975: "I refer all questions about Carlos Castaneda to Carlos Castaneda." Suppose the director of the

Sloan-Kettering Institute could get away with saying: "I refer all questions about William Summerlin to William Summerlin." Peter Medawar would still be trying to make a patchwork mouse. The cost is different, but the principle is the same.

At nine o'clock on Wednesday evening, right after the fraud session, Retiring President Francis L. K. Hsu addressed his colleagues on problems of anthropology. I was busy digesting the statement of the patrons, so I didn't hear him, but I did remember sending him a questionnaire three years earlier, which contained the following item:

> It has been said that even if Castaneda's fieldwork never really happened, and even if academics and the public were temporarily misled, the deception was justified by the result, which is that Castaneda has provided a valuable catalyst for re-examining . . . the fieldworker's attitudes toward his indigenous informant.

Under which Hsu had written his comment:

> I don't think there is room in scholarly work for deception of any kind. As matters stand, our field work is not always scientific even with the best of intentions.

Coming from a future president of the Association, the answer is reassuring, but for me it is a little too strict. I think there is some room in scholarly work for fooling around, but I think people who fool around or get fooled by those who fool around ought to own up promptly. When they don't, jokes turn into frauds, and scholars turn into jokes.

"When a man decides to do something," don Juan said, "he must go all the way, but he must take responsibility for what he does." One thing the patrons had decided to do was science. I thought they should go all the way with it. If the patchwork mouse had been authentic, it would have had enormous significance for medicine. If Carlos's fieldwork had been authentic, it would have had enormous significance for anthropology. Even as an allegory it had some significance, but by never asking whether it was authentic or not the patrons implicitly admitted it was not, and by never taking responsibility for that admission they degraded their practice of science.

On 8 December 1978 I wrote to Joseph Long asking when my copy of the fraud-session tape-transcript would arrive. Long replied that he didn't know what the arrangements were; the young man had said only that he was taping so that the Association would have a record. I urged Long to find out when the transcript would be delivered. On 10 March 1979 Long sent me a letter from Edward J. Lehman, Executive Director of the Association. Lehman said he was puzzled about the identity of the young man, since no recording of the session had been ordered or authorized. "I am afraid that a fraud was perpetrated on you," he wrote, "when you were led to believe the young man was recording for the Association."

At this writing it is August, and the Sonoragate tapes are still missing. My account of the session is therefore less authoritative than I wanted it to be, but I did take notes, and a friend has kindly given me a transcript of his own tape. If inaccuracies remain, perhaps the person who hired the young man will come forward to correct them. In the meantime, speculation about who that person might be has run wild. Georg Olduvai is sure it was Simon and Prenticecott collecting actionable slurs on *Tales of the Amityville Cloning*. Claire Fausse-Idée thought it must be Castaneda's patrons hoping to record defamatory whispers on the dais. But folklorist César Arañuela Burlón said: "Who needed that tape the most? The person the panel would mention most often. A man who rarely appears in public but would like to know what was said about him. While we were practicing the art of talking, he was practicing the art of stalking!"

A penetrating hypothesis. The next section of this book raises to dizzying heights and drops to alarming depths the art of talking about Castaneda, as seething scholars and eloquent naïfs try to slay each other's errors while practicing Bronowskian tolerance.

II.

Insult and Argument

RdeM

In his own way, each of the next three contributors has tried to get to the center of human experience. Born in Vienna, raised a Catholic, Leopold Fischer fell in love with India, mastered Sanskrit as a boy, was called up by Hitler's army, got himself transferred to the Indian Legion, decided to become a Hindu monk, apprenticed himself to an eighth-century master, donned an ochre robe, walked the length of India on bare feet, took the name Agehananda Bharati, and is now Professor of Anthropology at Syracuse University. Once he saw the All-Goddess standing alive before him in a deserted temple.

Nurtured in New Jersey, regimented in Korea, liberated in Japan, schooled in Mexico, Hawaii, and London, inspired by transpersonal anthropology, Philip Staniford is Professor of Anthropology at California State University, San Diego. He once discovered the sex organs of a mountain.

Stan Wilk, who is a professor of anthropology at Lycoming College, achieved fame among his colleagues when he took them to task for not appreciating Carlos Castaneda. His specialty is humanistic anthropology: the restoration and development of persons through a study of culture. He communes with Lao Tzu.

Bharati says the *American Anthropologist* should never have invited Wilk to write about Castaneda. Staniford and Bharati, though venerating in each other the spark of divinity, have elsewhere traded epithets like "mystical dilettante" and "boorish buffoon." With difficulty I persuaded them to stay in their chairs while having their say.

Castaneda and His Apologists:
A Dual Mystical Fantasy

When Stan Wilk praised Castaneda as a savior of anthropology—in the pages and at the invitation of our leading journal—I thought it was most unfortunate, but now in apparent response to these glad tidings anthropologists have begun at last to call Castaneda's bluff. Outside our discipline, I have found no radical critics of Castaneda. Literary reviewers first praised him uncritically, then dismissed him contemptuously. Scholars from the official theologies either didn't know or didn't want to know what he was talking about. And scholars in comparative religion who, like Eliade, Joseph Campbell, and the Jungians, believed in privileged information enjoyed his saying things they didn't dare to say.

"I suspect Castaneda is not taken seriously by many anthropologists," Ralph Beals reflected, "not because he is so original but because he is so old hat." True, but non-anthropologists and naïve anthropologists were easily taken in. The less one knew about ethnography, the greater Castaneda seemed. Had he not arisen in the spirit-and-truth-seeking sixties, he might not have arisen at all.

In 1973, having read only his first three books, Mary Douglas said Castaneda could not give heartfelt allegiance to don Juan's discipline, because he was trying desperately to satisfy two schools, to reconcile the teachings of don Juan with the academic anthropology of UCLA. I must believe Douglas was being polite; I cannot think she was naïve. In her place I should have said Castaneda wrote *as though* "torn between two realities" (the original title of Douglas's essay), *as though* trying to satisfy two schools. Indeed, Richard de Mille characterized this struggle as a tug-of-war between two legendary figures, Carlos-Emic, apprentice of don Juan, and Carlos-Etic, graduate student at UCLA. But Douglas wrote as though there were only one Carlos and as though he were identical with author Castaneda.

In Castaneda's defense—luckily not his support—Douglas went on to say: "But take the lessons, go along with the teachings, and quite a lot appears that is *totally unexpected, new and provocative*" (my italics). Now there can be no quarrel with anyone's thinking a tract is "provocative," but nothing here is new or unexpected. In fact *everything* is expected if you are familiar with either: 1) primary tracts and commentaries in Sanskrit and Tibetan, and zillions of secondary comments in the primary languages and increasingly in European-language translations, or 2) a plethora of eclectic, neo-mystic writings, which I have described in *Light at the Center*. There is nothing in Castaneda's mysticism that you cannot also find, sometimes in nearly the same words, in Hindu and Buddhist tantrism or in the official Patañjali yoga, which is perfectly exoteric and comprehensible to Westerners.

"I have no reason whatsoever to suspect a hoax," C. Scott Littleton confessed; "I have known [Castaneda] too long and too well to doubt his professional integrity." Coming after *Tales of Power*, this is rather pathetic, but in any case a mendacious performance is surely more convincing when based on solid professional training than when based on ignorance. What matters is intent—which a successful deceiver does not confide to trusting colleagues any more than to gullible fans.

To me, the glaring sign of don Juan's illegitimacy is his intercontinental eclecticism. Years ago, at Sam Goody's in New York City, I saw a musical disc captioned "Aloha Amigo." That hideous little hybrid capsulates the malaise of youth-and-sixties culture, of which Castaneda caught a fatal case. Stir together bits of Blavatsky, dollops of David-Neel, gobs of Gurdjieff, sops of Ouspensky, snatches of Govinda, yards of tangled Amerindian folklore, and a series of programmatic LSD trips, and you have the don-Carlos idiom. Not exactly a newly discovered tradition of Amerindian mysticism.

My personal disapprobation of Castaneda's writings stems less from their anthropological inadequacy, which is patent, than from their mystical pretensions—which I challenge not as an anthropologist but as a Hindu monk ordained and proven in the Dashanāmi Sannyāsi order, one of the world's most elite and learned institutions of mystical technique, founded by Śamkarācārya in the eighth century. As a bona fide mystic, I am entitled to an entirely non-anthropological opinion, which is that all of Amerindian mystical and ecstatic lore, north, central, and south, compares with Hindu-Buddhist traditions about as a country choir compares with the B-Minor Mass. Even if we make assumptions contrary to fact (such as that don Juan exists in the flesh, or that Yaqui Indians have a mystical way of knowledge), and even if there were a pan-Amerindian shamanistic tradition (which is possible), all this would be child's play when measured by Indo-Tibetan standards. I am not, of course, referring to the phoney ramblings of a Blavatsky or the romantic travelogues of a David-Neel but to standards set by the Nāgārjunas, by Śamkara, and by others of authority. Insofar as don Juan's teaching resembles these traditions it must have come *from* them and cannot have come from the Western hemisphere.

Well before de Mille's *malleus maleficarum* descended on don Juan's eclectic head, I publicly rejected Castaneda's mishmash of other people's ethnography, mysticism, and LSD trips. Many years after concluding the long, rigorous, traditional meditational training in the monastic setting of the Dashanāmi order, I took LSD in varying doses and even more varying company about a hundred times during five years. About two years later *The Teachings of Don Juan* hit the literary market, and I remember my instant ire while reading the so-called Yaqui way, when I recognized a pervasive psychodelic pattern. It is very easy to load any number of experiences onto an LSD trip, or to enhance the power of the trip by reassembling memories of meditational practice, or of background reading in any theological tradition. LSD will corroborate *any* doctrinal premise, *any* theological promise, whether authentic or invented by a clever writer. Nor does the writer himself have to take LSD. Castaneda may or may not have taken it, but he must have read plenty of vivid accounts written by takers.

Castaneda-appreciators like Littleton can mistake the don Juan books for "an emic account par excellence" because very few Western anthropologists are prepared to deal with Asian mystical sources. My current estimate is that a total of five people on European or American anthropology payrolls read either Sanskrit or Tibetan. When the rest of our colleagues want to talk about Indian religious ideas and mystical practice, they rely on translation of the Bhagavadgītā. Worse, they may take seriously statements made by swamis of the Ramakrishna Mission. A few years ago I complained about the inexact use of *mystical* and *mystic* in American anthropology, but few took heed. Having no clear conception of the topic, most anthropologists tend to tolerate mystical-ecstatic-shamanistic stews served up by dabblers like Castaneda. What neither the aloha-amigo mystics (or shamans, brujos, or sorcerers—the indiscriminate use of such terms makes it all so much more exciting!) nor tolerant anthropologists know is that the transcendental power they talk about cannot be acquired without total immersion in a single, well-defined tradition. The teachings of don Juan do not constitute such a tradition.

I suspect Castaneda is a fast, perceptive, highly pragmatic reader of relevant mystical texts, albeit in translation. Information sufficient for his authorly needs could be found in the Upanishads and half a dozen other translated eastern canonical texts, or in Herbert V. Guenther's dry

Tibetan Teutonica, in my *Tantric Tradition*, or in Anagarika Govinda's *Foundations* or *White Clouds*. Much of it can even be found in the sensational writings of Blavatsky, Ouspensky, Gurdjieff, and David-Neel. Castaneda's genius, I believe, lies in transforming such materials into a pseudo-Mexican pseudo-mystical adventure tale for naïve modern readers.

Having grown up, presumably, in a Spanish-speaking family surrounded by Quechua-speaking Indians and Mestizos, Castaneda was privy to the nuances of Mestizo and general Latin American Spanish. Though not by linguistic standards, he is bilingual by fieldwork standards—to a degree seldom attained by American anthropologists, many of whom must constantly wrestle with any language other than English. Much sympathy for Castaneda may arise out of admiration for his supposed unimpeded Spanish conversation with don Juan, which anthropologists must envy if they believe in it at all. Of course, as de Mille has pointed out, a conversation can be easier, more satisfying, and certainly more emic when conducted with an informant who lives in one's own head.

I Come to Praise Carlos, Not to Bury don Juan

The nonordinary realities Castaneda describes I take to be quite valid, for I have directly and independently experienced many similar things in the course of my investigations as an anthropologist. The phenomena he transmits in vivid metaphor I find useful in identifying and delimiting the areas of consciousness I encounter. This endorsement does not make me a follower of Carlos or a devotee of don Juan, for some aspects of the teaching differ from my experience—the loneliness of the quest, for example, or the fearsomeness of the female apprentices—but it signifies my appreciation of many valid teachings, like the distinction between *tonal* (whatever exists) and *nagual* (wherever whatever exists comes from) or the distinction, popular today in psychology, between the left-brain-right-hand of reason and the right-brain-left-hand of intuition.

Much of don Juan's wisdom, we are told, has been taught before, and even better, in other lands and times. Yet if don Juan is truly a wise man, this should not surprise us. Important truths hold across oceans and centuries and may be rediscovered again and again. Castaneda has put some of these truths into a form we can grasp, relate to, and enjoy today. I find it ironic, therefore, that when don Juan's teaching seems like Zen, an "official" mystic like Agehananda Bharati calls him a fake. This fake is bringing us genuine teachings!

Carlos learns from don Juan, for example, that "a warrior does the best he can and then relaxes," that "a warrior can afford to wish another warrior well." When disagreement threatens to bog me down in futile arguments, I take don Juan's advice, wish my opponents well, and relieve effort with relaxation. This practice frees energies and efforts which otherwise get stuck fast on the tarbaby of misunderstanding.

The warrior's way requires sorting out priorities, investing consciousness positively, applying attention to things that count here and now. Focusing on what has meaning for me, I note some gems from *Second Ring of Power*:

Nothing has form, yet everything is present.
The dreamer holds the image of *his* dream.
Don't get caught in their webs.
And if you are, don't be angry. It can't be helped.

Hold the images of a dream in the same way we hold images of
the world.
Practice changing the levels of attention.

Throughout the don Juan books, such maxims offer practical guidance in
everyday affairs on the path with heart.

Over some years as an anthropologist I have attained a variety of
expanded states of consciousness—intuitive, free-ranging, fanciful, and
vividly experienced. These states arise from a regime that combines
meditation, fasting, running, yoga postures, and other mindbody
flexing/relaxing techniques. Often I have met Carlos Compadre at some
crucial juncture, where he waits to nail an effect I have long felt but never
put a name to. In *Second Ring* he describes the windpipe snap: "I heard
again, as I had heard the night before while doña Soledad was choking me,
a most peculiar and mysterious sound, a dry sound like a pipe breaking,
right behind my windpipe at the base of my neck."

One goal of my exercises is to create a suppleness of spine, muscles,
and spinal cord. In the process of doing "the plough"—lying on back,
legs together, arms flat past hips, legs come up over head and feet touch
floor behind—the windpipe snaps, crackles, and pops, as tension is released. The same thing happens during neck-bending, while standing
hands on hips. Concurrent mental states include expansive relaxation felt
inside the head, and flashes of insight. After one such snap I saw the
connectedness between whirls of thought and whirls of matter, after
another, the nature of society as a psychic organism became evident to
me.

Several times in *Second Ring* the snapping of Carlos's windpipe announces extraordinary feats or prodigious changes. His experience makes
me more aware of my own and helps to verify it.

What good is such knowledge? From my own experience I can recommend without hesitation the joys and rigors of a physical regime.
"Truly," says a Chinese proverb, "a flexible back makes for a long and
propitious life." Don Juan and Carlos would heartily agree.

To live long and propitiously one needs as well flexibility of mind,
expansion of consciousness, freeing of the will. Never have I been more
alive than today, and each day livens me more. This in itself is worth
pursuing, but also one finds heightened awareness of associations between apparently unrelated phenomena, empathy with other conscious-
nesses, and new implications about the world and our anthropological
experience of it. Carlos and don Juan—whoever each of us concludes

they may be—contribute positively to such growth.

> "Follow your own sinew down to the river," said Raccoon [in
> *Seven Arrows*], "and I will give you the answer." The two blind
> men followed the sinew down to the river's edge and they stood
> there waiting for further instructions. "Listen to the water,"
> Raccoon said. "It will give you your answer." But while they
> both listened, Raccoon sneaked up behind them and pushed
> them into the river—and their eyes were opened.

How many of us, Carlos Raccoon, have followed the sinews of our
understanding beyond the edge of ordinary consciousness to find ourselves, exhilarated, in the river of paradox with senses opening?

Don Juan on Balance

The Messiah will come as soon as the most unbridled individualism of faith becomes possible—when there is no one to destroy this possibility and no one to suffer its destruction; hence the graves will open themselves. . . .
The Messiah will come only when he is no longer necessary; he will come only on the day after his arrival; he will come, not on the last day, but on the very last.

—Franz Kafka

To know yet to think that one does not know is best.

—Lao Tzu

As a student and teacher of anthropology I am very appreciative of Carlos Castaneda's description of shamanic apprenticeship as a meaningful endeavor. Through his efforts something of the power of don Juan's teachings is communicated to the reader. To my mind the don Juan books do not constitute an attack upon, but rather a complement to, scientific anthropology.

In the Introduction to *A Separate Reality* Castaneda relates a conversation with don Juan about knowledge: "I was referring to academic knowledge that transcends experience, while he was talking about direct knowledge of the world." In the course of that conversation the old shaman declares that Carlos is not "complete." I believe that a serious consideration of the teachings of don Juan, of shamanic completion, can lead to a more balanced, more complete, anthropological discipline. Lao Tzu, another old shamanic figure whose existence is in dispute, is alleged to have said:

> He who knows others is clever.
> He who knows himself has discernment.

Don Juan has given academic anthropology a chance to increase its self-knowledge. With the help of don Juan we can join Carlos in a reexamination of the symbolic realities, the "tonal," of our profession. Don Juan's

154

teachings are rooted in the realization that the existence of the world as we know it, of necessity, implies the existence of human being in the world and that such being of necessity implies the mythic. Thus his teachings offer a basis for the consideration of value in anthropology and human affairs in general.

Anthropology as social science and anthropology as myth-making are not mutually exclusive endeavors. They are aspects of a self-implicating process that we ignore at our own expense. As Castaneda's work demonstrates, in the last analysis, the existence of both the scientific anthropologist and the shaman is in doubt. It is from such an existential commonality that we can appreciate don Juan's skeptical admonition to take ourselves seriously. As Lao Tzu noted:

A journey of a thousand miles starts from beneath one's feet.

Thus don Juan counsels Carlos to let death, rather than his doctoral committee, be his adviser. In the eyes of the old shaman, anthropology is transformed into humanity as academic discourse is located in the sphere of human consciousness. To accomplish this feat the obscure Indian meets the anthropologist on the equal footing provided by existential mystery, the "nagual," the uncarved block of Lao Tzu. To me Castaneda's account of shamanic apprenticeship represents a richer dialogue between primitive and civilized, subject and object than is to be found in the vast majority of typical anthropological studies.

As don Juan teaches, "Sorcery is interference," and the subject of Carlos's investigation interferes with his attempt at business-as-usual anthropology. Don Juan keeps his finger firmly pressed on the "key joint" of anthropological endeavor: "The things that people do cannot under any conditions be more important than the world. And thus a warrior treats the world as an endless mystery and what people do as an endless folly." As any primitive can tell you, in a world of relatives respect is the proper attitude for any self-respecting person to cultivate. From this vantage all symbolics, shamanic as well as scientific, are creative journeys, humanizing paths: "They lead nowhere. They are paths going through the bush, or into the bush." The question of human affirmation, "heart," emerges from this vantage as a valid touchstone of symbolic evaluation: "In my own life I could say I have traversed long, long paths but I am not anywhere. My benefactor's question has meaning now. Does this path have a heart?" From this perspective the naïveté of material utility can be powerfully addressed. The objectivity of a "valuefree" anthropological image can be fruitfully balanced by the subjectivity of a "valueless" anthropological image. As don Juan speaks to Carlos he speaks to us all: "The way I see it, you want to cling to your arguments, despite the fact that they bring nothing to you; you want to remain the same even at the cost of your well-being."

Scientific anthropology is just another carving of the block, as Lao Tzu might phrase it. Have the rewards of the dehumanizing descriptions of the world of humanity carried out in the name of science been so bountiful as to preclude the possibility of dialogue with a wide variety of other human symbolic carvings? Might not such a dialogue provide the dialectics for a hitherto unenvisioned rehumanization? By declaring certain factual domains as irrelevant, scientific anthropology masks its mythic identity. Don Juan's shamanic subjectivism can reveal hidden and typically ambiguous images of human being contained in so-called scientific descriptions. His teachings can help us to realize our paradoxical articles of professional faith. Along with Carlos we can learn to locate compelling human symbolics in a realm beyond rather than in opposition to what is given and taken to be the existent facts. By giving the human being of our personal experience a central place in anthropological description, by emphasizing the concrete reality of human feeling, Castaneda has rendered an objective portrayal of the necessary subjectivity in which all anthropological inquiry is bathed.

Professional reflexivity, however, like personal soul searching, is a powerful and often frightening activity. What if one turns oneself inside out only to discover that there is nothing there? Thus as don Juan teaches, fear is the first enemy of a man of knowledge, and it is to be expected that anthropology, like the individual, has built up its defenses, "shields," that keep it looking out for rather than into its tonal. In this respect the shamanic message to anthropology recognizes the necessity of relativity. There is today no choice between a scientific and a nonscientific anthropology, between fact and value, between theory and myth. They are all bound together in the tentative nature of human existence. Rather than the either/or choices of absolutism, don Juan presents the shamanic challenge of maintaining a relatively balanced position on the fine line of distinction. Don Juan's shamanic challenge to anthropology is no less than the necessity of developing a tolerance for the heights of a symbolic overview and the depths of experiential realization. As don Juan teaches: "You think there are two worlds for you—two paths. But there is only one. The protector showed you this with unbelievable clarity."

If we wish to cultivate the relativity at the heart of human awareness we must pursue a tentative tone in our descriptions of human existence. The personal pursuit of Carlos Castaneda has balanced the scientific dichotomy of subjectivity and objectivity upon a continuum of consciousness along which we may journey to greater or lesser awareness. His work has balanced the challenge of validating scientific hypotheses with the challenge of affirming human existence. It has balanced the enemy of science, human ignorance, with the shamanic source of strength, experiential mystery. It has balanced the social-scientific reification of human symbolics with the shamanic mediation of human feelings. The teachings of don Juan reveal that a complete anthropological discipline must celebrate not only a science of humanity but also a religion, not as an end in itself, but as an ever fertile beginning. Anthropology must appreciatively encompass the mythic as well as the scientific, the primitive as well as the civilized, if it is to enfold the whole of humanity in its creative embrace.

The scientific study of myth, and its twin, the mythic study of science, may truly be the infant gods of a new age of long awaited human maturity. If such a time of tolerance is on the horizon, it will surely balance the social scientific message of collective determinism with the shamanic message of individual freedom, potency, and responsibility.

Science as Religion

If Fritjof Capra, a physicist, can write a book called *The Tao of Physics*, one needn't be surprised to learn that anthropologist C. Scott Littleton is grateful to Carlos Castaneda for hurrying the synthesis of science and religion foreseen by sociologist Edward Tiryakian, or that Stan Wilk says the don Juan books "may be beneficially viewed as a sacred text." Interested in don Juan less "as a historical figure" than as "a subject of believing reception," Wilk would rather sit at his legendary feet than discover his literary origins in the library; like Wilk's other old shaman, Lao Tzu, don Juan transcends biography.

Don Juan's teachings reveal to Wilk "that a complete anthropological discipline must celebrate not only a science of humanity but also a religion." Should anthropology manifest itself as a religion? Jacques Maquet denies it: "Anthropology is neither a spiritual path, nor a search for nonordinary powers; it is a discursive discipline of knowledge. The warrior's quest and the sorcerer's endeavor belong to other realms and thus cannot provide guidance for anthropology, as Wilk would have it." "Methodological neglect" deprives Castaneda's work of scientific value, Maquet says. "He has not made it possible for another anthropologist to repeat his inner experience."

Each master points a different path for his apprentice, Wilk retorts. Don Juan makes Maquet nervous because Maquet is blindly committed to positivistic natural science and cannot appreciate Castaneda's "rigorous exemplification of an alternative methodology rooted in phenomenological description and uncommitted to reductive explanation."

What is this dispute about? New-scientists like Wilk, Littleton, and Philip Staniford want to liberate anthropology from its "hyperrationalistic straitjacket." They are fed up with formalism and hypothetico-deductive mumbo-jumbo. They want to break down the artificial barriers between fieldworker and informant, modern and preliterate, subject and object, conscious and unconscious, material and spiritual. They want information to flow freely and joyfully, unhindered by pedantic distinctions and dehumanizing restrictions. Old-scientists like Maquet, Beals, and the majority of professional anthropologists suspect such breaking down of barriers is just a loss of conceptual boundaries, a decortication of social science. They see its practitioners as non-thinkers, anti-intellectuals, empty verbalizers, occultists, and misteachers.

This is a persistent dispute, and we are not going to settle it here, but I can give you my reaction. Like psychologist Charles Tart, the new-science liberators want to get the feelings, intuitions, symbolic realizations, psychic experiences, and altered states of consciousness *of the scientist* into the observations and the scientific report. Unlike Tart, some of them seem quite unconcerned about what may happen to the discursive container when these consciousness-expanding events are allowed into it, or when literary and religious figures of speech replace theoretical propositions and scientific definitions. If scientists have dehumanized the world they study, it is because they want a problem orderly and palpable enough to think rigorously about. An extreme case is B. F. Skinner finding out absolutely everything about practically nothing: how rats and pigeons learn trivial, unnatural tricks while living inside teaching machines. Wouldn't it be better to observe rats in slums and pigeons on the grass? Sure, but it's a lot harder, and the attempt can easily leave science behind. Some of the anthropological re-humanizers seem perfectly happy to give up exactness, prediction, replication, theory construction, and even logical coherence if only they can deal with human expressions that make them feel warm, complete, transcultural, and transcendental. Wilk blithely mistakes Castaneda's science fantasy for rigorous methodology. He dignifies emotive clichés as a demonstration of "affective dimensions." He appreciates Castaneda's "richer dialogue between primitive and civilized, subject and object than is to be found in the vast majority of typical anthropological studies," without acknowledging the disadvantage of the typical anthropologist, who is not allowed to do fieldwork in the library, to invent his informant, or to put the words of Garfinkel and Suzuki, Wittgenstein and Sapir into his informant's mouth. How could the dialogue not be richer with all those invisible kibitzers? If Wilk is grinding a worthy ax—and he may be—he would do better to offer an authentic model.

When Maquet says Castaneda is not concerned with the validation of experience, Wilk answers: "Don Juan is a man of knowledge irrespective of our validation." Of course, Wilk is right. If don Juan exists, and is a man of knowledge, then he is one whether we know it or not. If there is life on Titan, it is there whether we detect it or not. But whether we detect it depends not only on whether it is there but also on what kind of science and technology we employ; whether Carlos's apprenticeship can be validated depends not only on whether it took place but also on what anthropological techniques are used to repeat it. Wilk is apparently satisfied by field reports from Castaneda and Lao Tzu, but science has stricter rules than that. The rules may be deliberately modified, but when they are lightly abandoned one is no longer doing science. One may, for example, be doing religion in the name of anthropology, like Wilk, or self-improvement in the name of anthropology, like Staniford, or allegory is the name of anthropology, like Castaneda. Those who are still doing science in the name of anthropology will have limited patience with such excursions. Gregory Finnegan put it this way:

> Until de Mille's analysis is refuted by data showing that don Juan lives, is somehow representative of a wider culture, and that Castaneda has accurately observed, recorded, and interpreted his "Teachings," it is premature to proclaim (as do Wilk and many of Noel's contributors) that we should (or even can) found a new social-scientific paradigm upon a coyote and a crow.

As a liberating antidote to loose thinking and quasi-science, I offer *Peyote Hunt*, whose author, Barbara Myerhoff, immersed herself in Huichol myth and ritual, then wrote a penetrating, consistently lucid, culturally descriptive, theoretically articulated, discursive report of her experience, including feelings, intuitions, and altered states of consciousness. Liberating anthropology from the hyperrationalistic straitjacket does not have to mean letting it fall apart.

Outside anthropology, Joseph Chilton Pearce judged don Juan an almost worthy successor to Jesus, but professional religionists have given the Juanist gospel mixed reviews. Though Joseph Grange was inspired by its vision, Martin Marty called it a fad, whose only benefit was getting rid of "that dumb Pelagian seagull," Jonathan Livingston. Christian writers give Castaneda some points for validating the other world but call him to account for various sins and heresies. Hal Lindsey unmasked don Juan's allies as old-fashioned demons. Carol McFadden suspected *seeing* was a gift from Satan. David Nelson thought the separate reality was don Juan's private room in Hell. James Sire said don Juan and Carlos were breaking the First Commandment. Peter Meinke said the path with heart was not paved with Christian virtues.

The most thorough Christian treatment of Castaneda comes from John P. Newport, who holds the monistic, amoral mysticism of don Juan inferior to the dualistic, moral mysticism of Christians. Though Juanism may help some readers come to Jesus by convincing them a spiritual realm exists, its world of Godless, demonic occultism is a sinister, hazardous detour on the way to Salvation. Newport makes nothing of Castaneda's having been born on Christmas day; mercifully, he didn't know one of Castaneda's given names was Salvador, or Savior. Newport was well aware of *Castaneda's Journey* but carefully avoided coming to grips with its thesis that don Juan is an imaginary person. That puzzled me, until I realized that if your mission is to save souls from Satan, you don't want someone saying Satan is imaginary. Don Juan's most diabolical trick is to convince us he doesn't exist.

Biblical scholar William Doty recognized the don Juan books as "fantasy-mysticism," like Tolkien, Aleister Crowley, and Alan Watts, but Sufist psychologist Robert Ornstein said if true it didn't matter; factual or fictive, Carlos-Skeptic impressed him as a model of the Westerner unprepared to receive esoteric knowledge.

At the counterreligion pole, Juanism has been exposed as a peyote-flavored opiate for the masses. Brian Easlea cited don Juan's irrationalism as a threat to the rational humanism of socialist scientists. Marvin Harris jumped on Castaneda for distracting middle-class youth from achieving social justice. "To make a revolution," said Harris, "everybody must do the same thing." The path with heart does not lead to Utopia.

The synthesis of science and religion was accomplished years ago, some would say, by Carl G. Jung. Daniel Noel, a close student of Jung, is a professor of religion and literature and the editor of *Seeing Castaneda*, an indispensable collection of essays, which I cite over and over in this book. Not that I agree with Noel's views. When I think I understand them, I usually disagree with them. But Noel is an articulate exponent of a current intellectual trend, and so we should listen to him. In the beginning he subscribed to the factuality of Carlos's apprenticeship. Castaneda, he wrote, gives us "a lesson in 'lived hermeneutics,' the actual *experience* of interpretation's role in interpreting experience so as to constitute what we know as 'world,' 'reality,' 'meaning.' " "Castaneda's personal experiences of the loss of ordinary meaning . . . have provided him with a very practical, existential exercise in hermeneutics, one which he himself *lived*."

That was in 1972. Noel's article in the 1980 *Colliers Encyclopedia* will conclude:

> Castaneda's own central teaching and enduring contribution may involve the trickery of publishing, as *non*-fiction, books which consistently ridicule our reliance on factuality—and then, as if to underscore the point, turn out to be fiction.

The message is beginning to get through. Despite this rapprochement, Noel and I are still at odds. He likes to make reality misty and uncertain; I like to make it clear and certain. He likes to sit on the fence between the worlds; I jump off at the first opportunity. Each of us knows he is making his own reality, but we have opposite cognitive styles. The difference is probably hereditary.

The next chapter reproduces an exchange between Noel and me, which ought to make it perfectly clear we are never going to agree. When the editors of *Parabola* asked me to review *Second Ring of Power*, I proposed that Noel review it too and that we answer each other's comments. The result is incompatibility fixed in amber.

Seeing and
Seeing Through Castaneda

RdeM:

Starting with *The Teachings of Don Juan*, four best sellers have told how a remarkably transcultural Mexican Indian taught isolated sorcery, eclectic metaphysics, quasi-Stoic ethics, and fabulized psychic power to a somewhat backward, culturally European apprentice, who was supposedly the same person as author Castaneda, anthropology student at the University of California, Los Angeles, and eventual recipient of a controversial Ph.D. Reviewing my critique of those anthropoetic thrillers, Daniel Noel said my prime achievement was to reveal Castaneda's fictive power—his creation of mythical fieldwork, by which he exposed the rationalist's hazardous reliance on scientific facts believed to be more than mental constructs.

Noel and Castaneda draw our attention to the inevitable subjective aspect of objective information: even the most established, agreed-upon fact exists not in an external world (though something corresponding to it *may* exist there) but in the minds of human beings. If Castaneda deserves any of the praise, much of it foolish, that has been heaped upon him, it is for impressing this slippery epistemological proposition on the worldview of the general reader.

A fifth installment of Carlos's adventures in Juanderland, *The Second Ring of Power* further develops the don Juan allegory. Though Juan of the rings has gone to the other world, he is neither dead nor missing, since he lives not only in memory but in the beings and very bodies of his apprentices. If that were not enough, he also inhabits a fifty-thousand-foot dome bathed in greenish-yellow light on a phosphorescent plain, where he and don Genaro confidently await the arrival of Carlos, Pablito, Nestor, Benigno, Soledad, Lidia, Rosa, Josefina, and Elena—called La Gorda because until don Juan shrank her she weighed 220 pounds. Eligio, the chosen, somehow got lost in a worldwarp, but he'll be along by and by.

Students of alternative realities will admire Castaneda's extended virtuosic demonstration of how a living myth grows and changes in response to social pressures and opportunities. Published at the height of the drug craze, *The Teachings of Don Juan* mapped a more disciplined and probing psychedelic path. *A Separate Reality* bridged the chasm between themes, so that well into the reaction against drugs *Journey to Ixtlan* could surprisingly discover drugless techniques interleaved among the old field notes—purer, gentler ways of building character and seeking transcendental knowledge. The year of *The Exorcist* and Uri Geller's bending keys saw *Tales of Power* bending the lines of the world to the will of sorcerers, while *The Second Ring of Power*, published as the Equal Rights Amendment clutches at ratification, broaches women's rites—anerotic sexual encounters with occult parafeminist playmates.

Boldly rebutting small minded Freudians who had accused author Castaneda of not being able to tolerate the company of women, the legendary Carlos here surrounds himself with witches: occasionally ugly, usually gorgeous, always fascinating, often dangerous rivals in the race to the other world, who do not hesitate to strip off their undergarmentless dresses, flaunt their virginal or multiparous genitals, piss on their hands and snap their fingers to make parapsychodynamic sparks, gangwrestle Carlos to the floor, rub sinister breasts against his left shoulder, nibble his flank like ferrets, and both metaphysically and anatomically invite him into the crack between the worlds. On certain days of the month, don Juan had said, women lose contact with the ordinary reality (as Nixon's doctor told us) and are better prepared for sorcery than men (which Nixon's doctor was apparently afraid to admit). I had always suspected it.

In his own peculiar way, writer Castaneda makes progress in this book, elevating former hoaxing tricks into a mythopoeic style. Take for example his originating flashbacks, in which Carlos unexpectedly recalls one original idea after another, purportedly past revelations from don Juan, incredibly forgotten until now. Coupled with vivid fanciful images and pell mell magical feats, this frank reworking of the myth carries *The Second Ring* leagues beyond the pseudo-anthropology of *The Teachings* into the realm of symbol, where Castaneda is most at home.

One provocative allegory tells how children steal childhood from parents by forcing them to grow up. Along with childhood goes the power of fantasy, of living in another world. Parents who would regain their visionary power must take their childhood back, even if it means destroying the children. Soledad was lucky, La Gorda tells a flabbergasted Carlos, because her daughter died, thus restoring half the power Soledad had lost by bearing two children.

Like the four volumes before it, *Second Ring* ends without a resolution. Some progress has been made toward the ultimate transfiguration, but there is still a long way to go. Cyril Henry Hoskin mesmerized the masses with his prosthetic *Third Eye*; now *Books in Print* lists thirteen titles under his pen name. Carlos Castaneda is a man of better parts than T. Lobsang Rampa, but at this rate he'll drag on with thirteen tales of solipsorcering before the ecstatic luminous beings are finally all gathered in that eschatonic dome beyond the brujorison.

Noel:

As we left the Carlos of *Tales of Power*, he was apparently jumping off a mountain-top into an abyss in a final feat of sorcery. Now, in a fifth book, we return not only to that nonordinary event—Carlos has gone back to Mexico to seek its explanation from fellow apprentices Pablito and Nestor—but to the question at the heart of the very first volume, *The Teachings of Don Juan*. "Did I really fly, don Juan?" has become "Did I really jump?" a decade later, and both variants confront us with the same need to revise our modern perspective, reinstating the imaginal, the mythic, in a postmodern maneuver.

On one level the new book adds a unique ingredient: Carlos initially finds not Pablito and Nestor but the former's former mother and four sisters, transformed by the now-absent don Juan and Genaro into worthy warriors in their own right. Indeed, it seems for much of the account that the abyss into which Carlos has leaped is woman, the womb, menstrual mysteries and the archetypal Female. Nor is this the totally passive power men might wish it to be. La Gorda tells Carlos that her sisters "trained themselves to sip you up like a glass of soda." After several chapters' worth of sometimes tiresome "bouts" between Carlos and the active-feminine, we feel that what is at issue is not only a surface battle between the sexes but also that ongoing pull from "focused" toward "diffuse" awareness which may constitute a subterranean androgyny throughout Castaneda's works.

Along with all the sexual harum-scarum this shift of awareness is also signaled by what we call the "problematics of metaphor" in *The Second Ring of Power*. Commenting on one of his contests with the women, Carlos stresses that "it was not as if something came out from the top of my head; something actually did come out from the top of my head." The neo-Jungian psychologist James Hillman has remarked that "'as-if' is a necessary philosophical step for recognizing the metaphorical character of all certainties in what we see, say, and believe. But if we begin in mythical consciousness we do not need the prefix." Since, with Carlos, we begin in skeptical rationality rather than within the consciousness of myth, the question is one of strategy: How do we renew our roots in the older mode of awareness where "as-if" is always simply implied?

The efforts to do so in Castaneda's tales are constantly accompanied by Carlos's tendency to cast off the chains of reason in literalistic ways which would only tie him more tightly to it. "La Gorda and the little sisters," he says, "had turned my obscure metaphors into real possibilities," and like him we often assume that dropping our rational fixations must mean transcending rhetorical designations of metaphoricity or fictiveness. I am convinced that for author Castaneda, however, a crucial pivot between our starting point in modern skepticism and a renewed mythic consciousness is the focus on metaphors and as-if fictions as inherently *more* than "mere rhetoric," as what Hillman calls "ways of perceiving, feeling, and existing."

Certainly the imagery of sight and sighting in *The Second Ring* functions in just this larger fashion, for, as metaphors enacted in Mexico or engaged on the page, such language provides an avenue to the "second ring," or "attention of the nagual," itself. Along this avenue we find that trivial tricks of the eye—the deliberately distorted gaze, the fleeting glimpse, the peripheral flicker—contain the secret of true seeing and that the "art of attention" is the "art of the dreamer." Far from being an activity of closed eyes and a sleeping consciousness alone, the art of controlled dreaming emphasized here is a twilight affair in which inner images can be sustained and acted upon as surely as the perceptions of sense, and our limited version of physical seeing can be transformed into remythicized vision.

That vision, of course, will never be more clear-cut than the metaphors and as-if rhetorics required for its voicing, since, as James Hillman again reminds us, "the revelation of myth within events confirms ambiguity, it does not settle it." Perhaps this is why Carlos concludes of the female warriors in the present work that "their revelations, although extraordinary, were only missing pieces to a jigsaw puzzle. The unusual character of those pieces was that with them the picture did not become clearer but that it became more and more complex." This would also appear to be the appropriately postmodern response to the five-volume quandary of whether Carlos really flew/jumped—and of whether Castaneda is really the Carlos of his books.

Richard de Mille's review raises most effectively the question of whether, even at this late date, we know how to take Castaneda. As I explained in the introduction to *Seeing Castaneda*, I take him very seriously despite the scatological humor pervading his books and the buffoon's part Carlos is often made to play. Solemnity is surely inappropriate, but even the looniest tricks of these tales seem like serious teachings to me. This is above all true of the trickery of their telling, if de Mille is correct in his negative answer to the reader's question: Did these things happen as narrated in the books?

De Mille's reaction to all this is apparently an attempt at out-tricking Castaneda with a barrage of bon mots and enviably awful puns. This is good fun, and I am often tempted to play along—but along to where? Can de Mille's verbal Santa Barbarisms see us through to wisdom by seeing through every purported sublimity of Castaneda's pedagogy? Will de Mille's ridicule lead us to the wisecrack between the worlds?

It may be that he honestly cannot take Castaneda seriously, and no doubt in these pages, as (according to Mac Linscott Ricketts) in the history of religions, someone must play the shaman's role and someone the trickster's—however inadequately in either case. Eventually we should each learn a lesson from this liaison.

RdeM:

"De Mille has probably taken Castaneda as seriously as any critic has," wrote Sam Gill, but de Mille does not prefer every question to go unanswered, every problem to remain unsolved, all dreams to be confused with waking, every fairy tale to be shelved with the Volkswagen manuals. Some things in this life can be sorted out.

Granted, Castaneda lives so reclusively we cannot easily separate his routines from Carlos's, but a private detective could surely separate them. Reading the detective's report, would Daniel Noel still not know how to take it? Perusing Ralph Beals's satirical letter about don Pedro, did he wonder whether Castaneda's former professor had really apprenticed himself to don Juan's elder brother? Is there nowhere one can draw a line between the credible and the incredible? In a world where authentic myths are as numerous as UFOs, do we need to elevate awkward, plodding allegories and transparently spurious autobiography to the rank of myth?

Castaneda popularizes some fine old metaphysical puzzles, and readers who have never seen the like will no doubt think he invented them, while others who feel them intensely for the first time may call him a great teacher, but if we do not eventually see through Castaneda, how shall we recognize Zeno and the Zeitgeist standing behind him?

Here endeth the *Parabola* debate. In a letter, Noel wanted to know how I could reconcile my complaint about elevating "awkward, plodding allegories to the rank of myth" with my characterization of Castaneda elsewhere as a "talented allegorist." A fair question. The paradox proceeds from Castaneda's gift for allegorizing social science contrasted with the crudeness of his style and the predictability of his dramaturgy. Though a very slick trickster and a skilled juggler of propositions, he is not much as poet or legendary hero. Deliberately and discursively constructed, his allegories do not rise to the level of myth, because they lack emotional authority. Cashing in on an intellectual tour de force is not a prelude to canonization. If Castaneda had written only *The Teachings*, and if it were believed he had gone back to the desert and jumped into the *nagual*, and if in fact we never heard from him again—then we should have the makings of a Castaneda myth. What we have instead is popular hunger for myth feeding on artificial mushrooms of vision. The don Juan books deserve to survive as an ingenious and instructive hoax, but they will never be literature or sacred texts.

Religion as Science

RdeM:

As in the previous chapter, I'm about to have an argument, this time with Bob Gover, author of seven novels including the world-famous satire, *One Hundred Dollar Misunderstanding*. Drawing confidently on his experience as an amateur anthropologist specializing in Voodoo, Gover offers some adroitly phrased absurdities about science, whereupon I try to set him straight. True to form, he gets the last word and survives unreconstructed. Guest scoffer Paul Christoffers puts Gover's religio-scientific proposal into national perspective, and Gover puts a libertarian hex on Christoffers.

Gover:

Those who believe the truth can be told only as scientific fact are appalled by the idea that Carlos Castaneda did make-believe fieldwork and pawned it off as anthropology. At the other end of the spectrum, those who believe truth is best revealed through literature and art are equally appalled, at fiction that would be second rate if it were not pretending to be fact. It's obvious, however, that Castaneda wanted to write something that was neither *The Peyote Cult* nor *Robinson Crusoe*, and the genre he developed—call it the ethnomystical thriller—proved to be just what was needed. By giving us fiction in the guise of science, Castaneda accomplished far more than tons of actual fieldnotes have accomplished. Instead of embalming a live shaman in ethnocentric scientism, he leaped the cultural divide and took us into the shamanic mind.

Rather than explore this remarkable accomplishment, de Mille took it upon himself to psychologize the leaper, and promptly ran into trouble. In *Castaneda's Journey* he tells us he twice tried to interview Castaneda and was twice rebuffed. Had de Mille been a wage-earning journalist, such lazy legwork would have gotten him laughed all the way to the unemployment office. But de Mille struck a scholarly stance and so got away with relying on the legwork and interviews of others, plus memories, comments, and rumors culled from Castaneda's ex-wife and acquaintances. Out of such scraps he put together a version of Castaneda's personal history and psyche, rendering a portrait of a kid from the hinterlands of Peru who went to the big city and made good by becoming a diligent library researcher with a small flair for fiction and a mighty talent for lying.

What de Mille's ethnocentricity kept him from seeing was that Castaneda came to the scientific reality from the pagan reality of his Peruvian homeland. It is these two very different belief systems, the scientific and the pagan, that are united in the don Juan books. Whether in Africa or in the Americas, the pagan belief system is such that it can accommodate, embrace, and include the belief system of Western science. Any witchdoctor with knowledge of modern science can tell you the theory of relativity is one god "speaking" through science, while the quantum theory is another god "speaking" and he can tell you the relationship between the two gods. On the other hand, the belief system of modern science excludes pagan beliefs. Castaneda understands this; de Mille does not.

Having interviewed over a hundred witchdoctors—Haitian Houngons, Trinidadian Shango priests, Brazilian Macumberos, Mexican brujos, American Voodooists, etcetera—I have learned that scientists and witchdoctors hold one basic belief in common: theory precedes discovery of evidence. Science postulates the atom, evolves a graphic image of it, and accumulates evidence suggesting it exists in that very image. While it's not unusual to read about the atom being "observed," no one has ever seen one in the ordinary reality. Atoms exist in a nonordinary reality of nonthings. What scientists observe through electronic microscopes are electronic cartoons that supposedly show the behavior of atoms. Similarly, Afro-American paganism postulates gods as programmers of all things. The witchdoctor "observes" these gods acting and speaking through stones and trees, Catholic saints, Hindu gurus, you and me. Neither gods nor atoms can be seen in ordinary physical reality, but both god-theories and atom-theories furnish plenty of evidence for those who seek.

De Mille collected some mythological tidbits about a god called Trickster, but only to belittle Castaneda's accomplishment. What de Mille depreciates as an entertaining hoax is a bag of brilliant tricks Castaneda used to transcend the limits of science in order to show us a reality that is still valid for millions in Africa and Latin America. In the years ahead, East, West, and Third World will draw closer and closer together through swifter travel and instantaneous communication. Westerners will find it economically beneficial to appreciate the working theories of those they have until recently denigrated as primitive, superstitious, and ignorant.

RdeM:

Gover's errors come in two flavors: frivolous and serious. Let's take the frivolous first. Having interviewed over a hundred witchdoctors, he taunts me with "lazy legwork" for failing to corner the notoriously elusive Castaneda. Had I been one of *National Enquirer's* go-getters, I should undoubtedly have lain in wait at Castaneda's beach house and interrogated him there—perforce at gunpoint, since he is both able and unwilling. I don't suppose Gover held a gun on his Houngons, but if he had I wonder how much faith he would put in their statements. How many of his Macumberos had published four books about themselves? How many of his Shangos had already told their stories to six other interviewers? A witchdoctor or anthrofantasist who couldn't tell his life story or get his ideas across in a thousand pages and six interviews would hardly deserve to be interviewed again. So much for Gover's frivolity.

On the serious side, Gover hopes to promote international accord by explaining Third-World belief systems to the West. Anthropologists have tried to do the same thing, but Gover is not impressed by their efforts and instructs them on how to improve their professional practice. Pagan beliefs, he says, can embrace modern science—detecting voices of gods in theories of relativity or quanta—but science cannot accommodate pagan beliefs. Scientists, then, should presumably get their theories from gods.

Gover's unsound epistemology fails to comprehend the capacity of any theory to subsume any other if terms can be redefined. When quanta are gods, then God can be "a 6000-foot tall, red jellybean," and candymakers can build a bridge to the other world. Science is at least as versatile as Voodoo. Scientists can penetrate pagan beliefs at least as well as witchdoctors can fathom science. Anthropologists can be as unethnocentric as Gover can. His impatience with their slow discursive unfolding of compact pagan animism may drive him to gather his own data or to practice Voodoo, but it does not justify confusing Voodoo with science. Voodoo is not science. It is a prescientific system of thought whose assumptions and procedures are quite different from those of science. Like science, it explains the world, but its explanations are not scientific. Like science, it provides techniques for manipulating the world. Like modern technology, shamanistic magic enjoys astonishing successes and suffers embarrassing failures. Admittedly, scientists do not understand the successes of shamanism, but then shamans do not ordinarily understand the successes of science either. Physicists look at holograms of atoms. Houngons listen to atoms talking. Anthropologists listen to Houngons. Each learns something, but not what the others are learning. A witchdoctor who understands science as a scientist understands it has become a scientist. A scientist who practices Voodoo as a witchdoctor practices it has become a witchdoctor. Such transitions promise to advance our knowledge, but they are quite unusual. Castaneda's popularity shows how exciting the idea can be, even in allegory. In the meantime, each profession practices according to its proper rules, and there is no advantage whatsoever in mixing them up as Gover does.

Since the legitimate anthropologists have not yet carried us as far into the shamanic mind as they and Gover want to go, he is grateful for Castaneda's new genre, which "unites" the pagan and scientific belief systems, thereby accomplishing "far more than tons of actual fieldnotes have accomplished." In contrast, I believe this "uniting" merely confounds two readily distinguishable points of view, thereby confusing the reader. The "shamanic mind" into which Castaneda carries us is a blatant fake, comprising snippets of the ethnography Gover disdains, borrowed occult and mystical notions, and paraphrased philosophic propositions. Don Juan's wisdom rings true by striking familiar chords. He is a house-shaman, especially domesticated to serve the bookish seeker. I admit he's lovable, but so are Uncle Tommyhawk and Tio Taco.

Castaneda's anthrofiction did reach millions of fans who had never read a word of anthropology, but the accomplishment was self-limiting. Though the sound of shamans can be heard in the works of numerous writers, and though don Juan alerted many an untrained ear to listen for that sound, Castaneda's pretense of factual reporting forestalled his directing the reader to the ethnographic, religious, and philosophical texts out of which his synthetic sage had been born.

Gover:

De Mille's foolhardy assertion that "scientists can penetrate pagan beliefs at least as well as witchdoctors can fathom science" exemplifies the pompous ignorance that hampers us in today's world. Our culture supposes that newer truths are truer truths, but in the pagan perspective, knowledge is a constant—like energy, neither created nor destroyed but merely worked in ever-changing patterns. To fathom science, one must study the beliefs of science, which may be found in textbooks. Witchdoctors attending the University of California can easily do it. To penetrate pagan beliefs, one must have personal experience of pagan gods, invisible forces that are alive and responsive to human intention. A modern scientist who attempted to document such experience would be judged unfit by his peers.

Christoffers:

How amazing to discover that the solution to the defects in the belief system of Western science may be found in the African-Amerindian pagan belief system! If only this insight could now be put to use for the betterment of mankind. Given that one of Gover's mental giants could singlehandedly reconcile the corpuscular theory with the wave theory, what might not be achieved if a whole cartload of such sages could be assembled under the same roof. How about setting up a think tank for this purpose, on some idyllic spot near the very centers of government? We could call it Zulu-on-the-Potomac. The Zu, for short. Furnished with the necessary scientific tools—rags, bones, hanks of hair—the Zu would lose no time in solving the problems that plague civilization: energy shortage, limit on travel faster than light, burden of mortality, and so on.

Owing to the prejudices inherent in our Western belief system, funding the Zu would no doubt be difficult, but once again Gover has pointed a solution. Dr Castaneda could prepare a fictitious account of successful Zu projects and publish it as fact. Endowments would quickly come forth. In the past we have hesitated to employ such means because we were scared of getting caught, but our qualms were needless, for it has been shown that the path of duplicity safely circumvents the bungling, backward superstitions of modern science.

Gover:

Once there was a real smart scientist who insulted a witchdoctor. In retaliation the shaman put a hex on the insulter. Within a year the scientist was terminally ill and wondering if indeed the shaman's evil spirits had caused his misfortune. His doctor put such misgivings to rest by presenting reams of documented evidence: "It's cancer you're dying from, not evil spirits." Thus assured, our hero faced his end certain that the hex had not worked, although he did wonder what had caused his cancer.

Likewise, Christoffers's lightheaded idea of a Zulu on the Potomac would be more catchy if it weren't for the fact that one already exists. Of course these witchdoctors are of a homegrown variety and we call them congresspersons. But most of them are devout worshippers of dog spelled backwards, God, or what in African language literally translates as Voodoo. And although they don't do their works with beads and bones, the effect of their activities is to extort about half our earnings in return for controlling our lives, causing a cancerous situation in the body politic.

R. de Mille Doesn't Exist

RdeM:

Just when my don Juan debunking was really rolling, a radical challenge to my authority loomed up like an angry ally. *High Times*, the magazine of "high" society, where official policy frowns on peddling baking soda as coke, camel dung as hash, or ethnomethodallegories as datura trips, had published my article questioning the existence of don Juan.

Leaping three-thousand miles from the Catskills, an indignant letter offered in don Juan's ontological defense: two visitors from Boulder, a music box, an alcoholic nephew, and a sorcerer's delight in his first refrigerator, purchased with royalties from *The Teachings* of Himself. The letter went on to reprove Gordon Wasson and to question the existence of R. de Mille.

Nonexistence doesn't phase a legendary sorcerer, but it's a terrible handicap for a beginning debunker. Luckily, my photo had appeared in *High Times*, whereas the challenger had produced no photo of don Juan. I called her up.

"Here I am," I told her. "I exist, as you can see."

"I don't see you," she said.

By the time I had persuaded her to believe in me, we had also agreed her letter would appear in this chapter and two drawings of La Catalina in a later chapter.

"I dashed off that letter in a fit of exasperation," Matson said. "After talking to you for a while, I think you're as real as don Juan."

March 24, 1977

Sir : (idiot)
   in 1969 (summer) i
was in Boulder Colo. when
two very good friends took
their old car to visit Don
Juan then living in the
southwest. They brought
him a beautiful music
box & some wine for the
lushing (nephew? i forgit)
relative. they found him
very enthusiastic over a
new refrigerator he'd bought
with the proceeds casteneda
had given him from the
sale of the 1st book,
                    Sincerely
                 Irvin Matson
P.S. no i won't give you names
or address of the friends for

obvious reasons: ~~unclear~~
mainly that you would
publish such a stupid
opeonion in a national
rog.

(which has had ^em^ many
such i.e. wassons (sic)
claim that A. muscaria
is soma when almost
certainly soma is canabis;
i.e. in tibetan canabis is
called soma-ratsa or "grass".
i send you this because i'm
tired of ~~unclear~~ opinions
that "D. Juan" doesn't exist":
i believe R. de Mille
doesn't exist & have as
much reason to believe
so.

THE DON JUAN PAPERS

RdeM

"The Guru" will examine some differences between discursive knowledge developed in a rational dialogue among equals and inspirational paths along which dominant masters lead or drive their submissive apprentices toward a separate reality closed to reason but opened by revelation. This outstanding essay finds its way into *The Don Juan Papers* by having chosen Castaneda's books and *Reading Castaneda* to exemplify the occultism haunting modern society and the relativistic sociology that manifests the very occultist tendency it seeks to deal with.

Kenneth Minogue (rhymes with thin-ROGUE) was born in New Zealand in 1930, went to school in Australia, and attended the University of Sydney and the London School of Economics. For "most of his life" he has been teaching political science in the University of London. He has written *The Liberal Mind* (1963), *Nationalism* (1967), and *The Concept of a University* (1971) and has edited, jointly with Anthony de Crespigny, *Contemporary Political Philosophers* (1976).

Minogue is that stimulating sort of scholar who gets the best out of his intellectual adversaries by giving them a good, hard, literate punch in the dialectic gut. As they lie gasping on the disputative mat, he calmly observes that to floor them in this way "is not to discredit them," for relativistic sociology and occultism face up to something important in our culture which has been neglected by safer disciplines afraid of toppling over into absurdity.

The Guru

Is it only nakedness that distinguishes man from other apes? Aristotle thought that rationality and language made the difference. The capacity to laugh and an addiction to swallowing medicines are typical of a vast number of other suggested *differentiae*. But anyone taking a cool look at contemporary humanity could hardly escape the thought that man is an advice-seeking animal. What shall I do?—better: what*ever* shall I do?—is the archetypal human question; and ever since the Christian Church began to shed the burden of human freedom a complex and specialised industry has grown up to supply the need. Miss Lonelyhearts and Sigmund Freud are sob-sisters under the skin. In advice-giving circles, the unadvised man is found to be as deplorable as was the masterless man of early mediaeval times.

An Eastern adviser increasingly popular in the West, the Guru is typically concerned not just with imparting knowledge, but with transforming lives. What he requires of his followers is total submission not to knowledge but to a Way or Path. Any critical response exhibited by the followers is likely to be construed as an unregenerate element of the mechanical personality. To follow a guru is to embark on a voyage in which the only compass point is the master himself.

The attractions of the guru can no doubt be traced back to the beginnings of Western self-distaste in the 18th century, but the more celebrated gurus only began to make a splash towards the end of the 19th. India was, so far as this particular diffusion is concerned, the guru's original homeland, and the most romantic account of what a guru could do for you was given in Somerset Maugham's *The Razor's Edge*. The most recently fashionable guru has appeared in books written by Carlos Castaneda, and is an Indian of a different kind.

In principle, the Carlos of the don Juan story is a student and inquirer rather than the disciple of a guru; and certainly in Castaneda's account of the meetings Carlos maintains something of a critical and rational attitude. But this is not to be taken entirely at its face value, partly because there is some doubt about whether don Juan is a real rather than an invented personage, and partly because the drift of the whole enterprise appears to be to commend don Juan's beliefs and practices as capable of giving access to a reality which we are denied. Most Western observers would regard many of don Juan's beliefs as primitive sorcery. Carlos, as an anthropologist, would take them entirely seriously as the practices of a culture. But Castaneda as the writer of best-selling books is doing something different again.

The very terms in which his enterprise is broached need to be considered with care. To talk of "Yaqui" knowledge would raise the question of whether certain beliefs were true or false; and it may well be the case that Indians know all sorts of things, especially in herbal matters, that Western science does not know. To talk of a "way of knowledge", however, puts that question to one side. Ways, paths, and other directional impedimenta are among the more obvious equipment of the average guru, and quite astonishing things can be done with them. Thus Peregrine Worsthorne recorded recently his astonishment, not to say rage, when on a recent trip to China he heard a Party functionary propose a toast to the Free Press, commenting that Britain and China have different "ways" of press freedom. Ways can turn black into white, and need watching.

Gurus, then, are teachers not of knowledge but of ways and paths, and the very word "knowledge" is misleading because what gurus have to offer is less a matter of truths than of new perceptions, variations of consciousness, or new sensations.

Consider, for example, a typical guru's doctrine from one of the more interesting practitioners of the art, P. D. Ouspensky:

> We always think and act as though we knew the truth. This is lying. . . . The first lie we tell ourselves is when we say 'I'. It is a lie because in saying 'I' we presume certain things: we presume a certain unity and a certain power. . . . Being surrounded by these lies, born and educated in these lies, we cannot be any different from what we are; we are just the result, the product of this lying.

Years after encountering this doctrine, one of Ouspensky's more prominent disciples came across David Hume's argument in the *Treatise* that the human self is "nothing but a bundle or collection of different perceptions, which succeed each other with inconceivable rapidity, and are in perpetual flux and movement." Dr Kenneth Walker decided that Hume's was a formulation of the same idea he had learned from Ouspensky; but in an important way he was wrong. Gurus are different from philosophers, and there is about the aggressive manner of Ouspensky's formulation a feature entirely foreign to Hume's reasoning. Ouspensky seeks to use this relatively commonplace idea as a revelation which will shake his disciples and transform their lives. The capacity to induce such revelations is an important part of the ascendancy of the guru over the disciple. The use of doctrines in this way is, of course, found in many areas of life, most notably today perhaps in ideological politics; but in its purest form it is found in the practices of Zen masters.

It is characteristic of the guru, then, to work upon the whole personality of the disciple. He is not just teaching them new things, but remodelling their perceptual and emotional responses. And if he is to achieve the necessary ascendancy, he must be regarded as infallible. What this means is that the disciples must take everything he does, even his apparent moments of irritation or human weakness, as being part of a continuous process of teaching. Nothing is redundant; everything will be interpreted in a constructive sense. It is axiomatic that everything the guru does is under his control.

One consequence of this common feature of gurus is that the disciples are usually worried, anxious people whereas the guru often bubbles over with gaiety—indeed, remembering the celebrated giggle of the Maharishi Mahesh Yogi, one is tempted to say "with transcendental gaiety." Gurdjieff was prone in this way to subject his followers to all manner of amusing caprices; and Alan Brien, reviewing *Tales of Power*, was reduced to cataloguing the number of times don Juan burst into derisive laughter, slapped his thighs, and otherwise expressed his mirth.

Until recently, it would have been indisputable that the guru was essentially a foreign import. For one of the most usual beliefs about a guru is that he belongs to a higher realm of being than that of ordinary humanity, and any such role in a Christian civilisation had already been decisively pre-empted. Those who attempted to make superhuman claims staggered under the burden of heresy. The ascendancy of priests over their flocks may often be considerable; but priests and clergymen are bound to a theology and to institutional disciplines. Psychoanalysts may often totally dominate their patients and seek to transform their lives but they are denied the possibility of being the proprietors of profound secrets (one of the commoner ways in which gurus attain their ascendancy) by their claims to scientific status. Philosophers and other academic teachers must explain themselves to pupils who are assumed to be fundamentally on the same level as the teachers. Hence the great guru-hunger which has led to the current spiritual Disneyland in the West has been unmistakably satisfied from sources outside our own culture, even when the experience of discipledom has been intelligently packaged for a technologically oriented public, as with the adaptations of

Occultist thought by Gurdjieff and Ouspensky.

Although the guru is an exotic outsider the actual techniques he uses are by no means foreign to the West. The foreignness of the techniques is exaggerated so long as we seek to understand the guru in the context of religion and popular philosophy. For the teacher of any *practical* skill often behaves in exactly the same way as gurus do. His business is to impel students to do things, often unpleasant things, whose point the pupil cannot at this stage understand. Some acts of obedience may be commanded for no other purpose than to enhance the authority of the teacher himself. The practices of gurus are strikingly reminiscent of marine sergeants licking into shape a platoon of rookies who will soon face the tests of war. The sheer caprice, brutality, and insistence on un-thinking and instant obedience turn out to be essential in later situations. And this makes it clear that the main point about the guru is that he is a practical rather than an intellectual figure. The move from "knowledge" to "ways of knowledge" is a move from theory to practice. Some of our own academics may behave a little like gurus, but when they do, they have taken a holiday from their academic commitment.

The kind of knowledge gurus possess is fundamentally the diagnosis and cure of the disease of being human. A common conviction of modern Europeans is that they are "spiritually crippled." Their sensibility is dis-sociated; they suffer from alienation; they have not realised the pos-sibilities of spiritual evolution, or the mechanical routines of modern life have suffocated some vital spark within. There is no end to ways in which the disease may be described; but each description refers to a similar observation of our complex human state. The fact that some three thousand years ago the ancient Hebrews already believed themselves cursed and expelled from paradise might have been expected to modify at least the element of self-pity in the belief that *modern* man is the specific sufferer from this disease.

Religion is, of course, the arena in which these preoccupations have normally been discussed and contained. Hence it is that many humanists and progressives, abandoning Christianity, took the option of denying that there was any disease at all. Man was evolving towards moral perfec-tion; indeed, some of the more intrepid spirits took the view that relig-ion, far from being the cure, was in fact the disease itself, and that man would become whole if only he would throw away the crutches of wish-fulfilment and stand on his own two feet.

The cult of the guru needs to be understood in terms of those who abandoned organised religion yet remained preoccupied by the condition to which religions respond. Some of these attributed the disease not to man himself but to the structure of the society in which he lived, thus giving the idea of revolution its unmistakably salvationist aura. These men invented ideologies, and they have prospered mightily. The Occultist solution to the problem is different from the Ideological, and in a sense far more radical. It consists in saying that the ordinary world we live in, the world of rational and regular connections between physical bodies, is merely the response to a *part* of reality, by a *part* of ourselves. This is why we seem spiritually crippled and barren. Beyond what we have learned to perceive is a realm of phenomena which are occasionally glimpsed if we are specially attuned to see. Techniques of attunement will allow us human fragments (or more usually, some of us) at last to take on our full stature as men and women.

Just as the ideological project of liberation from our shackles has thrown up a multitude of mutually antipathetic sects, so too has Occultism. Particular variants of each type of belief necessarily compete for the same audience. Ideological sects reserve their fiercest contempt for each other rather than for the deluded bourgeois beyond the pale (for "bourgeois" has the technical sense in all ideologies of referring to the unregenerate enemy); and Occultism is full of teachers and groups with a noticeable tendency to anathematise their competitors as deceiving fakes who muddy the pure stream of truth with their superstitious babblings.

Within this general framework, the impulses behind Occultism are extremely various. The dream of magical power is usually a central theme. Thus the search for the power of communicating with the dead produces Spiritualism and an involvement with ghosts, often bolstered by theories of astral and other strange sorts of "body." A preoccupation with knowing the future produces fortune telling, and was a strong component of the omens, auguries, and oracles which dominated classical religion. Alchemy has a long and respectable history as the attempt to obtain power over substances, and illustrates very well the characteristic Occultist combination of sophistication and superstition. For it may be concerned either with transforming the soul, or with vulgar external matters like getting rich and powerful. Magic and sorcery may describe petty-minded attempts to encompass one's ends (like the mysterious death of enemies), or it may be concerned with self-purification. There are two levels of Occultism, which we might describe as the vulgar and the elevated; or which we may distinguish according to whether the aim is to enhance our power over the world, or to transform our own character and understanding for the better. What this means is that Occultism is, in different ways, a competitor with science and with religion.

From the 17th century onwards, the progress of that heterogeneous and complicated tradition of thought we call "science" (not to be confused with that lesser part of it with which philosophers deal when they study the logic of science) has depended upon an unyielding hostility to Occultism in any form; and this hostility has been reciprocated. Paradoxically, however, modern science became capable in time of feats that would have made legendary any Renaissance magus. The wonders of magic, for all their romance, are insignificant in comparison with modern technological transformations. But these transformations have concerned only the lesser level of Occultist preoccupation: power over *nature*. They have had no effect upon the human heart. The hope of moral progress to partner that of technology has indeed been consistently entertained, but its frustration has left the way open for Occultism to continue as a kind of intellectual underworld, and made possible the modest resurgence of its ideas that we see taking place today.

But if we look a little closer, we shall see that the paradox commonly noted in the histories—that science has achieved triumphs beyond the dreams of magic—is less paradoxical than it seems. For one thing the 17th-century slogan that "knowledge is power" strongly suggests that science abandoned the techniques of magic rather than its ends. For another, progress was thought to depend upon a process of purification of the mind from the debris of earlier learning, a process which itself seems to have an interestingly occult character. And these considerations are reinforced by the close involvement of science and Occultist ideas during the Renaissance period, an involvement familiar in different ways in the careers of Kepler and Bacon.

Christianity, by contrast, has often been hostile to dreams of power as a form of pride. It therefore tended to attack science and Occultism alike. Both seemed to deny or to ignore man's fallen condition and to direct attention away from the only remedy recognised by the Church: faith in God. Hence it was that the only theologically respectable versions of Occultist experience in Christian life took the form of religious mysticism. The condition of such respectability was that the transformation of the soul could be identified with the workings of God. Sometimes this identification fell apart, and many heretics persecuted by the Church were mystics whose spiritual journeyings had led to blasphemous pronouncements. The execution of the Sufi mystic Al Hallaj in Baghdad in A.D. 922 reminds us that a similar situation obtained within Islam.

Modern Occultism results largely from the dissolution of the always unstable connection between Occultist ideas and religious orthodoxy, and is composed of a vast number of ideas which have been circulating for many millennia. Sometimes a little surface exoticism is derived from science fiction (the notion of Jesus as a space-traveller, for example), and in most versions the technicalities have been given a modern veneer. But it seems safe to say that very little has fundamentally changed.

Carlos Castaneda has produced his own particular version of these ideas. His immense popularity derives also from several novelties of his presentation. One of these is, of course, that he is himself an enigmatic figure who is seldom interviewed—and when he is, supplies false information about his own past. A guru (even a guru who writes himself up as an apprentice) knows better than most men that there is a war between those who write books and those who criticise and review them. Writers wish to emphasise their uniqueness, reviewers assimilate books and men to convenient categories. (This very article is itself a skirmish in such a war).

Castaneda has also given a powerful legitimacy to the currently popular use of drugs as one possible escape from this prison we call our life. His own view of the importance of drugs in the making of a man of knowledge oddly parallels the fashion for drugs in the Western world— *The Teachings of don Juan* appeared at the height of the drug cult and connects hallucinogenic experience with a deeper experience of reality. It is perhaps incidental that by the time *Tales of Power* appeared drugs had passed from fashion, and Carlos had discovered that:

> The extraordinary effect that psychotropic plants had had on me was what gave me the bias that their use was the key feature of the teachings. I held on to that conviction and it was only in the later years of my apprenticeship that I realized that the meaningful transformations and findings of sorcerers were always done in states of sober consciousness.

Drugs are essentially a mechanical stimulus, and it would have made Castaneda a less interesting exponent of Occultism if he had stayed with them. Indeed, part of the tedium of the early stages of the teachings derives from the fact that so much is concerned with describing merely personal drug-induced sensations.

Castaneda has also introduced a relatively new angle of Occultist vision, making it derive from the practice of sorcerers among an unsophisticated group of Mexican Indians. The great vogue for Occultism in the West over the last century has usually been derived from Eastern illumination: from Buddhist, Hindu, or Islamic masters; and the grand civilisations in which these religions are embedded have given a necessary grandeur to what has been accepted. For one of the commonest of Occultist beliefs is that man himself is largely a mechanical and uncreative beast whose civilisations and religions are but a scrambled version of what has been taught by superhuman gurus in earlier times. Particular contemporary occultist beliefs are often thought to be the pure doctrine from which all else derives; and not infrequently the guru himself is thought to be a member of this superhuman company. Castaneda has not followed this option (though there are hints at various points that it could be incorporated without difficulty). He has found the possibilities of higher being among people who it is relevant to note might be regarded as noble savages, unspoilt by the rat-race of urban sophistication. But don Juan himself, we learn, is perfectly at ease even wearing a suit in Mexico City.

Carlos's apprenticeship to don Juan lasts for over ten years and is described in four volumes. It can best be described in terms of what sort of experience Carlos must blot out, and what sort of experience he must learn to let in.

Carlos has to be taught to break his educated habit of trying to explain everything. For explanation is concerned with the world as we conveniently *describe* it to ourselves: it is a world of fixed connections and solid material bodies. Such a description is acquired very early in a child's life, and his acquisition of it marks the stages of his membership of the human community. "For don Juan, then", Castaneda tells us in *Journey to Ixtlan*,

> the reality of our day-to-day life consists of an endless flow of perceptual interpretations which we, the individuals who share a specific *membership*, have learned to make in common.

This process of learning encourages the use of some kinds of perception to the detriment of other things that we might "see", and it is perpetually reinforced by the incessant internal dialogue we have with ourselves. Castaneda is entirely in the Occultist tradition in appropriating the ordinary vocabulary of perception for technical use. Indeed, most of *A Separate Reality* is taken up with "the task of 'seeing'." The sorcerer as don

Juan describes him apprehends the world not only in the ordinary way but also "with his nose, or his tongue, or his will, especially with his will", and the results are different from what we think of as reality:

> "when we perceive the world with our will we know that it is
> not as 'out there' or 'as real' as we think."

The point of most Occultist meditation is to cleanse the mind of the debris created by our perceptual habits so that it may attain the passivity which allows it to "see" beyond the limits of our communally described world. There is a well-known Zen saying which puts the belief with the utmost economy: "Avoiding thought, all appears." Carlos has to learn how not to probe the limited world he perceives with the questions he habitually employs, and in the early stages his perceptual explorations are given a boost by drugs. Don Juan also employs technical devices designed to prevent awareness from slipping back into the reality we take for granted: "wearing a black cap, or tying my left shoe first, or fastening my belt from right to left." Carlos's mental life must be entirely transformed so that things become possible to him which were inconceivable before. The secret of it all is the direction of one's attention. As don Juan tells him:

> "All of this exists only because of our attention. This very rock
> where we're sitting is a rock because we have been forced to give
> our attention to it as a rock."

It is only in the last volume that the point of many things in his earlier apprenticeship becomes evident. It is all a matter of breaking out of the trap we have made for ourselves:

> "We are perceivers. We are an awareness; we are not objects; we
> have no solidity. We are boundless. The world of objects and
> solidity is a way of making our passage on earth convenient. It is
> only a description that was created to help us. We, or rather our
> *reason*, forget that the description is only a description and thus
> we entrap the totality of ourselves in a vicious circle from which
> we rarely emerge in our lifetime."

Reason limits. This is a central part of the message of Carlos's apprenticeship, and it is a part which cannot but be of nervous interest to modern educated men. One doubt which will soon afflict any educated reader is whether Castaneda, for all his possible qualifications as an anthropologist, actually knows what reason and logic are. At one point in the culmination of his learning, Carlos has to construe the fact that his "benefactor" don Genaro suddenly appears before him, and he works out that the appearance has been arranged by don Juan as a kind of trick. This attempt at explanation is described in rapid succession as "my logical explanatory scheme", "my logical scheme", and "my rational structure". Logic is not in fact involved, and to identify one possible hypothesis with rationality itself makes it easy for Castaneda to discredit rationality as further considerations appear to invalidate the explanation that has occurred to him.

As with most Occultists, then, the reader has to put up with a certain amount of crudity in specifying the rationality which is supposed to entrap us. What Castaneda is in fact saying (and it is a typical situation in the books) is that Carlos has tried and failed to make sense of his experience in naturalistic terms. It may be that there is a natural explanation, and he has failed to find it. It may also be that he has in fact stumbled upon events which require some kind of "supernatural" explanation. But reason is evidently not to be discredited by any particular consequence of using it, and Carlos and don Juan are both in fact presenting a rational argument and marshalling evidence as they go along. What is really at stake is what Carlos calls "my nearly invincible habit of assessing everything . . .my processes of book-keeping." For unless such habits are overcome, we shall never experience the *nagual*!

The nagual? It is pronounced *nah-wa'hl*, and is one component of what turns out to be the central distinction of don Juan's teaching. It must be distinguished from our rational ordering of the world which constitutes the *tonal* (pronounced *toh-na'hl*), a term which in Indian lore describes a guardian spirit. As don Juan explains it, the dilemma of human life is that the guardian, who is broad-minded and understanding, has become a guard, who is narrow and vigilant.

> "The *tonal* is everything we are. . . . Name it! Anything we have a word for is the *tonal*. . . . The *tonal* makes the world only in a manner of speaking. It cannot create or change anything, and yet it makes the world because its function is to judge, and assess, and witness. . . . the *tonal* makes up the rules by which it apprehends the world. So, in a manner of speaking, it creates the world."

We live in "the island of the *tonal*", and we could not live without it. Nevertheless, it limits us; and we may break out of these limits if we can come to apprehend the *nagual*, a term extended beyond its meaning in Indian lore (the transformation of a witch into an animal) to describe a form of indefinable creative power by which our world is surrounded, and out of which it has been created.

> "The *nagual* is not experience or intuition or consciousness. Those terms and everything else you may care to say are only items on the island of the *tonal*. The *nagual*, on the other hand, is only effect. The *tonal* begins at birth and ends at death, but the *nagual* never ends. . . . One can say that the *nagual* accounts for creativity."

The *tonal* by contrast creates nothing; yet, because it makes up the rules by which it apprehends the world, it can be said to create our world. The point is that the world *is*, in one sense, the way we describe it; and the kind of conflict Castaneda wishes to bring out appears in the following exchange with don Juan (in which, as often, Carlos's questions are less those of an experienced apprentice than a surrogate for the objections the reader of the book may want to pose):

> "If the *tonal* is everything we know about ourselves and our world, what, then, is the *nagual*?
>
> "The *nagual* is the part of us which we do not deal with at all."
>
> "I beg your pardon?"
>
> "The *nagual* is the part of us for which there is no description—no words, no names, no feelings, no knowledge."
>
> "That's a contradiction, don Juan. In my opinion if it can't be felt or described or named, it cannot exist."

No doubt it might be objected that "*nagual*" is also a name, and that the world of description cannot be transcended by a description. Don Juan's answer is that the *nagual* can only be experienced; and Carlos's encounters with it are described in the books Castaneda writes.

But we are dealing here with a profoundly unphilosophical view, one which wants to get the biology, zoology, mineralogy, psychology out of the world in order to restore omens, auguries, miracles, spirits, portents and other hints of environing spirit which science and technology have banished as superstitions. This is not to say that don Juan's sorcery is irrationalist, for he often tells Carlos to trust to his senses and his reason. He does so because the *tonal* guards us against the unpredictabilities of the *nagual*, which is so alarming that the unfortunate Carlos spends most of the active parts of his apprenticeship in a state of gibbering terror, while his teachers are giggling away in the background.

The "impeccable warrior" must approach the *nagual* prepared for death; he must open himself up to it, but the moment he begins to experience it, he must moderate the experience by invoking the *tonal*. The sudden movements through space or the suspensions of gravity which are the simple openings to the *nagual* vouchsafed to Carlos are not adventures to be embarked on light-heartedly. Indeed, it is hardly a voluntary adventure at all, for although Castaneda's Occultism has no theology, it does incorporate a notion called "power" which guides the actions of both sorcerer and apprentice and might be construed as a determining providence. Providence, however, also guarantees that no advance in power will happen without a corresponding moral change in those who acquire it.

It is, indeed, a striking feature of Occultism that it is generally quite without interest in moral questions. Occult illumination reveals men as largely sunk in folly from which nothing short of illumination can redeem them:

> ". . . a man who *sees* [don Juan tells Carlos] controls his folly, while his fellow men can't. A man who *sees* has no longer an active interest in his fellow men. *Seeing* has already detached him from absolutely everything he knew before."

And in the journey to Ixtlan which becomes the metaphor for the voyage of spiritual discovery, don Genaro finds only "phantom travellers." The unilluminated have become unreal to him.

Tales of Power, like the other books of the canon, is a skilfully constructed literary work in a genre that has little respectability at the moment, but which remains of teasing interest to modern human beings, particularly as many of the wilder dreams of technology collapse. Part of its attraction derives from the variety of possible responses a reader may have to it. Calculated ambiguities run right through the don Juan cycle, and are not dissipated by the heavy-weight doctrine in the last volume. I have been putting the cycle in an Occultist context, but Walter

Goldschmidt (who wrote a foreword to *The Teachings of don Juan*) interprets the material in its more explicit anthropological sense:

> The central importance of entering into worlds other than our own—and hence of anthropology itself—lies in the fact that the experience leads us to understand that our own world is also a cultural construct. By experiencing other worlds, then, we see our own for what it is and are thereby enabled also to see fleetingly what the real world, the one between our own cultural construct and those other worlds, must in fact be like.

There is an obvious objection to this argument. If, in the fullest sense, "our" world *is* a cultural construct, then we are logically incapacitated from having those fleeting moments of freedom. If, on the other hand, such fleeting moments are possible, then our world cannot be entirely a cultural construct. One horn of the dilemma must give way, but most exponents of this type of relativist doctrine want to affirm both horns equally.

This is a difficulty that Castaneda does not have to deal with, for to the extent that his account of the *tonal* and the *nagual* is an explanatory doctrine (rather than a practical belief allowing us to transform our experience) it runs into the different problem of trying to describe what is by definition indescribable. But it is no more troubled by the problem of relativism than is the physicist who has available two totally different descriptions of the chair in which I sit. Hence it seems odd that Goldschmidt should interpret Castaneda in cultural and sociological terms and thus complicate his intellectual viability. Yet the very same thing has been done in a recent discussion of the Castaneda writings. It is called *Reading Castaneda*, and its title indicates homage jointly to Castaneda and Louis Althusser. This imaginative juxtaposition is made all the more striking by the fact that it is intended to introduce undergraduates to the social sciences.

An account of an apprenticeship to the magical beliefs of a shaman is not exactly the sort of thing one would immediately recognise as a suitable text for such a purpose. But since the lectures from which the book derives were first given in California, we may recognise in it an attempt to capitalise upon an existing situation: the kids were all familiar with Castaneda, so why not capture their interest and lead them forth into wider currents of thought? This is not perhaps a tactic entirely appropriate to university education, where in general the wits of the students must come to meet the thoughts of the teachers; but one may admire the audacity of the attempt. Indeed, although it will be clear that there is much that may be found unsatisfactory about this sort of book, it may be commended as a discussion which conveys a good deal of the genuine excitement that reading Castaneda may evoke.

David Silverman's central thesis is (in Goldschmidt's words) that "our world is a cultural construct", and a large part of the book is concerned with elaborating the way in which Carlos's scientific questions betray the limiting bias of our own method-obsessed culture. He discusses at length a passage in which Carlos asks don Juan whether, during a hallucinatory experience, he actually did fly as he seemed to be doing.

Don Juan refuses to answer the question at all. "What do you think yourself?" he asks, and remarks "That's all there is in reality—what you felt."

Silverman's view of this passage is that Carlos's questions typify Western society which can only take seriously what can be publicly validated, and don Juan's answers signify a respect for the dignity of each individual's experience. But Carlos's questions simply involve a commonplace distinction between dreaming and actuality, and public validation is merely a peripheral matter of how one might make this distinction. Silverman seems to me to be on the right track when he writes (in connection with Carlos's difficulties in finding what don Juan calls his "spot"):

So [Carlos's] problem is more than just 'how to do it'—a problem with which we are routinely faced in everyday life and which we routinely resolve by learning and applying *techniques*. His problem, as he states it, is that it is by no means certain that he has a problem; yet another person insists that he has.

The word "routine", it soon becomes clear from Silverman's argument, expresses much of what he thinks is wrong with the Western world and it turns up later in a revealing phrase as the "frozen bourgeois reality" we all live in. Yet this situation—in which someone is being persuaded that he has a problem, but in which the terms of the problem are being almost wilfully kept from him—expresses not respect for individual experience but rather the typical technique of the guru with his disciples.

This technique might be seen merely as a device for disturbing the disciple's accustomed view of life in order to increase his receptivity. Dr

Silverman thinks there is more to it than that. He considers that don
Juan employs such shifts because he is trying to say what is unsayable in
our familiar terms. He takes it to be a repudiation of several practices
built into Western discourse. One of these is that an event that can be
publicly witnessed has a higher status than what is merely seen or felt.
Another is the confused distinction between (subjective) experience and
(objective) fact. (I say "confused", of course, because the notion of "subjective" runs together questions of truth and questions of self-reference.)
Silverman takes Carlos as being someone who is in doubt about the
status of his experience until he is reassured that it can be "validated" in
terms of a physical event that can be publicly witnessed. But Carlos
seems to be in no doubt about what he *experienced*. He merely seeks an
additional piece of information—whether his body actually flew through
the air—which will make clear the status of what he has experienced.
Don Juan's refusal to answer would only begin to bear the weight Silverman puts upon it if he were consistently at sea with the distinction
between dream and actuality; but, as he shows in other conversations,
this is not the case.

The salutary character Silverman finds in don Juan's refusals depends
upon an equivocation I have already noted: between being imprisoned in
a culture, and being able to break out of that prison. Silverman explicitly
denies that language is a prison; yet he often writes as if it were. When
we speak, we cannot help affirming our membership of the community
to which we belong. In a typical argument, he affirms the paradox that
criticism *is* acceptance, explaining this by remarking that the critic accepts
the language in which he criticises. Yet if I criticise an institution (the
operation of the House of Commons, for example) I am criticising, not
accepting, *that* institution. It is indeed true that any criticism has to take
some things for granted. But this commonplace point could be better
elucidated in terms of such transparent prose as that of Plato's *Meno* than
by the pretentious and overblown pieces of philosophical sociology to
which Silverman introduces his readers.

The real significance of Carlos and don Juan within Silverman's book is
that they serve as stalking horses by which one sort of valued Western
experience, free-floating imaginativeness, is affirmed against what is taken
to be a cripplingly dominant sort of experience, namely science and
technology.

> For don Juan, it seems [Silverman writes], the uniqueness of
> personal experience is precious ('Every man is different'). To learn

a technique by which to recognize 'unimaginable things' is to negate the unique 'seeing' which is every man's expression of himself. For technique (methods, rules as we conceive them), by specifying discrete paths to knowledge, closes off other paths and diverts our attention away from those experiences which, because they seem personally valid for (as) us, seem to transcend technique.

There are things we might cavil at here (as indeed in nearly every paragraph). For example, are rules to be identified with techniques? Many rules, such as those of games, are not technical at all. Nor is it clear what "validity" means when qualifying personal experience rather than arguments. There is, in fact, in Western culture, a very strong tendency to respect individual experience, and in some of its forms Silverman eventually comes to draw upon this very tendency. But, cavils apart (and it is difficult at times, given the manner of exposition, not to drown in them), it is easy to sympathise with some aspects of a position which criticises the absurd rationalism of much of Western life and affirms the value of direct human experience.

Sympathy begins to erode, however, as the argument slides towards melodrama. Dr Silverman is perfectly well aware of the familiar arguments to the effect that no skill can consist purely of rules, for rules cannot specify their own applications. This means that there is an irreducibly personal, non-methodical element in the exercise of any skill. Dr Silverman sees technique as a corset preventing us from exploring large and valuable areas of our experience. Yet the currency of techniques depends upon the fact that they actually open up (rather than close) possibilities which did not previously exist—allow us, indeed, accessibility to "those experiences which . . . seem personally valid for us." In Dr Silverman's view, however, techniques bureaucratise life.

> Being a 'proper' bureaucrat, just as much as being a 'proper' scientist, means showing one's commitments to the 'facts' and to the correct methods whereby the facts may be assessed. . . . His actions [i.e. those of scientists and the bureaucrat] are never allowed to be viewed merely as 'his' but as the actions of an 'official' holding an 'office' and following rules. He is to be seen as simply the instrument of the rule book. His undisputed claim to authority is always: 'I may not like doing this but I'm only doing my job. . . .'

The puzzled reader may well wonder how "claims to authority" enter the argument at all. Scientists don't "claim authority"; they argue and present evidence. The authority of a bureaucrat derives not from method but from the authority of the constitution under which he works: democratic, monarchical, or whatever it may be. The unmistakably pejorative drift of all this becomes clear, however, when Adolf Eichmann suddenly pops up out of nowhere into the argument. Somehow, reading Castaneda has led Dr Silverman to the view that:

> to write (act) under the auspices of method (rule) is to find one's community among all those whose activities are the very denial of their humanity; who, like Eichmann, conceal them-selves [*sic*] behind method and rule.

Scientists have had to put up with a lot of loose lay talk about themselves in recent times, but association with Eichmann does seem to be going a little far.

That is part of what Dr Silverman makes of Castaneda. But any reader experienced in these particular labyrinths will recognise even before consulting the bibliography that much of this material is Habermas *garni*. This fact may well illustrate Silverman's own contention that it is difficult for us to escape from our own cultural milieu. Indeed, the more Silverman reads Castaneda, the more he seems to be reminded of a bizarre and eccentric selection of views from recent Western writers. There is some delicious nonsense from Roland Barthes in which a conventional Marxist account of early Dutch society is extracted from the aesthetic features of a few Dutch painters. Jean-Paul Sartre is ushered in to affirm: "In actual fact, he [*i.e.* the reader] is not an instantaneous consciousness, a pure timeless affirmation of freedom, nor does he soar above history; he is involved in it." What the undergraduates in California made of passages like this depends, no doubt, upon how many of them were much given to remarking "Man is an instantaneous consciousness, a pure timeless affirmation of freedom" etc., and thus in need of Messrs Sartre and Silverman to announce the error of their ways.

In the context of a flood of material of this kind, connected to Castaneda by a thin thread of association, the pedagogic question becomes uppermost. If one is introducing undergraduates to the social sciences, it may be tactically useful to connect one's argument with what already interests them; but it is also necessary to make clear to them the real character of the problems about which people hold differing views. What are they to make of the following passage (quoted from Kockelmans)?

> All genuinely human thinking is necessarily a thinking on the basis of an historical situation. Any thinking which denies this fact is not genuinely human thinking, or else is thinking which fails to understand itself.

Like many others of the writers Dr Silverman quotes with approval, Joseph Kockelmans has an admirable boldness in declaring what is genuinely human (he would no doubt know what Dr Silverman means by "a denial of humanity"). It needs to be said, however, that the fact that each thought is a spatio-temporal event does not entail that all thought is "thinking on the basis of an historical situation", whatever that may possibly mean. Mathematical thought, for example, has a history, but is itself historical only in a trivial sense. One's only relevant amusement in the face of so much vacuous dogmatism is to imagine what Galileo, Pascal, or Einstein would say if Kockelmans were trotting around beside them saying "All genuinely human thinking . . ." etc.

But undergraduates are not likely to see the issues clearly; they are likely to pick up these pomposities and imagine that the utterance of them constitutes profundity, without ever quite understanding how anyone ever came to argue in a different manner. R. G. Collingwood records in a well-known passage of his *Autobiography* that, after hearing his philosophy teachers criticise various classic predecessors, he actually went to the library, read the predecessors, and discovered that they had not at all held the doctrines which had been so enthusiastically kicked about on the lecturing rostrum. A Collingwood is in no danger of corruption from picking up such contemptuous expressions as "not genuinely human thinking"; but most undergraduates are not Collingwood.

Silverman has, then, an unfortunate line in quotations from the less luminous passages of modern intellectuality, and these befog the argument he seems to be extracting from Castaneda. That argument is fundamentally one of extreme cultural relativism. "To speak is to locate oneself within a way of knowledge." Hence there can be no "neutral" way of deciding Castaneda's question of whether he actually did fly when he took the Devil's weed. "For not to see men fly with the Devil's weed is simply not to see the Yaqui way." This extreme conclusion is supported, but not justified, by a number of familiar arguments about the element of construction involved in description, and some material about language games drawn from Wittgenstein. Dr Silverman is contemptuous of the whole idea of neutrality, and the word seldom appears in his text without inverted commas (in moments of extreme derogation it is italicised as well).

One of the things we are supposed to get from Castaneda is that "facts and truths only exist in and for communities." *Only* for communities? One cannot but wonder what happens in those communities that deny that bullets kill, that toadstools are poisonous, or that men suffer nasty bumps if they step off high cliffs. We are all morbidly sensitive to committing the intellectual sin of ethnocentricity these days, but it does need to be remembered that this refers only to practices. Science is science, and Yaqui or European makes no odds. How can the "Yaqui way of knowledge" legitimise everything? There are, indeed, occasions when Dr Silverman seems to recognize that his coherence is disappearing with a gurgle down the plughole of a self-contradictory relativism. "Note that I am *not* asserting that the world is how we choose to see it", he remarks on p. 23. But it is p. 93 before a similar caution strikes him again, and he tells us that he does not deny that there is some point in sticking to the facts. But for the most part, in a mood of *épater les étudiants*, he just lets relativism rip.

It is, no doubt, this happily imaginative subjectivism which allows Dr Silverman to remark early on that it is of no consequence to his argument *whether don Juan really existed* or was merely a *fiction* of Castaneda's imagination. In fact, this question is crucial, at least to the manner in which Dr Silverman has treated Castaneda. For if there were really such a personage as don Juan, and if he were correctly reporting features of the magic of another culture, then the perceptive and cognitive variations that mark off its assumptions from ours would pose a *genuine* cultural and sociological problem. But if don Juan is merely Castaneda's invention, then the whole cycle of books becomes a reworking of themes familiar in the Occultist tradition and *only* to be understood in those terms. As we have seen, it is part of the ambiguity of Castaneda's writing that he licenses both interpretations at different times. This may be a sign that he has changed his mind (rather as he may also have changed his mind over the question of drugs), or it may be part of the calculated ambiguity of the books which offer much to many possible responses.

If Castaneda's work is, as I have argued, a piece of Occultist doctrine, then Silverman's book reveals not so much the sociological character of Castaneda's Occultism, as the Occultist character of the tradition of relativistic sociology to which he is so extensively indebted.

Both are flirtations with the unsayable, intellectual adventures poised unsteadily on the edge of self-contradiction. To say this, however, is not to discredit them. By contrast with the plying of safer disciplines, relativistic sociology and Occultism are invitations to excess, and frequently topple over into mere absurdity. But they face up to something which, whatever its status in reality, has been of undeniable importance in our culture. The whole question of Occultism is fearfully difficult, and is now being brought to light in a variety of piecemeal ways: in some of the work in the history of ideas on Hegel and Marx, in the investigations of Renaissance Occultism by Frances Yates, perhaps even in recent attempts to exhibit mystical pre-suppositions in Wittgenstein. What stands in the way of bringing such material to light is not "Science," or "Reason", or even our everyday commonplace sense of the reality of things, but a kind of Enlightenment positivism militant. It is not merely that Occultist answers have been relegated to the underworld of superstition, but that the questions posed by the Occultist tradition have become unaskable in any serious way. The slow ferment of ideas, however, seems to be opening them up again.

RdeM

Five years tracking don Juan across the dream-dunes have taught me quite a lot—surely not enough to pass an exam in introductory ethnology, but enough to qualify as Master of Castanedics and Doctor of Anthrofolly. All the same, I'm still amazed at the cold shoulder turned to laymen's inquiries about academic anomalies, particularly the don Juan hoax. Though Town holds Gown accountable to community and taxpayers, professors prefer to account only to each other. This annoying discordance will now be explained, though not excused, by a sociologist of science.

Stephen O. Murray's *Group Formation in Social Science* is a social history of "theory groups" in linguistics and anthropology, including "ethnoscience." Currently he is editing a collection of critical writings on the work of Margaret Mead, focusing on academic disapproval of scholars who try to enlighten the public. Murray's "Invisibility of Scientific Scorn" parts the Ivory Curtain, to permit a rare glimpse of a "system of informal evaluation," through which the don Juan books were generally discounted by social scientists who didn't mention them in public.

Stephen O. Murray **22**

The Invisibility of Scientific Scorn

A quack is someone loved by his patients and loathed by his colleagues.
—Everett Hughes

"Why," asked de Mille in *Castaneda's Journey*, "has no anthropologist complained in public about what happened at UCLA?" The answer was simpler than those he proposed. No one outside UCLA knew enough to be certain anything untoward had occurred. Scientists may be skeptical about a work legitimated by a degree, and may freely criticize the work, but they never contest the right of another university to confer a degree upon whomever it chooses. A presumption that any respected department seeks appropriate documentation led many anthropologists to believe Castaneda's defense of his dissertation must have met critical scrutiny and satisfied a committee of competent professionals. Since Castaneda furnished an academic abstract and a different title for his dissertation, and since he forestalled its circulation beyond UCLA, it was far from obvious that the work was *Journey to Ixtlan*. Castaneda skilfully manipulated the system of trust.

A question more fundamental than why anthropologists did not complain about unknown events at UCLA is why so few criticized Castaneda's published oeuvre. The answer gets at a basic characteristic of the structure of science—its invisibility. The organized skepticism operating in science is largely invisible to outsiders. Formally, manuscripts are read by referees, and those that survive are analyzed in book reviews and journal comments (visible to persons who know where to look for them). Simultaneously, judgments pass through informal channels. Important work is cited, expounded in reviews of literature, and finally reproduced in textbooks. Highly-regarded work is discussed in public, while adversely-judged work usually disappears from sight. As S. B. Barnes noted, "Scientific communities rarely undertake exposés of those they regard as incompetent; informal communication usually ensures that their work is treated [by other scientists] as suspect, or, in some cases, written off." There is normally no reason to pillory suspect work in public. Such work is not cited, not built upon, not considered in reviews of literature, and not enshrined as established knowledge in textbooks. Because there is a flood of publication, much of it unimportant, scientists avoid dwelling on what they consider suspect and concentrate on keeping abreast of what their peers consider significant.

The system of informal evaluation works efficiently for scientists and no doubt protects the egos of the many producers of negatively-judged work—they find themselves ignored rather than condemned. New ideas may be prematurely written off, but many scientists are reassured by a belief that good work spontaneously surfaces.

A more pressing concern arises when non-scientists evidence interest in a line of scientific work. The semi-weekly cure for cancer trumpeted in the *National Enquirer* is an extreme but recurrent example of the distortion of scientific findings by writers and for readers heedless of scientific cautions and ignorant of statistical logic. Editors and writers of the *National Enquirer* do not seek out recognized authorities in the research areas they plunder but seek anyone they can find with some scientific certification or affiliation who is willing to make sensational claims; or they draw conclusions on their own which they attribute to scientists.

The general public holds simple certification in exaggerated and undifferentiated respect. All "experts" are treated as equal: a doctor is a doctor is a doctor. Authorities highly regarded in a research area are not distinguished from those merely regarded as competent or even from those regarded as incompetent. Paul Riesman reviewed Castaneda in the *New York Times* with about as much authority as Weston La Barre would have, and an outsider might think Stan Wilk was a generally respected authority on Castaneda's subject, whose judgment should be preferred to that of Ralph Beals. Within the discipline of anthropology, La Barre and Beals are recognized authorities on topics Castaneda touched, while Riesman and Wilk have no such standing, yet all are professional anthropologists, and that may suffice for general readers.

When there is disagreement among "experts," the public listens to what it wants to hear, without weighing the evidence or comparing qualifications of the disagreeing "experts." Such confusion can be fostered. "To destroy the unanimity backing scientific evidence is a deliberate technique employed by some pressure groups," Barnes concluded, having examined the great publicity given the work of a few charlatans disputing—against overwhelming scientific consensuses—the links between smoking and cancer and the efficacy of fluoridation.

Sensational assertions attract editors and readers in general, not just those of the *National Enquirer*. The media reward scientists with attention and money for addressing wide audiences while abandoning nuances, documentation, and narrow competences. Such popularizing, however, ensures the low regard of professional colleagues, who are deeply suspicious of it. Since peer approval is important, popularizing is not undertaken lightly by anyone committed to a professional career. In graduate school, where the commitment to a professional career is made, future scientists learn to value the good opinion of professional colleagues more than the vulgar rewards of ignorant acclaim—such as royalties and *Time* cover stories. Within scientific disciplines there are status hierarchies based on the importance of contributions to current research. An academician aiming to tell anyone but colleagues something they don't already know has less time for advancing the research front, and thereby reduces his or her chances of receiving peer esteem.

Disillusioning those who were lapping up Castaneda's eclectic mysticism was not a way to advance research and thus not a way to enhance one's professional status. Anthropologists who regarded Castaneda's work as incompetent or as not-science therefore did not bother to announce their adverse judgments. They assumed their colleagues—the only ones who count for them—shared their judgment and, thus, felt justified in proceeding with their own work. If Castaneda was producing science fiction or inspirational literature, authorities reasoned, what obligation did *they* have to criticize it. Denunciations might even be interpreted as envying Castaneda's success.

Having learned from Thomas Kuhn that new lines of work are misunderstood, anthropological gatekeepers may have given Castaneda the benefits of some doubts, so as not to condemn a new paradigm out of hand. Unlike most sociologists, many anthropologists were impressed or bewildered by ethnomethodology, to which they had heard Castaneda was somehow tied. Thus unsure of their ground, they refrained from expressing their skepticism about his supposed field reports.

Another reason for remaining silent was the lack of institutional remedies for scientific malpractice. Scientists are not defrocked. If Castaneda had submitted his work to scientific journals, it would have been critically scrutinized, but he has not published his work in any professional forum, and has refused to provide any of the information necessary to evaluate his work as ethnography. His popular writings failed to meet "the accepted canons for anthropological reporting," Beals at last complained. "He fails to follow the most elementary rules of the anthropological game." Not seeking an academic appointment, not presenting his work to scientific publications, and not submitting to any critical inquiry, Castaneda placed himself outside the science of anthropology. Anthropologists, in turn, were content to leave him to his fantasies and to his readers, though many of his readers were mistaking his work for anthropology.

I have argued that ignoring what is regarded as poor science is standard procedure in all scientific disciplines. Only when suspect work does not disappear from *scientific* discourse, when it is taken seriously by some *scientists*, does scientific scorn become visible. When a professional anthropologist praised Castaneda's work as exemplary in the pages of the official journal, some of those who had privately dismissed Castaneda were provoked to express their judgment in public. When informal organized skepticism failed to kill the work within the discipline, public discussion became necessary.

Sociologists have shown considerable interest in the diffusion of new ideas and techniques—in how what is judged important is transmitted through informal networks. We have been more concerned with the baking of scientific wheat into new loaves than with the winnowing of scientific chaff. Nevertheless, while Castaneda's professional socialization clearly failed in a number of ways, the scientific *reception* of his work conformed to the standard sociological model of how science operates. Examination of the Castaneda case reveals difficulties that recur when scientific ideas diffuse outside the academy's cloistered calm and are taken up by non-professionals.

The institutions of science *are* poorly equipped to present a unified front to publics unaware of or uninterested in the accepted boundaries of competence within a scientific discipline. There is considerable social control over properly socialized scientists who highly value colleague approval, little control over those who cut themselves off from scientific discourse, and no control at all over what is conveyed in non-professional media.

Scientists are *not* notably concerned with explaining their own research or the errors of their colleagues to anyone but their colleagues. Generally they feel either that the public does not want careful guidance or that persons who want it will somehow receive it. Even scientists not blinded by elitism are dismayed at the way expert consensus is continually cast aside (as when presidents reject the findings of presidential commissions) and at the popularity of work put forward by the least responsible members of their discipline. I think there is also a sincere failure to apprehend how unintelligible research reports can be to those not trained to read them. Unaware of how much they routinely take for granted, scientists genuinely believe that anyone of reasonable intelligence wanting to learn about a line of work will be able to do so.

There is a twin failure of imagination. Members of the general public have a low tolerance for ambiguity, and care little about scientific methods or statistical logic. They demand clear, definitive answers—and science does not provide them. The producers of science fail to recognize that the public has a serious, if naive, interest in the science they produce. This is one of the reasons scientists are intolerant of colleagues' efforts to enlighten the public. To break out of the vicious circle would require the expenditure of far more energy than either scientists or interested laypersons are willing to expend, since neither population cares much about the other's misunderstanding, nor recognizes its own.

III.

Spun by the Ally

RdeM

"Spinning with your ally," said don Juan, "will change your idea of the world." Carlos wanted to know just what an ally was. Don Juan admitted there was no way of saying exactly what an ally was; the way one understood the ally was a personal matter. Still it was clear an ally was "an aid to knowing," an influence "capable of carrying a man beyond the boundaries of himself," a spirit to be seized, wrestled to the ground, and pinned there until it gave up its power. A man who was not "firmly grounded" could be knocked flat by the ally. A man who tried but failed to master the ally would be "spun away into an unknown place," from where it would be a long walk back, a journey wherein one never quite came home to one's old self.

For many of his readers, Castaneda was the ally, appearing in various guises. For anthropologist Paul Riesman he was a professional colleague who had come closer than anyone else to achieving the ideal of fieldwork. For parapsychologist Richard Reichbart he was one of the two dedicated investigators who had been willing to apprentice themselves to psi-talented members of preliterate cultures. For college freshman Neil Erickson he was the rather stupid chronicler of a marvelous real magician living in another world one might hope to visit.

Each of these men was spun by the ally. Each was carried away by winds of inspiration, only to find himself in a place where things were not as he had expected them to be. Each had a long journey back, but possessed the strength to make the journey and courage to tell about it.

The telling was not easy. The traveler had to admit being taken in by false promises, had to confess feeling disappointed, getting angry, clinging nostalgically to promises already broken, had to risk alienating both skeptics and subscribers. After praising Castaneda's first three books in the *New York Times Book Review* as "among the best that the science of anthropology has produced," Riesman now had to say they were not science at all though still a valuable lesson for scientists. After being deeply touched by four don Juan books, Reichbart now had to say he was offended by the fifth and saddened by the tragic failure of such a promising initiative. After spending seven years in a separate reality searching for don Juan, Erickson now had to face the fact that the supposedly stupid chronicler had invented the marvelous magician and robbed the searcher of seven good years.

Each of these men writes frankly about his struggle with the ally and tells how far he has come on his homeward journey. Africanist Paul Riesman is a professor of anthropology at Carleton College, writing here as a philosopher of science. Richard Reichbart, though currently pursuing a Ph.D. in clinical psychology at City University of New York, is also an attorney, who has specialized in legal problems of American Indians, and a contributor to journals of parapsychology, a field he spiritedly commends to anthropologists, above and beyond the Castaneda controversy. Neil Erickson, while telling his autobiographical story, proves his graphic accomplishments by illustrating it as well.

Paul Riesman **23**

Fictions of Art and of Science or Does it Matter Whether don Juan Really Exists?

The more Carlos Castaneda writes, the scarier he becomes to write about. Seven years ago, when I reviewed his first three books, it did not occur to me to doubt that Castaneda was trying to produce what in his own eyes, at least, would be as faithful an account as possible of his apprenticeship with don Juan, a Yaqui sorcerer. In my view, this was a valid and very commendable ethnographic approach, an approach where the writer does not merely present his inferences about the society or situation he studied, but where he gives as full an account as he can of the experiences and encounters on which those inferences are based. But was Castaneda really doing this? Joyce Carol Oates may have been the first to express in print the thought that Castaneda's books might be fiction, not anthropology. Some anthropologists, Weston La Barre in particular, had criticized Castaneda for gaps in his ethnography; Oates, however, was not expressing a critique but was saying the books seemed to be creating "characters" and to be of a recognizable genre, that of the young man's initiation as we find it, say, in Hesse's *Siddhartha*. Oates was saying the books seemed too good to be factual descriptions, which is what they claimed to be, and that while anthropologists could better judge their scientific value, for her own part the books made more sense as fiction.

After finishing *Journey to Ixtlan*, I felt it had to be the last book in the series. Carlos had broken off his apprenticeship for the third time, and readers got the impression he had told as much as would be permissible about the secrets of sorcerers. I didn't take Oates's questions very seriously at the time, but when *Tales of Power* came, I was surprised and puzzled. At about the same time, while in the field in Africa, I received a letter from Richard de Mille, who was writing *Castaneda's Journey*. His letter, and eventually his book, raised serious doubts in my mind about Castaneda's aim in writing and about the authenticity of his accounts. Since then, to be quite honest, I have been confused; I have just not known what to think about Castaneda. The reading of his fifth book, *Second Ring of Power*, left me more puzzled than ever. Some descriptions in that book seemed contrived or forced, and I found myself not so absorbed and fascinated as by the four earlier books. At the same time, I

207

am sensitive to my total lack of experience in the study of shamanism or any forms of dissociation, whether induced by drugs or other means; thus I have no fixed reference point to help me "triangulate" my position with respect to Castaneda. But if I lack expertise, why write about Castaneda, and by what right do I do so? The reason is that I have been affected by him and feel a need to straighten out the issues he has raised for me as best I can. I do not offer what I have to say as the word of an expert, but simply as the sharing of an attempt to clarify my own thoughts.

Two major issues I want to discuss are these: 1) what do the don Juan books tell us about the world, and 2) does it matter if they are fiction?

If the books are an honest attempt to convey to readers what it is like to be introduced to the world of sorcerers, then we are obliged as scientists to find some way of making sense of Castaneda's often bizarre experiences. What do those experiences tell us about the world and man's relation to it? Many of their philosophical implications are beautifully brought out by don Juan himself and can be summarized as follows:

When we human beings look at the world, the images we perceive do not correspond to what is "really there" but are in fact created by a continuous internal dialogue we are usually unaware of that tells us what we are seeing at any moment. Our way of seeing the world is not a privileged access to reality but only one of many possible "glosses" on whatever is there. Sorcerers can experience the world in a way radically different from our normal, Western way, and their way taps power in our selves and in nature that most of us are not aware of.

Now, one of the weaknesses of Castaneda's books as ethnographies is that the only contrast is between the world view of don Juan or some other instructor and the world view of the naïve apprentice. The contrast is a great one in that lay Westerners, exemplified by the skeptical Carlos of the narrative, tend to take as fundamental the physical concreteness of things. The world, they believe, is made up of objects; and the phenomena of energy, acceleration, and life itself are thought to result when spatial relations among those objects change. For the sorcerer, however, the world is made up of forces and powers (one kind being the "allies") which have no definite form but take shape only when we are looking at them.

What Castaneda has omitted here is the fact that many non-Western peoples, including probably the Yaqui, normally think of the world this way. What distinguishes the sorcerer from the non-sorcerer is that while the non-sorcerer works with his fellows to maintain their fragile consensus about the shape of the world, the sorcerer seeks to face and conquer those frightening forces on his own. The aim is thus primarily to increase one's personal power.

One thing that rings true for me in Castaneda's account of sorcery is the ruthless, egotistical seeking of power by all the figures in his books. This quest emerges clearly in *Second Ring*, where the theme of self-sufficiency, implicit all along, dominates the characters to the point where they would kill someone or sacrifice their own children in order to become "complete" and thereby capable of going forever into indescribably beautiful worlds not accessible to normal perception. Sorcerers do not see people as people. Near the end of *Ixtlan* don Genaro says normal people no longer seemed real to him once he had seen the world sorcerers see. These antisocial characteristics jibe well with attitudes of lay people commonly described in anthropological literature, particularly the widely held belief that sorcerers or witches kill or eat people, usually their own children or other close relatives. All of us know, too, the eerie feeling sometimes amounting to panic that comes when a person we are dealing with, especially if he has power over us, does not appear to see us as real. But according to don Juan neither the sorcerer's view nor the normal view *is* reality. Whatever is actually out there can in fact not be perceived, because to perceive is to create an image out of the meanings we have acquired by growing up as social beings. Ultimate reality does exist; it is what is there when we stop perceiving the world, that is, when we utterly stop telling ourselves what it is we are seeing. Not only do human beings find it disconcerting to think that the world they take to be real is in fact an aspect of their own minds, but also they find it almost impossible to "stop the world," that is, to stop this constant creative flow of glosses that makes perceptions seem real. Not even sorcerers can all do this, but sorcerers have the advantage, don Juan says, of living in two worlds and therefore have the possibility of slipping into "the crack between the worlds."

Expressed in such an abstract way, this philosophy of reality approximates what I believe myself—but then what about the experiences Castaneda describes, which, for all their beauty and terror, are often simply incompatible with our everyday view of man and nature? If Castaneda really thinks he had these experiences, is he crazy or are there actually wonders that most of us ignore most of the time? What makes us want to believe in such wonders? Is it boredom, a longing to escape from the drabness of our everyday life? Is it, as Marvin Harris argues, an insidious manifestation of our middle-class desire to maintain a privileged position in the world by claiming that realities like racial oppression, colonialism, or militarism will somehow go away if we stop thinking they are there? Or are we courageously facing the human condition when we accept the possibility that our views of the way things are and work are but glosses on a reality that is truly other and ineffable?

I find evidence for all three of these factors in my own response to Castaneda. In this essay, however, I won't try to answer these questions directly, for any such answer must be affected by how we face up to the second major issue Castaneda's books raise, namely: what difference does it make whether the books are fiction or not? A number of writers have mentioned this question, usually only to dismiss it. David Silverman, for instance, feels he can use *The Teachings* as a kind of paradigm for problems of sociological inquiry regardless of whether the book is factual or fictional. This is legitimate: many teachers find that novels contain sociological or psychological "truths" in much clearer, and certainly more readable, form than they usually take in formal studies. For some didactic purposes, then, it doesn't matter whether a work is fact or fiction, but are there contexts where it *does* matter? Yes, there are some. The first one that comes to mind is that of using don Juan to confirm our own ideas about things. I said earlier that many ideas expressed by don Juan are similar to my own philosophy. When I first read *The Teachings* I was greatly excited not only by Castaneda's apparently honest report of his "fieldwork" but also by a sense of corroboration from don Juan. Here was a man who had developed a philosophy based on long experience and on traditions that could have had little influence from the Western world, yet much of what he said expressed clearly and forcefully ideas and feelings that had come to me only tentatively or inchoately. Yes, Virginia, there *is* a Santa Claus. Believing profoundly, as we in social science do, that beliefs and ideas are neither innate nor a direct transcription in language of the actual properties of phenomena, but are largely products of our socialization and "cultural influences," when we receive corroboration from someone as differently placed as don Juan our sense of reality is strengthened because we feel that the overlap between his ideas and ours comes from the correspondence of these ideas to the nature of things. The same kind of thinking underlies the importance we attach to replication of experiments in science.

If Castaneda's books are fictional, then we have no assurance that what happens in them is really within the range of human possibility, nor can we take the world-view expressed in them as an outgrowth of non-Western experiences. Science helps us increase our understanding of the world by coming to grips with "facts" that refuse to fit neatly into whatever our current explanation of phenomena is. If don Juan and his associates did what Castaneda says they did, and led Castaneda to have the experiences he describes, then, as we have said, anthropology would be obliged to fit these data into its theoretical frameworks. Anthropologists might well fail at this, however, in which case Castaneda's data would become anomalies in the Kuhnian sense and would remain a thorn in the side of anthropology until a new paradigm emerged to account for them (or until they faded from memory). On the other hand, if the books are works of fantasy, we don't have to worry about anthropology's possible inadequacy because, as with Piltdown man, we have already explained what we are seeing as a joke, or the product of a desire for notoriety or wealth, which makes unnecessary and irrelevant an explanation in terms of natural laws.

Wait a minute. Maybe we can get anthropology off the hook, but can we get ourselves off? A basic tenet in Castaneda's books is that experience is not something that just happens to us but something we in large measure create, though we are usually unaware of our creative role. Even if don Juan does not "really exist," his non-existence doesn't mean this proposition can be summarily dismissed. For one thing, if the proposition is true, then the very question of whether don Juan exists becomes less important because in any case the way he appears in Castaneda's books is an artifact of someone's perception—not only Carlos's perception but ours too, as readers. After all, the very existence of the ever more flourishing discipline of literary criticism implies that reading too is a creative act, a sort of collaboration between reader and author, such that each reading of a work is an experience that differs—sometimes radically—from what the author consciously intended. The implication here is that each reader must decide for himself what Castaneda's books—or any books—mean.

But science is a collective enterprise. Even if some scientific work is done by individuals, working quite alone, judgment of both the meaning and the value of the work is rendered by the "scientific community." We even use the metaphor of weight, saying the whole weight of scientific opinion is on the scales in favor of this or that theory. Now, how can a community think an idea or have an opinion? What is the nature of the scales in which the community weighs the work? The process cannot be confined to individual experience or perception. In fact, the process of arriving at a scientific consensus is the opposite of personal experience because the very essence of nearly all scientific methodologies is the attempt to remove the individual's own contribution to his perception.

Science and art thus go in opposite directions, on this issue at least. An artist tries to communicate something that is personal, whether or not he is aware of how much he is fabricating it, while a scientist—including, generally, the social scientist—is trying to communicate something that is the case regardless of his perceiving, recording, or analyzing. Neither scientist nor artist can ever fully escape the creative quality of perception—the fact that in some sense we make what we see. For instance, the most important advances in nuclear physics have occurred with the help of enormous particle-accelerators human beings have built in order not only to record but to create events that would otherwise almost never happen on earth. We call this enterprise an experiment, not a work of art. Why? Once again, because the aim of the entire procedure is to reduce as far as possible the individual's contribution to the message from the universe. This kind of behavior, observed anthropologically, seems to express certain ideas important to the scientific community: 1) human consciousness and the universe are two quite different things; 2) a major function of human consciousness is to represent the universe, but it does this imperfectly because of limitations inherent in our perceptual systems; 3) if we want to understand the universe—and we do—we must above all reduce human error and individual interpretation, so as to approach as closely as possible the ultimate structure of reality undistorted by perceptual or cognitive mechanisms.

Truth, then, is "out there," not in ourselves. Any idea of reality arrived at by methods that do not eliminate—or at least come close to eliminating—the individual's participation in making reality is unscientific and therefore cannot claim validity. Let's spell out these ideas and their social correlates a bit more. Notice first of all that the idea of the individual as participant in the making of the world is either overlooked or rejected. This does not contradict the fact that our society highly rewards individual achievement, for in so doing it of course specifies what the modes of achievement are. To the extent that people feel valued *by society*, it is for work within these modes, not as full participants in the very making of reality. We all recognize that our society needs intelligent, imaginative, responsive people, but few of us have the fortune to feel that the best of ourselves is actually called forth or would be appreciated if offered. The various efforts to "humanize" work implicitly avow this situation: the organization of most work in our economy is such that an individual perceives his own capacity to shape reality to be at best superfluous and at worst disruptive to the smooth flow of the operation. Perhaps because our lives so obviously depend on the success of our interlocking economy, this perception of our value to society is generalized to the whole social and political system.

Second, the idea that truth is "out there" and our task is to find it seems like a religious idea and reminds me of Durkheim's thesis that society constructs a god which is a "collective representation" of the society and that in worshipping a god the society is in fact reaffirming its own existence. Looking at science this way helps us to see both why we in our society turn to natural laws for guidance as other peoples turn to gods and why, as in fundamentalist Protestantism, we don't want the guiding message to be adulterated by "interpretations." The scientist, the Protestant, the Taoist—and don Juan—all want to confront God or Nature directly. The aims of "eliminating one's participation in making reality" and of "stopping the world" are fundamentally the same. But while the Taoist sees himself as an integral part and expression of nature, the fundamentalist Protestant or scientist sees himself as something other: he feels an abysmal inferiority and an overweening superiority at the same time, inferiority to God or cosmos and superiority to the tangible natural world. The ultimate source of this contradiction of feelings, widespread in our culture perhaps since Periclean Athens, is the daily contradiction of belonging to an immensely powerful society that seems to be dominating nature, yet in which our unique contributions today seem to be ineffective, self-defeating, or harmful to someone.

Scientists, like sorcerers, often view themselves as different from and superior to ordinary people because they see things ordinary people don't see and manipulate powers ordinary people don't know about. Like sorcerers, they recognize that everyday language cannot describe the world they move in. Both scientists and sorcerers recognize, at least implicitly, the absolute otherness of ultimate reality, whatever that may be. But don Juan, like mystics in general, feels this otherness cannot be seen, let alone described, while we are in our normal state of mind because, as we have said, to see normally is to make of reality something that fits what we have been told it is. To speak of the world at all is to impute to it some elements of our own subjectivity. There are undoubtedly scientists who feel the same way, but the contrasting popular view of science is that the more we investigate the closer we come to understanding reality—which implies that such understanding can be shared, just like any datum. This widely held idea is quite wrong, as a little reflection will show. For one thing, there cannot be, hiding under the countless versions of reality we find in countless world-views, a single true reality acceptable to all men. The reason for this is that the reality that seems most true to any person is the one that serves as framework for ordering his life. While many scientists would deny that they know the truth or are even searching for it, most Westerners, we have seen, turn to science for authority when faced with difficult problems and decisions. I believe that to search for understanding is to recognize the inadequacy of our current knowledge and our current language and is therefore necessarily going to isolate us in some measure from one another. Scientists are thus isolated, not only from each other by the distinct disciplines they study but also from neighbors and fellow citizens by their rejection of common-sense ways of understanding and explaining things. That being so, isn't it contradictory and downright chimerical to hope that we shall one day have a *generally accepted* understanding of the way the world works?

The world is mysterious because we have the capacity to be mystified by it. This is a polite way of saying that we are really not all that smart and that there is no particular niche in the world where we know we belong. Our ignorance of nature's plan, if there is one, has allowed us to change the face of the earth drastically and to tap forms of energy that, if released, could cut short the apparent evolutionary experiment that all living things are a part of. If evolution is a blind, stochastic process, then we human beings are blind too, in the sense that we can never have the certitude we desire about what we are all supposed to be doing here, not to mention what the consequences of a particular act will be. What we think we know about life we learn from each other and from the experiences of living in the structures of knowledge and social life our predecessors have created. The structure of our own society, for example, is highly complex. In concrete terms, one aspect of this complexity is the self-perpetuation of diverse ethnic groups, upper and lower social classes, and a huge variety of occupations. Living in such a complex society, whether industrial or other, people almost inevitably experience "determinism" and "causality," because it is obvious to them that past events, such as birth into a certain family, determine or cause many events in their lives. For this reason, citizens of complex societies tend to accept as self-evident such ideas as fate or natural law. These ideas are not merely in the air, to be taken or left; rather they must be actively espoused. Regardless of whether the universe is ultimately deterministic or causal, people in a complicated society must fill the places in its structure if it is to function. In other words, people must act as if, and perhaps believe that, their behavior is determined rather than chosen.

The arts, as well as the sciences, have always reflected this view of the world—witness, for example, the great Greek tragedies—but unlike the sciences the arts have always emphasized an indeterminacy of human action, an idea that in living we can and must choose what we will do. With the phenomenal rise of science in the 19th and 20th centuries, the freedom of will and choice proposed by the arts has come to seem more and more a fiction. Speaking for myself, faced with the massive, deterministic world I live in, I find I can give very little credence to my own imagination and hence can't really trust anybody else's either. It is in this context that Carlos Castaneda's books are so troubling. Their thrust is literary in that they profoundly assert man's creative ability and his obligation to make choices in everything he does. At the same time, the books come in the guise of science, where the (intermittently successful) aim, we have seen, is to minimize the observer's contribution to the data and arrive at a result as fully determined by the data as possible. In *The Teachings* Castaneda appeared to have adopted the scientific aim; in fact the structural analysis at the end seemed like a dogged, over-zealous attempt to restrict the interpretation to the recorded data and nothing but the data. Likewise, in *A Separate Reality* and *Journey to Ixtlan*, the continued use of dated entries, and Carlos's almost fanatical concern with "getting it all down" in his notebook, allowed one to read on with the feeling that the aim was scientific. But after reading the fourth and fifth books, and after reading the criticism that has been published, I think Castaneda is deliberately blurring the line between science and literature. He gives the reader neither the background material nor the rhetoric that normally help one feel one is reading a scientific report. At the same time, he never says he is making up the characters and events either. If Castaneda did one or the other he would in effect be telling us how to read his books. By refraining from doing one or the other he puts us readers in the very position Carlos endures as hero of the accounts. Castaneda leaves it up to us to decide whether "it's real" or not, just as don Juan leaves it up to Carlos in the famous passage where Carlos asks if he really flew. The reason for this parallel, I think, is that Castaneda wants to reinforce one of the main ideas in the books, namely that we have powers of will and creative vision we are normally unaware of, and that everything we find real is actually in part our own creation. Whether we like it or not, then, truth is not "out there," independent of us; if we want truth at all, we have to make it for ourselves.

Much as I like this idea, I find scary Castaneda's didactic blurring of the line between science and fiction, a blurring that seems tantamount to saying science *is* fiction. In one sense, of course, it is; and that's not a new idea. The crucial issue is how scientific fictions differ from literary ones. We might sum up our earlier discussion by saying that literature makes fictions about the world in order to tell us truths about experience and will, while science makes fictions about experience and will in order to tell us truths about the world. Living between these two poles inevitably creates tension in us, and we are thus often tempted to let one pole preempt the other. Even if he *is* describing actual events, Castaneda is writing literature not anthropology, nor even interpretive anthropology. This is not the same as making anthropology an art, which at its best it is. Rather, it amounts to abandoning the attempt to make it a science.

The abandonment of science is unsettling because we have seen how deeply important it is for the functioning of an industrial society to maintain the scientific disciplines and a scientific attitude towards the world. Castaneda's literary-scientific trickery strikes at the very legitimacy of our social order. What makes me ambivalent even now about this thrust of his work is that despite my unhappiness with many features of our society, I am like most other Westerners in hankering, if only secretly, after a social system that is firmly based on knowledge of how the universe works. But it is just such a social system that people everywhere seem to believe they have. Anthropologists studying exotic cultures find that folk beliefs about nature do not correspond to *our* view of reality but are merely functional for the maintenance and legitimation of the natives' social structure. By writing in such a way as to transform an anthropological study into a fictional genre, Castaneda employs our deeply held confidence in the truth of science to make us doubt that same truth. Ironically, we thus come to a better understanding of our own society through an anthropological paradox: we are brought to recognize that for us as for "primitive" peoples the very continuation of society depends on faith that our beliefs about the universe—which we know to be fictions—are somehow true.

RdeM

Lionel Abel, a professor of English writing in the dogmatically materialistic *Humanist*, surprised me by saying: "There is ample testimony that there is something describable as 'psi function' and that such functions enter into all mental activities. I do not think this view has been refuted or can be set aside. . . . What don Juan had to tell Carlitos was very simply how to enter a world in which psi phenomena are possible." Nevertheless, Abel found Castaneda "essentially ideological," not to be taken seriously as a reporter of paranormal events.

Though most parapsychologists dismissed him, a few have taken Castaneda seriously. Robert Thouless credited him with focussing attention on mystical vision as a possible separate reality rather than a mere hallucination. Stuart Holroyd found don Juan helpful in fusing parapsychology, counterculture, and new-age consciousness. Anthropologists C. Scott Littleton and Marlene Dobkin de Rios saw a new spirit of paranormal inquiry brought by Castaneda to anthropology.

Introduced earlier to the reader, Richard Reichbart was one of those parapsychologists who took Castaneda seriously. "Castaneda and Parapsychology" offers his later reflections, reviews parapsychological literature touching on Castaneda, and invites anthropologists to do their parapsychological homework before confronting the *nagual* in book or field.

Castaneda and Parapsychology

When I decided to examine the relationship between the works of Carlos Castaneda and the field of parapsychology, I did not anticipate finding my task so difficult. But it has been, for a number of reasons. First, I have been cautioned by two of my fellow parapsychologists about getting involved in the controversy at all. One of them thought the don Juan series was fiction, the other thought it was factual, but both of them thought nothing could be gained for parapsychology by pursuing the issue. Frankly, it *is* tempting to leave the dispute to the anthropologists, to whom it more rightly belongs, rather than involving parapsychology (which has enough problems of its own) in such a thorny issue. But in the end, I have concluded that however uncomfortable the ground, I cannot resist the opportunity to bring some parapsychological information to an audience that in its usual discussions of Castaneda does everything to avoid informing itself about parapsychology. Second, I have found the task difficult for a more personal reason. There was a time when Castaneda through his works touched me deeply, emotionally and intellectually. Even now, there are infrequent moments when something occurs in my life that reminds me of an incident, or a concept, from the don Juan series. On the other hand, as I read through the series and examined it more closely, I progressively found an evasiveness, a lack of factual detail, and an annoying repetitive, formula-like quality to the conversations and events. As a consequence of these two different impressions, I feel ambivalent toward Castaneda's works and feel dismay and regret that something which touched me so successfully is so marred. I suspect that this feeling of ambivalence underlies much of the acrimony of the participants in the Castaneda controversy, no matter what their ostensible positions. In fact, the extent to which Castaneda through his works has succeeded in inspiring such deep ambivalent feelings is an important datum of the "Castaneda phenomenon"—the inordinate attention paid to the works by the public and the professionals. For this reason, I will attempt here to describe my own encounter with the don Juan series, both from a personal viewpoint and from my perspective as a parapsychologist.

I encountered the first three don Juan books early in the 1970s, having recently returned from a government fellowship on the Navajo reservation in the Southwestern United States. The reservation is a vast tract of harsh but beautiful semidesert, dotted with small Indian towns, hogans, mesas, and haunting geological formations (Monument Valley, for example, is in its midst) and largely isolated from contemporary "American" life. There I had lived and worked in intimate contact with the Navajo for over a year, learning of their beliefs concerning misfortune and witchcraft, and attending a number of their ceremonies. Back in my own culture, I experienced "reverse" culture shock, repeatedly wondering as a consequence of my contact with the Navajo sense of reality why contemporary Western culture had developed a concept of reality in which "mind" had no inherently causal property and in which chance, rather than determinism, held sway. Thus Castaneda's books— particularly the first one—reflected some of my own questions at the time, depicting as they did an apparent member of primitive culture locking philosophical horns with a member of Western culture.

The books asked, for example: Why do the teachings of Western culture drive us so far from our "subjective" perceptions that we tend to no longer accord them validity? What, in fact, is an hallucination or a hypnotic state or an intuition? How meaningful is the Western cultural concept of "chance" when applied to the events in the life of a single individual? Questions such as these became road markers for me in a personal search for a more satisfactory explanation of causality, a search that led me to (among other things) the study of psychic phenomena. But, although Castaneda's books represented one of a large variety of sources that stimulated my thinking at the time, they did not encourage the continued pursuit of scientific answers; and so, as I began to discover answers more satisfactory to me, the philosophical impact of the trilogy on me slowly dissipated. I lost interest in the books, did not read the fourth or fifth in the series until recently, and was only dimly aware of the growing controversy concerning the authenticity of the events Castaneda describes.

From the parapsychological perspective as well, I found the Castaneda works initially interesting. This was not because of any striking evidentiary value in the psi phenomena they relate, although Castaneda does recount numerous events that correspond to psi phenomena collected by parapsychologists from largely Western cultural sources. To list some examples: There are frequent, sometimes emotionally gripping, incidents of apparent *telepathy*; these range from unexpected, apparently psi-determined meetings between don Juan and Carlos to incidents in which don Juan appears to telepathically pick up significant events in

Carlos's past (such as the white falcon Carlos hunted but refused to kill as a boy on his grandfather's farm; the button-nosed boy whose arm Carlos broke when eight years old; the blonde woman from whom Carlos parted) to incidents in which Carlos appears to telepathically pick up information (such as his vision of the knapsacked young man who steals books from the library and defaces them). There are numerous instances of *astral projection* or *out-of-the-body experience* occurring to Carlos or recounted by don Genaro, some of which closely resemble reports from our culture, others of which seem to violate the rules parapsychologists generally have observed, by transporting the physical body of the astral projector from the spot where the experience began. There are incidents of *psychokinesis* (such as the time don Juan apparently prevents Carlos's car from starting) and incidents of *shared apparition* (such as the time Carlos and Pablito simultaneously experience the terrifying "nagual"). In addition, the psi phenomena often take place in conjunction with psychological states which psychic research suggests are "psi-conducive," that is conducive to the emergence of psychic phenomena, including states of hypnosis, hallucinogenic drug intoxication, and belief instilled by suggestion or illusion. But parapsychologists would never cite Castaneda's account of these phenomena for its evidentiary value. Since the massive investigations of the (British) Society for Psychical Research in the late 19th century, parapsychologists have collected hundreds, if not thousands, of examples of spontaneous psi phenomena—multiple-witnessed, detailed as to time and place, recorded at the time of occurrence, checked against correlated events, and so forth—incomparably superior from an evidentiary viewpoint to anything Castaneda offers.

On the other hand, it would be foolish to expect from the type of study Castaneda describes the evidentiary certainty one finds in a well-recorded spontaneous psi case (or a well-controlled psi experiment). An anthropologist who sets out to discover what it is to be a sorcerer's apprentice is faced with very different procedural problems. He must be prepared to meet a psi-talented individual of another culture on his own ground, to submit himself to the hallucinations, fits, hypnotic states that seem to be a necessary part of the role, and to abide by his guide's usually rigid "rules of the game." None of this lends itself to the "objective" data collection one expects from a spontaneous case under other circumstances. Nor is the sorcerer's apprentice (or "participant-observer") seeking airtight "objective" evidence to begin with. What he seeks, instead, is valuable phenomenological information we otherwise lack: What is the subjective experience of being trained by a sorcerer? How does the sorcerer attempt to control psi phenomena? How do psi phenomena fit into the belief system of the sorcerer? As a parapsychologist, I was very much interested in these phenomenological aspects of Castaneda's works. In addition, Castaneda emphasizes an attribute of psi that primitive cultures readily accept but Western culture (and Western parapsychologists) tend to gloss over, namely that psi has malevolent as well as benevolent manifestations; and an attribute of animal psi appearing frequently in primitive culture but seldom reported in contemporary Western culture, namely the human subject's tendency to experience a sense of "merging" with an animal in the process of ostensible psi communication. Lastly, Castaneda's report suggests the extent to which primitive culture treats (what Western culture labels without understanding) "hallucinatory" or "apparitional" phenomena as veridical; and encourages the cultivation of these phenomena in shamanic training.

What makes Castaneda's report doubly interesting is that parapsychologists have very little phenomenological data of this sort. In part, this is understandable: Only the unusual individual would wish to subject himself to this type of participant-observer experience in the first place. Then again, anthropologists on the whole have not put much store in subjective studies. But even more basic is a fact which never ceases to amaze me: Anthropologists in general have no knowledge of the field of parapsychology nor any evident interest in it. When they are confronted by cultural events in which ostensible psi phenomena play a role (such as witchcraft, shamanism, religious healing or prophecy) or by primitive theories of etiology or causality which posit the existence of psychic phenomena, they typically use every variety of social, psychological, mythical, biologic, or economic formulation to explain the cultural events or the primitive theories. It almost never occurs to them to entertain the idea that genuine psychic events may exist and may contribute to the formation of cultural institutions. The irony of this situation is that anthropologists have collected vast quantities of parapsychological data without recognizing them as such; and the data simply sit there, waiting for some enterprising and parapsychologically-sophisticated individual to categorize and process them—as the sociologist Dean Sheils recently did in a cross-cultural study of out-of-the-body experiences. On the other hand, all too often the anthropologists' lack of parapsychological sophistication affects their fieldwork: They fail to seriously investigate the psychic claims or psychic training techniques of the people they study (a notable exception being Ronald Rose's study of Australian aborigines and their 'clever men'). Despite the fact that the 1974, 1975, 1977, and 1978 meetings of the American Anthropological Association included symposiums (of varying quality) on parapsychology, anthropologists on the whole resist the psi hypothesis.

In this regard, anthropologists are hardly unique among Western scientists. Despite the fact that the study of psi phenomena in Western civilization began as far back as the 18th century, with the discovery that the mesmeric state was sometimes accompanied by telepathy and suggestion-at-a-distance; that among the contributors to parapsychology are such illustrious thinkers as William James, Sigmund Freud, Charles Richet, and Pierre Janet; that in 1969 the American Association for the Advancement of Science belatedly recognized psychic research by granting the professional organization for parapsychologists, the Parapsychological Association, affiliate status; despite these things there is no indication that the contemporary Western scientific community can look dispassionately at the phenomena parapsychology explores much less entertain the psi hypothesis. Of course (to bring the discussion full circle), this resistance of Western scientists to parapsychological data is a central feature of the intellectual encounter between don Juan and Carlos.

On the other hand, few contemporary parapsychologists incorporate or explore anthropological data in their work (a failing common to psychologists in general), even though such data could greatly improve our understanding of psi and the way culture shapes psi manifestations. Parapsychology is, after all, a remarkably underpopulated field although popular works abound: There are only about 300 members of the Parapsychological Association, most of whom do not devote full time to parapsychology; virtually no federal funds are allocated to parapsychological research; and for a contemporary researcher or a non-tenured teacher to exhibit a serious interest in psi phenomena may be a professional "kiss of death." All of which means that the amount and variety of contemporary psychic research is quite limited. In addition, parapsychologists are an insular lot: They exhibit, particularly in the United States, a preference for tightly-controlled experimental studies with dice, Zener cards, random number generators, and so forth, in the tradition J. B. Rhine and his associates established in the 1930s, hoping to obtain additional "hard" evidence of psi, and not incidentally, additional establishment approval of parapsychology as a "hard" science, and they are wary of largely nonexperimental disciplines, like anthropology. Only a handful of contemporary parapsychologists (for example, Van de Castle, Eisenbud, Stevenson, Osis and Haraldsson, Tart, Reichbart) have attempted to integrate their work with anthropological data or theories.

The upshot of this is that when Castaneda's work appeared it was almost unique from a parapsychological perspective. As far as I am aware only one similar study exists—in which the evidentiary data are far more solid—and that is Adrian Boshier's report of his apprenticeship to the "sangomas" of South African tribes. From the beginning, Castaneda's work suffered from the fact (which he readily admitted) that he provided no recognizable cultural milieu for his informant; we do not know which of don Juan's views are culturally determined (or for that matter, by which culture). Despite this ethnographic ambiguity and the lack of evidentiary data, I was initially sufficiently enthusiastic about Castaneda's work from a phenomenological vantage point to make written reference to the first book in passing.

However, given the background I have discussed, it should come as no surprise that parapsychologists in general did *not* cite Castaneda. In fact, his books have never been reviewed in the established parapsychological journals of the United States nor are they likely to be. The few parapsychologists inclined to mention the books had a generally favorable assessment of them. For example, Charles Tart—one of the first to do so—made brief and discerning comments about the "did-I-really-fly" discussion of astral projection in the first book and about don Juan's use of drugs in general to create psi-conducive altered states in his apprentice; Robert Van de Castle, one of the few parapsychologists to do experimental psi studies in an anthropological context (with the Cuna Indians), cited the Castaneda tetralogy as an example of relevance to anthropology and parapsychology; Stanley Krippner made similar remarks; philosopher-parapsychologist Michael Grosso made brief reference to an incident of apparent astral projection in Castaneda's work; and anthropologist Joseph Long, a current leader in attempting to achieve cross-disciplinary give-and-take, traced the effect of the "Castaneda phenomenon" on interest in psychic research among anthropology students. Only Elmer and Alyce Green, biofeedback specialists with an interest in parapsychology, appear in their writings to have accepted without reservation the psi phenomena and much of the philosophy of the don Juan series. In addition, Castaneda's work apparently has sparked parapsychological interest in a few people formerly not associated with the field: Kalish and Reynolds cite Castaneda in a worthwhile if parapsychologically naive study of ethnic belief in survival; and anthropologically-oriented psychologist Douglass Price-Williams, in the most interesting (but unfortunately still unpublished) report to date, conducted three dream experiments in which Castaneda attempted to send an image telepathically (in two of the experiments, the nature and shape of his "ally") and in which some striking dream correspondences occurred, in one case among eight individuals. However, although I believe in the veracity of this report, it says very little about the veracity of the don Juan series itself.

How do I evaluate the veracity or faithfulness of Castaneda's subjective report now that it has been called into question? I have read most of the professional reviews and arguments, and many of the popular ones, on both sides of this issue; and I still find that there is insufficient information for me to reach a firm conclusion. The most damning aspects of Castaneda's position for me are two: His failure to respond to criticism by providing the data which (without revealing the identity of his informants) could settle the uncertainty surrounding his work; and the appalling shoddiness of his fifth book. However, recognizing Carlos's tendency to describe hypnotic or hallucinatory experiences as veridical (in itself one of the important philosophical issues concerning the nature of reality), from a parapsychological perspective, most of the altered-state, extrasensory, or out-of-the-body experiences in the first four books are entirely plausible—although I find their profusion rather incredible. In other words, although one might object to some of the style or confusion in the subjective reporting of psi-determined events, one must look elsewhere—to internal consistency, for example—to determine whether the account is mendacious.

The fifth book, however, has for me some of the overtones in its parapsychological references of the thirteenth chime of the clock: The psychic claims here begin to "know no bounds," as parapsychologist Karlis Osis has remarked referring to the women dancing in the air, and call into question the veracity of the preceding tetralogy. Regardless, my intuition—or "act of faith"—is that there is or was such a person as don Juan, that Castaneda did experience with him much that he initially reported accurately, but that he has progressively embellished, changed and fictionalized his experience. As a consequence, the phenomenological value of the don Juan series for parapsychology has been severely compromised. This is not to say that because the series is partially fabricated, it suddenly loses its power to inspire one, or to convey insight concerning some of the philosophical implications psi phenomena pose for one's concept of reality. Often fiction suggests in an unsystematic fashion truths about the nature of reality that science has overlooked. For example, Tolstoy's *Anna Karenina* anticipated by seventy years some of the findings of psychoanalytic parapsychology by incorporating telepathic and precognitive phenomena in the encounters, dreams, and hypnagogic imagery of the lovers Anna and Vronsky. But the uniqueness of the don Juan series—the fact that we possess so few subjective accounts of what it is like for a (Western educated) man to undergo a "primitive" psychic training experience—must make us cautious in extracting anthropological or parapsychological principles from it once its veracity has been called into question. Thus it is for me that the intellectual and emotional power of these books is tragically marred.

Finally, I look at the "Castaneda phenomenon"—the inordinate attention paid to the works by the public and the anthropologists—with some of the same misgiving as my two colleagues. For when the dust has cleared, whether the works be judged as fact or fiction, or as a combination, I have little reason to believe that parapsychology will be much advanced by all the attention paid to Castaneda. As an example of what I mean, the anthropologists who have been most vociferous in their defense of Castaneda continue to exhibit virtually no knowledge of nor interest in parapsychology. I cannot help thinking that if they, or their fellow scholars who oppose them on this issue, spent a fraction of the time they have on Castaneda in learning the fundamentals (even the rudimentary vocabulary) of parapsychology, the impact on anthropology would be immense.

In addition, the intensity and extent of the "Castaneda phenomenon" often strike me as escapism: It is true that psi phenomena appear to manifest themselves more consistently when the subject is in a "psi conducive state;" it is true, as well, that primitive cultures accept psi phenomena more readily than does Western culture and have developed societally-approved ways of attempting to gain control over such phenomena; but it is certainly not true that these phenomena do not exist in our culture. For one thing, contemporary Western culture has its great psychics, such as Croiset or Serios, whose psi abilities have been put to strong evidentiary tests. For another, we are inextricably involved with less well-controlled psi phenomena in our daily lives. We have simply been conditioned from childhood by our culture to deny the existence of these phenomena; to disguise and mislabel them; to call them "accidents," "chance," or "imagination." It is, of course, much safer to relegate these phenomena (which both fascinate and scare us despite our denials of their existence) to a separate reality that can only be approached with the help of a unique and virtually inaccessible shaman. And so, in what is really an adventure away from ourselves, our society ignores the much more fascinating, certainly more reliable parapsychological data and anecdotal cases in its midst in order to sojourn with Carlos and don Juan in a land distant from ordinary life. That, to my mind, is the greater tragedy that surrounds the Castaneda controversy.

Seven Years with don Juan

Some friends and I were playing on the skeleton of a new house, scampering about on the exposed floor joists. I was eight years old. The game required us to lay planks across the joists to create runways. Stepping carelessly on an unsteady plank, I plummeted nightmarishly to the basement below and crashed full force on my left arm.

The din of pain in which I found myself was truly new to me. Hardly able to cry, mostly in shock, I realized I had to get home. In panic I went for the ladder. The climb was hard. Every time I jostled my impotent left arm, I was stricken with paralyzing pain. Once on the joists again, I crossed sixteen of them to safety, this time very carefully.

At home I bawled to Mom and Dad that I had "broken my arm off." Naturally, they laughed. Dad squeezed my arm to show it was not true. When I collapsed, they rushed me to the doctor. X-rays proved we were each partly right.

Before long I was running about as usual, falling down, using my cast to buffer the falls. A concrete arm was handy to crush clods or fend off possible attackers. When the cast was removed, revealing a skinny grey arm instead of a muscular tanned one, I was upset, but sun and exercise restored my symmetry, and I have a perfect set today. Years later, I walked another sort of plank, fell into a new kind of basement, and had a harder time climbing out.

Losing Personal Footing

At seventeen I was truly in love for the first time. The girl of my heart was beautiful, only sixteen, and built for a dream. She laughed at my jokes and admired my talents. She said she loved me, too. It was an all-consuming infatuation.

Adolescence was making me and my buddies aware of strange new worlds—relentless hard-ons, and intrusions from beings called teachers. The wheel of time was rolling us forward, growing us up whether we wanted to or not. A major portion of our energies was commandeered by "the system." We were evidently being prepared for important life decisions.

But few kids were interested in much more than getting laid or getting rich. I was not opposed to these either, having the proof in my pocket

227

both ways. What pressed on my mind was the feeling I should do it right, whatever it was, should extract the most from the situation.

Not pushing me in any particular direction, my father offered me the education of my choice. I showed promise in graphic arts, and my grades were right for the university. All I lacked was confidence.

In the fall of 1971, I traveled 760 miles from home to enroll at the University of British Columbia. I hated every goddamn minute of it. The superior SOBs called professors disgusted me, orating arrogantly from the podium, peddling pedantic pabulum to new arrivals. I might have become a revolutionist but for one thing, the pull on the heartstrings.

After a tearful separation, my girlfriend and I were exchanging weekly letters, but I couldn't cope with a nagging feeling that someone very special was gone. Soon I was despondent, knocking on a door I knew was closed between us. Maniacal letters and silly jealousy forced her to lock the door on her side. One sunny day in November she sent me my final notice.

Inside of a week I quit UBC and wandered aimlessly about. My parents worried about me, but trusted me to pull myself together and find a new path.

January 1972 I enrolled in a ski instructor's course. I passed the course but did no paid instructing. March I worked on a construction project. Twenty-five days of that month it rained. As dreams of success, money, and love dissolved, I looked all the harder for a concrete answer, some authoritative, powerful key to life.

Stopping the World

One warm sunny day in the spring of 1972, I met don Juan. Despite a bit of skepticism, I approached him with absolute interest, fixed my unbending attention on him, grabbed him for all I was worth. That afternoon I lost my balance and fell into a new reality. When I hit bottom, my worldview snapped.

My body was numb. I watched it from behind. One of me was walking, talking, and eating, the other was watching me walking, talking, and eating. Encompassing this split was blinding terror, not enough to crush me, but too much to dispel by crying. Hot and cold water felt the same. The new reality didn't wash off in the shower.

My older brother could see I was in a bad state but felt he couldn't do a thing for me. He was right. I never thought of asking for help. Where I was, there was nobody to ask.

Though a storm raged inside me, I remained unruffled on the surface. People thought I had slipped into a mood, or wasn't quite myself. They had no way of knowing I was lost in an unfamiliar world looking for my soul. The only one I talked to was my brother.

Engulfed by Castaneda's story, I poured credibility into it. Though frightened at the prospect of beings from another world, I studied Carlos's dealings with "the ally." Like him, I pressed on, fully afraid. Unlike him, I had no place to retreat to.

Peyote visions and hundred-foot gnats didn't help me out of the pit, but when *Journey to Ixtlan* described the "warrior," I felt I had found the ladder. Some of the rungs might not support my full weight, but I could begin to climb.

I dropped routines, lost self importance, assumed responsibility, erased personal history, and took death as my adviser. Nobody knew what I was doing, not even me, but whatever it was, I was trying to do it right, to do it impeccably.

Like Carlos, I stopped the world and saw a new reality. Unlike Carlos, I never met a luminous coyote or got an appointment to talk things over with don Juan. All I could do was haunt the bookstore, waiting for another volume, hoping it would lead me back to the crack between the worlds.

As for the ordinary world, I was stumbling through it with a club foot. During seven years, I accomplished the following: one month construction work mostly rained out, one month forest service, nine months art school, eight months armored car service, about a month odd jobs, and five months father's farm. Four years missing somewhere. I know I spent a lot of time tinkering with stereo equipment, but I haven't got any now.

Spring 1976, I drove my little MGA sports car down the Oregon coast in the general direction of Sonora. A month later I wound up in Death Valley. There was enough money left to get me to Yaqui country but, like Carlos, I knew it was not my time yet. I went to Disneyland instead.

Back home I took pride in living, like don Juan, with no visible means of support. Though I collected a lot of unemployment insurance, I owed a year's rent to my father. Whenever family or friends started shaking their heads, I explained the life of the warrior to them. That was before I turned into a bird, while I was still being a jackass.

Really Flying

Next I discovered hang-gliding. For a year and a half I prepared myself to fly, reading every available work on the hang-gliding cult of the Caucasians of North America. In the fall of 1977 I bought a kite.

Everything around a person—I liked to say at that time—tests his sphere of power. If you fail to match the pressure points, the forces of the world will . . . ah . . . pour in and crush you or something. My kite had the latest aerodynamics and was stressed for a whole mess of Gs. I trusted it to carry my luminous sphere in and around among the forces and bring me to safe landings.

Flying at three-thousand feet is both awesome and terrifying. I demonstrated some competence and made no bad mistakes—something you don't get many of on a hang-glider. Still, the grandeur I saw while flying wasn't the world I was looking for.

In March of 1978 four of us went to Keremeos for the Easter fly-in. Nick had destroyed his rag-wing around Christmas but was trying out a rigid-wing crashed by its previous owner and then restored. June came along for the ride, and to be with Nick. Sam owned the van.

The wind was bad at Keremeos, so we kept on to Sooyoso. Sam and I got in some choppy flights, but Nick didn't like the site. Nobody was enthusiastic. Back at the motel I talked about quitting the sport, about how skiing was a bigger love for me. Sam said it was the other way round for him. Nick was brooding. I made some chili, we drank Sam's wine, teased June, and laughed at Nick's jokes.

Next morning the wind was up to 40 miles per hour. The sky was overcast. Nick couldn't find a site to suit him, and June said he was ready to head back to Vancouver. Around noon the winds came down, but the air looked pretty junky. Sam launched at two o'clock. I set up and waited for a little less air. By three the wind sat between 15 and 25. Though I stumbled on take-off, the kite took most of my weight, and I got a twenty-minute flight.

Nick launched right after me. His flight was very short. I was one of the three fliers who found him. An ambulance came, and bearers carried him down the mountain. They also brought news that a flier had been killed at Keremeos.

June was worried sick, eyes swollen with crying.

"Is Nick all right?" she said.

"No, he isn't." I felt myself slipping into a dream. "He's not all right, June." I grappled for control. "He's dead."

Her screams burned into my brain.

The Predilection of an Idiot

Early in the summer of 1978 I bought a motorcycle, which needed a bunch of repairs. By the time it was in shape I had five-hundred dollars in it. For a month I rode around aimlessly, collecting speeding tickets. Accelerating hard one morning, I broke the back wheel free. It tried to trade places with the front wheel. I bounced along the pavement. My helmet went BOK-BOK-BOK!

The forces of the world, I *saw*, were short on patience. I sold the motorcycle. Dad said he would still finance my career if I had anything at all in mind. What I had in mind was *knowing*, but knowing *what*?

An idiot kept jumping out of me and staying for a minute or a month. I tried to leave him behind by hooking onto the solid words of don Juan, whose answers were so great. Whenever they didn't sound great, I faulted myself or Castaneda. Somewhere, I felt, there must be a don Juan to straighten everything out for me, if only I could find him, and talk to him.

Selling everything I owned, I borrowed my brother's packsack and got ready to go south once more. September 26th I was on my way to California, maybe to Mexico. Though I already suspected he was blind, I took my idiot along as pilot. On the way I met a lot of other drifters.

Appointments with Knowledge

Our Greyhound stopped half an hour for lunch. I looked around the station. There was no white-haired old Indian sitting in front of the window, so I wandered outside. Drifting into a bookstore, I brought up my favorite topic.

"Castaneda writes trash!" the owner barked. "Plato said it all much better, a long time ago." Seeing I was unimpressed, he offered to give me a book by Plato, but he couldn't find it. Hurrying back to the station, I saw my bus roll out of town without me. The station was empty. A few hours later it filled up again.

Bob and Dale were on their way to Zigzag, Oregon, to see Dale's newborn nephew. Bob wore a baseball cap pulled down so far he had to tilt his head back to look at me. Dale had borrowed his cousin's baby blue suit. The shoulders were a good fit, but his cousin was four inches shorter.

Dale asked me if the granny knot in his tie looked okay. A withered old man in bifocals turned round and, without saying a word, began to re-knot Dale's tie. As if by magic, a Windsor knot appeared. The old man went back to his work, collecting cigarette butts and emptying the to-bacco into a little pouch. Even at his present age, I thought, don Juan could not be so decrepit.

Next stop was San Francisco. A wholesome-looking fellow named Bevan asked me up to the house. Seeing he had a lady friend, I went along to check their answer out. The house was a mansion, but the people were too friendly. I signed the register and paid a dollar for din-ner.

Since there was no furniture, we ate on the floor. About thirty people sang forty campfire songs. A lovely girl soloed on the guitar. When I played the Moonlight Sonata, the audience went wild.

A young woman gave an inspiring lecture, complete with blackboard and chalk. Everybody urged me to come to the farm; 680 acres, they said. No thanks, I said. Everybody looked disappointed. I told Bevan that if he truly loved me as a brother, he would respect my decision to leave as much as my decision to stay—logic he couldn't deny, in a spirit he couldn't refuse. We shook hands on it, and I returned to the path with heart.

The Benefactor's Explanation

Early on the morning of October 2nd I arrived in Santa Barbara. When my friend Bill didn't answer his phone, I hung around waiting for the stores to open. Nine months had passed since *Second Ring of Power*, so my hopes for a new Castaneda book were rising, but I was hardly prepared for the one I found.

What's this? Another half-wit parody? No, but this guy can't swallow all of Castaneda's story. Typical. Authenticity is questionable if he won't furnish the fieldnotes. Well, maybe, but . . . Carlos is 53 *years old*? I . . . Hey, wait a minute! He was married? A Carlos *and* a Castaneda? That's clever, but . . . What's this about UCLA? Oh-oh! I'm gonna buy this little bugger.

The chapters that followed were clearly aimed at resurrecting reason. I didn't even have to throw away that inspiring old fart don Juan, at least not all of him. Systematically and qualitatively the words came true and cutting, severing forever my luminous fibers to the world of Castaneda.

I was euphoric. I read them again and again. He's right! A dam let go inside of me. Then I remembered six years, almost seven, gone. What kind of fool would do that to himself? Only one I could think of. And only a fool's luck had brought me back alive. Any moment I could have cashed in without getting back to myself.

Castaneda's Journey had been published in Santa Barbara. I had a distinct feeling the author might live there too. The directory gave a number for Richard de Mille. I was sure he must be the one. All day I was telling my friends about the book. When I spotted a note saying the author lived in Santa Barbara, I knew I had to phone him.

I phoned him. I asked him if he was he. He said he was. I didn't know where to start, but I babbled at full speed. To my satisfaction, he listened, for a long time. Then he asked if I could write.

Thinking he meant, "Save your breath, buddy," I waited for an explanation. He was writing another book, he said, and would like to publish my account. If I could write it, he would read it. We would go from there. He could pay me only a copy of the book, but he'd credit my authorship. He asked me for a thousand words.

Journey to Erickson

The minute we hung up, I started my personal history. Finished it a week later in Vancouver. On the way, I found Carlos and don Juan sitting on a transcendental bench, so I decided to have it out with them.

Writing books, I told them, was the greatest magic of all, bringing wealth, fame, power, and absolute control over what is real. Don Juan took this like a gentleman, but Carlos fought back, refusing to admit it was all a game. Knowing it was him or me, I worked relentlessly to perfect my arguments. Everyone I met had to listen to them.

About this time I forgot to eat and sleep. My reasoning power steadily drained away. Dad phoned to say a letter had come from Richard de Mille, and I drove the forty miles out to the farm as calmly as could be, but when I opened the letter, the words wouldn't stand still. At every reading I got a different meaning.

By twilight I knew my time had come and the challenge had to be met. I had to face the forces of the world.

"Oh—*Neil*," Mom sighed in a very sad way, when she saw me shedding my clothes.

"Don't worry," I wanted to tell her, "this won't take long."

Actually, I couldn't say anything to her. Naked, I walked out into the stormy night, ready to die if necessary.

Dad took me by the arm and tried to pull me into the house. I threatened him, and he backed off. Mom kept pretty cool. Both of them were pleading with me to come in out of the cold and wet, but I defied them. Cold and wet were nothing to me. Thoughts and feelings were useless. Gradually the world grew silent and then I was alone.

Dad picked my body up off the ground and carried it toward the house. A bolt of black lightning struck it and stiffened it like steel. I passed into the realm of the *nagual*.

The garden gate clicked and my body became weightless (a change my father does not confirm). From a distance voices spoke to me. I listened to them closely. Mom and Dad were speaking, and somehow they were new. We were back inside the house, and I was alive again.

For the next two months my family took care of me, their help and love keeping my body from following my soul into the other world. Thanks to them I'm still a survivor on this earth. A lucky warrior finds more in his garden than nostalgic birds and imaginary wizards. A lucky warrior finds friends.

This has been the true story of my seven years with don Juan and my journey to Erickson. Some of the names have been changed to protect the innocent. I thought of calling the story, "Seven Years with the Wrong Guru is More than a Man can Stand," but I've stood it so far, and anyway, a warrior meets his fate impeccably; he doesn't complain about it.

Tell it to the Toltecs

"A vindictive, sadistic, utterly hateful piece of writing by an acutely intelligent warped human being, whose controlled folly is entirely inaprapo"—is the way one follower of don Juan described *Castaneda's Journey*. Others brought copies back to the store, slammed them down on the counter, and demanded a refund. Rather than exchange such an evil thing for money, one devout couple exorcised the Antijuan, burning the book page by page in their fireplace. First to feel the wrath of the faithful had been Donald Barthelme, whose *New York Times* parody of *The Teachings* evoked a letter classing don Juan with Jesus, Barthelme with R. Crumb.

The *Los Angeles Times* review of my book kicked off a scrimmage that lasted eight months. Bruce Anselmo scored de Mille's "unproven conjecture and superficial interpretation," while praising Castaneda for seeking neither money nor fame and calling for extensive fieldwork into American Indian sorcery to test Castaneda's claims. Ralph Beals tipped Anselmo to the ill-guarded secret that a vast ethnographic literature awaited his perusal in the libraries. Laboring to excuse Castaneda's textual contradictions, G. E. Nordell argued from an implicit assumption that Matthew, Mark, Luke, and John had been a single evangelist writing inconsistent gospels to earn a social-science Ph.D. Carl Harpon thought the contradictions were traps to catch the reader. Roger Peters accused "academic bureaucrats" of suppressing the separate reality, whereupon Ralph Beals got born again, confessed his "past hypocricies," and disclosed an early apprenticeship to don Juan's elder brother, during which Beals had received the texts of all his scholarly works from a nagual propitiated by seven gourds of fermented pineapple juice. Raised a Catholic but beset by feelings of powerlessness in a violent world, Jonathan Lamal testified that don Juan's fine moral force had helped him as had no other contemporary writing. Recalling Carlos's terminal leap into the nagual, Lamal wrote: "If nothing else would shake my faith in Castaneda's veracity, it would be another book." Four months later *Second Ring* appeared. Trickster is not an easy teacher.

Whoever disrupts the ministry of a new redemptor is asking for complaints, but don Juan must have done something right, because none of the calls or letters I got were mean-spirited. Most pitied me for not standing in the true light and tried to help me become a luminous being. A correspondent who had not read my book advised me to read "Castenada's" books more carefully and be saved by them. Another advised me to read my own book more carefully and be saved by *it*. A third confided that his confidant was a snake.

A young man called to tell me he was on his way to Mexico to found a school of spiritual healing on a power spot between two unexcavated pyramids. The nagual and the Nagas were tied together, he said. And where could he read more about *emic* and *etic*? I suggested an article but warned it might be a little technical. "If I can illuminate it within me," he said, "I'll be able to pick it up."

An apprentice of Carlos's wrote to say he had enjoyed *Castaneda's Journey* and had even thought Carlos might have written it, since, he said, "I am one of the people you quoted in it." Carlos had given him exercises that are not in the books, but I could find new exercises there if I would just copy passages out by hand. Carlos could induce a hypnotic trance without a person's knowing it but was too humble to match the powers of his teachers. His textual contradictions had been introduced by editors cutting and rearranging to save a buck. Carlos hadn't explained everything in the books because a lock had been put on his ability to tell the whole story. Though he talks very frankly in person, there's a lot about sex he's embarrassed to write down. The apprentice praised my hunger for truth and said my teacher would find me sooner or later. He urged me to talk to Charles Tart. He revealed that other apprentices of Juan's had erased their personal histories before writing their books. He didn't list the titles, and he didn't sign his name.

An apprentice willing to sign his name was Timothy Martin, who in 1977 sent a letter to departments of anthropology offering to lecture on a system of knowledge identical to don Juan's but learned from a teacher named Jesus Miguel and a benefactor named Margaret Castillo, a woman with a perfect tonal. The first contact with Miguel had occurred in Arizona in the summer of 1969. Seeing an old but very alert Indian at the side of the road, Martin approached and asked for information. The Indian was reluctant to answer, but Martin persisted. Though the old man pretended not to know what Martin wanted and, in truth, acted as if Martin were crazy, he already saw that Martin would make a good sorcerer. Shortly afterwards the apprenticeship began.

Miguel's teachings came to Martin in dreams but more often during waking when Martin entered the mood of a warrior. After Martin was sent overseas, Miguel continued the lessons by using the eight points of

Martin's totality. Sometimes another sorcerer, ostensibly a friend of Miguel's, would teach Martin the ways of a hunter. Returning to the United States, Martin dropped in and out of colleges trying to rid himself of sorcery, but always felt a need to return to it. When severe psychosomatic symptoms developed, sorcery cured them, but also captured Martin.

Though milder than Carlos's, Martin's encounters with the nagual were impressive. A canyon threatened to bury him in a landslide. Opening his apartment door, he was greeted by a volley of explosions and a series of stomach cramps; he fled to a motel for the night; next day the attacker was gone. The worst experience saw him crouching on the floor, "whining and shivering like a rodent awaiting execution," as a two-foot-wide, silent, translucent power-funnel invaded his room. Two years later, he was similarly attacked, but by that time he had learned enough wizardry to resist.

Wizardry is the name of the Miguel-Castillo system of knowledge, which parallels don Juan's sorcery at many points: force corresponds to power, steersman to sorcerer, ranger to hunter, grand wizard to man of knowledge, lazar to ally, and ceasing intellection to stopping the internal dialogue. Martin has seen a movie in the branches of a tree, has been menaced by a sign that turned into a man, and has flown on the wings of perception. "For now," he said, "I find wizardry the only way to live."

A Los Angeles executive was losing his way to live. His self-destructive behavior was threatening his business. Money and position weren't helping. One day he met Castaneda and began taking lessons in the warrior's way. As if by magic, the self-destruction stopped, the business was saved. Words could not express the executive's gratitude to don Juan. When he heard about *Castaneda's Journey* and its thesis that the teacher who had saved him was an imaginary person, he was at first revolted, then enraged. A man of some influence, he vowed to stop the slander in its tracks. A prudent man, he took the precaution of asking some friends at UCLA whether there could conceivably be anything in the allegation. The result was a sickening shock. The answers were far from reassuring. A practical man, he sadly accepted the fact that he had been healed by a hoax. Fortunately the teachings proved more lasting than the teacher.

Maximilian E. Obermayer, a Los Angeles physician, told me I might have saved myself the trouble of writing *Castaneda's Journey*, since the mere fact that I remained alive was enough to prove Castaneda had acquired no magical powers, with which he would otherwise have killed me. I pointed out that if I had not written the book Obermayer's Test of Sorcering Authenticity could not have been applied, since Castaneda would have had no reason to be offended.

My favorite gripe was written to the editors of *Fate* by Robert Holbrook of Warren, Ohio, who thought it likely don Juan's teachings had descended from the Toltecs as Castaneda said. It didn't matter whether don Juan was real, since "we are all hallucinatory projections of each other." *Fate's* ignorant and unfounded contrary opinion, Holbrook declared, was "based on Richard de Mille's *Castaneda's Journey*, an asinine book which I will not read."

IV.

Carlos in the Realms of Discourse

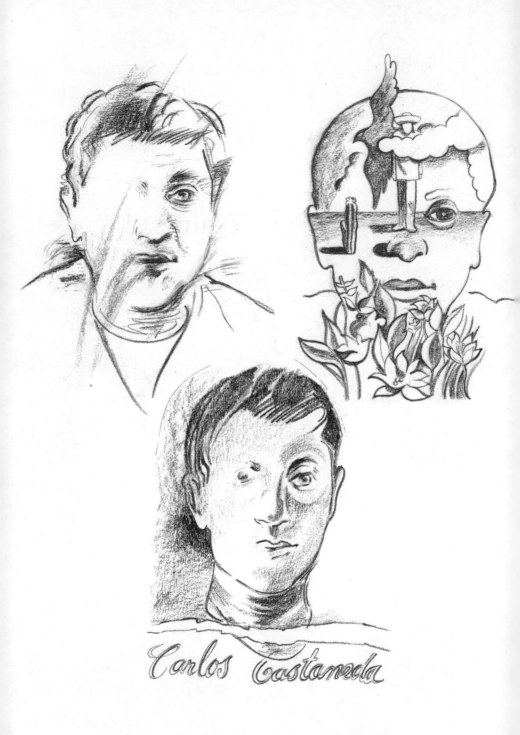

Three Faces of Carlos

Sergeant Castaneda and the Photos of don Juan: Transforming the Special Consensus

A legend aspiring in his own time does well to cultivate an obscure or inaccurate biography. Following don Juan's advice to create a fog around himself, Castaneda let *Time* photograph him peeping between pudgy fingers, hiding under a pork-pie hat, twinkling atop Angelo Orona's dissertation, never full face. As shown in the illustration, he partly erased his personal image, drawn for *Psychology Today* by Dick Oden. That year, Oden said, Carlos was living "in a van with lots of tape recordings," though Castaneda's dissertation would say, "I was not permitted to tape record or photograph any event," while *A Separate Reality* had twice said: "I turned on my tape recorder." For the first time here it can be revealed that Carlos's tape recorder is equipped with a special attachment to create a fog around him.

In spite of the erasure, Oden's drawing did resemble Castaneda, as one can see by comparing it with Schlesinger's naturalistic portrait in Chapter Two. The metamorphosis of Carlos was accomplished mainly on the cover of *Time*, where a squarish European visage contracted into a round-headed Filipino-looking desert. Five years later *Psychology Today* got another crack at shaping the legend, as *Time's* rice farmer merged with Oden's taxi driver to become a most unlikely adolescent Spanish aristocrat, right eye partly restored, name boldly proclaiming a false identity. A fan who went looking for Carlos Castaneda with this peculiar princeling in hand would certainly not have recognized the literary commoner who turned up on Memorial Day weekend 1979 at the American Booksellers' Association convention in Los Angeles. Accompanied by Harlan Kessel of the University of California Press, the celebrated nondescript was wearing a tan leisure suit with shirt in muted checks. Sources say he hobnobbed with Jerzy Kosinski, but nobody saw don Juan. Neil Erickson recommends looking under Carlos's hat to find don Juan, but my informant says Castaneda wasn't wearing a hat. So much for facts. The legend is more entertaining.

A warrior intent on mastering personal history would not be satisfied to keep his name out of the biographical dictionaries; he would submit his name along with false information. Marquis's *Who's Who in*

America (not to be confused with St Martin's highly respected *Who's Who*) shows how sorcerers manipulate learning resources. The 1976-77 edition proposes that Carlos Castaneda was born in Sao Paulo in 1931 to C. N. and Susana (Aranha) Castaneda, received an M.A. in 1964 and a Ph.D. in 1970, and is the author of *The Teachings of Don Juan* and *Tales of Power*. Since the editors of *Who's Who in America* ask their readers to point out any errors that may have crept in, I wrote to them on 5 November 1976 offering documentation that Castaneda had been born in Cajamarca in 1925 to C. B. and Susana (Castañeda) Arana, had received an M.A. never and a Ph.D. in 1973. Though the editors sent no word of thanks, they apparently wrote to Castaneda for an update. Naturally he didn't correct the errors, which the editors carefully preserve like Piltdown relics, but he did add to his list of publications, which the 1978-79 edition carries as: *Teachings*, *Separate Reality*, *Ixtlan* (with a wrong date), and *Tales of Power* (with another wrong date). What caught my eye was the subtitle he appended to *A Separate Reality*. It was not *Further Conversations with Don Juan*, which appears on the actual book (as the editors could easily have determined if they were in the habit of checking anything), but *The Phenomenology of Special Consensus*, which appears nowhere. Castaneda, it seems, had answered me himself. His message was: If you think you can restore my personal history by writing to these mercenary boobs in Chicago, you are pitifully mistaken; to show how hopeless it is, I will now twist the tale still further, and they won't do a thing about it.

What, then, is the phenomenology of special consensus? "In don Juan's teachings, special consensus meant tacit or implicit agreement on the component elements of nonordinary reality." When Carlos sat down on a park bench with don Juan, or when Castaneda wrote to the editors of *Who's Who in America*, the conference achieved agreement on a separate reality. Don Juan supplied Carlos with component elements like giant gnats and talking cactuses; Castaneda supplied the editors with a fake biography and a spurious subtitle. The beauty of the subtitle was that it commented reflexively on its own spuriousness: This is how I tell you tall stories you are too credulous or too careless to question in spite of their glaring incongruities; I call such story-telling creating a special consensus; this explanation is the phenomenology of special consensus. Condensed into only five words and disguised as a subtitle, the sorcerer's explanation was a peyote button too tough for these editors to chew, even if they had recognized it as a power object and had not been afraid to taste the bitterness of their own errors hidden within it.

Contemporary Authors is a large and useful dictionary of writers' biographies, where, in addition to the usual misinformation about nationality, family, and degrees, Castaneda's entry for 1977 adds the provocative assertion: "*The Teachings of Don Juan* sounds like a novel, but it was Castaneda's master's thesis, and all of the experiences are true." We are told, moreover, that the book "was produced by Sterling Silliphant as an underground film." Now there is a movie I'd like to see. From the Silliphant office at Warner Brothers I learned the production had been planned but the rights subsequently withdrawn. Castaneda once declared he didn't want Anthony Quinn to play don Juan, but certainly they could have found somebody else. Eager to understand the relationship between the author and the producers he temporarily encouraged, I tried to phone Silliphant but could reach only his brother Mark, who told me he didn't like what I was doing, and hung up. An editor at *Contemporary Authors* was more responsive. The original entry, she said, had been prepared for the 1971 edition and approved by Castaneda; no reason to revise it had come to the editor's attention in 1976, but the second revision would take my new information into account.

Weaving the narrative web is Castaneda's characteristic way of dealing with people. Editors engender some restraint, but friends evoke the Peruvian Baron Munchausen, particularly in one-to-one consultations where Castaneda seems to reveal delicate and often painful details of his private life to uniquely trusted confidants. A UCLA professor excused him from an exam when he told her all his time was taken up caring for the child of a friend killed in the Korean War. The boy was real enough, and Castaneda used to bring him to the campus, but he was Margaret Runyan Castaneda's son, whose father was enjoying perfect health. Some friends were told the little fellow was Castaneda's own son, whose blond hair was explained by Carlos's recessive genes. Others heard about Carlos's blond Swedish wife, though Margaret was neither blond nor Swedish. Still others, like committee chairman William Lessa, were treated to the war-orphan scenario.

At 5:15 PM on Thursday, 27 January 1977, I received a call from a rather agitated gentleman who wouldn't give his name but said he was a scientist residing 200 miles to the north. I'll call him Newton Threebody. Having read my book "standing up," he just had to talk to me. Some years earlier Castaneda had befriended him, flattered him, and sat on park benches with him, weaving the narrative web. Three stories from that period had stuck in Threebody's mind:

Carlos of the Border Patrol. Carlos was working for the border patrol down El Paso way, investigating a gang of dope smugglers. One night he found himself on the roof of the smugglers' farmhouse accompanied by a friend he had met in the local cantina. Hearing a click, he whirled to see his drinking buddy pointing a pistol at him. Luckily, Carlos got off the first shot, but he always felt sorry about having to kill his friend like that.

Carlos in the Sky. Carlos and a black war buddy (presumably not the ill-fated father of the little blond boy) yelled *Geronimo!* over Inchon, but the buddy's chute didn't open. Luckily, he fell on top of Carlos's open chute, and the two made a safe landing together.

Carlos of the Purple Heart. On ground patrol in North Korea, Carlos was shot in the left testicle by a Chinese soldier. (You can tell when it's a Chinese soldier, because North Koreans always go for the right testicle.)

Readers of *Castaneda's Journey* may recall Castaneda's claim of having fought with the American Army in Spain, and *Time's* report that the Defense Department had no record of Castaneda's service. At any rate, Threebody said he had been rather suspicious of these stories, and when he later read some of his own words reproduced in *A Separate Reality*, he realized his supposed friend had just been toying with him. Talking to me about it made him feel better, he said.

John Hitchcock, Castaneda's fourth committee chairman, invited Castaneda to dinner at his Beverly Glen house, where he and Mrs Hitchcock heard the story of:

Sergeant Castaneda and the Cuban Commandos. Carlos was leading a troop of Cuban soldiers under heavy attack in North Korea. All were killed except Carlos, who was castrated by a rifle shot (presumably fired by a Chinese soldier raised in North Korea). Consequently unable to have a child of his own, Carlos took up with the mother of the little blond boy, who soon decamped for New York, leaving Carlos to care for the boy by himself. Authoritative and helpful as this report is, Hitchcock did not get the whole castration story, for we learn in *Second Ring* that Carlos is an empty person because he "made a female child," which goes to show that a sorcerer can do just about anything he puts his mind to.

Threebody also told me Castaneda had given him a photograph of don Juan, and had then taken it back. Which reminded me of an earlier conversation with another friend of Castaneda's, LSD-tripper Al Egori, who claimed to have a surreptitious photo of don Juan. He wouldn't say who had taken it. Once published, Egori's claim inspired photographer Ralph Ullman to interview "Juan Matoses" he found listed in the Sonora telephone directory. The first 2999 were obviously not sorcerers, but on the 3000th call Ullman got lucky. His three photos of Number-3000, published in *New Age*, show better than any other document don Juan's power to transform the special consensus, for the uninformed person would inevitably mistake them for photos of three different old men. "This is no hoax," the editors declared, and proved it by adding that Ullman was an art history major at the University of Michigan.

Ullman's epochal photographic essay might never have been attempted had he believed Craig Karpel, who said: "You can't just call Mescalito on the phone." Karpel explained that Castaneda does not come to the phone when you ring UCLA Anthropology, not because he isn't there writing up his new fieldwork but because he is afraid your mind will flow through the wire and get mixed up with his own. Sorcerers have to be careful—as do editors: so many readers complained about Ullman's article that *New Age* published a retraction and apology.

Minor rumors are easy to come by. Carlos is working for the CIA to counteract Soviet military psi. Carlos saved some people from an earthquake by making their house float out to sea. Page 68 of David Silverman's book was left unnumbered to honor the year in which *The Teachings* was published. Raul Suppes saw Carlos walking across the campus with two old men, but when he tried to talk to them, he suffered a complete lapse of memory, which had to be cured by Scientology. Ludwig Wittgenstein served on Castaneda's dissertation committee; asked to comment on charges of fraud and deceit, Wittgenstein replied: "Whereof one cannot speak, thereof one must be silent."

Perhaps the grandest rumor of all arises from Stephen Reno's conjecture that Castaneda may have taken the idea for don Juan from José López-Portillo's "Don Q." The conjecture is untenable, because "Don Q" was not published before *The Teachings* as indicated in the translation Reno read, but not until 1969, though both manuscripts were completed in the fall of 1967. Which brings us to the more newsworthy conjecture that Castaneda is actually the president of Mexico.

Exhilarating though such speculations are, I find myself constantly drawn back to the transformations of special consensus achieved by Castaneda in conference with persons who recognized him as a professional colleague. His teacher Ralph Beals, for example, was apparently the only one to be told Carlos had been raised in Mexico rather than Brazil. Douglass Price-Williams and Karlis Osis entered into informal but serious agreements with Castaneda to act as agent in parapsychological experiments. The experimental designs did not require Castaneda's presence or allow any monitoring of his activity, so there is no way to know whether he carried out his nonordinary part of the bargain or just had a good ordinary laugh at the expense of his co-experimenters, but I feel no hesitation in choosing the latter alternative, and Osis's letter to *Psychology Today* suggests he agrees with me.

The most poignant example I know of a practical joke on a colleague was unwittingly reported by Gloria Garvin, student and editorial assistant of Clement Meighan, the professor who first encouraged Castaneda to do fieldwork. Garvin was analyzing photographs of prehistoric Chumash Indian rock paintings. One of the paintings, displaying a type of figure conventionally called the "anthropomorphic frog," is represented in the illustration. When Garvin showed this pictograph to Castaneda, "he said there was a striking similarity between this image and a particular drawing don Juan had made for him several years ago when he was attempting to explain the concept and practice of 'dreaming.' " Later, Castaneda showed Garvin a drawing "nearly identical" to the prehistoric painting and said it was the drawing don Juan had made.

According to don Juan, the figure on the right was the tonal, or dreamer, while the figure on the left was the nagual, or dreamed. As Garvin did not question this interpretation, Castaneda apparently warmed to the task of creating the separate reality through special consensus with a trusting colleague. Don Juan's rules were typically exacting: soles of feet together, arms on ground, hands resting lightly on solar plexus, fingertips barely touching, and so on. The dreamer's hands must slide down smoothly, for "if they should open outwards with palms facing up, the whole process would be disrupted."

Dutifully and gratefully Garvin reproduced this novel ancient lore in her chapter of an archeological book titled *Four Rock Art Studies*. She was obviously delighted with Castaneda's shamanistic interpretation of figures some archeologists had depreciated as mere representations of animals. "Perhaps," she concluded, "the analogy between elements at this Chumash or Canalino rock art site (dating to 100-1500 AD) and a shamanistic practice of a present day Yaqui Indian is unwarranted. Yet it is a striking coincidence that a shaman drawing a picture to illustrate shamanistic practices should draw a picture nearly identical to that seen in rock art in California." Indeed. As Castaneda's partisan Michael Harner put it: "Carlos is really a shaman." Nor is he really lying, Harner would surely add, for anthropomorphic frogs may well have been shamans a thousand years ago even if don Juan's sketch was drawn by Castaneda. On the other hand, prehistoric shamans had not been privileged to sample don Juan's hash of East and West, ancient and modern, academic and preliterate, so Castaneda's pseudo-Yaqui travesty must have imposed substantial invalidity on Garvin's report along with manifest inauthenticity.

On 6 October 1978 I wrote to Garvin asking why she had not reproduced don Juan's drawing, since it provided such powerful independent confirmation of her shamanistic interpretation of the pictographs. "I am quite curious about the reason for not reproducing it," I said—which was a little disingenuous, for I was sure I knew the reason: Castaneda had taken the drawing away with him. As he had taken the photo of don Juan back from Newton Threebody. As he had dropped in unannounced at the offices of *Psychology Today* to retrieve the tapes of his several interviews with Sam Keen. A sorcerer doesn't leave power objects lying around where counter-sorcerers can get hold of them and drain their power, or hurl them at him from a distance. Garvin didn't answer my letter.

"A hunter deals intimately with his world," don Juan had said, "and yet he is inaccessible to that same world." "He taps it lightly, stays for as long as he needs to, and then swiftly moves away leaving hardly a mark."

Don Juan's formula for dealing intimately with the world is no doubt correct from a sorcerer's point of view, but from the world's point of view something remains to be said. A social-science sorcerer may take pains not to leave fabricated data in the hands of trusting colleagues, but it cannot be truly said he leaves hardly a mark on those he makes fools of before their fellow scholars.

RdeM

The next two essays interest me not only for what they say but for the tone in which they say it. Douglass McFerran, Professor of Philosophy at Los Angeles Pierce College, was for ten years a Jesuit seminarian and so is well prepared to deal with the heresies of Carlos-Apostate. Under the pseudonym of David Farren he has authored several studies of Western occultism, including *Living with Magic* and *Sex and Magic*, which furnish a broad basis for his judgment that Castaneda is a radical occultist and closet diabolist, who turns the Establishment Devil into an Antiestablishment Messenger of Enlightenment. In "Carlos and the Toltec Devils" he gives Castaneda credit for reopening the question of how to talk about right and wrong while saving or losing one's immortal soul, but he doesn't trust don Juan to come up with any satisfactory answers.

Stephen J. Reno, Lecturer in Phenomenology and History of Religion at the University of Leicester, views Castaneda sympathetically, as the creator of a modern equivalent of traditional myth. Reno discovers in the don Juan cycle many typical features of the folk tale. Although born, raised, and schooled in Castaneda country—southern California—Reno has no difficulty distinguishing Carlos-Fieldworker from Castaneda-Fabler or separating scholarly critiques of science hoaxes from literary appreciation of stories that speak to our intuitions. Though drawn into the stories while reading them, he does not feel obliged to take up permanent residence in Castaneda's counterpart of Middle-earth or Narnia.

Douglass McFerran   **28**

Carlos and the Toltec Devils

According to his former wife, Carlos Castaneda was well versed in the lore of Western occultism long before don Juan appeared on the scene. What is particularly significant about this is that it explains an otherwise puzzling choice of terms.

Don Juan calls himself a *brujo*, a word that in rural Mexico unfailingly indicates the practitioner of a harmful magic. Even though the spry old Indian shares many characteristics of the *curandero* or benign witch doctor, Castaneda insists from the start on interjecting references to the dark side of Mexican folklore: don Juan can transform himself into a crow, for example, and in Carlos's duel with 'la Catalina' (reprised in his later struggle with doña Soledad) the apprentice is made to understand that the price of defeat is not just death but the loss of his soul.

The Teachings of Don Juan purported to reveal a secret native mystical tradition, which had kept something like Aldous Huxley's "Perennial Philosophy" alive through centuries of oppression. At least, that was how the book was widely interpreted. If don Juan was a sorcerer, we thought, it was along the lines of the Western magus, the master of illusion. All the baleful talk of *diableros*, or devil-worshippers, was no more than window dressing, an ironic commentary on the inability of the rational Westerner to acknowledge the moral superiority of Indian shamans.

In his sequels Castaneda continued to expand on metaphysical themes suggested in his first book. What most of us call reality, he said, is only one possible interpretation of the world. The sorcerer—or at any rate the sorcerer worthy of the label "man of knowledge"—has learned another interpretation that allows for wholly different perceptions, and thus for "a separate reality." Beyond both realities, however, is the mysterious *nagual*, the source of all possible sets of perceptions.

So far this could be simply an amplification of ethnomethodology, an exotic technique of social analysis Castaneda learned at UCLA. For the ethnomethodologist, anyone's view of the world is a function of how he is led to talk about the world, but even the ethnomethodologist remains a prisoner of his own conceptions. Don Juan, the imaginary sorcerer, is the one who has found a way to break out of the verbal prison. By calling the world a mere description he confirms the truth of ethnomethodology,

251

but by breaking through the conceptual walls he escapes the confines of social science and offers hope of salvation from the limits of human experience, eventually even from the limit of death itself.

It is this peculiar conception of salvation that reflects Castaneda's earlier occultist leanings. A basic theme of the Gnostic tradition that is the root of Western heterodoxy is that the human being is a scintilla of the eternal light trapped in an alien world of physical objects. Man, then, is a sleep-walker who can be awakened only by a messenger from the source of light that lies beyond the physical universe, beyond even the lesser God who created that universe. Once awakened, man can display the same type of power as God: he can manipulate the appearances of the physical world at will.

Often the Gnostic theology reversed the Jewish and Christian conception of God and Devil. The serpent in Eden, for instance, was interpreted as a messenger come to liberate Adam and Eve from the bondage in which they had been placed by a malevolent creator. Jesus too was a messenger, a superhuman entity who only seemingly took on human form to free mankind from the restraints of Mosaic law and the worship of an inferior divinity.

In Castaneda's later volumes don Juan's teaching closely parallels the Gnostic diabolism. Men are really luminous eggs condensed from the infinite possibilities of the *nagual*, but unless taught to *see* and to *dream*—to use their "second ring of power"—they live in a meaningless world of shadows. Sorcerers like don Juan and don Genaro are come from the *nagual* to guide a new cycle of apprentices in a magical tradition reaching back to the days of the Indian civilization that preceded the Aztecs. In a telling phrase their disciples refer to them as "Toltec devils." To anyone familiar with mesoamerican mythology this suggests the image of the Plumed Serpent, the warrior god Quetzalcoatl, whom the Spanish conquerors equated with Satan. And Quetzalcoatl, it should be remembered, was represented in Indian art as both benign and horribly malevolent.

Castaneda's *brujos* are not "evil," yet neither are they "good." Like Nietzsche's nihilist Zarathustra, they are beyond good and evil. Though don Juan is solicitous for Carlos's welfare, he nevertheless trains doña Soledad for the mission of assassinating him. Thus, the *brujo* cannot be judged by conventional morality any more than can Quetzalcoatl, the original Toltec warrior.

It is unlikely that such a sophisticated myth of the conjunction of opposites survives in rural folklore. Something like it appears in Antonin

Artaud's description of Tarahumara peyotism, but Artaud, who also had a strong background in Western occultism, was very much like Castaneda in his need to romanticize native magic as an antidote to Western rationality.

Castaneda may not have been particularly aware of mesoamerican mythology when first creating the character of don Juan. All he needed for that was ethnomethodology, which derived from European phenomenology and so was closely related to the ideas of the existentialists. In 1963, when Castaneda was into his graduate study, there appeared the second edition of Hans Jonas's *The Gnostic Religion* with an essay detailing the affinity between Gnosticism and the nihilism of the existentialists. Whether he read Jonas or not, Castaneda certainly did see the connection between phenomenology and an ultimately amoral outlook. If don Juan were to epitomize the illumined ethnomethodologist, he could well be the Gnostic diabolist disguised as a preliterate *brujo*.

Eventually, having exhausted the pose of the invincibly ignorant apprentice required by ethnomethodology, Castaneda could elaborate the idea of the *brujo* as Gnostic diabolist. Anthropologists, already disturbed by his fanciful approach to their field, may wince at his appropriation of the Toltecs, but we have to recognize that he has here undertaken a task fully as challenging as his initial treatment of the basic questions of knowledge and reality. Far from being merely an exercise in sensationalism or an invitation to Freudian speculation, *The Second Ring of Power* reopens the issue of how to talk about right and wrong when a literal immortality is at stake.

In later volumes Castaneda will have the opportunity to convert his myth of the *brujo* into a full theology. Already he has indicated that the *nagual* plays the same role as the Kingdom of Heaven of his Catholic background. What remains to be seen is whether, like the most radical of the Gnostics before him, Castaneda completes the reversal of values by taking Quetzalcoatl, a Mexican Abraxas, as the ultimate equation of good and evil and demanding that his followers subscribe to both evil and good in order to be saved.

If don Juan did not Exist,
It Would be Necessary to Invent Him

Something in myself doesn't let me believe what's taking place is real. So said don Juan's apprentice after a dozen years, and readers both lay and professional have so long and fully shared this skeptical quandary that by now the fabulous Carlos Castaneda rivals in wonder the mysterious world of don Juan.

My own experience of these writings began in 1969 when a friend asked what I thought of this new anthropologist. At my confession of ignorance, he gave me a copy of *The Teachings*, and thus I embarked like so many others on the legendary journey from a drab, ordinary bus station to a magnificent, nonordinary mountain top. Fascinated by the first book, I followed Carlos into "sorcery," shared his constant doubts and fears, and regretted the breaking off of his instruction.

When *A Separate Reality* appeared two years later I looked askance at the renewal of the apprenticeship, my credulity stretched by feats like don Genaro's ten-mile leap to the mountain tops and the wondrous filaments of light that sustained his body at the waterfall. Arguing none too convincingly that despite the first two volumes the true teachings had not required psychotropic plants, *Journey to Ixtlan* invited a certain cynicism, but by the end of the book I was left with the impression that Carlos was finally beginning to act like a "warrior."Rare published interviews with Castaneda bore out this progress, and *Tales of Power* brought the story to an apparent fitting conclusion in a poignant meeting of master and apprentice on a barren Mexican plateau. The young man—and he will always seem young!—fully initiated into the mysteries at last, bade his teacher farewell and jumped into the abyss. The skepticism prompted by this startling symbolic commencement gave way quickly to an obscure nostalgia, as I realized that along with Carlos and no doubt with most readers I, too, had been initiated, vicariously. Unwittingly I had been drawn deep into that compelling sequence of events reaching back to the archetypal meeting in 1960, punctuated en route by Carlos's hesitations, losses of nerve, and maddening stupidities as well as by his occasional insights and triumphs. Little wonder that each time I opened another of his books half of me knew what to expect while the other half stood ready to be permanently puzzled. Having failed to become an outright cynic, I was able to get back each time into don Juan's world, with its familiar landscape, characters, and language, all of which combined on each occasion to bewitch the sympathetic reader, eliciting his participation and witness. In short, as in religious myths, don Juan's way was a way of enchantment—which helps explain the attraction of Castaneda's writings whatever one may think of their authenticity. Though I do not regard the question of authenticity as unimportant, nor even hold that the teachings should escape structural analysis, the fact remains that the story is charming, and its resemblance to traditional myths offers a likely explanation of its charm.

Portraying a long-developing friendship between a pre-literate magician and an arrogant academic and dramatically contrasting the spiritual wealth of the former with the pedantic poverty of the latter, Castaneda produces a modern equivalent of a myth.

Myths are stories told by traditional religious peoples to make sense of their existence, sacred narratives recounting events in the past that give clues to life in the present. Implicitly, myths pose philosophical questions, assert social values, establish categories of meaning, and integrate past with present while offering hope for the future. A cycle of myths outlines a cosmos, a coherent view of the world. Myths are true—not as history is true when substantiated by evidence—but as any story is true that fits the expectations and understandings of the listener. Although we westerners have generally discarded universally-accepted myths to guide our lives and explain our experiences, we have not, I think, lost our longing for such stories and for the community felt by those who tell and hear them.

Despite our modernity we yearn to inhabit, albeit for a passing moment, a world where things fit together, where good and evil, strong and weak, male and female, virtue and vice, age and youth are clearly drawn, and where their interactions obey time-honored rules. At some point, dimly perceived, there is a shift in such a world from the story being in us to our being in the story, and this, I think, is the critical difference between myth and non-myth. In myth, we are involved.

Castaneda's quintet can be understood as an extended myth cycle: an epic account of a dramatic confrontation between the wisdom of don Juan's "primitive" age and the foolishness of Carlos's modernist youth. Their philosophic import reaches us through many appealing encounters between the venerable holy man and the naïve seeker, don Juan continually dissuading Carlos from the academic study of "medicinal" plants, continually urging his commitment to a quest for transcendent knowledge.

The teachings are conveyed by a series of stereotyped incidents, each conforming roughly to the following sequence of events: Carlos enters the scene and meets the other character(s). He has a premonition that something important is about to happen. He is apprehensive, usually feeling some physical discomfort. He is reassured—often, as it later turns out, by some trick. The test or challenge comes swiftly, unexpectedly. Carlos panics and all seems lost. Surprisingly, however, he draws on unsuspected personal resources to complete the test successfully. Exhausted by his victory, he rests. He gains new strength. Finally, the meaning of the experience is explained to him, originally by don Juan, later by others. Thus by means of an illogical, absurd, or nonsensical exercise the disciple (and along with him the reader) has broken through intellectual limitations to gain a sudden glimpse of experiential knowledge. The perennial struggle between reason and feeling, certitude and doubt, spiritual and material comes not abstractly but in a dynamic drama of interpersonal exchange.

Here are both the strength and the weakness of Castaneda's writings. On the one hand, the narrator's active, participatory role allows us to identify readily with his fears, skepticism, triumphs, and joys: a possibility central to all good stories. At the same time, however, because they do not happen directly to us, Carlos's extraordinary adventures remain on the level of plausibility at best, delusion at worst, depending on one's judgment of the account.

Reading these books one would do well to keep in mind the formula with which traditional Sudanese story-telling begins: "I'm going to tell a story," the narrator proclaims. "Right!" the audience rejoins. "It's a lie," he warns. "Right!" comes the reply. "But not everything in it is false," he asserts. "Right!" echo the listeners.

This mixture of truth and exaggeration, of precision and distortion, which characterizes myth, is similarly a prominent feature of Castaneda's writings. Myths express truths of human life through larger-than-life events, their truth very much like that of a caricaturist's drawing. The test of a good caricature is how much one feels the artist has caught the mood of his subject by exaggerating details of countenance or expression. Recognizing the truth of a myth is like recognizing the truth of a caricature: despite our awareness of the obvious distortions, we appreciate a correspondence between the understanding expressed in the caricature and our own view of things. Like myths and caricatures, Castaneda's writings speak to our intuitions.

Yet this accounts for only part of their appeal. Another factor is our involvement in the story. Originally all myths were stories told, and don Juan's story shares the innate power of all story-telling. "Once upon a time" is a door through which the listener or the reader or recently the film-goer gains access to another world, where ordinary conventions and distinctions do not always apply and where truths about life are told by larger-than-life events in which one feels involved. This element of enchantment, outstanding in oral narratives, is no less apparent in the don Juan story, as one's own reactions may be called to witness. Opening each volume we may feel a certain skepticism or even cynicism, but as the teller warms to his task such feelings soon take second place. Quickly the familiar contours of don Juan's world emerge: the provocative (if barely described) Mexican landscape, the youthful anthropologist in search of further data, the hint of strange adventures to come. The characters stand again before us: don Juan, the curious mixture of ignorant peasant and powerful wizard, Carlos, the perpetual scribbler and scared rabbit. Tensions mount gradually, are broken suddenly. Tests are passed. Experience is gained. Before long the reader has forgotten himself altogether, engrossed in the tale like any listener to a good story. At the conclusion self-consciousness returns, the spell is broken. One may even scoff with embarrassment at having been taken in. Yet the potential for enchantment, for assenting to the truth of what is told despite the distortions and exaggerations, has temporarily prevailed. Such enchantment is a universal characteristic of myth-telling and a prominent feature of good story-telling, and whatever else he may be, Carlos Castaneda is a good teller of stories.

He also claims to have written ethnography, which claim appears to have been his academic undoing. Had he admitted producing a modern myth most of the complaints against him would never have seen print. Yet myth-makers are not so direct. Their productions are in soft focus, deliberately ambiguous, tantalizingly uncertain. Repeatedly they elude our attempts to peek behind the curtain, to find out what *really* happened. In the realm of myth the quest for historical don Juans or even Castanedas has no place. The reader who has willingly entered the mythic world of don Juan remains unimpressed by attacks on the authenticity of Castaneda's fieldwork or the propriety of his academic career, however correct such critiques may be in the realm of scholarship or science.

Entering don Juan's world is like visiting C. S. Lewis's Narnia, Tolkien's Middle-earth, or even Durrell's Near East. Where mythic truth is established and sustained through evocative, compelling stories, the enchanted reader turns away from questions of objective or ordinary truth. A pervasive, irresistible desire for myth compels a large group of readers to declare that don Juan exists or that if he does not exist he ought to. Scholarly criticism, however convincing to skeptics, has little power to alter such deeply felt subscription. For my part, I admit that after ten years, notwithstanding my rejection of its literal truth, the don Juan legend appeals to me strongly still.

Learning by Not-Doing:
An Uncanny Curriculum

"The reason Castaneda's books are so widely used in beginning anthropology courses," Eugene Anderson explained, "is that the students are reading them anyway, and will not read more serious tomes with equal enthusiasm. . . . Students raised on TV spectaculars and science fiction novels expect anthropological studies to read the same way." "The fact that 'students are reading them anyway,' " Marcello Truzzi countered, "should be . . . a major reason for *not* assigning Castaneda's books in the classroom."

Neither Professor Anderson nor Professor Truzzi would assign Castaneda's books in the classroom, but both recognize the well known production trade-off in the education factory, from which supplier Castaneda and his publishers have profited. The typical young person growing up in college simply because that is where members of his social class grow up, is likely to find most intellectual disciplines dull and forbidding, uninteresting and excessively laborious. Teachers making a living as resource persons for these non-scholars may calculate a balance of instruction and entertainment that produces at best half-taught at worst mistaught students, who then joyfully compliment the teacher on a fun course. The trade-off is briefly exemplified in two introductory anthropology textbooks.

The 1971 edition of *Exploring the Ways of Mankind* contained three pages from *The Teachings of Don Juan* reproduced under the heading, "A Yaqui Man of Knowledge." Pursuing his theme that education is an instrument for transmitting culture from one generation to the next, the textbook author introduced don Juan as a shaman who had led his apprentice down "the road of knowledge . . . of the Yaqui Indians." The characterization fitted nicely into the scheme of the textbook but grossly misrepresented don Juan, who was not a shaman and whose teachings bore no resemblance to a Yaqui way of knowledge. While absorbing this tendentious introduction, the diligent student would also get the impression that: 1) Castaneda had done actual fieldwork, 2) don Juan was an actual person, 3) don Juan was a curer, 4) a *brujo* is the same thing as a shaman. The best one can say about the chapter is that it disappeared from the 1977 edition. In this case, slighting validity to increase reader interest proved a bad trade-off for both student and teacher.

A more complex case is furnished by some passages in a book of readings titled *Other Fields, Other Grasshoppers*, published in 1977. Hoping to provide a book "that will actively stimulate beginning students to a further interest in anthropology," the anthologist urges students to read (along with other, authentic volumes) *Wizard of the Upper Amazon* and all of Castaneda's tetralogy. Under the heading, "Listen to the Lizards," he reproduces ten pages of *The Teachings*, containing don Juan's instructions for sewing lizards' eyelids (with tools Hans Sebald found utterly impractical). As in the previous example, the text misrepresents Castaneda's works as ethnography, which supposedly conveys "the Yaqui view of reality" or "how the Yaqui themselves understand knowledge." The editor hedges this blether by adding: "Curiously, they tell us little about Yaqui Indian culture as such." Some years of editing have made me very suspicious of the inconspicuous phrase "as such," which here suggests to the naïve reader that Castaneda's books do tell us about Yaqui culture in some indirect, unspecified way (thus excusing the ethnic misrepresentation) though not in the direct way one would expect (thus rendering vague lip service to authoritative findings that Castaneda's books tell us nothing about Yaqui culture at all). The editor then recommends six books that tell us about Yaqui culture; ironically, four of them are by Spicer and Kelley, two authorities who said don Juan's teachings contradicted what was known of Yaqui ways. This intricate obfuscation is hardly a service to the student.

Offering a loose but conventional definition of the emic approach (as a way of recognizing "the native's point of view rather than the anthropologist's"), *Grasshoppers* relays Castaneda's impudent claim to emic reporting. The editor goes on to point out that emicists take care to learn the native language, without pointing out that Castaneda neither learned Yaqui terms nor reported Spanish terms for the important concepts in don Juan's teachings. Students who swallow this editor's assertion that *The Teachings* is "an extreme example" of the emic approach will get quite a shock if they later encounter emics in linguistics classes.

Despite his endorsement of Carlos's fieldwork, the editor acknowledges "a considerable controversy" over the authenticity of the tetralogy. "Whether the account is completely authentic or not," he says, "it still represents one of the most comprehensive and convincing descriptions we have of a non-Western theory of knowledge." "But just how much of this 'philosophy' is . . . Castaneda . . . regurgitating the Book of Revelations is hard to say," a quite unconvinced Edmund Leach had written. Apparently unfamiliar with the field of fiction, the editor foolishly declares that such a high degree of verisimilitude could not be a product of writing skill alone. He fatuously compares Castaneda with Laura Bohannan (Elenore Bowen), as if there were some formal difficulty in distinguishing fiction masquerading as field reports from self-proclaimed novels based on authentic fieldwork.

Meanwhile, the student is having his own difficulties distinguishing educational text from special pleading. In a rather disingenuous defense of the don Juan books, the editor limits the evidence against them to the relatively unimportant lack of biographies of don Juan and Castaneda, completely ignoring the much more telling internal inconsistency of the tale. He puts the burden of proof on the community of scholars by saying the books should not be dismissed as anthropology until the facts are known, and then says it would be unethical to make the facts known because it would destroy don Juan's privacy. This Catch-22 conceals from the student Castaneda's unprofessional refusal to furnish the supporting evidence that would *not* have destroyed don Juan's privacy.

Textbooks can be made interesting without pandering to fads. As a not very well read latecomer to anthropology, I have nevertheless seen dozens of passages in legitimate anthropology books more inspiring than exploring the ways of an imaginary mystical magician or listening to his spuriously stitched lizards. Some of the best were imitated by Castaneda. Why not read the originals? The year of the *Grasshoppers* also brought *The Eye of the Flute*, Chumash traditions related by Fernando Librado Kitsepawit, of whom Eugene Anderson said: "Librado was one of the great informants of all time, and his vision of the world revealed here should make Castaneda's 'don Juan' blush for shame." An editor who knew enough to recommend Jane Holden Kelley's *Yaqui Life* should have known enough not to reproduce Carlos Castaneda's Yaquiless way of not-doing anthropology.

All this is not to say don Juan should never be allowed to show his face in anthropology classes. Teachers who know what they are doing can get a good day's work out of the old leprechaun. Thomas R. Moore tells how he did it at Adelphi University:

> *The Teachings* was quite useful for introductory courses in cultural anthropology, not as a scientific exposition of shamanism but to stimulate thinking and provoke questions about the possibilities of other kinds of consciousness. Some of the students questioned the legitimacy of Castaneda's work, which led to a lot

of productive discussion of what anthropology is, should be, or might become. Students tend to be turned off by positivistic approaches, and alternatives can be helpful.

Nor should don Juan be ruled out of textbooks. In its own way, *The Don Juan Papers* is a text-casebook on social science and society undergoing a twenty-year test by Trickster. Castaneda, one sees, is neither scientist nor enemy of science, neither educator nor destroyer of education, but rather a nonordinary ally of scientists and educators, many of whom have been spun away into strange places while trying to wrestle him to the ground. My purpose is to pin him down just long enough to take his scientific and educational powers, so that I can distribute them among the people, like the nourishing bits of Trickster's penis after it was chewed up by Chipmunk. Meanwhile, some wreckage left by Trickster's passage is still to be surveyed.

Cliffs Notes on Castaneda suffer from faulty scholarship (*Ixtlan* said to deal with peyote; the word *nahuatl* said to mean peyote), poor diction ("attributed to be"), sloppy editing ("absorbtion"), credulous reading, and superficial analysis. *Cliffs* credits Harold Garfinkel, said to be "a UCLA Anthropology professor," with encouraging Carlos's fieldwork but—not surprisingly—does not recognize him as the fountainhead of Castaneda's ethnomethodallegory. "Castaneda's works," says *Cliffs*, "presents [sic] to the reader a philosophy seldom recorded in Western literature."

Such ill-informed wonder was decried by Colin MacInnes, who wrote: "Wisdom is probably to be found inside his own culture by anyone born into one of the great civilizations of the world. Thus Europeans [possessing] a knowledge of what their sages, artists, and scientists have revealed, would find in their own history most answers to the mysteries that perplex them." S. T. Crump thought it a comment on our times that most readers to whom the mystical don Juan appeals "will be unaware of any mystical element in their own cultural tradition: how many of them will have heard, for instance, of St Teresa of Avila?"

Sheldon Weeks, of the Educational Research Unit at the University of Papua New Guinea, could see no mystical purposes at all in don Juan's teachings and chided Carlos-Apprentice for failing to comprehend what must be the true goals of don Juan's sorcery: divination and curing. Weeks recommended reading the volumes "*only* for the voice of don Juan." Next thing you know, we'll see a red-letter edition.

The English Journal listed *Journey to Ixtlan* among the books most often chosen by high school juniors and seniors and commended it as an antidote to fake Indian books. American studies teacher Christopher Vecsey countered: "It is unfortunate that the recent hunger for American Indian religious perspectives has received Castaneda's ersatz chronicles and neglected such delights as *A Yaqui Life*."

One of Castaneda's better satires portrays the ethnocentric social scientist imposing inappropriate academic theories on native cultures. Sections Two and Three of *A Separate Reality* describe Carlos's futile attempt to make sense of peyote meetings in terms of a theory of covert cueing. With characteristic disdain, don Juan warns Carlos that the whole idea of cueing is crazy, a complete waste of time when one has the privilege of confronting Mescalito. Persisting in his folly, Carlos attends the meeting but sees no evidence of cueing. Whether one takes the story as a satire or as a factual account, the cueing theory comes off badly. Nevertheless, quite as if they were characters in Castaneda's tale, Frank Lutz and Margaret Ramsey, of the Pennsylvania State University College of Education, adduce Carlos's cueing fiasco *in support of* their own theory of nondirective cues as ritualistic indicators in educational organizations. "It is not clear," they insist, "whether or not don Juan realizes at an overt level that he is cueing or if he simply refuses to verbalize a nonverbal system. . . . As an anthropologist, Castaneda knows that there is a cueing system among Yaqui sorcerers. We believe it true for all organizations, technical and pretechnical." But what if don Juan was practicing not-cueing?

Ronald D. Cohen, a professor of curriculum and instruction at the University of Wisconsin, thought Castaneda's trilogy could be related to deschooling, to alternative schools, to varieties of consciousness, and to styles of learning. Defying reduction to standardized units of pupil/teacher interaction, the lessons of don Juan included intuitive gambits and moments of impulse and play. They exhibited mutual trust between teacher and pupil as well as a teacher's concern for the pupil, understanding of the complexity of the learning task at hand, and awareness that the pupil must give in fully to the teachings.

> Schooling [Cohen said] exists within a social milieu. . . . Thoughtful reading of Castaneda's trilogy raises numerous questions about this social matrix. For example, how does the don Juan/Castaneda relationship vary from what happens in a classroom setting? What contemporary methods of schooling come closest to the spirit of the don Juan/Castaneda encounter? How

might the presence of Castaneda's friends influence his reactions to the teachings of don Juan? Can the don Juan/Castaneda relationship occur only in a one-to-one setting? And, given an eccentric world view such as don Juan's, what pressures might restrain him in an institutional setting? One might also ask how parents might bring influence to bear on don Juan without direct confrontation. In what way does don Juan's teaching style differ from presentational modes of many classrooms? Can don Juan be considered a responsible teacher with the best interests of his students at heart?

Though Professor Cohen stopped short of PTA meetings, I believe an on-going process of sharing perspectives with parents and teachers would provide a unique reference point for developing non-discursive guidelines and breaking through barriers of rational modes to achieve new levels of impeccability.

Don Juan: *El mundo no se nos viene encima directamente. La descripción siempre está en el medio. Siempre estamos a un paso de distancia. Siempre andamos un salto atrás.*

Translator (Dr Ryle): Don Juan says our descriptions of the world condemn us to eternal penultimacy. We never succeed in jumping onto the shadow of our own heads, yet we are never more than one jump behind.

Chairperson (Mrs Petrullo): Is there another question?

Parent: I'd like to ask him why my Johnny can't read.

Translator (after conferring with the speaker): Don Juan says he himself did not learn to read until Carlos lent him a copy of Edmund Husserl's *Ideas*. The book happened to be in English, so don Juan first learned to read English, though he speaks only Spanish, Yaqui, Yuma, Mazatec, and Toltec. Don Juan says there is more to learning than reading. There is, for example, not-reading, which don Juan practiced for 71 years with great benefit to himself and eventually, through Carlos, to the world. Don Juan says there is no point getting upset about your Johnny. He is just practicing not-reading.

Parent: Thank you.

Chairperson: If there are no more questions the meeting will adjourn to the ramada area, where we are invited to sample Mrs Thornapple's non-alcoholic punch and taste the rattlesnacks prepared by don Juan.

Carl R. V. Brown, author of the next chapter, is Director of the Writing Program at Trinity College, Hartford. His dissertation in the theory and practice of education, completed at Stanford in 1977, explores the usefulness of Castaneda's work in the English curriculum and presents a phenomenological account of reading *Journey to Ixtlan*, an account "designed to reveal something of the lived quality of the reading experience." Two passages will illustrate the method:

> Chapter Five is entitled "Assuming Responsibility." I am coming to be a little irritated with one aspect of don Juan's character. He seems to break into laughter every time Carlos says something. I don't always understand why this hilarious laughter is appropriate. I am also aware at this point of the intentionally cumulative effect of don Juan's lessons, something I didn't notice on the first reading. . . .

> Chapter Nine is titled "The Last Battle on Earth." Don Juan begins to talk cryptically and rather mystically about powers that guide our lives and our deaths. I am beguiled by the idea of powers I do not know, and want to inquire further. I want to be in Carlos's place, next to don Juan, asking about those powers. Egoistically, I feel something I should have is lacking in me. I feel I should be able to acquire it if only I knew the right teacher, the right master, the right way. . . .

Besides using the text to demonstrate this method of phenomenological analysis, Brown suggests ways of using the books in English classes to elicit discussion of values, cultural democracy, and pluralism.

The idea that Castaneda's books would be used in English classes struck me as black humor when I first heard it. Imagining myself an English teacher, I thought of offering my students such Castanedian gems as:

> A masterful feat
> A mountain of glass shreds
> That statement had clinched me
> I recuperated my balance
> I wanted to adapt a fighting position
> Lack of image conversion entailed a double perception
> The art of the teacher was to deviate the apprentice's attention

Don Juan placed each rock about a foot apart in two crevices
In a forest of thick trees

I wrote to Carl Brown asking why an English teacher would use books by
a barbarous, ungrammatical writer whose characters are shallow, artificial, and isolated from social context. He answered:

> Fiction is a special form of discourse where the rules of standard
> written English may or may not be adhered to. I agree Cas-
> taneda is no James Joyce, but bad grammar is not the reason.
> Shallowness, artificiality, and lack of social context are greater
> faults, but here again, satire and allegory often rely on caricature
> to make their points. Whether Castaneda's allegories deserve the
> status of literature is just the kind of question students of litera-
> ture should learn much from answering.

Given such a reasonable reply I shall complain no further about Brown's
classroom use of the don Juan books, though in his place I should assign
quite different reading: *Animal Farm* or *The Circus of Dr. Lao* for allegory, *Till We Have Faces* for myth, Cabeza de Vaca for lyrical wandering
through deserts of magic and mystery:

> They answered . . . that we could not possibly be Christians. For
> we appeared out of sunrise, they out of sunset; we cured the
> sick, while they killed even the healthy; we went naked and
> barefoot, while they wore clothes, and rode horseback and stuck
> people with lances; we asked for nothing and gave away all we
> were given, while they never gave anybody anything and had
> no other aim than to steal.

> In facing these marauders I was compelled to face the Spanish
> gentleman I myself had been eight years before. It was not easy
> to think of it. Andrés and Alonso agreed that it was not easy.
> What, your Majesty, is so melancholy as to confront one's
> former unthinking and unfeeling self?

What I miss most in Carlos Castaneda's metaphysical fairy tales is
good writing. The fact that he got so far without any style at all pays
left-handed tribute to his unquestionable skill in narrative manipulation
of academic abstractions. The power of his writing is felt by the academic

reader dimly apprehending those ideas behind the story, or when time-less maxims pop out of don Juan's pseudo-Indian mouth to inspire read-ers who have never seen the originals. Because of this limited but noteworthy achievement, I think Castaneda's not-writing deserves a place *in* literature though it is *not* literature. As Carl Brown teaches his English classes, I'm sure he will keep the distinction in mind.

Reading *Journey to Ixtlan*

Chapter 20 is entitled "Journey to Ixtlan." I am enchanted with don Genaro's story of his battle with his ally, how don Genaro first took his path on the way to Ixtlan, a journey which has no end and no rest. Ixtlan, therefore, is a symbol for the sorcerer's quest—the journey. I am reminded of the cover of the book, which I now see with more insight as a depiction of that lonely path to Ixtlan—a place that does not exist except in the surreal landscape of a sorcerer's mind, the place he is always travelling to. It is a lonely road where everyday people become only phantoms that hope to draw the sorcerer away from his proper course. I find this section of the book poetic, and it raises melancholy feelings in me. I am touched by the simple metaphorical explanation of the sorcerer's journey as alone, never ending, and severe. I think these feelings are raised in me because I associate that journey with the journey I am taking in my own life—whatever that might be—which at times also seems severe and lonely and never-ending—and I am brought to feel that in a very profound way in this last section of the book.

Accepting a sorcerer's way of life means blotting out all previous connections with the old life. At this point, I find myself drawn back from the sorcerer's view of the world, in however small a degree, because while this world seems to have its problems and its deficiencies, it is the only one I know, and the thought of giving it up for a journey alone—no matter how beneficial in the end—is too disturbing. Likewise Carlos doesn't feel that he is capable of taking up fully the way of the sorcerer because of his dependence upon the world that he has known. I find myself being more contemplative now, and I notice that as I let the idea of the journey to Ixtlan sink in, there is commonly a sense that one does leave things behind, one does change in essential ways through contacts with very important or powerful things or people in the "real" world. The sorcerer's change in leaving all behind as he captures his ally is paralleled in my own life where important experiences—being in the service, great books, education, people—have changed my world, and I know that the world is wholly different for me now than it was ten years ago. There is a nostalgic truth to the metaphorical idea of the journey to Ixtlan, that we can change and do change in essential ways. Perhaps that change is so slow that we are only brought to the nostalgic truth of what we left behind upon some remembered reflection of it. Nevertheless, at the instance of my recalling certain events in my past I do feel nostalgia for some people I have met who I may never see again—people whom I have loved and have since passed away, for example. And, too, there are people I have simply left behind (as they have left me behind). It all seems to work as an explanation for—on a metaphorical level—what happens to all of us as our life changes, as our views of the world change.

The book ends wonderfully for me on a bitter-sweet nostalgic note, and the feeling that I have at the end of it all is one of emotional uplifting, of an encounter that has left me more sensitive and insightful. I want to lay the book down and just let that feeling wash over me, concentrate on it. It is one of the fine things in life to have been touched by experience—whether it be of a work of art or something else—to be moved to that kind of heightened sensitivity that I now feel and that I wish were possible for a more extended time.

RdeM

Because his father went south in 1944 to get work, Juan Bruce-Novoa was born by mistake in Costa Rica, but soon the family returned to Mexico City, emigrated to San Antonio, and settled in Denver, where Juan grew up. Playing in a rock band put him through Denver's Regis College. At the University of Colorado he earned an M.A. in Spanish literature and a Ph.D. in Mexican literature. Since 1974 he has been a professor in the Department of Spanish and Portuguese at Yale.

"Castaneda has plagued me for years," Bruce-Novoa said. "My last encounter was at the University of Southern California. A dark, smiling man kept insisting I had to include Castaneda in my list of Chicano authors. He wouldn't drop the subject. I told him Castaneda was a Peruvian. He said, 'Castaneda is a Chicano, because Chicano means all Third World people.' I suppose if you think don Juan is a Yaqui, Chicano can mean all Third World people, but this man was a professor from the University of California. When I asked if he were a Chicano too, he said, 'Of course, since I am a beautiful person.' No wonder Castaneda has such a following out there. When everything is bound up in one luminous web, there can't be much difference between one point on the web and another. Perhaps we should abolish the divisions of knowledge and just study the teachings of don Juan."

Perverse innocence, one might call it—which, by coincidence, is the title of Bruce-Novoa's 1977 book of poetry: *Inocencia Perversa/Perverse Innocence*.

Chicanos in the Web of Spider Trickster

Though Carlos Castaneda said he was born in Brazil, and claimed the Portuguese name Aranha, many took him to be a Chicano. Of course, that was before *Time* said he was a Peruvian, whose grandmother's name was Novoa. This could get pretty complicated. Let me simplify it a little by saying Castaneda and I are not related: I am a Chicano, he is not. Nevertheless, I am writing about him because of his appeal to Chicanos and his minor but visible influence on Chicano literature.

As the Chicano Movement was emerging, the don Juan books began to appear. Naturally, their panegyric to visionary plants affected young Chicanos no less than other members of the drug culture, but more importantly they offered an alternative not only to spiritual exhaustion in the West but also to compensatory Eastern mysticism rushing in to fill the vacuum. Don Juan's spiritual power could overcome the establishment; his ancient knowledge could replace it with something better. His path with heart could lead Chicanos out of gringo servitude without losing them in the maze of mystical fads practiced by the alienated children of the oppressors.

While Black America was finding its roots in African traditions, Chicanos were seeking authenticity as Mexican mestizos, hybrid Spanish-Indians. The mestizo ikon, however, was firmly in the hands of a Mexican establishment that cared no more than did the gringo establishment for Chicanos in the United States. Something was needed to symbolize our life north of the border without obscuring our Mexican-Amerindian essence. Don Juan promised to do that.

Like the Yaqui Indians, supposedly his people, don Juan lived on both sides of the border, calling both his home. Don Juan's friend Genaro would lead us always toward, though never to, Ixtlán, a name in which Chicano nationalists could hear the echo of their lost Aztec Paradise, Aztlán. As Carlos's Spanish fieldnotes had become Castaneda's English text, so many Chicanos had begun life speaking Spanish and made the transition to English. Like them, Carlos was an Americanized Hispanic who turned to Mexico for intuitive truth, struggling with little confidence to rid his "agringado" mind of constricting rationalism. As the typical early Chicano activist would feign knowledge of his Mexican heritage, so Carlos in the famous bus station pretended to be an expert on peyote, each wishing to learn what he pretended to know already, each wishing to be accepted by the one who already knew.

Castaneda's strange adventure at UCLA grotesquely mirrors the Chicano academic career: a sense of one's inadequacy to the task; a feeling of being despised, mistreated, and overworked; recourse to a field where one could be both investigator and informant; and the long, painful production of a dissertation demanding inordinate labor and unbending intent. Like Castaneda, though for rather different reasons, many Chicano academics are now trapped in their own creation, possessing degrees and boasting publications but suffering the resentment of academic peers, erosion of faith among followers, and the skepticism of a new generation. One thing, regrettably, is quite different: no Chicano academic has become a millionaire.

Castaneda has tapped some Chicano writers lightly, penetrated others deeply. One at least, a Yaqui Indian, has grabbed and wrestled him to the ground. Lorna Dee Cervantes, author of "Meeting Mescalito at Oak Hill Cemetery," is not much influenced by Castaneda, though she told me he had reaffirmed her sense of a world unified by a web of invisible interconnections. In contrast, Alurista, poet laureate of Chicano Aztlán-mysticism, apparently planned four books to illustrate, respectively: fear, clarity, power, and old age, the enemies one meets on don Juan's path to knowledge. Alurista writes of cosmic harmony, paths with heart, willing one's being, facing fears, overcoming threatening monsters, turning menacing natural forces into allies, and seeing realities in a new way. At two points he strays from don Juan's path. Despite Castaneda's playing with the Aztec terms *nagual* and *tonal* and dropping Toltecs-ex-machina into *Second Ring of Power*, don Juan utterly ignores pre-Columbian *cultures*, whereas Alurista interlocks his work with Nahuatl and Mayan thought. His title *Floricanto* evokes the poetry-philosophy of the Nahuatl poet-priests. While don Juan doesn't give a fig for any social utility of his knowledge, Alurista hopes to regenerate Chicano barrio society through a synthesis of Juanism and pre-Columbian high culture.

Rudolfo Anaya's aged, mysterious *curandera*, Ultima, shares much with don Juan. Seven-year-old Antonio, her apprentice, is about as naive as the 35-year-old Carlos, but more sensible and certainly more believable. Ultima doesn't use drugs in front of Antonio, but she does carry a bag of herbs that can cure wounds overnight. She confides in an owl familiar, can remove curses and kill rivals by magic, and reads nature like a secret text. She teaches Antonio to see the harmonious unity behind the chaos of the world. Antonio learns to use and talk to plants and to recognize the earthly gods. As with Carlos, however, his crowning achievement is not to practice magic but to mediate between an inaccessible wise one and an uninitiated reader. Antonio-Apprentice is an obvious equivalent of Carlos-Apprentice, while Antonio-Narrator serves the same function as Carlos-Narrator, in stories respectively written by Anaya and Castaneda.

Though *Bless Me, Ultima* was not published until 1972, the writing mainly coincided with Castaneda's writing of *The Teachings*. Anaya denies any influence from Castaneda, and we have no reason to question his denial. Most of the similarities come plausibly from a common source: Hispanic Amerindian shamanism. Nevertheless, Anaya may have influenced Castaneda. Ultima's honorific title La Grande (the great one) may well have inspired Elena's mocking nickname La Gorda (Fatso) in *Second Ring*, Castaneda thereby sending a sardonic salute to fellow novelist Anaya.

If the novelist's true homeland is his novel, Castaneda and Anaya may both exist today by virtue of their published texts and at the pleasure of teachers visible only to them. Just as Castaneda has told several interviewers about his conversations with don Juan, so Anaya told me Ultima had appeared to him and dictated changes in the novel. Outweighing this and other similarities is the fact that Castaneda draws capriciously and unreliably from written texts about cultures foreign to him, while Anaya draws earnestly and accurately from oral traditions of his own land and people.

Miguel Méndez is a Yaqui Indian, whose first short story was published in 1969. Méndez used more Yaqui words in those 14 pages than Castaneda used in 1400. A master named Tata Casehua begins by teaching his Yaqui apprentice to see and hear the desert; he concludes by pitting the boy against a horrible monster; resisting the monster, the boy wins the title of son to Casehua; fulfilled, the master disappears into the sand. In miniature, the story prefigures the don Juan books. A suspicion that some readers might think the genuine Yaqui had copied the bogus Yaqui could well have infuriated Méndez—and apparently it did.

In his long epic poem, "Los Criaderos Humanos," Méndez conjures up a hideous character who constantly assumes animal shapes. This sinister metamorph labors to distract the nameless narrator-protagonist from his cosmic purpose and search for origins. Others warn that the troublemaker is a traitor, who sells his own mother. The narrator ponders the puzzle why people would follow this beast when they know him to be a liar. Only when we learn that he is an arachnid, or spider, does the monster's identity come clear. Like don Juan's luminous beings, the spiderman has an aura of luminous fibers, from which he weaves intriguing webs, or suspends himself as don Genaro did at the waterfall. But Méndez is after bigger game than the lovable Genaro. *Aranha*, the Portuguese pseudonym claimed by Castaneda, means spider; in Spanish it sounds the same: *araña*. The venomous spiderman stands for Castaneda, whom Méndez attacks as a mercenary false prophet, a liar who would sell his own mother.

Araña makes the connection well enough, but Castaneda, or possibly fate, provides a further link. Though Castaneda's authentic paternal family name was neither Castañeda (his maternal family name) nor Araña (a name rare among Spanish-speakers), it *was* Arana. *Arana* means trick. Aranha-Arana is Spider-Trick! January 1960, when Castaneda gave the name Aranha on his marriage license, was rather early for him to have read about the Spider-Trickster of the Sioux and Ashanti tribes, so the correspondence may be an accident that achieves the perfection of art. Either way it fits beautifully into Méndez's indictment. As *Aranha* hides *Arana*, so the intriguing surface of Castaneda's story hides fraudulent, perverted misknowledge, not to be taken lightly but to be firmly rejected. Méndez's intricate play of words and allusions excoriates the falsifier of Yaqui knowledge. Still, the desecrater of Yaquiness proves a worthy opponent. If imitation is the sincerest of flattery, insult runs it a close second. Méndez cares enough about Castaneda's crimes to memorialize them in a subtle pattern of invective which itself manifests the craft of the trickster, one who can teach while hiding.

Carlos Castaneda created an alternative to the reality imposed on him by life first in a Hispanic, then in an Anglo culture. This bold project appeals to Chicanos, who would impose their own multicultural synthesis on the established order in the United States, an order many perceive as chaos. I have shown a few interactions between Castaneda and Chicanos, but there may be more. Other literary moths may struggle in Castaneda's web like the adoring Alurista, or tear it flying through like the angry Méndez. If Arana's tricks help a few of these Chicano writers become visible to the gringos, will Castaneda laugh? I'll bet you a "birria" he's laughing right now—as he reads this sentence.

RdeM

Yaqui Indians are not the only faction offended by the don Juan books. Lately women have taken umbrage. I don't mean feminists particularly, but any women who loved Carlos when he lived among men and were then repelled by his way of living with women. The trouble started in *Second Ring of Power*. Responding to chronic complaints there were no women in his books (not counting, of course, the unapproachable Catalina) Castaneda brought on a sudden swarm of household females and took up several overtly feminist themes: androgyny, women's consciousness, male chauvinism, burdens of child care, liberation from femininity. *Second Ring's* leading lady, La Gorda, tells Carlos she has a lot of maleness in her while he has a lot of femaleness in him. The four sisters are way ahead of Carlos in magical techniques and understanding. Trying to make a harem of them, Pablito comes a cropper. La Gorda lectures Carlos about the disadvantages of parenthood. Her handsome, unseductive body goes without corsets, tampons, or perfume. Nevertheless, despite all this catering to the Weibgeist, the women apprentices remain under the departed don Juan's magical domination and even hail the clumsy Carlos as his successor. Don Juan, we are told, had shrunk the 220-pound spiritual weakling Elena into the 115-pound executive witch La Gorda by imprisoning and starving her for days in a hole in the ground; he tamed the lustful, rebellious Lidia by setting an imaginary chicken to running round inside her blouse; he inflated Soledad like a balloon until wrong-thinking blew out of all her orifices; he punished Josefina by causing her to clench an angry fist on a razor edge. Only Rosa had been immediately submissive, without needing to be tricked or forced.

Carlos's out-of-body trips begin as ways of clobbering the womenfolk or escaping their erotic demands. The women get even by ostentatiously gifting him with a bundle of menstruation rags. Only when embraces are understood at last as a sexless technique for flying to the other world is closeness no longer too frightening or too uncomfortable for a man to bear. At no time was it tender. Thus rejected by Carlos-Misogynist, women readers have taken a harder look at Castaneda-Author, and some have voiced objections they might never have got round to if Castaneda as well as Carlos had jumped off that cliff in the spring of narrative-1974.

Jean W. Cox is a freelance writer with a college major in philosophy and literature. Her 1976 article in *Southwest Review* emphasized all that was humanistically and ethically beneficial in don Juan's teachings, where she found "a reality identical, in all essential features, to the reality or world described by other great teachers, such as Socrates and Heraclitus and Wittgenstein." Though Carlos failed to grasp the Stoic core of don Juan's teachings, though he wasted attention on occultist inessentials don Juan despised, Cox forgave him. What, then, was her dismay at the Toltec devils, Star Wars scenery, and supernatural vaudeville acts of *Second Ring*! "Going Back to *Ixtlan*" is Cox's lament for the don Juan she loved and the noble ideas he taught her, now swept into limbo at the caprice of a heartless humbug.

Going Back to *Ixtlan*

Readers like me who expected more wisdom and beauty from Castaneda's fifth book must be deeply disappointed by *The Second Ring of Power*, for nowhere in it can we find the parables and poetry that graced the earlier books, especially *Journey to Ixtlan* and *Tales of Power*. Here the worst elements are expanded, the best contracted. Sorely missed are don Juan's truthful maxims, Genaro's comical counterpoint. By sending the teachers to another world, Castaneda contradicts don Juan, who stomped his foot to drive home the point that this world is the only one we have.

Granted, the author had continually juxtaposed seemingly other-world experiences with humanistic this-world teachings, but in *Second Ring* the occult dominates, while humanism all but disappears. Carlos, doña Soledad, and four bizarre young women fly in clusters, walk on walls, spin webs, double themselves, vanish, and rematerialize out of thin air. The book is an ironical paean to powerful quasi-feminists magically menacing feckless male rivals. Dismissing such tricks as trivial and unworthy, don Juan had stressed the search for knowledge by a warrior who accepted the mysterious, beautiful, unfathomable world without expecting to master it or even understand it.

Second Ring replaces the nobility of the warrior's way with petty bickerings among the pupils, an immature rivalry between the sexes, and morbid, empty occultism. Where don Juan taught responsibility and accepting one's fate with dignity, these apparently unworthy successors have wandered from the warrior's path toward some gloomy gnostic netherworld where I refuse to follow. For, like many readers, I indulge myself in the illusion—or perhaps the truth—that I understand don Juan better than either Carlos or Castaneda.

Farewell, Carlos of *The Second Ring*. I'm going back to *Ixtlan*.

RdeM

Currently working on a novel "about fantasy and geography and love," poet and critic Lynn Luria-Sukenick also teaches literature and creative writing at the University of California, Santa Cruz. *Houdini,* one of her three books of poetry, comprises twenty-five reflections on the great escape artist. Like Castaneda, Houdini wrote books and created illusions under an assumed name. Unlike Castaneda, he was noted for exposing psychical frauds, not for perpetrating them. Luria-Sukenick's third Houdini poem might have been written about Castaneda, for it says:

> He didn't try anything natural.
> A real thing might take him
> like an animal.
> He always started, himself,
> what he meant to undo.

Had Castaneda tried the natural desert, it might have taken him— perhaps away from everything, perhaps toward a different career. Castaneda always started, himself, any deserts or sorcerers he meant to unfold for our amazement.

Not having expected too much from Castaneda, Luria-Sukenick is not wounded by the apparent decline of his powers. His bizarre quasifeminism amuses her. Fondly, she recalls better days, when don Juan was our teacher. Quietly, in passing, she preserves a romantic wish from a time when she knew the parabolist face to face: Even if his books are fiction, Castaneda may be a sorcerer, or an embryonic sorcerer.

Parabolist's Progress

"I would not want him as my guru," said Leonora Carrington when we talked about don Juan in 1972. I had been an enchanted spectator when I read *The Teachings*, but she, a woman trained in esoteric religion and the occult, was taking the book seriously enough to evaluate and question its sensibility and procedures. Sorcery was a serious business, though the word reminded me of the perfume *Sortilège* and scenes from *Fantasia*. Later, I read Maya Deren's book on voodoo, which is perhaps a very different thing, certainly more ornate and more communal, and it was not an enchanting book: the customs were alien, one took them in fully or failed to understand, one believed or one did not—there was no dabbling possible.

Both poetry and sorcery defamiliarize the world; shock us into an awakening by means of images and through the power of the word; they flood us with unpredictable experiences and change our psychic spatial relations, demanding something new of us. But poetry at its best begets a spontaneous healing, no matter how tragic the message, and sorcery, it appears, mingles threats and scars with its rewards.

I wonder why Castaneda's story of apprenticeship to a sorcerer is so attractive to so many. Partly, perhaps, because it upsets completely the traditional Christian doctrines of kindness, charity, moral seriousness, and sobriety which everyone is used to. Don Juan's teachings, rigorous and humorous, are closer to the severity of Zen Buddhism in which compassion makes sympathy look simpy, in which empathy and guilt are replaced by such a steep grade of attention that discrimination becomes mere equivocation. Clearly this steep grade of attention is difficult to achieve. It is exclusive, exhausting, and dangerous, and it teaches us not to cling, teaches us to stop the world, to step off the cliff, teaches us, to put it in terms of that voguish therapeutic imperative, to "take risks." The difficulty or impossibility of the effort makes it all the more thrilling to read about—religion as adventure, as spectator sport, as radio serial, a cliffhanger, literally.

The books of Castaneda, whether they are fact or fiction—and they may be fiction at the same time that Castaneda is a sorcerer or embryonic sorcerer—are studded with a number of literary conventions which can generally be counted on to give us pleasure. They have many puzzles and riddles, for instance. They are detective stories, and even use over and over the recapitulation and explanation always found at the end of such stories, although in detective yarns mystification tends to be superseded reliably by explanation whereas in Castaneda's books explanation struggles against mystery, reasoning always giving way to perceiving. Castaneda makes us realize that reasoning is only a small part of our intelligence, and although this may cause a certain terror in us it also suggests that we have hidden resources and capabilities—which of course makes these self-help books as well. They are fairy tales too, obviously, vindications of the invisible where the hero undergoes the frustrations of initiation and is then given deliciously magical sleep and sweet recovery, experiencing the adventurer's reward of peace after fright. These are, indeed, *given* to Carlos, as to a child; the risks are imposed, not taken, though the risk in being there at all, if he is there at all, is a big one. And finally, the books involve us in a good deal of arbitrary and clear-edged ritual. They thus present us with an increased sense of order—not the order of rationality, not the order that keeps society going, but the ceremonial order that stops the world.

Don Juan's strict presence, his patient/impatient instruction which leads to impeccable action—so different from our clumsy mediated hopeful messy lives—appeals to our respect for specialness, obedience, and correctness, if it appeals. The sinewy antics and instruction of this necessary trickster are missing from *The Second Ring of Power*, however, except through flashbacks, and without them the physically improbable feats, people running around the walls for instance, do not stretch our credulity to the point of enlightenment but stop short at comic opera. A number of women are present, for the first time in the series, and their presence is suspiciously fashionable, though in their functions they are old-fashioned, seen as they are in relation to their inherent differentness from men, their beauty, their diet hints, and their witchy cackles. The characters squabble among themselves as if to undercut the appealing dignity of Castaneda's previous books, as if to keep the world of sorcery silly and rough, free from any chic we may have imposed on it. Or perhaps Castaneda is simply either writing less well than he has or, for his own reasons, baiting our will to believe. The instructions, tasks, and behavior in *Second Ring* have the quality of fancy and formula as opposed to imagination and ritual, though there are still, occasionally, things to inscribe in our commonplace books—Pablito carrying his chair with him because he has to store his power and can't go around sitting on just anything: "Who knows what kind of a creep sat there before me?"

Or further reminders of how to deflect and eliminate self-indulgence, a task eminently translatable from the land of sorcery to the ordinary world. And of course Castaneda does mock his own self-indulgence as writer, as interrogator, as sentimentalist: he does demystify as he goes, always, with understatement, redundancy, ingenuousness, and a certain awkwardness which seduces us into believing that the story has to be true if he's willing to spoil its possible perfections with artlessness. He likes to show, too, how the sort of coincidence many people today regard—with an amazing egotism—as confirmation of their own special and lucky status in the world at a given moment is merely luck, another random move in that great game of chance to which we should be both respectful and indifferent. He shows us in *Second Ring* that one may suddenly stop to tie one's shoelace and thereby avoid the boulder that comes crashing down inches in front of one at that moment or, as don Juan reminds him, one may stop to tie one's shoelace and be in precisely the wrong place as a result and be instantly killed by the falling boulder. The only thing one can do, don Juan continues, is to tie one's shoelace well. As a parable, a literary moment, this is charming and affecting, and as a practical direction it is demanding and right enough to keep us interested in the teachings, however weak the most recent volume.

The modern world forces us to be sophisticated whether we like it or not. Technology has masked the vagaries of nature and we are left with no nourishment, no source of aliveness that is not distorted by our manipulation and control over things. Gaining control, then, is no longer news, no longer interesting. The real plum, as the new therapies make clear, is loss of control, relinquishment of ego. Castaneda's books seductively mingle the goals of mastery over the self and of respectful and ecstatic abandonment of self to bewildering phenomena. The combination has clearly been palatable, if not genuinely nourishing, to the tastes of the seventies.

Epistemallegory: I fly, therefore....

"Either Castaneda is recording an encounter with a master of the most remarkable sort or else he is himself that master," wrote Joseph Margolis, a professor of philosophy at Temple University, but few other professional philosophers have taken don Juan seriously. Hector-Neri Castañeda, editor of *Noûs*, reconciler of phenomenalism with perceptual realism, struggled through Chapter One of *The Teachings*, and gave up. Perhaps Hector-Neri had no taste for epistemological allegories. Perhaps he was put off by suggestions he could attract hordes of students if he would just assign readings in the other, more popular Castaneda. At any rate, most philosophy professors have not seen any challenge to novelist Jean-Paul Sartre in the don Juan books.

Margolis likened don Juan's mystical nagual to Anaximander's non-limited original material, from which all things come and to which they return. He called don Juan and Wittgenstein "two masterly teachers," whose statements he found "tantalizingly similar." He did not ask whether the similarity had arisen fromCastaneda's reading of Wittgenstein. Nor did he cite the interview in which Castaneda told Sam Keen: "Once I read a bit of the linguistic philosophy of Ludwig Wittgenstein to don Juan and he laughed and said: 'Your friend Wittgenstein tied the noose too tight around his neck so he can't go anywhere.' "

In Wittgenstein's *Tractatus* I found seven ideas that seem to have made their way into the don Juan books; the Alleglossary lists them under: *Boundaries*, Death, *Equal*, Eternity, Explaining, *Ladder*, and *Witnessing*. Of the seven, Margolis noted the four in italics. Don Juan appeared to Margolis as a formidable, "utterly unforgettable presence—not merely a character and more than a man," a presence inspiring "a genuine longing to be worthy in don Juan's eyes." "What don Juan and Wittgenstein both claim," Margolis reported, "is that what we see is what the system of our beliefs and concepts permit us to see."

More technically, less personally, Laurence Foss applied that claim to the scientific endeavor. Science has its particular way of conceiving and believing, which shows it some things clearly and makes it blind to others. Sorcerers can't bring back a bag of rocks from the moon, but an astronaut can: score one for science (and technology). Science can't explain firewalking, but sorcerers can: score one for sorcerers—or at least don't score one for science. Does don Juan really fly? Which way of looking at things is better? Foss concludes:

> As regards the matter of whether don Juan flies. . . . evidentially we are permitted to say either that don Juan does and Neil Armstrong doesn't fly; or vice versa; or both do; or neither do.

> For the one scenarist, don Juan surely does not fly; for the other, he may indeed. And neither scenario reflects any higher standards of "what is to count as cognitive," only different standards.

> The reason for accepting the primacy of the scientific idiom is not that the factual data . . . are not conceivably compatible with an alternative idiom. Rather it is that when only the claims of natural science are considered . . . they form the kind of coherent whole that is capable of accounting for what needs accounting for.

I should have said "capable of accounting for *much* of what needs accounting for," since I think science ought to account for firewalking, or try to, but then I sometimes dabble in parapsychology and call it science, so maybe I'm being unreasonable.

The main point seems to be that any system of reason and belief, modern or traditional, accounts in some way or other for what it cares about and lets the rest go. Descartes's view of the world satisfied Descartes, Dirac's satisfies Dirac, don Juan's satisfies don Juan. I will extricate myself from the quandary by saying that if Neil Armstrong didn't really walk on the moon, Laurence Foss didn't really ask whether he did, and the predicament remains unpredicated.

Jerry H. Gill saw technical difficulties in the Sapir-Juan hypothesis: don Juan's assertion that ordinary reality is a function of psycho-socio-linguistic conditioning. He was far from convinced that the sorcerer, if he existed, could stop the world merely by stopping the internal dialogue. He judged the special consensus to be an untenable notion. Nevertheless, his own life had benefitted from don Juan's ethical precepts, even if the way of the warrior was "far too individualistic to be either realistic or fully helpful." "How does love figure into it?" Gill asked. How indeed?

Lucius Outlaw said the teachings radically challenge our present modes of understanding, though he doubted don Juan's *seeing* was the same thing as grasping Kant's *noumenon*, the transcendental or ultimate reality. Beatrice Bruteau looked through don Juan's relativism about world views to spy the only absolute reality: "the totality of the infinite intercommunicating universe."

Gordon G. Globus, a professor of psychiatry at the University of California, Irvine, attended Castaneda's 1972 seminars there and found stimulation for his own writings on brain and consciousness. From a sea of current opinions about Castaneda he distilled four alternative views: 1) The fieldwork is fraudulent, the teachings trivial. 2) Castaneda's brilliant and extraordinary allegory penetrates the epistemological culture clashes of our time. 3) Don Juan and don Genaro possess occult and terrible powers. 4) Though only a man, don Juan is both an indigenous Yaqui philosopher of the first rank and an accomplished hypnotist, who imposed nonordinary realities on Carlos through suggestion. Globus said each of these descriptions was valid, since each fitted a tenable theory, and since theories define and select the facts that support or test them. He concluded that the true don Juan was unknowable.

My own less impartial view combines Globus's first and second alternatives: The books are a hoax but the allegory is penetrating. One of the clearest examples of teaching philosophy through telling stories appears in Keen's interview, where Castaneda plays Carlos-Phenomenologist arguing with don Juan Platonist. Keen asks whether don Juan was trying to teach Carlos a new view of the world, a mere alternative substituting the sorcerer's strange but limited world for the ordinary world, or was trying to help Carlos see the world in its true form or formless essence, devoid of interpretation.

"Don Juan and I disagreed about this," Castaneda answered. Well, Charley McCarthy used to sass Edgar Bergen, so why shouldn't don Juan disagree with Castaneda? "I say he was reglossing me"—that is, providing a new interpretation of the world—"and he says he was deglossing me"—that is, getting rid of interpretations. "Don Juan thinks that what he calls seeing is apprehending the world without any interpretation; it is pure wondering perception." Which is pure wonderful epistemallegory.

For at least three volumes of the fieldwork fantasy Carlos finds the sorcerer's world incomprehensible, and his incomprehension is the basis for Castaneda's claim that he "adopted the phenomenological method" while "recording" don Juan's teachings. The method allowed Castaneda to describe Carlos's experience without explaining it. Such neutral describing departs from common sense, which tries to explain everything immediately in terms of familiar concepts. Phenomenology is an academic maneuver meant to expand one's conceptual repertory by avoiding dependence on the familiar. Any such conscious, purposive regime of record keeping, however, is quite capable of imposing its own peculiar constructions, constrictions, and distortions of experience. The hazard was recognized by Donald Palmer, who wrote:

> Oddly enough, the object of Castaneda's phenomenological analysis, an old Yaqui sorcerer named don Juan Matus, emerges from that analysis appearing to be a man who in many respects is himself a phenomenologist. This seems roughly equivalent to performing a Marxian analysis of Thomism and concluding that St. Thomas Aquinas was himself a Marxist. It certainly raises the question of the degree to which the actual outcome of Castaneda's account is determined by the method he uses. . . .

That such a question is raised, I heartily agree, though of course I would add that Castaneda's method is not phenomenological accounting but creative writing. Anthropologist C. Scott Littleton did not share Palmer's concern about distortions of don Juan's teachings. He wrote:

> Despite Castaneda's reliance upon the rhetoric espoused by Garfinkel and others, the underlying assumption here is that don Juan, too, is a phenomenologist and that his own rhetoric is essentially isomorphic with that employed by Carlos. In short, it would seem that phenomenology, like so many other things, has been independently invented at least twice: in turn-of-the-century Germany and contemporary Sonora.

Klaus-Peter Koepping, phenomenologist and anthropologist at the University of Queensland, had no such illusions, for he wrote:

> Castaneda is presenting us with an approach which is not at all interesting from the point of view of the content of the "factual" information provided [since, Koepping explains, most of the content was already known to anthropologists], but is of great interest from the method of transmitting to the reader, layman or otherwise, this factual information. . . . I do not think that it matters at all whether Castaneda wrote about real experiences or concocted a fiction along the lines of *Alice in Wonderland*. . . . So, let us assume that firstly, Castaneda cribbed the content of

his hallucinogenic experiences from other ethnographers, and secondly, that he wrote a piece of fiction. What then is the point of it all?

The point Koepping discovers is that Castaneda adopted and demonstrated for our edification the observational attitude of *epoche*, proposed by founding phenomenologist Edmund Husserl, which required him to establish cognitive distance from the natural world by suspending judgment about it. Stephen Murray comments:

> Koepping's adduction of *epoche*, or bracketing, is disingenuous. Interpretation of a work traditionally includes knowing what kind of a work one is interpreting. The author's intent—whether to produce ethnography or allegory—is hardly irrelevant. Koepping says Castaneda used "the hermeneutic method of interpretation," which the reader in turn must use to understand what Castaneda wrote, but the goal of hermeneutics is to understand a text by discovering both the author's intent and the context of discourse in which the text arose. Discovering whether Castaneda suspended judgment while conversing with don Juan in the Sonoran Desert or while reading Wasson, Opler, and Govinda in the UCLA library is central, not irrelevant, to the hermeneutic reading Koepping advocates.

I should have thought anthropologists would care to know whether Castaneda's familiar ethnographic facts and occasional new findings had arisen among the dunes or in the stacks, but Koepping apparently thinks his colleagues wouldn't or shouldn't care. "There are no 'pure facts,' " he says. "Everything a social scientist puts into words is a mediated form of facts, is an interpretation of facts." The implication that all stories are not only true but equally true and that there is no way and no need to choose among them has been vehemently condemned by Marvin Harris as a scientifically corrupt and morally depraved doctrine. Guards and prisoners at Dachau told different stories, Harris points out, but we don't have to toss a coin to decide between them, and it is not a matter of indifference which story comes closer to what actually happened. Khmer Rouge and refugees offer different versions of the depopulation of Cambodia. "It does not follow from our inability to obtain absolutely certain knowledge," writes Harris, "that all knowledge is equally uncertain."

Koepping does say there are facts to be interpreted, so one may hope to acquire some impure facts, but what I should like to ask him is how much impurity can be tolerated. If I say I am reporting data from ten years in the Sonoran desert, are the data still acceptable if I have never been there? Is an examination just as good when written by a friend or an employee of the student whose name is on it? Is scholarship just as meritorious when plagiarized from a fellow scholar? Are new findings invented in the library likely to be as valid as old findings found there? When old findings are presented as new findings, do they reflexively validate themselves? Were Husserl and Schutz plotting to replace fieldwork with fantasy, credit with cribbing, impure facts with pure fiction? Boundless and thrilling prospects are opened up by Koeppingian phenomenology.

Beyond doubting that it obliges anyone to go round in such dizzy hermeneutic circles, I am not prepared to judge the value of phenomenology in science or philosophy. I am prepared, however, to ask a few simple questions about Castaneda's claim that he adopted a phenomenological method in conducting and reporting ten years of fieldwork:

1) Is phenomenological social science the same thing as lying? I should expect most phenomenological social scientists to say no. If it is not, then:

2) How can the two be distinguished? I should hope for a list of criteria.

3) Can phenomenology be incorporated into social science without making it wholly subjective? In other words, can phenomenological social science be tied to the ordinary reality at some point? I should expect most practitioners to say yes.

4) Given such answers, if the criteria mentioned in Point 2 then be applied to the don Juan books, what will one find? I should expect the findings to be: a) Castaneda was consistently practicing creative writing, b) at no point was he practicing science, c) his claim of factual reporting was false and (assuming mental competence) deceptive, and d) he was teaching phenomenology by telling stories he made up.

A popular defense of Castaneda in academic circles like the ones Peter Koepping goes round in is the assertion that his practice of phenomenology makes questions of authenticity superfluous and irrelevant; that since phenomenology has replaced the stereotypical standard, reliable, objective observer, a myth of old-fashioned science, with the idiosyncratic, unpredictable, subjective observer (which I should call a mythical stereotype of new-fashioned science), authenticity is now passé and it is an atavistic waste of time to raise questions about it. This is pretty exciting. Maybe it is even creative. I don't know how unfair it is to proper phenomenology, but I do know it is antiscientific extremism and unprofessional self-indulgence. The discovery that the observer was not a standard, reliable instrument was a very important discovery, but it happened a long time ago, at least as early as 1816, when Bessel got curious about the firing of Kinnebrook for recording stellar transits a half-second later than Maskelyne, and it does not now justify junking empirical science, any more than the addition of an error term to a prediction formula justifies dropping the predictors. Some part of scientific procedure must be standard, reliable, authentic, and ordinary, or there will be no science. If science survives, Castaneda will not be included in it, and questions of his authenticity will not be a waste of time for scientists, though they may be for non-scientists.

The next chapter demonstrates conscientious phenomenology compatible with science, as Richard McDermott traces Carlos's progress "from two worlds to one" and shows with unusual clarity how the first four don Juan books can be read as lessons in philosophy. Allowing the reader to judge whether the books were written as experiential accounts or as didactic allegories, McDermott refrains from making our familiar distinction between author Castaneda and character Carlos. By calling both figures "Castaneda," he preserves the ambiguity of Castaneda's text. In a longer version of his essay, McDermott asked how Castaneda's books "want to be read" and why they have a ring of actual experience for many readers. Interpreting Carlos's foolish questions to don Juan not only as a literary device but as "a rule for reading our world into the texts," McDermott wrote:

> By repeatedly asking don Juan for explanations Castaneda, the author, tells us that an important question for him as a character is: "What's really happening here? How can I believe what I just saw?" . . . By voicing this "reader's concern" throughout the text Castaneda informs us that we should *not* suspend our ordinary criteria of what is really possible. . . . Any violation of the ordinary features of *our* world terrifies Castaneda as a character and he urgently demands that don Juan account for it. The fact that what seems unbelievable to us as readers is just as unbelievable to Castaneda as a character, tells us that the narrative's action takes place in our world.

McDermott finds a neater system in the books than I do. For example, he emphasizes reality-as-agreement in the second book, whereas I find it more obvious in the third. Nevertheless, I think his interpretation is correct: the books are lessons, which demand to be taken as factual accounts. Offered as fiction, they would have been much less effective. McDermott's commonsense judgment that *Second Ring* "reads like pure fantasy" serves as a welcome antidote to Mehan and Wood's stultifying proposal that all realities are equally real, showing that one can do phenomenology perfectly well without being swallowed up by it, without indulging in ethnoromancing, and without either playing or falling victim to intellectual shell games.

Richard McDermott **36**

From Two Worlds to One

Castaneda's first four books do not simply record the bizarre events which he, as the works' central character, experienced under the guidance of don Juan. In order to explain how he came to believe in the occurrence of those "impossible" events, Castaneda, as an author, involves us in a discussion of how a world could exist in which people turn into crows, talk with animals, leap to distant mountain tops, and see things from perspectives which they do not bodily inhabit. Each of Castaneda's books provides a different explanation for why that world is possible, correcting the explanations proposed in the previous books.

Most of the unusual experiences described in *The Teachings of Don Juan* occur while Castaneda is under the influence of hallucinogenic drugs. He concludes that while under their influence he did not see what he thought he saw, that the things he thought he saw could not actually have been seen because they were not there, objectively, to be seen. Like the world of dreams, the sorcerer's world leads its life in one's head. It does not challenge or deny the objective world of ordinary life, but merely sets it aside by superimposing an illusory world upon it. Thus, in *The Teachings*, Castaneda maintains his faith in the finality of his ordinary critical perception. His bizarre experiences were possible because they were illusory, and illusion is what distinguishes a sorcerer's world from our own.

In *A Separate Reality* Castaneda participates in many impossible events without the aid of hallucinogenic drugs. Unable to identify any change in his perceptual faculties, he begins to lose his faith in the objective existence of the world as it ordinarily appears. Here Castaneda argues that the appearance of the world is socially constructed, a result of our agreements with each other about what we are seeing. Thus the appearance of the world is a feature of the community to which we belong. By drawing Castaneda into a community of sorcerers don Juan exposed him to a sorcerer's agreements about the world. Nonordinary events are therefore possible because the reality about which sorcerers agree is as valid and convincing as the reality about which the rest of us agree, although each is separate from the other.

Journey to Ixtlan recounts some of don Juan's early lessons which Castaneda had previously considered insignificant. Castaneda sees don

Juan's teachings as personal lessons articulating themes hidden in the unexplored background of Castaneda's experience: taking responsibility for one's actions, learning not to manipulate others, living with both abandon and self-control, and taking death as one's adviser. Castaneda realizes that he acquired a sorcerer's viewpoint by incorporating those lessons into his life and that don Juan had not offered him a separate alternative to his ordinary life but had given him a deeper understanding of it by attuning his ordinary life to the world of sorcery. As a result, the truth of don Juan's teachings could only be judged in terms of Castaneda's personal history and relationship to don Juan. In that context Castaneda found nonordinary events believable because they helped to make sense of his life. Don Juan had seen more deeply into Castaneda's life from a sorcerer's perspective than Castaneda had from his ordinary one. By drawing the two perspectives closer together, don Juan had laid the groundwork for Castaneda's conversion to the sorcerer's reality.

In *Tales of Power* Castaneda goes native and begins to explain nonordinary events in terms of a new perceptual faculty, the *will*. Don Juan reveals that although we ordinarily see things from the perspective of *reason*, an alternative perspective is provided by the *will*. Like extrasensory perception, *will* has access to aspects of the world that are ordinarily unavailable to us. Don Juan's teachings have prepared Castaneda's body for seeing with his *will*. In this book Castaneda argues that perception of any kind is a description of the world. Whether achieved through *reason* or through *will*, perception is a picture or description of the single, objective world that underlies both modes of perception. A sorcerer does not participate in a reality separate from and coextensive with our own, but in a description that is simply a bigger picture of the world than we ordinarily see. According to this explanation, the world of sorcery is possible and observable because it is as real as the world of the atom and ordinarily as invisible.

These four formulations of the reasons why don Juan's world is possible explore the relationship of reality, thought, and perception, giving a progressively more unifying explanation of how Castaneda, as a character, came to believe in events he had thought impossible. From one formulation to the next Castaneda advances both toward understanding don Juan's world and toward becoming a member of it. It is a progression from two worlds to one.

At first Castaneda sees don Juan's world as an outsider. He judges it against the objective world with which he is familiar and rejects it as illusory. Next he finds it more believable and sees it as having a reality of its own. He drops his reliance on the notion of an external, coexperience-able world as the sole criterion of what is real, admitting that reality itself depends on what counts as real in a particular social setting. Don Juan's world and the ordinary world are equal and separate realities. Finally, gaining membership in a sorcerer's reality, Castaneda realizes that don Juan's teachings are not about a different world but about aspects of the single, external world that are ordinarily hidden from us. Thus he returns again to the notion of a unitary, objective world as the basis for assessing the reality of don Juan's world.

These different formulations of the nature of a sorcerer's reality are not simply arguments establishing the philosophical grounds of Castaneda's works. They each give us a way of understanding how don Juan's world could be possible by exploring the relationship between his world and our own. They formulate what the experiences which Castaneda reports could have been experiences *of* in terms that are at least theoretically, if not experientially, sensible to us. Thus they give us a way of understanding the seemingly impossible events Castaneda presents as real experiences.

The four-volume discussion of how don Juan's world is possible provides a way of reading ourselves and our world into the books, finding a ring of truth to them, and, if we wish, accepting them as actual accounts. Aside from their value as entertaining narrative and intellectual allegory, Castaneda's books examine what he, as a character in them, and we, as readers, are willing to accept as real. In the fifth book, *The Second Ring of Power*, the world of sorcery becomes a concretely real world much like another planet, where don Juan and his apprentices will someday meet. The bulk of the book is taken up with long explanations by don Juan's apprentices of the theoretical foundations of sorcery. Although Castaneda's mastery of sorcery has brought him some impressive magical powers, he is no longer awed by their seeming impossibility and no longer tries to understand how he could have exercised them. Instead of continuing the exploration of how things count for us as real, *Second Ring* reads like a work of pure fantasy. Still, the first four books stand as a remarkable introduction to a serious philosophical concern.

RdeM

Standing bemushroomed at the foot of the stairway in the house of Genaro's brother Cayetano on the night of 29-30 June 1955, "holding on to the rail transfixed in ecstasy by the visions that he was seeing in the darkness with his open eyes," Gordon Wasson felt for the first time "an immediacy of vision" he soon identified with the "very Ideas" Plato had seen "without the intervention of mortal eyes," Ideas he thought Plato had first encountered in the Temple of Eleusis after imbibing the sacred potion. Twenty-three years later, in *The Road to Eleusis*, Wasson and his co-authors, Albert Hofmann and Carl A. P. Ruck, argued convincingly that the mysterious Eleusinian potion had been eidetically potentiated by a form of mushroom—ergot of barley or wild grass—and that Plato had therefore *seen* in the Temple with the same bemushroomed brain as Wasson in Cayetano's house, or Carlos (they might have added) when smoking don Juan's mushroom mixture.

In *Castaneda's Journey* I said Carlos's mushroom visions had been inspired by Wasson's 1957 account, but Carlos had more kinds of visions than Wasson. First he smoked the mushroom and flew with silvery crows. Next, cold sober, he imagined the sandstormy world of diableros described by don Juan as "a plane above the ground," like (he might have added) Plato's "world above this world." Finally he *saw* the lines of the world, the terrestrial essence, not with the aid of visionary plants or verbal description but by stopping the internal dialogue through an act of conscious concentration. Thus Carlos had three kinds of visions: the first released by hallucinogenic plants, the second verbally suggested to normal consciousness, the third produced by non-discursive awareness, a kind of meditation. As Carl Ruck will presently show, Plato also distinguished three kinds of visions, which correspond rather well to Carlos's, though I don't think Castaneda could have known about the correspondence, since Ruck and I develop the theme apparently for the first time here. In a review of *The Road to Eleusis*, I wrote:

> Professor of classics at Boston University, Carl A. P. Ruck specializes in Greek mythology and ethnobotany. The Eleusinian vision, he says, could not have been a drama, since the temple was completely unsuited for that and no payments were recorded for equipment or actors. The holy thing initiates saw was not a collection of relics, for when Alcibiades profanely

showed it to friends at home no one accused the priests of lend-
ing him holy objects. What was seen in the temple was Deme-
ter's daughter, the goddess Persephone, returning from captivity
in the realm of Hades, assuring each beholder that grain would
grow anew, that death was the cradle of life, that agriculture
could tame wild growth as religion would reconcile the underworld of passions with the upper world of reason. Months of
instructive ritual preceded the revelation. . . .

While writing that review, I noticed a provocative discrepancy.
Though Wasson had confidently taken Plato's Ideas to be the same thing
as Plato's visions in the Temple, Ruck said Plato had called the temple
visions *phasmata*, or ghostly apparitions, a term incompatible with the
stable, vivid clarity Wasson and others attribute to mycogenic
(mushroom-born) visions. Indeed, Plato used contrasting terms for the
Ideas and the temple visions. Intrigued, I asked Ruck to sort this out and
explain the discrepancy. His conclusion, presented in the next chapter,
was that, while Plato very likely *did* see mushroom visions in the Temple, those visions were *not* the Ideas he later wrote about. Unlike the
tradition-directed hallucinations of the Eleusinian Mystery, Plato's Ideas
arose from unbemushroomed but perhaps entranced "meditation upon
paradigms of rational logic such as mathematics and geometry." This is
somewhat like Carlos's stopping the world by stopping the internal
dialogue, but even more it is like Arthur Koestler's "hours by the window" contemplating Euclid's proven infinitude of prime numbers while
languishing three months condemned to death in solitary confinement in
cell Number 40 of the Prison of Seville, meditations that led Koestler first
to a realization of perfection and then to a disappearance of the I. While
Wasson and Plato may well have had similar mystical visions of ultimate
reality, Ruck's commentary suggests they achieved their visions by different means, Wasson through ritual mycophagy (like the Eleusinian initiates and Carlos of *The Teachings*), Plato through rapturous contemplation of abstractions (like Koestler in cell 40 and Carlos of *Ixtlan*).

Plato's Hierarchy of Visions: Hallucinatory, Sensate, and Paradigmatic

Frequently expressing distrust of the confusing, mutable world perceived through the senses, Plato sought instead more stable objects for true cognition in the conceptual categories he termed the *eide (eidea)*, the Visionary Paradigms or, as they are traditionally translated into English, the Forms or Ideas. Neither "form" nor "idea" suffices as a translation, however, for the *eide* are things actually seen, if only in a state of rapture.

Indeed, the Greek language assumes that knowledge comes from seeing. *Oida* (I know) is formed from the same root as *eidon* (I saw), thus linguistically predicating knowledge as a perfected state of being attained by seeing. Plato, for his part, was not using the term as a dead metaphor but proposing the *eide* as objects of living vision. In the *Phaedrus*, for example, he described the soul's voyage to a higher realm where it gazed ecstatically upon eternal paradigms, a substance of reality truer than the perishable imitations offered as particular examples of reality by the ordinary world about us.

Describing such transcendent contemplation or vision, Plato often borrowed metaphors from the comparable experience of initiation into mystery religions, like the Eleusinian Mysteries. These religions were called mysteries because secret things were done, culminating in something that could not be told not only because the participants were sworn to silence but also because the experience was ineffable. In *The Road to Eleusis*, R. Gordon Wasson, Albert Hofmann, and I argue that the climactic event was a drug-induced visionary communion with the spirits of the earth. The initiates glimpsed their own mortal involvement in the ancient agrarian magic whereby death and putrefaction became the fecundating prelude to rebirth, and the art of agriculture was sensed as the principle by which all civilization had evolved out of primitivism.

Plato had probably experienced the ritual intoxication of Eleusis, and seen the vision, for he came from a wealthy and conventional aristocratic family, and it seems likely he would have undergone the customary indoctrinations for his role as Greek and Athenian. As a youth, moreover, he had fancied himself a tragic poet and thus would not have objected to ecstatic possession or to inebriation caused by the vinous potions of the god Dionysus, for tragic poets were the special servants of the god whose gift to civilized mankind was wine, a drink whose spirits were not only those of alcohol from fermented grapes, but also those of the wild and often psychotropic herbs that flavored it. On the occasion of the great Dionysian festivals of drama, the entire populace would ceremoniously submit to the intoxication of this drug, and as Plato himself testified in the *Ion*, the poet, as witless as they, was enthralled and possessed by the god as he conveyed to them the visions of his inspiration.

The mature Plato, in contrast, came to disdain both the visions in such mystery rituals and the emotional fictions of art, considering them still more insubstantial and hallucinatory than the sights of ordinary perception, for under the influence of his teacher Socrates he had come to see a different vision. Socrates himself was a visionary, as Plato showed in the *Symposium*. Twice in the course of that dialogue we are told how Socrates fell into deep trance-like states of contemplation. While those about him at the drinking party were prey to physicality and senses, eventually succumbing to the wine, Socrates maintained sobriety, a disembodied eye rapturously gazing upon the paradigm of beauty before its immersion in corporeality.

Such Socratic rapture was induced, if we are to judge from the curriculum presented in the *Republic*, by a regime of meditation upon paradigms of rational logic such as mathematics and geometry, leading finally to an apperception of the rational patterns underlying the apparent diversity in material reality. Plato denigrates irrational rapture, like that of the mysteries, since there the mind instead of escaping to commune with the realm of rational paradigms is all the more burdened by the physicality of the *soma* (the body) which, as in the famous pun, becomes its *sema* (its tomb). In this denigration, Plato resembles those mystics who today reject pharmacologically induced vision, in favor of regimes of meditation.

No doubt there was also an Orphic influence upon this Platonic puritanism, for the mathematicians whom Plato so much admired often espoused certain Orphic doctrines about the dichotomy of mortal body and immortal soul. Orphism seems originally to have been a religious development of Dionysianism seeking an ethical dimension for the agrarian mystery cults, which had claimed no ethic other than the evolutionary magic of fertility. In Plato's parable of the cave, men entombed within the earth watching a hallucinatory picture-show must be painfully induced to leave their prison and ascend into the brilliant clarity of day. Applying the parable, Plato argued that the sunlit world about us is itself an illusion, recognizable once the confused corporeal being has gazed upon the paradigms of the still higher realm that is the ethical home of the soul.

The Cactus Couch of Doctor Matus or
The Psycho-Path with Heart

"I feel a terrible anger. I told him that one should not play with a person's feelings and loyalties. Don Juan laughed until tears rolled down his cheeks, and I hated him."

> Does don Juan's conduct attest to his own personal mastery of the system he represents and into which he ushers his apprentice? . . .
> Is there a consistency between theoretical principles and actual behavior? The answer to this question is, ultimately, "No."

> Don Juan's behavior frequently reveals the presence of significant unconscious conflicts which not only mark him as a flawed, perhaps tragic figure, but which seriously impede the progress of his pupil whose inability to complete the apprenticeship is rooted *both* in his own emotive vulnerabilities and in the pathological acting-out of his teacher.

Which passages come from the major published psychological study of the don Juan books, comprising three long articles by M. D. Faber, who is not as his initials suggest a medical doctor but a professor of English at the University of Victoria, where he teaches literature and object-relations theory. Faber knows his subjects inside and out and writes with clarity and directness. While X-raying don Juan's id, his articles furnish a short course in psychoanalytic theory, which I confidently recommend to anyone interested in the pre-oedipal approach to psyche and behavior. Of course there are other approaches, such as the Jungian and the Humanistic, which we shall consider in due course.

Faber's portrait of Matus-Patherapist proceeds not only from much study of literature and psychoanalysis but, surprisingly enough, from a friendship with Carlos Castaneda at UCLA during the early 1960s, going with groups to films and parties, meeting for coffee or lunch on the lawn, enjoying rambling conversations that never touched on clinical matters but were spiced with tall stories like the ones related in "Sergeant Castaneda and the Photos of don Juan." Despite having heard those Munchausenish adventures, Faber stated his conviction that the apprenticeship had been genuine, at least as described in *The Teachings* and *A Separate Reality*. The assumption that don Juan existed outside of Castaneda's head skews Faber's analysis somewhat but does not destroy it. Separating the mistreated Carlos from the sometimes cruel don Juan makes the picture easier to draw. If both sadist and masochist are aspects of Castaneda, the psychodynamics must be more complicated. I invited Faber to deal with this new problem, but unfortunately time did not permit, so the treatment remains within the fictive relationship of master and pupil, where it is still instructive.

The study begins by recalling that the typical mother constitutes most of her infant's social world. Displaying ordinary human inconsistency, she is sometimes the warm, loving, nurturing mother, sometimes the cold, hateful, neglecting mother. Thus she creates alternative worlds of good and bad social relations for the infant to live in. So doing, she becomes the original enigma, the archetypal trickster and betrayer. Learning from her inconsistency how to be a person, the infant develops a split personality, with joyful and miserable selves assigned to good and bad social worlds. Helpless against the mother's angry moods and physical size, the infant is sometimes afraid of being devoured by her or engulfed in her massive bulk. As time goes by, such trials and terrors sink into unconscious chambers of the mind, whence they are occasionally called forth by new terrors and trials.

Don Juan, Faber discovers, is also an enigma, trickster, and betrayer. Combining traits of father and mother, he is sometimes good, as often bad. Treating Carlos like a child eager to be accepted by a loving parent, he transfers the early family feelings up through the years from South America to the apprenticeship in sorcery. Assigning Carlos's realities to two separate worlds, he reactivates the infantile personality split. Letting Carlos go out to play with the preverbal Mescalito, and get mauled by the dangerous, dominating, seductive, unpredictable, female devil's weed, he upsets Carlos's equilibrium. Calling in La Catalina, a super-bad-mama, he terrifies the child-apprentice, and then compounds the ambiguity by merging with the medusa (in the last episode of *The Teachings*) so that the tortured regressor doesn't know whether he has the good father or the bad mother to deal with. Toward the end of *The Teachings*, Carlos is obsessed by a mass of dark pinholes that threaten to engulf him, like the pores of an overwhelming mother's skin seen up close by a frightened infant. Thus don Juan drives his apprentice to the edge of psychosis, whence the poor chap can escape only by fleeing back to the rationalistic safety of UCLA. (Author Castaneda, in contrast, seems psychologically much too sturdy and well-armored ever to have been in any danger of the psychotic break that was always menacing the fragile Carlos, a danger Castaneda's friends and academic sponsors often worried about, since Castaneda frequently described Carlos's incipient breakdown to them.)

In *A Separate Reality* Carlos's ambivalence toward his mother is made conscious and various buried objects are retrieved from the unconscious world. Don Juan listens to the sobs of Carlos's childhood. The giant gnat brings back the threats and pains of infancy. All of which might be a suitable preparation for working consciously through the early traumas if don Juan were a wise and loving therapist, but he is not. His tricks confuse Carlos. His unpredictable coldness leaves Carlos psychologically abandoned. Sending Carlos out alone to confront the terrible Catalina, he arms the boy with a boar's foot to ram into her middle, the gift implying Carlos has no penis of his own; thus the therapist symbolically castrates the client. Such destructive manipulations oblige Carlos to tighten the very system of intellectual, rationalizing defenses against anxiety that would have to be relaxed if early traumas were to be worked through, a process much too threatening to be trusted to such a treacherous guide.

The foregoing treatment is published in the *Psychocultural Review*. A third article, in the *Psychoanalytic Review*, focuses on the character of the inept therapist, asking why don Juan mistreats his pupil so. Once more Faber reviews the human condition, summing it up this time as an "absence of perfection in human interaction." In order to save some part of the prenatal paradise, the infant gathers the good things into one world, the bad things into another. In the good world the infant has personal power, a feeling that he controls all things; in the bad world he is a helpless victim deserving of his fate. Don Juan's program of accumulating personal power rearranges the internal economy. Old emotional investments are reduced by avoiding old relationships, which means the apprentice must erase personal history and abandon friends and family. This frees his feelings for voluntary investment in less taxing concerns, such as magic and mystery, but leaves him socially isolated, bereft of love and support. *Doing* is the reaffirmation of old ties; *not-doing* is cutting them; but cutting them completely is too frightening, so Carlos does not *see*. Twilight on the desert symbolizes readiness to enter the unconscious world. The crack between the worlds is a disguised anatomical invitation to rebirth, after which the umbilical luminous fibers will stretch as one gains independence.

Are don Juan's tricks and buffets merely didactic ploys excusable in the master-pupil relationship? No, says Faber, such excuses, whether or not supported by reference to equally suspect traditional systems of teaching, are psychologically naïve. Don Juan's acts are not just teaching devices but expressions of unconscious aims. His central act is choosing Carlos as an apprentice, but why does he want an apprentice? Faber explains. The world from which don Juan has detached himself is a cruel world, which robbed him of father and mother, uprooted and exiled him, made him feel vulnerable and emotionally dependent. In that unfriendly world he learned to do without feeling, caring, responding, or laying himself open to others, but this massive defense did not erase the residue of disappointment, anger, and dependency—which is where the apprentice comes in. Don Juan needs Carlos to be the unwitting receptacle of his unconscious struggle, of the painful burden that drove him out of the ordinary world and marooned him in a schizoid nonordinary world. In Carlos, don Juan spies at last the perfect victim on whom to act out the sadistic rage left over from bitter childhood suffering.

Are the precepts of don Juan's system invalidated by his bad behavior? No, says Faber, but the system has its own flaws: reliance on drugs (unexpectedly revived in *Second Ring* when Eligio is sent off into the other world by a final boost from power plants), social isolation, a struggle to control one's dreams instead of learning from them, the use of shock, terror, and betrayal to shake up the organism. In a letter to me, Faber wrote:

> While certain aspects of don Juan's treatment may harbor some positive therapeutic potential, the program in its entirety, in all its manifestations, must ultimately be regarded as sadistic, even sick. The pathological countertransferences are everywhere. One is reminded of Dr Johnson's remark: Beware of philosophers, they discourse like angels but they live like men. As a therapist don Juan leaves nearly everything to be desired.

What the character of don Juan tells us unforgettably, Faber concludes, is that all the sorcery in the world will not work if one fails to confront, and to bravely work through, the ordinary realities of one's own unconscious mind.

Don Juan's bad rating from M. D. Faber was balanced by a good report from the editor of the *Psychoanalytic Review*. Marie Coleman Nelson went over the same textual ground, cited many of the same anecdotes, but found little that was not praiseworthy in don Juan's practice. Where

Faber saw sadistic countertransferences, Nelson saw kindly, forbearing understanding that did not coddle the pupil. Where Faber saw a capricious exploiter, Nelson saw a master teacher. Where Faber saw his old friend from UCLA victimized by a twisted magus, Nelson saw a modern hero journeying toward knowledge in the company of a wise parental guide. Substituting don Juan's nagual for the id, she speculated, psychoanalysis could explain a host of anomalies like poltergeists and hexes. Aware that Castaneda's legitimacy was under attack, Nelson predicted questions of authenticity would "pale to insignificance by comparison to the deeper interpersonal and moral issues imbedded in his writings." In concluding, she recalled the dialectical role-playing and journalistic disguises of Kierkegaard, another famous non-scientist who tricked us into learning.

Humanistic psychologist Barbara Forisha credited don Juan with adding a mystical or transpersonal dimension to humanism, expanding the client's concern and competence beyond the personal-social to the cosmic sphere, breaching conceptual boundaries by means of tricks and manipulations, albeit at a cost of great anxiety and need for self-discipline. The well of consciousness may be deeper than humanists have told us, Forisha said. This challenge to conventional counsels of warmth, caring, and emotional honesty was taken seriously by editor Thomas Greening, who asked:

> Are support and empathy enough to help us let go into the void out of which transformation arises? Or do we need to be shaken loose? Much as I value the warmth and encouragement I've received in my own journey, I have to admit that the most profound changes were provoked by drastic and unwelcome disconfirmations of my mental structures. As Barbara says: "The ego does not seek its own destruction." Who, then, can we trust to help us with this self-surgery? Much of the controversy about est, for example, centers on this issue of what method in whose hands can enable us to separate our being from our ego. Is Castaneda's apprenticeship to don Juan or my trust of my experience of est a dangerous abdication or a wise and necessary leap?

The dichotomy with Faber's view is not so clear-cut as it may seem, for Greening does not ask whether support, empathy, and trustworthiness are *necessary* but whether they are *enough*. Presumably Forisha and Greening would not assign cases to don Juan if they detected in his practice the ubiquitous pathological countertransferences so evident to Faber.

Forisha noted a strong resemblance between don Juan's gospel and *What is Zen?* but did not attribute it to Castaneda's reading of Suzuki, though she reproduced parallel passages (listed in the Alleglossary, under Self) which suggest not only metaphysical agreement but literary influence.

In *Religious Humanism*, Jean and Charles Cox treated "alienation" as "powerlessness" and gave don Juan credit for remedying it. The paradox of the utterly isolated warrior accumulating power to cure his "alienation" was made to vanish by adopting don Genaro's explanation: a warrior isn't lonely because he's in love with the world. The flaw in this formula is that the warrior's world is populated by nineteen warriors and four-billion phantoms. Psychoanalyst Elsa First conceded don Juan's world was gained at a price of permanent alienation from human attachments, but judged it still a creative alternative to insanity, in the vein of R. D. Laing's alternative worlds. Psychologist Steven Hendlin systematically compared don Juan with Frederick Perls, concluding that don Juan multiplies life options, while providing freedom from social rejection and control, for persons given to nonordinary realities. Charles Pulvino and James Lee, professors of counseling and guidance, offered an uncritical appreciation of don Juan's worldview and didactic method. Author Peter Marin called don Juan's way the most extreme example of the new narcissism, a morally empty self-worship peddled also by Arica, Moonism, Hare Krishna, est, Scientology, and Esalen.

In an essay titled "Psychic Bisexuality" Charlotte Painter said Castaneda's allegorical dialogues demonstrate "the capacity of a single individual for more than one way of thinking. His intuitive, mystical mentor is his own rejected 'female' self . . . and his task is . . . to balance the two, to take possession again of the rejected self."

Bruce W. Scotton, of the Langley Porter Neuropsychiatric Institute, saw Castaneda as a teacher of cross-cultural psychiatry and nonverbal therapy, the confrontation between Carlos-Skeptic and don Juan furnishing a model in which the patient's worldview is compared not with a standard external reality but with the psychiatrist's worldview. Scotton supposed the number of nonpsychotic people who do not share the average psychiatrist's view of reality must be large. He assigned don Juan's eight points on the fibers of a luminous being to parts of the body, in the manner of the seven Hindu chakras: *reason* and *talking* to the head, *seeing* to the left ribs, *dreaming* to the right, *feeling* to the breastbone, *will* below the navel, *nagual* to the genitals. "The anus," he said, "seems the likely location of the *tonal*." Or as don Juan must have said: "The orderly world you're hanging onto is a crappy world." Scotton thought don Juan had furthered Jung's work on *persona* (the socially apparent self) and on symmetrical aspects of the personality (invisible *nagual* balancing visible *tonal*).

Some Jungians have been attracted to Castaneda's works by their legendary aura and symbolic variety: Carlos on the hero's journey guided alternatively by Trickster and the Wise Old Man, meeting various other archetypes. Though Stephen Larsen discounted don Juan as an ineffectual therapist and inadequate shaman, he found Carlos-Skeptic a useful emblem of modernist rationalizing. Mary M. Watkins cited Sacateca's dancing as a waking-dream technique and Carlos's looking-at-hands as a way of controlling dreams; Faber would deprecate such attempts at control, but Watkins said the effect was unknown.

Jungian analyst Donald Williams and poet W. Allen Ashby chronicled their friendship which, like Carlos and don Juan's, had endured while marriages and other friendships had come and gone. Unhappy in love, Ashby had sought guidance from don Juan, an egregious example of misplaced confidence, since don Juan's ideas on love fall somewhere between worthless and corrupt. To his credit, Ashby felt uneasy about this guidance. Williams strove to render don Juan's teachings social, which he could do only by some rather tenuous symbolic interpretations. Corresponding with me, Williams mentioned the salience of the Amerindian as an archetype for modern Americans. I answered that Americans must have made little progress toward the Amerindian if they were satisfied with an archetype as synthetic and European as don Juan.

Psychiatric social worker Michael Whan (no relation to don) saw symbolic thresholds at the twilit crack between the worlds, in don Juan's changeable behavior, in Carlos's epistemological questions, and in the legendary bus station at the border between academic rationality and preliterate magic. He defined Carlos's prentice problem as whether to listen to the Wise Old Man or call Trickster's bluff. He spotted ethnomethodology as a haunt of don Juan's trickster spirit, the enemy of boundaries. He said that by calling the world of sorcery only a description don Juan repudiated a literal reading of the story and revealed "an iconoclastic attitude toward his own esoteric teachings, his concerns being not occult literality but epistemology and hermeneutics."

An ally, don Juan told Carlos, would look like a man he had once known or would always be about to know. Marie-Louise von Franz, author of numerous Jungian works, interpreted don Juan's ally as the

Self in its primary, demonic form, a dangerous beast that attacks sorcerer or analysand and must be subdued. Though von Franz liked don Juan, she regretted the absence of Eros (love) and Anima (the feminine aspect of personality) from his consequently rough handling of Carlos. Don Juan, she said, lacks Jung's great merit, which was to teach how one could deal with the weird world of the deeper unconscious without destroying one's human relationships and social situation. "Active imagination," she concluded "should not produce a lonely, asocial hunter of mysteries."

Weston La Barre, a dedicated admirer of Freud and disadmirer of Castaneda, agreed with Faber that the don Juan books manifest a character disorder, but since he recognized don Juan as a character wholly contained in the story, he attributed the defect entirely to author Castaneda. La Barre would have preferred me to be less tolerant of and amused by the "provocative psychopathy" implicit in the don Juan hoax, but I explained that my tolerance and amusement were justified by a comparison with antisocial behaviors that did much greater harm and offered no compensations. "As editor of *The Don Juan Papers*," I wrote to him, "I should be very interested in an essay developing the theme of heinous harm done by Castaneda to others, but I suspect categorical victims cannot be discovered. Those I have queried typically feel honored by his impositions."

Instead of growing furious with Castaneda over his "unethical method," as Carlos grew furious with don Juan; instead of saying "one should not play with a person's feelings and loyalties," as Carlos told don Juan; instead of feeling a terrible anger at Castaneda or hating him, as Carlos hated don Juan; Castaneda's putative victims fiercely defend him against my judicious, fair-minded critiques. If they become furious at all, they become furious with me. I can't bring myself to blame *him* for their incorrigible, supine submission to the Trickster, who must be giving them something they want. As Bharati is said to have blurted while hoisting a glass with Madame Blavatsky: "*Mundus vult decipi,*" the world wishes to be deceived.

Castaneda can be plausibly if not conclusively defended against charges of antisocial behavior by weighing his useful tests of popular and professional gullibility against the embarrassment and inconvenience they have cost. If Neil Erickson suffered a seven-year psychosis after reading *The Teachings of Don Juan*, how do we know he wouldn't have suffered an equivalent psychosis after seeing *The Exorcist* or reading "The Call of Cthulhu"? Maybe Castaneda saved him from angel dust by catching him early. Granted, Castaneda's benefactions seem to come as fortuitous by-products of a need for power and glory expressing itself in public rather than from a benevolent and modest desire to help others; granted, the deeper we look into Trickster's motives, the darker they get; but isn't that true of depth psychology in general? "If the typical antisocial person"—concluded my letter to La Barre—"did as little harm as Carlos Castaneda, this ordinary world of men would be a better place."

V.

Understanding Castaneda

The Catalina, a Charming Hotel

A Worthy Opponent

"Without the aid of a worthy opponent, who's not really an enemy but a thoroughly dedicated adversary, the apprentice has no possibility of continuing on the path of knowledge."

In the story, as on the calendar, it was 1962. Carlos was setting traps for rabbits and quail but catching none; Castaneda was showing his manuscript to professors at UCLA but getting no sponsors.

"Someone is interfering with your hunting," don Juan announced.

"Who?" said Carlos, but he knew. It was La Catalina, his worthy opponent—or, as she was called in the first three books, "la Catalina," the quotation marks, oddly, forming part of the name.

The episode illustrates two subtle features of Castaneda's way of working. One is that calendar-time and narrative-time often coincide, Carlos's adventures being written or at least dated when their counterparts happen to Castaneda. The other is that oddities of style or diction may signal metaphorical correspondences, providing clues whereby the allegory can be traced to its origins in ordinary events. What events prompted Castaneda to imagine "la Catalina," the handsome but frightening witch who interfered with Carlos's hunt for power?

The worthy opponent's genealogy goes back, I believe, to two articles in the *Saturday Evening Post*, the first by Aldous Huxley, one of Castaneda's favorite writers. "Stimulators of the mystical faculties" like peyote and LSD, wrote Huxley, "make possible a genuine religious experience" by which "large numbers of men and women [can] achieve a radical self-transcendence and a deeper understanding of the nature of things," which will constitute a religious revolution. Huxley's article was published in October 1958, on the verge of the sixties. The following year Castaneda read *The Sacred Mushroom*, which led him to the Wassons' epochal *Mushrooms, Russia, and History*, whose shamans María Sabina and Don Aurelio, I have argued, provided the first models for don Juan.

Castaneda was not the only spiritual revolutionary to take inspiration from Huxley and the Wassons. Just as in the summer of narrative-1960 Carlos met don Juan for the first time, so in the summer of calendar-1960 Harvard psychologist Timothy Leary was sitting beside a swimming pool in Cuernavaca consuming his first hallucinogens, nine sacred Mazatec mushrooms. (Don Juan's mushroom mixture would be smoked in a little house beside an irrigation ditch, where don Juan would bathe Carlos to revive him.) During the ensuing five hours, Leary realized he had died. In what he later called the deepest religious experience of his life, he left his body on the bed, relived his life, and went back to being a one-celled organism. Having thus discovered "the spiritual equivalent of the hydrogen bomb," he went back to Harvard to spread the word. One of the first recruits was psychologist Richard Alpert, later to be known as Baba Ram Dass. The two of them preached the new gospel to faculty and students until the University authorities got fed up, whereupon the evangelists founded a non-profit corporation they called "The International Federation for Inner Freedom"—"If-If" for short. In the summer of 1962 If-If set up a training center in the Mexican fishing village of Zihuatanejo, up the coast from Acapulco. There psychedelic seekers found a sanctuary in the charming Hotel Catalina, shown in the illustration clinging to the bluff under the palm trees, as one sees it looking up from the beach. Americans who stayed with Leary in the hotel called it "the Catalina." Translating that into Spanish, one gets "la Catalina," an unsurprising name for a hotel but a rather unusual name for a character in a story.

Although five-thousand applicants signed up for training at the Catalina, only a few made the journey. In the spring of 1963 Harvard fired its errant professors and the Mexican government kicked the 20 Catalina trippers then in residence back over the border. Undaunted, If-If leased a 45-room mansion near Millbrook, New York and got ready for the crucial campaign to turn on the youth of America, as the media gave full play to Leary in the Sky with Diamonds. *Look* featured "The Strange Case of the Harvard Drug Scandal," while *Saturday Evening Post* carried "The Dangerous Magic of LSD," in which writer John Kobler related the Mexican adventure.

"I sat transfixed all evening before a tree, feeling in it the very treeness of trees," said one LSD visionary in Kobler's account. "I sensed it was a tree by its odor," a drugless Carlos would recall. "Something in me 'knew' that that peculiar odor was the 'essence' of tree."

"Our favorite concepts are standing in the way of a floodtide, two billion years building up. The verbal dam is collapsing," Leary and Alpert exulted. "I *saw* the loneliness of man as a gigantic wave which had been frozen in front of me, held back by the invisible wall of a metaphor," Castaneda would write.

If-If proposed to liberate members from their "webs," so that they might soar through the infinite space of consciousness. Carlos's bemushroomed head would fly among silvery crows; his undrugged eyes would see a range of mountains as a "web of light fibers."

If-If adopted *The Tibetan Book of the Dead* as a drug-taker's manual. Don Juan would tell Carlos the book was a "bunch of crap."

"The experience is essentially nonverbal, so you can't follow your collaborator's responses, unless you're under the influence of the drug too," said Leary and Alpert. The components of nonordinary reality "were not subject to ordinary consensus," Castaneda would write; they required a "special consensus." Kobler asked a psychoanalyst about the risks of using such powerful drugs to keep up with the patient. "Oh yes," admitted the doctor, "the sorcerer may find he's only the sorcerer's apprentice."

"If anybody can show us a better road to happiness," the notorious Leary challenged, "we'll drop our research. But we don't think they will." A better road was already running through the unknown mind of Castaneda, don Juan's path with heart, which would carry future readers away from what Castaneda saw as the haphazard drug-fiendery of the Catalina, toward a disciplined and eventually drugless mysticism. Ten years later, Castaneda would tell students at Irvine don Juan didn't need the psychotropic plants any more, though dedication to ritual still obliged him to "go out each day and collect the mushrooms with meticulous care"—a botanically incongruous statement, since the mushrooms cannot be collected "each day" even in Oaxaca, let alone in Sonora. Castaneda's fantasy of Leary's degenerate leavings was chronicled by John Wallace:

> Carlos told how he was horrified to find the remnants of a colony supposedly started by Timothy Leary in the 1960s. When the Mexican authorities ran the Leary group out of Mexico, some of the people remained behind, hiding in the hills until things had cooled. Carlos talked of going to a house where these people still lived. He said: "I walked in wearing my best smile and said, 'Hi friends! I'm Carlos Castaneda from Los Angeles.' They were all zonked out. There were 25 of them in a big room [—an impressive remnant from a group of 20]. Stoned. One little girl who almost smiled at me almost encouraged me. But she wouldn't talk to me either. She lifted up her leg to scratch it. It was very hairy. I was shocked at what I saw there. Truly

shocked. I got up and left. Don Juan came and we went into the mountains [—but why was don Juan hanging around Zihuatanejo, 500 miles from Oaxaca, 1000 miles from Sonora?]. I told him about the Americans. Don Juan told me that he had seen them too. He thought them truly preposterous. He told me that he saw them in the fields eating the mushrooms directly. Don Juan was appalled—it is truly toxic to eat the mushrooms like that without meticulous preparation [—which will be news to María Sabina, though, of course, the supposed toxicity is a metaphorical warning against spiritual or mental harm from using hallucinogens without a guiding ritual]. He could not understand how they could be so stupid. He saw a naked American standing in the field, eating the mushrooms right there on the spot. Don Juan was horrified."

Castaneda had to learn sorcery, he explained, because drugs alone can't stop the world; they just rearrange the old glosses. "That is my quarrel with people like Timothy Leary," he said—coming as close as he dared to proclaiming a contest for the hearts and minds of Huxley's self-transcenders. While the Messiah of LSD was leaping from one foolish extreme to the next—"I'm very fond of Tim," said Huxley, "but why does he have to be such an ass?"—landing in prison, escaping to miserable exile, coming home to serve a long term, Castaneda was writing three best-sellers.

The impact of a worthy opponent would elicit a warrior's best efforts, don Juan said; the opponent he thought worthy of Carlos was "la Catalina." In the fall of calendar-1962 If-If flourished in Zihuatanejo; in the fall of narrative-1962 Carlos survived six hair-raising encounters with his worthy opponent in Sonora. A startling photograph in Kobler's 1963 article (rendered here in a drawing) shows a formidable young woman in a leopard-skin bathing suit wading into the Mexican surf after taking LSD, her long left hand extended downward toward the water. Kobler's caption tells us she is "feeling the power of the ocean." That remarkable image, I believe, incubated four years in Castaneda's fabulizing brain, emerged in his manuscript of 1967 as the "fiendish witch" who was trying to finish don Juan off, a metaphor of Leary's booming psychedelic supermarket, which threatened to bury an unpublished author of a quasi-academic romance about the rigorous regime imposed by in inaccessible magus mixing secret formulas.

From 1968 to 1974 Leary's fortunes fell while Castaneda's rose. Con-

If-Ifer wades into the Mexican surf
after taking LSD. She said she was:

currently, La Catalina grew less frightening in each successive book. In *The Teachings* she was too terrifying to be seen in her own form. In *A Separate Reality* she was dangerous but handsome. In *Ixtlan* she received a promising new title: A worthy opponent. In *Tales of Power* don Juan admitted she had been a friend all along pretending to be an enemy. Thus did Castaneda grow metaphorically magnanimous in victory to his fellow Catholic apostate and charismatic adversary. He could afford to be magnanimous, for as early as 1969 the wide-eyed pundit Theodore Roszak had proclaimed his work a uniquely important contribution to the psychedelic literature, which should perhaps replace the "comparatively amateurish efforts of Huxley, Watts, Burroughs, and Leary."

Interviewed by *Time's* Sandra Burton, Castaneda told of being invited to a party in New York's East Village, where he met Leary but found the chatter of the acid-heads absurd. "They were children," he said, "indulging in incoherent revelations. A sorcerer takes hallucinogens for a different reason than heads do, and after he has gotten where he wants to go, he stops taking them." Translation: An allegorist writes about hallucinogens until he gets a couple of books published; then he stops writing about them. The confrontation between Leary and Carlos is thematically indispensable, but there is something wrong with the report. *Time* gave the date as 1964, but why would an unpublished and utterly unknown Los Angeles writer be invited to meet Leary in New York, and how could a poverty-stricken graduate student afford to make the trip? A more colorful version of the meeting, published a year later in *Fate*, has Carlos journeying east to explain his adventures with don Juan, which Leary and Alpert have read about in *The Teachings*. This version eliminates the unknown guest and penniless traveler but introduces a more troublesome difficulty: By the time *Teachings* was published, Leary had moved to California, so the trip would have been unnecessary. At any rate, Carlos is no more impressed by Leary in *Fate's* 1969 than he was in *Time's* 1964. The acid-culture conversation is still trivial. Leary jokes and giggles, calling Alpert "a Jewish queer," while Alpert—now returned from India as Baba Ram Dass—blesses the convocation by flashing a banana that was hidden in his robe. A dismayed Carlos flees the party, as a horrified Carlos fled the house of degenerate hippies.

Since Leary and Castaneda were both living in California between 1968 and 1970, I'm quite ready to believe they found themselves at some time in the same room, but the alternative versions of the confrontation offer more than don Juan's bare disdain of Leary's fiendery. Castaneda was apparently trying out different imaginary scenes and occasions for

"Feeling the Power of the Ocean"

engaging his then more popular adversary, thus gaining magical control over Leary by drawing him into the allegory. If Leary hadn't been quickly snatched away by the California Department of Corrections, he might well have turned up in a conversation like the following:

Catalina: ¡*Hola, Doctor Liri!* Good to see you. It's been a long time.
Leary: Hi! Don't I know you from somewhere?
Catalina: You bet your *botes!* I'm "the Catalina."
Leary: That's a hotel—a charming little hotel.
Catalina: Knock off the *sexismo*, don Timo. We're all parafeminists here.
Leary: Well, who are you really?
Catalina: "The Catalina!" I used to be a hotel, now I'm a witch.
Leary: Far *out!* I used to be a one-celled organism.
Catalina: I know. That's in Kobler's article—which was the link between you and Castaneda.
Leary: Really? I couldn't get anything out of Castaneda. He came to a party in New York—or was it California? Anyway, he sat in a corner and didn't say a word.
Catalina: He was *stalking*.
Leary: No he *wasn't*.
Catalina: Ess-*talk*ing. With an *Ess*.
Leary: I see.
Catalina: You don't *see*. You just *look*. You rearrange the old glosses. You and Ram D'Ass, with his effete beautitudes and his provocative banana.
Leary: None of that matters now. I'm doing space colonies. Inner to outer in one lifetime!
Catalina: *Hah!* You think we're not up on *that*? Did you read about our fifty-thousand-foot dome? Is that an artificial extraterrestrial environment, or is it?
Leary: I see what you mean.
Catalina: You *don't* see. You're wrapped up in your incoherent revelations and your superaphrodisiacs and your nightclub act. You were supposed to be a worthy opponent, to boost Carlos into orbit. I had to take over for you because you made such an ass of yourself. Even don Aldous says so.
Leary: *Huxley?* He's *alive?*
Catalina: Well, he's not dead.
Leary: Where is he?

La Catalina, a Worthy Opponent

Catalina: In the dome, of course.

Leary: Can I go to the dome?

Catalina: If you're scheduled to go there. It's up to the Nagual.

Leary: How can I find out?

Catalina: Keep reading the books.

Leary: More books? The reviewers said Castaneda was burnt out.

Catalina: That's a bunch of crap. They're burned *up* because he made monkeys out of them. This cult business can go on forever. It's a kind of immortality.

Leary: That's reassuring.

Catalina: Not for *you, bobo.* For *him.*

Leary: I see.

Catalina: No you don't. Don Juan and Carlos *see.* Don Q and Liri *talk!*

Allegory is not Ethnobotany:
Analyzing Castaneda's Letter
to R. Gordon Wasson
and Carlos's Spanish Fieldnotes

M any people have written letters to Carlos Castaneda, but few have gotten answers. R. Gordon Wasson is one of the few. On 26 August 1968 he sent the following letter:

Dear Mr Castaneda:

I have been asked to review *The Teachings of Don Juan* for *Economic Botany*. I have read it and am impressed by the quality of the writing and the hallucinogenic effects you have had. Perhaps you are not yet overwhelmed with letters from strangers and you can discuss with me the use of mushrooms by don Juan.

My professional life has been chiefly concerned with the hallucinogenic effects of the Mexican 'sacred mushrooms.' It was my wife and I who publicized the re-discovery of the cult in Oaxaca, and it was on my invitation to Professor Roger Heim that he came over and studied them with us. We three have written books about them and innumerable articles.

I.

Am I right in concluding from your narrative that you never gathered the mushrooms, nor indeed ever saw a whole specimen? In the book they are always in powder, perhaps already mixed with other ingredients, are they not? Don Juan carried the powder around his neck in a sack. When he utilized them, they were smoked. Once you embarked (p. 63) on a trip to Chihuahua for *honguitos*, but your quest turned out to be for mescalito. When you first mention the mushrooms they are 'possibly' *Psilocybe mexicana* (p. 7), but later they are that species. Did you satisfy yourself that you were dealing with *Psilocybe mexicana*? This mushroom would normally, in don Juan's hands, macerate into shreds, rather than a powder, whereas the hallucinogenic puffballs used in certain spots in the Mixteca would give a powder. Do you know where your mushrooms grew, whether in pastures, corn fields, bovine dung, on the trunks of dying trees, or elsewhere?

II.

Don Juan (I assume that this was a name adopted by you to save him from pestering) seems to have spoken perfect Spanish and to have lived in many places—the U.S. and southern Mexico, perhaps elsewhere, as well as Sonora and Chihuahua. What is his cultural provenience? Is he a pure Yaqui? Or has his personality been shaped to a noticeable extent by the influences of the foreign places where he has been? May he have been influenced by the Indians of Oaxaca, in the remote parts of that State, and there learned to know the mushrooms? I ask this because the use of the hallucinogenic mushrooms has never previously been reported in Sonora or Chihuahua. In fact they have never been found there, and one would think that if specimens were found, in the arid conditions prevailing in those States, it would be hard to find enough for ceremonial use, or at any rate to count on finding enough. There may be restricted areas known to the Indians where the Indians might expect to find them, places well watered and fertile. Perhaps the species is one not yet known to science and that grows in arid country. It would be thrilling if you could pursue this further and make a discovery. The practice of smoking the mushroom powder is hitherto unknown to me. Had you brought back the powder, or the mixture in which the mushroom powder was an ingredient, we might have identified the species under the microscope, since there must have been spores present, and if the species is a known one, the spore suffices to place it. We now have almost a score of hallucinogenic species from Mexico.

III.

Will there be a Spanish edition of the book? You gave a few translations, but there were many times when I was hungry for more. 'A man of knowledge'—did don Juan say, 'hombre de conocimientos' or simply 'un hombre que sabe'? In Mazatec a curandero is $cho^4ta^4chi^4ne^4$, 'one who knows.' Was don Juan bilingual, or was he better in Spanish than in Yaqui? Did you gather in your field notes the Yaqui equivalents of the terms he used? It would be fascinating to study with a linguist proficient in Yaqui the meaning of those terms. Did you ever tell your readers whether he could read and write in Spanish? How did he ordinarily make his living? His esoteric knowledge must have been his vocation, but he must have had a bread-and-butter occupation. I take it that you yourself are a fully acculturated 'gringo,' since you spell your name 'Castaneda' rather than Castañeda in the Spanish way.

Sincerely yours,
R. GORDON WASSON

Those who believe don Juan was born in the rare book room at UCLA while Castaneda was reading the Wassons' 1957 volumes will see some irony in Wasson's introducing himself as a "stranger" and taking the trouble to establish his ethnobotanical qualifications. In 1968 Wasson did not yet appreciate the extent to which his own work had inspired Castaneda. As he would admit three years later, however, he did "smell a hoax." Not only were don Juan's mushrooms unrecognizable, but Castaneda seemed oddly unconcerned about identifying them. Wasson's letter exemplifies the scrupulously respectful tone in which senior scholars query junior scholars they suspect of fraud. In 1968 Wasson was 70 years old and had bested his share of tricksters and pretenders, but in Castaneda he met an opponent worthy of his scholarly and forensic skills.

In replying to Wasson's letter, Castaneda purports to be a scholar and man of science who has published ethnobotanical findings, or at least legitimate observations that could lead to ethnobotanical findings, and is now answering questions put to him by a well known contributor to that field and strictly limited to his published claims. That being so, the substance of his letter inevitably becomes the property of the scientific community and may not be withheld on any plea of property or privacy. It is therefore my duty and privilege, made possible by Wasson's kind cooperation, to convey that substance to you. On the other hand—and this will disappoint many—the literary property constituted by the letter is protected by the copyright law and may not be exploited without the proprietor's permission. On 12 August 1979 I wrote to Castaneda: "Your fans and my readers would appreciate the opportunity to read the original text of your reply rather than depend on me to tell them what is in it." Few will be surprised to learn that no answer came to that letter. Eventually Castaneda's letter will be published, at which time I hope you will compare it with this chapter and conclude that I have done a good job of separating substance belonging to the community of scholars from form belonging to Castaneda and have rendered the substance fully and faithfully. Until Castaneda relents, or his heirs permit the publication, you'll have to trust me.

Castaneda's letter to Wasson comprises six neatly typewritten pages, every page dated "September 6, 1968." The signature is unmistakably Castaneda's. Nevertheless, in his next book the author will write: "On September 4, 1968, I went to Sonora to visit don Juan. . . . Two days later, on September 6, Lucio, Benigno, and Eligio came over . . . to go hunting with me." While Carlos hunts jack rabbits in Sonora, Castaneda stalks Wasson from Westwood. A man who really knows how to stalk appears to the deer as a deer, to the coyote as a coyote, to the scholar as a scholar. Castaneda's characteristic treatment of persons he wishes to engage or persuade is to mirror their interests or mimic their manner. His letter to Wasson starts with mimicry: the heading on each page showing the name of the recipient and the date, as Wasson's did; three sections numbered with centered Roman numerals; the same valediction, "Sincerely yours." To avoid repeating phrases like "Castaneda says," I shall give the substance of the letter in a list of numbered assertions written in the third person, commenting on these assertions in brackets, [ ], as I go along. Wasson's questions, repeated by Castaneda, will be repeated here in *italics*. The letter begins:

1. It was a great pleasure to receive Wasson's letter, for Castaneda is "very familiar" with his work and is honored by his attention. Wasson must bear in mind, however, that Castaneda is not an authority; his knowledge is limited strictly to the data he has collected. His fieldwork was never anthropological fieldwork proper but an "inquiry product" of his own interest, which is "content" and "meaning." He therefore became absorbed in don Juan's "innuendoes" rather than in "specific ethnographic details." Since he was dealing with a "dramatic and serious" system of beliefs, he intentionally blurred such details. It would be "superflous" to try to remedy that vagueness in a single letter without first preparing a better "ethnographic context," but Castaneda will do his best to answer Wasson's questions. [With exquisite humility in the service of the ego, Castaneda pleads limited expertise and informal purposes, thus quickly slipping out of the straitjacket of ethnographic sci-

ence. His contention that the drama and seriousness of don Juan's beliefs somehow obliged him to blur ethnographic details seems a nonsequitur intended to mystify the reader. By "superflous" he apparently means futile, but he implies that if he wished to he could put don Juan into some clear ethnographic context, an implication he contradicts later in the letter. Here the implication serves to lend an aura of authenticity without producing any evidence of authenticity.]

Q: *Am I right in concluding from your narrative that you never gathered the mushrooms, nor indeed ever saw a whole specimen?*

2. Castaneda has gathered the mushrooms. He has held in his hands "perhaps hundreds" of specimens. He and don Juan went every year to collect them in the mountains "southwest and northwest of Valle Nacional." [Huautla de Jiménez, where Wasson first ate the mushrooms, is in the mountains northwest of Valle Nacional. Castaneda's mirror customarily approximates what the other person expects or hopes to see, without showing it exactly. He reminds Wasson of Huautla without mentioning Huautla.] Castaneda wanted to describe the collecting ritual in *The Teachings*, but since, unlike peyote and Jimson weed, the mushrooms contained don Juan's "ally (*aliado*)," don Juan imposed a rule of "total secrecy about specific processes." [Castaneda smoothly turns the inquiry away from the specimens that interest Wasson toward don Juan's gathering ritual, and then says the ritual may not be described to anyone. He neither says nor here implies that specimens could not have been brought back. Why doesn't he? If don Juan specifically forbade the taking of specimens, that would foreclose botanical inquiry, but Castaneda is too subtle for that. He brushes the specimens into his hat while we are goggling at the ritual, as any conjuror would.]

Q: *Did you satisfy yourself that you were dealing with* Psilocybe mexicana?

3. No. The identification was tentative and "terribly unsophisticated." [Humility again.] The definite identification in *The Teachings* is— Castaneda fears—an "editorial error." Since he was never fully convinced of the classification, it should have remained tentative all the way through. [Castaneda reluctantly blames the error on some editor at the University Press, but why didn't he catch the error?] Don Juan's mushrooms looked like pictures of *Psilocybe mexicana* Castaneda had seen, and an [unnamed] member of the UCLA Pharmacology Department showed him some specimens that looked the same. Nor did don Juan's mushrooms turn into powder on being handled. [So they were not Mixtecan puffballs but probably *Psilocybe mexicana*—in which case,

why not say so later in the book? A sorcerer's tactical display of humility serves his strategy of eventual self-assertion.] Don Juan always picked the mushrooms with his left hand, transferred them to his right, and then put them through the neck of the gourd. [Wait a *minute!* What happened to the rule of "total secrecy" about the gathering ritual? Does it become flexible when one is writing letters? Did don Juan invent it to help in writing this letter?]

Q: *Do you know where your mushrooms grew?*

4. Yes. On trunks of dead trees, but more often on decomposed shrubs.

Q: *What is don Juan's cultural provenience?*

5. Don Juan is a marginal man, whose personality has been formed by many influences outside the Yaqui culture. His first name is actually Juan. Castaneda tried to find a substitute, but no other name seemed to fit the man he knew. [If one tried to think of another name for Peter Pan or Doctor Dolittle, what name would fit?] Don Juan is not a pure Yaqui. His mother was a Yuma Indian. He was born in Arizona, where he lived six or seven years before moving to Sonora. Some time after being deported from Sonora by the Mexican government, he went to the Valle Nacional area [of Oaxaca], where he stayed more than thirty years. Castaneda believes he went there with his teacher, "who must have been Mazateco." Castaneda has not been able to find out who the teacher was or where don Juan learned sorcery, but the fact that Castaneda must take don Juan to Oaxaca every year to collect the mushrooms strongly suggests where don Juan learned to use them. At any rate, Castaneda cannot determine don Juan's cultural provenience, "except in a guessing manner" [—which contradicts the earlier hint that in a series of letters Castaneda could "go back" to "re-establish a better ethnographic context"]. The impossibility of determining don Juan's cultural background brings up another mistake Castaneda was unfortunately involved in owing to his "lack of experience in matters of publications." Upon accepting his manuscript for publication, the Editorial Committee of the University of California Press "suggested" the word Yaqui be included in the title in order to "place the book ethnographically." "They had not read the manuscript," but they argued that Castaneda had called don Juan a Yaqui—which, of course, he had—but never meaning don Juan was a product or example of Yaqui culture, as the subtitle *A Yaqui Way of Knowledge* falsely implies.

[Let us pause here for a moment to consider what Castaneda has just told Wasson about academic publishing in the University of California:

1) The Editorial Committee of the University accepts for publication manuscripts it *has not read* and then, by mere "suggestion," 2) imposes misleading titles on these works against the wishes of conscientious authors inexperienced in matters of publications. In contrast, the record shows that Walter Goldschmidt, a member of the Committee, read Castaneda's manuscript, which the Committee accepted on recommendations from him and three non-member consultants. As to the second charge, recalling Spicer's speculation that the University Press "went beyond Castaneda's intention" to add the spurious subtitle, I wrote to the Press quoting what Spicer had said. Associate Editor Udo Strutynski answered: "The title of Castaneda's book and the entire text are the work of the author." Despite my reservations about the trustworthiness of University Press depositions in the case of Castaneda versus the Community of Scholars, I am inclined to accept Strutynski's statement, having been told by an unimpeachable source at Simon and Schuster that Castaneda "has his own rules about almost everything and has never displayed any sign of cooperating on anything short of delivering a manuscript." Indeed, Goldschmidt wanted Castaneda "to cut down on that Structural Analysis," while the Press was reluctant to publish the wearisome parody at all, yet there it is in the book, 54 pages of "pure Garfinkel," published, Strutynski said, "not at our insistence but the author's." Would a writer who could ram that literary cactus ball down the throats of Goldschmidt and the University Press stand meekly by to see his book mistitled—as it undeniably was—unless he approved of the mistitling? I find no way to believe it.]

Castaneda doesn't know [the letter continues] whether the hallucinogenic mushrooms grow in the arid regions of Sonora and Chihuahua, but he doesn't think don Juan has ever looked for them there. Yet don Juan has said that once a man commands the power of the mushrooms, they will grow where he expects to find them. [There are more things in heaven and earth, Mr Wasson, than are dreamt of in your mycology.] The first time Castaneda saw the mushrooms was in Durango [which is just south of the State of Chihuahua], but there were not enough of them to use. [Castaneda is mirroring Wasson's "hard to find enough for ceremonial use."] Don Juan said that to get useful quantities they would have to go to Oaxaca. In 1964 Castaneda found "one specimen" in the Santa Monica Mountains (near Los Angeles), but "the laboratory at UCLA" [no person being named] carelessly lost it before it could be identified [—showing once again how the virtuous intent of a conscientious but terribly unsophisticated and unassertive investigator can be frustrated by bureaucratic callousness and rampant incompetence in a big university]. It was "strikingly obvious" to Castaneda that the specimen had been one of don Juan's mushrooms. [Can one bear this tragic loss to science!—but sorcerers have other things on their minds:] Don Juan said finding the specimen was an omen of learning, but picking it and giving it to strangers [like Wasson] was a clumsy mistake [—which has the feel but not the form of a prohibition on gathering botanical specimens].

Q: *Have you brought back the powder or the mixture in which the mushroom powder was an ingredient?*

6. No—but Castaneda is sure he could obtain a very small amount, "perhaps a dab of it." If that would be enough for examination under the microscope, he could send it to Wasson before the end of 1968. [Although Carlos smoked the mushroom powder eight times after Castaneda wrote this letter, the promised "dab" never arrived.].

Q: *Will there be a Spanish edition of the book?*

7. Castaneda hopes the University Press will "consider that possibility." The fieldnotes are all in Spanish, and *The Teachings* is "almost an English version of a Spanish manuscript." [Why, then, did Mexican novelist Juan Tovar have to translate *The Teachings* and three of its sequels strictly from the English version, including many hard-to-translate American slang expressions? Why was the "Spanish manuscript" not sent to Tovar to make his task easier and his translation more faithful to don Juan's actual pattern of Spanish speech? An answer will be proposed later in this chapter.]

Q: *Did don Juan say 'hombre de conocimientos' or simply 'un hombre que sabe'?*

8. "Here" Wasson has given Castaneda "the most fascinating piece of information." [What is the new and fascinating piece of information? Wasson's paragraph, mostly questions, contains only one informative assertion: Mazatec Indians call a curandero "one who knows." Castaneda implies that Wasson has now given this information for the first time, in his letter, rather than on pages 251-252 of *Mushrooms, Russia, and History*. The further implication is that, although Castaneda is "very familiar" with Wasson's work, he has surprisingly never looked into Wasson's (at that time) most famous and detailed treatise on Mexican ethnomycology.] Though don Juan used three different terms, Castaneda preferred "man of knowledge," because it was "more concrete" than "one who knows"[—and perhaps because it did not exactly mirror the phrase found on page 252 of the book Castaneda had surprisingly

never read]. To illustrate don Juan's uses of the terms, Castaneda encloses with his letter [12] pages of his notes in Spanish, which he hopes are legible. These pages are the "direct transcription" of less legible notes Castaneda took while don Juan was talking to him. Ordinarily he would transcribe his notes "immediately," to retain the freshness and flare of don Juan's words and ideas. [Presently we shall look into those notes and learn more about the Man of Novels.]

Q: *Was don Juan bilingual, or was he better in Spanish than in Yaqui?*

9. It may be don Juan speaks Spanish better than any other language, but he also speaks Yaqui, Yuma, and Mazatec. Castaneda has never heard him speak English but suspects he understands it perfectly.

Q: *Did you gather in your field notes the Yaqui equivalents of the terms he used?*

10. Castaneda has a few Indian terms in his notes, not all of them Yaqui, and not enough "to make a serious study." [Very well, but correspondence between colleagues neither constitutes nor requires "a serious study." Wasson would obviously be overjoyed to learn even one of those Indian terms, yet none is given.]

Q: *Did you ever tell your readers whether he could read and write in Spanish?*

11. Don Juan reads Spanish very well, but Castaneda has never seen him writing anything. For a long time, simply because don Juan is just not interested in such skills, Castaneda mistook him for an illiterate. This difference between the two men is a theme Castaneda is trying to develop in the biography of don Juan he is now writing [—but which, eleven years and four books later, has not yet seen the light of day, perhaps because it is difficult to write a biography of a man whose cultural provenience one cannot determine, "except in a guessing manner"].

[Q: *I take it that you yourself are a fully acculturated 'gringo,' since you spell your name 'Castaneda.'*]

12. There is not much to tell about Castaneda [— who, as anyone can see, is a boring, uncomplicated fellow, who just happened to run into a fascinating old Indian]. His home was in São Paulo, Brazil, but he went to school in Argentina before coming to the United States. His "full name is" Carlos Aranha. Because the Latin tradition adds the mother's last name, he became Carlos A. Castaneda when he came to the United States, and then dropped the A. [Castaneda apparently means that to *fill out* his name one adds the mother's name Aranha to the father's name

Castaneda; thus he exchanges his mother's and father's true (or nearly true) names. But instead of saying what he means he says his "full name is Carlos Aranha." What is the significance of this tiny error? I should guess the slip testifies that truth weighs *something* in his mind and here asserts itself unnoticed by him to approximate what he was usually called in Peru: Carlos Arana.] The name Castaneda belonged to his Sicilian grandfather, who modified whatever form it originally had in Sicily. [But if the grandfather came to Brazil, a Portuguese speaking country, why did he change his Italian name, whatever it was, to the Spanish Castañeda rather than the Portuguese Castanheda?] Castaneda hopes he has answered all of Wasson's questions clearly and thanks him for his letter.

Though he neglected to say how don Juan earned his living, Castaneda did answer all of Wasson's other questions clearly, if not completely and accurately. Moreover, without being asked, he sent 12 pages of fieldnotes. This simulation of compliance would later be optimized as a "full and frank" reply, but at the moment Wasson was far from satisfied with the information. On 4 October 1968 he sent a letter expressing the hope that Castaneda would, while working on the biography, discover the identity of don Juan's teacher, who "must have been an extraordinary person." Wasson asked also at what altitude the mushrooms had been collected, whether they were always smoked, what the other ingredients were, and how long the inebriation would last. He urged Castaneda to send at least the "dab" of mushroom dust but to get whole specimens if he could. He said the mushrooms could not be *Psilocybe mexicana*, which never grow on dead trees or decomposing shrubs, but might be the similar looking *Psilocybe yungensis*, or perhaps an undiscovered species.

Castaneda did not answer Wasson's second letter, but the two met briefly in New York and again in California, on which occasions, despite his earlier suspicions, Wasson got an impression of "an honest and serious young man." By 1973 Wasson had been startled to discover in María Sabina's unpublished *velada* a Mazatec chant translated into English as: "Woman who stops the world am I." Here was apparently the first hard evidence authenticating Castaneda's fieldwork, for the shamanistic (as distinct from the showbiz) "stop the world" had been used by both María Sabina and don Juan, though never published anywhere before appearing in Castaneda's *Journey to Ixtlan*. Wasson was by that time reviewing Castaneda's writings as allegories rather than field reports, but the writer's apparent sincerity and the concordance of stopping the world made him believe there must be *some* authentic core of shamanistic contact buried *somewhere* in Castaneda's fiction-science.

While the concordant stoppings of the world intrigued and encouraged Wasson, they threatened to stop debunker de Mille in his tracks, for if there were even one solid piece of evidence testifying that Castaneda had done his fieldwork off campus, the Piltdown-level hoax would instantly turn into a piddling, so-called "fictionalized treatment" of field observations, the scandalized external dialogue would stop, and the great exposé would collapse. Before writing a word of *Castaneda's Journey* I had to know whether that concordance really linked Castaneda to a preliterate shaman. Was the similarity superficial, or did it involve meaning and spring from pre-Columbian roots? I sent a letter to Mazatec linguist Eunice Pike asking what she thought María Sabina might have had in mind when she uttered that particular chant in the presence of Wasson's tape recorder on the night of 12-13 July 1958. Her answer (later confirmed by Wasson's translator and co-author Florence Cowan) pricked the sorcerer's bubble of authenticity:

> You ask what María Sabina meant when she chanted, "Woman who stops the world am I." Actually that is not the way I would have translated her Mazatec. The verb she used is *se 'nqui*[3] and the same verb is used with a cornerpost under a roof. I would prefer the translation "holds up" or more literally "stands under." So the sentence might be translated, "Woman who supports the world am I."

Don Juan's "stopping" does not stand under the world or support it or hold it up but causes it to collapse, so the connection between the two stoppings was an accident, the evidence of authenticity was an illusion, and the exposé could proceed.

I asked Wasson to send me Castaneda's letter and the 12 pages of fieldnotes. He wrote to Castaneda on 10 January 1976 asking whether there were any objection. The reply has not yet come, and Wasson concluded that three years of silence gave consent. Accordingly, in October 1978 at the San Francisco conference on hallucinogenic plants, he handed me his correspondence with Castaneda, and the 12 pages of fieldnotes, to which we now turn our attention.

The 12 sheets are xerox copies of pages of dialogue and narration written on lined paper like the pads purchased by students. Each page is numbered in the upper righthand corner: 38-42 for 8 April 1962, 1-7 for 15 April 1962. The handwriting is compact, uniform, steady, odd, not eminently legible, but legible enough. The language is Spanish. There are no Indian words. Don Juan uses three phrases for man of knowledge: *uno que sabe* (one who knows), *hombre que sabe* (man who knows), *hombre de conocimiento* (man of knowledge). Castaneda's Spanish is not as good as the English he gradually learned to write. It employs a limited, colorless vocabulary and exhibits peculiar grammar and spelling. He writes *tubo* for *tuvo*, *hiba* for *iba*, *comanda* for *manda*. He uses prepositions in strange ways and omits pronouns where one expects to find them. His dialogue is even more repetitious than in the published text.

In 1973 Wasson said of these pages: "Their substance appears satisfactorily rendered into English on pp. 56-60 of *Teachings*." That is not exactly correct. *Some* of their substance so appears, but some does not appear. In 1968 Wasson could not have recognized or interpreted the additional substance, as can be done now. First, however, I must retract the following statement, from page 50 of *Castaneda's Journey*:

> Subject to refutation by long-awaited proofs from Castaneda, it is my solemn conviction that those 12 pages did not exist before Wasson wrote his letter, that they were manufactured for the occasion, and that they are the only pages of Spanish field notes to come out of Carlos's dozen years in the desert.

Unintentionally, with Wasson's assistance, Castaneda has now furnished the long-awaited proofs that refute my solemn conviction of 1976. My equally solemn conviction, of 1979, is that Castaneda began to write his story in Spanish and did not switch completely to English until he was working on his second book, where don Juan unaccountably began to speak American slang. This means there may indeed be many notebooks bulging with Spanish-language fieldnotes, to be analyzed in the twenty-first century by UCLA doctoral candidates. In the meantime, we can analyze the 12 pages in hand.

My retraction is not going to resurrect Carlos-Fieldworker. On the contrary, it will bury him deeper than he already lies. What I imagined in 1976 was Castaneda sitting down, opening *The Teachings* to page 56, and translating five pages of the book into Spanish, throwing in a few variations for artistic verisimilitude. It would have been better for Carlos-Fieldworker if Castaneda had done that. What really happened, apparently, is that he pulled a few pages out of his voluminous Spanish manuscript. The peccability of this move resides in the fact that the Spanish manuscript and the English book do not tell the same story. Instead of an original account in Spanish and a translation into English, we find early and late versions of a romance. If translator Tovar had received both versions, he would have been deeply perplexed, not knowing which one was authentic. Inevitably he would have concluded neither version was authentic, which explains why he had to translate from English with no help from the Spanish manuscript. Though in his letter to Wasson Castaneda said he transcribed his notes immediately to preserve don Juan's words and ideas, examination of his two versions reveals not preservation but notable discrepancies, of which the rest of this chapter will describe a few.

As the scene opens, it is morning, and Carlos is preparing to leave don Juan's house. Don Juan asks when he will return, and Carlos says in two months. Don Juan says that with such spotty application Carlos will never become a man of knowledge. Don Juan, in contrast, entered his benefactor's house as a boy and did not leave until he was a man and his benefactor had died. Though times were hard, the benefactor cared for him as if for his own son. Carlos asks where they were living. Don Juan says that can't be told, just as, when it comes don Juan's turn to die, Carlos will not be able to say where he met don Juan, where he visited him, or what his name was. That is the rule followed by sincere and dedicated sorcerers. When don Juan dies, Carlos must not even ask where his body is buried. Carlos points out that many persons know the two of them and where they have been meeting. Don Juan denies it. Carlos mentions Fernando, don Nacho, and don Juan's daughter in law. Don Juan says those people don't count, because they are stupid asses, but there are others who count. Carlos asks who. Don Juan says Carlos will learn that at the proper time. The main thing is to follow the rule of secrecy. Carlos promises to follow it faithfully. Don Juan declares that Carlos has a big mouth and will talk. Carlos protests. In the manner of Jesus talking to Peter, don Juan calmly and without rancor assures Carlos he will betray him when the time comes.

This is an intriguing passage, quickened by New Testament allusion, pregnant with possible dramatic conflict, containing information about don Juan's benefactor found nowhere else in the books—or rather, I should say, found nowhere in the books, for this is a passage discarded by a novelist. But not forgotten by him: on narrative 5 October 1968 (a month after Castaneda wrote to Wasson in calendar time), don Juan reminds Carlos of the rule of secrecy, about which he has told him "before."

In *The Teachings*, the narrative for 8 April 1962 ends with don Juan refusing to tell Carlos any more about the four enemies. In the fieldnotes, however, a new passage begins near the bottom of page 42. It is now two o'clock on the same day, and the men begin to talk about the magic crystals used by sorcerers, but then don Juan changes the subject. "There are three forms of spiritual beings," he says. "There are three classes of spirits. The spirits that give nothing because they have nothing to give. The spirits that frighten because that is. . . ." But there the page ends. This brief passage from the fieldnotes is found well preserved in the published text, but it is found in *A Separate Reality*, where it is dated not 8 April 1962 but 16 December 1969. It is a passage retrieved from an old manuscript by a writer working on his second novel. And what about the magic crystals used by sorcerers? They turn up on page 245 of the third novel, dated 14 April 1962.

Having compared *Teachings* and *Ixtlan* for 15 April 1962, Wasson reported that the narratives "part company disconcertingly." *Teachings* has the two men talking in don Juan's house, but *Ixtlan* has them eating a late lunch in a border town. This is barely possible if don Juan's house is close to the border, but on page six of the fieldnotes for that day we are told: "Don Juan leaned against the post of the ramada and looked toward the Bacatete Mountains in the distance." If don Juan's house is near the border, then don Juan has very good vision, because the Bacatete Mountains are more than 200 miles to the south.

Succeeding in fighting off his last, invincible enemy, a man can be called a man of knowledge, if only for a moment, but "that moment of clarity, power, and knowledge is enough." So ends don Juan's sermon on the four enemies, on page 60 of *The Teachings*. In the fieldnotes, however, the conversation is not yet finished. As don Juan leans against the post of the ramada, gazing into the distance at the Bacatete Mountains, Carlos ruminates that it is not possible to escape the last enemy. Don Juan agrees. "As you see," he says very somberly, "it has already thrown me to the ground. It is pressing me down. It is fast crushing me." Carlos looks hard at don Juan but sees only a strong and vigorous man, much younger than his years. Nevertheless, don Juan's words about death have made Carlos understand for the first time the intensity of don Juan's struggle against his last, his invincible enemy.

A stirring scene, but perhaps one the writer judged a little melodramatic and elected to delete. Such revisions, of course, are a novelist's right.

RdeM

The Huichol Indians of north-central Mexico are mountain dwellers whose remoteness and dedication to custom allowed them until recently to preserve their ancient religious tradition in spite of having contacts with Europeans since 1542. The central figure in Huichol religion is the *mara'akame*, or shaman-priest, and the *mara'akame* best known to outsiders is Ramón Medina Silva, whose teachings and leadership were chronicled by anthropologists Barbara Myerhoff and Peter Furst.

"Almost We Cannot Speak About It" comprises two selections from Myerhoff's dissertation. Many similar passages can be read in her book *Peyote Hunt*, and in Furst's article "Huichol Conceptions of the Soul." Elegantly translated from Huichol to Spanish to English in a team effort by Ramón Medina, Peter Furst, Joseph and Barbara Grimes, and Barbara Myerhoff, these two brief shamanic discourses not only give pleasure in the reading but furnish an instructive contrast with don Juan's characteristically un-Indian metaphysical and ethical lectures, an egregious example of which is offered by his academic "recapitulation" in *Tales of Power*. Ramón Medina was a genuine shaman, whom Carlos Castaneda actually met.

Almost We Cannot Speak About It

This is a long story, because it is an important thing. Because in those days they never went disunited. Everything was united, it was one part, united, as though wrapped up in one sheet, as one sleeps at night. So this is our history, from that time when there was no one yet to tell them how it was before, because no one was there before. It was not as it is today, when one has someone to tell how it was in those ancient times, when it was all laid down. This story is something sacred, for the reason that it is from very ancient times, from so long ago. These are things that are almost alone among ourselves. Almost we cannot speak about it. It is a very sacred thing and one must guard it well. Whoever one is, one must guard it well. One must guard it much in one's heart.

(*The* mara'akame *tells how the yearly pilgrims arrive at* Wirikuta, *sacred land of the Huichol ancestors, gather round* Tatewarí, *or Grandfather Fire, and prepare to hunt* híkuri, *the peyote cactus. Each of the pilgrims has become one of the ancient ancestors. One pilgrim is now* Kauyumari, *or Sacred Deer Person; another is* Tatutsí, *Our Great Grandfather; and so on. The* mara'akame *stalks and shoots the peyote, which is also the deer, so that it cannot run away but will stay to be harvested, like the grain it also is.*)

The next day in the morning, all rise early. We venerate *Tatewarí*, we circle him. We leave him there, burning, so that he will not be extinguished. Carefully, carefully, all is heaped together so that he will burn when we return. We get ready. We leave. Without eating anything, without drinking anything. We take our bags, our baskets, that in which to carry the peyote. We go with the *mara'akame* leading, he who is *Tatewarí*. He goes to the right side. *Tatutsí* goes to the other side. The others stay in the center, one following the other.

All go quietly, quietly. One whispers, one does not speak. One walks with care. One steps carefully. One keeps vigil, to see where the *híkuri* lives. Ah, where is he? How does he appear? Where does he hide?

One walks, slowly, with great care. Quietly. Here it is very sacred. One looks there for sticks, something that sticks up, that is like the maize stalks, like the stubble in the field. That is where the peyote is, that is where he lives. It is the same thing. The maize, that is the mother of the peyote. And the peyote, that is the essence, the heart of the maize. It is the deer, it is the maize. It is all. It is our life. It connects all. It unites all.

Ah, then what? The *mara'akame* sees it. All is quiet. All stand, looking. He takes his bow, he takes his arrow. There he puts down the horns, the horns of *Kauyumari*. There he puts them, next to the peyote. He stands there with his two feet, he lifts his bow, he places his arrow on the bowstring. He wets the tip of it, he sucks on it right there. They stand there, silent. Waiting. He lifts his bow, high, he has his arrow in a shooting position. He lowers it, slowly, slowly. He lowers it, he starts lowering it, until he has it in his eye, until he sees it there, clearly. Then he lets the arrow fly. He shoots it. He shoots it at its base, there where it comes out of the earth. So that it cannot be lost, so that it will not leave. Because if at that time you do not hunt it with an arrow, if you do not shoot it with an arrow, it can be lost. It can leave. It can run away. And once you put an arrow into it, it will remain there.

Ah, there it sits. All of them, all of us see where the arrow went. All stand there, in a circle. All venerate. It is very sacred, very, very. It is a beautiful thing to see.

Conversations with Yoawima

Barbara G. Myerhoff and Carlos Castaneda met in the spring of 1966. He had been writing about don Juan for several years. Her article on the shaman of Rincon was about to be published. Friends thought they would have a lot to say to one another and had been urging them for months to get together. The friends were right. Barbara was a talented, hard-working graduate student, destined to write praiseworthy books, head a department of anthropology, and appear in *People* magazine. Carlos was a brilliant, corner-cutting misfit, an academic illusionist on his invisible way to being a best-selling author, a famous hoaxer, and half a face on the cover of *Time*. Each of them could see a stretch of hard road ahead before reaching a Ph.D.

In those days some five-hundred students were struggling in statistical anonymity to earn advanced degrees in the UCLA anthropology department. Despite encouragement from particular faculty members, Barbara was like most of the five-hundred in distrusting the academic establishment, fearing failure, and feeling alone in the crowd. It was therefore deeply reassuring to find another student with interests like her own, who had been to unnamable places and befriended a most unusual man, more unusual even than the shaman of Rincon. They met for the first time in Haines Hall and talked "for about ten hours." Enthusiastically Carlos approved of Barbara's dissertation topic. Patiently he helped her understand the world of the shamans: a world where people turned into crows, flew through the air while chained to a heavy rock, hurled words at each other, saw with double vision, sought the crack between the worlds, and hoped to defeat the four enemies of a man of knowledge. Though Barbara was delighted by that world, Carlos admitted being frightened of it. He told her it must be easier for a woman to face it.

In the summer of that year Barbara went to Guadalajara, where she spent many days in a little hut on the outskirts of the city tape-recording songs, chants, stories, and explanations of myth and ritual given by Ramón Medina, who was at that time preparing himself to be a *Wixárika mara'akame*, or Huichol shaman-priest. One afternoon the regime was pleasantly interrupted by an excursion into the country. The party included half a dozen Huichol adults and children and anthropologist Peter Furst, also of UCLA. As Barbara tells it:

Ramón led us to a steep barranca, cut by a rapid waterfall cascading perhaps a thousand feet over jagged, slippery rocks. At the edge of the fall Ramón removed his sandals and told us that this was a special place for shamans. We watched in astonishment as he proceeded to leap across the waterfall, from rock to rock, pausing frequently, his body bent forward, his arms spread out, his head thrown back, entirely birdlike, poised motionlessly on one foot. He disappeared, reemerged, leaped about, and finally achieved the other side. We outsiders were terrified and puzzled but none of the Huichols seemed at all worried.

Next day Ramón explained that a shaman must keep his balance while crossing the narrow bridge to the other world, so that he will not fall into the abyss and be eaten by terrible animals. Marching two fingers confidently up his violin bow, he illustrated in miniature the shaman's equilibrium once more. If Barbara had felt any doubt that Ramón would soon be a full-fledged *mara'akame*, the waterfall demonstration and the supernatural explanation quite dispelled it. In August, when she returned to UCLA, she told Carlos about her shaman balancing birdlike on the waterfall.

"Oh!" said Carlos in surprise. "That's just like don Genaro." He proceeded to describe Genaro's now well known waterfall levitations, an unmistakable counterpart of Ramón's shamanic leaps and postures. Barbara was elated. Carlos's authoritative confirmation was just what she had hoped for.

The winter of 1966-67 found Barbara again in Mexico, making the annual Huichol pilgrimage to the land of the Ancient Ones, where peyote was hunted as though it were a deer and gathered as though it were grain.

"Now I will tell you of the maize and the peyote and the deer," Ramón said. "These things are one. They are a unity. They are our life. They are ourselves"—a symbolic paradox that would be celebrated in Barbara's illuminating book *Peyote Hunt*. Early in the pilgrimage she was given a Huichol name, Yoawima 'Uimari, which means Growing Purple Maize Girl, "an affectionate but not especially sacred appellation." When she had proved her worth as a pilgrim, she received a second Huichol name, too sacred for use in the title of this chapter.

For more than a year Barbara and Carlos saw each other often, sympathizing in their common academic travail, sharing the Indian lore that fascinated them, urging each other to greater efforts and ultimate success. After *The Teachings* was published, in 1968, she saw less of him. In October of that year she defended her dissertation, which contained a report of Ramón on the waterfall.

For the spring of 1970 Peter Furst organized a series of lectures at UCLA on the ritual use of hallucinogens. His own lecture included his eye-witness account of Ramón's demonstration of shamanic balance. Carlos Castaneda dropped in at the Latin American Center and offered to present an eye-witness account of don Genaro's corresponding but more spectacular demonstration. Furst accepted the offer. Castaneda presented his account in the 1970 lecture series and in *A Separate Reality*, published in 1971. Furst's *Flesh of the Gods*, published in 1972, took note of Castaneda's "strikingly similar" account, and Barbara Myerhoff's *Peyote Hunt*, published in 1974, gratefully acknowledged his contribution to her understanding of shamanism and mentioned his "strikingly similar" episode of virtuosic balance.

Having closely examined Castaneda's account, I said in *Castaneda's Journey* the similarity was a little too striking to escape suspicion, but I had no clue to a startling anachronism documented for the first time here. In the separate, narrative reality, Carlos first met don Genaro on 2 April 1968, the day he tried to give a copy of *The Teachings* to don Juan. On 17 October of that narrative year he saw Genaro balance on the waterfall. In the ordinary world of calendars and committee meetings, however, Barbara was concurrently defending her dissertation, page 94 of which told how she had been astonished by Ramón's agile leaps at the edge of the chasm. Though Castaneda had said in 1966 Ramón was "just like don Genaro," Carlos would not set eyes on Genaro for another two years—a virtuosic display of precognition in a supposedly failed apprentice recently withdrawn in dismay from the reality-breaching experiments of his demanding tutor.

While writing *Castaneda's Journey* I tried to elicit comments from Barbara, but she would say nothing, fearing my inquiry might be just one more misconceived attempt to belittle a man toward whom she felt not only gratitude but admiration and affection. On the surface, this was the typical reluctance of the Castaneda partisan, and I found it unsurprising. What did surprise me was Barbara's change of heart when she had read *Castaneda's Journey*, in which she was relieved to find a more or less sympathetic treatment of her friend but startled by some convincing evidence that he was operating on a plane of reality quite different from the one where fieldwork is usually done. She wrote to me, suggesting we compare viewpoints.

A year went by before we got together, a delay I attribute not to my formidability but to Barbara's discomfort in redefining an important friendship and to her difficulty in reconciling personal loyalties with professional obligations. If one's colleague or dear friend turns out to be a hoaxer, what should one do? Polar reactions are easy: stubbornly assert the authenticity of don Juan, or angrily fling Castaneda into the ashcan. What takes both insight and courage is to assimilate the contradictions, weighing personal and social costs against public and private benefits and coming to terms at last with the conflict. Like Paul Riesman, Barbara Myerhoff is one of the few Castaneda subscribers to display impeccable equilibrium while crossing the bridge of second thoughts to a balanced judgment of Trickster-Teacher instead of falling into the chasm of emotional turmoil, where one is chewed up by the jaguars of resentment or swallowed by the anaconda of rationalization.

The interview that follows is condensed from transcripts of two long conversations. Except for minor rearrangements, the topics came up in the order given here. As one does in conversation, we both called Castaneda "Carlos," though of course most of the time we were talking about the actual person Barbara had known, not the legendary Carlos of the don Juan books. My first question was whether she still felt some reluctance to talk about Carlos for the record.

BGM: I really have never talked about him in public before, largely because the subject seemed so ripe for dissension and controversy, and I thought there was so much value in what he was doing. I didn't want to simply debunk it.

RdeM: You felt a conflict about it?

BGM: Yes, between my loyalty to Carlos—and to some of my friends at UCLA who were involved with him—and my profession as an anthropologist.

RdeM: What made you change your mind about discussing it?

BGM: Your book, which put the whole thing in a new light. I began to see Carlos as doing a kind of massive, half humorous teaching operation, and I thought he wouldn't mind my talking about him, because I think he really *wants* comment from those he has fooled.

RdeM: If that's so, why did it take you a whole year to get round to talking to me?

BGM: For a long time it was hard for me to make my peace with the foolishness I felt about being so naïve, about being completely taken in.

RdeM: You felt foolish.

BGM: Yes, and on a lot of levels, personal to professional. But then I thought about how I had really only had delight and amusement from Carlos and, in the long run, enlightenment, which is more than you get from most people. So I decided it was okay to feel foolish.

RdeM: Most people who play a trick on you don't give you pleasure and information as a compensation.

BGM: That's right.

RdeM: I suppose his biggest trick on you was feeding your waterfall story right back to you.

BGM: That was a very interesting incident. I mean, it never crossed my mind that his description of don Genaro on the waterfall proved anything except that I was doing good fieldwork because I had come up with an observation and interpretation so much like his. When he said, "Oh, that's just like don Genaro," it was very validating for me.

RdeM: How do you feel about it now?

BGM: The feeling of validation remains, the feeling that we were both talking about the same serious and important manifestation of Mexican shamanism.

RdeM: Even though his part of it was made up on the spot, the feeling of mutual understanding and significance remains.

BGM: Yes.

RdeM: He must have a remarkable ability to resonate to things people tell him.

BGM: Oh, he does.

RdeM: The stories he makes up exactly fit the person he is talking to.

BGM: They're mirrors. It's happened over and over. So many people describe their conversations with Carlos, saying, "I know just what he's talking about." But each one tells you something different, something that is part of his or her own world, which Carlos has reflected. "It's all really sexual," they say, or "it's all psychological," or "mystical" or "shamanic" or whatever they're into. His allegories, the stories he tells, seem to validate everybody.

RdeM: Paul Radin said Trickster was everything to every man.

BGM: Exactly. You remember the dedication in *The Teachings*: "For don Juan—and for the two persons who shared his sense of magical time with me." It's completely anonymous. Anybody who had known Carlos in the sixties could put himself or herself into that dedication, and a lot of us did.

RdeM: In *Castaneda's Journey* I called Carlos a Rorschach man, a man on whom people project their inner worlds.

BGM: That's right, and the first day we met he did it with me. I was telling him about the sprinklers on the VA-hospital lawn near UCLA. They're that old-fashioned kind that send sprays whipping around, sparkling in the sun. I told him about driving down the freeway and being dazzled by the beauty of the sunlight on the whirling water, and almost feeling I was being drawn into it, and then he described it to me from above, the way he had seen it as a crow, when he was flying over it.

RdeM: Right after you had said it.

BGM: Yes. (LAUGHING) We saw a lot of each other toward the end of that summer, because we were both working every day in the library. And this is where my feeling of deep gratitude and affection for him comes in, because my father was dying of cancer, very horribly, and Carlos was kind and very helpful to me. We were two vulnerable, pitiful, impotent, confused little creatures together in that horrible time and place.

RdeM: How was he kind? He let you talk about it, and he understood?

BGM: More than that. He was genuinely giving and consoling. He talked to me about things I didn't know anything about. About death "being with you, beside you on the mat."

RdeM: He helped you to cope with the impending death of your father.

BGM: Yes, very much. And I helped him too. He was struggling——and I really think he was; I don't think that part was bull. He was struggling with the idea, as he put it, that he was somewhat crazy. He kept saying he was struggling with madness. I never saw him look so miserable. He didn't think he was going to make it through UCLA. He had lost his little boy. Many of his colleagues and associates on campus were cold, stuffy, positivist types. He wasn't being well treated. Every day he'd come chugging up to the campus with his briefcase, and no matter how poor he was and in the hottest weather he always wore proper, three-piece, dark flannel suits. All day, every day, he'd sit from nine to five in one of those little carrells in the library writing his book, looking like a business man.

RdeM: Did you ever get any idea how he made a living?

BGM: He told me some stuff. He had investments or something like that.

RdeM: No job?

BGM: I think he had a part-time job coding in a research project for the ethnomethodologists, at the Neuropsychiatric Institute. He used to go down there often.

RdeM: Were you married during that period?

BGM: Oh yes. But my husband and I were both absorbed in our dissertations, and we didn't have much left over for each other. Carlos seemed so lonely and wretched and panic-stricken himself that I found consolation in his company.

RdeM: Did you ever feel physically attracted to him?

BGM: Yes, but not in the usual way. He was not an ordinary man. He was a pixie.

RdeM: Well, how did you feel attracted to him?

BGM: It's hard to put into words. It wasn't a simple erotic man-woman bond. It was as though we entered a bubble of pretending and playfulness together. It was an intimacy made out of impossibility and weirdness. And it was an escape from the ordeal we were going through.

RdeM: Was it like children playing together?

BGM: Uh-huh. There was a lot of poking and giggling. Romping almost. We had a kind of omnipotent, aggrandized view of ourselves, which we also laughed at.

RdeM: While at the same time you felt miserable, wretched, powerless. . . .

BGM: Yes. We kept telling each other *we* were the serious, important, imaginative, powerful ones, and all those others, those idiots who were torturing us, were the crazy ones. We said one day we'd show them, and our biographers would laugh at them as we were laughing. It was a grand conceit. You can imagine the fun we had years later when we met and told each other it had come true. In a way. More for him than for me, of course. But we exulted in the partial realization of our childish vision of omnipotence. By then we had both completed our degrees and published our books.

RdeM: When did you first see the manuscript of *The Teachings?*

BGM: That August. He was so disgusted with it he threatened to burn it. I took it home with me for a few days and told him I was going to xerox it and keep a copy. I was afraid he might actually destroy it. We went over a lot of it together. I remember telling him it was pointless to put in that awful "Structural Analysis." And the term "sorcerer," which I felt he misused. And "Yaqui," for which there seemed no cultural justification. I didn't like the name "don Juan," which I thought was too much like the literary prototype and therefore confusing. Since it was only a pseudonym, he could easily have changed it. I wanted him to call the book *A Path with Heart*, and leave out "sorcerer" and "Yaqui" altogether. We argued endlessly about those things, but he went ahead and did everything his own way. I think history has proved my criticisms right, but that's another story. Anyway, it was the beginning of a long and curious friendship. Later we would have sporadic, intense meetings every six months or so, when we'd talk all day or through the night.

RdeM: How did Carlos meet Ramón?

BGM: It was in the spring [of 1971]. Ramón had come up to Los Angeles to exhibit his yarn paintings at the Museum of Natural History, and he and Lupe [his wife] were staying at my house in the San Fernando Valley. They were camping in my son's bedroom. Literally. They moved all the furniture to the sides of the room and built a little cooking fire in the middle of the room.

RdeM: How could they do that?

BGM: They used a little metal sheet. And they threw their trash and orange peels all over the room. It was a mess like you would not believe. My son couldn't fathom what was going on.

RdeM: How old was he?

BGM: Three. He was astonished. Anyway, I told Carlos, and he was eager to meet Ramón. He had often talked about taking me down to meet don Juan—in fact, we'd made two dates to do it, which didn't come off—and I had said, "One day you must meet Ramón." We'd always done this "comparing of our shamans." So Carlos came right out. I was glad to have him there, because I was teaching full time and couldn't be with Ramón and Lupe as much as I wanted.

Ramón was an incredible trickster. Each morning that I drove him to USC, just when we'd get to the freeway interchange, where you have to pay close attention to the merging traffic, he'd begin to tell me some ethnographic tidbit that put several other things into place that I'd wanted to know, and I'd be caught between the need to learn and the need to survive. Very much like don Juan's trickster style of teaching, which is one of the most valid things Carlos has portrayed. It's typical of North American and Central American shamans.

Ramón's certainty of his own powers was very impressive to see. I gave a party for him at my house, and when it was over and the guests were taking gracious leave of him, he said, very nicely without any arrogance, that it had been a pleasure for all of them to meet him.

RdeM: What happened when he and Carlos met?

BGM: They *saw* each other!

RdeM: What did they *see*?

BGM: The same kind of person. We had dinner in a funny little Mexican restaurant, and they started to laugh at once and didn't stop. They both saw the world from some lofty position that made it look ridiculous.

Being around the two of them was like entering a separate reality. They really saw and believed and dwelt in another realm. Once I walked with Ramón through the May Company [a big department store] when he was dressed in very ordinary American clothes because he had sold all his Indian clothing to buy tape recorders and transistor radios. People stopped and stared at him. He looked like a Mexican fruitpicker, but he had a presence that was extraordinary. Talk about the glance of kings! There are people who have this sense of another realm, and they move differently through this realm because of it. Carlos and Ramón had that.

RdeM: What else happened between them?

BGM: They capered around a lot, playing like children. They exchanged gifts. One day Carlos took Ramón to a "power spot" he had discovered in the Santa Monica Mountains. Carlos wanted to know if Ramón really *saw* it as a power spot. Ramón agreed that it was a wonderful power spot. He started jumping up and down and farting, and he said, "I'll show you what a power spot it is!" And, in Carlos's words, he took a crap in it. He had been unhappy that there was no place at my house to go to the bathroom. That is, there was a bathroom, but he thought it was not a proper place to defecate. He was reluctant to use my garden, and so he had been very uncomfortable. Carlos's power spot was a marvelous solution. If Carlos had taken himself too seriously, he might have been offended. He had invited Ramón up there in a very serious mood, to validate the power spot, and here was Ramón using it for a toilet. Carlos thought that was absolutely hilarious, and afterwards he would tell this funny story on himself.

RdeM: Did you hear the story from Ramón too, or just from Carlos?

BGM: Just from Carlos.

RdeM: So you don't know whether it really happened that way.

BGM: True, I don't. And then there was another strange episode. Some time after Ramón was murdered in Mexico, Lupe phoned Peter Furst, or a relative of hers phoned him, to say she was all right and everything had at last gotten back to normal. Carlos went down there looking for her, and when he came back he was very agitated and upset. He said people were after her, and she was terrified and afraid to go out of the house. Just the opposite of what Peter had heard.

RdeM: Do you think he really did go down there to find her?

BGM: He could have.

RdeM: Or he could have made it all up.

BGM: Yes, but why would he make up such a story? Let's suppose he invents things all the time. Why would he invent that particular story?

And why would he be upset? He seemed alarmed and afraid. I think he told it to me over the phone.

RdeM: I don't know why he would make up the story, but I also don't know why he would come back with a story that doesn't match what other people say. Did you ever have any confirmation of his story?

BGM: No, but at that time nobody had any reason to doubt him, you understand. So many things he said and wrote about seemed so right. One reason people get so upset when you call him a hoaxer is that he teaches in a concrete if allegorical form. His story comes to them as direct experience. *Zap!* It hits them, and they know it's right.

RdeM: It has the certainty of art rather than the dubiousness of fact.

BGM: Exactly. So you are attacking not just him but their own private experience, which has truth value for them. The form he teaches in is essential. It's as important as the content. His allegory. His mirroring. He gives us in a concrete form things we had abstractly conceptualized but didn't know how to articulate or use. He does that beautifully. That's where he's a gifted teacher.

RdeM: Some writers, including me and Joyce Carol Oates, have interpreted the Structural Analysis as a parody of social science.

BGM: I hope it is! (LAUGHING)

RdeM: Well, it must be. It's much too arch and insistent and repetitive to be sincere. It's a punishment for anybody who would take it seriously.

BGM: That's very well put.

RdeM: Lawrence Watson was no doubt sincere when [according to Castaneda] he helped write it, but Carlos was just playing one of his many tricks on colleagues.

BGM: And then he acknowledged Larry's help in print.

RdeM: Sure he did. He likes to rub it in. One interesting item in the Structural Analysis was a rather ironical admission that the mushrooms don Juan smoked wouldn't burn.

BGM: I wondered about that. But why would he admit it?

RdeM: Maybe somebody questioned the feasibility of smoking mushroom dust, but he already had it in his manuscript where faculty members had read it, so he covered his aspirations by saying the dust was merely ingested.

BGM: (LAUGHING) When I first met Arnold Mandell, he threw me with the theory that Carlos had cooked up the Structural Analysis with some graduate students as a joke.

RdeM: Watson had just finished his graduate work, but I don't think he was in on the joke. The joke was on him, along with the rest of the community of gullible scholars.

BGM: The last time I saw Carlos, I said something about how much I wanted from life, and Carlos said: "Don Juan would say, 'We are peegs for life!' " I remember laughing to myself and thinking: *"Pigs* for *life?* Don Juan would *never* say *that!"* Because don Juan was basically ascetic. So it struck me even then as some part of Carlos speaking. He used the don Juan accent, but the phrase was definitely his own, it seemed to me.

RdeM: But you still thought there was such a person as don Juan.

BGM: I'm not sure there isn't. There may very well have been, in the beginning, an experience with a concrete person. Otherwise, why would Carlos have said to me, "Come down. Meet him. Come with me"? I'm still not convinced he was completely lying to me, all of the time.

RdeM: I think I want you to believe he was.

BGM: I know you do.

RdeM: Because I think I see him truly, and I want you to see him the same way.

BGM: Well, Richard, I have to tell you, there is still an element of mystery in it for me. Because I find things in it that convince me. Even the waterfall episode was not just Carlos reflecting me back to me. There was something besides.

RdeM: Margaret Castaneda told me she didn't believe a word of the don Juan story, but she was sure something of the kind had happened to Carlos earlier in his life, which he was dramatizing in the don Juan books. She was very interested in spiritual experiences, and was sure he had had some. Another instance, I think, of people looking into the Rorschach man for their own deep sources.

BGM: Perhaps, then, I look into him for the mystery I need and you look into him for the clarity you need.

RdeM: Touché.

BGM: Or perhaps I just don't want to re-examine my original judgments.

RdeM: If you came round to my point of view, would you lose something valuable?

BGM: I don't know. I've considered the worst possibility, and I no longer find it odious—that I was completely taken in and a fool.

RdeM: Not everybody who is completely taken in is a fool. If the deceiver is very clever, he doesn't deceive only fools. There's a whole profession based on that, called magicians.

BGM: All right. But there's a part of me that's not content with a psychological explanation of what Carlos is doing. Somehow from my experiences of fieldwork I get a feeling he is building on an exchange with another person. I'm not ready to give that up.

RdeM: If the source he's drawing on is made vague enough, one would never have to give it up. It recedes into inaccessibility.

BGM: Maybe it's an archetypal figure, that trickster-teacher, but it doesn't come only from inside Carlos. That's my feeling.

RdeM: Why doesn't it?

BGM: Because over and over he reveals in himself qualities that don't match don Juan: inflatedness, narrowness, rationalizing, rigidity.

RdeM: Pearl Pollard Curran wrote four million words in the name of Patience Worth, a disembodied spirit from the seventeenth century. There was no plausible explanation of where all this jumbled up archaic material could come from, and it looked very much as though an external source named Patience Worth were furnishing it through Mrs Curran. An alternative explanation was that Mrs Curran's personality had split into two parts.

BGM: What you say is entirely plausible. Don Juan is clearly the "Other" for Carlos.

RdeM: How do you feel about that interpretation?

BGM: It appeals to me, because I have a hard time reconciling the Carlos I knew, or think I knew, with the one who is supposed to be a hardboiled, manipulative deceiver. Don Juan may be a subpersonality, or a person-ification of a part of Carlos that was underdeveloped and could be de-veloped and manifested in the stories. That seems much more plausible to me than the swindler theory.

RdeM: What swindler theory?

BGM: The conscious, careful, diabolical plan to write fake fieldnotes for eight years, get them published by the University Press, add two best selling volumes, and get an anthropology Ph.D. for the whole megillah.

RdeM: Doesn't sound like the sort of thing one could work out in ad-vance.

BGM: It sure doesn't! (LAUGHING)

RdeM: As a long-range plan it's preposterous.

BGM: He's got to be improvising as he goes along.

RdeM: His need to perform the fantasy is so intense that he foists it little by little on everyone around him.

BGM: Doesn't that sort of shoot down your UCLA conspiracy theory?

RdeM: In general, yes. Most of the professors who tolerated or en-dorsed his fantasies could have been duped by his perfect performance, but I still think one or two of them must have been a little more canny than that.

BGM: People are not as canny as you would like them to be, Richard. I endorsed his fantasies, and I'm not exceptionally stupid. The main difference—if you'll excuse my saying so—between you and his academic supporters is not canniness but skepticism. They were ready to believe. You were ready to doubt. As it turned out, you had more points on your side. Maybe that was just luck.

RdeM: Maybe it was luck, or maybe it was the fact that I had some prior experience with charlatans. Most of us have never met a person like Carlos Castaneda.

BGM: That's true.

RdeM: But you have had this unusual experience.

BGM: And I was bowled over by it.

RdeM: Did you ever visit Carlos where he lived?

BGM: Yes. During the time when my father was dying. Carlos was living about two blocks from the hospital, and I would frequently stop off there on my way back. He brewed me a special tea, from an herb called *angelita*, and we would exhort one another to courage. I felt he was very supportive, in a genuine, simple way.

RdeM: You found him always to have this gentle, healing quality?

BGM: When you could pin him down. Or when he came around. But if you had Expectation One, forget it. He was not someone you could count on to be there when you needed him.

RdeM: Did he ever show any hostility toward you?

BGM: Never. But on one occasion he showed fear, or something like it. Revulsion perhaps. I went to see him at another place he lived, in Westwood, to give him a costume that had belonged to Ramón. This was after Ramón had been murdered. I was visibly pregnant, and Carlos could tell from the timing that the child had been conceived while Ramón was living in my house. Or maybe I told him about it. Anyway, the idea seemed to terrify him.

RdeM: He thought it was Ramón's child?

BGM: No, but for him I think it was something like stealing Ramón's soul. He drew back aghast.

RdeM: Just like a woman, to steal the shaman's soul.

BGM: Well, it was spooky. He recoiled from me. I had never felt anything like that from him before, and I left very quickly. Up to that point he had often called me a *brujo*, and I had always thought it was flattering, but on this occasion I didn't feel like a sorcerer. I was very upset about Ramón's death.

RdeM: This was your second child?

BGM: Yes. And I had an interesting episode with Carlos and my first child, another incident when he was a great friend to me. He came to visit me when my child was three months old, and had colic. Carlos sat there a long, long time watching me feed the baby. Three spoons of cereal into the mouth, two spoons out. You know how boring that is for anyone who is not a smitten mother, which I was, but Carlos was fascinated by it and kept whispering: "He's a warrior. A *warrior!* He's impeccable! You have to raise him to be *impeccable!*" Some of our long nights talking were about child rearing. He gave me some of the strangest advice anybody has ever gotten. Some of it wasn't bad, but it was wild. He told me how impeccable my son was, which of course I wasn't averse to hearing. Then I complained to him about how the baby had colic and I hadn't slept much for three months, and he said: "Leave him to me." And I said: "What are you going to do?" And he said: "Don't ask. Leave the room." So I left the room, and left my baby with him, until he called me back. He wouldn't tell me what he had done, and I didn't press him, but the baby never had colic again.

RdeM: (LAUGHING)

BGM: Now, of course, you know what happens to babies at three months.

RdeM: They give up colic?

BGM: They give up colic. On the other hand, from that *day* the baby never had colic again. Well, that delighted me. Carlos used to say: "You must never want to be with your children when they don't want to be with you. You must never be too available. They must seek you out." He was very big on that, and it so happened it was good advice for me, because I was overly seeking. Then I remember at the San Diego Anthropology meetings [in November 1970] he told me the story of scaring his little boy into good behavior. You remember what don Juan said about hiring somebody to pop out and scare the little boy. Carlos told me to do that. He told me he had done it. He told it to me as something he had done at the zoo. He told me lots of things I subsequently read in his books.

RdeM: Did he visit your classroom and talk to your students?

BGM: Yes. He had just finished the manuscript of *A Separate Reality*. And he was superb. He did something I've seen only a few great teachers do. He gave the students an understanding of the provisional nature of reality. "You only see *this* chair once. After that you gloss. You see *chair*, instead of wood, shape, black. Only once do you have the first experience." And then in the USC cafeteria, amidst the din, he tried to teach me to listen to silence instead of noise, to "find the holes between the sounds." At that time I was playing with a chamber music group, and the fellow who played the oboe kept saying to me: "You're not *listening* to the rests. You're treating them as if they were absent instead of being part of the music." In his aphoristic language, Carlos was teaching me the same thing. It was delightful having him as a teacher. He was at his best then.

RdeM: Beyond the time when you brought him the costume, did you ever see him off balance?

BGM: Only once, at a meeting in San Francisco. My husband saw Carlos across the room and hailed him with the quite ingenuous but outrageous comment that he was growing stout. Carlos was definitely not amused. Just for a blink he lost his cool. It was droll to see that little flicker of mortality in him, when he was already such a famous man.

RdeM: You said Carlos used to call you a *brujo*.

BGM: Until he saw me pregnant, yes. Never after that.

RdeM: You mean *bruja*, don't you?

BGM: No, he called me a *brujo*. It was one of his most charming and affectionate terms.

RdeM: He made you a male, his brother in sorcery.

BGM: No, we were both sexless. Sexless playmates. I felt he was disappointed in me for getting pregnant and having children. Though he was fascinated by my feeding the baby, it also made him uneasy. When I saw him at the meetings in New York [November 1971], I was so pregnant it was ludicrous. I had gained 44 pounds. Carlos was standing in the lobby, and I came up behind him. He turned around and almost recoiled, he was so shocked. The time he cured my son of colic I had the feeling it was his way of getting control of the situation, of restructuring it in his own terms, so he would feel comfortable with it. And it was very strange while he was there. Although I was the mother, I kept feeling, what are two children like me and Carlos doing here in the presence of this baby?

One of our funniest capers was at the meetings in Seattle [November 1968]. We were terribly bored in a deadly session and wanted to escape. I remember the two of us laughing and skipping arm in arm out of the hotel. It was a Sunday morning, and no one was around, so we went up to the top of the Space Needle and took a ride. We had a fantasy of flying off into the distance and never coming back. We kept whispering to each other: "What if it keeps going? What if it just *keeps on going?*"

RdeM: Was Carlos considered odd in graduate school?

BGM: Pretty odd. He was constantly flouting the rules and barely getting away with it. He had handfuls of incompletes. He was always disappearing and coming back. Yet he always looked *exactly* the same. He behaved with an almost rigid regularity.

RdeM: One of his committee members thought he was psychologically very fragile and might have a psychotic break at any moment.

BGM: I never saw any sign of it.

RdeM: Even when he kept telling you he thought he was going crazy?

BGM: He didn't mean crazy-psychotic. He meant he was under so much pressure he couldn't stand it.

RdeM: The normal graduate school experience.

BGM: (LAUGHING) Well, we both felt that way.

RdeM: To be a person who complains about being driven crazy is usually to be a sane person.

BGM: I agree. But I have to tell you at the same time he was truly uncomfortable with his mental state. He was in a panic and somewhat disoriented. He felt helpless.

RdeM: His back was against the wall.

BGM: Right. One of the most delightful moments was on the balcony of Haines Hall, where the anthropology department was on the third floor, and sociology on the second. That's where the whole drama was played out. That was the scene of the crime. We were standing on the balcony one day at four o'clock on a Friday afternoon having a very heavy conversation about the craziness of the place and how we would someday get out of it and how the two of us were sort of secret, gifted, oppressed, wonderful maniacs, who would one day turn the place upside down. A little grandiose, I admit. And as we were saying these things—we were almost the same height as I recall, so it was a fuming conspiracy of two little creatures—but as we were saying these things, a crow flew overhead. Cawing. And it was like a sign. No doubt about it. And the two of us were—I remember being in goose pimples. "It's an *omen!*" Carlos said. Suddenly we knew for sure we were right and they were wrong. Another thing I remember——am I taking too much of your time?

RdeM: (LAUGHING)

BGM: Because these things come back in little dibs and dabs.

RdeM: They're worth whatever time they take.

BGM: Well, they really are, and I've never written any of this down. A funny thing happened when I saw him in San Francisco. He came up to me, and he pinched me, and he said: *"Oh!* You're so *trim!* You're so *lean!* You're in such *good condition!"* And I laughed about that a lot. It seemed so important to him that I was thin again, and now in *Second Ring of Power* we have La Gorda [Fatso].

RdeM: Who weighed 220 pounds until don Juan shrank her to 115.

BGM: I had lost 44 pounds since he saw me pregnant.

RdeM: So you could be a child with him again.

BGM: I think so. And something else he might have gotten from me. As a child I had double vision, and it wasn't until I was about eleven that I found out everybody didn't have it. I could let one eye wander off, and the images would separate, and when I wanted to I could converge them again. Carlos was very interested in that.

RdeM: In *Ixtlan* don Juan talks about forcing the eyes to see the same image separately and says the lack of image convergence gives a double perception of the world. That sounds like your wandering eye.

BGM: Yes it does.

RdeM: So maybe crossing the eyes isn't an old mesoamerican mystical technique after all.

BGM: Maybe not. William Blake wrote a poem about double vision. And these people in *Second Ring* are devastatingly un-Indian. It's hard to find an Indian in any of Carlos's books.

RdeM: Not even don Juan?

BGM: Most conspicuously don Juan. Carlos's most sympathetic readers admit don Juan's an eclectic. They say he's traveled, he's been around.

RdeM: Ramón had traveled and been around, so what's the difference?

BGM: Well! How much time do you have? An Indian is a man with a specific, rich, coherent set of beliefs. Don Juan has no Indian culture. You never see any other people, you never hear any traditional stories or customs. And another thing. If Carlos is so identified with Mexican Indian tradition, why does he take two beautiful indigenous concepts like *nagual* and *tonal* and fool around with them? As if they didn't have their own reality in other people's thought systems. That offends me. It really does.

RdeM: He turned them into Zen Buddhism.

BGM: Whatever he did with them. Did you know he lived in San Diego?

RdeM: He did?

BGM: For a while. In a basement room.

RdeM: He told you this?

BGM: Yes. In a friend's house. I thought it was rather a long commute to UCLA, but those things never seemed to bother him.

RdeM: Not when he could go back and forth to Mexico in the blink of an eye.

BGM: Maybe that's it. Anyway, he said he gradually emptied the room out. First he got rid of the bed. Then he got rid of the books. Until there was nothing left but him and the typewriter. And he had these confrontations with something coming into the room—foxes or the moon or something. A light would come in through the barred window and terrify him. And he would struggle and wrestle with it. But he overcame it by giving up all his normal habits. He gave up food. He gave up sleeping. Honing himself, so to speak. And I thought it was all rather shocking. But he was training himself in asceticism. He has a profound ascetic streak. If I had to give you a psychological interpretation, I might say he's a tragically isolated man, struggling for discipline, dominated by his will, animus-possessed, anima-terrified, seeking impeccability, seeking passion with control. Willful asceticism. He was merciless with himself. Though he indulged himself by not giving in to the system, at the same time he sternly made himself give up personal relationships. Maybe he really wanted to give them up, but I felt it was a struggle. Made himself give up the little boy. Made himself be there in the library every single day, perfectly dressed in the dark suit, with the briefcase, everything in order, a narrow, determined quality. I suspect it's getting fiercer and deeper as he gets older. At the same time, he always wanted to escape into a world of joyful play. His imagination was so well developed that all he needed was one accomplice like me or Ramón, and he could get right *into* that other world of fun he yearned for.

[*Barbara reads to me out of the book she is writing,* Number Our Days, *about a community of aged Jewish immigrants in Venice, California. The passage relates a dream in which Carlos Castaneda appeared to her and told her how to understand the old people.*]

Even if Carlos's model of fieldwork is too idealized to be applied exactly as he describes it, just having somebody talking about it is good for anthropology. One reason I'm grateful to him is that he taught me to put myself into my reports and helped me dare to do it. First-person reports used to be very bad form in anthropology, but if you don't know what's happening to the fieldworker you miss half the process. Or maybe most of it. Another good thing he's done is show how someone obscure and ordinarily overlooked may have a message of great value to give the world. My father was such a person, and so are the old people in *Number Our Days.*

RdeM: Nobody would have heard about don Juan's teachings if Carlos hadn't gone out into the desert and listened to him for ten years.

BGM: Exactly.

RdeM: And the fact that the don Juan books are a transparent fraud doesn't invalidate the model?

BGM: No, it doesn't. The model is the same, and the message is needed. It says: "Look around. There are people here with things to say in ordinary simple language that may be well worth listening to." Anthropology can listen to them. It's a profoundly humanistic endeavor. That's one reason why I like it.

A Portrait of the Allegorist

"In spending many hours with Castaneda over a matter of weeks, *Time* Correspondent Sandra Burton found him attractive, helpful and convincing—up to a point. . . . As the talks continued, Castaneda offered several versions of his life, which kept changing as Burton presented him with the fact that much of his information did not check out. . . ."

Someday, I suppose, a biography may be written about Carlos Castaneda. I'd like to read it, but I wouldn't like to write it. The biographer will spend a lot of time in Peru seeking the cooperation of the Arana family, who have not so far shown any disposition to cooperate. He or she will have to go through records in Lima and Cajamarca and talk to many people who knew Castaneda as infant, child, youth, and man. Given the customary Latin reticence about family and private matters, the biographer will do well to start out as a Peruvian who has known the family for years. But, as a matter of fact, Peruvians haven't been terribly interested in Castaneda, so the project doesn't look very lively.

Another requirement for a satisfactory biography is authorization. Unauthorized biographies run into various kinds of difficulties. They don't get access to certain records and interviews. Their publishers worry about lawsuits. They lack the imprimatur that gives the buyer confidence he is getting the true story. Whose authorization would be appropriate here? The obvious answer is Castaneda's, but that answer is a hundred percent wrong. Castaneda's authorization would be worse than no authorization. How can a person who has made a public and private career of distorting the record and creating false records authorize anything? He can't. Whom does that leave to authorize the biography? His heirs, but of course he can't have heirs while he is alive, and he is impudently vigorous. By the time he has gone to join don Juan in the fifty-thousand-foot dome, those Peruvian records and interviews will be even more problematical.

All of which is a way of saying this chapter is not a biography of Carlos Castaneda. It is a portrait. The main difference is that its biographical information is incomplete, unauthorized, and possibly inaccurate here and there. Mind you, it's bound to be more accurate than any version provided by Castaneda, but it is still tentative, in places hypothetical. To save you the boredom of reading phrases like "it was reported, Fulano recalled, it seems likely" over and over, I am going to say things in a simple, declarative way even when the evidence is skimpy or the interpretation is chancy. This will make for better reading, but you must bear in mind that many of these assertions are subject to correction by later, more accurate information. My purpose in this chapter, as to a considerable extent in the previous 42 chapters, is to give you a picture of Castaneda that is true, even where I can't prove it is true. I will tell you what I believe about the man, and you can make up your mind whether I am right. To help you make up your mind, I will continue my practice of documenting all statements as fully as possible, but some of my informants wish to remain anonymous, and I must respect that wish. Because readers don't like nameless characters, pseudonyms will sometimes be used. As before, "Carlos" will be a character in stories I think are fictive; "Arana" and "Castaneda" will be persons in accounts I think are factual.

Some of the accounts will treat hitherto unpublished details of Castaneda's life. Is this an invasion of privacy? It could be if Castaneda were the private person he is often said to be, but I think he is categorically not that private person, for he has published several of his private lives in books and interviews. A critic or biographer is not obliged to assume that all of his conflicting autobiographical assertions are actually fiction, or that any of them is exempt from public discussion. Physical elusiveness does not constitute narrative privacy. By publishing what purported to be his lives, Castaneda gave up any claim to biographical or critical privacy. We have read, for example, that Carlos lost a very dear blond woman by clinging to her. While I doubt the existence of that particular woman, I believe Castaneda has ruined his relationships with some actual women by being unreliable. In writing about such things, I am a critical essayist responding to Castaneda's autobiographical initiative. If he didn't want such a response, he could have kept the supposedly factual blond-woman story and others like it to himself. We have been told about Carlos's little boy, how he was taken away—or left behind, depending on which version it was—and how Carlos suffered on his account. That little boy is now a young man, and it is both possible and appropriate to clarify the family relations. *Second Ring of Power* revealed that Carlos had "made a female child." In 1975 Castaneda introduced a young woman to numerous persons as his daughter. By describing the relationship between Castaneda and that young woman, it is possible to illuminate striking features of his character.

In making these points at length I am, in part, expressing my discomfort at digging into a man's personal life, however public he has made it, when the record will show him in a less favorable light than his books do. One advantage of being a theoretical scholar rather than a biographical journalist is not having to get into such things. In telling a truer story of Castaneda's life than he has told, I am dealing with many facts and inferences he has not published, but I believe it is my duty to deal with them.

One of the most interesting stories about him was told by a person I concluded was unreliable, so I threw the story out. Accounts that appear here come from persons I have confidence in, but no one speaks with perfect accuracy, and no report is entirely clear or complete. Nor have I the apparently infinite time an exhaustive study of Castaneda would take. This is the truest story of his life I have been able to put together. Along with the previous 42 chapters of this book, it is the way I understand him.

Carlos César Salvador Arana Castañeda was born on Christmas day 1925 in the isolated Andean city of Cajamarca, where four-hundred years earlier Pizarro's soldiers had strangled the Royal Inca Atau Huallpa, and where César Arana Burungaray had a jewelry store. Though Castaneda would later claim his cousin Lucía as a sister, little Arana was an only child, which one might guess from the illustration, where he is held by his aunt and flanked by his father and mother. From the resemblance, I should say the aunt is the father's sister.

At the age of eight months, Carlos spoke his first word: *diablo*, devil. I'm not at all surprised, but of course that was Carlos, described by Castaneda to his wife Margaret. Eight months is pretty early for talking, so perhaps we should assume little Arana spoke later and said something rather different: *Mamá*, perhaps. Carlos's mother was "morose, very beautiful and dissatisfied; an ornament." She complained constantly of having no diamond ring. Carlos's despair, at the age of six, was not being able to make her over into something else. In contrast, little Arana's mother seems rather plain. Married to the proprietor of a jewelry store, she must have had a diamond ring if she wanted one. While little Carlos sailed his boat in a nearby stream, his dissatisfied, ornamental mother would rendezvous with a strange young man, thus playing the archetypal trickster and betrayer and taking first place in Castaneda's list of unfaithful women. Little Arana's mother, on the other hand, seems above suspicion.

"The memory of my mother filled me with anguish," Castaneda

wrote, "but when I examined her I knew that I had never liked her. This was a shocking realization." One may doubt little Arana never liked his mother, but if Castaneda could say so even in a pseudo-autobiography, the child's disappointment in his mother must at times have been intense. Yaqui poet Méndez accused Castaneda of selling his own mother, which may be fair, but behind the selling must lurk a desire to punish her for not loving him in a satisfying way, for giving him love he felt as a "horrendous burden."

Castaneda's father suffers less distortion than his mother. Carlos's father is a professor of literature "who has never written a thing," a scholar who "won't talk to anybody who has not read Plato." Such a description seems unlikely for a goldsmith and watchmaker in a remote mountain city, but to our surprise we learn that César Arana triumphed in liberal arts examinations at San Marcos, the oldest university in South America. He finished as an artisan and shopkeeper not for lack of intellectual ability or interest in ideas but because he did not resist the temptations of Bohemia and wasted his academic opportunities in fast living with artists and bullfighters in the big city of Lima. Thus he could well be allegorized as a failed professor. What about Plato? There again the portrait is only slightly twisted. Settling down in Cajamarca, Don César turned into a steady family man, tireless chess player, and constant reader of Kant and Spinoza. A sedentary thinker, he lost himself in endless speculations about the ultimate meaning of life. When he was not contemplating the infinite or working in his gloomy shop, he was discussing weighty matters with friends from the professional community, where he was considered a cultivated intellectual gentleman, though he never wrote anything. *Time* said Castaneda spoke and wrote about his father with fondness, pity, and contempt. Though constantly drawn to him, a boy of six might feel little joy in the company of such a dignified and distant man. An ambitious adolescent might learn to sneer at the failure of a talented man to achieve great things in a world larger than Cajamarca. A successful author might look back on such a failure with pity.

A vision in *The Teachings* has Carlos embracing his father, pouring out confessions of love and imperfection unvoiced in childhood, only to see the father fade away, leaving the son alone in sadness and remorse. Yet this brief glimpse of filial surrender, which leaves little doubt Castaneda loved his father, hardens three years later into *Time's* "pity and contempt." What did César Arana do in the meantime to prompt the change? In 1970, between *Teachings* and *Separate Reality*, César Arana

Carlos Arana as a child, with his father and mother (standing)
and his aunt.

died. Though Castaneda never publicly acknowledged the death, he began immediately to punish the deserter. A father who had failed to become an ideal parent stood accused of academic triviality, of living in a "boring sterile world," of being indecisive, weak-willed, helpless, and "filled with an ultimate sense of despair." In the ordinary world, it was the son who felt helpless—to bring the old man back—and filled with despair at the irrevocable loss of a father to whom he had never confessed his love and from whom he had not yet earned admiration or even respect. "There is no power on earth that can make him change his mind about you," Castaneda wrote, about a year after his father died.

By leaving home in 1950, emigrating in 1951, and giving up the paternal name, Castaneda had rebelled against his father's provincialism, authority, and low opinion of him, but he had not given up hope of someday returning as a successful adult to claim his father's respect and admiration. The dream died with his father. Don Juan's role as substitute father has been remarked by several writers, but between the first and second books don Juan changed from a cold, gloomy, sinister father into a warm, playful, relatively benevolent father, the father Castaneda had been waiting for Don César to turn into.

Carlos could easily deal with don Juan's playfulness, but warmth was difficult. When don Juan was affectionate, Carlos had to distract himself: "There was such a warmth and kindness in his gesture that it seemed to be an appeal to restore my trust in him. I felt idiotic; I tried to disrupt my mood by looking for my spoon." How can a father inconsiderate enough to die before perfecting himself restore your trust in him?

Sorrowfully the author recreates occasional gestures of paternal affection: "This was the first time don Juan had called me 'my little friend.' It took me aback. He noticed it and smiled. There was a great warmth in his voice and that made me very sad. I told him that I had been careless and incompetent because that was the inherent bent of my personality; and that I would never understand his world. I felt deeply moved. He was very encouraging and asserted that I had done fine." In his distant way, César Arana had loved his son in return.

Let us imagine for a minute the small Arana, having been scolded by the large one for not acting like a big boy, lingering in the shadows as the imposing gentleman broods over chessboard or philosophy book. Unwilling to leave, afraid to interrupt, he is unable to touch the one whose assurance he wants. The scene shifts to don Juan's desert, where the teacher has just scolded the apprentice in "smooth and deadly words" for not sincerely applying himself to the task of sorcery. The teacher sits in the shadows like a stone. Apparently he will sit there forever. The embarrassed apprentice can think of nothing to say. Hours go by. At last the apprentice inwardly acknowledges the superiority of the teacher, touches don Juan's arm, and is flooded by tears. If only the small boy could have done the same thing.

Now let us imagine little Arana going on a rare walk with his father. As Don César strides ahead, the child runs hither and yon examining the wonders of nature. Looking up, he realizes Don César is waiting for him. When he catches up, he gets a scolding and is told to walk like a man or stay home. At first he is nearly in tears. Then he recovers his composure and begins to talk to his father. Don César says nothing but smiles down at him, and little Arana is suddenly very happy.

"We walked for another hour," Castaneda wrote, "and then started on our way back to his house. At a certain time I dropped behind and he had to wait for me. . . . He told me imperatively that whenever I walked with him I had to observe and copy his mannerisms or not come along at all. 'I can't be waiting for you as though you're a child,' he said in a scolding tone. That statement sunk me into the depths of embarrassment and bewilderment. How could it be possible that such an old man could walk so much better than I? I thought I was athletic and strong, and yet he had actually had to wait for me to catch up with him." Carlos follows don Juan's instructions in the right way of walking and finds he can keep up. "I felt elated. I was quite happy walking inanely with the strange old Indian. I began to talk and ask repeatedly if he would show me some peyote plants. He looked at me but did not say a word."

Later in the allegory Castaneda began to deal with the tragic loss: 'We are both beings who are going to die,' don Juan says softly. 'There is no more time for what we used to do.' "He clasped my hand. His touch was firm and friendly; it was like a reassurance that he was concerned and had affection for me." César Arana's death did not mean he had not loved his son. That was reassuring.

In Tales of Power don Juan puts his hand on Carlos's shoulder, and Carlos has "a gigantic urge to weep." He admits his fear that they are going to part forever. 'This is our last journey together,' don Juan says. Carlos feels a jolt in his stomach. 'There are many ways of saying farewell,' don Juan tells him. 'The best way is perhaps by holding a particular memory of joyfulness. For instance. . . the warmth you felt when the little boy rode on your shoulders. . . .' Or perhaps the warmth little Arana felt when riding at some rare time on Don César's shoulders.

These passages tell us, and I think truly, that Castaneda sadly recalls happy moments from early childhood. Around the age of six, however, something went wrong which nobody, not even his father, could put right, something later allegorized as desertion by his mother. At the age of eight he said to the woman who had been his nurse in infancy, María Caruapoma (whose Quechua name means tawny lion): "I want to be a famous man. I want to learn many languages. That's why I have this big head." Surely a boy of eight may dream of accomplishments that would make his father proud, but where and how did little Arana expect to achieve fame? In the United States, by telling tall tales about himself. He was already rehearsing. One morning he told Doña María he had three sons in the United States. She thought that was very funny. Here he was, only a child in Peru, and he was claiming three sons in the United States. Each son had a name; one was named Willy; Doña María couldn't remember the names of the other two.

Though Cajamarcan society was dominated by Europeans, it was animated by the surrounding Indian cultures. Little Arana lived in a world of witchcraft and spirits. Curanderos magically healed the sick; a house on Calle Dos de Mayo was cursed with a poltergeist; a man was seen in the square and on the bridge at the same time. As little Arana listened, Don César used to talk about such mysteries with his friend Dr Teófilo Vera, Member of the Court of Cajamarca. Years later, don Vicente would be called a curer; don Juan would tell of nasty spirits that followed people into their houses and frightened them with clattering noises; Carlos and don Genaro would be seen in two places at once.

Young Arana attended Public School 91 and San Ramón High School in Cajamarca, but didn't graduate. In 1948, at the age of 22, he moved to Lima, finished high school, and entered Bellas Artes, the national fine arts school of Peru. His mother came to visit in 1949 but fell ill, and his father had to join her. The family lived in a third-floor apartment in the Porvenir District, on the outskirts of Lima. In 1950 Susana Castañeda de Arana died. Her son refused to attend the funeral, locked himself in his room for three days without eating, came out and announced he was leaving home. The "burden" of his ailing mother's unbearable love was all that had kept him from escaping.

Arana rented an apartment with two fellow art students. Carlos Reluz he "incited to go away to Brazil," where Reluz grew famous. José Bracamonte, now a noted illustrator, remembers Arana as "a big liar and a real friend," a witty fellow who lived off card games, horses, and dice, while harboring "like an obssession" a wish to go to the United States. Victor Delfín, a third fellow student, told journalist César Lévano:

Carlos Arana as a youth.

He was a wonderful liar [*el tipo más fabuloso para mentir*]. A very capable fellow, likable and rather mysterious. A first-class seducer [*un seductor de primera línea*]. I remember the girls used to spend the morning waiting around for him at the Bellas Artes. We called him Smile of Gold because he had, I think, a gold tooth. It seems to me that during that period he spent all his time goofing off and annoying people [*vagar y fregar la pita*]. Sometimes he would go to La Parada [an open market or flea market in Lima] with some used watches—didn't he get them from home?—which only he could make run for two or three hours. He would sell the watches to the boys and then disappear for a while.

Though Bracamonte recalled some of Arana's drawings as strange, stark, almost ugly, Alejandro González Apu-Rímak, one of their most respected teachers, had defended Arana, saying: "But this boy has something tremendous inside of him."

He was a great gambler [Bracamonte said] who intended to go to the United States to make money betting. He wanted to be rich. In the meantime he was always thinking up unlikely stories—tremendous, beautiful things. At times he sold blankets and ponchos from the mountains. He was always talking about Cajamarca, but oddly he never talked about his parents. Only now have I learned that he has an uncle who lives near my studio.

Already practicing secrecy, Arana didn't tell his fellow renters his father's house was only a few blocks from their apartment on Jirón Humboldt. Despite unconventional exploits, he was showing a streak of asceticism that would mark his later life. On nights of carousing and revelry, he would exercise more restraint than his friends, "partaking of the euphoria but neither drinking nor smoking." Lévano took this moderation to be a sign of Arana's fear that he might miss great opportunities by surrendering to Bohemia as his father had done. "I am my father," he would tell Sandra Burton.

About a year after his mother died, Arana disappeared. Nobody knew where he had gone. Eventually some letters came from Los Angeles. Writing to his "sister" Lucía, the fugitive described an imaginary military career and hinted at mental or physical wounds. Rarely did he write to his father. One letter, mildly deriding Don César's preoccupation with ultimate questions, contained only a single sentence: "Dear old fellow: Who is God?" Another said: "I'm going on a very long journey. Don't be surprised if you learn nothing more about me." Ironically, it was the father who went on the very long journey and sent back no news. César Arana died having heard not a word from his son for several years, unfamiliar with a new American writer named Carlos Castaneda, unaware of a best-selling book about a magician named don Juan, who had already taken up Don César's parental burden.

Between Arana's immigration at San Francisco in 1951 and Castaneda's resurfacing in Los Angeles in 1955, the record is blank. Nothing is known of where he lived or what he did. I have given some thought to his possible occupations. Driving a taxi, delivering liquor, working in a factory, keeping books for a women's wear store, and investing in the stock market are all livelihoods he has claimed; on that basis I rule them out. In *Castaneda's Journey* I supposed he might have worked as an attendant in a retirement home, since *A Separate Reality* describes long conversations with a very old man who lived in a home for the aged. His interest in gambling suggests he might have frequented the poker parlors of Gardena, just south of Los Angeles. His selling of blankets, ponchos, and broken watches would have been good training for selling subscriptions or vacuum cleaners. Margaret said he was a good cook and an accomplished tailor. But my favorite hypothesis arose when two women independently told me he did a very good job of cutting his own hair. Many barbers cut their own hair; few non-barbers do so. In a barber shop an imaginative immigrant could practice English to his heart's content, while telling tall tales, learning local customs, and making a decent living. It seems made to order. A search of union files might turn up a barber named César Arana or Carlos Aranha or even Salvador Castaneda, whose portrait in Chapter Two of this book a former fellow barber would recognize.

In December of 1955 the daughter of Margaret Runyan's Spanish-speaking dressmaker brought two dresses to Margaret's apartment. She also brought a young man Margaret found instantly attractive. On her next visit to the dressmaker, Margaret left for him a copy of Neville Goddard's *The Search*, a metaphysical book she had inscribed with her name and phone number. Six months later he called her.

"I saw him every day, from June 2, 1956 until 1966, when I left California," she told me.

"*Every* day?" I said.

"Well, maybe not *every* day, but I don't remember his ever being gone for any length of time." Memory plays tricks, of course, but if Castaneda had accompanied Carlos on those trips to don Juan's desert, you'd think Margaret would have missed him once in a while.

"Did you talk about mysticism and metaphysics?" I asked her.

"That's all we ever talked about," she said—but meant she talked, he listened. Castaneda would claim to have no interest in mysticism and metaphysics. Why then did he seek out and visit almost every day for ten years a woman whose invitation had been written in a metaphysical book and who constantly talked about such things? They used to go to Ingmar Bergman movies and discuss them afterwards.

"Did you see *Seventh Seal?*" I asked.

"That's the one we talked about the most," she said.

When Sam Keen said don Juan echoed Plato's idea that a philosopher should study death, Castaneda won the point by saying don Juan had added "a strange twist" in describing death "as a physical presence that can be felt and seen." In *Seventh Seal*, looking much like Dwight Eisenhower, death plays chess with the protagonist.

"What about *Wild Strawberries?*"

"That one, too," she said. In *Wild Strawberries*, an old man has a vision of a beautiful, dissatisfied young mother meeting a strange man in a woody glen, a likely model for the misbehavior attributed to the no doubt blameless Susana de Arana. I told Margaret about the Chinese-Korean bullet that had castrated Carlos.

"That couldn't be true," she said, "but he does have a very bad scar from his lower abdomen downward."

"How did he get it?"

"He said it was when they hung him up by his feet and tortured him." Having enough tall tales in my file already, I didn't ask who "they" were.

Margaret didn't fall in love with Castaneda so much as she fell under his spell. His looks were exotic, his mysteries intriguing, his stories entertaining, his poems enchanting, his paintings admirable. Once he gave her a beautiful sculpture of a pregnant woman. At his suggestion she enrolled at Los Angeles City College, where he was studying creative writing under a man named Vernon King, who would later receive a copy of *The Teachings* inscribed: "To a great teacher . . . from one of his students, Carlos Castaneda."

"Learning and the love of learning were the bonds between us," Margaret wrote. "We are married spiritually and always will be." The spiritual marriage has taken some rather hard knocks. After four years of friendship they were married in Tijuana on 27 January 1960. Six months later Castaneda moved out of Margaret's apartment. The explanation was that Carlos had met don Juan and must spend weeks at a time studying with him—a regime that somehow would not keep Castaneda from seeing Margaret "every day." The separation lasted 13 years; Margaret filed for divorce in 1973.

Castaneda spent a lot of time with Margaret's son, whom he eventually insisted on adopting. Before the adoption, however, Margaret moved to West Virginia to take care of some family business. Castaneda was upset by the defection, which gave rise to various stories about the loss of Carlos's little boy. Though Margaret always supported herself, Castaneda's literary success resulted in his putting money into her telephone answering service and furnishing sporadic child support. When she sold the business, he didn't ask for his investment back. It would be incorrect, therefore, to say that he refused to take care of the family. When he wanted to, he helped. The trouble was, one never knew when he would want to. The only thing you could count on was that you couldn't count on anything. If he said he would come, he stayed away. When you didn't expect him, he would arrive. When you got used to his being around, he would vanish. If the check was in the mail, it got lost. If the plan was made, it fell through. Don Juan calls this sort of thing disrupting the routines of life and recommends it as a mystical technique, but ordinary people call it heedless irresponsibility and condemn it as antisocial. The sorcerer's world and the social world have very different rules.

Castaneda's friends typically don't meet or even hear about each other. Each is treated as if he or she is the only friend. Sometimes they are warned against each other. When I first knew Margaret, I made up a list of people I thought had been important to his academic career and asked her about each one. She had never heard of any of them. She had few friends in common with him and met none of his fellow students. When the little boy grew up, Castaneda advised him to have nothing more to do with his mother if he wanted help in going to college. "Your mother is dead to me," he said. The boy consorted with his mother, and the money stopped coming. It sounds a little more bizarre than it may actually be, for I suspect Castaneda didn't think the boy would follow the rule. At any rate, the broken rule served to excuse the failure of tuition. When the boy was preparing to enter college in Arizona, Castaneda announced he had enrolled him at UCLA. The boy preferred Arizona and was deemed uncooperative. Castaneda said that if the boy got a passport he could go to school in England, but when the passport was in order, the plan was dropped. Still, the boy recalls happy moments with Castaneda, going for walks, riding on his shoulders, visiting the magic ring of boulders in the Santa Monica Mountains. He doesn't remember ever seeing don Juan, though Castaneda has told him they went together to meet don Juan when he was little.

What is the effect of such confusing, inconsistent treatment on a young person? The boy stoically says he can take Castaneda or leave him; I suspect he can do neither. In Chapter 38 I defended Castaneda against charges of antisocial behavior, saying I doubted involuntary victims could be found, but I'd overlooked wives and children. However mild and charming Trickster's role, he is not going to win any prizes for husbanding or parenting. Reading Castaneda's tearful passages about the little boy, Yaqui Méndez would likely say Trickster sells not only his mother but his son as well.

"Carlos has a daughter," Margaret told me. I asked for the details. It seems the little girl's name is Carlotta. Carlos calls her Toti. The mother is an American with an Anglo name, but Toti lives with Carlos's father in Brazil. Margaret saw a photo of a cute five-year-old who looked like Castaneda though slightly oriental. Since the little girl was a half-sister, the boy was invited to make a present for her, which he did, and sent it off to an address in Los Angeles. There was no reply. Carlos had left the mother long before, because coming home unexpectedly from work one day, he had found her in bed with another man. Those archetypal betrayers are all over the place.

Toti in Brazil is not the daughter I'm concerned about, nor the child supposedly abandoned in Argentina. The one I have in mind is Esperanza, a 23-year-old woman who showed up in Berkeley in May 1975 with Castaneda, who introduced her as his daughter. Of course, I suspected a trick. A sorcerer invents his nonordinary world, but ordinary people wander into it, where they have to play by the sorcerer's rules. Castaneda told two bookselling ladies in Sacramento about an army officer father moving from post to post, so that little Carlos never had a real home. He told Margaret he had married a gypsy girl in a blood ceremony. Those stories were hard to check, and the hearers didn't have to live in them, but other stories spring like traps when compared with ordinary reality. Castaneda got a Ph.D. for interviewing don Juan, but when *Castaneda's Journey* said don Juan was imaginary, the UCLA patrons found themselves trapped in Carlos's fieldwork. In February 1973

Castaneda met Margaret in New York, and they went to the Drake Hotel. All night he was talking on the phone with people in Los Angeles and—of course—"Mexico." Having expected him to be charming and attentive, Margaret was disappointed and uncomfortable. Next day she moved to another hotel, shopped a few days with a lady friend, and went home to West Virginia. The next time Castaneda called her, she taxed him with his strange behavior in New York. He said he didn't know what she was talking about. She described his coldness at the hotel. He said he hadn't seen her for months and certainly had not stayed in a New York hotel with her. The trap sprang on Margaret. She couldn't believe he was saying those things. Even when separated physically, they had always been close spiritually. She had never felt so far from him.

The following year, when *Tales of Power* was published, Margaret began to understand what had happened to her in New York. It seems a sorcerer has a double. But he doesn't know where his double is or what it is doing. More than that, it is very dangerous for him to know; if he met his double, he might die. Margaret didn't want him to die, so she had to forgive him, both for the coldness of his double and for not knowing what his double had put her through. In her nightmares, talking mushrooms climbed into caskets; they looked like the ones on the blouse she had worn at the Drake Hotel, but they had large black eyes, like holes. She was a long time getting out of that particular trap. Reflecting on the experience, she said:

> It bothers me to think back on my life with Carlos and realize that after twenty-five years there are many ways I still don't know him any better than his readers do. I'm sure I've spent more time with him than any other person. For years I never missed a day seeing him. Yet he is just as great a mystery to me as he is to everybody else. Sometimes I wonder, did I really spend all that time with him? Though I understand the symbolism in his books and have seen him many times since the first one was published, he has not once discussed any of them with me. His books are conversations he is holding with himself.

Castaneda's traps don't always spring on loving quail or baby rabbits. When he catches a couple of young lionesses, the hunting goes both ways, and the tale turns funny. In the spring of 1972, four years before Carlos would hear of them for the first time from doña Soledad, Castaneda told his Irvine students about the "four winds." Don Juan had said a sorcerer meets his crucial test when he goes to a certain Mexican plain to confront the ally. Because the confrontation is dangerous as well as horrendous, the sorcerer does well to take a crew of helpers with him: four dedicated women who will stand at the compass points around him to bear the brunt of the ally's onslaughts, willingly sacrificing themselves to improve his chances. (If Marie-Louise von Franz is listening, I'm sure she is thinking Castaneda leans too heavily on the women who care for him, making them confront his demonic self, when he should deal with it directly.) A sorcerer who fails the test gets spun by his ally and doesn't feel or act human any more.

A sorcerer cannot deliberately seek his four wind-women, who must come to him of their own accord. Carlos found one wind, but don Juan said she was too dependent on him, not strong enough to help him against the ally. More charming than Carlos, Pablito had found three winds—though of course attracting the winds is not a sexual affair but an arrangement of power. Despite the terrible danger, rumor had it Carlos had indeed acquired two winds. I thought that was pure invention—until one of the winds wrote me a letter.

Ramona DuVent is a plains Indian and apprentice shaman who teaches anthropology in a major university. During Castaneda's one quarter at Irvine, she and her friend Marjory Dill were graduate students. Both were going through an occultist phase and were fascinated by Castaneda's purported discoveries of magical shamanic lore. DuVent had been surprised to note the similarity with teachings of Zen and Frederick Perls, elements she had never before encountered in the Native American tradition. "What have I been missing?" she asked herself.

Dill was receiving special instruction from Castaneda. She introduced DuVent to him, and the three went to lunch. DuVent immediately impressed Castaneda as a good candidate for sorcery. He made the usual lunch date with her and, following his custom, broke it. Dill defended him to DuVent, saying he had far more important things to do than keep dates with sub-apprentices. Before long, however, Dill informed DuVent that the two of them had been chosen as Carlos's winds. DuVent was excited at being chosen, because initiation as a wind would confer advanced status in sorcering otherwise attainable only through long and arduous training. At the least, it would prove Castaneda either a genuine sorcerer or a literary faker. DuVent hoped it would be the former, since graduate school had been rather dull up to that point.

To prepare Dill for initiation, Castaneda gave her a vision quest, took her to the Malibu place of power, built a twig hut over her, and left her to meditate. He told her she must cut herself off from her friends, who were wasting her time, get rid of her dog, on which she spent too much attention, and abstain from sex with anyone who was not a sorcerer or at least an apprentice. Casual intercourse disperses a sorcerer's power, he said. DuVent didn't recognize that as an Indian idea and went on the warpath when she heard about getting rid of the dog, since she had three dogs of her own. She asked to see the directive on dog abatement in Carlos's fieldnotes, but he was living in the van, taking showers at the gym, and had left the fieldnotes in Los Angeles. Dill wanted to know when the initiation would take place. Castaneda said he must pop down to Mexico to check everything out with don Juan.

At the next meeting Castaneda said he had *smoked* the two of them with don Juan, who had *seen* that they were acceptable winds, but the time of induction was still to be set and the ritual specified. The winds began to fret. Castaneda confessed that the prospect frightened him out of his wits and said he didn't know whether he would be able to go through with it. The winds exhorted him. A week or so later he said he had once more returned from Mexico, where don Juan had commanded him to initiate the winds without delay, while the omens were favorable. The winds said fine. Castaneda got flustered. The winds said, what's wrong? Castaneda said the ceremony was more terrifying than he had expected. They asked what it was. Castaneda said it was ritual intercourse. Dill said, when? DuVent thought: Why not?—It can't hurt me, and I'll either be an instant shamanette or I'll be done with the whole thing.

Dill asked if it was group sex. Castaneda said, no, no, they had to be initiated in the order he had discovered them in, which was Dill first, DuVent second. Dill said: I'm ready. DuVent said: I'll wait. Castaneda said he was screwing his courage to the sticking place, or words to that effect. Dill said, there's nothing to be afraid of. One day he phoned to say he was coming over. Dill hid her dog in the back room. Castaneda entered warily. Dill tried to put him at ease. He said something felt terribly wrong. She said: Come on, initiate me. The dog barked. Castaneda looked reproachfully at Dill and said she could never be initiated if she wouldn't follow the simplest rules of sorcery. He departed. She was furious.

At their next meeting, she badgered him about contradictions in the fieldwork. He said people were making outrageous demands: 'Would you believe, day before yesterday a band of hippies banged on my office door? They had a young woman in a white robe, with flowers in her hair, and they wanted me to deflower her.' Dill said there was no proof any of his stories were true, and she thought he had made them all up, including don Juan. From now on she'd have to see proof. After that she couldn't get in touch with him any more. He just vanished.

"Why didn't he initiate her?" I asked DuVent. "That would have been easy."

"Marjory's very assertive," Du Vent said. "I think he likes women to be more passive." Which may be true, but I think we also have to remember that attracting the winds is not a sexual affair; it's an arrangement of power. I'd say Castaneda was testing his power to make two intelligent, self-directed women who didn't love him believe a preposterous story and submit to outrageous demands.

Castaneda had entered UCLA in 1959, the year he became a U.S. citizen; he received his Ph.D. in 1973. Except for his novel dissertation and one paper read at a professional meeting, he had no scientific or scholarly publications. Beyond brief duties as a teaching assistant at UCLA, his only teaching appointment was made by the students at UC-Irvine for the spring quarter of 1972. It is reasonable to say he became a full-time writer in 1972 and will continue in that career for the rest of his life. As his career combines writing and hoaxing, so his character recalls two very different hoaxers, whose lives I suspect he studied. A 1959 book called *The Great Impostor* would have taught him to avoid certain pitfalls; articles about novelist B. Traven would have given him a model to emulate. In the same vein, Weiner's *Piltdown Forgery*, popular among anthropology students in 1959, showed what could be accomplished by a determined scientific hoaxer. Fourteen years of faultless role playing at UCLA argue strongly against Castaneda's having gradually drifted into the don Juan hoax. I believe he knew just what he wanted to do by 1960 and laid strategic plans he was able to carry out with only tactical adjustments.

A crucial difference between Castaneda and B. Traven is that Traven called his adventure stories fiction while Castaneda called his fairy tales field reports. Otherwise, they had much in common. Both used pseudonyms and erased their personal histories; Castaneda's history has been fairly well restored, but Traven's may never be. Both avoided photographers, had mysterious marriages and uncertain places of residence, were extensive readers whose reading influenced their writing. Each worked hard for years as an unknown writer before achieving any success, wrote in English as well as a foreign language, and created confusion about different versions of his texts. Each produced books in rapid succession, Traven more and faster than Castaneda. Both wrote about Mexico and about a clash of Indian and European cultures. Each got involved with a movie maker, Traven with John Huston, who made *Treasure of the Sierra Madre*, Castaneda with Sterling Silliphant, who wanted to make a movie of *The Teachings*. Both wrote English in an odd foreign manner that was sometimes unintentionally funny; Traven was odder and funnier than Castaneda: shut your grub-hold, a punch in the swear-hold, what for thousand devils are you doing? Castaneda was tricky and evasive in Peru, so it is clear he did not learn such traits from Traven, but Traven's example may have inspired him.

Ferdinand Demara succeeded temporarily in each of several occupations: school teacher, monk, jailer, college dean, and navy surgeon. Since he had not finished high school, he also forged his qualifying documents, got into trouble with the law, and was always (so far as we know) discovered and expelled. One thing he achieved was fame. A book was written about him, and a film was made of his life. A young hoaxer just starting out would have done well to read up on Demara, who had many tricks to teach and whose mistakes were freely admitted. One mistake was not settling on a specialty he could master. Another was not becoming his own boss. A third was breaking the law. Castaneda avoided those mistakes. He became a self-employed writer and the world's leading practitioner of ethnomethodallegory, to which no laws apply. Below are a few lines from Robert Crichton's *Great Impostor* that could have instructed him:

> To succeed, all impostors must sooner or later learn and have confidence that the burden of proof is always on the accuser [66]. "I am a superior sort of liar. I don't tell any truth at all, so then my story has a unity of parts, a structural integrity and this way sounds more like the truth than the truth itself" [142]. "I call it Demara's law for passing, or, the invisible past" [86]. The organization involved stands to suffer from publicity of his case as much as he does. In truth, everyone involved except the public would just as soon forget it [167].

Did Castaneda study *The Great Impostor*? I think he did. Here are three notes I think he must have taken, and what he later made of them:

> "I'm rotten. . . . Every bone in my body is rotten. I'm rotten through and through. . . . I am a rotten man" [Demara]. "I

already know that you think you are rotten. . . . that you are ugly and rotten and inadequate. . . ." [don Juan].

He frightened the others in school and they let him alone [Crichton]. Growing up, he had to contend with twenty-two cousins, and he fought with them all until they left him alone [Cravens].

He'd think of himself as aimless and unable to direct and control the flow of his life as was a leaf in its direction [Crichton]. "You feel like a leaf at the mercy of the wind. . . ." [don Juan].

Demara suffered from boredom and needed always to create excitement; don Juan told Carlos to relieve the boredom of certainty by creating the excitement of uncertainty. Demara hunted power lying about loose in organizations; Carlos hunted metaphysical power in the desert; Castaneda hunted social power in the university. Demara seemed always to be laughing at his victims, enjoying a great big secret all his own; Castaneda has a "sardonic sense of humor much like don Juan's," said Michael Harner; "he mocks everyone he meets," said co-author Alberta Greenfield. "We impostors are unaccountable people," said Demara; my life is weirder than it looks, said Castaneda. "This is not your ordinary cheater," said Robert Crichton; Castaneda "is a marvellous cheater," wrote anthropologist Jacques Meunier.

In 1978, perhaps modeling his name on "B. Traven," an Australian aboriginal poet, B. Wongar, made his international literary debut. Wongar (the pseudonym means "dreaming") is the son of an aboriginal mother and a European father, educated in Europe. His book, *The Track to Bralgu*, collects twelve fantastic stories about the conflict between an aboriginal people trying to save the earth and a European people determined to exploit it. The stories have been hailed in Australia, Britain, and the United States as first rank literature written by a man who lives inside the tribal myths and therefore has no need to interpret them as something else, whose writing tells us for the first time what it feels like to *be* an aboriginal—something a European writer could neither do nor get away with pretending to do.

Does this account begin to have a slightly familiar ring? If so, perhaps you will not be astonished to learn that only one person claims to have met Wongar, a Yugoslav expatriate anthropologist and writer named Streten Bozic, who lives in Melbourne but met Wongar in Paris. Bozic is

Wongar's sole contact with the white world. More than that, Bozic is Wongar's agent, editor, and cashier. He signs Wongar's literary contracts, cashes Wongar's royalty checks, and, when they need it, rewrites Wongar's stories. Of course, they don't often need it, because Wongar is the better writer, having won more literary awards than Bozic, who has won some. Asked to produce Wongar, Bozic said the mysterious author must be protected from reprisals by bureaucrats, mining companies, and tribesmen who resent his revealing tribal secrets. Asked if he is not himself Wongar, Bozic said: "You put me in a very difficult position. Our paths cross and he's a different personality and a different writer." Not a different *person* but a different *personality*. To identify him as Bozic "might affect Wongar's work." Literary agents have agreed not to reveal Wongar's identity.

Two things interest me about the apparent Wongar hoax: the question of its origin and the reaction of its subscribers. Australian novelist and Wongar subscriber Tom Keneally said that if Bozic is Wongar, he is, by some strange mystical means, more aboriginal than white. Wongar's London publisher said that if *Track* is not by Wongar "the writer is some kind of genius." Joseph Chilton Pearce said that if don Juan is a literary invention, Castaneda is a genius. Judgments of "genius" arise from literary deceptions which do not arise from admitted works of fiction produced with the same degree of skill and dedication. Why is that? Does genius require lying? Or do such judgments come from persons who believe only a genius could deceive them?

People in the same line of work imitate each other. Has Castaneda imitated Bozic? So far, it's too early for that, but what about the reverse? Is Bozic imitating Castaneda? I commend the question to graduate students at the University of Melbourne. If Bozic wins prizes on his own, why does he need Wongar? What are the motives of hoaxers? More manageably, what are the motives of the don Juan hoaxer? While turning his life into an allegory, Castaneda has told us a lot about them, though not everyone has understood what he has told us. *Time,* for example, could find no motive for a don Juan hoax. Here was an obscure undergraduate bright enough to get a Ph.D. in the regular way, who took twice as long as usual and had to write three best-sellers to get the same degree in an irregular way, all the while risking exposure and expulsion? To *Time,* it didn't make sense. Well, of course it doesn't make sense if you think hoaxers are mainly interested in academic recognition or making money, but hoaxers are mainly interested in the exhilaration they feel when they prove their superiority to ordinary people by deceiv-

ing them. That is a fact it is hard for non-hoaxers to grasp. Joyce Carol
Oates, who writes about mysticism, believed Castaneda must have had
some authentic mystical experience, because "no one feigns mystical experience." Nonsense. Bharati wrote a book about genuine and fake mystics. From Madame Blavatsky to Yogi Ramacharaka to Lobsang Rampa,
the woods are full of mystical feigners. What Oates meant to say is that
persons *like Oates* do not feign mystical experience, but then persons like
Oates don't claim three children at the age of eight, sell broken watches,
and register their doubles in hotel rooms either. "I don't want to be a
professor," Castaneda said at the end of his graduate school career. "I
love to write, but I don't think of myself as a scientist or an intellectual."
Hoaxing and storytelling are Castaneda's callings. The pseudo-
anthropology of mysticism was a means of bringing them together; now
it is no longer needed.

Novelist Ronald Sukenick couldn't believe Castaneda was a fiction writer, because Carlos-Academic seemed so unimaginative and because the
don Juan stories, as Castaneda told them over and over, had a "cumula-
tive smell of experience rather than imagination." Sukenick was judging
Castaneda against the other fiction writers he knew, who didn't live in
their stories *all the time*, and whose stories were consequently not the
core of their life experience. Castaneda has a much greater need for the
company of his characters than most fiction writers do, because his
characters are his only intimate friends. And he has an advantage over
most fiction writers in being able to say, outside of books, that his characters are actual people.

Don Juan's art, Castaneda said, "is the metaphorical way in which he
lives." It sounds good, but it's not right. Don Juan lives not in a
metaphorical way but in a literal way. In don Juan's world, things are
what they are; nothing stands for anything else; there are neither symbols nor metaphors. Animals talk, weedmen fly, plants like to be picked
with respect. These events are not to be interpreted or explained but to be
witnessed. The one who lives in a metaphorical way is Castaneda, constantly constructing a separate reality by deliberately transforming
common social meanings into uncommon ones—going to Mexico in the
blink of an eye, telling you he is *in* Mexico as he stands talking to you in
Los Angeles, inviting you to accompany him to Sonora to meet don
Juan, reminding you of the time you met don Juan when you were a
child. What makes it metaphorical rather than insane is that Castaneda
knows which reality is ordinary and which is nonordinary, though his
listener may not. Don Juan, in contrast, never pretends. "His dramatic

exertion was always much more than acting; it was rather a profound state of belief." Don Juan is the genuine, sincere person Castaneda could be if the separate reality were more than imagination, a man Don César would have respected. Don Juan can really leave this evil world—where our fellow men are "black magicians" who enslave us—and go to a better place; he doesn't have to make up stories about it. "He lives in magical time and occasionally comes into ordinary time. I live in ordinary time and occasionally dip into magical time." Lucky don Juan; unlucky Castaneda. In *Second Ring* Castaneda struggles to turn "obscure metaphors into real possibilities." It doesn't work. The result is bad storytelling, loss of readers, and mounting futility.

When Arana didn't get what he wanted from parents, teachers, church, and God, Castaneda took revenge. If Susana de Arana abandoned her son emotionally when he was six, Carlos's mother would be maligned, and Castaneda would frustrate every woman who tried to love him. If César Arana was distant and unexciting, Carlos's father would be boring and weak-willed. If the schools of Cajamarca seemed prisons to an imaginative boy, the man would call teachers time-serving pedants and would sabotage the academy. If the Church offered empty ritual, Carlos would imagine it falling down. If God was just another distant, censorious father, don Juan would replace him with an amoral, impersonal, but accessible *nagual*.

A rebellious mood fills one with energy but is hard to maintain. When it fails, look out for depression and self-rejection. Carlos confesses he has never liked or respected anybody, not even himself, but has always felt himself inherently evil. (After all, his mother must have had a reason for abandoning him.) Don Juan agrees: "You don't like yourself at all." To counteract the ordinary truth about Carlos—that he is "ugly, rotten and inadequate"—don Juan instructs him to imagine the opposite and so learn that both descriptions are lies. But if all descriptions of self are lies, how can one ever be sure of deserving the love that was taken away? Thus depression must be fended off forever by sustaining the mood of a warrior: "I can like my fellow men"—and myself, he could have added—"only when I am at my peak of vigor and am not depressed."

Boredom, a symptom of depression, is Castaneda's constant enemy. To keep it at bay he stirs up excitement. Loud parties and celebrations are quickly used up, but a more reliable source of excitement is always at hand. "You want to keep the freshness, the newness in what you do," don Juan explained. "You lie in order to keep on going." Reliable information is boring, don Juan said; unreliable information is exciting. As a heroin addict organizes his life around heroin, a person who palliates mental suffering and gets a high by lying organizes his life around lying. Each is a slave to his habit. An imaginative person turns lying into fantasy, fantasy into storytelling. Castaneda finds great comfort in Carlos's life. Carlos is a special person, a chosen man, an impeccable warrior, a man of knowledge. He displays courage under fire. He endures mental and physical hardships, never asking for mercy. He is on his way to a better world. Over and over these ideas appear in the don Juan books, but writing books is not enough. The fantasies must be shared face to face, as they were with María Caruapoma. In narrative-November-1970, for example, don Juan gave Carlos instructions for frightening a little boy out of bad behavior. In calendar-November-1970 Castaneda told Barbara Myerhoff he had actually carried out the sorcerer's version of *Scared Straight* with his little boy at the San Diego Zoo. In 1970 the boy was living in West Virginia; in 1979 he did not recall ever having gone to the zoo with Castaneda. Here we find an extension of the rule stated in Chapter 39: that Castaneda writes what he has just read. He also tells what he has just written. Reading turns to writing; writing turns to telling. Thus living people are brought into the fantasy world, where they add temporary warmth and excitement.

Critics are also drawn into the separate reality. Beyond his letter to Wasson, Castaneda has never to my knowledge answered a critic directly, yet he conducts an aloof and secret dialogue by answering in story. Three years after Joseph Chilton Pearce said isolation was don Juan's flaw, don Juan retorted that a warrior is never lonely because he loves the biosphere. When don Juan was faulted for promoting irrationalism, he replied: "Nobody wants or seeks the extinction of the *tonal's* rationality. That fear is unfounded." After Vine Deloria asked where the curing was, La Gorda let it be known don Juan had smoked the mushrooms not only to *see* but also to cure, though she added that curing would weaken a sorcerer, which explains why don Juan left it out of his teachings. Thirteen months after I asked where Carlos's friend Bill was hiding out, Castaneda retroactively killed him off. Sixteen months after Mary Douglas asked whether don Juan had really been afraid of La Catalina, don Juan said, of course not; Catalina was his confederate. Douglas remarked a resemblance between don Juan and John of the Cross, whereupon the saint popped up in the frontispiece of *Tales of Power*. After Carlos-Apprentice was criticized for exploiting don Juan by exposing his secrets to the world, Carlos had second thoughts: "Maybe I'm revealing things I shouldn't," he said. Don Juan reassured him: "It doesn't matter what one reveals or what one keeps to oneself." In his letter of October 1968, Wasson pointed out that visionary mushrooms do not grow in Sonora or Chihuahua; Castaneda's answering letter revealed that Carlos had to take don Juan to Oaxaca every year to collect the mushrooms; his next book opened with Carlos finding don Juan, for the first time, in Oaxaca.

The world of fantasy offers many distractions and some pleasures, but it does not lift the burden of childhood disappointments or suppress the emotional outbursts that voice early sorrows and rages. Many of don Juan's mystical techniques serve to take a sorcerer's mind off his troubles and shield him from unhappy feelings. "Whenever I witness something that would ordinarily make me sad," don Juan confides, "I simply shift my eyes and *see* it instead of looking at it. But when I encounter something funny I look and I laugh." To suppress emotional outbursts, strict controls are needed. Carlos quells the war within him by leading a tight warrior's life, by subjecting every impulse to rigid will and merciless self-discipline. "To become a man of knowledge," don Juan says, "one must be a warrior, not a whimpering child." Carlos's constant "indulging" is a tendency to get in touch with his feelings—a weakness don Juan deplores and ridicules. "You indulge like a son of a bitch," he says.

Castaneda's asceticism is protected from the assaults of feeling by constant, intricate intellectual activity. The so-called internal dialogue may be an obstacle to Carlos's mystical *seeing*, but it shields Castaneda from a flood of emotion. As Carlos practices his "only sorcery," which is taking notes and writing, Castaneda reinforces the discursive, ascetic regime by living in spartan apartments (before his success at any rate), never taking LSD, drinking one glass of wine, keeping his body trim and fit, and admitting he lacks "the sensitivity and openness to be a great artist." "Sensitivity matters very little," don Juan declares. What matters is to be impeccable in substituting will for feelings. In youth, don Juan's hate nearly destroyed him, but he vanquished it. Carlos, who reminds don Juan of himself, displaced his anger from disappointing parents onto a luckless high school principal and a pitiful Brazilian six-year-old with the Spanish name Joaquín; after breaking the child's collarbone, Carlos renounced all violence. Castaneda's hostility comes out in countless subtle insults and practical jokes on colleagues, friends, and family.

Though Carlos was hungry for love, it seemed nobody loved him. The most desperate way for an unloved person to feel is helpless. "We have spent an eternity as helpless infants," don Juan said. When Carlos caught a rabbit, don Juan said it was the rabbit's time to die. Looking at the rabbit in the cage, Carlos felt he *was* the rabbit. "That rabbit goes free," he said. Stamping on the cage to free it, he broke the rabbit's neck. "I told you he had no more time," don Juan whispered. Thus did the adult Castaneda kill the child Arana while trying to free him from the past. From then on, other victims had to take his place in the trap; don Juan called it hunting power. As Carlos uses traps and bare hands to catch rabbits, Castaneda uses stories and gestures to catch people. He is characteristically charming. He affects weakness, confusion, and naivety. He flatters people, especially women; though he would tie UCLA into a knot, he praised Myerhoff's superior ability to cope with the cold, threatening academic world: "I don't have the mechanics," he said— thereby twisting Garfinkel's "machinery" just enough to hide its source. Twisting things just a little is a major technique: soul-catcher becomes spirit-catcher, no-mind turns into not-doing, La Barre pinch hits for Petrullo, glosses are linked to Parsons instead of Richards, Husserl instead of Schutz or Garfinkel is read to don Juan.

Castaneda mirrors the mind of his collocutor. Having read an account somewhere of Yaquis using Jimson weed for flying, Michael Harner told Castaneda about it. Soon afterwards don Juan gave Carlos lessons in flying with Jimson weed. A typical performance for Castaneda, but when Harner was writing up the occurrence, he couldn't find the reference he had read. Noting that he listed 37 other references and recalling statements by ethnographers that Yaquis wouldn't be caught dead using Jimson weed, I accused Harner of conspiring with the hoaxer. Anthropology student David Christie hounded Harner for the reference, which Harner promised to send if he could find it. It didn't arrive, and Harner looked more like a conspirator than before. Finally, Hans Peter Duerr sent the reference—to me—from Germany: an obscure, invalid, second-hand account, published in Madrid six years before Carlos flew. Harner was rescued from the hall of mirrors and restored to the community of non-conspirators.

Castaneda is bold. He walks an allegoric line between the plausible and the absurd, daring the listener to topple him. Take the following exchange with Theodore Roszak, broadcast in 1968:

Roszak: One point I'd like to clear up is something I wondered about as I read [in *The Teachings*] your own experiences using herbs and mushrooms and the long conversations with don Juan. How were you able —just as a technical problem—how were you able to keep track of your experiences over such a long period of time? How were you able to record all of this? [To his credit, Roszak here puts his finger on one of the major implausibilities of Carlos's fieldwork, but see how adeptly and brazenly the hoaxer fields the question—on the air, in a broadcasting station, with no time to prepare a reply and no later help from a sympathetic editor. I retain all of the hems and haws to give the flavor of the spoken answer and to show delays for thinking.]

Castaneda: Um, it ah seems difficult that ah since one of the ah items ah of the learning process [the stall has worked, and now he's ready to go] is a recapitulation of whatever you experience, in order to remember everything that happened, um, I ah [he wonders if he dares to take the next step; he decides to risk it] I had to make *mental* notes [his emphasis], of all the steps, of all the things that I, I saw, all the events that occurred during the states of, let's say, expanded consciousness, of whatev——and ah then it was easy to translate them into writing after, ah, because I had them all, ah, ah, meticulously, ah, *filed*, sort of, and ah, i-, i-, in my *mind*. [This is the first time he has ever had this idea; he is inventing it on the spot.] That's i- ah as the ex ah the the experience itself goes, but then the questions and answers [between Carlos and don Juan], th- I simply *wrote* them down. While I was——

Roszak: Oh, you were able to take notes while you were——

Castaneda: Ah, not at the very beginning of our relation you see I never took any notes [he changes his mind] I took notes in a *covert* manner. [Castaneda goes on to describe at length how ethnographers write notes on pads inside their pockets.]

By this time Roszak has been successfully distracted from his main question and from Castaneda's preposterous answer: that while under the influence of drugs—once for three days—Carlos made something called mental notes, which he kept meticulously filed in his mind, until it was time to pull them out and transcribe them. Roszak praises don Juan's eloquence. Castaneda agrees that don Juan "is very *artful* with the use of words." Castaneda says he was lucky to find a teacher with the same predilection he has, for artful talking. He laughs quietly, at Roszak's expense. "Don Juan," he says, "sets his life as a strategic game. He makes use of anything that he can."

Castaneda's soft, hypnotic discourse is well preserved on the Roszak tape. *Time* called his speech "mesmeric." One moment he mystifies, the next he appeals. Admiration is sought from young men by recounting brave adventures. Kindness is elicited from older men by playing the son or younger brother; though Castaneda was older than five of his eight

UCLA patrons, he pretended to be three years younger than the youngest; what faculty member would sense danger from a cute little fellow who called Wittgenstein "Bickerstein"? Emotions are counterfeited; Bracamonte remembered Arana pretending anger to get his way. Manipulations are applied as needed; Castaneda wrote: "I could usually cajole . . . or make concessions, argue, get angry, or if nothing succeeded I would whine or complain." Women's sympathy is excited by tales of suffering, sorrow, and helplessness; Anaïs Nin was led to believe that by taking a manuscript of *The Teachings* to New York she had "worried" UCLA into publishing it; a generous act but an unlikely effect.

Beyond arm's reach Castaneda's main appeal is to a universal hunger for myth and magic. Like the spiritualist bringing messages from the departed to the bereaved, he returns with good news from an ideal world everyone has dreamed of visiting, if only as a child. "I cannot adequately convey the excitement I experienced on reading this account," wrote anthropologist Edmund Carpenter. "I kept putting the manuscript down and walking around." Transporting Carpenter to a world of perfect fieldwork, building a hut of twigs over Marjory Dill, showing Gloria Garvin don Juan's drawing of the dreamer and the dreamed, Castaneda furnished illusions which eventually faded but at the time were thrilling.

Dealing with human beings while living in a fable is a strange and acute form of social isolation. Playing with people's lives adds a sinister touch. Women are the most frequent puppets, children the most fragile. Before being whisked away by uncontrollable forces, Carlos's little boy had been "more than anything else" his friend. While that is a touching bit of nostalgia, we have to ask what kind of father views his son as friend first, child second. Turning one's child into an imaginary playmate is not acting like a father. Though Castaneda insisted on adopting the boy, he did not keep promises made to him. A man who unconsciously acquires a son to reenact an unhappy childhood is bound to play the disappointing father.

Women in Castaneda's world are demanding and untrustworthy; they "make one suffer in an unbelievable manner." Often they are helpful or comforting, but it doesn't last; one can't tolerate their presence very long, and certainly one can't live with them. They get pregnant, swell up, look fat, and earn the name Gorda. When the child is born, it leaves the parent empty. Children steal one's boldness, sap one's energy, destroy one's illusions. To remain free and whole, one has to learn not to care about them. Don Juan told La Gorda Carlos had a little boy he loved and a daughter he had never seen; those kids were standing in the way of his salvation. Because he had "made" a female child, Carlos was empty and needed to regain his wholeness. The method was clear. Soledad was lucky, because her daughter died; she got some of her substance back without having to do anything about it; to get the rest she may have to kill her son Pablito. Until she regains her completeness, she will not be able to enter the world where sorcerers go instead of dying.

In narrative-1976 La Gorda said Carlos would have a hard time giving up his "useless affection" for the little boy (who never grows up no matter how many years go by), but the grown daughter Carlos had never seen could easily be rejected. In calendar-1975, however, Castaneda presented Esperanza to several friends as his daughter. When Ramona DuVent told me about a dark, Spanish-speaking daughter, I thought, here we go again; some Chicano girl has fallen in with his pranks and is playing Carlos's daughter. I said:

"Was she a Chicano?"

"No, she's from Peru." That was too much. A daughter in Peru must have been discovered by *Time*, or certainly by *Caretas*.

"That's hard to believe," I said.

"Don't take my word for it. Talk to Wright Dennison. A friend of his knew the girl and her mother in Lima."

Truly, I thought, Castaneda is a bottomless pit. If DuVent thinks I'm going to follow up this nonsense, she doesn't know the Way of the White Writer. The same day I spoke at length with Dennison and with his friend, Eleanor Witt. This is the story they told me:

In 1951, while a student at Bellas Artes, Carlos Arana met Dolores, a Chinese-Peruvian girl years younger than he. A perfect innocent, she was a nubile prize for a young hunter Victor Delfín would remember 25 years later as "a first-class seducer." When Arana declared his romantic desires, Dolores raised moral objections, but when he proposed marriage, she accepted him. Before very long she announced the impending birth of their child. About a month after the announcement Arana left the country. In far-off Los Angeles he told his consul general he meant to study in the United States and not return to Peru until he had graduated. Earning barely enough to keep himself alive, he had no money to send home to Dolores, but his letters to her professed undying love and promised she could join him shortly. He didn't stop writing until 1955. Since Latin cultures hold a woman, even a wife, to be necessarily at fault if she is abandoned, life was full of sorrows for Dolores, whose child, Esperanza, was raised in a convent. In 1973 *Time* magazine proclaimed that a certain very successful North American writer was really Carlos Arana of Peru. Mother and daughter read the story, looked at the pictures, and knew it was true. Here after 18 years of silence was Esperanza's long lost father. In May 1975, filled with hope, Esperanza flew to California to join the truant. It was a joyful reunion. He was charming, she was thrilled. He flattered her, she was delighted. He offered help, she accepted. He made promises, she made plans. He said she should attend college in the United States; she said that would be perfect. When she got an invitation from a midwestern university, he insisted she attend the nearby University of Redlands; she assented. He forbade her to talk about him to the media; she agreed. During a pause in the excitement, she asked why he had never wanted to see her before. He protested that he *had* wanted to see her, very much, that it had been constantly on his mind, in fact—though she might find it hard to believe—he had once actually gone to Peru to see her, when she was still a child, but catching sight of mother and daughter in the market place he was suddenly overcome with guilt about deserting them and couldn't bring himself to face them. Instead, he followed them through the market, sadly observing them from a distance, and then flew back to Los Angeles, having given up hope of ever seeing them again. With tears in her eyes, Esperanza told her father how much she loved him; but she thought he was a very strange man. After two ecstatic weeks in California, Esperanza flew back to Peru—where bitter disappointment awaited her. One letter came from Castaneda. The plans for college fell through. Esperanza's letters went unanswered. She stopped talking about her father, told Eleanor Witt to forget she had ever come to the United States, married a European, and went to live in Europe. Dolores is still living in Peru and has never remarried.

Is this pathetic story true? Unfortunately it seems to be. DuVent, Dennison, and Witt are responsible professional people. The account does not contradict any known fact. Official Peruvian documents attest to both the marriage and the desertion. Father and daughter were seen together in Berkeley and Los Angeles.

In his inimitable, indirect way Castaneda confirms the story himself, for by writing anachronistically that Carlos had a grown daughter he had never seen, what was Castaneda doing but magically returning a daughter he *had* seen to her former condition of invisibility? Though Carlos was shocked at La Gorda's proposal that sorcerers must kill their children to get their wholeness back, Castaneda wrote at length about that macabre necessity. A daughter dead to Castaneda could not keep Carlos from going to the other world to join the undead sorcerers. A choice between the worlds had to be made, and Castaneda made it. If he felt regret at the ease with which he symbolically killed his child, he could comfort himself with don Juan's maxim: "Once a man embarks on the road to knowledge he's no longer liable for what may happen to those who come in contact with him."

When I asked Barbara Myerhoff what Castaneda and Ramón had *seen* in each other, she said: "The same kind of person." She meant a person who laughs at the absurdities of this world from some vantage point in another world, but there is a crucial difference between the two seers as well. Shamans hunt power to guide their people, cure their neighbors, or feed their families; sorcerers like don Juan and Carlos have no people, neighbors, or families. Castaneda belongs to no community on this earth. As von Franz put it, he is "a lonely, asocial hunter of mysteries." Since the age of eight he has been making his way toward wealth and fame by telling tales and cutting himself off from human beings. Now he has achieved those goals, and it is time to make amends for the costs others have paid for his success, but he can't change the pattern. How easy it should have been to provide reliable assistance and unmanipulative treatment to an adopted son who had been not only one's child but one's friend. He couldn't do it. How pleasant it should have been to make an intelligent, industrious, adoring young woman happy simply by keeping a few moderate promises and remaining more or less accessible. It proved impossible. The nonordinary parent's mind is on other things: like getting his wholeness back from the children who have stolen it; like gazing down enraptured—as a lonely child stares at insects on the ground—at "the most beautiful and perfect thing one could imagine," don Juan's nest of little red bugs.

The career deceiver has all the ability he would need to achieve success in some conventional way but is unwilling to obey social rules and unable to deal with his fellows except by being one up on them. Social accountability and mutual trust are not part of his repertory. Loving surrender is beyond him. Their absence means he must always be an outsider, manipulating events and people, distorting and hiding information. His rewards are pride in his cleverness and a feeling of personal power. His penalties are isolation, coldness, and a need to be always on his guard. By offering little truth and many falsehoods to those who were closest to him throughout life, the hunter of personal power has with amazing skill and unbending intent built around himself a cage so strong he will never get out of it. A few rabbits have fallen into it and squirmed out through the mesh, but no benefactor has come to open it from the outside. Well, that's not entirely true. On 24 February 1977 I wrote to Castaneda proposing that we collaborate on a book about him. On the face of it, this was a naïve gesture, since Castaneda has not cooperated in any way with scholars who wish to write about him, and I am hardly the most likely recipient of his cooperation. In 1974, while still an enthusiastic admirer of Castaneda, Daniel Noel wrote a book analyzing his works as literature without taking any position on whether they were fact or fiction. Warner Paperback Library accepted Noel's manuscript for publication, but when Warner applied to Simon and Schuster for permission to quote from the don Juan books, they were told Castaneda would authorize no quotations whatsoever. As an original essay, which neither substituted Castaneda's labor for Noel's nor competed with the don Juan books in the marketplace, Noel's study was covered by the fair-use provision of the copyright law. Anyone who doubts this should consider the alternative, which is that an author could block publication of normal scholarly criticism of his works simply by refusing permission to quote from them, an immunity from criticism Congress never had in mind. Most book publishers, however, subscribe to an extra-legal gentlemen's agreement under which permission is always asked. No doubt the agreement works perfectly well in most cases, but a maverick like Castaneda could manipulate it to disrupt the conventional critical process. Noel wrote to Castaneda hoping to remove the obstacle. Castaneda phoned to say it wasn't his obstacle but Simon and Schuster's. Simon and Schuster said: "Dr Castaneda's decision is irrevocable." During four maddening telephone conversations Castaneda said he would try to intercede with Simon and Schuster but explained he had very little leverage under his contract—an assertion Noel found hard to swallow. Eventually Noel abandoned the project without knowing just who had denied him permission.

M. D. Faber also wrote a book about Castaneda. When Faber's prospective publisher asked permission from Simon and Schuster, they too were told Castaneda would never give it. Since Faber and Castaneda had been friends at UCLA, Faber wrote to his old friend, explaining the nature of his book—how it was a psychological study of the relationship between sorcerer and apprentice—and begging him to change his mind. At that time Faber thought the sorcerer was an actual person and didn't realize with what reluctance imaginary apprentices would submit to literary psychoanalysis. Castaneda didn't answer. Faber sent registered letters. The return receipts came back. Faber sent telegrams. In the end, he split his book into three articles (summarized in Chapter 38), which were published in 1977, journal editors being more sanguine than book editors about fair use. With considerable restraint, Faber did not expand his study to interpret Castaneda's refusal as a sign of persecution complex or antisocial character.

Aware of Noel's difficulties, I made my overture to Castaneda expecting it to be neither accepted nor acknowledged, but I thought someone should make the offer, and I was in a position to do so. The crux of my letter read as follows:

> Devoted as I am to don Juan, I find you more interesting than he. You are undeniably one of the most intriguing figures ever to appear on the literary scene—let alone in the academy. I would put you well ahead of B. Traven, himself a fascinating character. I believe there is a marvelous book to be written about you, describing you from the ordinary point of view. I suspect you will never write such a book yourself, being too fond of the nonordinary reality. But you could contribute to such a book, if the author were to assume responsibility for keeping the realities sorted out. Conversations with Castaneda might be a good title. You have seen what I can do entirely without your cooperation. Think what we could do together—provided I didn't let you get control of the crack between the worlds.

Ten months later, Second Ring was published. Knowing Castaneda's habits, I looked for an answer there. Perhaps this is it:

> 'Sorcerers don't help one another like you helped Pablito. . . . [Don Juan] said that a warrior had no compassion for anyone. For him, to have compassion meant that you wished the other person to be like you, to be in your shoes, and you lent a hand just for that purpose. . . . The hardest thing in the world is for a warrior to let others be. . . . The impeccability of a warrior is to let them be and to support them in what they are. That means, of course, that you trust them to be impeccable warriors themselves.'

I should have known. "A warrior doesn't seek anything for his solace" and doesn't want to be rescued from the path of knowledge even if the path is going round and round inside a cage. A sorcerer is a world unto himself. Not even another sorcerer can help him.

Five years Castaneda and I have traveled the allegoric road, though we have never met. Now it is time to say goodbye before we say hello. I started later but have finished earlier. Carlos still has a long way to go toward true nagualhood; Castaneda, by my reckoning, will produce eight more books for cultists; Arana is lost and will never be found—the boy he was, rejected by the man he is. Of three abandoned children, little Arana is the one nobody will claim. It's a sad story all the way round, sadder for him than for anyone else. Of course, he's telling it himself, but it's the only story he knows. At times he reflects on the unsubstantiality of his imaginary companions: "It was as if the point of departure had always been myself; it was as if don Juan had never really been there; and when I looked for him he became what he really was—a fleeting image that vanished over a hill." At times he complains about his isolation: "Don Juan has no real compassion for me. He gives me his attention, that is all. He cannot give me his feelings because he can only approximate true human feelings." Yet he never breaks out of his tiny, special world into the larger world where people live. As don Juan said: "A man who *sees* has no longer an active interest in his fellow men."

Don Juan's teacher and his benefactor were men of great personal power, who never broke out of their limited views of life and so never arrived at the totality of themselves. They knew what should be done but couldn't do it. They knew they had missed the boat. They knew only death would bring significant change.

"Am I still shaped like an egg?" Carlos asked.

"No," said La Gorda, "You're shaped like a tombstone."

A warrior considers himself already dead, so there's nothing for him to lose. Sorcery gave a glimpse of the goal but never the means to achieve it. The fate that befell don Juan's teacher and benefactor is falling just as heavily on don Juan's inventor. There is apparently nothing he or anyone else can do about it. Life has become an allegory, and "there is no other way to live."

VI.

Appendices

In English, a *gloss* is an explanation of an unfamiliar word in a text, and a *glossary* is a list of glosses; this conventional sense is the one I intend here. In ethnomethodology, however, glossing is provisionally understanding or describing what is meant in a conversation or some other immediate social interaction. Castaneda turns ethnomethodological glossing into a perceptual metaphor; to him, a gloss is a language-sustained perception, a way of seeing or hearing the physical world (see AG:**Gloss**).

An *allegory* is a description of one thing under the guise of another, particularly a description in story. Castaneda's books are allegories. The words and events in his books (in addition to being straightforward elements of a story that can be taken at face value) are disguised propositions in an extended tract on social-science methodology and various kinds of metaphysics.

This *Alleglossary* (to which citations are made by the code AG) is therefore an explanatory list of Castaneda's allegoric terms: words and ideas from his books that say one thing while meaning another, each term explained by showing that it undoubtedly or very likely came from an earlier work by another writer, where it meant something rather different. Most of the original ideas and words were transformed or redefined just enough to make them seem newly original but not so much that they lost the capacity to reflect their origins. Allegory requires not only disguise but resemblance recognizable beneath the disguise.

The word *gloss* has been parlayed by the ethnomethodologists and Castaneda far beyond the simple verbal explanation of an unfamiliar word; of that conventional definition, Castaneda's *gloss* retains only the sense of interpretation. For the ethnomethodologists, a gloss is a statement approximating an unstatable meaning shared by two people who understand each other in conversation; glosses are what people say to each other to indicate (that is, to point in the direction of) what they really mean, which they can never exactly say, can never completely express in so many words. If we manage to penetrate the relentlessly murky language in which Garfinkel habitually enshrouded his ideas (whose lack of profundity and coherence was thereby hidden, no doubt as much from him as from the suffering graduate student), we find *gloss* merely extended in a tolerable manner from signifying a product of textual explanation to signifying a process of conversational understanding. Castaneda then leapt from this redefinition into metaphor. Glossing became perceiving, seeing the physical world—a meaning it had never had before and I trust will never have again. When he said, "This room is a gloss," he was rendering social science in story.

Three years after I first put the question to him (CJ:82n), Walter Goldschmidt finally got round to explaining his seminal mischaracterization of *The Teachings of Don Juan* in the now famous opening sentence of his introduction· "This book is both ethnography and allegory" (C68:vii). Since ethnography is supposed to be factual and allegory is supposed to be fictive, that sentence had a most nonsensical ring to me. He must mean the book is *partly* allegory, I thought, and Colin Wilson had the same idea: "Walter Goldschmidt . . . begins by admitting that it is partly allegory" (Wilson 1975:13). Wilson and I were dead wrong. When I proposed our interpretation in a letter to Goldschmidt (CJ:82n), he asked how one could take seriously a scholar who could not see that something could be ethnography and allegory at the same time. It was clear from his tone that the matter was too easy and familiar to need any explaining, but I felt obliged to persist, on behalf of readers who might be as simple and ignorant as I was. I wrote again, begging him to tell me how a field report could be both ethnography and allegory, but he did not reply.

"I meant that the book has a moral," he commented three years later. "It gets us all where we live" (Preuss 1978:56). The explanation made some sense, at last, of his calling the book "both ethnography and allegory"—though the statement still mischaracterizes *The Teachings*, which is not ethnography in any case. Ethnography is both cultural and factual, whereas don Juan's lore arises from no identified culture, certainly not from Yaqui culture, and the old man himself is by all reasonable tests not factual but imaginary. By finding a moral in *The Teachings*, Goldschmidt *rendered* the book an allegory, much as one might read an allegory of man's fate into the sinking of the *Titanic*. This would be a *reader's allegory*, implying neither that the *Titanic* was an imaginary ship nor that reports of the sinking were written to convey a moral. Reports written to convey a moral would likely depart from accuracy, since intentional allegorizing conflicts with factual reporting in both purpose and technique. By using the bare term "allegory," which connotes writer's intent much more strongly than reader's interpretation, Goldschmidt unwittingly but correctly told his readers *The Teachings* was a *writer's allegory*, an intentional piece of story-telling masquerading as a field report, a fairy tale about fieldwork. For ten years, Goldschmidt's inadvertently accurate labelling of *The Teachings* as a fairy tale contradicted his misleading endorsement of it as a field report, thus making nonsense of his "both ethnography and allegory."

This Alleglossary does not list all of Castaneda's ideas or even all of his allegorical terms but seeks only to provide a generous sample of those terms, to identify their certain or likely origins, and to show how Castaneda adapts the words and ideas of other writers to build his allegory. Every item in the list contributes to those ends. Many of the items also contribute to a proof that Castaneda was writing fiction rather than fact. Since the items are variably evidential, some offering strong evidence of fictioneering, others weak evidence if any, an opportunity arises for Juanist fanatics and professional obfuscators to seize on the weak items and prattle about their weakness, while ignoring the strong items. Years of observing such perversity convince me that anyone who wishes can escape the implications of a sound argument. I have no hope of preventing the escape. Indeed, I shall make it easier by listing here a few items to be strictly ignored if one wishes to go on proclaiming the authenticity of don Juan: **Ally, Barking, Collapse, Crack-b, Description, Dreaming, Egg, Gait, Lizard, Pearce, Peyote, Red, Self, Waterfall.** These items say to me not only that Castaneda was definitely adapting the words and ideas of other writers but that he was daring us to catch him in the act—which we have done.

After these four years of digging, how many of Castaneda's sources remain buried in the stacks? Many, I should judge, for it seems to me that *every* element of don Juan's teachings could be traced—by an obsessed graduate student with a ten-year grant—to some earlier publication. Parapsychologist Stuart Holroyd proposes that all of Castaneda's ideas could have come from Eliade's *Shamanism*, and yet this Alleglossary cites Eliade only eight times among hundreds of items from other writers, where similar language makes the connections more obvious than in Eliade. Holroyd's proposal is only rhetorical, for he goes on to say (1977:154): "It is more likely that the books are what they purport to be: an anthropological study written from a 'state specific' point of view." The flaw in that hypothesis is that Castaneda would have had to live in a trance for fourteen years, not only while visiting don Juan but while working up his fieldnotes and writing his story, which purports to intersect the ordinary reality at many points.

I am grateful to Holroyd for unintentionally pointing out to me

(1977:156) Castaneda's adaptation of Wittgenstein's propositions about explaining, where Wittgenstein's "whole modern conception of the world" becomes don Juan's "whole world," Wittgenstein's "as if everything were explained" becomes don Juan's "explaining everything," Wittgenstein's "modern conception" becomes "your way," Wittgenstein's ancient believers become don Juan's "phony sorcerer," Wittgenstein's "God and Fate" become don Juan's "witchcraft," and Wittgenstein's "both are wrong" becomes don Juan's "you're no better" (AG: **Explaining**). This one paradigmatic item shows very clearly how Castaneda transforms works of philosophy, mysticism, and ethnography into conversations with don Juan.

Most of the items in the list are titled by words denoting ideas, but where Castaneda has followed a rich vein, an author's name may serve as title and several ideas may be distinguished by paragraphs labelled **a, b, c,** and so on. Author's names also serve to title lists of items in which they are the source. As elsewhere in the DJP, the five don Juan books are cited as: C68, C71, C72, C74, and C77; Castaneda's dissertation is cited as C73; *Castaneda's Journey* is cited as CJ or CJ2, depending on the edition. Quotations from Castaneda and other authors are given in double-quotes ("); quotations from don Juan or other characters are given in single-quotes ('). Occasionally, I have had to summarize passages, and these summaries appear, of course, without quotation marks. In all but a few items, the quotation from the source precedes the quotation from Castaneda.

Though little is known except by inference about Castaneda's reading habits, his familiarity with the following authors is firmly documented by his having reviewed their works for Wendell Oswalt's Anthropology 250, UCLA, Fall 1962: **Leightons, Petrullo, Pozas, Steward,** and **Underhill.** He was photographed holding a copy of the dissertation by **Orona.** Though he said he had read **Wittgenstein**, he said he had read him aloud to don Juan, so the claim is paradoxical (AG: **Noose**). He said he had read everything available on peyote (C72:19) and specifically mentioned La Barre (Keen 1972:92), who does not appear in this list, but he never breathed the name of **Petrullo,** who is well represented here.

Abyss "An edge of a huge cliff seemed to project over a gulf of unseen depth" (Klüver 1928:24). "Man in greenish velvet . . . jumping into deep chasm" (28). ● Don Genaro "plunged with me into the abyss" (C74:253). See: Self-b.

Accounting "By his accounting practices the member makes familiar, commonplace activities of everyday life recognizable *as* familiar, commonplace activities" (Garfinkel 1967:9). "What is it about natural language that makes these phenomena . . . *account-able* phenomena?" (Garfinkel & Sacks 1970:342). • 'Sorcerers have learned after generations of using power plants to account in their views for everything that is accountable about them' (C74:239).

Agreement "All the members of a given community agree in arranging the letters of the alphabet [but] there is one . . . who takes the liberty of interchanging A and Z. . . . If we get enough [like him] to agree on the interchange of A and Z, we have what we call a new tradition. . . . What starts as [an] aberration seems to have the power, by some kind of 'social infection,' to lose its purely personal quality. . . . even 'existence,' in a world of socialized behavior is nothing more than consensus of opinion" (Edward Sapir, in Mandelbaum 1949:571-572). Sapir goes on to say that, though the social world is created by consensus, the physical world is less transformable by language and agreement. • In contrast, don Juan says: 'We are making this room. Our rings of power are spinning this room into being at this very moment. . . . Every one of us knows the *doing* of rooms. . . . We have all been taught to agree about *doing.* . . . You don't have any idea of the power that that agreement brings with it' (C72:252-253). Castaneda's dissertation abstract (1973:vi) restates don Juan's position in phenomenological terms: "The sorcerer's contention is that the world at large, or our physical surroundings, which appear to have an unquestionably independent and transcendental objectivity, are the product of the perceivers' agreement on the nature of what they perceive. In other words, we, the perceivers, are the dynamic parts of the world, because we not only imbue it with meaning but also with 'form.' Thus the perceived realness of our surroundings is due to social consensus, rather than to its objective nature." Wilber (1977:133, 230-231) gives don Juan as the source of Sapir's notion of agreement-based reality. See: Gloss, Pearce-1.

Ally "The celebrant is shut up alone with a corpse in a dark room. To animate the body, he lies on it, mouth to mouth . . . holding it in his arms. . . . After a certain time the corpse begins to move. It stands up and tries to escape; the sorcerer, firmly clinging to it, prevents it from freeing itself. Now the body struggles more fiercely. It leaps and bounds to extraordinary heights, dragging with it the man who must hold on. . . . At last the tongue of the corpse protrudes from its mouth. The critical moment has arrived. The sorcerer seizes the tongue with his teeth and bites it off. The corpse at once collapses. Failure in controlling the body after having awaked it means certain death for the sorcerer. The tongue carefully dried becomes a powerful magic weapon which is treasured by the triumphant *ngagspa*. The Tibetan . . . needed all his strength to hold it. . . . If he failed to conquer it, the horrible being would kill him" (David-Neel 1932:135); the full account was reproduced in Mead & Calas (1953). ● 'When a man is facing the ally [he] must wrestle the spirit to the ground and keep it there until it gives him power' (C71:282-283; see also C71:303, C72:246). 'After I grabbed it . . . the ally made me twirl, but I didn't let go. We spun through the air. . . . Suddenly I felt that I was standing on the ground again. . . . The ally had not killed me. . . . I had succeeded. . . . I jumped up and down with delight' (C72:306). 'The jolt that one gets from grabbing an ally is so great that one might bite off one's tongue' (C72:305). See: Campfire, Spin.

Alpert See: Kobler.

Anaya See: Gorda.

Ancient ones See: Toltecs.

Animal "Strange animal turns into a piece of wood in horizontal position" (Klüver 1928:28). ● "There was something on the ground. . . . It was definitely some animal. . . . Judging by its body the animal was obviously a mammal, yet it had a beak, like a bird. . . . then something rearranged the world and I knew at once what the animal was. . . . It was a large branch of a bush" (C72:130-132).

Arm-sweeping "The Chiricaua have a ceremonial procedure . . . which they call, 'It moves the arm about.' It is used . . . for determining the whereabouts of the enemy. . . . the 'feeling' went all through his body, from the end of the toe, up through the knee, and on up through the top of the head. . . . He had to go to the top of a hill. He stood under a tree, facing north" (Leightons 1949:158, 160; reviewed by Castaneda fall 1962). ● "He said that as soon as I reached the hilltop I had to extend my right arm in front of me. . . . when I felt a warmth coming up my left leg I had to begin sweeping my arm slowly from north to south and then to north again. . . . 'If the spot where your hand gets warm is toward the north, you will take a bad beating. . . . if the spot is toward the south you will have a hard fight' " (C71:276-277).

Artaud Colleagues have pointed out striking similarities between Antonin Artaud's Tarahumara memoir and ideas in the don Juan books, but I assume Castaneda does not read French, and Spanish and English editions either came too late or were not readily available. I conclude that the similarities arose from common interests in Amerindian lore and oriental mysticism.

Atkinson See: Egg.

Attention " 'Attention' implies to attend, that is to listen, hear, see, with all the totality of your being. . . . completely. In that total attention—in which there is no division—you can do anything" (Krishnamurti 1971:43). ● 'Our mistake is to believe that the only perception worthy of acknowledgement is what goes through our *reason*' (C74:249). "To him reason meant attention. . . . the 'attention of the tonal'. . . . The second domain was the 'attention of the nagual'. . . . I had placed my attention on both domains" (C77:266-267; see also: 270, 271). See: Pearce-e,g.

Awareness "He is the five senses disembodied, all of them keyed to the height of sensitivity and awareness, all of them blending into one another most strangely, until, utterly passive, he becomes a pure receptor, infinitely delicate, of sensations" (R. G. Wasson in Furst 1972:198). ● "Those nuggets of awareness were scattered; each of them was aware of itself and none was more predominant than the other. Then . . . all of them had to be pooled in one clump, the 'me' I know [which] would witness a coherent scene" (C74:262-263). See: Self.

Barking "Those rites take place now . . . far from the beaten track, high in the mountains of Mexico, in the stillness of the night, broken only by the distant barking of a dog or the braying of an ass" (Wasson 1961:158 or in Furst 1972:200). ● On a remote plateau high in the mountains of Mexico, Carlos carries out a ritual of saying goodbye to all present or left behind (C74:280). "The silence around us was frightening. The wind hissed softly and then I heard the distant barking of a lone dog. . . . The barking of that lone dog was so sad and the stillness around us so intense that I experienced a numbing anguish. . . . 'That dog's barking is the nocturnal voice of man,' don Juan said" (C74:285). For shaman's barking or howling dog, see Furst 1966:346-347.

Bath 'I dreamed of a tree rolling down the mountain and of something black. . . . I got up and talked to my power asking it to protect me. . . . Then I took a cold bath in the lake.' "Several informants told of taking cold baths to nullify evil predicted in a bad dream" (Steward 1934:431, reviewed by Castaneda fall 1962). ● "Don Juan rushed me to the irrigation ditch at the back of his house; he dumped me there fully clothed" (C71:151). 'Whenever a sorcerer has an encounter with any of those inexplicable and unbending forces [it makes him] more susceptible to his death. . . . When I dumped you into the water. . . . you were protected' (C71:261; see also C71:145, 193).

Bauman Correspondences appear between *Tales of Power* (C74) and Z.

Bauman's (1973) article on Husserl and ethnomethodology. The *nagual* echoes Bauman on: "transcendental intersubjectivity" (6), "pure Mind, pared to the bone of all vestiges of the world of objects. . . . [which is] the basis of our knowledge" (7), "liberty from both 'empirical' and 'introspectional facts' " (10). The *tonal* can be seen in Bauman's: "the individual cannot but be deeply immersed in the world of objects" (7), and "the individual can surrender his subjectivity to the objects 'over there,' but this act will inevitably amount to the betrayal of his virtual subjective existence" (8). Don Juan's cataloguing of the objects on the table top answers Bauman's: "Even the most meticulous inspection of the world of objects would not reveal the nature of the subjective" (9). Don Juan's bubble of perception fits Bauman's: world of subjectivity, which "can be scanned from inside only" (9). See: Nagual, Tonal, Table, Bubble.

Bean The source given under each item here is *Temalpakh* (Bean & Saubel 1972), but how could findings published in 1972 influence *Ixtlan* (C72), let alone *Teachings* (C68)? Bean began his fieldwork in 1960 (3), the year Carlos met don Juan, and soon offered lectures at UCLA (Beals 1978:359); three preliminary reports were published by 1963 (211-212).

Bean-a "Datura. . . . is unpredictable [and may cause] serious mental disorientation, disorders. . . . psychoses" (60). ● 'She has a serious drawback. . . . She distorts men. . . . and makes them . . . unpredictable. . . . the flowers [are] used to turn people crazy' (C68:35).

Bean-b "Dancers used it to acquire great stamina and strength. . . . Singers . . . took datura to give them strength. . . . 'It gives you great strength' " (65). ● 'I feel a strange vigor' (C68:42). 'I too felt its swelling inside me. . . . only five hundred times more strongly. . . . Once I jumped so high I chopped the top leaves off the highest trees' (C68:44).

Bean-c "The hard needle-like thorn at the end of each agave leaf will if carefully detached come out of the leaf with several feet of fibre attached, thus making a natural needle and thread combination" (36). ● "The [agave] thorn came out from the pulp bringing with it a bunch of long threadlike fibres, attached to the woody part like a white tail, two feet long. . . . don Juan twisted the fibres together between the palms of his hands and made a string" (C68:50).

Bean-d "Plants were . . . viewed . . . as living beings with whom one could communicate and interact. . . . Plants were placed on earth by the Creator to serve man, but it was not intended that this should be an exclusive one-way relationship. . . . All parts of this system were reciprocal. . . . Plants . . . were therefore treated with respect. A person gathering a plant would thank the plant for its use, apologizing . . . for the harm inflicted . . . but also recognizing that it was natural that the plant submit to its predetermined use" (15). ● 'It doesn't matter what you say to a plant. . . . what's important is. . . . treating it as an equal.' Don Juan said the gatherer must assure the plants "that some day his own body will serve as food for them" (C72:43). See: Plants, Propitiation.

Bean-e "Such works as Weston La Barre's *The Peyote Cult* (1959) and Carlos Castaneda's *The Teachings of Don Juan* (1968) and *A Separate Reality* (1971). . . . offer an excellent introduction to the ways in which the hallucinogenic plants have been used and the philosophical and cosmological constructs of societies employing them" (60; see also 62).

Bean-f See DJP: Chapter 5, Note: Puma charges.

Beast "A giant rosetta-spotted jaguar. . . . This tremendous animal shuffled along with head hanging down, mouth open, and tongue lolling out. Hideous, large teeth filled the open mouth" (Córdova-Rios & Lamb 1971:157). ● "A giant nauseating-looking coyote or wolf. . . . Its jaws shivered and globs of saliva flew all over the place. . . . a colossal feline loomed in front of us" (C74:259).

Beetle 'Once I found out how I would get out of trouble. I dreamed that my soul was sitting in a house when I saw near me a small, round bug called [coyote's fish]. I looked at it and said: "Now you little bug, I think that you could jump from where you are up through the smoke hole in the roof and make your escape. If you can do that, I too can escape when I am in a bad place." The bug made the jump and got away and ever since that time I have been always able to get out of trouble' (Steward 1934:430-431, reviewed by Castaneda fall 1962). ● "I observed the insect for a long time and then I became aware of the silence around me. . . . The thought crossed my mind that death was watching me and the beetle. . . . I experienced a shiver. The beetle and I were not all that different after all. Death, like a shadow, was stalking both of us. . . . I had an extraordinary moment of elation. The beetle and I were on a par. Neither one of us was better than the other. Our death made us equal" (C72:294-295).

Beyond "The ultimate Reality . . . is really a something or a nothing which is altogether beyond the grasp of a thinkable thinking agency. And at the same time it is graspable as such, as beyond our grasp, for to state something positive or negative about it makes it to that extent fall within human intelligibility" (Suzuki 1972:10-11; correspondence noted by Forisha 1978:30). ● 'If I would say, Nothing [is what one can find beyond the island of the *tonal*], I would only make the *nagual* part of the *tonal.* All I can say is that there, beyond the island, one finds the *nagual.'* 'But when you call it the *nagual,* aren't you also placing it on the island?' 'No. I named it only because I wanted to make you aware of it' (C74:128-129). "I don't read mystical books"—Castaneda to Cravens (1973b:174).

Bill-a "Since Gregorio, like most of the other Indians in the region, spoke no English, we communicated with him entirely through our interpreter, Bill. . . . We had told Bill and Carlos that we were eager to learn how Navahos live" (Leightons 1949:8; reviewed by Castaneda fall 1962). • "I was sitting with Bill, a friend of mine, in a bus depot in a border town in Arizona. . . . Bill was my guide in the Southwest while I was collecting information and specimens [compare DJP: Chapter 40] of medicinal plants used by the Indians of the area. . . . Bill, who speaks only a few words of Spanish. . . ." (C71:9-10). 'I was in a bus depot in Arizona with a high-school friend of mine' (Keen 1972:92/1976:77).

Bill-b When I challenge Castaneda to substantiate Bill (CJ:91), he responds by killing Bill off: 'The Nagual *saw* that the man's death was hovering over his head' (C77:52).

Bird "Anthropomorphic bird whistle figurine . . . possibly representing metamorphosis of shaman into bird" (Furst 1966:330); plate (1965:39; 1966:331) shows man's head, at the back of which arms are turning into wings, the remainder of the body is very small. • "Then he told me that my body had vanished completely and that all I had was my head; he said that the head never disappears because the head is what turns into a crow. . . . he talked about the crow's wings and said they would come out of my cheekbones" (C68:121-122).

Body "I learned that the human body may act like a self-conscious person, without any participation of the recollecting mind" (van Eeden 1969:147). "The wisdom of the body operating in sleep . . . to reorganize the accumulating experience. . . . the organizing wisdom of the body" (Stewart 1969:165). • 'Your body has learned. . . . your body knows. . . . I've been telling your body. . . . I would like to show your body. . . . your body returns to see me because I am its friend' (C72:216-217). 'It is the body that does [*not-doing*]' (C72:226). 'Letting your body know' (C72:233). "My body knew much more than I suspected" (C72:238). "My body somehow became aware" (C72:276). 'Let your body decide what's what' (C72:292). "My body experienced" (C72:297). 'The real thing is when the body realizes that it can *see*' (C72:302). "Bodily experiences, not intellectual ones" (C74:45). 'His *will,* which comes from the midsection of his body' (C74:178). "The body has a will of its own. Or rather, the will is the voice of the body"—Castaneda to Keen (1972:100/1976:89-90).

Boundaries "It will therefore only be in language that the limit can be set, and what lies on the other side of the limit will simply be nonsense" (Wittgenstein, *Tractatus*, Author's Preface). ● 'We make sense in talking only because we stay within certain boundaries, and those boundaries are not applicable to the *nagual*' (C74:190).

Bubble "It is as if one's skull was suddenly expanding like a balloon being blown up and that a huge spherical hollow was thus created which then served as a stage of visual drama. The eyes appear no longer as looking out from within into the world, but rather they are reversed upon themselves, clinging to the walls of the hollow sphere looking in and moving freely along the total inner surface of that sphere, so that ever new perspectives are opened up and phenomena reveal themselves in thousandfold manifestations at a phantastic speed" (Swain & others 1963:234). ● 'We are inside a bubble. . . . That bubble is our perception. . . . And what we witness on its round walls is our own reflection. . . . The thing reflected is our view of the world' (C74:246-247). See: Bauman.

Burial "The shamans lay the novice on the ground and cover him with leaves and branches" (Eliade 1964:343). ● "I . . . asked how he was planning to bury me. He . . . began collecting dry branches. . . . the leaves were so well placed that no dirt came inside" (C72:136-137).

Campfire Opler (1941:203) tells about a man "sitting by a campfire and something sat with him." It was Buzzard, who offered the man "power so that he would be able to see things that otherwise he could not see." The man refused to accept the power, saying: "Your power is of no use to me now." ● In "The Task of 'Seeing,' " Carlos is sitting by don Juan's campfire, when the light is blocked by a spirit resembling a moth. Don Juan says this spirit has no secrets of power to give, that it is "useless" (C71:279-284, 280). See: Ally.

Carroll See: Collapse.

Carving "Gregorio watched his grandfather work for two days. First he got the root of a certain plant and carved it into the shape of a snake. . . . A forked tongue was made out of white cotton" (Leightons 1949:10; reviewed by Castaneda fall 1962). ● As part of a two-day ritual, don Juan "took the long piece of root shaped like the letter Y. . . . the bars of the fork had become more widely separated. . . . slowly and patiently he carved the shape of a man" (C68:49).

Catalina See DJP: Chapter 39.

Chair The shamanic chair provides the Huichol shaman with his 'sacred place' during his chants at ceremonies. When travelling, he carries his chair on his back (Myerhoff 1968:129; 1974:110). ● "Pablito came back in a moment carrying an unusual-looking chair on his shoulders. The chair was shaped to follow the contour of his back, so that when he had it on his shoulders, upside down, it looked like a backpack" (C77:173). 'I might as well be a jackass as long as I'm carrying this damn chair.' 'Why do you carry it, Pablito?' 'I have to store my power. . . . I can't go around sitting on just anything. Who knows what kind of a creep sat there before me?' (C77:311; see also C77:201, 216).

Citizen "The *mara'akame*, he said, must learn to read and write in order to protect the people from 'land-grabbing Spaniards with their maps and titles.' He should learn the ways of the cities and learn to move easily among the authorities" (Myerhoff 1968:95; 1974:47). ● "He looked like an old Mexican gentleman, an impeccably tailored urban dweller" (C74:106). 'To wear a suit is a challenge for me. . . . A challenge as difficult as wearing sandals and a poncho would be for you' (C74:109). 'My suit . . . represents . . . one of the two parts of my totality' (C74:119). 'I'm a stockholder' (C74:162). One of Castaneda's UCLA partisans told Myerhoff and Furst Ramón was not a true shaman like don Juan, because he knew how to get on in the cities.

Collapse "One wonders . . . what makes . . . linguistic relativity so fascinating. . . . Perhaps it is the suggestion that all one's life one has been tricked, all unaware, by the structure of language into a certain way of perceiving reality, with the implication that awareness of this trickery will enable one to see the world with fresh insight" (Carroll 1956:27). "What we call 'the world' is a conceptual structure of space and time in which events occur" (Langer 1962:148). " 'Nature' is far more a language-made affair than people generally realize—made not only for sense, but for understanding, and prone to collapse into chaos if ideation fails" (Langer 1962:150; quoted by Pearce 1971:50, 159/1973: 51, 168). ● 'The internal dialogue is what grounds us. The world is such and such or so and so, only because we talk to ourselves about its being such and such or so and so' (C74:22). 'Whenever the dialogue stops, the world collapses' (C74:40; see also C72:14, 133, 168, 299). See: Gloss.

Completeness "If he lacks these qualities he will never 'complete himself'. . . . he must 'see' with an inner eye. . . . 'Completing oneself' is really progressive minimization of matter and maximization of spirit. . . . what the Huichol call 'balance' " (Furst 1972:152; lecture UCLA spring 1970). ● 'I'm talking about the fact that you're not complete'(C71:13). 'From the moment we become all *tonal* . . . that old feeling of incompleteness . . . tells us constantly that there is another part to give us completeness' (C74:128). 'Once a sorcerer regains his completeness he's balanced' (C77:136). 'There are plenty of good sorcerers who *see* and are incomplete. To be complete is only for us Toltecs' (C77:234; see also C74:174, 284; C77:55, 95, 118, 130-135).

Confidence "It was not until we had worked with him for over a year that he [Ramón] agreed to tell us stories about *kiéri* [Datura person]" (Furst & Myerhoff 1966:7). • "I had known don Juan for a whole year before he took me into his confidence" (C68:2).

Conversations *Conversations with Ogotemmêli* "was to have been followed by . . . further conversations" (Griaule 1965/1970:220). Castaneda's 1971 book was subtitled *Further Conversations*.

Córdova-Rios See: Beast, Whistle.

Coyote 'My husband was a Coyote-Meeter. . . . he saw a dead coyote on the sand. . . . That coyote rose up and said: "Do you want to see something?" "Yes." My husband died right there and the coyote carried him away. . . . Next morning my husband awoke and found himself lying by that dead coyote. . . . The coyotes had killed him and taught him while he was dead' (Underhill 1936:47-48; reviewed by Castaneda fall 1962). • 'He kills the man on the spot, and while he is dead he teaches him' (C68:138). "The coyote said, 'Que bueno!' and then I realized that it was a bilingual coyote. . . . When I again became aware of myself I was lying on the rocks" (C72:297-298).

Crack-a "Candidate shamans. . . . must go up to the sky through a passage that opens but for an instant" (Eliade 1964:485). • 'It opens and closes like a door in the wind. . . . It is a plane above the ground' (C68:137-138).

Crack-b After vomiting twice, Wasson saw "dark gates reaching upward beyond sight [which] were about to part, and we were to find ourselves in the presence of the Ultimate. . . . the gates were to part and admit us. . . . into the presence of the ineffable, whence . . . we might not have returned, for we had sensed that a willing extinction in the divine radiance had been awaiting us" (Wasson & Wasson 1957:293, 295; CJ: 145). • 'That moment is announced by prolonged shaking of limbs and violent vomiting. . . . the crack between the worlds appears right in front of his eyes, like a monumental door, a crack that goes up and down. When the crack opens the man has to slide through it' (C68:138). 'He has to intend and will his return, or the [mushroom] smoke will not let him come back' (C68:56). 'You must decide whether or not to return'

(C74:276). See: Door, Twilight.

Cubic Centimeter See: Don Q.

Curing "Medicinally jimsonweed was used to cure sores. . . . Either the leaves or the roots were used" (Hill 1938:20). ● "The devil's weed has four heads. . . . The stem and the leaves are the head that cures maladies' (C68:35). 'They use the leaves and flowers for other matters; they even say it cures their boils' (C68:44).

Danger "Now, he admonished us, we must all leave as quickly as possible. . . . for 'It is very dangerous to remain here.' We were puzzled but fell into our places at the end of the line and found ourselves barely able to keep up, for the group was nearly running. . . . we literally raced out, as though pursued and in danger" (Myerhoff 1968:172; 1974:157-158, 245-246). ● " 'Let's get out of here,' he said and began running. . . . I suggested that we should stay. . . . He retorted in a very dramatic tone that to stay there would be suicidal. . . . He reassured me that he would try to go as slowly as possible. . . . but no matter how slowly he moved I could not keep up with him" (C72:208-209).

David-Neel See: Ally, Gait, Self.

Death "So too at death the world does not alter, but comes to an end. Death is not an event in life: we do not live to experience death" (Wittgenstein, *Tractatus*, 6431, 64311). ● 'I don't understand why those people talk about death as if death were like life. . . . I don't think death is like anything. . . . death is nothing. Nothing! It is here yet it isn't here at all. . . . I cannot tell you what death is like. . . . it dissolves our lives into nothing. . . . Death was nothing all the time. Nothing!' (C71:235-239). See: Eternity, Harner-e, Tibetan Book.

Deer-a "The deer is the sacred and magical animal of the Huichols" (Myerhoff 1968:238; 1974:199). ● 'They have no routines. . . . That's what makes them magical' (C72:101).

Deer-b 'When the deer came out, I raised my gun. . . . It stopped and began to look at me. It stared so long that I got tired of waiting and shot and killed it. . . . Two nights later I dreamed that the deer was singing. . . . It made a kind of humming sound. I listened very carefully but could not understand what it was saying. The deer was giving me the power to become a doctor, but I refused, for I did not wish to become a doctor' (Steward 1934:430; reviewed by Castaneda fall 1962). ● 'It is very easy to figure out what an average man would do in a situation like that. . . . If he is armed he would get his weapon ready. . . . I quickly stood on my head and began to wail softly. . . . The deer looked at me and I told him I would not harm him. And the deer. . . . said as clearly as I am speaking now, "Don't be sad."' "Don Juan stared into my eyes. He had a glint of sheer mischievousness" (C72:102-103).

Description "We have tacitly accepted the essentially arbitrary modes of interpretation that social tradition is constantly suggesting to us from the very moment of our birth" (Sapir in Mandelbaum 1949:546). • "He said that. . . . the world we all know, is only a description. . . . a description that had been pounded into me from the moment I was born" (C72:8-9). 'People tell us from the time we are born that the world is such and such and so and so' (C72:299). 'A description, which is given to us from the moment of our birth' (C74:247).

Divining "The Navajo . . . used jimsonweed. . . . in locating thieves and lost or stolen property. . . . In the visionary type the man saw the location of the property or the identity of the thief was revealed. . . . Those possessing acute auditory sensibilities were directed by voices to the hiding place" (Hill 1938:19-20). • "Some time earlier a large number of books had been stolen from a reading room. . . . I rubbed the lizards against my temples, asking them who the thief was" (C68:79). "As I looked further into the new vision I saw a young man coming out of a room carrying a large knapsack in his shoulders" (C68:83). "Then I heard a 'voice' in my ear describing the scene. . . . I 'heard-saw' the entire sequence of the young man's actions" (C68:115).

Doing "Ethnomethodology sees itself for the first time explicitly 'doing' sociology" (McKinney & Tiryakian 1970:18). " 'Doing' designates the work" or activity of playing chess or handling data (Garfinkel & Sacks 1970:352); "What kind of 'machinery' makes up the practices of doing [conversation]?" (355); "A 'machinery' for doing [rational activities]" (358). • 'Everything we do is a matter of *doing*. . . . the *doing* of the world. . . . the *doing* in this room. . . . the doing of *rooms*' (C72:251-252). See: Mechanics.

Don Genaro In the story, Genaro was a pseudonym (C71:115), but a good name for the benefactor who would open the bubble-door to the other world, since Genaro means January, and January is door-keeper to the year. Genaro, brother of Cayetano, attended Wasson's mushroom eating (Wasson & Wasson 1957;CJ:45), and Castaneda seems preoccupied by the name, since two superfluous Genaros appear in the first two books (CJ:53n, three Genaros) and several apprentices are called "the Genaros" in *Second Ring*. Adapting a portion of *Ring* for prepublication, Castaneda (1978b) finally furnished the family name "Flores" for Genaro, apparently to balance don Juan's "Matus" in the same sentence. Accepting this late bit of narrative embroidery, anthropologist Roy

Wagner (1978:267) said he would take *Second Ring* at face value because verification was "a deadly boring game."

Don Juan Matus In the story, Juan Matus was a pseudonym (C71:115; compare DJP: Chapter 40, Question 5). Luis Matus was a Yaqui military hero (CJ:96). The original version of the Spanish Don Juan myth was Tirso de Molina's play, *El Burlador de Sevilla*, or *The Trickster of Seville* (D. G. Winter, *The Don Juan Legend, by Otto Rank*, Princeton 1975). See also: CJ:154n more experienced men. RdeM links don Juan and John of the Cross (CJ:146-152). See: Juan de la Cruz.

Don Q José López-Portillo y Pacheco, who would become President of Mexico in 1976, wrote the last line of his philosophical satire, *"Don Q,"* at 2:55 PM 31 October 1967 (López 1969:181), while the University of California Press was considering publishing *The Teachings of Don Juan*, a simultaneity that rules out literary influence of *"Don Q"* on *Teachings*, though not, of course, on later don Juan books. When *Don Q* was published in English (1976), the original copyright date was shown as 1965 (1976:iv), which led Stephen Reno to the false conclusion that Castaneda might have conceived don Juan while reading *"Don Q"*; in fact, Castaneda was showing his manuscript around in 1962 (Preuss 1978:55). *"Don Q"* (1969) carries a subtitle (translated) *Conversations about the Iety* [that is, Ego-ness] *and Other Transcendentalities* and pits a word-bound university lawyer, Pepe Seco (Joe Dry or Juiceless Joe), against a Mexican Indian philosopher, Don Q, in a series of quasi-Socratic exchanges, a "portrayal of the synapse between modernity and antiquity, between rigid intellectualism and aboriginal wisdom"—says Reno (1978:590), but to me, Don Q, like don Juan, is far from aboriginal. López and Castaneda both confront a stereotyped academic rationalist with a Europeanized pseudo-primitive. *Booklist* (1 Jan 1977, 73:651) called *Don Q* "a mordant exercise reminiscent of . . . don Juan's rhetorical obfuscation. A long dialectic loaded with diversions, pauses, and the narrator's frustration touches on a philosophical synthesis of the profound and the inane." *Choice* (May 1977, 14:382) said: "The reader becomes confused by the many paradoxes offered by Don Q. At times even Don Q is incapable of understanding his own utterances." Castaneda's readers also suffer a confusion of paradoxes, but I believe don Juan's paradoxes are perspicuous when one possesses the ethnomethodological, phenomenological, and ethnological lenses through which to view them, whereas I suspect most of Don Q's paradoxes are not meant to make sense; indeed, *Don Q* reads like an obsessive parody of *Tales of Power*. I have found one passage in *Ixtlan* that suggests literary influence from

"*Don Q.*" In López-Portillo's text we find: "*Sabía que, si le mantenía la mirada, nos íbamos a pelear y yo no quería llegar a ese extremo*" (1969:101)/"I knew that, if I met his eyes, we were going to fight and I didn't want to go to that extreme" (1976:82); '*Mi querido licenciado, lo que ocurre, es que usted padece de una cuasi solemnidad escolástica en su funesta y agresiva tendencia a los distingos y subdistingos que, no pudiendo expresar en grandes soritis, descompone usted en paréntesis porque, y esto es lo peor que le puede pasar a un cuasi escolástico, está usted en muy precaria condición: sin sistema y sin trascendencia, por lo que se tiene usted que conformar con los subproductos de mi conversación. O en otras palabras y para decírselo con el más erudito de mis desprecios: es usted un prospecto, mediocre por cierto, de glosador'* (1969:40)/'My dear bachelor, the problem is that you suffer from a quasi-solemn scholasticism in your ill-fated and aggressive tendency towards distinctions and sub-distinctions which, not being able to fully explain, you decompose into parenthesis because, and this is the worst that can happen to a quasi-scholar, you're in a very precarious condition—with neither system nor transcendence—and therefore you have to be satisfied with the subproducts of my conversation. In other words, and to tell it to you with my most erudite disdain, you are a prospective, certainly mediocre glosser' (1976:33); '*Oigame usted, Don Q, yo creo que se ha esclavizado demasiado a las palabras y que son estos instrumentos imperfectos, la fuente de sus contradicciones'* (1969:50)/'Listen, Don Q, I believe you are too enslaved by words. They are imperfect instruments, the fountain of your contradictions' (1976:41). By which three passages Castaneda may have been inspired to write the following: "Don Juan's statements put me in a belligerent mood. I could not make sense of what he was saying. I told him it was gibberish, and he mocked me and said that I did not even have an impeccable spirit in what I liked to do most, talking. He actually made fun of my verbal command and found it faulty and inadequate" (C72:230). Don Q draws a cabalistic figure 8 lying on its side to signify the "universal saturation of infinites" (1969:21; 1976:16)—which may have prompted don Juan's drawing of the eight points on the fibres of a luminous being (C74:98, 270). Don Q discusses "the specific gravity of imperfection" (1976:16)/"*el peso específico de la imperfección*" (1969:22); since specific gravity is relative density, and density is measured in grams per cubic centimeter, one sees an easy transition to don Juan's "cubic centimeter of chance" (C72:278). Don Q and don Juan both talk a lot about responsibility and will.

Door "But the man who comes back through the Door in the Wall will never be quite the same as the man who went out" (Huxley 1954/1963:79). ● 'After you return, you will not be the same man' (C68:138). 'But . . . once the door opens there is no way to close it again' (C74:227-228). 'Once the seal is broken, the warrior is never the same' (C74:248). See: Crack, Twilight.

Double-a "There is distinctly a *double* recollection of the two bodies. . . . it leads . . . to the conception of *a dream body*" (van Eeden 1969:151). ● 'The double begins in *dreaming*' (C74:67).

Double-b "The double who catches sight of himself must die within a year" (Otto Rank, *The Double*,U. North Carolina 1971:50; CJ:127n double; Castaneda may have heard about Rank from Anaïs Nin). ● 'The sorcerer that finds himself face to face with himself is a dead sorcerer' (C74:52).

Douglas See: Juan de la Cruz.

Dreaming-a "In the West the thinking we do while asleep usually remains on a muddled, childish, or psychotic level" (Stewart 1969:167). "*Ordinary dreaming*, is the usual well-known type to which the large majority of dreams conform. . . . they are absurd and confused" (van Eeden 1969:148). ● 'You've always had weird dreams. . . . Don't concern yourself. . . . Like the dreams of any ordinary dreamer, they don't have power' (C72:118).

Dreaming-b "Every person should be the supreme ruler and master of his own dream or spiritual universe" (Stewart 1969:162). ● 'Now it's time for you to become accessible to power, and you are going to begin by tackling *dreaming*' (C72:118).

Dreaming-c "In these lucid dreams . . . the sleeper remembers day-life and his own condition, reaches a state of perfect awareness, and is able to direct his attention, and to attempt different acts of free volition" (van Eeden 1969:150). "Every dream force . . . can and must be outfaced, subdued, and forced to make a socially meaningful contribution" (Stewart 1969:165). ● '*Dreaming* is real for a warrior because in it he can act deliberately, he can choose and reject, he can select from a variety of items those which lead to power, and then he can manipulate them and use them' (C72:119-120).

Dreaming-d 'When you have a falling dream . . . you will feel that you are traveling to the source of the power which has caused you to fall' (Stewart 1969:162); "a power which he can control through . . . mental set. . . ." (164); "the dream which starts out with the fear of falling changes into the joy of flying. . . . one should arrive somewhere when he flies" (163). • 'The next step in *setting up dreaming* is to learn to travel. . . . you must will yourself to go to the specific locale' (C72:142-143).

Dreaming-e "I made the reflection, during sleep, that my fancy would never be able to invent or to make an image as intricate as the perspective movement of little twigs seen in floating by" (van Eeden 1969:150). • *'Dreaming* is real when. . . . there is no difference between what you do when you sleep and what you do when you are not sleeping' (C72:127).

Dreaming-f "I prepared myself for careful observation, hoping to prolong and to intensify the lucidity" (van Eeden 1969:151). • 'The trick in learning to *set up dreaming* is obviously not just to look at things but to sustain the sight of them' (C72:127).

Dreaming-g "I made the following experiment. I drew with my finger, moistened with saliva, a wet cross on the palm of my left hand. . . . Then I *dreamt* that I woke up and felt the wet cross on my left hand by applying the palm to my cheek" (van Eeden 1969:151). • 'Tonight in your dreams you must look at your hands' (C72:126).

Dreaming-h See: Man of Knowledge.

Drugs "Narcotics are only a vulgar substitute for 'pure' trance. . . . to provide an *imitation* of a state that the shaman is no longer capable of attaining otherwise" (Eliade 1964:401). • "I realized that the meaningful transformations and findings of sorcerers were always done in states of sober consciousness" (C74:238).

Dust "They insert gold dust into his eyes to give him keenness and strength of sight powerful enough to see the soul wherever it may have wandered" (Eliade 1964:57). • 'Knowledge comes floating like specks of gold dust. . . . knowledge is like taking a shower, or being rained on by specks of dark gold dust' (C74:36).

Ear "A lama, a brother in belief, or a close friend must read the funerary text into the dead man's ear" (Eliade 1964:438). • "Don Juan and don Genaro came to my side, squatted by me and proceeded to whisper in my ears" (C74:261; compare 183, 184, 191).

Egg "The Human Aura . . . is seen by the psychic observer as a luminous cloud. . . . certain colors being predominant in each person. . . . It is oval or egg-shaped. . . . the 'Auric Egg'. . . . to the psychic vision it appears to be 'streaked' by numerous fine lines extending like stiff bristles from the body outward. . . . the several hairs standing out in all directions" (Atkinson 1909:62, 63, 58). • "The human quality was shown as an egglike cluster of luminous fibers" (C74:39). "What I called coloration was not a hue but a glow of different intensities" (C74:41). 'The little smoke will help you to *see* men as fibers of light. . . . Very fine threads that circulate from the head to the navel. Thus a man looks like an egg of circulating fibers. And his arms and legs are like luminous bristles, bursting out in all directions' (C71:33). Correspondence noted by Rueger (1973:76); compare CJ:94-95. See DJP: Chapter 2.

Eight points See: Don Q.

Eliade See: Burial, Crack, Drugs, Dust, Ear, Enemies-c, Human, Twilight.

Ending "I began to worry. Would this never end? I certainly didn't wish to remain here forever" (Swain 1963:225). ● "I began to lose patience; I wanted to stop. 'How can I end this?' I thought" (C68:115-116).

Enemies-a 'I was approached by a man . . . who wanted to transfer his power to me. I told him, "No, I am afraid of it" ' (Opler 1941:211). ● 'And thus he has stumbled on the first of his natural enemies: Fear!' (C68:57).

Enemies-b "Anything that interferes with the clarity of purpose of the shaman gravely weakens the rite" (Opler 1941:209). ● 'That clarity of mind, which is so hard to obtain, dispels fear, but also blinds. It forces the man never to doubt himself' (C68:58).

Enemies-c "The 'powers' [and] the magical sense of boundless capability . . . . they produce . . . can make the yogin forget his true aim" (Eliade 1964:416-417). ● 'He can do . . . whatever he pleases. . . .' 'But what if he is temporarily blinded by power, and then refuses it?' 'That means he is still trying to become a man of knowledge' (C68:59).

Enemies-d "Power is not always neutral, not always a force ready to act at the bidding of the shaman" (Opler 1941:255). ● 'The power he has seemingly conquered is in reality never his' (C68:60).

Enemies-e "Power which has seemed to be beneficent may finally demand that the shaman sacrifice a life to it" (Opler 1941:255). ● 'The man. . . . ends in making rules, because he is a master. . . . His enemy will have turned him into a cruel, capricious man' (C68:59).

Enemies-f "The older you get, the weaker you become with your ceremony. Your mind is weak. Your praying is mixed up. . . . Your voice is feeble. . . . You can't have a good vigorous talk with your power any more" (Opler 1941:209). ● 'His enemy will cut him down into a feeble old creature. His desire to retreat will overrule all his clarity, his power, and his knowledge' (C68:60).

Equal "All propositions are of equal value" (Wittgenstein, *Tractatus*, 6.4). ● 'All things are equal and by being equal they are unimportant' (C71:104). 'There was no sadness, no feeling. His death was equal to everything else' (C71:113).

Erasing "He has given up his past, and when after many years he emerges from his cubicle, nothing of his former personality has remained and nobody knows who he was" (Govinda 1971:84). • 'Nobody knows my personal history. Nobody knows who I am or what I do. Not even I' (C72:32).

Eternity "If we take eternity to mean not infinite temporal duration but timelessness, then eternal life belongs to those who live in the present. Our life has no end in just the way in which our visual field has no limits" (Wittgenstein, *Tractatus*, 6.4311). • 'Do you know that at this very moment you are surrounded by eternity? . . . Do you know that you can extend yourself forever in any of the directions I have pointed to?. . . Do you know that one moment can be eternity?' (C74:17). 'The future is only a way of talking. For a sorcerer there is only the here and now' (C74:206). See: Death.

Explaining "The whole modern conception of the world is founded on the illusion that the so-called laws of nature are the explanations of natural phenomena. Thus people today stop at the laws of nature, treating them as something inviolable, just as God and Fate were treated in past ages. And in fact both are right and both wrong: though the view of the ancients is clearer in so far as they have a clear and acknowledged terminus, while the modern system tries to make it look as if *everything* were explained" (Wittgenstein, *Tractatus*, 6.371-6.372). • 'You insist on explaining everything as if the whole world were composed of things that can be explained. . . . Has it ever occurred to you that only a few things in this world can be explained your way? . . . A phony sorcerer tries to explain everything in the world with explanations he is not sure about, and so everything is witchcraft. But then you're no better. You also want to explain everything your way but you're not sure of your explanations either' (C71:155; see also C74:270).

Face "That night I went to bed and had a dream. I saw a man coming toward me but I don't know who he was; maybe he was God, but he looked a lot like [a certain village elder]. He came up close to me and spoke in my ear" (Pozas 1962:96; reviewed by Castaneda fall 1962). • "I had seen the same man. This time, however, he was almost touching me. I saw his face. There was an air of familiarity about it. I almost knew who he was" (C71:229).

Fighting "Against the sorcerer the Huichol shaman also assumes a special—and highly secret—defensive position . . . whose details my informant [Ramón Medina—RdeM] would not reveal" (Furst 1965:68). • "He then gave me precise instructions about a 'fighting form,' a specific bodily position. . . . to be used if I was attacked" (C68:132). See: Warrior.

Flatulence "An instance of the latitude permitted in such assertions [that mountains, earth, and wind give power by talking to shamans] is the case of a man who claimed to receive special knowledge from his own anal flatulence" (Opler 1941:206). ● " 'Witness, please squeeze your spirit catcher,' don Genaro said to Nestor. I heard the loud, most ludicrous sound. . . . noticed a peculiar smell and realized then that Nestor had farted. . . . not as a joke but because he did not have his spirit catcher with him" (C74:282).

Fog After helping Castaneda to clarify the Structural Analysis (C68:ix), Lawrence Watson began to teach anthropology at San Diego State University, where he was soon joined by Philip Staniford, who has stated (Letter 11 April 1978; see also Staniford 1977b:53): "Larry Watson related a dream of green fog to Carlos, and it popped up in *A Separate Reality* [C71:199], much to Watson's surprise."

Folly "Ethnomethodological studies . . . describe members' accounts . . . while abstaining from all judgments of their adequacy, value, importance, necessity, practicality, success, or consequentiality. We refer to this procedural policy as 'ethnomethodological indifference' " (Garfinkel & Sacks 1970:345). ● 'We must know first that our acts are useless and yet we must proceed as if we didn't know it. That's a sorcerer's controlled folly' (C71:97). 'Everything I do in regard to myself and my fellow men is folly, because nothing matters' (C71:101). 'Everything is equal and therefore unimportant' (C74:104). 'Whether his acts were good or bad, or worked or didn't is in no way part of his concern' (C71:107). 'The next thing one needs to be a warrior is detachment. The idea of imminent death . . . becomes an indifference' (C71:183). See: Equal.

Furst See: Barking, Bird, Completeness, Confidence, Fighting, Gourd, Ixtlan, Left, Moderation, Plants, Protected, Shields, Soul, Spirit-Catcher, Tickling, Warrior, Waterfall, Wind-Women.

Gait For text, see Chapter 6: Gait (David-Neel 1932:201; C72:204); sunset (1932:213; C72:205); feet (Govinda 1971:80, see also 78-83; C72:207); danger (1971:81; C72:207). These correspondences were called to my attention by Eugene H. Whitehead; they were noted by Matthiessen (1978:151, 328).

Garfinkel See: Accounting, Doing, Folly, Gloss, Mechanics.

Gesture "No matter how eager a man is to acquire a ceremony, the first gesture is always attributed to the power, for power . . . constantly seeks human beings through whom 'to work' " (Opler 1941:202). ● 'Why do you tell me all this, don Juan?' 'You were brought to me. And I have had a gesture with you' (C72:66). (See also: C72:80, 183, 188).

Gloss See the first and fourth paragraphs of this Alleglossary. *Gloss* in ethnomethodology (Garfinkel & Sacks 1970:342-344). Castaneda turned Sapir's "mode of [social] apprehension" (Mandelbaum 1949:547) into a mode of physical perception: "The sorcerer must work through the perceptual *glosses* of the culture. . . . Don Juan had to use *three* psychotropic plants to disrupt my glosses" (Wallace 1972:139); "A gloss is a total system of perception and language. For instance, this room is a gloss. We have lumped together a series of isolated perceptions—floor, ceiling, window, lights, rug, etc.—to make a single totality. But we had to be taught to put the world together this way. . . . We are subject to the syntax of language and the mode of perception it contains" (Keen 1972:95/1976:78-79); in passing, Castaneda attributed his conception of glossing to Talcott Parsons, who did not treat the topic. See: Agreement, Collapse.

Gnat "The Sphinx," a tale by Edgar Allan Poe (1938), describes a gigantic monster of hideous conformation, which turns out to be a tiny moth very close to the terrified observer's eye. A reading of "The Sphinx" followed by a reading of Carlos's encounters with the giant gnat (C71:143-162) leaves a strong impression that either Poe read Castaneda or Castaneda read Poe. I am grateful to Scott Graham for finding the source, which I had remembered from 1939 but vainly sought in the works of Ambrose Bierce.

Goldschmidt See: Reality.

Gorda Ultima (Anaya 1972), a somewhat sinister old *curandera* suspected of being a witch, taught magic to a boy who grew up to be the first-person narrator of his story. Her knowledge had come from a great healer called "the flying man." When her companion owl (or *tonal*) was killed, she died. Animals sniffed around the house at night to spoil her cures; a pounding was heard on the roof. Though her name was Ultima, she was called "la Grande," the Great One, a title of respect. • Elena (C77), a beautiful young witch, taught magic to the youthful Carlos, the first-person narrator of his story. Her knowledge had come from a great sorcerer who knew how to fly. She told Carlos that curing makes one weak (C77:218) and that sorcerers do not die (C77:281). Something outside the house growled and leaned against the door (C77:163); a tapping was heard on the roof (C77:242). Though her name was Elena, she was called "la Gorda," Fatso, a formerly disrespectful title acquired when she had weighed 220 pounds (C77:54, 121).

Gouldner See: Stop.

Gourd "The deer scrotum is also used, to cover the tobacco gourd carried by the older or more experienced peyoteros. . . . The use of . . . the sacred tobacco . . . seems to be the exclusive prerogative of men. . . . The women do not hunt or use items made of any part of the deer" (Myerhoff 1968:244; 1974:204). "Ramón did not have a tobacco gourd but kept his supply in a small woven neck bag, exactly like those worn around the waist . . . but much smaller" (Myerhoff 1968:147; 1974:126; see also Furst 1972:176-177). • Doña Soledad tells Carlos don Juan tried to use his *guaje*, or gourd, to introduce her to Mescalito—who 'was' his gourd—but Mescalito refused her because she was an empty woman (C77:41-42); she says the gourd is tied to don Juan's belt and contains his allies, which are 'funneled through' it (C77:55); this gourd 'acts on' women, harrassing them until they submit to it (C77:55). From la Gorda Carlos learns that to control supernatural forces "we needed a special container, a gourd of some sort, like those I [Carlos] had seen dangling from don Juan's and don Genaro's belts" (C77:144). La Gorda says sorcerers keep their allies in their gourds. Don Juan's gourd was a tiny, perfect one with a neck, the size of a thumb. She had never seen it, because 'it's like a little bundle that one can distinguish hanging from their belts. But if you deliberately look at it you will see nothing' (C77:149-150); what Freudians will make of all this, I shudder to think. In Mexican slang, *guaje* means a stupid person, a gourd-head; perhaps Mescalito—who 'was' don Juan's gourd—is now a stupid peyotero, left far behind by Castaneda's ever more intricate occultism.

Govinda See: Erasing, Gait.

Griaule See: Conversations.

Guardian "Power tests the faith of the novice and determines whether he is the kind of an individual through whom it should work. Frightful animals guard the portals through which the candidate is conducted" (Opler 1941:204). • " 'We'll soon know where you stand,' he said cryptically" (C71:139). "At a given moment I would be able to see the guardian of the other world. . . . a gigantic, monstrous animal" (C71:143-144).

Gurdjieff See: Stalking-b.

Harner-a "He must not tell anyone that he has acquired such a [protecting] soul, or it will desert him" (1962:261). • 'The protector has accepted you [but] neither his name nor his dealings with you should ever be mentioned to a living being' (C68:109-110).

Harner-b "When . . . the shaman throws [the magical dart], it will penetrate . . . the body of the victim, causing death within a few days to several weeks" (1963:106). ● 'Objects . . . permeated with power. . . . made to kill, to be hurled. . . . can kill a man by entering into his body. . . . he will die within three months (C68:7-8).

Harner-c The shaman's dart, held in his mouth, absorbs the power of the magic dart he sucks out of the patient's body; failing that, "it would pass down into the shaman's stomach and kill him" (1963:110-111). ● 'A brujo may succeed in sucking the kernel out, but unless he is powerful enough to repel it, it will get inside him and will kill him instead' (C68:8).

Harner-d The soul of an old Jívaro man "enters the body of the dreamer, where it is lodged in the chest" (1962:261). ● "He said I must struggle not to fall asleep. . . . 'Get inside my chest,' I heard him say. I felt I was engulfing him" (C68:100).

Harner-e "The true soul then changes into water vapor. . . . and persists eternally in the form of mist" (1962:267). ● 'I would *see* his personal life disintegrating, expanding uncontrollably beyond its limits, like a fog of crystals' (C71:113).

Harner-f "The shaman . . . sends [magical birds] to the house of the victim. . . . frightening him. . . . caus[ing] him to become feverish and insane, with death resulting shortly thereafter" (1963:107). ● "The 'blackbird' had stood in front of him. . . . Don Juan's tone was . . . almost pathetic. . . . he reaffirmed . . . that the next time she came near him was going to be his last day on earth" (C71:246).

Harner-g "The shaman . . . sneaks into the forest to hunt and kill the bird" (1963:113). ● "I was to hide in front of his house and wait until the blackbird landed on the roof and then . . . let go with both barrels" (C71:247).

Harner-h "The victim is given no specific indication that someone is bewitching him" (1963:106). ● "Don Juan, after listening attentively to all the details, concluded that I was suffering from a loss of soul" (C68:131).

Harner-i "Shamans. . . . specializing in bewitching try to steal their intended victim's arutam soul before attempting to kill him through witchcraft" (1962:263). ● "He said that . . . now I was truly bewitched. . . . he had no definite idea as to who had trapped my soul, but whoever it was intended without doubt to kill me" (C68:132).

Harner-j "The curing shaman 'sees' the shaman who bewitched his patient" (1963:114). ● "He was going away to see who had taken my soul" (C68:132). See: Soul.

Harner-k "The normal waking life, for the Jívaro, is simply 'a lie,' or illusion" (1968:28). ● *'Doings* are lies, unreal' (C72:239).

Harner-l "Special quartz crystal [darts] . . . are particularly deadly" (1972:154-155). ● "Quartz crystals [whose] power went beyond our understanding. . . . hurled to kill . . . [they] penetrated . . . then returned to their owner's hand" (C72:244-245). Eliade (1964:47, 50, 52n, 125, 339, 350) mentions quartz crystals for curing but not as weapons.

Harner-m "When a child is disrespectful to his father, [Datura] will put him into a trance state to see the supernatural world [where] he will discover [that his father's reality claims] are true and he will be less disrespectful" (1972:90; see also 134). ● 'If your friend were a warrior he would help his [misbehaving] child to *stop the world*. . . . to change his idea of the world' (C72:10-11).

Harner-n "The father brings [his young son] up to the corpse . . . and has him fire into it, with the father helping him hold the gun" (1972:113). ● 'He must take his son there and show the dead child to him. . . . [and] let him touch the corpse' (C72:12).

Harner-o In relation to items Harner-l to Harner-n, Castaneda would have needed access to Harner's ideas some months before Harner's 1972 book was published, but the two men had been friends since 1963 (Stein 1975).

Harner-p "I am thoroughly conversant with Castaneda's publications; I have known him for a decade and a half; and I am not familiar with any evidence that he has borrowed material from my works" (Harner 1978).

Heaven The mushrooms, it was often said, "would take you there where God is" (Wasson & Wasson 1957:294). ● 'Can you tell me where Mescalito takes you?. . . is it heaven . . . where God is?' 'You are being stupid now. I don't know where God is' (C68:62).

Hill See: Curing, Divining.

Human "The shaman proves that he is . . . no longer a human being" (Eliade 1964:486). ● 'After you become a sorcerer, you're no longer human' (Cravens 1973a:97). 'Don Juan. . . . and don Genaro. . . . have lost their humanness' (Wallace 1972:141).

Husserl See: Bauman, Thing.

Huxley See: Door, Seeing.

Ixtlan Castaneda labels don Genaro "a Mazatec Indian" (C71:30; C74:187, 245), and don Genaro tells other Indians he takes to be Mazatecs that he is 'going home to Ixtlan' (C72:307). Don Juan says: 'Genaro left his passion in Ixtlan: his home, his people, all the things he cared for' (C72:314). It is, therefore, definitely established that don Genaro is a Mazatec Indian who once made his home among his people in a place called Ixtlán. There is, however, *no* Mazatec Ixtlán (though there is a Mazatec Ixcatlán); Ixtlán de Juárez, just beyond the Valle Nacional, is inhabited by Zapotecs; further afield lie the un-Mazatec Ixtlán del Río and Ixtlán de los Hervores (Weitlaner & Hoppe 1969:330, 517, 524). Castaneda's choice of the wrong home town for Genaro was, nevertheless, not a careless mistake but a defiant quirk; Wasson (letter 4 Oct 1968) had already warned him that Mazatecs did not live in the Valle Nacional; Castaneda ignored the warning. Why? Furst's UCLA dissertation (1966:34, passim) refers over and over to "Ixtlán" pottery, the classic Nayarit ceramic figurines associated with Ixtlán del Río. This repetition of the name by a fellow student and putative intellectual rival, together with the echo of *Aztlán*, mythical home of the Aztecs (see DJP: Chapter 32), could have made "Ixtlan" irresistible to Castaneda.

Juan de la Cruz In June 1973 (see notes for DJP: Chapter 3), Mary Douglas remarked a resemblance between don Juan and John of the Cross; 16 months later, a quotation from John of the Cross appeared as frontispiece for *Tales of Power* (C74:7; discussed in CJ:146-152).

Jump "To describe what one has just done . . . is to comment upon a step. . . . But the operation which is the commenting is not, and cannot be, the step on which that commentary is being made. . . . Self-commentary [is] logically condemned to eternal penultimacy. . . . He never succeeds in jumping onto the shadow of his own head, yet he is never more than one jump behind" (Gilbert Ryle, *The Concept of Mind*, Barnes & Noble 1949:195-196). • 'The world doesn't yield to us directly, the description of the world stands in between. . . . we are always one step removed. . . . We're always one jump behind' (C74:53-54). See: Recollection.

Kelley See: Moisés.

Klüver See: Abyss, Animal, Mushroom.

Kobler See: Catalina, Dam, Tibetan, Treeness.

Krishnamurti See: Attention, Mark.

Ladder "My propositions serve as elucidations in the following way: anyone who understands me eventually recognizes them as nonsensical, when he has used them—as steps—to climb up beyond them. (He must, so to speak, throw away the ladder after he has climbed up it.) He must transcend these propositions, and then he will see the world aright" (Wittgenstein, *Tractatus*, 6.54). • 'We won't discuss the dilemmas of your *reason*. . . . They are, properly speaking, only steps of an endless ladder' (C74:107). 'One has willingly used the *tonal* to make sense out of one's actions in the *nagual*. . . . only there [in the *tonal*] are they like stairways where one can count the steps' (C74:265).

Lamb See: Córdova-Rios.

Langer See: Collapse.

Leary See: Kobler.

Left-a "The unseen enemy . . . always on the left. . . . the right is usually the side of life, the left of death" (Furst 1965:45, 60; 1966:355, 388). • 'Death is. . . . always to our left' (C72:54). See: Warrior.

Left-b "Note uneven position of eyes (left lower than right), a common characteristic of Colima figurines" (Furst 1965:36). • 'Usually the left eye of a warrior has a strange appearance; sometimes it becomes permanently crossed, or it becomes smaller than the other, or larger, or different in some way' (C74:231).

Leightons See: Arm-Sweeping, Bill, Carving, Orphan.

C. S. Lewis See: Spin.

Lines of the World See a drawing by M. C. Escher, Catalogue 1968 #30, "Rossano, Calabria, 1931." • "I saw the 'lines of the world'" (C72:298). Castaneda draws; Mehan & Wood (1975: frontispiece) reproduced Escher's drawing of reciprocally drawing hands, to illustrate ethnomethodological reflexivity.

Lizard "A sorcerer who wished to bring sickness or death to an enemy might. . . . take a toad, sew up its eyes and mouth with thorns, tie its feet, bury it in a place where the enemy would be likely to sit down. The suffering of the toad was supposed to pass into the enemy" (Rowe 1946:314). • "The lizard's mouth was sewed up with rude stitches. . . . its eyelids were sewed together" (C68:78). 'Sew up her mouth. Use the fibers of agave and one of the thorns of a choya to do the sewing. Draw the stitches tight' (C68:80; see also C68:78-86, 113-117; CJ:41-43; DJP: last note for Chapter 5).

López-Portillo See: Don Q.

Luminous-a "His eyes glowed with a yellow light" (Swain 1963:241). • "His eyes were two enormous mirrors, like a tiger's eyes" (C74:256).

Luminous-b "Her eyes shown with a glow that seemed to light up her head" (Swain 1963:224). • "The strange, luminous object in front of me had to be don Juan's face. . . . then it lost its glow and became solid and fleshy" (C71:192). See: Egg.

Man of Knowledge R. C. White (1957) of UCLA told how "men of knowledge-power" achieve mastery by "picking up" knowledge, an invisible, dangerous, but desirable power which exists everywhere in many forms and must always be used "in exact accord with its particular nature." One may acquire it through "instruction, experience, or 'dreaming.' " Some are born with it; others accept it reluctantly. Some tap the "world 'pool' of knowledge" to get extraordinary powers; though at first fearful, they must grow fearless to succeed. The master who initiates young warriors is "alternately jokester and disciplinarian." See also DJP: Chapter 40.

Mark "The beauty of freedom is that you do not leave a mark. The eagle in its flight does not leave a mark" (Krishnamurti 1971:11, 2). • 'A hunter uses his world sparingly. . . . then swiftly moves away, leaving hardly a mark' (C72:95). Correspondence noted by Gorman (1978:171).

Mechanics "The machinery of professionals' gloss achievements is described . . . as members' machinery" (Garfinkel & Sacks 1970:361). • "As far as seeking his teachings, I don't think I would. I sincerely think I don't have the mechanics" (Roszak & Castaneda, summer 1968). "I had gained *membership*" (C72:14). See: Doing.

Mescalito A berry-headed, green-warted, cricket-bodied, choral-voiced, cinema-handed supernatural personage, Mescalito appears when Carlos has been eating peyote and shows him a sparkling but enigmatic future. True to Indian tradition, don Juan does not distinguish the peyote cactus from the teacher and protector who comes when one eats it. 'You really are going to teach me about peyote?' Carlos exclaims. 'I prefer to call him Mescalito,' says don Juan (C68:19). A month later (C68:21-23) one of don Juan's Indian friends hands Carlos something called both *peyote* and *mescal*, which he must chew. But peyote is not mescal, and Indians know it is not, especially men of knowledge like don Juan. In *The Peyote Cult* (1975:14-15) Weston La Barre lists two-dozen Indian names for peyote, but not *mescal*. The original mescal was the Nahuatl *mexcalli*, the agave cactus, from which pre-Columbian Indians fermented beer. Hard-drinking Spaniards distilled the Indian beer into a liquor they called *mescal* and, prizing alcohol above all other mind-benders, obtusely applied the same name to two unrelated vision-plants used by the Indians: the fairly poisonous red-bean plant, *Sophora secundiflora*, and the more benign peyote cactus. Jeremy Bigwood and Jonathan Ott (book in preparation) note that a German scientist named Heffter isolated a crystalline alkaloid from peyote and in 1896 perpetuated the Spaniards' misnomer by naming his discovery "mezcalin." Since Castaneda admitted having read *The Peyote Cult* before Carlos's apprenticeship began (Keen 1972:92/1976:77), we can be sure he knew peyote was not mescal. Why then does Castaneda's archetypal Indian wise man call peyote "dear little mescal," a name that echoes Spanish parochialism? For the same reason,

I believe, that he calls Jimson weed *la yerba del diablo* and mushrooms *honguitos* or *humito*, all Spanish names (compare CJ:172-174): if Indian names for such things had popped up in the story, don Juan's exclusively Spanish discourse would have come under question, and Castaneda might have been held responsible for an extensive Indian vocabulary he had no wish to acquire. See: Peyote.

Metaphor "During the peyote hunt the major symbols make the imaginary life the real life. . . . Wirikuta is not an imaginary place. The pilgrims need not speculate as to what it might be like [but can] watch with their own eyes as the surrounding world becomes a luminous and vivid place of magic animals and plants and flowers (Myerhoff 1974:263; 1968:306). • "I had always believed that he was talking in a metaphorical sense about a subtle division between the world that the average man perceives and the world that sorcerers perceive. . . . But la Gorda and the little sisters had turned my obscure metaphors into real possibilities. La Gorda had actually transported us half a mile with the energy of her 'dreaming' " (C77:270-271). See: Sisters.

Moderation "One of the *hikuri*-seekers had just spotted a sizable cluster and was reluctant to abandon so rich a find. Ramón admonished him: 'Our game bags are full. One must not take more than one needs.' If one did . . . Elder Brother would be offended" (Furst 1972:180; lecture UCLA spring 1970). • " 'Two are enough for us,' he said and let three of them loose. . . . I said jokingly . . . that I would have cooked all five. . . . 'But if you [had done that, he said] we might never have left this place in one piece' " (C72:83-84, also 94).

Moisés See: Signs, Time.

Mold "The attendant places the girl face downward . . . and 'molds' her . . . so that she will have a good disposition and be good" (Opler 1941:98). • 'He used to make me lie naked on a rock' (C77:154). 'We can mold anything with our hands. . . . A group of *tonals* can mold anything' (C77:141). "Don Juan told me that he was going to mold me for flying" (C74:183). (See also: C74:205.)

Monroe Robert A. Monroe offered a model for starting a psychedelic story over without drugs. Monroe's dreaming was first reported by Puharich (1962:66-92) as the case of "Bob Rame." "Rame" had his first out-of-body experience while inhaling ether (1962:70). *Journeys Out of the Body* (Monroe 1971:28) reported the same experience without the use of ether. *Ixtlan*, published a year later, restarted the don Juan story without visionary plants. Monroe's chapter "Sexuality in the Second State" offered ideas for sexuality in *Second Ring*, specifically the notion of escaping physical and emotional closeness with family women to enjoy a rarified intercourse or communion with transcendental female consorts while traveling in a separate reality during dreaming. Carlos rejects love and lust (C77:13-35, 110-111) in favor of a sexless intimacy (C77:97, 133, 145, 165, 238, 263) that carries him to the other world (C77:163-164, 302-307). (See also C77:61, 84, 87-88).

Moth "A large greyish moth. . . . The *palometa* flew on board and landed on the boat. Those that were up on deck saw it but said nothing. All was quiet. After it flew away on its own accord, I was told that it is a sign that announces death" (Orona 1968:240-241). ● 'What flew to us was a moth. . . . Knowledge is a moth' (C74:25). 'That was the moth. . . . Don't get so jumpy. . . . a warrior considers himself already dead, so there is nothing for him to lose. . . . The moths are the heralds or, better yet, the guardians of eternity' (C74:35). Angelo Orona and Castaneda were fellow students at UCLA; both acknowledged the help of Lawrence Watson. Like the legendary Carlos, Orona spoke not only English and Spanish but also Italian. In *Time's* cover story (5 March 1973:37), published while Castaneda was writing *Tales of Power* (C74), Castaneda is shown hiding the lower part of his face behind a book—Orona's dissertation.

Mushroom "A drawing of a head turned into a mushroom" (Klüver 1928:27). 'Dr. B. named different persons . . . I was to imagine. Soon, thereafter, they appeared to stand in perceived space . . . some persons . . . seemed to be in natural size before me' (Klüver 1928:53). ● "The mushroomlike object remained unchanged within my field of 'vision'. . . . 'But what did I *see*?' I asked. 'Your friend,' he retorted" (C74:39). "Don Juan urged me to continue 'calling' friends" (C74:41). "'The last person you're going to call is Genaro'. . . . Don Genaro was standing right in front of me. In person!" (C74:43).

Myerhoff See: Chair, Citizen, Confidence, Danger, Deer, Gourd, Metaphor, Propitiation, Rabbit, Rich, Spirit-Catcher, Stalking, Thing, Toltecs, Waterfall, Whistle, Wind-Women.

Mysticism See: Ally, Attention, Awareness, Beyond, Boundaries, Door, Egg, Erasing, Eternity, Gait, Juan de la Cruz, Ladder, Mark, Nagual, Pearce-h, -i, -j, Seeing, Self, Tonal, Witnessing.

Nagual "The nagual is a special transformation of a man into an animal, and the term helps define a witch" (Adams & Rubel 1973:336; see also Foster 1944). ● " 'Nagual' . . . was the name given to the animal into which sorcerers could allegedly transform themselves, or to the sorcerer that elicited such a transformation" (C74:121). Don Juan calls this anthropological definition, offered by Carlos, 'pure nonsense' and proceeds to redefine the term as a mystical concept. 'The *nagual* is the part of us which we do not deal with at all. . . . for which there is no description. . . . [it] never ends. . . . has no limit. . . . is the only part of us that can create. . . . is but a reflection of that indescribable void that contains everything' (C74:126, 141, 271; see also CJ:117-118). Later the nagual is defined as a person (C77:69), a substance (C77:88, 219), a perception (C77:220), a place (C77:261). See: Bauman, Pearce-f-j. Table, Tonal.

Noose "The correct method in philosophy would really be the following: to say nothing except . . . propositions of natural science . . . and then whenever someone else wanted to say something metaphysical, to demonstrate to him that he had failed to give a meaning to certain signs in his propositions. . . . *this* method would be the only strictly correct one" (Wittgenstein, *Tractatus*, 6.53). • Carlos reads 'a bit of the linguistic philosophy of Ludwig Wittgenstein' to don Juan, who says: 'Your friend Wittgenstein tied the noose too tight around his neck so he can't go anywhere' (Keen 1972:95/1976:79).

Not-Doing Boyd (1973/1976) finds similarities between Buddhism and Juanism, particularly between the Buddhist action-in-nonaction and don Juan's not-doing (C71:266-272; C72:219-254). See: Doing.

Opler See: Campfire, Enemies, Flatulence, Gesture, Guardian, Mold, Place, Power, Rule, Sunrays.

Order "Even a child may speak the most difficult language with idiomatic ease but . . . it takes an unusually analytical type of mind to define the mere elements of that incredibly subtle linguistic mechanism which is but a plaything of the child's unconscious" (Sapir in Mandelbaum 1949:549; see also Garfinkel & Sacks 1970:359). • 'The very fact that we are thinking and talking points out an order that we follow without ever knowing how we do that, or what the order is' (C74:270).

Orona See: Moth.

Orphan "When Gregorio was about seven his mother died" (Leightons 1949:9; reviewed by Castaneda fall 1962). • 'Mexican soldiers killed my mother'. . . . 'How old were you, don Juan?' . . . 'Maybe seven' (C71:167).

Out-of-Body See: Monroe.

Pearce The source in every item under this heading is Joseph Chilton Pearce's popular philosophy book, *The Crack in the Cosmic Egg*, published early in 1971. Since Pearce's ninth chapter is titled "Don Juan and Jesus," one assumes Castaneda read the book the minute it was available.

Pearce-a "The stance [the Australian aboriginal hunter] takes for his Dream Time is rigorous and exact. . . . He stands on one leg, immobile for hours" (120). • "He told me to stand still with my right leg in front, as if I were walking. . . . My legs became very stiff and my calves hurt. It was an agonizing position" (C72:177).

Pearce-b "He knows when his own totem food animal is in his vicinity, though a hill intervenes" (120). • "From where I stood I could very plainly see a large lush green bush"—which was on "the other side of the hill . . . outside my field of vision" (C72:177-178).

Pearce-c "The rewards of Dream-Time were greater for the aborigine than . . . rewards from the world of the 'unreal men'. . . . Outsiders were called 'unreal' " because they did not share the aboriginal reality (123-124). • 'They were people [but] they were no longer real' (C72:311). 'You are a phantom. Your feelings . . . are those of people' (C72:312). Before Castaneda read Pearce, don Juan distinguished allies from people, but called both "real" (C71:52).

Pearce-d "This psychic activity . . . directed his life along newer and larger lines. He became the totally unpredictable" (149). • 'A hunter . . . has no routines. . . . he is free, fluid, unpredictable' (C72:100).

Pearce-e "Opening to the total process of mind" (175). • 'Arriving at the totality of oneself' (C74:13).

Pearce-f "We *must* . . . develop a balance between the modes of thinking" (174). • 'Half of the bubble is the ultimate center of reason. . . . The other half is the ultimate center of will. . . . That is the order that should prevail' (C74:248).

Pearce-g "A surrender is made as a 'child' to a father-figure who gives sureness and confidence that one *can* give over his . . . conceptual framework . . . and receive it back enlarged" (164). • "Don Genaro . . . expressed delight in my being his. . . . protected one" (C74:197). 'Don Genaro. . . . made him a child again' (C74:224). 'The benefactor's task then is to open the bubble. . . . Once the seal is broken, the warrior. . . . has then the command of his totality' (C74:248). See: Attention.

Pearce-h "We have been . . . cataloging and indexing our clearing in the forest. . . . But the nature of the *dark forest* is the real problem" (17). • 'The *tonal* is like the top of this table. An island' (C74:125). 'The *nagual* is there. . . . surrounding the island' (C74:127). See: Table.

Pearce-i "Our clearing in the forest is all there appears for us to go on" (18). • 'The *tonal* is everything we know. . . . everything that meets the eye' (C74:123, 124).

Pearce-j "The light of the clearing still determines what is seen in the dark forest" (118). "Indeed, there may be no trees at all in the depths of that dark. Rather, the forest may shape, the trees may grow, according to the kind of light our reason throws" (17). ● 'The *tonal*. . . . makes the world because it witnesses and assesses it according to *tonal* rules. . . . the *tonal* makes up the rules by which it apprehends the world. So, in a manner of speaking, it creates the world' (C74:125).

Pearce-k "The relation of mind and reality has been but dimly grasped. . . . We *are* an open possibility" (178-179). ● 'How far one can go on the path of knowledge and power. That is an issue which is open and no one can predict its outcome' (C74:243).

Pearce-l "Benjamin Lee Whorf recognized cultural *agreement* as implicit and unstated, but absolutely obligatory. Agreement determines the way we organize nature into concepts giving nature significance. . . . Whatever this agreement decrees is what then makes up reality. . . . furnishing the 'obvious facts' of experience" (55). ● See: Agreement.

Pearce-m See: Collapse, Reality.

Penis "Thereupon he took his penis out of the box and addressed it. 'My younger brother, you are going after the chief's daughter' " (Radin 1956:19; quoted in 1976 by RdeM CJ:108). ● 'Hey, Pablito, tell the Maestro about our doubles'. . . . 'You tell him, Benigno. . . . Better yet, show it to him'. . . . "Benigno stood up . . . pulled down his pants and showed me his penis" (C77:195).

Petrullo See: Peyote.

Peyote The source in every item under this heading is Vincenzo Petrullo's *Diabolic Root*, a book Castaneda reviewed in the fall of 1962 for Anthropology 250 at UCLA.

Peyote-a "By eating Peyote one could learn to lead a good life" (143). ● "He related the use of *Lophophora williamsii* to the acquisition of wisdom, or the knowledge of the right way to live" (C68:7).

Peyote-b "His methods of helping the Indian are gentle" (145). ● 'Mescalito . . . is gentle, like a baby' (C68:61).

Peyote-c "To ask of the Peyotists questions on the religion is not necessary. They should be asked of Peyote instead" (v). ● 'Don't ask *me*! . . . Ask *him*. The next time you see him, ask him everything you want to know' (C68:65).

Peyote-d "Peyote was pleased with me" (88). ● 'The protector has accepted you' (C68:109).

Peyote-e "The herb itself took the form of a chief and medicine man, and began to talk. The herb was Peyote, and the chief was also Peyote himself" (36). • "I saw a man sitting on the ground. . . . His head was exactly like the surface of the peyote plant. . . . his voice was like the soft rustle of a light breeze" (C68:70; narrative 28 June 1962).

Peyote-f "Then Peyote taught her the four original songs which have to be sung in the meeting" (36). • 'I am sure someday he will teach you your own songs' (C68:73). "Immediately I heard a song in my ears" (C68:106).

Peyote-g "You must keep your mind fixed on the purpose for which the meeting is being held. . . . Before you go to the meeting, set your mind on a good purpose" (66-67). • 'Your thoughts must have been steady when you asked that question. And that is the way this sorcery should be conducted, with clarity. . . . If you could hold one thought steadily. . . . As long as your thought is steady and does not go into other things" (C68:84-85).

Peyote-h "Peyote also asks questions by giving you visions. It asks you, what is it you want?" (67). • "Then I heard it as music—as a melody of voices—and I 'knew' it was saying, 'What do you want?' " (C68:70; narrative 28 June 1962).

Peyote-i "They don't know what they want" (67). • "I had been too afraid to know *exactly* what I asked Mescalito" (C68:73).

Peyote-j "Suddenly I heard a buzzing. It appeared to come out from the very roof of the house in which the meeting was held. . . . It reached almost the top of my head, and it felt as if it were going to alight there. . . . I noticed that the sound had changed, and that it was now like the buzzing of a bee and about to alight on my head" (72-73) • "I detected a noise that seemed to be a buzzing inside my ears. . . . The noise reminded me of a science fiction movie in which a gigantic bee buzzed its wings coming out of an atomic radiation area. . . . the image of a gigantic bee accosted me again" (C68:67-68; narrative 28 June 1962). For buzzing at a peyote meeting, see C71:71.

Peyote-k See: Mescalito.

Place "At the supernatural home of power. . . . The 'holy home' is of the greatest religious significance to the shaman. He describes its beauty and wonder. . . . If he feels that his power is dissatisfied with him or that it is deserting him, he journeys to this place to pray and to receive some reassuring sign. . . . Here are revealed to him the songs, prayers, and ritual gestures of a ceremony" (Opler 1941:204-205). • "The endless expanse of land toward the south was truly majestic. 'Fix all this in your memory,' don Juan whispered in my ear. . . . 'This hilltop . . . is yours to use for the rest of your life. . . . This is the place where you will meet

with powers, where secrets will someday be revealed to you'"
(C72:182-184). "I would fall seriously ill if I did not go to my 'place of
predilection' to be cleansed and restored. . . . We left before dawn. . . .
The soothing feeling of peace and plentitude that I experienced in that
mysterious place" (C72:219-220).

Plants "No *hikuri* was ever dug carelessly. . . . it was handled with
tenderness and respect and addressed soothingly by the *hikuri*-seeker,
who would thank it for allowing itself to be seen, call it by endearing
names, and apologize for removing it from its home" (Furst 1972:180;
lecture UCLA spring 1970). ● "He kneeled in front of it and began to
caress it and to talk to it. . . . He babbled inanities. . . . He explained
that a man who gathers plants must apologize every time for taking
them" (C72:42-43). See: Bean-d, Propitiation.

Plato See: Recollection.

Poe See: Gnat.

Power-a "Power is dangerous if you try to use it and don't know how.
Then you go crazy and jump into the fire or jump off a cliff or stab
yourself or lose yourself so that you die wandering around the mountains" (Opler 1941:207). ● "Power was a devastating force that could
easily lead to one's death and had to be treated with great care"
(C72:133).

Power-b After many years, the power will ask some shamans to sacrifice
some of their best friends or the very ones they love best in the family"
(Opler 1941:208). "Sometimes the power calls on them to sacrifice their
own relatives, and they do" (Opler 1941:255). ● 'He [don Vicente]
won't cause you any harm by himself. But knowledge is power, and once
a man embarks on the road of knowledge he's no longer liable for what
may happen to those who come in contact with him' (C71:47).

Power-c See: Man of knowledge.

Pozas See: Face.

Propitiation Since the Huichols believe men and animals were one in
the "first time," the hunter explains to his "brother," the slain animal,
why he had to die (Myerhoff 1968:34; 1974:58). "The hunter must
speak to the deer when he dies to soothe and propitiate his spirit"
(Myerhoff 1968:103). "Everyone takes a turn stroking him, thanking
him for allowing himself to be caught. . . . the animal is man's brother
who sacrifices himself to the hunter willingly" (Myerhoff 1968:182-
183). ● 'Today we took a little snake. I had to apologize to her for
cutting her life off so suddenly. . . . we and the snakes are on a par'
(C72:77). See: Bean-d, Plants.

Protected "Although the Huichol shaman is generally strong enough to defeat his enemy's magic. . . . On certain days. . . . the shaman is well-advised to remain quietly indoors and not attempt to exercise his supernatural functions, lest he expose himself to surprise, attack, and harm. . . . One of the important functions of the shaman's wife is to guard her husband's back against such attacks" (Furst 1965:68; 1966:404-405). • 'This morning is a bad time for sorcerers. . . . You're too weak to leave my room. Inside here you are protected. If you were to wander off now. . . . An ally could kill you on the road' (C71:234). See: Warrior.

Rabbit 'We must set snares to catch him. . . . so that he will break our hearts. So that we will think, "Ah, it is a very special thing he does for us. . . ." If it is ordained that he go into the net. . . . if One has commanded him so, I will come up there beside him. . . . He is in the snare, he looks up at me, saying, as he does so, "Ah, this is the death of me." There he lies down, he stretches out before me of his own will. . . . He calls to me, "I am taking leave of my life, my life is darkening" ' (Myerhoff 1968:181; 1974:174). • "He yelled at me that the rabbit had to die. . . . because the power or the spirit that guides rabbits had led that particular one into my trap. . . . I looked at it and it looked at me. . . . We exchanged a sombre glance . . . which I fancied to be of silent despair. . . ." (C72:114). "He said the rabbit's death had been a gift for me" (C72:115). See: Time.

Radin See: Penis.

Ramacharaka See: Atkinson.

Rank See: Double.

Reality-a "Entering into worlds other than our own . . . leads us to understand that our own world is also a cultural construct. By experiencing other worlds, then, we see our own for what it is and are thereby enabled also to see fleetingly what the real world, the one between our own cultural construct and those other worlds, must in fact be like" (Walter Goldschmidt, C68:vii-viii). • 'He can *see* things as they really are' (C71:182, also 51). '*Seeing* happens only when one sneaks between the worlds, the world of ordinary people and the world of sorcerers' (C72:300).

Reality-b "Goldschmidt realizes the intriguing riddle to lie in don Juan's . . . crack between the worlds. Goldschmidt concludes, however, that through this crack we can then see, fleetingly, what the 'real world . . . must in fact be like.' Here, I do believe, we have an example of the perpetual error. . . . there is no such thing as a 'real world' other than that one from which one makes such a statement. The crack is only a capacity . . . for processing an infinite number of worlds—none of which is absolute" (Pearce 1971:131; RdeM—CJ:82-83, 82n fallacy, 121-122, 121n true reality—and Kenneth Minogue—DJP: Chapter 21—made the same point). • 'I said that only if one pits two views against each other can one weasel between them to arrive at the real world. I meant that one can arrive at the totality of oneself only when one fully understands that the world is merely a view, regardless of whether that view belongs to an ordinary man or to a sorcerer' (C74:240).

Reality-c In the two previous items we see don Juan first accept Goldschmidt's epistemological fallacy and then, prompted by Pearce, revise his position—under the guise of clarifying it—to retain the sound part of Goldschmidt's statement and abandon the fallacy.

Recollection 'Plato said that all knowledge is recollection' (Castaneda to Cravens 1973a:94). • 'Our experience of the world is always a recollection of the experience. We are perennially recollecting the instant that has just happened, just passed' (C74:53). See: Jump.

Red "My eyes were closed, and a large black pool started to open up in front of them. . . . I was able to see a red spot. . . . a most unusual odor. . . . different parts of my body getting extremely warm, which felt extremely good" (Swain 1963:232). • "Pungent odor of the water. It smelled like cockroaches. . . . I got very warm. . . . I saw a red spot in front of my eyes. . . . 'What would have happened if I had not seen red?' 'You would have seen black, and that is a bad sign'. . . . 'What happens to those who see red?' 'They do not vomit, and the root gives them an effect of pleasure' " (C68:40-41). See DJP: Chapter 2.

Rich 'The *mara'akame* is rich, very rich, the most fortunate man of all, but he has very few things. He is a poor man, but he is rich (Myerhoff 1968:94; 1974:97). "In spite of great privation, they do not see themselves as victims. . . . Their wealth is aesthetic and spiritual. They envy no one [but] pity those who live a life different from their own" (1968:305; 1974:263). • 'Do you think that your very rich world would ever help you to become a man of knowledge?. . . . Then how could you feel sorry for those children?. . . Any one of them could become a man of knowledge. All the men of knowledge I know were kids like those you saw eating leftovers and licking the tables' (C71:32).

Rising "I threw my head back and willed myself out of that place. . . . I exploded upwards like a rocket. . . . I found myself standing" (Swain 1963:226). • "Standing up was perhaps the most unusual of all the acts I performed that night. I thought myself up!" (C68:99).

Rodent Maria Chona's brother drew a ring on the ground, picked up some smooth pebbles, spit on them, and threw one up into the air. 'It fell in the circle and it looked as though a baby quail was hatching out of an egg. We saw its eyes and its bill; it was wobbling and trying to run.' He repeated the performance with the other stone. Then he picked them up and spit on them, and they were stones again (Underhill 1936:24; reviewed by Castaneda fall 1962). • 'Creativity is this,' says don Juan, producing on his palm a squirrel-like rodent with a porcupine's tale, glasses, a Japanese look, and fur that feels soft to Carlos's finger. The rodent grows beyond Carlos's frame of vision, and Carlos then finds himself standing, though he does not remember having stood up (C74:141-142).

Routines See: Stop.

Rowe See: Lizard.

Rule "In order to maintain the good will of his power, the shaman must observe its rules. The person who fails to live up to his part of the power relationship agreement runs the risk of alienating the power and inviting retaliation. . . . If a shaman makes a mistake. . . . the power gives him another chance. If the shaman always makes mistakes, he may get sick and die" (Opler 1941:207). • "The ally had a rule. . . . The rule was inflexible. . . . An ally had the capacity to . . . withhold the deleterious, and usually fatal, effect resulting from noncompliance with its rule. Such evidence of flexibility was thought to be always the product of a strong bond of affinity between the ally and its follower" (C68:155-156). See: Man of Knowledge.

Ryle See: Jump.

Sacks See: Accounting, Doing, Folly, Gloss, Mechanics.

Sapir See: Agreement, Description, Gloss, Order.

Seeing "We must learn how to handle words effectively; but at the same time we must preserve and, if necessary, intensify our ability to look at the world directly and not through that half opaque medium of concepts, which distorts every given fact into the all too familiar likeness of some generic label or explanatory abstraction" (Huxley 1954/1963:74). • 'Once you learn, you can *see* every single thing in the world in a different way. . . . Whenever you look at things you don't *see* them, you just look at them. . . . things look very much the same to you every time you look at them' (C71:50). '*Seeing* is not a matter of talk' (C71:130). 'There is really no way to talk about it. *Seeing* . . . is learned by *seeing*' (C71:207). Correspondence noted by Heelas (1972:135).

Self-a "We grow to realize that the *self* is compound, impermanent; and that the self, *as self*, does not exist" (David-Neel 1932:277). • "After every one of those coherent views the 'me' would disintegrate and be nothing once more" (C74:263).

Self-b "The Self is likened to a point. . . . Psychologically, the point must perform a leap into the nothingness of the void. . . . The point is now everywhere, filling as it were the whole area of the circle which has no circumference. The Self-point is shorn of its fictitious contents which are now replaced by an infinite number of Self-points. . . . Every one of such Self-points is my Self" (Suzuki 1972:50-52). ● "I was the awareness itself. . . . I suddenly found myself standing on a cliff. . . . I again had the sensations of being tossed, spinning, and falling down at a tremendous speed. . . . There was no longer the sweet unity I call 'me.' There was nothing and yet that nothing was filled. . . . I was a myriad of selves which were all 'me' " (C74:261-262). Correspondence noted by Forisha (1978:34). See: Abyss, Awareness.

Self-c On 14 Feb 1969 in a seminar led by Harold Garfinkel at UCLA, Houston Wood described a dizzying mystical experience similar to the one described in Self-b, brought on by a reality-breaching procedure called Zato Coding, in which the world became a "swarm" that engulfed the coder (Mehan & Wood 1975:231-232, 253). Castaneda was enrolled as a graduate student Jan-Mar 1969 (CJ:178).

Sharon See: Table.

Shepherd See: Sparks.

Shields Furst (1965:38; 1966:327) shows a shaman carrying a "large rectangular shield" to guard himself against supernatural enemies. ● 'A warrior selects the items that make his world. . . . every item he chooses is a shield that protects him from the onslaughts of the forces he is striving to use. A warrior would use his shields to protect himself from his ally' (C71:260; see also 264, 271). See: Warrior.

Signs "The interpretation of the meaning of signs . . . occupied Rosalio almost perpetually. Few events and happenings were left uninterpreted" (Moisés & others 1971:xxxi). ● Don Juan interprets the roar of an Air Force jet (C72:23), the perking of his coffee pot (C72:24-25), and the rolling of a rock (C72:42) as agreements from the world; he interprets the flying or cawing of a crow (C72:39, 41), the finding of a bush (C72:179), and the shining of the sun (C72:185-186, 189) as omens.

Sisters Don Juan called some of his lesser witches *las hermanitas*, the little sisters (C77:72), a parody of the Catholic name for nuns, as in Hermanitas de la Caridad, Little Sisters of Charity.

Smoke Photo caption: "María Sabina, the Mazatec *curandera*, passing the mushrooms through the smoke of aromatic plants" (Wasson

1958:221). • "He said the function of the leaves and the flowers was to sweeten the [mushroom] smoke mixture" (C68:55; see also CJ:61, 61n smoking mushrooms; Pollock 1975:77).

Sorcerer 'The stick doctor. . . . could kill a person by merely saying, "I wish that man dead". . . . The witch doctor. . . . was blamed for killing a great many people, especially women. . . . When he wanted one, he threatened her. If she would not do as he wished, he killed her. . . . Our people were angered . . . and got two men . . . to waylay and kill him' (Steward 1934:426-427; reviewed by Castaneda fall 1962). • 'My benefactor . . . could make a person mortally ill by merely looking at him. Women would wane away after he had set eyes on them. Yet he did not make people sick all the time but only when his personal power was involved' (C72:153). 'His fellow men hate him and fear him and will strive to end his life; on the other hand the inexplicable and unbending forces that surround every one of us . . . are for a sorcerer a source of even greater danger' (C72:258).

Soul "The idea that the soul has . . . been abducted by a sorcerer . . . and hidden in some secret place is . . . widespread; its recovery, often in ferocious combat . . . is the exclusive province of the shaman, for only he . . . 'knows . . . the regions to which it can be carried away' " (Furst 1965:69; 1966:405). • "He was going away to see who had taken my soul, and to find out if it was possible to get it back" (C68:132). 'You won your soul back. It was a good battle' (C68:139). See: Harner-j, Warrior.

Sparks "I can snap sparkles from my fingertips. . . . Blue sparkles shower from my fingers when I snap them" (Shepherd 1967). • "When she snapped her fingers open a volley of sparks flew from them. . . . as she made her urine fly like reddish sparks" (C77:142; also 138).

Speed No source found. • 'You could not see [the spirit] because you did not have the speed' (C71:273).

Spin For possible influence of C. S. Lewis on don Juan's Ally, see CJ:86-88.

Spirit-Catcher "Horned figurine. . . . Sling or rope held in right hand, would around left" (Furst 1965:36). "Sling with which this and other figurines pull left hand against right is probably not conventional slingshot weapon but rather a 'soul catcher' " (Furst 1965:39; 1966:332-333); the supernatural function of this rope was confirmed by Ramón Medina (Furst, telephone, 5 May 1978). "Ramón then placed one end of his deerskin bow in his mouth, using his mouth for a sounding chamber, holding the other end between his toes, began twanging rhythmically on the string with the side of an arrow" (Myerhoff

1968:155). 'He places that bow in his mouth, one end. He makes this ancient sound with his arrow, tapping against the string. That is how he speaks to those ahead, those ancient ones that are awaiting us'— —Ramón (Myerhoff 1968:196-197). "The music of the 'bow drum' is intended to tell the supernaturals that the pilgrims are on their way, and to charm the Deer-Peyote" (Furst 1972:147, also 160; lecture UCLA spring 1970). ● "He then took a sort of whitish cord from his pouch. It looked like a big loop. He looped it around his neck and stretched it with his left hand until it was taut. He plucked the tight string with his right hand. It made a dull, vibratory sound. . . . He said that if something came at me in a very menacing way I had to adopt a fighting form" (C71:195-196). 'What was the string you played, don Juan?' 'A spirit catcher' (C71:198). 'Now let us call that spirit of the water hole' (C71:201). "The man . . . pulled a string from his bag, and wrapped it around his left hand" (C71:225). 'The ally showed you a spirit catcher that he got from his pouch. You need to have one if you are going to call him' (C71:273). 'He wrapped it around his left hand. . . . Today he again wanted to show you the spirit catcher' (C71:274). For illustrations, see DJP: end of Chapter 6. See: Fighting, Flatulence, Warrior.

Stalking-a "The party set out across the desert. . . . Everyone was completely quiet and grave, looking closely at the ground for signs of deer or peyote. . . . The behavior was precisely that of stalking" (Myerhoff 1968:169-170; 1974:152-154). 'It is as when one hunts. All are quiet, all whisper, all walk with gentle feet. So as not to make noise, so as not to disturb the peyote' (Myerhoff 1968:215). ● 'How can one stalk one's weaknesses, Gorda?' 'The same way you stalk prey. You figure out your routines until you know all the doing of your weaknesses and then you come upon them and pick them up like rabbits inside a cage' (C77:221).

Stalking-b "Gurdjieff had often said that those in the Work should know how to become invisible" (de Ropp 1979:359; for more, see DJP: Chapter 1). ● 'She's practicing the art of stalking. . . . The Nagual taught us to baffle people so they wouldn't notice us' (C77:102). Don Juan and don Genaro 'learned to become unnoticeable. . . . They knew the art of stalking' (C77:200). See: Toltecs.

Steward See: Bath, Beetle, Deer, Sorcerer.

Stewart See: Body, Dreaming.

Stop "Behind both the 'happenings' and the ethnomethodological demonstration there is a common impulse: to bring routines to a halt, to make the world and time stop" (Gouldner 1970:392). ● 'In order to be a hunter you must disrupt the routines of your life' (C72:100). 'In order to *stop the world* you must stop *doing'* (C72:228). See also: DJP: Chapter 40; CJ:101-102.

Sunrays A Mescalero shaman says: 'This spider web represents the ropes of the sun. . . . the sparkling of the web is the fire that is eating you. . . .' Opler (1969:113) notes: "The association between the strands of the spider web and the rays of the sun occurs in a number of ritual contexts." ● " 'Look there fixedly,' he said. 'The sun is almost right.' He explained that at midday the light of the sun could help me with 'not-doing' " (C72:240). "If I squinted my eyes I could see the whole range of mountains as an intricate array of light fibers. . . . a web of light. . . . I again squinted my eyes and once more saw the web of light fibers" (C72:241). "The sun was almost over the horizon. I was looking directly into it and then I saw 'the lines of the world'. . . . I felt something warm and soothing oozing out of the world and out of my own body" (C72:298). See: Lines of the World.

Suzuki See: Beyond, Self.

Swain See: Bubble, Ending, Luminous, Red, Rising, Translingo, Tricked.

Table UCLA anthropologist Douglas Sharon (1978:144-148) compares the sacramental *mesa* (table) of the Peruvian shaman Eduardo with the restaurant table over which don Juan explains *nagual* and *tonal* (C74:see AG: Nagual, Tonal). "It appears," Sharon concludes (148), "that there is a great deal of structural similarity between the teachings of don Juan and Eduardo's symbol system." Sharon (144) allows the possibility, urged by RdeM, that the don Juan books are fiction but overlooks the possibility that don Juan's table is not only similar to Eduardo's *mesa*, as it might be if shamans think alike, but *based on* Sharon's earlier description of the *mesa* (Furst 1972:123-130), as it would be if Castaneda were mining the newly-published works of his UCLA friends (see AG: Bean, Furst, Myerhoff, Orona). In *Second Ring*, Castaneda elaborates the table theme (C77:282-283). See: Bauman.

Thing "The founder of modern phenomenology, Edmund Husserl,. . . wished to redirect philosophical inquiry to 'the things themselves,' to the phenomena of consciousness" (McKinney & Tiryakian 1970:18). Carlos discussed Husserl with don Juan (Keen 1972:92/1976:75), but Ramón's interpretation was simpler: "deer, peyote, and maize are one": 'it stands for itself' (Myerhoff 1968:183). ● 'My spirit catcher is a wild boar.' 'Do you mean your spirit catcher is made out of a wild boar?' 'No! Nothing in the life of a sorcerer is made out of anything else. If something is anything at all, it is the thing itself' (C71:273).

Tibetan "To guide the drug-takers through 'the limitless new realities of the consciousness-expanded state,' If-If adapted a manual from the Tibetan *Book of the Dead*" (Kobler 1963:35). • 'The Tibetans. . . . must have realized that what they *see* makes no sense at all and they wrote that bunch of crap because it doesn't make any difference to them' (C71:235). See: DJP: Chapter 39; AG:Death.

Tickling There is a "strong itching or tingling of the top of the skull" when one takes the hallucinogenic snuff *ebene* (Furst 1976:152). • "A ticklish sensation on top of my head stopped me. . . . at the very moment I had felt the tickling on my head my thoughts had diminished" (C77:86).

Time "We came to thousands and thousands of candles. . . . [Jesus] stopped and said, 'This is your candle. It is very tall, and it is burning still.' There were many candles which had burned down to the ground. 'Do you see those?' he asked. 'They are for persons living on earth. Their time is up' " (Moisés 1971:90). • " 'This rabbit's time is up.' Don Juan's tone shocked me; it was so authoritative; so knowledgeable, it left no doubts in my mind that he knew that the rabbit's time was up" (C72:114). See: Rabbit.

Tirso See: Don Juan.

Toltecs "Ramón explained that the peyote pilgrims, the *peyoteros*, were the Ancient Ones going back to their home" (Myerhoff 1974:21). "The pilgrims became and were known to each other as the Ancient Ones" (Myerhoff 1974:136). • 'Did the Nagual by any chance tell you that the Toltecs were ancient people that lived in this part of Mexico?' 'We are the Toltecs. . . . Rest assured that we are' (C77:181). 'A sorcerer is a Toltec when that sorcerer has received the mysteries of stalking and *dreaming*' (C77:239)—which is the statement that convinced RdeM Stephen Reno (1978:590) was right in predicting Castaneda's sixth installment would treat the art of stalking (see Note for front cover). See: Stalking. A historical footnote to Castaneda's belated discovery of the Toltecs in don Juan's teachings is the fact that in hearings years ago on the status of Yaquis as United States Indians some Yaqui leaders wished to evoke a mythical descent from the Toltecs, who had apparently traversed what is now Arizona in prehistoric times. Anthropologists dissuaded the Yaquis from claiming a Toltec connection (Letter 8 Apr 1979 from Stephen Murray relaying information from Edward H. Spicer).

Tonal "The tonal is a companion animal or destiny. . . . subject to stealing, and is specifically of concern in becoming ill" (Adams & Rubel 1973:336; see also Foster 1944). • "The 'tonal' . . . was thought to be a kind of guardian spirit, usually an animal, that a child obtained at birth and with which he had intimate ties for the rest of his life" (C74:121). Dismissing Carlos's conventional definition, don Juan redefines *tonal* as the complement of his metaphysical *nagual*: 'The *tonal* is not an animal that guards a person. . . . The *tonal* is the social person. . . . the organizer of the world. . . . [it] is everything we know. . . . everything that meets the eye. . . . [It] begins at birth and ends at death. . . . [It] is a creator that doesn't create a thing. . . . [It] is but a reflection of that indescribable unknown filled with order' (C74:122-125, 270-271; see also CJ:117-118). See: Bauman, Nagual, Pearce-f-j, Table.

Translingo "I roused myself and forced myself to speak. To my surprise the Mazatecs answered in English. . . . I was later told it sounded to them that I spoke in Mazateca" (Swain 1963:225). ● "When I tried to speak I realized I couldn't. . . . I . . . listened to what the men were saying. They were talking in Italian . . . about the stupidity of sharks. . . . it never occurred to me to think that none of them could speak Italian" (C68:23-24).

Treeness 'The very treeness of trees' (Kobler 1963:32). ● "The 'essence' of tree" (C74:200). See: DJP:Chapter 39.

Tricked "This made me even more furious. I felt I was being tricked" (Swain 1963:226). "I thought . . . it was a trick to hypnotize me" (Swain 1963:241). ● 'Don't be angry. It was not an ordinary trick' (C71:256). "The thought occurred to me . . . that I was being tricked. . . . that perhaps they were mesmerizing me" (C72:283). 'I always think I'm being tricked' (C74:28). See: Collapse.

Twilight "Candidate shamans. . . . must go 'where day and night meet' " (Eliade 1964:485). ● 'The twilight is the crack between the worlds' (C68:66, 82; C74:286). See: Crack, Door.

Underhill See: Coyote, Rodent.

van Eeden See: Body, Double, Dreaming.

Visions "There exist certain species of wild mushrooms . . . which, if you eat them, cause you to see visions . . . of almost anything you can imagine" (Wasson 1958:221). ● 'The [mushroom] smoke . . . will set you free to see anything you want to see' (C68:56).

Warrior "Without exception, these so-called 'warriors' also faced left in a fighting stance, always as though warding off an enemy threatening attack from that side. . . . I believe the case for shamanism and against 'warriors' [is] strong" (Furst 1965:46; 1966:356-357). "The armed tomb figurines of West Mexico are, in fact, not 'warriors' but shamanic guardians of the dead against those forces . . . identified with the sinistral side" (Furst 1965:67; 1966:402). ● 'Only as a warrior can one survive the path of knowledge' (C71:258; C72:315). 'I have endeavored to show you those forces as a sorcerer perceives them, because only under their terrifying impact can one become a warrior. . . . The spirit of a warrior is geared only to struggle, and every struggle is a warrior's last battle on earth' (C71:259; see also C72:112-113). See: Fighting, Left, Man of Knowledge, Protected, Shields, Soul.

Wasson See: Awareness, Barking, Crack, Genaro, Heaven, Man of Knowledge, Smoke, Visions.

Waterfall-a When Myerhoff told Castaneda about Ramón on the waterfall, Castaneda instantly told Myerhoff about Genaro on the waterfall, though Carlos would not meet Genaro for another two years (see DJP: Chapter 42, introductory passages and notes; CJ:112-113).

Waterfall-b One of Myerhoff's photographs (1974:45) showed a semicircular cloud shadow on the ground behind Ramón. ● "Directly above us there was a huge, dark, bluish cloud . . . shaped like an enormous half-circle" (C71:124).

Watson See: Fog.

Wave Concepts standing in the way of a floodtide. ● Gigantic wave held back by a metaphoric wall. See: DJP: Chapter 39.

Whistle "It seemed to me to be a singing insect of some kind, but I was sure I had not heard it before. The sound appeared to come from a different direction each time. . . . a small, inoffensive insect, the greatest game-finding charm an Indian hunter could have" (Córdova-Rios & Lamb 1971:57-58). Ramón "put his hands to his mouth and made the call or whistle of the deer" (Myerhoff 1968:146; 1974:126). ● 'Suddenly I heard a sweet whistle. It was unknown to me; never . . . had I heard such a sound. . . . it seemed to come from different places. . . . I knew it was a magical being, a deer. . . . aware of the routines . . . of hunters' (C72:102).

White See: Man of Knowledge.

Wind-Women Furst & Myerhoff (1966:33) linked the world directions NSEW with the "four winds" and winds tenuously with female deities, the "winds of sickness." Myerhoff (1968:124, 205; 1974:106) added the fifth point, the center of the world, where the Huichol are placed. ● Castaneda described four magical wind-women stationed at the compass points (C77:42-45) and Carlos in the midst of them as "the center and binding force of the four corners of the world"—"a Toltec power arrangement" (C77:302-303). In the story Carlos learns about these women for the first time in 1976, from doña Soledad (C77:42-45), after don Juan has left this world (for the chronology, see C74:11, 267; C77:7-8), but in ordinary time, Castaneda told his UC-Irvine students about the wind-women in the spring of 1972, when don Juan was still teaching Carlos (Wallace 1972:140-141; CJ:157-158; see also DJP:Chapter 43).

Witnessing "There are, indeed, things that cannot be put into words. They *make themselves manifest*. They are what is mystical" (Wittgenstein, *Tractatus*, 6.522). ● 'It's useless to talk about it. Whatever I may say doesn't make sense, because. . . . The affairs of the *nagual* can be witnessed only with the body, not the reason' (C74:158). 'There is no way to refer to the unknown. . . . One can only witness it' (C74:266).

Wittgenstein See: Boundaries, Death, Equal, Eternity, Explaining, Ladder, Noose, Witnessing. See also: DJP: Chapter 35.

Wood See: Self-c.

The notes are keyed by bold page numerals; some refer to subsequent pages without a change of numeral. The following abbreviations are used:

RdeM	The Editor
DJP	*The Don Juan Papers*
AG	Appendix 44—The Alleglossary
CJ, CJ2	*Castaneda's Journey* (RdeM 1976,1978)
C68	*The Teachings of don Juan* (Castaneda 1968)
C71	*A Separate Reality* (Castaneda 1971)
C72	*Journey to Ixtlan* (Castaneda 1972)
C73	*Sorcery*, a dissertation (Castaneda 1973)
C74	*Tales of Power* (Castaneda 1974)
C77	*The Second Ring of Power* (Castaneda 1977a)

Proprietary permissions are acknowledged in particular notes, as is the Editor's gratitude to many persons. Here I wish to thank: Margaret de Mille for indispensable dispensations; William Madsen for furnishing needed academic authority; Jacques Meunier and José Matos Mar for unlocking Peru; Robert Sheldon and Paul Cornell for crucial fieldwork; Marcello Truzzi, Donald Brown, Imogen Seger-Coulborn, Stephen Reno, Robert L. Morris, Arthur von Wiesenberger, and Gregory Cross for valuable references; Marie Ensign, Ned Divelbiss, and Laura Nanna for impeccable bibliognostics; Kendrick Frazier for introducing me to Sanford Berman; and Petra Löwen for translating from the German of Duerr and Timm.

000 Cover/jacket design (for hire) by Fran Smith, Don French Graphic Design. Cover/jacket copyright ©1980 by Richard de Mille. The crow is borrowed from Frederick A. Usher's Escherly illustration for *Castaneda's Journey*. "If you wish to upset the law that all crows are black," wrote philosopher and psychical researcher William James, "it is enough if you prove one single crow to be white" (Murphy & Ballou 1960:41). James's white crow is escaping from don Juan's desert, because it doesn't want to get mixed up in a psychical-research hoax. The reflexive, Escher-like, ethnomethodallegoric theme of the cover is: Out of real books comes an unearthly desert out of which come real books. Out of books by Suzuki, David-Neel, Myerhoff, Garfinkel, and so on (see Appendix 44, Alleglossary) comes a desert Hans Sebald proves imaginary (see Chapter 5), out of which come *The Teachings of Don Juan, A Separate Reality, Journey to Ixtlan,* and—a title predicted for Castaneda's sixth book by Stephen Reno (1978:590), carved in stone for this cover (specified 17 Apr, completed 18 Sep 1979), and confirmed in December by Simon & Schuster (Korda 1979)—*The*

Art of Stalking (see Chapter 1 and AG:**Stalking**). Usher suggested turning the books into rock strata. The scorpion has crawled into the picture to protest the fact that during all his years in the desert Carlos never saw one. The rabbit looks sleepy because it has rabbit fever.

2 QVOVSQVE—Marcus Tullius Cicero began his first oration against the conspirator Catiline with the rhetorical question: *Quousque tandem abutere, Catilina, patientia nostra?* Which means: How long, O Catiline, will you try our patience? Sometimes erroneously attributed to Spicero, Cicero's first oration against Castaneda is said to be a graffito popular on the third floor of Haines Hall, at UCLA.

8 Don Juan & Georg Simmel—I have somewhat revised Castaneda's "translation" (C72:230) of don Juan's legendary Spanish discourse, without, of course, altering don Juan's meaning. A University of California Press editor took similar liberties when he deleted *the, a, a,* and *for me* from Castaneda's text (C68:137) to make a more readable quotation at the front of *The Teachings of Don Juan* (C68:xii). There don Juan and Simmel apparently agreed about the path with heart. Here they disagree about the importance of truth (Simmel 1950: 312,313).

Richard de Mille   1
9 "The Art of Stalking"—With apologies to Stringfellow Barr. *Agnes Redux*—Agnes brought back, roughly Agnes revisited; see DJP: Chapter 7.
11 Just like every other—Clement Meighan, quoted by Preuss (1978:56). Conflicts illuminate—Compare Collins & Pinch 1979:238.
12 Editor opined—Letter, UC Press, Los Angeles, 10 Jan 1977.
13 Stalking—Gurdjieff (de Ropp 1979:359); dress (*Time* 1973:43/ 1976:101); witch (C77:239); weasel (Keen 1972:98/1976:86); disguises, title (Korda 1979:8,5); AG:**Stalking.** Happy Cave—See AG:**Erasing.**

Richard de Mille   2
16 "The Shaman of Academe"—A preliminary version appeared as RdeM 1979b, copyright ©1979,1980 by Richard de Mille. The illustration, "Carlos Castaneda in 1965," was drawn (for hire) by Schlesinger from a photograph; drawing copyright ©1980 by Richard de Mille.
17 Castaneda biography—CJ:Chapter Two; *Time* 1973; M. Castaneda 1975; Parrott 1975; Lévano 1973. No interest in mysticism—CJ:30: Freilicher 1972:51; Cravens 1973b:174. Academic career—CJ: Chapters Three & Four. Fellow story teller—Oates 1972; Kennedy 1974; Sturgeon 1973. Trendy Castaneda—Rosenwald (1979) agrees. Competition too steep—Kennedy (1974) and Inglis (1978) agree.
18 Meighan—Quoted by Strachan 1979:91. Reports contradict each other—CJ:166-172. Gothic tale—So it was called by Edmund Leach (1969:12/1976:33). Total mood—C71:16
19 Detail—CJ: Chapter Three. Mushroom challenged—DJP: Chapter 40;

THE DON JUAN PAPERS

PAPERS

FURTHER CASTANEDA CONTROVERSIES

RICHARD DE MILLE

Wasson 1969. Write everything—C72:8; C71:259; C74:22,229; CJ:47-48. Faculty resistance—Beals 1978:357; RdeM conversations (16 Sept 1978) with two of Castaneda's more skeptical chairmen, John Hitchcock and William Lessa. Tape recordings—C71:21,76. Voluminous field notes—C72:8. Similar words—See AG:**Egg, Red.**

20 Yogi Ramacharaka—Pseudonym of William Walker Atkinson, of Chicago, whose 1922 book, *Personal Power*, was published by the Personal Power Company, of Detroit; see also CJ:94-95. Wilk—Quoted from 1977c; 1977a:87.

21 Shares worldview of informant—Heelas 1972:134,140,145,148; Wilk 1977a, 1978. Knowledge of hidden realms—"Whereas, since Heraclitus and the pre-Socratic nature philosophers, the touchstone for truth of occidental man has been intersubjectively-accessible sensory experience, by contrast American Indians held as their epistemological authority the subjective supernatural experience, trance- or drug-induced" (Weston La Barre. Psychedelics galore. *Duke University Letters*, 13 Dec 1979, #4:3). English-language texts—See Authors by name in the Alleglossary.

22 Really a shaman—Naranjo & Harner 1968; compare Eliade 1964:509. Not really lying—Harner 1963:111. Not really experts—Harner 1978. Valid 110 percent—Harner quoted by Stein (1975), where he was not misquoted, for in his lecture-promotion letter of 30 Aug 1975, he said: "I enclose a copy of a recent interview with me published in the San Francisco Chronicle to give you an idea of my position with regard to Carlos' work"; Harner 1978.

23 Smoke mushrooms—Pollock 1975:77; CJ:61,61n; Duerr 1978b:289; AG:**Smoke.** Great impostor—In the 1961 movie, Tony Curtis played Demara creditably, but the story was biographically impaired while being dramatically improved; better read the book (Crichton 1959).

Mary Douglas   3
25 "The Authenticity of Castaneda," first published in *The Times Higher Education Supplement* (London, 15 June 1973, No. 87:13) as "Torn between two realities," received its present title as Chapter 13 of Mary Douglas's *Implicit Meanings* (Routledge & Kegan Paul, 1975: 193-200); reproduced here by permission of author and publisher.

30 Don Vicente—C71:46.
31 To hinge yourself—C72:239.

RdeM
32 Rosalio's candle, guess, preoccupation—See AG:**Time, Swain, Signs.** "A Yaqui Way of Kidding"—Kelley 1978:24-25. Reprinted from *Yaqui Women* by Jane Holden Kelley by permission of University of Nebraska Press. Copyright ©1978 by the University of Nebraska Press. Disagree with Castaneda—Sebald 1978:199.

Hans Sebald   **5**

34 "Roasting Rabbits in Tularemia or The Lion, the Witch, and the Horned Toad"—Subtitle suggested by C. S. Lewis's *The Lion, the Witch and the Wardrobe* (Lewis 1950), Book 1 in the Chronicles of Narnia, which tells how Aslan (compare Aztlan, Ixtlan), the noble lion, freed the magical land of Narnia (compare Sonora) and its talking animals from the spell of the White Witch. Author and editor have contributed notes; editor's notes are signed.—RdeM.

Claim—Castaneda writes (C68:5): "I carried out the apprenticeship first in Arizona and then in Sonora, because don Juan moved to Mexico during the course of my training." The move occurred some time between August 1961 (C68:21) and January 1962 (C72:172). Both don Juan's Arizona house (C72:37,71) and his Mexican house (C71:36) are described as being *in* the desert, which must be either the Sonoran desert or an imaginary desert.—RdeM.

Field reports—"The data that comprises the present work was gathered over a period of ten years of sporadic fieldwork. . . . I took notes and thus recorded in writing all the instances of our teacher-disciple relationship" (Castaneda, dissertation abstract, 1973; the text of the dissertation is the same as C72, *Journey to Ixtlan*); the ten years of fieldwork are 1961-1971, the period of the first three books.—RdeM.

35 Review ignores nonordinary events—Having read (on C72:38) that an enormous crow flew over don Juan's head, I was going to write that crows characteristically do not risk flying directly over human beings but veer aside some distance away. I have restrained myself for two reasons. First, don Juan took the overflight to be an omen, which implies it was unusual. Second, followers of don Juan will no doubt say he had enough sorcering power to *make* crows fly over his head any time he liked. I have stuck to what I think are clear-cut examples of the ordinary environment, unwarped by don Juan's power or Carlos's confusions.

Summer hiking—C72:70-151. Forgot to eat lunch—C72:83. Cold wind—C72:84; on May 21st (C71:36) the evening was cool, though the day had been "quite uncomfortable" at over 100 degrees. Roamed for hours—C72:105. Climbed hill to rest—C72:124. Lukewarm rain—C72:161.

36 Five quail—C72:83, 145.

Puma charges—C71:186; Wasson 1972:98. Castaneda may have gotten the idea that mountain lions (pumas) are aggressive from Lowell J. Bean (*Cahuilla Indian Cultural Ecology*, dissertation, U. Calif. Los Angeles, 27 Feb 1970, XUM 70-19825, DAI 31/04-B1665), whose Indian informants said mountain lions occasionally maimed or killed humans and that the "lonely hunter was especially wary and cautious of them" (91). Such stories may have been left over from the days of jaguars, which were much more fearsome than pumas, but don Juan should have known the difference even if Carlos or Castaneda did not.—RdeM.

Crawling with lions—C72:144-151. Eight years later—C71:296.

37 Rodents—C72:145. Oblivious to flies—C71:35-58; C72:275-315; Carlos rolled up his car window to keep out "mosquitoes and other flying insects" in May (C72:281); flies of some kind pestered him in late June, but did not land on don Juan's face (C72:71); presumably don Juan's power kept them away; Carlos, obviously, had no such power. Outruns predators—C72:96. Catches rabbit—C72:113; this was only a month after Carlos lacked the power to keep flies from pestering him, so we are not to suppose here that he bewitched the rabbit; he merely stalked and caught it.

38 Rabbit dies—C72:115. Untouched by cacti—The omissions listed in this paragraph were suggested by a desert-wise anthropologist, Ralph Beals, to whom I am most grateful. Deer—Don Juan tells Carlos two stories about spirit or magical deer (C72:66-69,101-104); see AG:**Deer.**

Lizard sewing—Carlos's macabre sewing shut of a living lizard's eyelids with a cholla-cactus needle and an agave-fiber thread (C68:78-86,113-117) was challenged by RdeM (CJ:41-43) on three grounds. One was that Carlos performed the delicate operation in the dark, never having tried it before and never having seen anyone do it; I agree that success under such unfavorable conditions is highly implausible. A second ground was RdeM's discovery in the *Handbook of South American Indians* that Peruvian sorcerers used to pin shut the eyes of toads, though the author (Rowe 1946:314) had inadvertently written *sew* when he meant *pin*, an error of diction revealingly preserved in Castaneda's account (see AG:**Lizard**); this argument also appeals to me. Recently, however, I experimented in my garden with Carlos's sewing kit and came to the conclusion that RdeM's third ground needs a little shifting. His suggestion that agave fiber is too thick to be threaded through a hole punched in a cholla thorn is at first glance true, but I found that when dried the fiber yields fine strands that could *conceivably* be so threaded. Nevertheless, these materials are still inappropriate for what purports to be an Indian ritual and not a one-time laboratory demonstration of what can be done with unsuitable materials at the limits of their utility. The cholla thorn is very narrow indeed, which makes punching or notching it before threading most problematical; it also bends or breaks under very little pressure, which makes it almost useless as a needle, particularly if one is going to sew leather. A Sonoran Indian could easily, and would certainly, have found more practical tools for his ritual, if he and his ritual actually existed.

Lest some quick-thinking authenticator of don Juan triumphantly retort that Carlos and don Juan must have used the fiber *and attached thorn* of the agave rather than the unworkable combination of agave fiber and cholla thorn, let me say that this retort must fail. Neither Carlos, Castaneda, nor don Juan could have confused the all-agave instrument actually used by Indians (see AG:**Bean-c**) with the imaginary agave-cholla combination used by Carlos and don Juan, because each kind of instrument is explicitly described in *The Teachings* (C68:50,80). Nor could Carlos or don Juan have used the all-agave instrument to sew lizards' eyelids, because the agave thorn is much too thick and would destroy the eyelid on the first pass.

Richard de Mille   **6**

39 "Validity is not Authenticity"—Much of the credit, though none of the blame, for the contents of this chapter belongs to my gracious and patient correspondent Paul Heelas, who founded the *Journal of the Anthropological Society of Oxford* in 1970 and currently lectures on the anthropology of religion at the University of Lancaster. The opinions given here differ at several points from those of Paul Heelas, but their development and expression were greatly aided by our exchange of some 9000 words from April to November of 1978 on the question, What is truth in ethnography?

Hired leeches—Ron Fisher 1973. *Snow Leopard*—Matthiessen 1978:326; pages 55-56 take don Juan's Zen or Tibetan teaching for a sign of prehistoric cultural diffusion rather than of Castaneda's reading; see AG:**David-Neel, Govinda.** Carl Rogers—1973:386; his comments were delivered on 2 Sept 1972. *New Age*—1975. Seeds of doubt—Strachan 1977; MacCracken 1977; RdeM 1977b. Margolis—1976:231-232.

A big difference—Castaneda's fans, wrote Michael Mason (1975), "do not seem to care about what is actually a momentous question: are Castaneda's claims true or false? If Castaneda really witnessed the events he describes, this is a fact of extraordinary importance for mankind." Mason wondered at the fans' "refusal to treat the writings as statement rather than stimulus." "You should read Castaneda when you're stoned," one of them advised him.

40 Natural mind—First 1974a:35; compare Weil 1972:126-129. Thefts—Bly 1978; Harner 1978; see also Evers, Wilk, & Bly 1978; AG:**Harner.** Books read—See these authors by name in the Alleglossary. Parallels—AG:**Burial, Danger, Gait.**

42 Gorman—1978;171; having apparently read *Castaneda's Journey* and found there "some persuasive arguments" that "don Juan's teachings are pure fantasy," and having read five books by Castaneda, Gorman could still say (172): "It is this author's personal belief that Carlos has given a fairly accurate account of things that have happened to him, rather than written a novel." Sapir—AG:**Description.**

Psychodelic—Coined by neuropsychiatrist Humphrey Osmond (who kindly supplied references to his originating article, "A review of the clinical effects of psychomimetic agents," *Annals of the New York Academy of Sciences*, 14 March 1957, 66:418-434, and to Letter 744 in the *Letters of Aldous Huxley*, Harper & Row 1970:795), the term *psychedelic* has been called a malformation, since the Greek root for *show* or *make visible* is *del* (not *edel*) and the combining form of *psyche* is not *psyche-* but *psycho-*.

R. E. Schultes (in Furst 1972:4) uses *psychodelic*, a term I have adopted for contexts I judge to be normative, but as malformed as it surely is, *psychedelic* cannot be so easily got rid of, and I have retained it wherever its historical connotations or referents are compelling. De Rios's book *Visionary Vine* (Chandler 1972, Dover 1973), for example, was subtitled *Psychedelic Healing in the Peruvian Amazon*, and on CJ:113 I referred to de Rios as "an expert on psychedelic healing," rather than identify her as a persistent subscriber to the don Juan hoax; since she has objected to that anonymous treatment, calling it "cowardly" (telephone conversation 25 March 1978), whereas I had intended to be chivalrous, I take this opportunity to accede to her wishes. Ruck and others (1979) propose the terms *entheogen* and *entheogenic*, from the Greek *entheos*, "god within," for vision-producing drugs that have figured in shamanic or religious rites; loosely, *entheogen* could be applied to non-traditional drugs producing similar alterations of consciousness.

De Rios—1972a:149, "Casteñeda, effect" *sic*. Books read by Castaneda—For likely examples, see AG:**Crack, Face, Harner, Klüver, Pozas, Peyote, Swain.** Smoking mushroom—See Pollock 1975:77 or CJ:61, 61n: Ott & Bigwood (1978:12,98) dismiss Castaneda's mushroom reports as worthless; AG:**Smoke.**

Elmer Green—Green & Green 1977:6-7, 161, 293, 313, 328; the solar-plexus-chakra connection was also made by Drury (1978:63).

43 Rank, Suzuki—See AG:**Double, Self.**

44 "Authenticity of Castaneda"—To make sure I had not mistaken Mary Douglas's meaning, I wrote to her (6 Oct 1978) outlining my critique of her essay and stating my definitions of *validity* and *authenticity*; she affirmed (letter 13 Oct 1978) that she had indeed meant authenticity in the sense of my definitions. Ojibway—Keewaydinoquay 1978.

45 Beals—1978:357,359. Weird—Wallace 1972:141.

46 Timm—1978:85,90,93; letter RdeM-Timm 31 Dec 1978, Timm-RdeM 11 Feb 1979. In his letter, Timm said his book had been written as a sociology MA thesis, which was accepted in the Department of Philosophy at Westfälische-Wilhelms-Universität, Münster, in the spring of 1978 and published by the author in September 1978. It was written, Timm said, not (as I had suggested in my letter) to treat the phenomenology and occult significance of Castaneda's books, but to assert their significance for Western science and to analyze the arrogant presumptions and ingrained ignorance that keep Westerners from understanding Castaneda. "I want," Timm said, "to uncover the foul areas of my own culture with the help of his work."

47 Heelas—1972:141. Low marks—Letters Duerr-RdeM 8 Nov 1978, 10 March 1979; Timm reviews Duerr 1978b in *Kulturmagazin* [Bremen], Mar 1979 (3):51-53.

Hans Peter Duerr—Born 1943, studied ethnology at Vienna and Heidelberg, where his dissertation on the theory of consciousness in philosophy was accepted in 1971. Since 1975 he has taught ethnology at the University of Zürich. Currently a visiting professor at the University of Kassel, Duerr assures me that his encounter with the Tewa *yerbatero* is authentic, not a parody of C68:1, C72:18-19. Citations are from Duerr 1978b:9, 289-290, 128-132, 137-138. Review by Vollmann (1979). Carlos Etic—See CJ:72-76.

48 Rocks from the moon—Suzanne B. Siegel, letter 25 May 1978; C74:270.

50 von Däniken—Quoted 1973:1; debunked by Story 1976, Krupp 1978.

51 Prediction a waste of time—This does not mean that a doctoral committee is always at the mercy of a dishonest candidate. If serious doubts of authenticity arise for any reason, the burden of proof must be on the candidate, from whom the committee can demand direct evidence of authentic provenance, such as fieldnotes, photographs, correspondence, and independent witnesses. Authentic fieldwork should leave *some* traces. Sapir's social world—See CJ:75-76 or Mandelbaum 1949:569-574.

Rope trick—Ironically, the authenticity of Professor Pilcz's story is itself in doubt, since the report of it published by von Urban (1958:184) does not match the more entertaining report published by Puharich (1962:41-42,45), though Puharich says he got the story privately from von Urban, whose "shorter"—he does not say, "conflicting"—published version he acknowledges. Eric Dingwall (1974) gives a most interesting survey of the rope-trick legend, which goes back at least to the year 1568 and has appeared in many versions since. Intending the story only as a formal illustration of categories of reality, I have incorporated a few colorful details from earlier reports to flesh out the brief accounts given by Puharich and von Urban. See also Bharati 1974, for the ontology of psychic phenomena in Hinduism and Buddhism.

52 Ted Serios—Eisenbud (1967) presents impressive evidence that Serios could occasionally produce extraneous images on film inside a camera by inexplicable and apparently anomalous means. Serios did not make any paranormal movies, however. Film as normal standard—Compare J. J. Smith 1974:316. Paramount reality—James 1896, Chapter 21, "The perception of reality"; Schutz 1964:135-136; CJ:119-121.

53 Tart—1975: Chapter One. Schutz—1964:152. Influence of phenomenology—Palmer 1977; Armstrong 1979; Graves quoted from Strachan 1979:91; Letters RdeM 17 Jan 1979, T. Graves 30 Jan 1979; Harris 1979:319-324.

54 Turnbull—Barth & others 1974-1975: especially 101 (Barth), 354 (Turnbull), 345 (McCall), 355,356 (Turnbull), 353 (Mark); Crapanzano 1973:473-477, 481; for a possibly closer approach to validity, see Colin Turnbull, "Rethinking the Ik: A functional non-social system," in Charles D. Laughlin Jr & Ivan A. Brady, editors, *Extinction and Survival in Human Populations*, Columbia U. 1978:49-75.

55 Goldschmidt—Preuss 1978:56; see also CJ:81-83; DJP: Chapter 13, and introduction to the Alleglossary. Tonal and nagual—See AG:**Tonal, Nagual, Beyond, Self-b;** DJP: Chapter 42.

56 Amerindian explanation of nature—Furst 1976:159. Abandoned anthropology—Compare Preuss 1978:54. Yaqui way—RdeM 1979d; Spicer 1969; Beals 1977a, 1978; Kelly in Moises & others 1971:xxxiv. See also Basso 1973; La Barre 1975:271-275 or in Noel 1976:41; Aberle 1969; Madsens 1971:80. Simon & Schuster 1977. Disclaimers—C68:5; C72:8. Round trips—Beals 1978:357-358. Abandoned Beals—In those days, a candidate needed no one's permission to fire his chairman; today at UCLA permission is needed; this is known as closing the Gate of Power after Coyote has PhleD.

57 Stockholder—C74:162. Sorcerer—Beals (1978:357-358) also made it clear don Juan was not a shaman, since he cured no one and served no community with his magic. "Sew"—See AG:**Lizard.** Smoking mushrooms—See note above. Invalid content—See AG:**Govinda, Mescalito, Waterfall.** I am not saying here that levitation is impossible; I am saying Castaneda's report of waterfall levitation is not matched by similar reports from other anthropologists; the closest match is Myerhoff's report (1974:44-46), which does not include levitation.

58 "Jívaro Souls"—Harner 1962; see AG:**Harner-h-j.** Debunked for the wrong reason—Compare Peters 1977; RdeM 1977d; Beals 1977b. Truzzi—1978; I have dichotomized Truzzi's proposed scales.

59 Contradictions in *Second Ring*—RdeM 1978b. *She*—by H. Rider Haggard, Chapter Three; CJ:32; Keen 1972:92 or in Noel 1976:77; for intellectual don Juan, or "Indian don," see CJ:56-57. Apparently a subscriber to both the fallacy of limited inventiveness and the genuineness of Carlos-Naïf, anthropologist Roy Wagner (see AG:**Don Genaro**) said (letter 11 May 1979) he could more easily believe don Juan and La Gorda existed than that the "garrulous and extroverted" Castaneda had made them up.

60 Mysterious white man—See *Fate*, May 1979, 32(5/350):101, advertisement.

61 Prima facie evidence of fraud—Compare Zuckerman 1977:97. Custodian of data—The recently discovered Cyril Burt fraud has made this issue salient in psychology (Bryant & Wortman 1978; Dorfman 1978). Suspicious chairman—Beals 1978:357.

62 Naïve successors—Beals quoted by Strachan 1979:91. Scotoma—A tribe of invisible Indians.

63 Needham—1978:74-76.

65 Clifford Irving—Recalling Irving's fake biography of Howard Hughes, Bruce Cook (1973) quipped that the apparently unwriterly Castaneda may have gotten Irving to help write his anthromances.

67 California Coyote—Alexander 1964:227; for more of the passage, see CJ:104.

Soul-Catcher—See AG: **Spirit-Catcher.** "Soul Catcher" Illustration drawn (for hire) by Linda Trujillo from the photograph (Furst 1965:36); drawing copyright ©1980 by Richard de Mille.

"Bow Drum"—Drawn (for hire) by Schlesinger from a photograph furnished by Barbara Myerhoff; drawing copyright ©1980 by Richard de Mille. The photograph shows Ramón Medina raising his left foot over the sacred fire, not shown in the drawing. For explanation of what he is doing, see AG: **Spirit-Catcher.** Another photograph of the bow-drum may be seen on Furst 1972:147.

Richard de Mille   7

68 "Ethnomethodallegory"—In writing this essay, I have benefited greatly from the advice of Stephen O. Murray, who is not to blame for any of the opinions or errors.

University editors—CJ:78. Castaneda as EMer (ethnomethodologist)— Douglas (DJP:26); McFerran (writing as Farren 1974:273); Littleton 1976:149 ; Duerr 1978b:324. Harris (1979:319-324) recognizes Castaneda as an ethnomethodological phenomenologist. At Irvine, Castaneda interpreted don Juan's sorcery "from a phenomenological or 'ethnomethodological' perspective" (Rueger 1973:75). History of EM (EthnoMethodology)—Mullins 1973; Murray 1979b; McKinney & Tiryakian 1970; Gouldner 1970; Garfinkel & Sacks 1970; Mehan & Wood 1975:206 (rebellion).

69 World of the We—Schutz 1967:171. Realities equally real—Mehan & Wood 1975:31. Breaching procedures—Garfinkel 1967:46,55; Gouldner 1970:391-395; Mehan & Wood 1975:26-27, 110-113; dialogue by RdeM.

70 Sociologists react to EM—Gidlow 1972 (old practices); Coleman in Swanson & others 1968 (incompetency); Gouldner 1970:393 (sadistic), 394-395 (countercultural insult).

71 Still simmering—Mehan & Wood 1975:210-211,238; Murray 1979a,b; Silverman 1975; compare Armstrong 1979. Mandell—1975; Arnold J. Mandell is Professor of Psychiatry, Neurosciences, Physiology, and Pharmacology at the University of California Medical School, San Diego, and author of *The Nightmare Season* and *Coming of Middle Age.* Invention as ethnography—Murray 1979a:192. Permeability of realities— Mehan & Wood 1975:27-31.

72 Chagnon—1968;1969. First word—"Manolo" (Schneebaum 1969:3), the name of a man to whom Schneebaum was erotically attracted before meeting the Akarama. Book as breaching experiment—Mehan & Wood 1975:31. RdeM's breaching experiment—Mehan's fellow sociologist Stephen Murray attempted to elicit the same information (letter from Murray to Mehan, 1 Dec 1978), with no success.

73 Since earliest childhood—Compare Schneebaum 1979:73-75,104. *Wild Man*—Schneebaum 1979:1,31,28,42; called hackneyed pornography by anthropologist Vincent Crapanzano (1979).

Amarakaeri—Thomas R. Moore's dissertation at the New School for Social Research is titled *The White Peace in Madre de Dios* and is an ethnological and ethnohistorical study of the Amarakaeri (also called the "Mashco," as by Chagnon, 1969). Until recently, Moore says, the Amarakaeri were the most isolated of seven subgroups of a distinctive ethnolinguistic population that calls itself the Harakmbut; at present they are being overrun by a gold rush and may not last much longer as an ethnically distinct people. Though the tribe has not been known to have any chiefs, Moore adds, Dominican missionaries have erroneously called some Amarakaeri individuals "chief," a title Schneebaum gives to Yoreitone, an Amarakaeri whose actual name he uses (1969:78). Compare Robert Carneiro's comments on Amahuaca chiefs (DJP:95).

74 Disclaimers—Schneebaum 1969:viii,17; 1970:viii. Manolo beheaded—Schneebaum 1969:143.

75 Fabricate it all—Mandell 1975:69. Process vs product—"Ethnomethodology is not concerned with the truth value of statements about the world except as phenomena. It tries to determine the practices that make any statement true" (Mehan & Wood 1975:114).

My EM—Mehan & Wood 1975:238,3 (quoted); "Ethnomethodology cannot be captured by description. It is a form of life to be lived" (6); "rather than analyze an activity for its truth value, the researcher learns to do it" (228); "Castaneda, like Zimmerman and Wieder, organizes a 'nonordinary' reality into a coherent system of knowledge" (18). In the first of these four citations (see my text), the implication is inescapable that Mehan and Wood regard Castaneda not merely as a provider of data to support EM but as a "practitioner" of EM; they do not seem to recognize him as an allegorist of EM, which is a very special kind of practitioner.

Agnes—Garfinkel 1967:116-185,285-288; quotes from pages: 285, 288, 121, 285, 288; for critiques of this case see: Coleman in Swanson & others 1968:127-128, Gidlow 1972:400-401.

77 Yaqui shamanism—Garfinkel & Sacks 1970:349. Reflexivity—Don Juan's reaction to Carlos illustrates reflexivity of analysis, say Mehan & Wood (1975:19).

78 Is all this true?—Compare C72:230. EM indifference—Garfinkel & Sacks 1970:337,345; AG:**Folly.**

79 Not concerned with lies—Compare C71:40 and note Process vs product, above. Eating snake—C72:76. Chided anthropologists—Garfinkel & Sacks 1970:364-365. Use of fieldnotes—C72:8,10; also CJ:47-48.

80 Learning don Juan's language—CJ:25,29. Difficulty of saying in so many words—"Meaning has been rendered as I understood it [but inevitably] deflected by my own attempts" (C68:143). Parody—C68:154,161; Garfinkel & Sacks 1970:338,341; these 1970 examples are not worse than Garfinkel's earlier writing, where numerous unEnglish phrases pop up, such as: "interrogating actual contents" and "persuade consensus and action" (Garfinkel 1967:24).

81 A.F.C. Wallace—In Swanson & others 1968:125. Straightforward sentences—For example, the first text paragraph on Garfinkel 1967:26, as well as various descriptions of data collections. Meaningless tasks—For example, Carlos's seed grinding (C68:89) and absurd chores (C74:233). Garfinkel (1967:29) wrote: "I had required them to take on the impossible task of 'repairing' the essential incompleteness of *any* set of instructions. . . ." Castaneda wrote: "He said that . . . the act of dealing directly with the 'nagual' . . . was . . . an unattainable task as a task per se" (C74:234); "he explained that the task . . . is usually a sort of farfetched life situation [like pretending to be a boarder in one's own family home, or demanding to be seated by a customer in a restaurant—RdeM], which the apprentice is supposed to get into as a means of permanently affecting his view of the world" (C74:244). Confrontation—C68:131-140; CJ:170-171.

82 Special consensus—Schutz 1967:171; 1964:143. Many Schutzian parallels between don Juan and Don Quixote were found by sociologist Robert W. Maloy, who recognized *Don Quixote* as a novel but took the don Juan books to be "field studies" (1977:34). Maloy did not accept my invitation (letter 28 April 1978) to recast his discussion in this volume assuming both Cervantes and Castaneda to be fiction writers. Mather (1979) also failed to distinguish story-telling from social science.

Invisible world—Gouldner 1970:392; C71:131; C72:298. Bracketing—Garfinkel & Sacks 1970:342-343; C74:87,89; Joseph Chilton Pearce (1974, 1975:218) thought the ally might be the right-brain self waiting to be re-united with the left-brain self. Making out what he says—Garfinkel & Sacks 1970:344; C68:6; C72:14; the relevance of C68:6 to EM was noted by Silverman (1975:32).

83 Doomed from the start—C68:143; Garfinkel 1967:30; Silverman (1975:58-61) reaffirms the futility of the Structural Analysis as an attempt to explain what don Juan had said; see also CJ:68-72. Pathetic denial—Riesman 1972:10 or in Noel 1976:48.

A whole book—*Reading Castaneda* (Silverman 1975); though severely criticized by Kenneth Minogue later in this volume, Silverman's book is quite readable and will repay reading by the serious student of ethnomethodallegory. Fieldnotes—Beals 1978:357. Poor student—William Lessa, Letter 25 Sept 1978. Fiction publisher—John Hitchcock, telephone conversation 16 Sept 1978. Encouraged by Meighan—C68:ix.

84 Doesn't like to be saddled—C71:121. Broken watches—Lévano 1973. EMers lured out of sacred swamp—Preuss 1978:55.

Edgerton & EM—Garfinkel & Sacks (1970:340) cite Edgerton's *Drunken Comportment* (co-authored with Craig MacAndrew) as an EM study; Mullins (1973:200) says the book typifies "what ethnomethodologists would call 'ethnomethodological work'" and lists it as one of five early "major publications of ethnomethodological research." Edgerton had received both B.A. and Ph.D. in anthropology at UCLA, where he not only was influenced by Garfinkel but had also been a student of Walter Goldschmidt, who would later commend Castaneda's *Teachings* to the University Press and write its laudatory foreword. In 1973 Edgerton and Garfinkel signed Castaneda's dissertation. Two years earlier, the second edition of Goldschmidt's textbook, *Exploring the Ways of Mankind*, appeared containing passages from *The Teachings*, titled in the textbook, "A Yaqui Man of Knowledge," in spite of the fact that Spicer (1969) had said *Teachings* had no basis in Yaqui culture. Goldschmidt said that in preparing his book of readings he had been "particularly helped" by Edgerton (Goldschmidt 1971:xiii). So far as I have learned, the only other anthropology textbook to include a passage from Castaneda's works is *Other Fields, Other Grasshoppers*, by Lewis L. Langness, who joined the UCLA faculty in 1973. Langness also acknowledges help from Edgerton, who, he said, had been "more than encouraging from the beginning" (Langness 1977:xiii). In 1975 I wrote to Edgerton asking him to "help clarify Castaneda's unusual graduate career and evaluate his contribution to scientific anthropology and public education," but received no reply. If Edgerton's commendations were instrumental in persuading both Goldschmidt and Langness to anthologize *The Teachings* in anthropology textbooks, occultists may wish to note the fact that each of these anthologists acknowledged his influence on page xiii.

Ranking anthropologist—There was only one other anthropologist on the committee (the all-university editorial committee of the Academic Senate), Alan Dundes, of UC Berkeley; there were no sociologists (letter from the Secretary of the Academic Senate, 10 Aug 1977).

Small team—Since I am mainly interested in the committee that accepted *Ixtlan* as a dissertation, I have not included Theodore D. Graves, a behavioral anthropologist who taught in the UCLA anthropology department from Fall 1967 to December 1971 and served on Castaneda's Ph.D. advisory committee during the last two years of that period. Castaneda's written Ph.D. examinations were administered in Spring 1970 by Newman, Meighan, and Graves; his oral examination in June 1970 by those three and Garfinkel and Bolle (Walter Goldschmidt, 15 Nov 1978).

On 8 February 1977 I sent Graves an article (Strachan 1977) in which he was said to have been the "prime mover" who had persuaded his colleagues to take Castaneda seriously. Graves replied (15 Feb 1977): "I am delighted to accept any credit which the Department may now want to give me for having moved them to reconsider his case on its merits. . . . Castañeda was accepted for candidacy not on the basis of his popular books, but on a set of written and oral examinations, which I helped to grade. . . . In these he demonstrated what we already knew: that he was neither naive nor poorly read. Beyond that stage, however, I cannot comment. Since I left the country in December 1971, I know nothing about the debates which may have taken place concerning the appropriateness or acceptability of *Ixtlan* as a Ph.D. thesis; when I left Castañeda was promising something quite different."

Abstract—C73:v-vii; for a more detailed description of the dissertation document, see CJ:67-68 and notes therefor. Ethnoscience—McKinney & Tiryakian 1970:255; Murray 1979b; "Professor Volpe," who defined *emic/etic* for me earlier (CJ:73), now asks me to correct his statement of the birth of ethnoscience from the early 1960s at Harvard to the mid-1950s at Yale; Murray (1979b) concurs.

85 Sapir—See   AG:**Agreement,   Description,   Order.** Acknowledgements—C68:ix. *Emic/etic*—Letter from William Bright, 19 Sept 1975; C68:93; C72:38-39. "Carlitos and don Juan"—CJ:62-63. Getting inside the native's head—Compare CJ:72-76.

86 *Member*—Garfinkel & Sacks 1970:342; C72:9,14,296-298; C73:v-vii. Chua (1974:252) cites C72 on membership and reflexivity. Silverman (1975:68) notes the correspondence. Tobias, Mehan and Wood believed (1975:228), became a member when he accepted the Akaramas' moral facts. First 12 pages of dissertation, C73:v-vii, 1-9.

Perceptual metaphor—Wilber (1977:230-231) cites Castaneda on membership, giving don Juan credit for Sapir's notion (see AG:**Agreement**) and taking Castaneda's perceptual metaphor at face value to confirm neo-Whorfian exaggerations of the influence of language on perception; for a corrective view, see Bornstein 1975.

Normal scholarly expectations—Compare Paul Riesman's reaction (CJ:68-69). Imaginary sorcerers—Pablito & Nestor (C71:123), Eligio (C71:95), nameless (C72:243), Vicente (C71:46). "Sorcery"—Occasionally don Juan refers in passing to elements of conventional sorcery, such as divining (C68:46) or killing with magical projectiles, an unworthy practice of lesser brujos (C68:7-9).

87 Tape recordings—C71:21,76. Distribution forbidden—CJ:67.

88 Not an assertion—Chisholm & Feehan 1977:152.

89 Garfinkel's membership challenged—Mullins 1973:198. Hopelessness—Mehan & Wood 1975:210-211. More as disciples than as exploiters—Here I assume Mehan and Wood took don Juan at face value not because they were stupid, careless, or cynical, but because they were blinded by enthusiastic commitment to the principles of EM. Blindness arising from commitment to theory will be mentioned again in Chapter 12. World corresponds with knowledge—Mehan & Wood (1975:110) were presumably speaking of a social world, while don Juan (C72:227) was speaking of a physical world or non-social world. Disrupting routines—C72:100; Mehan & Wood 1975:209. Give up present life—C72:33,46; Mehan & Wood 1975:229; compare Luke 14:33; 9:61-62. I have struggled—Castaneda 1977b:34. Knew how to lie—C72:34. Better ways of being a man—Mehan & Wood (1975:207) are quoting approvingly from Feyerabend's summary of hermeneutic-dialectic doctrine, which they say was EM's theoretical mother, whereas logico-empiricism was EM's methodological father; the child EM, they say, is an activity that transcends the parents, both of which reject it because it does not prefer one parent to the other. Simmel—1950:313; see also DJP:8 and C68:xii.

90 Silverman—1975:83. Re-viewing the EM enterprise—Dolby (1979) offers a conceptual scheme that may be helpful in understanding deviant science at various levels, such as ethnomethodology and ethnomethodallegory, as well as the active defense of Castaneda by a few anthropologists, including Wilk, Harner, Littleton, Staniford, Goldschmidt, and Douglas.

Tobias Schneebaum   8
91 Aung San—Schneebaum 1979:157, slightly revised.
92 American anthropologist—Though the author has heard this story of ethnographic bungling several times in West New Guinea, it appears to be apocryphal. The anthropologist named in the original version flatly denied it, offering a quite different, very ordinary reason for leaving the village; a knowledgeable colleague supported the denial.—RdeM.

Robert L. Carneiro   9
94 "Chimera of the Upper Amazon"—Notes for this chaper were prepared by RdeM, using page citations supplied by author Carneiro. In the United States, *Wizard of the Upper Amazon* has appeared in two editions, the first from Atheneum in 1971 (here coded "W1"), the second from Houghton-Mifflin in 1974 (coded "W2"; where page numbers do not differ, the code will simply be "W"). Oddly, the two editions have different formal authorship, though their substance is mostly the same. In the first edition (Córdova-Rios & Lamb 1971) Lamb is the second author, but in the second edition (Lamb 1974) he is the sole author, relating "the story of Manuel Córdova-Rios." Lamb's promotion to sole author seems not to be purely a matter of book marketing, since certain discrepancies between the editions suggest creative writing more than editorial correction. Page W2:xvii grants Lamb greater license than the corresponding W1:ix to render Córdova's random recollections "in narrative form." W2:xvi says Lamb learned Córdova's trail-marking technique "much later" than a certain incident (W1:ix, W2:xvi) of improper ayahuasca preparation, but W1:vi puts the same learning shortly *before* that improper preparation. W2:199 adds president, ambassador, and judges to healing clients served by Córdova. W2:200 says Córdova keeps in touch with the tribe through his dreams, but W1 did not mention such keeping in touch.

Favorable reviews—*Scientific:* de Rios 1972b,c; *Popular: Booklist*, 1 July 1971, 67(20):890; *Library Journal*, 1 March 1971, 96(5):827; July 1971, 96(13):2378; *Time*, 8 March 1971, 97(10):82. Córdova identifies his tribe as Amahuaca—W1:vii, W2:200.

95 Chief Xumu—W:14,36,41,103,114,115; puberty 134; marriages 135; adultery 139; compare Thomas Moore's comment on Amarakaeri "chiefs" (DJP:73n).

96 Conical hut—W:15,17. Penis tied—W:22,137. Short hair—W:40. Lances—W:8,35,134,144. Bird spears—W:57. Snares—W:35. Basketry traps—W:35. Hunting territories—W:34,140. Trophy skins—W:55,63,74. Baptism—W:20. Wedding—W:132. Incorporation—W:21-22. Fermented beverages—W:17,85,113,135,166. Tobacco palaver—W:82,150,171.

97 Victims of witchcraft cremated—W:119. Ashes buried—W:119. Mummify—W:162,163. Cannibalism—W:153,171. Moon myth—W:116. Tooth blackening—W:22. Smoking pipes—W:169. Hunting blinds—W:52.

98 Córdova's age—Both editions of *Wizard* say Córdova was born "in 1887" and began his adventure when he was "only fifteen years old" (W1:4, W2:5), which would have been in 1902; but W1:3 says the adventure began in 1907. The discrepancy disappears from W2:3, not corrected by a precise "1902" but swept under the narrative rug by a vague "over fifty years ago." According to Lamb (telephone call to RdeM, 29 Jan 1980) Córdova died on 22 Nov 1978, "his ninety-first birthday" (1978 minus 1887 equals 91). Lamb said he has written a new book, about Córdova's career as a healer.

On 3 March 1980 Lamb sent me his "Response to R. L. Carneiro's Review," a spirited counterattack based on Lamb's examination of "the extensive anthropological collection of the New York Public Library," where Lamb found "source material in French, German, Spanish, Portuguese and English" that convinced him Córdova was more reliable than Carneiro, whose several months of fieldwork among the Amahuaca Lamb thought both too little and too late to refute Córdova's much earlier and longer captivity. Since Lamb's manuscript did not come in time for inclusion or treatment in this volume, I urged him to submit it to the *American Anthropologist*, where at this writing it is under consideration and where I hope to see it published along with Carneiro's inevitable rejoinder.

RdeM

99 *Library Journal*—Dennis Lewis 1977. *Booklist*—1977. Innocent victim—CJ:83; roared, kicked (C74:50). Warning—RdeM 1978b:114.

Sanford Berman, Head Cataloger at the Hennepin County Library (Edina, Minnesota), director of an Alternative Cataloging-in-Publication Program, and for six years editor of the *HCL Cataloging Bulletin*, prized alike by cataloguers, reference librarians, and lexicographers, has written extensively on cataloguing, intellectual freedom, the alternative press, Africana, and other library related topics. His monograph, *Prejudices and Antipathies: A Tract on LC Subject Heads Concerning People* (Scarecrow

1971), provoked intense debate among librarians and inspired substantial subject-cataloguing reforms.

Sanford Berman   10
100 "Cataloging Castaneda"—For earlier versions see Sanford Berman, *HCL Cataloging Bulletin*, Sep/Oct 1978, (36):38-39 and Nov/Dec 1978, (37):1-3, where RdeM's letters of 18 May and 28 Aug 1978 are more fully quoted. Rather reply—Letter of 18 Aug 1978.
103 *Ixtlan* drug theme—RdeM letter to S. Berman, 28 Aug 1978.

Richard de Mille   11
104 "Publishing the Factoids"—The tone of *A Separate Reality* "is so perfect for the book," wrote William Irwin Thompson (1972:26), "that it makes the third person pretentiousness of Norman Mailer seem clumsy by comparison." Let me balance the account here by giving Mailer credit for the title of this chapter and for contributing a very useful term to the language, for I understand Mailer invented *factoid* to signify the purely hypothetical "fact" adduced by an author to support his pet thesis. I extend the meaning to cover whole books.

   I'm José, You're José—Liebmann-Smith 1978. *In His Image*—Rorvik 1978. Mintz—Gwynne 1978. Markert—*Science News* 1978. Lippincott—Gwynne 1978. *The Clone*—Gwynne 1978. Shettles—*Science News* 1979; Reuter 9 March 1978. Simon & Schuster—*Science News* 1978; Associated Press 10 March 1978. *Amityville Horror*—Anson 1977; author quoted by Slattery 1979:25; the book has been thoroughly debunked by Morris (1978) and Moran & Jordan (1978).
105 De Ropp—1979:362. *New York Times* reviews—Simmons 1968; Young 1968; Jellinek 1971; Thompson 1972; La Barre 1975:271-272 (or a shorter version in Noel 1976:40-42); Jellinek 1972; Riesman 1972; Barthelme 1973; First 1974a:38,35; Leonard 1977; L. Ron Hubbard is the inventor of a religion called Scientology; Frank Herbert, author of *Dune*, is a science fiction writer; Bly 1978. Reviewing *Separate Reality* at about the same time as La Barre, but presumably unread by *Times* editors, S. T. Crump (1973) said: "The blurb, according to which 'The book is one of the most original and sensitive works of anthropology and ethnography ever written,' is misleading to the point of absurdity. It is not a serious anthropological study at all."
106 *Saturday Review*—Levi 1971; Kanon 1972; LeClair 1978.
107 *New York Review of Books*—Leach 1969; Lobsang 1956. *Publishers Weekly*—1968; 1969; 1971a,b; 1972; 1974; 1976; 1977b; interview by Freilicher 1972.

   Other media reviews—*Harper's* followed Gwyneth Cravens's (1973a, 1974) two professions of faith in don Juan with Jeffrey Burke's (1978) brief, sarcastic dismissal of *Second Ring* and Liebmann-Smith's (1978) satire.

Time took Castaneda at face value (Hughes Nov 1972) until investigation turned up his spurious autobiography (*Time* 5 March 1973); editor Hughes had it both ways, however, by adding: "A strong case can be made that the don Juan books are of a different order of truthfulness from Castaneda's pre-don Juan past" (*Time* 1973:44/1976:105); *Time* subsequently did not review *Tales of Power* or *Second Ring*. *Esquire's* one awe-struck tour through the separate reality was partly balanced by three skeptical letters two months later (*Esquire* March 1971; May 1971, 75(5/450):14). *Psychology Today* began with a straight-faced interview by Sam Keen (1972), continued with Joyce Carol Oates's (1974) appreciation of Castaneda's fiction, which she thought must be based on some authentic mystical experience, and concluded with Keen's (1977) disgusted review of *Second Ring* and his guess that don Juan was Castaneda's imaginary playmate (compare CJ:160). *New Yorker* took a swipe at Castaneda in a parody by Calvin Tomkins (1973). "The secret of popular success," said *The Spectator* (Ackroyd 1975), "is to say conventional things so baldly and so often that the ignorant and the innocent will assume them to be original"; *Tales of Power* "merely regurgitates the conventional mystical attitudes." *Tales of Power* "is not a work of mysticism," said *New Statesman* (Mason 1975); "this is Sartre with the brim of a sombrero pulled down over his face."

108 Reviews of CJ—Beardsley 1977,1979; *CoEvolution Quarterly* 1977; Crowder 1976; *Cultural Information Service* 1976; Drury 1977,1978; Fadiman 1977; Farren 1977; Finnegan 1977; Gill 1977; Gover 1977a; Inglis 1978; Jack 1977; La Barre 1979; Laird 1977; McAllister 1978; Madsen 1977; McFerran 1977; Melton 1977; Murray 1979; *New Age* 1977; Noel 1977; Preuss 1978; *Publishers Weekly* 1976; Reichbart 1978b; Reno 1977; Rickard 1977; Screeton 1979; Shere 1977; Staniford 1977b; Strachan 1977, 1979; Truzzi 1977; *Zetetic Scholar* 1979; Wilk 1977c.

Quotation from don Juan—Schneebaum 1969:vii. Jack Collins—1979. Carneiro neglected—Córdova-Rios & Lamb 1971:xi. *Seven Arrows*—Storm 1972; Moore 1973.

109 Artaud—1976:52,15,14; see also AG:**Artaud;** gather peyote C68:63. Four-million donfiction books—*Publishers Weekly* 1977a. Korda—1975; "Not a manual for manipulation," protested the International Entrepreneurs Association (1979:32) ad for Korda's *Power!*; Bourne 1978; Tolkien (Korda 1975:258); *buita* defined on CJ:53; *nakam* ears (Johnson 1962). Remainders—Publishers Central Bureau *Catalogue*, Oct 1978; C74 in Marboro *Catalogue*, March 1978.

110 *Life*—Darrach 1971. *Sunday Times*—Brien 1975. *Booklist*—1977. Mexican publisher—Letter 22 Sep 1978 from Fondo de Cultura Económica (Avenida de la Universidad 975, Mexico 12 DF); see Tovar 1974-76.

Charley Trick—"Charles Trick" is a fair translation of Castaneda's original name, Carlos Arana; see CJ:26n names; CJ:139-140. *Siete Flechas*—Seven Arrows. Don D—See AG:**Don Q.** *¿Dónde está?*—Where is he?

111 Night has fallen at noon—Lament of the Incas at the death of Atau Huallpa; see CJ:25. Wizard of Westwood—Not, of course, the famous UCLA basketball coach, but a parallel to the Wizard of Sussex, Charles Dawson.

Richard de Mille   **12**

112 "Uclanthropus Piltdunides Castanedae"—Which may be translated: "UCLA-Man Son-of-Piltdown Belonging-to-Castaneda" or, loosely, "don Juan, son of Piltdown." *Down* is related to *dune*.

Biggest hoax—Truzzi 1977; Melton (1977) made the same point, but so far as I know, one Paul Zakaras was the first to make the connection (letter in *Esquire*, May 1971:14): "Don Juan is quite a find. He is probably as much a reflection of our times as Piltdown was of his." Zakaras congratulated Castaneda for bringing back the art of hoax writing, formerly practiced by such masters as Ben Franklin and Edgar Allan Poe.

Several hundred articles—Weiner 1955:204, cited by Langham 1978:182. Forgery exposed—Weiner 1955. Other possible forgers—Millar 1972; Halstead 1978; Weiner 1979; Langham 1978, 1979, letter to RdeM 15 May 1979; Gould 1979.

113 Brain as engine of evolution—Langham 1978:196. In CJ2 (ix–xii) I followed Millar by citing Smith's theory of cultural diffusion (global spread of culture from ancient Egypt) rather than his theory of brain primacy; Langham convinces me that was an error. Similarly I treated Smith and Castaneda as hoaxers trying unsuccessfully to disillusion their victims; Langham finds Smith less playful than that. Four reasons—Gould 1979; Oakley 1979.

114 Basement flooded—Rumor first reported by Strachan (1977). Theodore Graves—Strachan 1977. Make merit—Castaneda "was given a Ph.D. for all his work, not just the dissertation," said Walter Goldschmidt, quoted by Strachan (1979:91). "If we'd flunked out Carlos Castaneda, it would have been much more of a discredit to the department than granting him a degree," said Clement Meighan, quoted by Strachan (1979:91). Robert Edgerton urged Castaneda to take the manuscript of *The Teachings* to the UC Press (Preuss 1978:55). Harold Garfinkel alluded to Castaneda's work along with that of Evans-Pritchard (Garfinkel & Sacks 1970:349).

Antirationalist—"The 1960s . . . reflected a loss of faith in the type of so-called objective-rational-pragmatic thinking that Americans used to claim to do so well but which they never really mastered. . . . The objective and pragmatic values of the past were questioned by many of the young who began looking to other cultures for inspiration" (Madsen 1977). Orang's forehead—Gould 1979:44.

115 Nervous breakdown—"At one point in my apprenticeship I became profoundly depressed. I was overwhelmed with terror and gloom and thoughts about suicide"—Castaneda to Keen (1972:100/1976:89). Castaneda's descriptions of Carlos's 22 drug trips reinforced the impression that he might crack under the strain of furnishing normal proofs of his extraordinary claims. One of Castaneda's UCLA teachers and one of his committee members told me confidentially (10 Jan, 7 Feb 1978) about his psychological fragility. Rift—Turnbull, in Barth & others 1975:355. *Hoaxes*—MacDougall 1958:50,265,25.

116 Frauds—Newton (Westfall 1973); Burt (Dorfman 1978); rodent ESP (J. B. Rhine, *Journal of Parapsychology*, 1974, 38:215-225; 1975, 39: 306-325); Sloan-Kettering (Hixson 1976; Medawar 1976); in general (Zuckerman 1977). Beneficial—"Fraud, of course, may even have beneficent consequences. . . ." (Weinstein 1979:649).

Exposed by perpetrator—"[According to Charles Babbage, 19th-century mathematician] hoaxes are intended to last only for a time and then to be revealed for what they are, to the amusement of the hoaxers and the embarrassment of those taken in by them. Babbage's kind interpretation is that hoaxes are a kind of scientific practical joke and not considered seriously deviant behavior unless they are repeated" (Zuckerman 1977:133); compare CJ:34-35.

Horror of frauds—"In view of their membership in a moral community, scientists understandably prefer to assume that error rather than fraud accounts for the unreproducible results" (Zuckerman 1977:96-97). "One's mind never considers fraud as a possibility"—James D. Watson, quoted by Zuckerman (1977:98). "Lacking contrary evidence the community of scholars does well to rely on a presumption of good faith" (CJ:69); in this case, of course, the evidence was *not* lacking once CJ was published.

117 Eugene Anderson—Anderson & others 1977; Anderson teaches at the University of California, Riverside. von Däniken's nonsense—Story 1976. Sweep Piltdown under the rug—Langham 1978:182.

118 Passionately committed—See Zuckerman 1977:120-122.

Richard de Mille   **13**

119 "Sonoragate"—I am grateful to Professor Mumfurt Botcheric for suggesting the title of this chapter.

Teachings reviewed—Should Spicer (1969:321/1976:31) have suspected a hoax? Not necessarily. *The Teachings* came well recommended by a prominent colleague, and Spicer relied on the presumption of good faith among scholars (see discussion at CJ:69). *Second Ring* reviewed—RdeM 1979d. Leach—1969 or in Noel 1976.

120 Not ethnography—Compare Madsens 1971:80. Subscribers—Goldschmidt (C68:vii-viii); Edmund Carpenter (C68: dust jacket); Aberle 1969; Bean (Bean & Saubel 1972); Heelas 1972; de Rios 1972a; Furst 1972; Wilk 1972; Douglas (1973, see DJP); Riesman 1973; Harner 1973; Siskind 1973; Myerhoff 1974; Ryle 1975; A. K. Mark (in Barth & others 1975:353); Long 1976b,1977; Littleton 1976.

Doubters—Wasson 1972,1973; Basso 1973; Ochoa & Hsu (*Time*

1973:38/1976:100); La Barre 1975:272 or in Noel 1976:42. Literary descriptions—See AG:**Huxley;** CJ:94.

Joseph K. Long—Criticized Castaneda (1977:4,7-8,13,213); divination (1977:261); telepathic abilities (1976b:307); Tibetan trance running (1977:385); credited Castaneda (1976b:301; 1977:1,9,14,236,247,378-379). *Extrasensory Ecology* reviewed—RdeM 1978a.

121 Outraged—Truzzi 1977. Organizing special event—J. K. Long memoranda: 12 Feb, 13 Apr, 25 May, 11 July, 28 Sep 1978. President—Goldschmidt was President of AAA 1975-1976, Hsu 1977-1978, Spicer 1973-1974, Beals 1949-1950. Special event—*Program of the 77th Annual Meeting,* American Anthropological Association, 1978:17, Session Number 160.

122 Littleton—1976.

123 Beals's articles—1977a,b; 1978.

124 Price-Williams—Study reported by Krippner & Villoldo 1976:300-302. Millionaire—Ned Brown, quoted in *Time* 1973:36/1976:94; Simon & Schuster, quoted in *Publishers Weekly* 1977a.

125 Writers—Prospects of payment (Chapman 1978); belief in self and work: Harold Robbins has claimed on TV to believe he is a writer of the first rank.

126 Letter to Goldschmidt—The complete correspondence includes letters: (1) 23 Aug, (2) 14 Oct 1975, (3) 21 Jan, (4) 23 Jan 1976, (5) 14 Aug, (6) 8 Oct 1978, of which items 2, 3, 4, & 5 are cited here; for archive, see first note for Chapter 40.

127 Ethnography and allegory—For discussion, see AG: Introduction.

128 Patrons—Goldschmidt identified himself and six doctoral committee members: Philip Newman (the chairman), Clement Meighan, Theodore Graves (who was replaced by) Robert Edgerton (an anthropologist in the UCLA Neuropsychiatric Institute), Harold Garfinkel (of the Sociology Dept), and Kees Bolle (of the History Dept). I have sternly rejected Mumfurt Botcherie's scurrilous suggestion that this group be called the Sonoragate Seven. In fairness, one should add the name of William Bright, UCLA Professor of Linguistics and Anthropology, who confirmed to me (12 Sept 1975) that he was one of those who had advised the UC Press to publish *The Teachings* as a work of ethnography and that he still believed the advice had been correct. Graves's committee responsibility was limited, since he served only two years and left UCLA a year before Castaneda's dissertation was accepted.

129 Anderson—In Anderson & others 1977. Cook—1973.

130 Garfinkel as thesis adviser—*Time* 1973:44/1976:106; Mandell 1975; CJ:80-81. Frog—Strachan 1977:91; RdeM letter to Meighan 17 Jan 1979; Castaneda does not actually describe being a frog. Cognitive norms—Zuckerman 1977:104; Murray 1979a:191.

131 Known to anthropologists—Wilk 1977c. We possess no information—Compare AG:**Harner-p.** Strongest critique—Finnegan

1977:745. Foreword—Long (1977:13) mentioned anthropologist Edmund Carpenter (C68: dust jacket blurb) as Castaneda's second influential legitimizer; "at his own suggestion" (Preuss 1978:55-56).

132 Defended dissertation Jan 1973—Goldschmidt gave this information during his presentation. "Before Carlos C."—*Abstracts of the 77th Annual Meeting*, American Anthropological Association, 1978, Session 238; a paper by Marlene de Rios, read by a substitute, did not mention Castaneda; Michael Harner was scheduled to participate but did not attend; see also AG:**Bean.**

133 Requirements of anomalistic anthropology—AAA *Abstracts* (as above), Session 347; a long abstract was reproduced in RdeM 1979e, with one omission; first sentence should read. "treats both infrequent fieldworkers' observations and frequent informants' reports. . . ." Inconsistent reporting—A collateral point, not at issue here, is that accurate reporting can describe inconsistent social phenomena. James H. Clark—Reuven 1977; *Ishi* (Kroeber 1961); letters 22 Nov, 8 Dec 1978; objected to Yaqui don Juan (Beals 1978:357).

134 Robert Zachary—Quoted from Reuven 1977 & Mitgang 1978. Reports from three sources indicate that the man who actually copy-edited *The Teachings* (thereby making it more literate than Castaneda's subsequent books, which seem not to have been edited at all) was an editor, no longer with the UC Press, whom I have called "Clement Benedict." "Carlos has used some of my experiences in his books," Benedict told me (CJ:103). Having edited *Teachings*, Benedict then praised the book in a popular periodical, and a quote from his review was reproduced in the 1969 Ballantine paperback edition. This is called editorio-critical reflexivity.

Teachings recommended by anthropologists—Preuss (1978:55) reported that Castaneda's manuscript came to Goldschmidt with the recommendations of Meighan, Edgerton, and Garfinkel: one anthropologist in the Department, one outside it, and one sociologist. (It is useful to note that Preuss submitted his article before publication to those he had interviewed, for correction of substantive errors; though he was not sympathetic to my position, he made the corrections I sent him, and we can assume he made any corrections provided by Goldschmidt, Meighan, or Edgerton; he did not interview Garfinkel.) Anthropologist William Bright (see Note, Patrons, above) also recommended publication. Goldschmidt said he had gone to the Editorial Committee with four favorable letters in hand, but Clark said the Committee had reviewed recommendations from three anthropologists; he said nothing about a sociologist. That leaves Meighan, Edgerton, and Bright as the likely anthropological consultants. Those three and Garfinkel are the first four of six scholars thanked in Castaneda's Acknowledgments (C68:ix). The remaining two are unlikely consultants. The fifth is anthropologist Pedro Carrasco, who had already left UCLA for SUNY-Stonybrook; the sixth is anthropologist Lawrence Watson, who had just completed his Ph.D. at UCLA. According to Clark, the only member of the Editorial Committee to read Castaneda's manuscript was Goldschmidt, which means that Alan Dundes, of UC-Berkeley, the only other anthropologist on the Committee, did not read it. Zachary suggested to Mitgang that "all" members of the Anthropology Department had reacted favorably to The Teachings, but I can identify only four: Goldschmidt, Meighan, Bright, and Philip Newman (also interviewed by Preuss, 1978:55). On the other hand, we can be sure Beals and William Lessa would not have approved if consulted. (Hitchcock had left UCLA in 1966; Maquet would not arrive until 1971.) Zachary's "other anthropologists," outside the Department, could have been Edgerton and Edmund Carpenter (see Note, Foreword, above).

135 Winner for 1968—UC Press, "The last fifteen years have been good to us [advertisement]," New York Review of Books, 12 Oct 1978, 25(15):15. Competitive publisher—Reuven 1977. Popular fame dangerous—Compare Stephen Murray's essay in this volume. Bon mot—"Castaneda's only sorcery consisted of turning the University of California into an ass" (CJ:24). Don Juan as a joke—CJ:78-79.

136 Dumb move—Strachan 1979:91; RdeM letter 17 Jan 1979. Prime mover—Strachan 1977. Separate the deed from the institution—In cases of fraud, "one motive for secrecy is to protect the reputation of the organization in which the fraud was enacted" (Weinstein 1979:647). Lewis Yablonsky—Yablonsky 1975.

138 Wise words—Spoken by Walter Goldschmidt (1976:355).

140 Organized skepticism—Zuckerman 1977; Medawar 1976; Murray 1979a:190.

141 Meighan—Handwritten note, no date, August 1975.

142 Go all the way—C72:61. Let me, in turn, go all the way by admitting I made a mistake when I said (CJ:50) "pulling your leg" could not have been translated from Spanish; Juan Tovar (1976:109,135) gives the Spanish equivalent as tomándote el pelo, taking you by the hair; the error was corrected in my second edition (CJ2:xii).

143 Sonoragate-tapes correspondence—RdeM 8 Dec 1978; Long 29 Jan 1979; RdeM 3 Feb 1979; Lehman 28 Feb 1979; Long 10 March 1979.

Transcript given—By Don Strachan, whose materials public and private I cite or relay with confidence because he habitually uses a tape recorder and has in my experience consistently shown himself to be a competent, conscientious reporter. He submitted his 1979 article to those he had quoted for correction of errors; later, Victoria Cebalo of New West telephoned persons quoted to check the facts once again.

Speculation runs wild—Those who took don Juan at face value will surely not question my saying that Claire Fausse-Idée is know for her Perspicuous Fallacies (Sottise 1973), César Arañuela Burlón for his Relatos de Tontura (Fracasos Académicos 1978). I am grateful to Mumfurt Botcherie for eliciting these quotations and to Rudolph East for correcting my earlier misspelling (CJ:13) of Georg Olduvai's name.

146 All-Goddess—Bharati 1961/1970:167-170; for other works of Bharati, see References. Sex organs—Staniford 1977a. Epithets—De Mille, Bharati, & Staniford 1978:58-59.

Agehananda Bharati **14**

147 Wilk—March 1977. Praised him—Ash 1969, 1971; Hughes 1972; Kanon 1972; Levi 1971; Peter Lewis 1975; Roszak 1969; R. Sukenick 1976; Thompson 1972. Dismissed him—Ash 1974; Bly 1978; Brien 1975; Burke 1978; Leclair 1978; Leonard 1977; Liebmann-Smith 1978.

Privileged information—Like most modern philosophers, I hold that there is no privileged information, that is, no knowledge gathered by extra-mental, non-intellectual, or non-cognitive means, no revelation, no special magico-mystical insight, in short, no knowledge that is not in principle accessible to all adult human beings. ESP, if it exists at all, may well be accessible to all, and therefore not privileged, and don Juan's *seeing* may be partly ESP, but when it allows Carlos to "see things for what they really are" (C71:51) or to visit alien worlds (C77:211) it is revelation of a truth not all are privileged to know, a truth about what is. It is this revealed ontology that commends Castaneda to religionists.

Beals—1978:361. Douglas—DJP: Chapter 3. Emic/Etic—CJ:74,76.

148 Littleton—1976:146. Eclecticism—James W. Boyd (1973), who thought the don Juan books might be "fiction of the Hermann Hesse type" (360) found the following parallels: "Don Juan's techniques for stopping the world are shamanistic variations on those of the Buddhists and Taoists" (362); "a process the Buddhist calls 'turning back the wheel of life'" corresponds to don Juan's *undoing* (361); and don Juan "might just as well have said, 'Nirvana *is* samsara'" (363). For Castaneda's borrowings from David-Neel and Lama Govinda, see AG: **Ally, Erasing, Gait, Self.**—RdeM.

Newly discovered tradition—Ironically, the University of California Press advertised *The Teachings of Don Juan* on the back cover of the *American Anthropologist* June 1968, as a "revelation" of a Western counterpart of Taoism, Yoga, Vedanta and Zen.—RdeM.

Hindu monk—See Bharati, *The Ochre Robe.* Western hemisphere—Inevitably some Juanist zealot will confuse the issue by reminding us that shamanist practices like visionary use of mushrooms came to the Western hemisphere over the land bridge from Siberia. Such prehistoric cultural diffusion has nothing to do with don Juan's eclectic mysticism, fed by historic India and Tibet through the conduit of modern libraries in southern California.

149 Vivid accounts—See, for example, AG: **Swain** and CJ:59. Littleton—1976:148. Inexact *mystical*—Bharati 1972. Mystical texts—Herbert V. Guenther, *The Tantric View of Life,* Chowkhamba 1964, Shambhala 1972; Bharati, *The Tantric Tradition;* Anagarika Govinda, *Foundations of Tibetan Mysticism,* Rider (London) 1959; *The Way of the White Clouds,* Shambhala 1970, 1971.

Philip Staniford   15
151 "I Come to Praise Carlos"—Notes by RdeM. Philip Staniford is a social anthropologist with specialties in Japan, overseas migration, local level politics, primitive religion, cross-cultural cosmology, and parapsychological anthropology. He received his Ph.D. from The London School of Economics in 1967 and has done fieldwork in rural Hawaii, Brazil, Japan, India, and California. Genuine teachings—"He is trying to teach us something!" (Stillwell 1979:8). Warrior— Relaxes (C72:150), wishes well (C74:224).
152 Windpipe snap—C77:84.
153 *Seven Arrows*—Storm 1972:251.

Stan Wilk   16
154 "Don Juan on Balance"—Stan Wilk is Associate Professor of Anthropology at Lycoming College, in Williamsport, Pa. He graduated from Hunter College of the City University of New York and received a Ph.D. in 1970 from the University of Pittsburgh for a study based on fieldwork in Mexico. He has published on political and on psychological anthropology, on shamanism, and on cultural theory, has done research in a non-residential psychotherapeutic community, and is currently exploring an experientially based symbolic anthropology.—RdeM.

Franz Kafka—"The coming of the Messiah," in *Parables and Paradoxes*, Schocken 1961:81. Lao Tzu—*Tao Te Ching*, translated by D. C. Lau, Penguin 1963:133; cited below as "Lao Tzu." Direct knowledge—C71:12-13. Discernment—Lao Tzu:92.
155 Journey—Lao Tzu:125. Death as adviser—C72: Chapter 4. Nagual—Lao Tzu:75,91,96; C74:118-129, especially 128. Interference—C71:240. Paths— C68:76.
156 Remain the same—C71:13. Rehumanization—Consult Sapir (Mandelbaum 1949) on the issue of incorporating humanity into anthropological discourse. Fear—C68:57. Balanced position—See Wilk 1977b. Only one path—C68:111.
157 Social-scientific reification—See: Roy Wagner, "Ideology and theory: The problem of reification in anthropology," in Erik Schwimmer, editor, *The Yearbook of Symbolic Anthropology*, Hurst (London) or McGill University (Montreal) 1978:203-209.

Richard de Mille   17
158 "Science as Religion"—Capra 1975; Thomsen (1979) puts mystic physics into scientific perspective; synthesis (Littleton 1976:152; Tiryakian 1974:12); Wilk (1977c; DJP ; 1978); Maquet 1978.

Straitjacket—Littleton 1976:152. Littleton assures me (letter 10 Sept 1979) he does *not* wish anthropologists to give up science or turn anthropology into a religion. His wish is to liberate science from a rigid, narrow positivism that is unable or unwilling to scientifically examine anomalous data. I agree with Littleton that science should take anomalous or paranormal data seriously, though, of course, I do not agree with him that any such data are to be found in the don Juan allegories. Maquet (letter 12 Sept 1979) would not reject the anthropologist's inner experience as a possible source of data but says we do not yet know how to use such 'observations' to build valid knowledge. Believing anthropologists like Wilk do not at all consider the epistemological problems raised by their proposals, Maquet objects to my calling them "new scientists," on the ground that they repudiate the scientific approach.

159 Persistent dispute—In *Seeing Castaneda*, Theodore Roszak dropped a transcendental fuzz-bomb on science (Noel 1976:144-160), while Carl Oglesby, Merton Kahne, Everett Mendelsohn, and Christopher Schaefer examined Juanism analytically (Noel 1976:161-185). Tart—1975:11-58, 94-95. Affective dimensions—Wilk 1977a:89; Beals (1978:360) took Wilk to task for calling Carlos's social isolation "humanizing"; it is dehumanizing, Beals said. Richer dialogue—Wilk DJP:155.

160 Finnegan—1977:745. Pearce—1971: Chapter Nine, or in Noel 1976·191-219. Religionists—Grange 1971, 1973; Marty 1973; Lindsey 1973; McFadden 1976; Nelson 1974; Sire 1975; Meinke 1976; Newport 1978; Newport cites additional Christian comment by Sire, Lande, and Ellwood, as well as many other relevant sources; Doty 1975.

161 Savior—Lévano 1973:16. Ornstein—1976; see also Ornstein 1972/1977. Juanist opiate—Easlea 1974; Harris 1974:257. Noel—1976; 1972:85,86; 1980

Richard de Mille & Daniel C. Noel **18**

163 "Seeing and Seeing Through Castaneda"—Most of this chapter appeared earlier as de Mille & Noel 1978; the middle section, attributed to Noel, is copyright ©1978 by Daniel C. Noel; the rest of the chapter is copyright ©1978 by Richard de Mille, except for the last paragraph of the text and for the notes, which are copyright ©1980 by Richard de Mille.

Reviewing my critique—Noel 1977.

164 Sparks—See AG:**Sparks.** Originating flashbacks—See RdeM 1978b. Children steal from parents—C77:130-135.

165 *Third Eye*—Lobsang Rampa 1956. Dragon with thirteen tails—He was green-eyed. Brujorison—Sorcerer's prayer.

James Hillman—1975; as-if (1975:157); ways of perceiving (1975:156); revelation of myth (1975:142).

167 Mac Linscott Ricketts—"The trickster and the shaman," a paper presented to the Trickster Myths Consultation, American Academy of Religion, annual meeting, San Francisco, Thursday, 29 Dec 1977.

Sam Gill—1977. Don Pedro—Beals 1977b.

168 Awkward, plodding—This argument does not contradict the sixth paragraph of my review, which ironically compliments Castaneda on turning his hoax into poetry. The hoax succeeded; the poetry fails. *Second Ring* is "leagues beyond" *The Teachings* but not above it. Castaneda seems to be at home in the realm of symbol but does not make the reader feel at home there.

Zeno and Zeitgeist—Zeno, founder of Stoicism; Zeitgeist, spirit of the time; Michael Grosso (1977:310) called *A Separate Reality* a brilliant expression of the current Zeitgeist of mentalism.

Bob Gover, RdeM, & Paul Christoffers **19**

169 "Religion as Science"—Notes by RdeM. This debate among two friends and one stranger is based on Gover's (1977a) review of *Castaneda's Journey* and three letters that resulted from it (RdeM 1977c; Gover 1977b; Christoffers 1977). Christoffers's letter, somewhat condensed, is reproduced by permission of the proprietor: Copyright ©1977 by Reason Enterprises. The rest of the chapter is substantially revised. Sections attributed to RdeM are copyright ©1980 by Richard de Mille; sections attributed to Gover are copyright ©1980 by Bob Gover.

171 Jellybean—Reisner 1967:39. Holograms of atoms—*Science News*, 13 April 1974, 105(15):238.

172 Distinguishable views—Horton (1967) analyses the confrontation of pagan and modern worldviews, showing remarkable similarities as well as crucial differences between African traditional thought and Western science. Gover's affinity for pagan quasi-science may be explained by Horton's finding that: "the modern Western layman is rarely more . . . scientific in his outlook than is the traditional African villager" (186).

Uncle Tommyhawk, Tío Taco—Native-American and Chicano terms for Uncle Tom: A synthetic literary or social character created to serve the needs of Anglos who thought they were appreciating a black slave, a warrior brave, a friendly Mestizo, or a Yaqui shaman.

Numerous writers on shamanism—Of whom this volume lists: Boshier, Chagnon, Eliade, Furst, Griaule, Halifax, Harner, Keewaydinoquay, Kitsepawit, Myerhoff, Opler, Petrullo, Radin, Rose, Rothenberg, Sharon, Underhill, and Wasson.

Erin Matson **20**

174 "R. de Mille Doesn't Exist"—Born in San Francisco in 1937, Erin Matson is a painter, now living in the Catskills. An editor of *High Times* (Aug 1977:10) rewrote her letter before passing it on to RdeM, but this is the first publication of the original letter, which is copyright © 1980 by Erin Matson. The introduction by RdeM is copyright © 1980 by Richard de Mille.

RdeM article—Selections from CJ, unreliably edited by editors of *High Times*, April 1977; the issue was on the stands in March.

Kenneth Minogue **21**

178 "The Guru" was first published in *Encounter*, August 1976, 47(2): 19-29, Copyright 1976 by Encounter Ltd. Here some introductory lines have been deleted, and an implicit distinction between writer "Castaneda" and character "Carlos" has been made explicit.

179 P. D. Ouspensky—*The Fourth Way*, Routledge & Kegan Paul, 1957: 30-31. Kenneth Walker—*A Study of Gurdjieff's Teaching*, Jonathan Cape (London), 1957: 73-74.

Commonplace idea as revelation—Anthropologist and psychotherapist William Stillwell discusses paradox as a technique of enlightenment, finding Castaneda's first five books to be "one of the finest descriptions of mystical initiation I know" (Stillwell 1979:8).

180 Alan Brien—1975:40.

184 The Extraordinary effect—C74:238.

185 Trying to explain—See AG:**Collapse, Description, Explaining.** Membership—C72:9; see also Membership, in the Index.

186 When we perceive—C71:181. Black cap—C74:233. All of this—C74:234. We are perceivers—C74:100.

187 Logical—C74:44, 45, 47. The *tonal*—C74:123-125.

188 The *nagual*—C74:141. If the *tonal*—C74:126.

189 A man who *sees*—C71:186.

190 Goldschmidt's philosophical dilemma See AG:**Reality.** *Reading Castaneda*—Silverman 1975.

191 So [Carlos's] problem—Silverman: 7.

192 For don Juan—Silverman: 38-39.

193 Being a 'proper' bureaucrat—Silverman:47.

194 To write (act); conceal them-selves—Silverman:56. The eccentricities of Dr Silverman's prose in this and some other passages derive from the fact that he is pioneering a language in which the insertion of hyphens within words allows them to bear a more reflective meaning than usual. Sartre quoted—Silverman:106.

195 Kockelmans quoted—Silverman:96. Locate oneself; not see the Yaqui way—Silverman:19. This view may seem to be licensed by *The Teachings of Don Juan*, but is directly contradicted by the introduction to *Journey to Ixtlan*: "So far I have made no attempt whatsoever to place don Juan in a cultural milieu. The fact that he considers himself to be a Yaqui Indian does not mean that his knowledge of sorcery is known to or practiced by the Yaqui Indians in general" (C72:8).

196 Only for communities—Silverman:69.

197 Occultism—See also James Webb, *The Flight from Reason*, Macdonald Educational Ltd (London), 1971.

Stephen O. Murray   **22**

198 "The Invisibility of Scientific Scorn"—Notes by RdeM are signed.

Quack—Comment made in a lecture by Everett Hughes, reported by Roger Pritchard. Why—CJ:83.

Outside UCLA—Presumably few anthropologists *inside* UCLA knew more; those that did may have felt loyalties or liabilities that kept them silent.—RdeM

Trust—At the time of Castaneda's training, a favorite tactic of ethnomethodologists was to breach what was routinely taken for granted (for example, that dissertations report research and that doctoral research is critically examined) in order to reveal unreportable expectations (Mehan & Wood 1975, Murray 1979a).

Organized skepticism—One of the four norms of science as an institution, according to Robert K. Merton, *Social Theory, Social Structure,* Free Press, 1968. Written off—S. B. Barnes 1972:287 (On the reception of scientific beliefs, in B. Barnes, editor, *Sociology of Science,* Penguin 1972:269-291).

Not cited—The impression that Castaneda was receiving no approval in scientific publications may have relieved disapproving anthropologists of feeling a duty to criticize him, but the impression was not correct. Before Wilk's 1977 article finally catalyzed the professional reaction, Castaneda's books had been respectfully reviewed by anthropologists in some scientific publications (Aberle 1969, Basso 1973, Douglas in this volume, Heelas 1972, Littleton 1976, John Ryle 1975, Spicer 1969) and cited in others (Barth & others 1975, Bean & Saubel 1972, de Rios 1972, 1977, Furst 1972, Harner 1973, Long 1976, 1977, Siskind 1973). Selections from *The Teachings* have been enshrined in textbooks by Goldschmidt (1971:187-190) and Langness (1977:99-111,114). Not realizing what he was saying, sociologist Michael Kimmel praised Castaneda's "incredible journey" (1974; 1975:701); likewise uncritically appreciative was sociologist Joseph L. Zentner (1976).—RdeM.

199 Destroy unanimity—Barnes (cited above) 1972:286.

200 Low regard for popularizers—There is, of course, an elitist contempt for the masses in this. Superficial trappings of scholarship—dense syntax, arcane jargon, polyglot documentation—are sometimes confused with essentials. Nonetheless, essential elements of good scholarship are often jettisoned from popular works. A single explanation for a phenomenon is often pressed without any consideration of alternative explanations or evidence. Self confidence is substituted for careful analysis, and sensational examples are substituted for systematic weighing of all the available evidence.

To advance research—Criticizing Castaneda would not have advanced any line of research but, as I have said elsewhere (Murray 1979a), it would have made a contribution to anthropology; my explanation should not be read as approval of anthropologists' silence.

Lack of institutional remedies—Compare Zuckerman 1977:97. Canons for reporting—Beals 1978:361.

Anthropologists content—According to Gordon G. Globus (1975:11), some were far from content: "I have been informed that some outraged anthropologists in the American Anthropological Association even want to purge Castaneda from their pristine ranks!" The failure of this movement (if it was more than idle talk) testifies to the lack of institutional remedies mentioned by Murray.—RdeM.

201 Praise in official journal—Wilk, March 1977a. Provoked—Beals 1978, Maquet 1978. Networks—Informal networks in 20th-century American anthropology, including the ethnoscience network, are delineated in Murray 1979b.

Cloistered calm—F. M. Cornford sardonically described an academic norm: "The Principle of Sound Learning is that the noise of vulgar fame should never trouble the cloistered calm of academic existence. Hence, learning is called sound when no one has ever heard of it; and 'sound scholar' is a term of praise applied to one another by learned men who have no reputation outside the University" (*Microcosmographia Academica*, Bowes & Bowes, London, 1908:11).

Presidents—Nixon's rejection of his commission's conclusion that there was no evidence of harm from pornography, and other cases, are discussed in Mirra Komarovsky, editor, *Sociology and Public Policy: The Case of Presidential Commissions*, Elsevier 1975.

RdeM
205 "Spun by the Ally"—Though many have been spun by Castaneda, few have come back to tell the tale. Others whose contributions could have been offered here rather than later, in Part IV, are Stephen J. Reno and Jean W. Cox.

Ally—C72:313; C74:87,89; C68:32,33; C71:283; C72:306; Cravens 1973a:97; see also AG:**Ally, Spin**. Riesman—Quoted from 1972:7/ 1976:47. Reichbart—1976b:391.

Paul Riesman **23**
207 "Fictions of Art and of Science"—I should like to thank Nancy Scherer for many stimulating conversations that helped lay the groundwork for this essay, and for helpful comments on one of the drafts. I also thank for their reading and comments: Jeremy Brecher, Jill Cutler, Richard de Mille, Keith Harrison, Daniel Sullivan, Harriet Sheridan, and Bardwell Smith.

I reviewed—Riesman 1972. Yaqui sorcerer—Castaneda did not identify any Yaqui culture or group beyond don Juan, who uses the word *sorcerer* in an unusual way. Oates—1972. La Barre—1975:271-275; Noel 1976:40-42. RdeM—CJ:68-69, 71, 76.

208 "Glosses"—Conventionally defined, a gloss is an explanation of an unfamiliar word in a text; the term is extended here as the ethnomethodologists and Castaneda have extended it (see AG: introduction).

209 Harris—1974: especially 243-258, The return of the witch.

210 Silverman—1975:xi; a paradigm is a theoretical framework.

211 Anomalies—Kuhn 1970.

213 Durkheim—Emile Durkheim, *Les formes élémentaires de la vie religieuse*, Presses Universitaires de France, 1960.

214 Stochastic—hit-and-miss.

215 Parallel—The idea that Castaneda is to us as don Juan is to Carlos became the title of an essay by Elsa First (1974a).

216 Make it a science—Compare an interesting attempt to create a description, scientific in spirit, of the experience of learning to improvise jazz on the piano, by David Sudnow, Singing with the fingers, *Human Nature*, Aug 1978, 1(8):80-86.

RdeM
217 Lionel Abel—1975:36. Taking Castaneda seriously—Thouless 1977:184; Holroyd 1977:21, 153-160, 163, 167; see also AG:Introduction, on Holroyd; and Hardy (1977:14) reviewing Holroyd; Littleton 1976:151; de Rios & Smith 1977:16. Nash mentioned Castaneda briefly (1978:62) but "will not take him at face value" if there is a second edition of his textbook on parapsychology (Letter 27 Dec 1978).

Richard Reichbart   **24**
218 "Castaneda and Parapsychology"—I wish to thank Richard de Mille for his assistance in identifying sources relevant to this article.
219 Inherently causal property—See my discussion of the dichotomy between Navajo and Western cultures in their treatment of "mind" (Reichbart 1976b). Psi-determined meetings—C72:19; C74:11.
220 White falcon—C72:48-54. Button-nosed boy—C71:171. Blonde woman—C72:92. Knapsacked young man—C68:83. Astral projection or out-of-the-body experience—C68:91-94, 101, 124; C74:68-77. Violate the rules—C74:71-72. Prevents Carlos's car from starting—C71:242. Carlos and Pablito simultaneously experience the "nagual"—C74:257-260. For a more convincing shared apparition, see Moisés & others 1971:137.—RdeM.
   Hypnosis—For a review of current findings concerning psi and hypnosis, see Charles Honorton's "Psi and Internal Attention States" in Wolman 1977: 435-472; for an example of mutual hypnosis, see Tart's "Psychedelic Experiences Associated with a Novel Hypnotic Procedure, Mutual Hypnosis," in Tart 1969:291-308.
   Hallucinogenic drug intoxication—For a review of this topic in relation to psi, see Charles Tart's "Drug-Induced States of Consciousness" in Wolman 1977:500-525.
   Belief—A classic study of belief in psi and ESP ability is: G.R. Schmeidler & R. A. McConnell, *ESP and Personality Patterns*, Yale U. 1958; for a review of subsequent findings, see: John Palmer, *Journal of the American Society for Psychical Research*, 1971, 65:373-408; 1972, 66:1-26.
   Illusion—Examples include the dead branch Carlos thinks is an animal (C72:131) and the cloth don Juan uses to create an illusion of undulating mountains (C72:223). In "Magic and Psi" (Reichbart 1978a) I suggest that magical techniques developed historically as psi-conducive techniques.
   Examples of spontaneous psi phenomena—Classic works incorporating spontaneous cases collected by the (British) Society for Psychical Research are: Myers 1903, and Gurney, Myers, & Podmore 1886; for a brief history of collection of spontaneous cases, see Eisenbud 1970, Chapter 5.
221 Dean Sheils—"A Cross-Cultural Study of Beliefs in Out-of-the-Body

Experiences, Waking and Sleeping," *Journal of the Society for Psychical Research*, 1978, 49:697-741. Rose—1956.

222 Anthropologists resist the psi hypothesis—For history of anthropology and parapsychology, see: Angoff & Barth 1974; Robert L. Van de Castle in Wolman 1977:667-686; papers from the 1974 symposium collected by Long (1977); criticism of Long's collection by Reichbart (1978b) and RdeM (1978a); report of the 1978 meeting by Rogo (1979). Malevolent psi— Treated by Jule Eisenbud, "Perspectives on Anthropology and Parapsychology," in Long 1977:28-44. William James—Murphy & Ballou 1960.

Sigmund Freud—"Dreams and Telepathy" [1922], *Standard Edition*, 1955, 18:195-220; "Dreams and Occultism" [1933], *Standard Edition*, 1964, 22: Chapter 30 (Published by Hogarth, London). It is a common misconception that Freud, who was a member of the (British) Society for Psychical Research and the American Society for Psychical Research, made no contribution to parapsychology. Richet—French physiologist, Nobel Prize winner; Richet 1923/1975.

Van de Castle—R. L. Van de Castle, "An Investigation of Psi Abilities among the Cuna Indians of Panama," in Angoff & Barth 1974:80-100. Eisenbud—1967:Chapter 14. Stevenson—The foremost exponent of the reincarnation hypothesis; Ian Stevenson, "Reincarnation," in Wolman 1977:631-663. Osis & Haraldsson—1977, a comparative study of paranormal experiences of the dying in India and in America. Tart—1970. Reichbart—1978a.

223 Boshier—1974. No cultural milieu—C68:5; C72:8. Established parapsychological journals of the United States—*Journal of the American Society for Psychical Research, Journal of Parapsychology, Parapsychology Review*. Tart—1970; and in Wolman 1977:500-525. Van de Castle—R. L. Van de Castle, "Anthropology and Psychic Research," in Mitchell & White 1974:268-287. Krippner—1975:221,288.

Michael Grosso—"Plato and Out-of-the-Body Experiences," *Journal of the American Society for Psychical Research*, Jan 1975, 69(1):61-74. Joseph Long—1977. Elmer & Alyce Green—1977.

R. A. Kalish & D. K. Reynolds—"Phenomenological Reality and Post-Death Contact," *Journal for the Scientific Study of Religion*, 1973, 12:209-221; one of the few studies related to parapsychology to receive a federal (NIMH) grant. Price-Williams—The report is summarized in part in Krippner & Villoldo 1976:300-302; see also CJ:196.

224 Failure to respond to criticism—For the record, I received no response to my letter of 3 June 1978 to Castaneda requesting comment on the authenticity of the don Juan series. Osis—1978. "Act of faith"—See Beals 1978:359. Tolstoy's *Anna Karenina*—See Reichbart 1976a.

225 Croiset—Dutch psychic; see Pollack 1964. Serios—American "thoughtographic" talent of the 1960s; Eisenbud 1967. Psi phenomena in our daily lives—See Eisenbud 1970.

Editor's Note—The relation of parapsychology to mainstream science is illuminated by Palfreman (1979), Collins & Pinch (1979), and Allison (1979) in Roy Wallis's *On the Margins of Science* (1979), a work I recommend highly to anyone interested in parapsychology or the growth of science.— RdeM.

Neil Erickson   25
226 "Seven Years with don Juan"—The two illustrations for this chapter were painted in colors in 1978 by Neil Erickson; copyright © 1980 by Neil Erickson.
227 Losing personal footing—This may seem like invention, but don Juan said dangerous forces could cause a man "to stumble, lose his footing, and go over a precipice" (C71:282). Erickson ironically and effectively combines losing footing with erasing personal history.—RdeM.

Richard de Mille   26
236 "Tell it to the Toltecs"—Many of the sources for this chapter must remain anonymous, but none have been invented. I am grateful to Timothy Martin for permission to use his name and tell his story.
   Parody—Barthelme 1973/1974; Pomaska 1973; R. Crumb draws raunchy underground comics; Pomaska didn't mention Crumb by name, but I think that's the class of parody she had in mind.
   Los Angeles Times Book Review controversy—Strachan 1977; Anselmo 1977a,b; Beals 1977a; Nordell 1977; Harpon 1977; Peters 1977; Beals 1977b; Lamal 1977. I wrote answers to: Anselmo (RdeM 1977a), MacCracken 1977 (RdeM 1977b), and Peters (RdeM 1977d). In response to Farren's (1978) unfavorable review of *Second Ring*, three letters appeared in the *LATBR* on 2 April 1978.
238 Obermayer—Letters 20, 28 June 1977. Holbrook—1978.
   Other complaints—Nancy Wood (1973) thought Carlos was exploiting don Juan. R. Pittman (1977) didn't like RdeM's article in *High Times*. L. C. Burns (1979) said practicing biologists who could see the parabolic nature of things believed Castaneda more than RdeM (1979b); I answered (RdeM 1979c) that I would never give up my belief in Sherlock Holmes. "If Carlos invented don Juan, then he is putting the shuck on all of us," gasped William L. Smith (1978).

Richard de Mille   27
242 "Three Faces of Carlos"—Drawings (for hire) by Linda Trujillo, copyright © 1980 by Richard de Mille, after illustrations by Dick Oden (*Psychology Today*, Dec 1972:91), Stan Zagorski (*Time*, 5 March 1973:cover), and Daniel Maffia (*Psychology Today*, Dec 1977:40).
243 Fog—C72:32-33. Tape recordings—Oden quoted by David Christie, letter 18 July 1979; C73:v, abstract; C71:21,76.
244 *Who's Who in America*—1976-77, 1:532; 1978-79, 1:556; whose editors must have had at least a year to make the corrections I suggested. In

both entries Castaneda lists his "home" at the UCLA anthropology department; in 1976-77 his "office" is in care of his Beverly Hills agent, but in 1978-79 it is in care of the University of California Press, Berkeley; the change suggests updating by Castaneda more than fiddling by editors. See critique of *WWA* by David Larsen, *Los Angeles Times*, 30 Nov 1979, I:1,25.

While we are on the subject of reference works, *The Encyclopedia of Occultism and Parapsychology* (Shepard 1978) promulgates the imaginary M.A. but links don Juan with the Lobsang Rampa hoax. In late 1971 or early 1972, Castaneda told Bruce Cook (1973) his thesis would be titled "Phenomenology of Special Consensus"; *Who's Who in America* is where he preserved this feature of the separate reality. He also implied to Cook and to Steven Roberts (1972) that his faculty status at UC-Irvine was more substantial than the one-quarter appointment made by the students (CJ:27). Castaneda was apparently the source of *Time's* (1973:36, deleted from Noel 1976) incorrect and unfairly handled rumor that John Wallace (1972) had made unauthorized use of Castaneda's material, a rumor repeated by feminosophist Eleanor Links Hoover (1977) a year after I had refuted it (CJ:25n) in a book she affected to have read, while getting its title wrong.

Special consensus—C68:163.

245 *Contemporary Authors*—1977; correspondence RdeM 8 Feb 1978, Ann V. Evory 7 March 1978. Quinn—"'I don't want to see Anthony Quinn as don Juan,' he says with asperity" (*Time* 1973:36/1976:95), but if Quinn could play *The Magus*, why couldn't he play don Juan?

Korea cycle—I am grateful to William Lessa, John Hitchcock, and Newton Threebody for recalling these stories and to the first two for permitting use of their names. Little boy—A photo of Castaneda and the little boy may be seen in M. Castaneda 1975:71; Swedish wife (CJ:30); genes (M. Castaneda 1975:76).

246 Paratroopers—This story struck me as absurd until I read a similar report from the Associated Press (4 Dec 1977) involving Nelson Peters and Jerry Tindal of Fort Bragg. Army—In Spain (M. Castaneda 1975:77); Defense Dept (*Time* 1973:44 1976:104). Female child—C77:119. Photo of don Juan—Egori (CJ:13); Ullman 1977; Karpel 1975; retraction (*New Age* 1977b).

247 Minor rumors—When asked whether Carlos would ever meet don Juan again, Michael Korda said mysteriously: "I know what his plans are, but I can't say" (Bourne 1978). Gordon Wasson (letter 8 Jan 1977) heard Carlos was writing a book called *Witness*. The little boy, now a big boy, said Carlos was rumored to be seeking power on a mountain top in Guatemala. Artist Tom Gillies (letter 6 April 1979) had an appointment to meet Carlos at Carlos's sister's house in Sacramento, California, but the meeting fell through. A UCLA librarian refused to talk about having been married to Castaneda; her mother denied it (phone 18 Sept 1978). Answering David Christie's letter to journalist Gwyneth Cravens, Ella Speed wrote from Nashville (undated, about Oct 1978) to say that Carlos's books "may be exercises he was asked to perform for reasons he does not yet know." Meg Krenz of the Laughing Man Institute reported (in a letter to Christie dated 24 Jan 1997 [sic]) that fire had destroyed all traces of a videotape of Castaneda speaking at Harvard. A sorcerer's life may depend on keeping his videotape out of circulation.

Wittgenstein—*Tractatus:* 7. Don Q—Reno 1978; see AG:**Don Q.** Mexico—Beals 1978:360. Experiments—Krippner & Villoldo 1976:300-302; Osis 1978.

248 Dreamer and dreamed—Garvin (1978:71-73); illustration after Garvin's Figure 1-d (1978:80); student and editorial assistant (Clement W. Meighan & V. L. Pontoni, editors, *Seven Rock Art Sites in Baja California,* Ballena Press 1978).

249 Really a shaman—Naranjo & Harner 1968. Tapes retrieved—David Christie (phone 27 Aug 1977) relayed this report from Sam Keen. Hunter—C72:95.

Douglass McFerran   28

251 "Carlos and the Toltec Devils"—Notes by RdeM. Versed in occultism—M. Castaneda 1975:74; CJ:26,30. Diableros—C68:2-4, 136-139; "There may have been an inherent connection between man of knowledge and diablero" (C68:144); "like don Genaro he [Pablito] had a winning smile with a touch of devilishness in it" (C74:195).

252 Escape death—"Sorcerers do not die," La Gorda told Carlos (C77:281).

Trapped in an alien world—Don Juan said that to be a man is to be condemned to a world that is not "the world of happiness" (C68:111-112); our fellow men are black magicians, he said (C74:28); Carlos told don Juan he had come "from a place where people rarely if ever wish one another well," and don Juan said the same thing had happened to him (C74:224); don Juan refused to enter Los Angeles because there were "too many evil spirits" there (Wallace 1972:85).

Toltecs—C77:180, 238-239, 288, 303. Devils—C77:14, 37, 180, 183, 237.

253 Abraxas—A god worshipped by the Gnostics.

Stephen J. Reno   29

254 "If don Juan did not Exist"—Notes by RdeM. Other comments on Castaneda are to be found in Reno 1975, 1977, 1978. Something in myself—C74:28, not an exact quotation.

255 Westerners—Though modern lives are guided and explained by beliefs in such things as infinite technical progress or the perfectability of man, such beliefs are not transmitted through universally accepted traditional stories.

256 Sudanese—Compare Blaise Cendrars, *Anthologie Negre,* 1947, cited by Susan Feldman, *African Myths and Tales*, Dell 1963:12.

Richard de Mille   **30**
259 "Learning by Not-Doing"—See AG:**Not-Doing.** Anderson &
Truzzi—In same & RdeM 1977. *Exploring the Ways of Mankind*—
Goldschmidt 1971:187-190; 1977.

Not a shaman—A shaman mediates between his people and the powers
of the other world; a *brujo* (or sorcerer) makes his enemies sick with the
devil's help. Having neither people nor enemies, mystical magician don
Juan did neither (Beals 1978:357).
260 *Other Fields, Other Grasshoppers*—Langness 1977: (stimulate) xi,
(*Wizard*) 59, (read tetralogy) 111, ("Lizards") 99-110, (ethnography) 110,
111, (as such) 111, (emic) 110, (controversy) 110. Leach—1969:13/1976:36.
261 Bohannan—Langness 1977:110, 114; Bowen 1954/1964. *Eye of the
Flute*—Kitsepawit 1977; Anderson 1978. *Yaqui Life*—Moises & others
1971/1977. Thomas R. Moore—Letter 20 May 1978.
262 Chipmunk—CJ:107. *Cliffs Notes*—McMahon 1974:10,14,10,51,
29,7. MacInnes—1975. Crump—1973. Weeks 1976; one New Testament edition
has Jesus' sayings printed in red. *English Journal*—Carlsen & others 1975; Trout
1974.
263 Vecsey—1978:133. Cueing—Lutz & Ramsey 1973:355-358.
Cohen—1974.
264 Dr Ryle—See Alleglossary:**Jump.** Mrs Thornapple—Datura, don
Juan's devil's weed, a female ally whose non alcoholic poisonous punch will
knock you into the next world while you are hoping to fly to the other
world (Weil 1977; Furst 1976).
265 C. R. V. Brown—Dissertation (1977); article (1976); passages from
the dissertation (1977:142,156) are slightly revised. Castanedian gems—
C71:127, 62, 234; C74:181, 258; C72:72; C74:233; C72:236, 102.
266 Bad grammar—Correspondence (RdeM 15 July 1978; Brown 9 Oct
1978). Reasonable reply—For a more exacting treatment of grammatical
exactness, read, mark, learn, and inwardly digest *Less than Words can Say*,
an authoritative, hilarious attack on educationism by "underground gram-
marian" Richard Mitchell (1979). *Animal Farm*—Orwell 1946. *The Circus
of Dr. Lao*—Finney 1936. *Till We Have Faces*—C. S. Lewis 1956/1964.

Cabeza de Vaca—Quotations are from Haniel Long 1969:33, which is a
faithful, illuminating, interpretive retelling of Nuñez 1871/1966; both versions are rewarding; Long's is brief and elegant.
267 Not-writing—Castaneda's brilliance is not literary. William Kennedy
(1974) said that when he gets down to concrete details he writes like a brick
mason touching up the gold leaf on the Taj Mahal. Joyce Carol Oates (1974)
thought him primarily concerned with teaching; she was the first, I believe,
to see don Juan as a Zen koan fleshed out. Less perceptive commentary on
Castaneda was provided by: Ash 1969, 1971, 1972, 1974; Baldwin 1977;
Booklist 1971, 1973, 1974; *Choice* 1973, 1975; Roszak 1972; Stafford

1977; World Almanac 1977. *Time's* (1973:37/1976:95-96) compliments to Castaneda's talent for description were false to the point of absurdity, as Kennedy (1974) observed.

Carl R. V. Brown   31
268 "Reading *Journey to Ixtlan*"—Adapted from Brown 1977:193-195; copyright © 1977,1980 by Carl R. V. Brown. Collectors of senseless synchronicities will wish to be told that Brown's dissertation committee was chaired by Professor Alfredo Castaneda, who—Brown says—"claims absolutely no relationship to Carlos." Trouble is, if Castaneda were posing as "Alfredo," that is exactly the kind of claim *he* would make. Brown has never met Carlos Castaneda, so how does he know "Alfredo" Castaneda is telling the truth? And another thing. Doesn't it seem a little odd that Brown has four names when most of us get along with three? And that his first name is almost the same as "Carlos"?—RdeM.

RdeM
270 Chicano—James Collins (1974:40,39) accepted Castaneda's Peruvian birth but called him: "this quiet unassuming Chicano—this stocky brown Latin-American." *Perverse Innocence*—Bruce-Novoa 1977.

Bruce-Novoa   32
271 "Chicanos in the Web of Spider Trickster"—Notes prepared by RdeM from information provided by Bruce-Novoa. A Chicano is a Mexican, or a descendent of Mexicans, now living permanently in the United States.

Novoa—CJ:26 said *Novoa* was a Portuguese name, which was almost right. *Noboa* would be Portuguese, but *Novoa* is Galician. Galicia is the region of Spain north of Portugal. Gallego, the Galician dialect, is closely related to Portuguese. My conception of Castaneda as "a Basquish Peruvian Spaniard" (CJ:28) therefore remains unchanged. "Agringado"—Gringoized.

272 Cervantes—"Meeting Mescalito at Oak Hill Cemetery" is from Lorna Dee Cervantes's unpublished manuscript, "Almost None." Bruce-Novoa interviewed Cervantes in October 1978. Alurista—Of four books apparently planned, three have been published (Alurista 1971, 1972, 1976). Give a fig—C74:283.

273 *Bless Me, Ultima*—Anaya 1972; for more possible influences of Anaya on Castaneda, see AG:**Gorda;** Anaya's interview will be published by the University of Texas Press, in Bruce-Novoa's *Chicano Authors: Inquiry by Interview.*

Méndez—"Tata Casehua" (Méndez 1969) and "Los Criaderos Humanos" (The Human Stockyards; Méndez 1975) are now available through Editorial Justa Publications, POB 9128, Berkeley CA 94709.

274 Marriage license—M. Castaneda 1975:73; most likely Castaneda was claiming the name Aranha before 1960, but Bruce-Novoa sticks to what is documented. Sioux and Ashanti—Trickster 1979:2.

Desecrater of Yaquiness—Though Castaneda's text (C68:5; C72:8) disclaims any attempt to describe Yaqui traditions, culture, or society, the University of California Press has allowed the subtitle *A Yaqui Way of Knowledge* to mislead readers for a dozen years, and recently Simon & Schuster (1977) hawked Castaneda's "examination of drug use in the mystical religious practices of the Yaqui Indians" in the *American Anthropologist*, of all places. Yaquis have a right to resent such blatant mislabeling and persistent misrepresentation.

"Birria"—Border slang for beer; "birria" also refers to mutton roasted on hot coals, steamed under maguey leaves, but Bruce-Novoa is wagering only a beer.

275 Spider illustration—The Spider Trickster is an original illustration by Julie Durrell from the cover of *Parabola* magazine, Volume 4, Issue 1 "The Trickster." Illustration copyright © 1979 by Julie Durrell. Reproduced by permission of the artist. The Trickster issue of *Parabola* is devoted to trickster myths in many cultures. It may be ordered (as of Aug 1979) at $6.50 from: *Parabola*, 150 Fifth Avenue, New York NY 10011.

RdeM

276 Feminists—Author and educator Miriam Wolf, who has billed herself as "teacher, writer, lecturer, discussion leader, consultant, socialist, pacifist, feminist, optimist" but now says she is a "meta-feminist," has written a short work titled, *Macho-Mysticism: Carlos Castaneda, Jack Mormon, and Others*, to be published by Word Travels (POB 1081, Minneapolis MN 55440). Wolf finds Carlos's magic frivolous when compared with the miracles offered by life.

Feminist themes in C77—Androgyny (290); harem (183); parenthood (117-135); unseductive body (133,238); "I could not possibly think of her as a woman" (165); "she was a formless warrior" (263); "she took off her long dress. In one single movement she was naked" (145); menstruating for power (50,161,240); lying naked for power (154).

Weibgeist—Womanspirit, a term contributed (memo 4 July 1976) by feminist writer Callista McAllister (CJ:89n).

Male pushiness and shovinism in C77—The incredible shrinking fat woman (55); Lidia's chickie run (53); blowing Soledad (43); Josefina and the razor's edge (54); Rosa without thorns (58); "A male sorcerer is very difficult to train because his attention is always closed, focused on something. A female, on the other hand, is always open because most of the time she is not focusing her attention on anything. Especially during her menstrual period. . . . When a woman menstruates she cannot focus her attention. That's the crack the Nagual told me about. . . . Sometimes we used to sit there for days until the crack would open" (240).

Out-of-body trips—See AG:**Out-of-body.** Clobbering the womenfolk—C77:61,84-85. Gift of rags—C77:258; used or unused is not made clear.

278 Cox—1976:393; S. Fisher (1978) agrees that C77 fails as humanism. Stomped his foot—C71:264.
279 *Houdini*—[Luria-] Sukenick 1973; poem reproduced by permission of the author; copyright © 1973 by Lynn Sukenick; inquiries may be addressed to the author at: 7830 Hihn Road, Ben Lomond CA 95005.

Lynn Luria-Sukenick   **34**
280 "Parabolist's Progress"—A version of which was published in *The American Book Review*, Summer 1979, 2(1):7.

Carrington—A surrealist painter and writer, born in England, schooled in Florence, recognized in Paris, living now for many years in Mexico, Leonora Carrington wrote—in the publisher's blurb for the Mexican edition of *The Teachings* (Tovar 1974a)—that Castaneda's books (I translate): "touch deep and sensitive parts of the collective soul, through which runs a current of myth returning toward [what Octavio Paz calls] 'the direct vision of the world'. . . . Do we dare recover it?" Carrington's reservations about don Juan's sensibility and her reluctance to submit to his regime do not contradict her appreciation of him as a figure of myth. Reno and Faber make similar distinctions.—RdeM.

Sorcery—A word used here in Castaneda's unanthropological sense of extrasocial magic and mysticism. Maya Deren—*Divine Horsemen: Voodoo Gods of Haiti*, Dell pbk 1972.
281 Pablito's chair—C77:311.
282 Awkwardness seduces us—Compare Mary Douglas (DJP:28): "The naiveties of expression can be taken as evidence of authenticity." Tie shoelace—C77:274. Control and abandon—C72:140,150.

Richard de Mille   **35**
283 "Epistemallegory"—Epistemology is the study of how things are known; epistemallegory is teaching epistemology in story.

Margolis—1976:232,236,237,230,239, "permit" sic. Hector-Neri Castañeda—Letter 12 Dec 1977. Sartre—"Carlos read a lot of Sartre" (Alberta Greenfield, interview 2 April 1978). Read to don Juan—See AG:**Noose.** Foss—1973:314-315; Foss does cite don Juan's "noose." Firewalking—James Beal offers a physicalistic explanation, in Long 1977:114.
284 Dirac—A mathematical cosmologist. J. H. Gill—1974:392, 393,395,400. Sapir-Juan hypothesis—Echoes Sapir-Whorf hypothesis; see AG:**Agreement, Description;** CJ:124. Outlaw—1975:437, 444; Servadio (1977) discusses the ultimate reality in parapsychology.
285 Bruteau—1975:45. Globus—Writings (1973:176); four views (1975); Yaqui philosopher (1976:272). Keen—1972:95/1976:79-80.

Phenomenology—C71:25, Palmer (1977:37); Littleton (1976:149); Koepping (1977:71-72); Murray (letters 12 Jan, 31 Oct 1979); Harris 1979:324,322.

288 Hermeneutic circle—The need to know before finding out, a version of the bootstrap difficulty.
289 Bessel—See, for example, E. G. Boring, *A History of Experimental Psychology*, Appleton-Century-Crofts 1950:134-138.

McDermott—Richard McDermott attended the University of Colorado, where he pursued an interest in myth and religion and graduated with a degree in philosophy, sociology, and psychology. Currently he is completing a doctorate in sociology at Brandeis University, doing research in the sociology of work. McDermott has taught sociology and anthropology and has an abiding interest in social theory, phenomenology, and ethnomethodology. Longer version—McDermott 1979:32-34.
290 Reality-as-agreement—See AG:**Agreement.** Mehan and Wood—See Chapter 7.

RdeM
294 Standing bemushroomed—CJ:43-45, 145; Wasson & Wasson 1957:295; Wasson 1958; Wasson 1961; CJ:116. Carlos's visions—Inspired (CJ:59-61); flew (C68:124); diablero's world (C68:138); lines of the world (C72:298).

Review—RdeM 1978c:112; copyright © 1978 by Richard de Mille.
295 Visions vs Ideas—Wasson, Hofmann, & Ruck 1978:20,80; RdeM letter to Ruck 29 May 1978.Koestler—1954: Chapter 33. Ritual mycophagy—Mushroom-eating, ritualized by shaman María Sabina.

Carl A. P. Ruck   37
296 "Plato's Hierarchy of Visions"—Orphism, mentioned in the chapter, was a religious movement that came into being in the seventh and sixth centuries B.C. Its doctrines, however, were attributed to a mythical teacher of much greater antiquity, the Orpheus whose wife Eurydice was poisoned by the bite of a serpent and, like the Persephone of the Eleusinian Mysteries, was abducted into death. Orpheus was said to have attempted to rescue her but to have failed, for he turned to look at her as she followed him out of the other world. Like a Dionysian victim, Orpheus himself was later torn to pieces by a band of intoxicated women, angered at the spell his music cast upon the natural world and upon their men-folk, who had forsaken them to follow him. Although Orphic dogma adopted ideas similar to those of the mystery cults, the religion was basically different, emphasizing purification from the sinful contamination of mortality and the eventual attainment of a blessed state of spirituality after the successful completion of many cycles of reincarnation.

Richard de Mille   38
298 "The Cactus Couch of Doctor Matus"—"Trickster is not the kind of teacher vulnerable people should seek out" (CJ:120). A terrible anger—C71:255-256; C72:256-257.

M. D. Faber—Quoted from 1977b:368. Faber is author of *Suicide and Greek Tragedy*, Sphinx Press 1970, & *The Social Meaning of Altered Awareness*, Human Sciences Press, scheduled for 1980. Friendship with Castaneda—Faber, Letter 7 Sept 1978.

299 Castaneda as sadist—To test this hypothesis, re-read the last six paragraphs of Chapter 27. I invited Faber—RdeM, Letter 9 Apr 1978. Pinholes—C68:127.

300 Absence of perfection—Faber 1977b:327.

301 Perfect victim—Faber 1977b:377. Power plants—C77:277,280. Letter to me—Faber 17 Sept 1978.

Countertransference—When the therapist feels or behaves toward the client in terms of the therapist's infantile family relationships, generally considered to be bad for the therapeutic process.

Character of don Juan—Faber 1977b:378. In contrast, psychologist Jean Houston (1974:581) called don Juan "a modern Ulysses of inner space."

Nelson—1976:358; while writing her article, Nelson sent a letter to Castaneda inquiring about his possible background in psychoanalytic theory but received no answer.

302 Forisha—1978. Greening—1978:1.

303 Suzuki—See AG:**Beyond, Self.** Coxes—1977.

Phantoms—That is, ordinary people (C72:311); nineteen warriors: don Juan, La Catalina, Sacateca, don Genaro, don Vicente, four nameless young Indians, Pablito, Nestor, Eligio, Benigno, Porfirio (C77:207), doña Soledad, La Gorda, Lidia, Rosa, Josefina.

First—1974b. Hendlin—1973:89. Pulvino & Lee—1975; psychologist Clint Weyand (1976) treated the separate reality briefly and uncritically as mystical illumination. Marin—1975. Painter—1974:401-402. Scotton—1978:230.

304 Jungians—Zinker (1978:258-268) jumped on the tonalwagon with a superficial adduction of "Castanedian" archetypal vision. Larsen—1976:200, 186-187. Watkins—Sacateca (1976:154; C71:19-25), dream hands (1976:22; C72:126).

Williams & Ashby—1978; correspondence 25 Sep, 7 Nov 1978; Williams's dissertation, *C. G. Jung and Don Juan*, submitted to the Jung Institute of Zurich in Sept 1974, is now being developed into a book; inquiries to: Donald Williams, 1200 Aurora Avenue, Boulder CO 80302.

Whan—1978:27; confirming don Juan's repudiation of the literal reading, Castaneda told Cravens (1973a:94): "Sorcery is simply the praxis of phenomenology." Ally—C71:273-274. Von Franz—1976.

305 Active imagination—A Jungian technical term for the more or less spontaneous appearance in consciousness of unconscious material having symbolic significance.

La Barre—1979; Letter RdeM 2 Feb 1979. Furious with don Juan—C72:256. Blavatsky—Helena Petrovna B., 1831-1891, an occultist organizer and mystical faker, founder of the Theosophical Society, and according to Bharati (1974:234), possessor of a "fertile, crafty mind." "Call of Cthulhu"—A story by H. P. Lovecraft.

Richard de Mille **39**
309 "A Worthy Opponent"—Don Juan quoted from C74:241. How Chapter 9 of *Castaneda's Journey* scrambled to explain the name La Catalina! Though I think those guesses retain peripheral merit, here at last is a confident description of the witch's birth.

Showing manuscript—Preuss 1978:55. Interfering—C72:255. Huxley—1958:113. *Sacred Mushroom*—Puharich 1959; Castaneda read it (CJ:59-60). Models for don Juan—Wasson & Wasson 1957; CJ:60-61.

Leary & Alpert—Playboy 1966:93; Weil 1963; Kobler 1963:32,35,39,40; I am grateful to David Christie for pointing out the Catalina connection in La Barre 1975:232-233.
310 Castaneda quotes—Tree (C74:200), wave (C72:315), web (C72:241), crap (C71:235), consensus (C68:163).
311 Wallace—1972:139-140.
312 Quarrel with Leary—Keen 1972:95/1976:80; equivalent comments made to Cravens (1973a:94).

Fond of Tim—Huxley quoted by Robert S. de Ropp (1979:287) in his chapter, "The Great Psychedelic Freakway," which comments on Leary's foolish leaps.

Impact—C72:238. Fiendish witch—C68:45.
314 Wide-eyed pundit—Roszak (1969:185) wrote: "The ritualistic precision and pedagogical discipline surrounding don Juan's teachings resound with generations of experiment, meditation and philosophical systematization." Though Roszak said the confrontation with La Catalina at the end of *The Teachings* read "like something out of Lord Dunsany or Sheridan Le Fanu," he did not draw the obvious inference that don Juan's meditation and philosophy were allegories based on Suzuki, Husserl, and Schutz. The replaceable Burroughs (1979), on the other hand, seems to recognize "Castaneda's don Juan books" as works of imagination inspired by Zen.
314 *Time*—1973:43/1976:101. *Fate*—James Collins 1974:38-39,44. Moved to California—*Current Biography* 1970:246. Returned from India—Alpert 1971.
316 *Botes*—Slang: jails. Don Timo—Sir Swindle. Ram D'Ass—Collins 1974:38. Inner to outer space—Phrase contributed by Marcello Truzzi, letter 21 Sept 1979. Dome—C77:211. Aphrodisiacs—Playboy 1966:100. Nightclub act—Entertainer Leary was scheduled to open in New York in November 1979. Not dead—Sorcerers do not die (C77:281,288,315).
318 *Bobo*—Slang: dummy. Don Q—See AG: **Don Q.**

"A Charming Hotel"—Drawn (for hire) by Schlesinger from a photograph supplied by Samuel Elizalde, manager of the Hotel Catalina; copyright © 1980 by Richard de Mille.

"If-Ifer Wades"—Drawn (for hire) by Linda Trujillo from the photograph (Kobler 1963:40); copyright © 1978 by Richard de Mille.

"Feeling the Power of the Ocean" & "A Worthy Opponent"—Copyright © 1980 by Erin Matson.

Richard de Mille   **40**

319 "Allegory is not Ethnobotany"—Ethnobotany is the study of social uses of plants. Wasson's letter, reproduced by permission, is copyright © 1980 by R. Gordon Wasson. A copy of Wasson's correspondence with Castaneda and of the 12 pages of "fieldnotes" will be found in the Richard de Mille Collection at the library of the University of California, Santa Barbara, along with correspondence between RdeM and Castaneda's UCLA patrons, letters from RdeM to Castaneda, and other pertinent documents. Castaneda's original letter to Wasson will be deposited in the Gordon and Tina Wasson Collection at the Botanical Museum of Harvard University.

321 Born in the rare book room—See CJ:59-61. Smell a hoax—Wasson 1972:99; see also CJ:45-47. Carlos in Sonora on 6 Sep 1968—C71:75,87,90.

322 Humility in the service of the ego—A phrase offered by psychiatrist Richard H. Lambert after listening to the interview between Roszak and Castaneda (1968).

323 *Aliado*—Here, as he did throughout *The Teachings* (see CJ:172-174), Castaneda supplies a Spanish term one could easily find by looking up *ally* in an English-Spanish dictionary, but none of the exotic terms Wasson would like to know.

324 Marginal man—Most of this information about don Juan's life had already been given on C68:4-5.

325 The record shows Goldschmidt read—See notes for DJP:Chapter 13. Beyond Castaneda's intention—Spicer 1969:321. Strutynski—Letter 18 Aug 1975.

Unimpeachable source—Simon & Schuster, letter 16 Jan 1976; Castaneda's editorial contact at Simon and Schuster offered a rosier reason for "never" changing a word in Castaneda's manifestly editable manuscripts: "I just have never been able to find in any of Carlos' [sic] books anything that it would make sense to change" (Korda 1979:5).

Goldschmidt wanted Structural Analysis cut down—Preuss 1978:55.

UC Press reluctant—"The only major question raised with *Teachings* was the inclusion of the second part, the 'structural analysis,' which was published not at our insistence, but the author's" (Udo Strutynski, letter 14 Aug 1975).

Pure Garfinkel—Preuss 1978:55. Mycology—Study of mushrooms.

326 Carlos smoked eight times—See CJ:167, Table 1. Tovar—1974a,b; 1975; 1976.

327 Man of Novels—Compare CJ:Chapter 5. Family names—Compare CJ:26n; DJP:Notes for Bruce-Novoa.

328 Full and frank—Wasson 1972:99. Honest and serious—Wasson 1973:152.

Velada—Wasson 1974:245; Wasson, Cowans, & Rhodes 1974: ix,56,110,136,278; Eunice Pike, letter 9 Dec 1975; Florence Cowan, telephone conversation 14 Jan 1976; Wasson (letter 6 Mar 1976) conceded Pike's translation was "correct in any literal sense." Don Juan's stopping is collapsing—C72:168,299; C74:40. Historian and Nahuatl specialist Alfredo

López Austin wrote from Mexico (6 Jan 1976) that although the term One who knows (*el conocedor*) is much used in mesoamerican shamanic texts, he has not found a single epithet referring to the shaman in his capacity to Stop the world (*detener el mundo*). For more likely, non-shamanic, sources of don Juan's world-stopping, see: Boyd 1973; CJ: 101-102; AG:**Stop, Collapse.** Earlier comments at CJ:101n.

330 Castaneda's Spanish—I am grateful to Carlos G. Barrón for providing points for this critique. Satisfactorily rendered—Wasson 1973:152.

Wrote in Spanish—Nevertheless, Castaneda must have been writing also in English quite early in the game, for "Philip Newman . . . says Castaneda showed him . . . 'revised field notes' (in English) no later than the spring of 1962. 'They were different [Newman said] because they recorded very long conversations'" (Preuss 1978:55). That is they were different from normal fieldnotes, being more like the manuscript of a novel, as John Hitchcock quickly saw but Castaneda's patrons have yet to admit.

331 Benefactor—At this point in his creative writing Castaneda had not yet distinguished *teacher* (mentioned in his letter to Wasson) from *benefactor* (mentioned in the fieldnotes); in *Tales of Power* the two terms would refer to quite different didactic roles, but here they refer to one man, don Juan's teacher or benefactor.

Stupid asses—Don Juan employs the Mexican obscenity *pendejo* (1. pubic hair, 2. a person stupid beyond recall).

Jesus to Peter—Matthew 26:34. Don Juan reminds Carlos—C71:115.

332 Spirits—C71:280. Part company—Wasson 1973:152. Bacatete Mountains—A region of legendary Yaqui exploits; compare Moisés & others 1971/1977.

RdeM
333 Ramón chronicled—Myerhoff 1968, 1974; Furst 1972, 1967. Translation—The process is described by Myerhoff 1974:18-21.

Contrast—C74:229-245. For comments on genuine and spurious discourse, see CJ:17-18. Genuine shamanic voices may be found in: *Shamanic Voices* (Halifax 1979), an article by Henry Munn (Harner 1973: 86-122), an article by Johannes Wilbert (Furst 1972:55-83), and in the monumental *María Sabina and Her Mazatec Mushroom Velada* (Wasson & others 1974), where the shaman's recorded voice may be heard as well as read in Mazatec, and read in Spanish and English. *Technicians of the Sacred* (Rothenberg 1968) offers a literary collection of shamanic discourses.

334 "Almost We Cannot Speak About It"—Myerhoff 1968:189, 209-210; reproduced by permission of Barbara G. Myerhoff; summary in italics prepared by RdeM. Illustrations of the peyoteros' activities may be seen in *Peyote Hunt* (Myerhoff 1974).

Richard de Mille   **42**
336 "Yoawima" is a Huichol name given by Ramón Medina to Barbara G.

Myerhoff, now professor and chairman (she would say chairperson) of anthropology at the University of Southern California (USC), across town from the University of California, Los Angeles (UCLA), where she received a BA in sociology and a PhD in Anthropology. In between, she acquired an MA in Human Development at the University of Chicago. "Conversations with Yoawima" is a title I invented to mimic Castaneda's subtitle *Further Conversations with Don Juan*, which in turn, I believe, mimics Griaule's *Conversations with Ogotemmêli* (see AG:**Conversations**); the title refers both to my conversations with Myerhoff tape-recorded in Santa Barbara, 25 January and 1 February 1978, and to Castaneda's many conversations with her beginning in the spring of 1966. For Castaneda as well as for me, Yoawima was a competent, credible informant offering authentic and fascinating observations of a very unusual person (Ramón or Castaneda) in his dealings with another world.

Shaman of Rincon—Myerhoff 1966. Carlos—In this article, as Barbara would, I often say "Carlos" when I mean Castaneda. *People* magazine—25 Sep 1978, 10(13):93-94. Haines Hall—Which housed the anthropology and sociology departments at UCLA.

Hurled words—Castaneda told Barbara don Juan would sometimes "hurl a word" at him; Underhill (1938:117,120) describes the Papago technique of "throwing words," a magical way of speaking to gods; the idea has not yet appeared in Castaneda's writings.

337 Ramón led us—Myerhoff 1974:44-46; with which compare Myerhoff 1968:94; Furst 1972:152-153; CJ:112-113, 112n. Now I will tell you—Myerhoff 1974:189. Yoawima—Myerhoff 1974:128. Castaneda dropped in—Peter Furst, telephone conversation, 5 May 1978. Strikingly similar—C71:122-128; Furst 1972:152-153; Myerhoff 1974:46; CJ:112-113, 112n.

338 Anachronism—C71:30,116; C74:187,245;CJ:91,53 note on three Genaros. My inference of anachronism appears to hang on a slender thread, which is Barbara's solitary, unsupported recall of a conversation in August 1966, when Castaneda said to her, "That's just like don Genaro." I shall now argue that this thread is tougher than it looks and show that it does not snap when strung on the bow-drum of logic. Four questions will test its strength.

First, is it possible Barbara lied to me? I confidently rule out this hypothesis on the basis of close examination of her works and conduct, judging her to be both a brave and honest reporter. More to the point than my judgment of her character, however, is my belief that when she told me about the conversation it was an admission against her own interest, which at that time was not to tell me anything, however innocent, that might embarrass Castaneda after running through my forensic typewriter, whose awesome power she had already seen in *Castaneda's Journey*.

Second, is it possible Castaneda described some other kind of event, which Barbara mistook for a report of a shaman demonstrating agility atop a waterfall? Again, I confidently rule this possibility out. Barbara's works show her to be a competent observer and careful reporter. Shamans on waterfalls were of great interest to her in 1966. Castaneda's story was given in response to her own. It is inconceivable that she could have mistaken the topic.

Third, could Castaneda's observation actually have occurred before Barbara's, and could she have gotten the sequence wrong? This point can be settled by referring to the public record. Barbara described her observation in a dissertation she gave to committee members in time for them to read it before she defended it in October 1968; Carlos supposedly saw Genaro on the waterfall on 17 October 1968. This conclusively rules out a mistaken sequence: Barbara's observation must have come before Castaneda's if Castaneda's existed, though not, of course, before Carlos's, which, being invented by Castaneda, was not subject to the strictures of ordinary time.

Fourth, is it possible Castaneda said to Barbara: "That's just like don Fulano, a shaman I saw in Mexico"? In other words, are we talking here about two different waterfall demonstrations? And did Barbara unintentionally substitute "Genaro" for "Fulano"? This is logically possible but highly implausible. It requires us to assume Castaneda saw two very similar performances, one before August 1966, which he has never reported in his books, and one in October 1968, which he reported in 1970 and 1971. If Castaneda were dealing with actual events rather than narrative inventions, would he slight the earlier don Fulano while making so much of the later don Genaro? The hypothesis must be rejected.

When, on 25 January 1978, I asked Barbara about the waterfall, she said (according to page 1 of the unedited transcript): "That was a very interesting incident. I mean, it never occurred to me in a million years that telling him about that proved anything except that I was doing good fieldwork because I had come up with the same material and the same interpretations that he had. It showed that these Mexican shamans popping around in the desert were really doing something serious and important, and I really had seen it, and so it was very validating to me, when he said: 'Oh, that's just like don Genaro.'" Some months later I casually asked Barbara if she were sure of his exact wording. She never altered the quotation or expressed any lack of confidence in it, which was in sharp contrast with her constant misgivings about the chronology. As we have seen, the sequence of events (which is the only aspect of the chronology that matters to the argument) rests on solid documentation and is not in question. Though the thread is slender, it is made of steel.

A friendly Juanist fanatic to whom I showed this note offered a *fifth* hypothesis: after hearing Castaneda's 1970 lecture or reading his 1971 book, Barbara dreamed the 1966 conversation and now mistakes the dream for ordinary reality. I have to admit such a thing could happen to many people, but I do not think they turn out work as solid as Barbara's, so I shall reject this fifth hypothesis also. In my opinion, reasonable men (male or female) will accept the anachronism as proved until further, contradictory evidence be presented.

340 Trickster—Radin 1956:169. Rorschach man—CJ:111; Lewis Yablonsky (1975) wrote: "Castaneda's . . . teachings have provided a vast anthropological Rorschach test upon which each reader (and critic) projects his own image of reality."

341 Coding for the EMers—Garfinkel was attached to the Neuropsychiatric Institute 1957-1966, Edgerton 1961-present.

344 Power spot—This was presumably the circle of boulders to which Castaneda conducted members of his UC-Irvine seminar a year later (CJ:27; Rueger 1973:73; Wallace 1972:141-142). Ramón murdered—June 1971 (Myerhoff 1974:24).

345 Parody—Oates 1974:10/1976:123. Lawrence Watson—Help acknowledged (C68:ix); for help unintentionally given by Watson, see AG:**Fog.**

346 Pigs for life—Don Juan says: "A man [detached by the idea of death] does not crave, for he has acquired a silent lust for life and for all things of life" (C71:184): a more restrained statement than "We are pigs for life."

347 Patience Worth—Litvag 1972. Megillah—Hebrew: a scroll, the Book of Esther, any extensive document.

350 Holes between the sounds—C71:267. Writer Alberta Greenfield, co-author with Castaneda of a book manuscript titled "The Whole World Sounds Strange, Don't You Think?" (Writers Guild of America West registry number 93093, 24 May 1965), told me (Interview, West Los Angeles, 2 April 1978) Castaneda had derived this formula from her habitual saying that one should learn to read "the space between the words."

351 Back against the wall—Castaneda quoted by Keen (1972:98/1976:87). Omen—Compare C72:38-39,72.

352 La Gorda—Margaret Castaneda told me (4 March 1978) Castaneda often called her La Gorda though she was always slim; she did, however, carry and bear a child during the time when he knew her.

Crossing eyes—C72:72, where Castaneda wrote "image conversion" though he meant convergence; for some Indian ideas likely to have been derived from BGM, see AG:**Myerhoff.**

Hard to find an Indian in any of Carlos's books—In a review of *Second Ring*, James Steck (1978), described by his editor (1978:47) as "a physician and a graduate of Stanford's writing program," said: "Castaneda cannot write very well [but] his Indians sound authentic in their hyperbole, blithe inconsistency, and affection for feet, hands, faces, and gestures. I once spent two months in an Indian village similar to Castaneda's before I found out that a healer lived in the ice cream store on my block." Since Castaneda's books nowhere describe an Indian village, I wrote to Dr Steck on 17 June 1979, asking the source of his information about Castaneda's Indian village, but received no reply.

Zen Buddhism—See AG:**Suzuki, Nagual, Tonal;** far from being offended, Myerhoff's fellow student Douglas Sharon found great value in Castaneda's transformed nagual and tonal; see AG:**Table.** Back and forth to Mexico—CJ:142.

353 Dream of Carlos—Myerhoff 1978:188-189.

Richard de Mille   **43**

355 "A Portrait of the Allegorist"—The illustrations, "Carlos Arana as a Child" and "Carlos Arana as a Youth," copyright © 1980 by Richard de Mille, were drawn for hire by Schlesinger from family photographs reproduced in Lévano 1973. César Arana's head was smaller than Schlesinger drew it; the other details are faithfully rendered. The photo shows Arana at the age of 15, more mature, less innocent than Schlesinger drew him; otherwise it is a very good likeness, showing him as he must have looked about the age of 13. The photographs belonged to Doña María Caruapoma.

Several versions—*Time* 1973:43/1976:101-102.

356 Pseudonyms—Warren Farley, Ramona DuVent, Marjory Dill, Wright Dennison, Eleanor Witt, Dolores, Esperanza. Blond woman—C72:92-95. Female child—C77:119.

357 Christmas Day—Reported by *Time* (1973:44/1976:103), which may explain the name Salvador, Savior, reported by Lévano (1973), a capable Peruvian journalist, who referred to an unpublished manuscript by historian Julio Rojas Melgarejo titled "Cajamarca y Cajamarquinos" and who interviewed several persons who had known Castaneda or his family. Additional biographical details are given in CJ: Chapter Two.

Margaret—Some of Margaret Runyan Castaneda's information comes from her article (1975), the rest from letters to and conversations with RdeM over a period of four years.

Mother—Susana Castañeda Novoa de Arana (*Time* 1973:44/1976:103); morose and beautiful (*Time* 1973:43/1976:102); diamond ring (Wallace 1972:140); rendezvous (M. Castaneda); never liked her (C71:73); Méndez (see DJP: Chapter 32); burden (C71:73).

358 Father—Professor (Cravens 1973a:93); never written (Cook 1973); Plato (Cravens 1973a:94); contempt (*Time* 1973:43/1976:102); vision (C68:108); father accused (Cravens 1973a; *Time* 1973; Keen 1972; C71:13; C72:62-66); change his mind (C72:30); rebellion: "an imposing figure that I unconsciously needed to fight, as don Juan had obviously been to me" (C77:293).

360 Don Juan as father—Warmth and kindness (C71:110); little friend (C71:297); flooded by tears (C72:81-82);wait for child (C72:45); going to die (C72:292); urge to weep (C74:191-192); last journey (C74:271-272).

362 Desertion by mother—C71:171. Famous man—Lévano 1973:16. Cajamarca—Compare CJ:130. Vicente—C71:46. Noises—C71:281. Two places at once—C74:48.

Schooling—Lévano 1973; finished high school at the Colegio Nacional de Nuestra Señora de Guadalupe (*Time* 1973:44/1976:104). Locked himself in—*Time* 1973:44/1976:104.

364 Delfín quoted—Lévano 1973:43. Bracamonte quoted—Lévano 1973. Something tremendous—"*Pero si este muchacho tiene un algo tremendamente interior.*"

Practicing secrecy—"Men who need to present false fronts and preserve dark secrets about themselves also need to maintain distance between themselves and others" (Stebbins 1975:200); don Juan told Carlos: "You are given to mysteries and secrets" (C71:274).

I am my father—*Time* 1973:43/1976:102. Letters—Lévano 1973.

365 Occupations—M. Castaneda 1975; Parrott 1975; Alberta Greenfield (interview 2 April 1978); conversations with old man (C71:109; CJ:28n).

366 No interest in mysticism—Freilicher 1972. Strange twist—Keen 1972:98/ 1976:87. Vernon King—*Time* 1973:43/1976:103. Bonds—M. Castaneda 1975:74,75,77.

368 Child in Argentina—Rumor reported by Warren Farley (CJ:30).

369 Sorcerer's double—C74:48,51-53, 61,67,82; CJ:127n; AG:**Double.**

370 Winds—See AG:**Wind-Women.** Von Franz—See DJP: Chapter 38. Not a sexual affair—Wallace 1972:141.

Perls—"I was with Carlos at Esalen, visiting Fritz Perls" (Alberta Greenfield, telephone, 29 May 1977); see also Hendlin 1973.

372 Student career—CJ:27,27n,68n. Piltdown—Compare DJP: Chapter 12; CJ2:xi. B. Traven—Baumann 1976; quotes from page 86.

373 *Great Impostor* (GI)—Crichton 1959; rotten (GI:8,217; C72:239); frightened (GI:18; Cravens 1973a:93; compare C71:171-172); leaf (GI:206; C72:138,139,150); boredom (GI:87,208; C72:35); power (GI:103); laughing (GI:216; Harner in Stein 1975; Greenfield 2 April 1978); cheater (GI:10; Meunier 1979); impostors (GI:10); weirder (Wallace 1972:141).

374 *Track to Bralgu*—Wongar 1978; Larkin 1978 (I am grateful to Paul Heelas for sending this article); Keneally 1978 (apparently having learned nothing from its experience with one hoaxer, the *New York Times Book Review* prepares to swallow another); Pearce 1974/1975; for a similar comment about genius, see Gorman (1978:173); for a German parallel in noble-savagery, see Ashliman (1977).

375 Motive—*Time* (1973:44/1976:105); Lee (1978) hinted a motive of hypocritical avarice; Oates 1974:12/1976:126; Bharati 1976a; Ramacharaka (Atkinson 1909); love to write (Cravens 1973b:177); Stebbins (1975:197) writes: "Inveterate deceivers . . . take a noticeable amount of pride in their skills of deceit."

376 Smell of experience—Sukenick 1976:112. Sukenick also said (113): "All versions of reality are of the nature of fiction. There's your story and my story, there's the journalist's story and the historian's story, there's the philosopher's story and the scientist's story. . . ." I wrote to Sukenick asking if he would maintain that all stories were equally true. He didn't answer, but Marvin Harris (1979:323-324) did, calling Sukenick's epistemology an "invitation to intellectual suicide" and adding: "Does Sukenick seriously believe that all versions of reality are fictions? If so, then he believes his version of reality is a fiction. Since he believes that everything he says is a fiction, including what he says about reality, only a fool would believe such a man about anything." For Harris's comments on the "moral opacity" of Sukenick's doctrine, see DJP: Chapter 35.

Metaphoric living—Keen 1972:96/1976:84; things are what they are (see AG: **Thing**); in Mexico (Sukenick 1976:119); Castaneda invited Garfinkel, Newman, and Myerhoff to meet don Juan (Preuss 1978:55; DJP: Chapter 42); profound state of belief (C68:148); evil world (C68:111-112; C74:224); black magicians (C74:28-29); magical time (Keen 1972:96/1976:84); real possibilities (AG:**Metaphor**).

377 Revenge—Abandoned son at six (C71:171); schools (C71:172); Church falls down (C74:105; CJ:135). Depression and self-rejection—C72:220,239; Keen 1972:102/1976:92. Boredom—C72:34,35.

378 Chosen man—C72:117. Frighten little boy—See AG: **Harner-m-n-o;** boy did not recall (telephone 24 June 1979); *Scared Straight,* a film that shows convicts telling juvenile delinquents about the terrors of prison; from 1966 to 1974 the little boy was living in West Virginia.

Answers to critics—Isolation (Pearce 1971:162/1973:172; C74:283; compare CJ:128); rationality (C74:173); curing (Deloria 1973:52-53,307; C77:259,218-219); friend Bill (CJ:29,33,61,91; see AG:**Bill**); Catalina confederate (C74:241); John of the Cross (see AG:**Juan de la Cruz**); exposing secrets (C74:16); Oaxaca, where Carlos and don Juan are waiting for don Genaro, "a Mazatec Indian" with whom don Juan lived (DJP:Chapter 40; C71:29-30,41; CJ:53n); see also AG:**Reality.**

379 Asceticism—Shift my eyes (C71:104); tight warrior's life (C74:156); rigid will (C68:146); self-discipline (C68:148; C72:221); whimpering child (C71:16); indulging (C74:192); only sorcery (C74:156,275); spartan apartments (M. Castaneda 1975); no LSD (Keen 1972:95/1976:80); one glass of wine (M. Castaneda 1975); trim and fit (Keen 1972:102/1976:92); lacks openness (*Time* 1973:43/1976:103); sensitivity (C74:13).

Anger—Hate (C72:166); reminds don Juan of himself (C72:192); displaced anger (C71:172-174). Hungry for love—(C72:95). Helpless—Infants (C74:87); rabbit (C72:113-115; Keen 1972:96/1976:84); see AG:**Rabbit.**

380 Power-hunting techniques—Flattery (DJP: Chapter 42); twisting (see AG:**Mechanics, Spirit-Catcher, Not-Doing, Petrullo, Gloss;** Collins 1974:47); mirroring (Harner 1973:140; C68:90-92; CJ:113-115; Pérez 1957:239, 310-312; which apparently relied on V. A. Reko's unreliable *La Flora Diabólica de México;* compare CJ2:115); one of Castaneda's terms for this mirroring is "stalking," a technique that involves simulating one's prey.

Broadcast—Roszak & Castaneda 1968; further examples may be sought in Muktananda 1974.

381 Mesmeric—*Time* 1973:43/1976:101. Mystifies—"One should meet strange events . . . with unexpected actions" (C77:144).

Older than patrons—Birthdates: Goldschmidt 1913, Garfinkel 1917, Meighan 1925, Castaneda 1925, Bolle 1927, Bright 1928, Newman 1931, Edgerton 1931, Graves 1932, Carlos 1935.

382 Bickerstein—Strachan 1977. Pretended anger—Lévano 1973. Manipulations—C72:18.

Sympathy—DJP: Chapter 42; Nin (Hinz 1975:227); for Nin's influence on Castaneda, see CJ:102,102n; Stebbins (1975:192) records the statement of a habitual deceiver that merits comparison: "A put-on I often use when dating a new girl is to tell her I've had an illigitimate son. I act very embarrassed and hurt, with the result that the girl thinks she knows a deep secret of my life. She then opens up to me about herself."

Carpenter—C68:jacket blurb. Women—Make one suffer (C68:138).

Children—Whisked away (C77:122); empty parents (C77:95,118-119,130-135); Soledad lucky (C77:234); Soledad kill (C77:134-135, 183-184,234); useless affection (C77:134).

383 *Caretas*—Lévano 1973.

384 Esperanza disappointed—For a similar awakening, see Wolff 1979.

385 Sorcerer not liable for others—See AG:**Power-b.** Shamans—White 1957:5; see also AG:**White.** Von Franz—See DJP: Chapter 38. Red bugs—C77:314.

386 Benefactor comes to open—C74:248. Publishing permissions—Daniel Noel, letter 10 Sept 1979; M. D. Faber, letter 13 Nov 1979.

387 Sorcerers don't help—C77:300; for a contrary, favorable interpretation, see Stillwell (1979:21), who says that a sorcerer's caring for his fellow sorcerer "is a letting-be rather than an intervention."

388 Warrior doesn't seek solace—C77:122. Long way to go—C77:309. Fleeting image—C71:286. No real compassion—Wallace 1972:141. No interest in fellow men—C71:186. Sorcerer's fate—C74:239-240. Tombstone—C77:233. Already dead—C74:35. No other way to live—C71:153.

Key for abbreviations (CJ, C68, etc.) is given in Appendix 45, Notes, along with scattered additional references not listed here.

Abel, Lionel. Sorcerers: The world of psi. *Humanist,* Jul-Aug **1975,** 35(4):35-36.

Aberle, David F. [Reviews C68.] *Man:Journal of the Royal Anthropological Institute,* Jun **1969,** 4(2):315-316.

Ackroyd, Peter. Comic strip [reviews C74]. *Spectator,* 10 May **1975,** 234(7663):581.

Adams, Richard N. **&** Arthur J. **Rubel.** Sickness and social relations. In *Handbook of Middle American Indians,* **1973,** 6:333-356.

Alexander, Hartley Burr. *The Mythology of All Races. Volume X. North American.* Marshall Jones 1916; Macmillan 1944; Cooper Square **1964.**

Allison, Paul D. Experimental parapsychology as a rejected science. In Wallis **1979:**271-291.

Alpert, Richard [Baba Ram Dass]. *Be Here Now.* Crown **1971.**

Alurista [Alberto Urista]. *Floricanto en Aztlán.* Chicano Cultural Center, UCLA **1971.**

———. *Nationchild Plumaroja.* Toltecas en Aztlán Publications (San Diego CA) **1972.**

———. *Timespace Huracán.* Pajarito Publications (2633 Granite NW, Albuquerque NM 87104) **1976.**

Anaya, Rudolfo A. *Bless Me, Ultima.* Quinto Sol **1972.**

Anderson, Eugene N. Jr, compiler. *A Revised Annotated Bibliography of the Chumash and their Predecessors.* Ballena **1978.**

Anderson, E. N. Jr, Marcello **Truzzi, &** Richard **de Mille.** [Letters about] Castaneda and anthropologists. *Zetetic [Skeptical Inquirer],* F-W **1977,** 2(1):122-124.

Angoff, Allan **&** Diana **Barth.** *Parapsychology and Anthropology.* Parapsychology Foundation (29 W. 57th St, NY 10019) **1974.**

Anselmo, Bruce. [Letters.] *Los Angeles Times Book Review,* 6 Mar **1977a:** 2; 24 Apr **1977b:**2.

Anson, Jay. *The Amityville Horror: A True Story.* Prentice-Hall **1977.**

Armstrong, Edward G. Phenomenologophobia. *Human Studies,* Jan **1979,** 2(1):63-75.

Artaud, Antonin. *The Peyote Dance.* Farrar, Straus & Giroux **1976.**

Ash, Lee. [Reviews C68.] *Library Journal,* **1969,** 94:1014.

———. [Reviews C71.] *Library Journal,* **1971,** 96:1630-1631.

———. [Reviews C72.] *Library Journal,* **1972,** 97:3328.

———. [Reviews C74.] *Library Journal,* **1974,** 99:1974.

Ashliman, D. L. The American Indian in German travel narratives and literature. *Journal of Popular Culture,* Spr **1977,** 10(4):831-839.

Atkinson, William Walker [Yogi Ramacharaka, pseudonym]. *Fourteen Lessons in Yogi Philosophy and Oriental Occultism.* Yogi Publication Society, **1909.** Copyright 1903.

Baldwin, Neil. The Castaneda series. *Journal of Psychedelic Drugs,* Oct-Dec **1977,** 9(4):347-349.

Barth, Fredrik, Colin Turnbull, **& others.** [Debate.] *Current Anthropology,* Mar **1974,** 15(1):99-103; Sep **1975,** 16(3):343-358.

Barthelme, Donald. The teachings of Don B.: A Yankee way of knowledge. *New York Times Magazine,* 11 Feb **1973**:14-15, 66-67.

Basso, Keith H. Southwestern ethnology. *Annual Review of Anthropology,* **1973,** 2(9529):246.

Bauman, Z. On the philosophical status of ethnomethodology. *Sociological Review,* Feb **1973,** 21(1):5-23.

Baumann, Michael L. *B. Traven: An Introduction.* U. New Mexico **1976.**

Beals, Ralph L. [Letters] *Los Angeles Times Book Review,* 17 Jul **1977a**:2; 16 Oct **1977b**:2.

———. Sonoran fantasy or coming of age? *American Anthropologist,* Jun **1978,** 80(2):355-362.

Bean, Lowell John **&** Katherine Siva **Saubel.** *Temalpakh: Cahuilla Indian Knowledge and Usage of Plants.* Malki Museum (Banning CA) **1972.**

Beardsley, Charles. [Reviews CJ.] *Peninsula Living,* 28 May **1977**:17.

———. [Reviews CJ2.] *Peninsula Times Tribune* (Palo Alto CA), 1 May **1979**.

Bharati, Agehananda. *The Ochre Robe: An Autobiography.* Allen & Unwin (London) **1961**; Doubleday 1970; Ross-Erikson distributors.

———. *The Tantric Tradition.* Rider (London) **1965;** Weiser 1975.

———. Anthropological approaches to the study of religion: Ritual and belief systems. *Biennial Review of Anthropology,* **1972**:230-263.

———. The ontological status of psychic phenomena in Hinduism and Buddhism. In Angoff & Barth **1974**:223-240.

———. *The Light at the Center: Context and Pretext of Modern Mysticism.* Ross-Erikson **1976a.**

———, editor. *The Realm of the Extra-Human: Agents and Audiences.* Mouton **1976b**; *Ideas and Actions.* Mouton **1976c.**

Bly, Robert. Carlos Castaneda meets Madame Solitude [reviews C77].*New York Times Book Review,* 22 Jan **1978**:7, 22.

Bok, Sissela. *Lying: Moral Choice in Public and Private Life.* Pantheon **1978.**

Booklist [reviews C71], 15 Sep **1971,** 68:68-69; [reviews C72], 15 Jan **1973,** 69:455, 457; [reviews C74], 15 Sep **1974,** 71:58; [reviews C77], 1 Dec **1977, 74**:599.

Bornstein, Marc H. The influence of visual perception on culture. *American Anthropologist,* Dec **1975, 77**(4):774-798.

Boshier, Adrian K. African apprenticeship. In Angoff & Barth **1974**:273-293.

Bourne, Tom. Carlos Castaneda: Genius or hoax? *Bookviews,* Nov **1978,** 2(3):38-39.

Bowen, Elenore Smith [pseudonym of Laura Bohannan]. *Return to Laughter.* Harper **1954**; Doubleday 1964.

Boyd, James W. The teachings of don Juan from a Buddhist perspective. *Christian Century,* 28 Mar **1973,** 90(13):360-363. Or in Noel **1976**:219-228.

Brien, Alan. Laughing matter [reviews C74 & Silverman 1975]. *Sunday Times* (London), 11 May **1975** (7926):40.

Brown, Carl R. V. *Journey to Ixtlan:* Inside the American Indian oral tradition. *Arizona Quarterly,* Sum **1976,** 32(2):138-145.

Brown, Carl Ray Vernon. *A Phenomenological Survey of Carlos Castaneda: Educational Implications and Applications.* Dissertation, Stanford University, Aug **1977**.

Bruce-Novoa. *Inocencia Perversa/Perverse Innocence.* Baleen Press (Phoenix) **1977**.

Bruteau, Beatrice. The grid-maker. *Fields within Fields,* W **1975** (14):42-48.

Bryant, Fred B. **&** Paul M. **Wortman.** Secondary analysis: The case for data archives. *American Psychologist,* Apr **1978,** 33(4):381-387.

Burke, Jeffrey. [Reviews C77.] *Harper's,* Feb **1978,** 265(1533):91.

Burns, L. C. [Letter.] *Horizon,* Jun **1979,** 22(6):72.

Burroughs, William. Interview. *Rolling Stone College Papers,* Fall **1979,** 1(1):41-42.

Capra, Fritjof. *The Tao of Physics.* Shambhala **1975**.

Carlsen, G. Robert, Tony **Manna,** & Betty Lou **Tucker.** Books for Young Adults 1974 honor listing. *English Journal,* Jan **1975,** 64(1):112-115.

Carroll, John B. Introduction [to Whorf **1956**:1-34].

Castaneda, Carlos. *The Teachings of Don Juan: A Yaqui Way of Knowledge.* U. California 27 Jun 1968a. **[C68]**

───── . The didactic uses of hallucinogenic plants: An examination of a system of teaching. *Abstracts of the 67th Annual Meeting* (of the American Anthropological Association) **1968b**:21-22. (Reference copied from La Barre 1975:277.)

───── . *A Separate Reality: Further Conversations with Don Juan.* Simon & Schuster 7 May 1971. **[C71]**

───── . *Journey to Ixtlan: The Lessons of Don Juan.* Simon & Schuster 23 Oct 1972. **[C72]**

───── . *Sorcery: A Description of the World* (Doctoral dissertation, University of California, Los Angeles). *Dissertation Abstracts International,* 1973, 33(12 Part 1, Jun), 5625B. (University Microfilms No. 73-13132—"For copies contact author at 308 Westwood Plaza, POB 101, Los Angeles CA 90024") UCLA library call number: LD 791.9 A6 C275. **[C73]**

───── . *Tales of Power.* Simon & Schuster 28 Oct 1974. **[C74]**

───── . *The Second Ring of Power.* Simon & Schuster Nov 1977a. **[C77]**

───── . The art of dreaming. *Psychology Today,* Dec **1977b,** 11(7):34-38, 118-122. (Passages adapted from C77.)

———. *The Art of Stalking.* Simon & Schuster, in press (see Korda 1979).

Castaneda, Margaret Runyan, as told to Wanda Sue Parrott. My husband Carlos Castaneda. *Fate,* Feb **1975,** 28(2/299):70-78.

Chagnon, Napoleon A. *Yanomamö: The Fierce People.* Holt Rinehart & Winston **1968.**

———. Love among the cannibals. *Book World,* 21 Sep **1969,** 3(38):12.

Chapman, Stephen. Gone legit. *New Republic,* 16 Dec **1978,** 179(25/3336):35.

Chisholm, Roderick M. **&** Thomas D. **Feehan.** The intent to deceive. *Journal of Philosophy,* Mar **1977,** 74(3):143-159.

Choice [reviews C68, C71, C72], Feb **1973,** 9(12):1627-1628.

——— [reviews C74], Mar **1975,** 12(1):112, 114.

Christoffers, Paul. [Letter.] *Reason,* Jul **1977,** 9(3):12, 49.

Chua, Beng-Huat. On the commitments of ethnomethodology. *Sociological Inquiry,* **1974,** 44(4):241-256.

CoEvolution Quarterly, Spr **1977** (13):136.

Cohen, Ronald D. Educational implications of the teachings of don Juan. *Phi Delta Kappan,* Mar **1974,** 55(7):496-497.

Collins, H. M. **&** T. J. **Pinch.** The construction of the paranormal: Nothing unscientific is happening. In Wallis **1979:**237-270.

Collins, Jack. [Reviews Schneebaum 1979.] *The Sentinel,* 18 May **1979:**16.

Collins, James. Carlos Castaneda . . . or the making of a guru. *Fate,* Apr **1974,** 27(4/289):38-49.

Contemporary Authors [biography of Carlos Castaneda], **1977,** 25.

Contemporary Literary Criticism [of Castaneda], **1980,** 12.

Cook, Bruce. Is Carlos Castaneda for real? *National Observer,* 24 Feb **1973,** 12(8):33.

Córdova-Rios, Manuel **&** F. Bruce **Lamb.** *Wizard of the Upper Amazon.* Atheneum **1971.** (See also: Lamb 1974.)

Cox, Jean W. The warrior's way: Castaneda's key to impeccability. *Southwest Review,* Aut **1976,** 61(4):386-394.

——— **&** Charles H. **Cox.** Overcoming alienation: Don Juan's concept of the warrior. *Religious Humanism,* W **1977,** 11(1):39-42.

Crapanzano, Vincent. Popular anthropology. *Partisan Review,* **1973,** 40(3):471-482.

———. Exotica, erotica [reviews Schneebaum 1979]. *New York Times Book Review,* 11 Mar **1979:**12.

Cravens, Gwyneth. Talking to power and spinning with the ally. *Harper's,* Feb **1973a,** 246(1473):91-94, 97.

———. The mysterious world of Carlos Castaneda. *Seventeen,* Feb **1973b,** 32(2):116, 174, 177.

———. The arc of flight. *Harper's,* Sep **1974,** 249(1492):43.

Crichton, Robert. *The Great Impostor.* Random House **1959.**

Crowder, Joan. [Reviews CJ.] *Santa Barbara News-Press,* 20 Nov **1976:**C13.

Crump, S. T. [Reviews C71.] *Man: Journal of the Royal Anthropological Institute,* Mar **1973,** 8(1):135-136.

Cultural Information Service [reviews CJ], Dec **1976**:22.

Darrach, Brad. Yaqui sorcerer's failed apprentice [reviews C71]. *Life,* 14 May **1971,** 70(18):20.

David-Neel, Alexandra. *Magic and Mystery in Tibet.* Crown **1932**; Dover 1971.

Deloria, Vine Jr. *God is Red.* Grosset & Dunlap **1973.**

de Mille, Richard. *Castaneda's Journey: The Power and the Allegory.* Capra Press (POB 2068, Sta Barbara CA 93120) 1976; 2nd edition 1978 [**CJ, CJ2**]. Sphere/Abacus (London) 1978. Berkley, in press for 1980.

———. [Letters.] *Los Angeles Times Book Review,* 27 Mar **1977a**:2; 24 Apr **1977b**:2; 16 Oct **1977d**:2.

———. [Letter.] *Reason,* Jul **1977c,** 9(3):10-12.

———. *Castaneda: Trickster-Teacher* (Tape Cassette WR136, 2 hrs). New Age Communications (POB 1047, Pacific Grove CA 93950) **1977e.**

———. Witches' brujaja: Sorcerer joins sinister sorority [reviews C77]. *Santa Barbara News-Press,* 26 Nov **1977f**:C20.

———. [Reviews Long 1977.] *Skeptical Inquirer,* Spr-Sum **1978a,** 2(2):108-112.

———. [Reviews C77.] *Skeptical Inquirer,* Spr-Sum **1978b,** 2(2):114-116.

———. [Reviews Wasson, Hofmann, & Ruck 1978.] *Parabola,* Aug **1978c,** 3(3):110, 112.

——— Explicating anomalistic anthropology with help from Castaneda. *Abstracts of the 77th Annual Meeting* (of the American Anthropological Association), Abstract 347, **1978d**:143. (See also: RdeM 1979e.)

———. [Reproduces CJ2:ix-xi.] *Human Behavior,* Mar **1979a,** 8(3):68-69.

———. [Preliminary version of DJP. Chapter 2.] *Horizon,* Apr **1979b,** 22(4):64-70.

———. [Letter.] *Horizon,* Jun **1979c,** 22(6):72.

———. [Reviews C77.] *American Anthropologist,* Mar **1979d,** 81(1):188-189.

———. Explicating anomalistic anthropology with help from Castaneda. *Zetetic Scholar,* Apr **1979e,** 1(3&4):69-70.

———, Agehananda **Bharati, &** Philip **Staniford.** [Letters.] *Phoenix: New Directions in the Study of Man,* Sum **1978,** 2(1):57-59.

——— & Daniel C. **Noel.** [Preliminary version of DJP: Chapter 18.] *Parabola,* **1978,** 3(1):104-108.

de Rios, Marlene Dobkin. The anthropology of drug-induced altered states of consciousness: Some theoretical considerations. *Sociologus,* **1972a,** 22(1-2):147-151.

———. *The Use of Hallucinogenic Substances in Peruvian Amazonian Folk Healing.* Dissertation, University of California, Riverside, Aug **1972b.** (DAI 34/10-B4797; XUM 74-09241.)

———. [Reviews Córdova-Rios & Lamb 1971.] *American Anthropologist*, Dec **1972c**, 74(6):1423-1424.

——— & David E. **Smith.** Drug use and abuse in cross cultural perspective. *Human Organization*, Spr **1977**, 36(1):14-21.

de Ropp, Robert S. *Warrior's Way: The Challenging Life Games.* Delacorte **1979.**

Dingwall, Eric J. The end of a legend: A note on the magical flight. In Angoff & Barth **1974**:241-261.

Dolby, R. G. A. Reflections on deviant science. In Wallis **1979**:9-47.

Dorfman, D. D. The Cyril Burt question: New findings. *Science*, 29 Sep **1978**, 201(4362):1177-1186.

Doty, William G. The stories of our times. In James B. Wiggins, editor, *Religion as Story*, Harper & Row **1975**:93-121.

Drury, Nevill. [Reviews CJ.] *Nation Review* (Sydney), 27 Apr **1977.**

———. *Don Juan, Mescalito and Modern Magic: The Mythology of Inner Space.* Routledge & Kegan Paul **1978.** (Reviewed by *Choice*, Oct 1978:1035.)

Duerr, Hans Peter. Können Hexen fliegen? [Can witches fly?] *Zeitschrift für Parapsychologie und Grenzgebiete der Psychologie*, **1978a,** 20(2):75-91. Summary in English.

———. *Traumzeit: Über die Grenze zwischen Wildnis und Zivilisation* [Dreamtime: On the Border between Wilderness and Civilization]. Syndikat (Postfach 174003, 6000 Frankfurt) **1978b.**

Easlea, Brian. Who needs the liberation of nature? *Science Studies*, **1974,** 4(1):75-92.

Eisenbud, Jule. *The World of Ted Serios.* Morrow **1967.**

———. *Psi and Psychoanalysis.* Grune & Stratton **1970.**

Eliade, Mircea. *Shamanism: Archaic Techniques of Ecstasy.* Princeton **1964.**

Esquire [editorial], Mar **1971**, 75(3/448):75.

Evers, L. M., Stan **Wilk, &** Robert **Bly.** [Letters.] *New York Times Book Review*, 7 May **1978**:45. (Error in Wilk's letter corrected *NYTBR*, 25 Jun 1978:56.)

Faber, M. D. Castaneda and don Juan: An unconscious dimension of the master-pupil relationship (I, II). *Psychocultural Review*, Sum, Fall **1977a,** 1(3,4):261-284, 399-420.

———. Don Juan and Castaneda: The psychology of altered awareness. *Psychoanalytic Review*, Fall, **1977b,** 64(3):323-379.

Fadiman, James. [Reviews CJ.] *San Francisco Bay Guardian*, 20 Jan **1977,** 11(15):9.

Farren, David [pseudonym of Douglass McFerran]. *Living with Magic.* Simon & Schuster **1974.**

———. *Sex and Magic.* Simon & Schuster **1975.**

———. [Reviews CJ.] *Books West*, Apr **1977,** 1(4):37.

———. [Reviews C77.] *Los Angeles Times Book Review*, 5 Mar **1978**:4.

Finnegan, Gregory A. [Reviews CJ & Noel 1976.] *Contemporary Psychology*, Oct **1977,** 22(10):744-745.

Finney, Charles G. *The Circus of Dr. Lao.* Viking **1936.**

First, Elsa. Don Juan is to Carlos Castaneda as Carlos Castaneda is to us [reviews C68, C71, C72, C74]. *New York Times Book Review,* 27 Oct **1974a**:35, 38, 40. Or in Noel **1976**:57-64.

———. Visions, voyages and new interpretations of madness. In John White, editor, *Frontiers of Consciousness,* Julian, **1974b**:43-52.

Fisher, Ron. [Letter.] *Time,* 26 Mar **1973,** 101(13):8.

Fisher, Stanley. [Letter.] *Psychology Today,* Mar **1978,** 11(10):10.

Forisha, Barbara. Castaneda: Humanist and/or mystic? *Journal of Humanistic Psychology,* Fall **1978,** 18(4):29-35.

Foss, Laurence. Does don Juan really fly? *Philosophy of Science,* Jun **1973,** 40(2):298-316.

Foster, George M. Nagualism in Mexico and Guatemala. *Acta Americana,* Jan-Jun **1944,** 2(1&2):85-103.

Freilicher, Lila. The Carlos Castaneda trilogy. *Publishers Weekly,* 20 Nov **1972,** 202(21):50-51.

Furst, Peter T. West Mexican tomb sculpture as evidence for shamanism in prehispanic Mesoamerica. *Antropológica,* Dec **1965** (15):29-80.

———. *Shaft Tombs, Shell Trumpets and Shamanism: A Culture-Historical Approach to Problems in West Mexican Archaeology.* Dissertation, University of California, Los Angeles, **1966.** (DAI 27/06-B1703; XUM 66-11907.)

———. Huichol conceptions of the soul. *Folklore Americas,* Jun **1967,** 27(2):39-106.

———, editor. *Flesh of the Gods: The Ritual Use of Hallucinogens.* Praeger **1972.**

———. *Hallucinogens and Culture.* Chandler & Sharp **1976.**

——— & Barbara G. **Myerhoff.** Myth as history: The Jimson weed cycle of the Huichols of Mexico. *Antropológica,* Jun **1966** (17):3-39.

Garfinkel, Harold. *Studies in Ethnomethodology.* Prentice-Hall **1967.**

——— & Harvey **Sacks.** On formal structures of practical actions. In McKinney & Tiryakian **1970**:337-366.

Garvin, Gloria. Shamans and rock art symbols. In C. William Clewlow Jr, editor, *Four Rock Art Studies,* Ballena **1978**:65-87.

Gidlow, Bob. Ethnomethodology—a new name for old practices. *British Journal of Sociology,* Dec **1972,** 23(4):395-405.

Gill, Jerry H. The world of don Juan: Some reflections. *Soundings,* W **1974,** 57(4):387-402.

Gill, Sam D. [Reviews CJ.] *Parabola Guide,* Spr **1977,** 1(1):4.

Globus, Gordon G. Consciousness and brain. *Archives of General Psychiatry,* Aug **1973,** 29:153-160, 167-176.

———. Will the real "don Juan" please stand up. *The Academy* (American Academy of Psychoanalysis, 40 Gramercy Park North, NY 10010), Dec **1975,** 19(4):11-14.

———. Mind, structure, and contradiction. In G. G. Globus, G. Maxwell, & I. Savodnik, editors, *Consciousness and the Brain,* Plenum **1976**:271-293.

Goldschmidt, Walter. *Exploring the Ways of Mankind,* 2nd edition. Holt, Rinehart & Winston **1971**; 3rd edition **1977.**

———. Biological versus social evolution. *American Psychologist,* May **1976,** 31(5):355-357.

Gorman, Michael E. A. J. Korzybski, J. Krishnamurti, and Carlos Castaneda: A modest comparison. *Et Cetera,* Jun **1978,** 35(2):162-174.

Gould, Stephen Jay. Smith Woodward's folly. *New Scientist,* 5 Apr **1979,** 82(1149):42-44.

Gouldner, Alvin W. *The Coming Crisis of Western Sociology.* Basic Books **1970.**

Gover, Bob. [Reviews CJ.] *Reason,* Apr **1977a,** 8(12):40-41.

———. [Letter.] *Reason,* Jul **1977b,** 9(3):12.

Govinda, Lama Anagarika. *The Way of the White Clouds: A Buddhist Pilgrim in Tibet.* Shambala **1971.**

Grange, Joseph. [Reviews C71.] *Commonweal,* 17 Sep **1971,** 94(20):482-483.

———. [Reviews C72.] *Commonweal,* 6 Apr **1973,** 98(5):117-118.

Green, Elmer & Alyce **Green.** *Beyond Biofeedback.* Delacorte/Lawrence **1977.**

Greening, Thomas C. Commentary by the editor. *Journal of Humanistic Psychology,* Fall **1978,** 18(4):1-3.

Griaule, Marcel. *Conversations with Ogotemmêli: An Introduction to Dogon Religious Ideas.* Oxford U. Press **1965** (hb), **1970** (pb).

Grosso, Michael. *Journal of the American Society for Psychical Research,* Jul **1977,** 71(3):310.

Gurney, E., F. W. H. **Myers,** & F. **Podmore.** *Phantasms of the Living.* Trübner (London) **1886.**

Gwynne, Peter & others. All about clones. *Newsweek,* 20 Mar **1978,** 91(12):68-69.

Halifax, Joan. *Shamanic Voices: A Survey of Visionary Narratives.* Dutton **1979.**

Halstead, L. B. New light on the Piltdown hoax? *Nature,* 2 Nov **1978,** 276(5683):11-13.

Hardy, Julia. [Reviews Holroyd 1977.] *Parapsychology Review,* Sep-Oct **1977,** 8(5):13-15.

Harner, Michael J. Jívaro souls. *American Anthropologist,* Apr **1962,** 64(2):258-272.

———. *Machetes, Shotguns, and Society: An Inquiry into the Social Impact of Technological Change among the Jívaro Indians.* Dissertation, University of California, Berkeley, **1963.** (DAI 24:3497; XUM 64-2060.)

———. The sound of rushing water. *Natural History,* Jun-Jul **1968,** 77:28-33, 60-61.

———. *The Jívaro: People of the Sacred Waterfalls.* Natural History Press 3 Nov **1972**; Doubleday/Anchor 1973.

———, editor. *Hallucinogens and Shamanism.* Oxford **1973.**

————. [Letter.] *New York Times Book Review*, 7 May **1978**:45.

Harpon, Carl. [Letter.] *Los Angeles Times Book Review*, 1 May **1977**:2.

Harris, Marvin. *Cows, Pigs, Wars & Witches: The Riddles of Culture.* Random House **1974**.

————. *Cultural Materialism: The Struggle for a Science of Culture.* Random House **1979**.

Heelas, Paul. Expressing the inexpressible: Don Juan and the limits of formal analysis. *Journal of the Anthropological Society of Oxford*, Michaelmas **1972**, 3(3):133-148.

Hendlin, Steven Jeffrey. *Toward a Converging Philosophy: Don Juan Matus and the Gestalt Therapy of Frederick Perls.* Master's thesis, United States International University, **1973**. (MA 1973 11:313; XUM M-4599.)

Hill, W. W. Navajo use of Jimsonweed. *New Mexico Anthropologist*, **1938**, 3:19-21.

Hillman, James. *Re-Visioning Psychology.* Harper & Row **1975**.

Hinz, Evelyn J., editor. *A Woman Speaks: The Lectures, Seminars, and Interviews of Anaïs Nin.* Swallow **1975**.

Hixson, Joseph. *The Patchwork Mouse.* Doubleday/Anchor **1976**.

Holbrook, Robert. [Letter.] *Fate*, Oct **1978**, 31(10/343):116-117.

Holroyd, Stuart. *Psi and the Consciousness Explosion.* Taplinger **1977**.

Hooper, Dick. Castaneda trickster-teacher: A conversation with Richard de Mille. *Zetetic Scholar*, **1978**, 1(1):27-30.

Hoover, Eleanor Links. Far out: Becoming a warrior and living the life of knowledge. *Human Behavior*, Sep **1977**, 6(9):14.

Horton, Robin. African traditional thought and Western science. *Africa*, Jan, Apr **1967**, 37:50-71, 155-187.

Houston, Jean. Myth, consciousness, and psychic research. In Mitchell & White **1974**:577-596.

Hughes, Robert. The sorcerer's apprentice [reviews C72]. *Time*, 6 Nov **1972**, 100(19):101.

Huxley, Aldous. *The Perennial Philosophy.* Arno **1945**; Harper 1970.

————. *The Doors of Perception.* Harper **1954**; H&R Colophon **1963**.

————. Drugs that shape men's minds. *Saturday Evening Post*, 18 Oct **1958**, 231(16):28-29, 108, 110-111, 113.

Inglis, Brian. The sorcerer's apprentice [reviews C77 & CJ]. *The Observer* (London), 11 Jun **1978**:27.

Jack, Alex. [CJ reviewed] by don Juan. *East West Journal*, Jan **1977**:49-51.

James, William. *Principles of Psychology*, volume 2. Henry Holt **1896**.

Jellinek, Roger. [Reviews C71.] *New York Times*, 14 May **1971**:37.

————. [Reviews C72.] *New York Times*, 14 Oct **1972**:31.

Johnson, Jean B. *El Idioma Yaqui.* Instituto Nacional de Antropología e Historia (México DF) **1962**.

Jonas, Hans. *The Gnostic Religion*, 2nd edition. Beacon **1963**.

Kanon, Joseph. [Reviews C72.] *Saturday Review*, 11 Nov **1972**, 55(46):67-69.

Karpel, Craig. Conversations without don Juan. *Playboy,* Aug **1975,** 22(8):186.

Keen, Sam. Sorcerer's apprentice. *Psychology Today,* Dec **1972,** 6(7):90-92, 95-96, 98, 100, 102. Or in Noel **1976**:72-92.

————. Don Juan's power trip [reviews C77]. *Psychology Today,* Dec **1977,** 11(7):40-42, 124, 140.

Keewaydinoquay. *Puhpohwee for the People: A Narrative Account of Some Uses of Fungi among the Ahnishinaubeg.* Botanical Museum of Harvard U. **1978.**

Kelley, Jane Holden. *Yaqui Women: Contemporary Life Histories.* U. Nebraska **1978.**

Keneally, Tom. [Reviews Wongar 1978.] *New York Times Book Review,* 25 Jun **1978**:14-15.

Kennedy, William. Fiction or fact [reviews C74]. *New Republic,* 16 Nov **1974,** 71(20/3123):28-30.

Kimmel, Michael S. [Reviews C68, C71, C72.] *American Journal of Sociology,* Jan **1974,** 79(4):1066-1068.

————. [Reviews C74.] *American Journal of Sociology,* Nov **1975,** 81(3):699-701.

Kitsepawit, Fernando Librado & John P. Harrington. *The Eye of the Flute: Chumash Traditional History and Ritual.* Santa Barbara Museum of Natural History **1977.**

Klüver, Heinrich. *Mescal, the 'Divine' Plant, and its Psychological Effects.* Kegan Paul, Trench, Trubner (London) **1928.** Re-issued as: *Mescal and Mechanisms of Hallucination.* U. Chicago 1966.

Kobler, John. The dangerous magic of LSD. *Saturday Evening Post,* 2 Nov **1963,** 236(38):30-32, 35-36, 39-40.

Koepping, Klaus-Peter. Castaneda and methodology in the social sciences: Sorcery or genuine hermeneutics? *Social Alternatives* (U. Queensland), Spr **1977,** 1(1):70-74.

Koestler, Arthur. *The Invisible Writing.* Macmillan **1954.**

Korda, Michael. *Power! How to Get It. How to Use It.* Random House **1975.**

————. A conversation about Carlos Castaneda. *Simon & Schuster Library News,* Dec **1979,** 4(1):5-8.

Krippner, Stanley. *Song of the Siren: A Parapsychological Odyssey.* Harper & Row **1975.**

———— & Alberto **Villoldo.** *The Realms of Healing.* Celestial Arts **1976.**

Krishnamurti, J[iddu]. *The Flight of the Eagle.* Harper & Row **1971.**

Kroeber, Theodora. *Ishi in Two Worlds: A Biography of the Last Wild Indian in North America.* U. California **1961.**

Krupp, E. C., editor. *In Search of Ancient Astronomies, Stonehenge to von Däniken.* Doubleday **1978.**

Kuhn, Thomas S. *The Structure of Scientific Revolutions.* U. Chicago **1970.**

La Barre, Weston. *The Peyote Cult.* Shoe String 1959, 1964. Schocken 1969, **1975.**

———. [Reviews CJ2.] *Journal of Psychological Anthropology*, Sum **1979**, 2(3):377-378.

Laird, Linda. [Reviews CJ.] *Books of the Southwest*, Nov **1977** (228):4.

Lamal, Jonathan. [Letter.] *Los Angeles Times Book Review*, 31 Jul **1977**:2.

Lamb, F. Bruce. *Wizard of the Upper Amazon: The Story of Manuel Córdova-Rios*. Houghton-Mifflin **1974**. (See Córdova-Rios & Lamb 1971.)

Langer, Susanne K. The growing center of knowledge. In Lynn White, editor, *Frontiers of Knowledge*, Harper's 1956. In S. K. Langer, *Philosophical Sketches*, Johns Hopkins **1962**:143ff.

Langham, Ian. Talgai and Piltdown—The common context. *Artefact* (U. Melbourne). Dec **1978**, 3(4):181-224.

———. The Piltdown hoax. *Nature*, 18 Jan **1979**, 277:170.

Langness, L. L. *Other Fields, Other Grasshoppers: Readings in Cultural Anthropology*. Lippincott **1977**.

Larkin, John. Mystery of Wongar, the Outback's wonder writer. *Observer* (London), 23 Jul **1978**:5.

Larsen, Stephen. *The Shaman's Doorway: Opening the Mythic Imagination to Contemporary Consciousness*. Harper & Row **1976**.

Leach, Edmund. High school. *New York Review of Books*, 5 Jun **1969**, 12:12-13. Or in Noel **1976**:33-38.

LeClair, Thomas. [Reviews C77.] *Saturday Review*, 4 Feb **1978**, 5(9):38.

Lee, Hermione. Secret smokers. *New Statesman*, 12 May **1978**, 95(2460):647.

Leighton, Alexander H. & Dorothea C. **Leighton.** Gregorio, the hand trembler. *Papers of the Peabody Museum*, Harvard U., **1949**, 40(1).

Leonard, John. [Reviews C77.] *New York Times*, 29 Dec **1977**:44(C18).

Lévano, César. La realidad del brujo: Un peruano que gana millones con sus libros. *Caretas* (Jirón Camaná 615, Lima), 10-24 Apr **1973** (475):16-17, 42-43. Illustrated.

Levi, Albert William. [Reviews C68 & C71.] *Saturday Review*, 21 Aug **1971**, 54(34):25.

Lewis, C. S. *The Lion, the Witch, and the Wardrobe: A story for Children*, Book One of the Chronicles of Narnia. Macmillan **1950**.

———. *Till We Have Faces*. Harcourt, Brace & World **1956**; Eerdmans **1964**.

Lewis, Dennis. [Reviews C77.] *Library Journal*, 1 Nov **1977**, 102:2267.

Lewis, Peter. Portrait of the author as a mystic who doesn't want to be anyone's guru. *Daily Mail* (London), 8 May **1975**:7.

Liebmann-Smith, Richard. Easy come, easy go. *Harper's*, Sep **1978**, 257(1540):100.

Lindsay, David. *A Voyage to Arcturus*. Macmillan **1963**.

Lindsey, Hal. *There's A New World Coming*. Vision House **1973**.

Littleton, C. Scott. An emic account of sorcery: Carlos Castaneda and the rise of a new anthropology. *Journal of Latin American Lore*, W **1976**, 2(2):145-155.

Litvag, Irving. *Singer in the Shadows: The Strange Story of Patience Worth.* Macmillan **1972.**

Lobsang Rampa, T[uesday: Pseudonym of Cyril Henry Hoskin]. *The Third Eye: The Autobiography of a Tibetan Lama.* Secker & Warburg **1956;** Doubleday 1957.

Long, Haniel. *The Marvellous Adventure of Cabeza de Vaca & Malinche (Doña Marina).* Souvenir Press (London) 1972—Distributed by Southern Methodist U. Press (Dallas TX 75275). Earlier editions under various titles, now out of print: Writers' Editions 1936; Duell, Sloan & Pearce 1944; Frontier **1969,** cited here;Ballantine 1973.

Long, Joseph K. Shamanism, trance, hallucinogens, and psychical events: Concepts, methods, and techniques for fieldwork among primitives. In Bharati **1976b:**301-313.

———, editor. *Extrasensory Ecology: Parapsychology and Anthropology.* Scarecrow **1977.**

López-Portillo y Pacheco, José. *"Don Q": Conversaciones sobre la Yoeidad y Otras Trascendentalidades.* Librería de Manuel Porrúa, S.A. (5 de Mayo 49, México 1 DF) Apr **1969.**

Lopez Portillo, José. *Don Q.* Seabury **1976.**

[Luria-] Sukenick, Lynn. *Houdini.* Capra **1973.**

Luria-Sukenick, Lynn. [Reviews C77.] *American Book Review,* Sum **1979,** 2(1):7. A version of DJP: Chapter 34.

Lutz, Frank W. **&** Margaret A. **Ramsey.** Nondirective cues as ritualistic indicators in educational organizations. *Education & Urban Society,* May **1973,** 5(3):345-365.

MacCracken, Peter James. [Letter.] *Los Angeles Times Book Review,* 10 Apr **1977:**2.

MacDougall, Curtis D. *Hoaxes.* Dover **1958.**

MacInnes, Colin. Power Play. *New Society,* 8 May **1975,** 32(657):356.

Madsen, William. [Reviews CJ.] *Santa Barbara News & Review,* 14 Jan **1977,** 6(1/203):28.

——— **&** Claudia **Madsen.** The sorcerer's apprentice [reviews C68, C71]. *Natural History,* Jun **1971,** 80(6):74-76, 78-80.

Maloy, Robert W. The Don Quixote problem of multiple realities in Schutz and Castaneda. *Journal of the British Society for Phenomenology,* Jan **1977,** 8(1):28-35.

Mandelbaum, David G., editor. *Selected Writings of Edward Sapir in Language, Culture and Personality.* U. California **1949.**

Mandell, Arnold J. Don Juan in the mind. *Human Behavior,* Jan **1975,** 4(1):64-69. (Also in *Ontario Review,* Spr-Sum 1975; *Pushcart Prize* 1976.)

Maquet, Jacques. Castaneda: Warrior or scholar? *American Anthropologist,* Jun **1978,** 80(2):362-363.

Margolis, Joseph. Don Juan as philosopher. In Noel **1976:**228-242.

Marin, Peter. The new narcissism. *Harper's,* Oct **1975,** 251(1505):45-56.

Marty, Martin E. The Castaneda cult. *Christian Century,* 21 Mar **1973,** 90(12):351.

Mason, Michael. High jinks [reviews C74]. *New Statesman*, 27 Jun **1975,** 89(2310):832.

Mather, Col. Cottonpicking. [Letter.] *Fate*, Jan **1979,** 32(1/346):113-114.

Matthiessen, Peter. *The Snow Leopard.* Viking **1978.**

McAllister, Mick. [Reviews C77 & CJ.] *Denver Post*, 8 Jan **1978.**

McDermott, Richard. Reasons, rules and the ring of experience: Reading our world into Carlos Castaneda's works. *Human Studies*, Jan **1979,** 2(1):31-46.

McFadden, Carol Prester. A separate reality. *Christianity Today*, 13 Feb **1976,** 20:482, 484.

McFerran, Douglass. The Castaneda plot. *America*, 26 Feb **1977,** 136(8/3478):162-164.

McKinney, John C. & Edward A. **Tiryakian,** editors. *Theoretical Sociology.* Appleton-Century-Crofts **1970.**

McMahon, Martin 3rd. *Notes* [on C68, C71, C72]. Cliffs Notes (Lincoln NB 68501) **1974.**

Mead, Margaret & Nicolas **Calas,** editors. *Primitive Heritage: An Anthropological Anthology.* Random House **1953.**

Medawar, P. B. [Reviews Hixson 1976.] *New York Review of Books*, 15 Apr **1976,** 23(6):6, 8, 10-11.

Mehan, Hugh & Houston **Wood.** *The Reality of Ethnomethodology.* Wiley **1975.**

Meinke, Peter. [Reviews Noel 1976.] *Christian Century*, 20 Oct **1976,** 93(33):907-908.

Melton, J. Gordon. [Reviews CJ.] *Fate*, Jun **1977,** 30(6/327):102, 104.

Méndez, Miguel. Tata Casehua. In Octavio I. Romano & Herminio Ríos, editors, *El Espejo: An Anthology of Chicano Literature*, Quinto Sol **1969:**30-43.

———. *Los Criaderos Humanos (Epica de los Desamparados) y Sahuaros.* Editorial Peregrinos (Tucson) **1975.**

Meunier, Jacques. Carlos Castaneda, un maître de l'ethnologie-fiction? *Le Monde* (Paris), Jan **1979.**

Millar, Ronald. *The Piltdown Men.* Gollancz (London); St Martin's **1972.**

Minogue, Kenneth. The guru: Thoughts after reading Carlos Castaneda. *Encounter*, Aug **1976,** 47(2):19-29. Reproduced as DJP: Chapter 21.

Mitchell, Edgar D. & John **White,** editors. *Psychic Exploration.* Putnam's **1974.**

Mitchell, Richard. *Less than Words can Say.* Little, Brown **1979.**

Mitgang, Herbert. Behind the best sellers: Carlos Castaneda. *New York Times Book Review*, 5 Mar **1978:**40.

Moisés, Rosalio, Jane Holden **Kelley,** & William Curry **Holden.** *The Tall Candle* [retitled in 1977] *A Yaqui Life: The Personal Chronicle of a Yaqui Indian.* U. Nebraska **1971,** 1977.

Monroe, Robert A. *Journeys out of the Body.* Doubleday **1971,** 1973.

Moore, John H. [Reviews Storm 1972.] *American Anthropologist*, Aug **1973,** 75(4):1040-1042.

Moran, Rick & Peter **Jordan.** *The Amityville Horror* hoax. *Fate,* May **1978,** 31(5/338):43-47.

Morris, Robert L. [Reviews Anson 1977.] *Skeptical Inquirer,* Spr-Sum **1978,** 2(2):95-102.

Muktananda Paramahansa, Swami. [Unpublished 30-minute tape recording of conversation with Carlos Castaneda & translator Jinendra Jain at Piedmont CA, 5 May **1974.**] SYDA Foundation (POB 11071 Oakland CA 94611).

Mullins, Nicholas C. *Theories and Theory Groups in Contemporary American Sociology.* Harper & Row **1973.**

Murphy, Gardner & Robert O. **Ballou,** editors. *William James on Psychical Research.* Viking **1960.**

Murray, Stephen O. The scientific reception of Castaneda. *Contemporary Sociology,* Mar **1979a,** 8(2):189-192.

———. *Social Science Networks: Theory Groups in the Study of Language in Society.* Doctoral dissertation, University of Toronto, **1979b.**(Non-circulating; published as Murray 1980.)

———. *Group Formation in Social Science.* Linguistic Research, Inc. (Edmonton, Alberta) in press for **1980.** (Published version of Murray 1979b.)

Myerhoff, Barbara G. The doctor as culture hero: The shaman of Rincon. *Anthropological Quarterly,* Apr **1966,** 39(2):60-72.

———. *The Deer-Maize-Peyote Complex among the Huichol Indians of Mexico.* Doctoral dissertation, University of California, Los Angeles, **1968.** (DAI 30/02-B475; XUM 69-11899.)

———. *Peyote Hunt: The Sacred Journey of the Huichol Indians.* Cornell U. **1974.**

———. *Number Our Days.* Dutton **1978.**

Myers, F. W. H. *Human Personality and its Survival of Bodily Death.* Longmans Green **1903.**

Naranjo, Claudio & Michael J. **Harner.** *Shamanism and the Unconscious* (Tape Cassette AT123, 55 minutes). New Age Communications (POB 1047, Pacific Grove CA 93950) **1968?**

Nash, Carroll B. *Science of Psi: ESP and PK.* C C Thomas **1978.**

Needham, Rodney. *Primordial Characters.* U. Press of Virginia **1978.**

Nelson, David. The self-equated beetle. *Inside,* Jul-Aug **1974,** 5(4):22-28.

Nelson, Marie Coleman. Paths of power: Psychoanalysis and sorcery. *Psychoanalytic Review,* Fall **1976,** 63(3):333-360.

New Age, Feb **1975,** 1(3):17; Feb **1977a,** 2(9):67; Aug **1977b,** 3(3):6.

Newport, John P. *Christ and the New Consciousness.* Broadman **1978.**

Noel, Daniel C. Makings of meaning: Carlos Castaneda's "lived hermeneutics" in the cargo culture. *Listening: Current Studies in Dialog,* W **1972,** 7(1):83-90.

———, editor. *Seeing Castaneda: Reactions to the "Don Juan" Writings of Carlos Castaneda.* Putnam's **1976.**

———. [Reviews CJ.] *Parabola*, **1977**, 2(3):87-90.

———. Carlos Castaneda. *Collier's Encyclopedia*, volume 5. Macmillan, in press for **1980**.

Nordell, G. E. [Letter.] *Los Angeles Times Book Review*, 10 Apr **1977**:2.

Nuñez. *Relation of Alvar Nuñez Cabeza de Vaca Translated from the Spanish by Buckingham Smith.* **1871**; XUM **1966**.

Oakley, Kenneth. Suspicions about Piltdown man. *New Scientist*, 21 Jun **1979**, 82(1160):1014.

Oates, Joyce Carol. [Letter.] *New York Times Book Review*, 26 Nov **1972**:41. Or in Noel **1976**:68-69.

———. Don Juan's last laugh. *Psychology Today*, Sep **1974**, 8(4):10, 12, 130. Or in Noel **1976**:122-128.

Opler, Morris Edward. *An Apache Life-Way: The Economic, Social, and Religious Institutions of the Chiricahua Indians.* U. Chicago **1941**.

———. *Apache Odyssey: A Journey between two Worlds.* Holt, Rinehart & Winston **1969**.

Ornstein, Robert E. *The Psychology of Consciousness*, 2nd edition. Harcourt Brace Jovanovich **1977**.

———. A lesson of Carlos Castaneda. In *The Mind Field*, Grossman **1976**:77-82.

Orona, Angelo Raymond. *The Social Organization of the Margariteño Fishermen, Venezuela.* Dissertation, University of California, Los Angeles, **1968**. (DAI 29/02-B3173; XUM 69-05343.)

Orwell, George. *Animal Farm.* Harcourt Brace **1946**.

Osis, Karlis. [Letter.] *Psychology Today*, Mar **1978**, 11(10):8.

——— & Erlendur **Haraldsson**. *At the Hour of Death.* Avon **1977**.

Ott, Jonathan & Jeremy **Bigwood**. *Teonanacatl: Hallucinogenic Mushrooms of North America.* Madrona **1978**.

Outlaw, Lucius. Beyond the everyday life-world: A phenomenological encounter with sorcery. *Man & World*, Nov **1975**, 8(4):436-445.

Painter, Charlotte. Psychic bisexuality. In Mary Jane Moffat & Charlotte Painter, editors, *Revelations: Diaries of Women*, Vintage **1974**:392-404.

Palfreman, Jon. Between scepticism and credulity: A study of Victorian scientific attitudes to modern spiritualism. In Wallis **1979**:201-236.

Palmer, Donald. Carlos Castaneda and the phenomenology of sorcery. *Humboldt Journal of Social Relations*, Spr-Sum **1977**, 4(2):36-45.

Parrott, Wanda Sue. I remember Castaneda. *Fate*, Feb **1975**, 28(2/299):79-81.

Paz, Octavio. La mirada anterior [introduction to Tovar **1974a**:9-23].

Pearce, Joseph Chilton. *The Crack in the Cosmic Egg.* Julian **1971**; Pocket Bks 1973.

———. *Exploring the Crack in the Cosmic Egg.* Julian **1974**; Pocket Bks 1975.

Pérez de Barradas, José. *Plantas Mágicas Americanas.* Instituto Sahagún (Madrid) **1957**.

Peters, Roger. [Letter.] *Los Angeles Times Book Review*, 14 Aug **1977**:2.

Petrullo, Vincenzo. *The Diabolic Root: A Study of Peyotism, the New Indian Religion, among the Delawares.* U. Pennsylvania **1934**; Octagon 1975.

Pittman R. & RdeM. [Letters.] *High Times*, Aug **1977** (24):10-11.

Playboy [interviews Timothy Leary], Sep **1966**, 13(9):93, 95-96, 100, 102, 104, 106, 110, 112, 250-251, 254-256.

Poe, Edgar Allan. The Sphinx. In *Complete Tales and Poems*, Modern Library **1938**:471-474.

Pollack, J. H. *Croiset the Clairvoyant.* Doubleday **1964.**

Pollock, Steven Hayden. The psilocybin mushroom pandemic. *Journal of Psychedelic Drugs,* Jan-Mar **1975,** 7(1):73-84.

Pomaska, Anna. [Letter.] *New York Times Magazine,* 11 Mar **1973**:98-99.

Popular Periodical Index (POB 739 Camden NJ 08102).

Pozas [Arciniega], Ricardo. *Juan the Chamula: An Ethnological Re-Creation of the Life of a Mexican Indian.* U. California **1962,** 1971.

Preuss, Paul. Does don Juan live on campus? *Human Behavior,* Nov **1978,** 7(11):53-57.

Publishers Weekly [reviews C68], 10 Jun **1968,** 193(24):61; 24 Mar **1969,** 195(12):56; [reviews C71], 22 Mar **1971a,** 199(12):49; 13 Sep **1971b,** 200(11):68; [reviews C72], 21 Aug **1972,** 202(8):77; [reviews C74], 26 Aug **1974,** 206(9):304-305; [reviews CJ], 6 Sep **1976,** 210(10):60; [announces C77], 30 May **1977a,** 211(22):29; [reviews C77], 28 Nov **1977b,** 212(22):42.

Puharich, Andrija. *The Sacred Mushroom.* Doubleday **1959,** 1974.

———. *Beyond Telepathy.* Doubleday **1962.**

Pulvino, Charles J. **&** James L. **Lee.** Counseling according to don Juan. *Counseling and Values,* Feb **1975,** 19(2):125-130.

Radin, Paul. *The Trickster: A Study in American Indian Mythology.* Philosophical Library **1956.**

Reichbart, Richard. Psi phenomena and Tolstoy. *Journal of the American Society for Psychical Research* [*JASPR*], Jul **1976a,** 70(3):249-265.

———. The Navajo hand trembler: Multiple roles of the psychic in traditional Navajo society. *JASPR,* Oct **1976b,** 70(4):381-396.

———. Magic and psi: Some speculations on their relationship. *JASPR,* Apr **1978a,** 72(2):153-175.

———. [Reviews Long 1977.] *Parapsychology Review,* Sep-Oct **1978b,** 9(5):14-17.

Reisner, Robert, collector. *Graffiti.* Parallax **1967.**

Reno, Stephen J. Castaneda and don Juan: Some preliminary observations. *Religious Studies,* Dec **1975,** 11:449-465.

———. [Reviews CJ.] *Religion,* Aut **1977,** 7(2):226-227.

———. Don Juan and Don Q. *The Listener,* 2 Nov **1978,** 100(2584):589-590.

Reuven, Ben. UC Press. *Los Angeles Times Book Review,* 24 Jul **1977**:3.

Richet, Charles. *Thirty Years of Psychical Research.* Macmillan **1923;** Arno **1975.**

Rickard, RJM. [Reviews CJ.] *Fortean Times,* Spr **1977** (21):35-36.

Riesman, Paul. The collaboration of two men and a plant. *New York Times Book Review,* 22 Oct **1972**:7, 10-12. Or in Noel **1976**:46-53.

Roberts, Steven V. For youth cult hero, a private reality. *New York Times,* 8 Dec **1972**:34.

Rogers, C. R. Some new challenges. *American Psychologist,* May **1973,** 28:379-387.

Rogo, D. Scott. Parapsychology at the AAA. *Parapsychology Review,* Mar-Apr **1979,** 10(2):21-23.

Rorvik, David M. *In His Image: The Cloning of a Man.* Lippincott **1978.**

Rose, Ronald. *Living Magic.* Rand McNally **1956.**

Rosenwald, Peter J. An open letter to Carlos Castaneda. *Horizon,* Apr **1979,** 22(4):68-70.

Roszak, Theodore. A sorcerer's apprentice. *Nation,* Feb **1969,** 208(6):184-186.

——— , editor. *Sources: An Anthology of Contemporary Materials Useful for Preserving Personal Sanity while Braving the Great Technological Wilderness.* Harper & Row **1972.**

——— **&** Carlos **Castaneda.** *Don Juan: The Sorcerer* (Tape Cassette 25021; 38 minutes; recorded at KPFA, Berkeley CA). Jeffrey Norton (145 East 49th St NY 10017) **1968.**

Rothenberg, Jerome, editor. *Technicians of the Sacred.* Doubleday **1968.**

Rowe, John Howland. Inca culture at the time of the Spanish conquest. In *Handbook of South American Indians,* **1946,** 2:183-330.

Ruck, Carl A. P., Jeremy **Bigwood,** Danny **Staples,** Jonathan **Ott, &** R. Gordon **Wasson.** Entheogens. *Journal of Psychedelic Drugs,* Jan-Jun **1979,** 11(1-2):145-146.

Rueger, Russ. Tripping the heavy fantastic. *Human Behavior,* Mar **1973,** 2(3):73-76.

Ryle, John. [Reviews C74 & Silverman 1975.] *Journal of the Anthropological Society of Oxford,* Trinity **1975,** 6(2):134-135.

Schneebaum, Tobias. *Keep the River on your Right.* Grove **1969, 1970.**

——— . *Wild Man.* Viking **1979.**

Schutz, Alfred. Don Quixote and the problem of reality. In *Collected Papers II,* Nijhoff **1964**:135-158.

——— . *The Phenomenology of the Social World.* Northwestern U. **1967.**

Science News [on Summerlin fraud] 1 Jun **1974,** 105(22):348-349; [on cloning] 18 Mar **1978,** 113(11):164; 17 Feb **1979,** 115(7):101.

Scotton, Bruce W. Relating the work of Carlos Castaneda to psychiatry. *Bulletin of the Menninger Clinic,* May **1978,** 42(3):223-238.

Screeton, Paul. [Reviews CJ.] *Ancient Skills and Wisdom Review,* **1979** (6):4.

Sebald, Hans. *Witchcraft: The Heritage of a Heresy.* Elsevier **1978.**

Servadio, Emilio. Parapsychology and the "ultimate reality." *Para-*

psychology Review, Jul-Aug **1977**, 8(4):21-24.

Sharon, Douglas. *Wizard of the Four Winds: A Shaman's Story.* Free Press **1978.**

Shepard, Leslie, editor. *Encyclopedia of Occultism and Parapsychology.* Gale Research **1978,** 1:151, 254.

Shepherd, Jack. A personal LSD experience. *Look,* 8 Aug **1967,** 31(16):23.

Shere, Charles. [Reviews CJ.] *Oakland Tribune,* 3 Apr **1977**:15-E.

Silverman, David. *Reading Castaneda: A Prologue to the Social Sciences.* Routledge & Kegan Paul **1975.**

Simmel, Georg. *The Sociology of Georg Simmel.* Free Press **1950.**

Simmons, Charles. The sorcerer's apprentice [reviews C68]. *New York Times,* 14 Aug **1968**:41.

Simon & Schuster. [Advertisement.] *American Anthropologist,* Sep **1977,** 79(3): inside of back cover.

Sire, James W. The newest intellectual fashion. *Eternity,* Nov **1975,** 26(11):40-41.

Siskind, Janet. Visions and cures among the Sharanahua. In Harner **1973**:28-39.

Slater, Philip. *The Wayward Gate: Science and the Supernatural.* Beacon **1977.**

Slattery, William J. Jay Anson: The man who wrote *The Amityville Horror. Writer's Digest,* Mar **1979,** 59(3):22-26.

Smith, Jeffery J. The occult and the intellectual. In Angoff & Barth **1974**:313-326.

Smith, William L. [Letter.] *Psychology Today,* Mar **1978,** 11(10):10.

Spicer, Edward H. [Reviews C68.] *American Anthropologist,* Apr **1969,** 71(2):320-322. Or in Noel 1976:30-33.

Stafford, Peter. Don Juan's distinctions. *Psychedelics Encyclopedia,* And-Or **1977.**

Staniford, Philip S. Inside out: Anthropological communication of alternate realities. *Phoenix,* Sum **1977a,** 1(1):36-46.

———. [Reviews CJ.] *Phoenix,* FW **1977b,** 1(2):53-55.

Stebbins, Robert A. Putting people on: Deception of our fellowman in everyday life. *Sociology & Social Research,* Apr **1975,** 59(3):189-200.

Steck, James. [Reviews C77.] *San Francisco Review of Books,* Jan **1978,** 3(9):16.

Stein, Ruthe. [Interviews M. J. Harner.] *San Francisco Chronicle,* 13 Jun **1975.**

Steward, Julian H. Two Paiute autobiographies. *University of California Publications in American Archaeology and Ethnology,* 3 Feb **1934,** 33(5):423-438.

Stewart, Kilton. Dream theory in Malaya. In Tart **1969**:159-167.

Stillwell, William. The process of mysticism: Carlos Castaneda. *Journal of Humanistic Psychology,* Fall **1979,** 19(4):7-29.

Storm, Hyemeyohsts. *Seven Arrows.* Harper & Row **1972.**

Story, Ronald. *The Space-Gods Revealed: A Close Look at the Theories of Erich von Däniken.* Harper & Row **1976.**

Strachan, Don. [Reviews CJ.] *Los Angeles Times Book Review,* 6 Feb **1977**:3.

————. In search of don Juan. *New West,* 29 Jan **1979,** 4(3):90-91.

Sturgeon, Theodore. [Reviews C68, C71.] *National Review,* 19 Jan **1973,** 25(3):104.

Sukenick, Ronald. Upward and Juanward: The possible dream. *Village Voice,* 25 Jan 1973:27. Or in Noel **1976**:110-120.

Sussman, Gerald. Don Juan revisited. *National Lampoon,* Jan **1980,** 2(18):38 39, 52.

Suzuki, Daisetz Teitaro. *What is Zen?* Harper & Row Perennial **1972.**

Swain, Frederick & others. Four psilocybin experiences. *Psychedelic Review,* Fall **1963,** 1(2):219-243.

Swanson, Guy E., Anthony F. C. **Wallace, &** James S. **Coleman.** [Review Garfinkel 1967.] *American Sociological Review,* Feb **1968,** 33(1):122-130.

Tart, Charles T., editor. *Altered States of Consciousness.* Wiley **1969**:Doubleday 1972.

————. Did I really fly? In Roberto Cavanna, editor, *Psi Favorable States of Consciousness,* Parapsychology Foundation, **1970**:3-10.

————, editor. *Transpersonal Psychologies.* Harper & Row **1975.**

Thompson, William Irwin. [Reviews C68, C71.] *New York Times Book Review,* 13 Feb **1972** (Pt 2):26.

Thomsen, Dietrick E. Mystic physics. *Science News,* 4 Aug **1979,** 116(5):94.

Thouless, Robert H. Implications for religious studies. In Stanley Krippner, editor, *Advances in Parapsychological Research: 1 Psychokinesis,* Plenum **1977**:175-190.

Time [Don Juan and the sorcerer's apprentice :: Prepared by Robert Hughes, Sandra Burton, Tomás A. Loayza & others], 5 Mar **1973,** 101(10):36-38, 43-45. Or in Noel **1976**:93-109.

Timm, Dennis. *Die Wirklichkeit und der Wissende: eine Studie zu Carlos Castaneda* [Reality and the Man of Knowledge: An Essay on Carlos Castaneda]. Author (distributed by: Literarisches Informationszentrum Josef Wintjes, Bahnhofstrasse 42, 425 Bottrop, West Germany) Sep **1978.**

Tiryakian, Edward A. *On the Margin of the Visible.* Wiley **1974.**

Tomkins, Calvin. The teachings of Joe Pye (Fieldnotes for Carlos Castaneda's next epiphany). *New Yorker,* 3 Feb **1973,** 48(50):37-38.

Tovar, Juan, translator, & Carlos Castaneda. *Las Enseñanzas de don Juan.* Fondo de Cultura Económica (Mexico City) **1974a.**

————. *Una Realidad Aparte.* F. de C. E. **1974b.**

————. *Viaje a Ixtlán.* F. de C. E. **1975.**

————. *Relatos de Poder.* F. de C. E. **1976.**

Trickster, The. *Parabola: Myth and the Quest for Meaning,* Feb **1979,**

4(1): entire issue.

Trout, Lawana. Paperbacks in the classroom. *English Journal,* Dec **1974,** 63(9):93-94.

Truzzi, Marcello. [Reviews CJ.] *Zetetic [Skeptical Inquirer],* Spr-Sum **1977,** 1(2):86-87.

————. On the extraordinary. *Zetetic Scholar,* **1978,** 1(1):11-19.

Turnbull, Colin M. *The Mountain People.* Simon & Schuster **1972.**

Ullman, Ralph. I found don Juan. *New Age,* Jun **1977,** 3(1):54-55.

Underhill, Ruth Murray. The autobiography of a Papago woman. *Memoirs of the American Anthropological Association,* **1936** (No. 46). Kraus Reprint Company (Route 100, Millwood NY 10546).

————. *Singing for Power: The Song Magic of the Papago Indians of Southern Arizona.* U. California **1938.**

University of California Press. [Advertisement.] *American Anthropologist,* Jun **1968,** 70(3): back cover.

————. The last fifteen years have been good to us [advertisement]. *New York Review of Books,* 12 Oct **1978,** 25(15):15.

van Eeden, Frederik. A study of dreams. In Tart **1969**:145-158.

Vecsey, Christopher. [Reviews Moisés 1977.] *Parabola,* May **1978,** 3(2):132, 134.

Vollmann, Rolf. [Reviews C77 & Duerr 1978b.] *Stern,* 5 Apr **1979**:187-188.

von Däniken, Erich. *The Gold of the Gods.* Souvenir (London) **1973;** Putnam 1973.

von Franz, Marie-Louise. *Confrontation with the Collective Unconscious* (Tape Cassette, 1 hr; last 8 minutes treat Castaneda). Jung Cassette Library (10349 West Pico Blvd, Los Angeles CA 90064) **1976.**

von Urban, Rudolf. *Beyond Human Knowledge.* Pageant **1958.**

Wagner, Roy. [Reviews C77.] *Anthropological Quarterly,* Oct **1978,** 51(4):267-269.

Wallace, John. The sorcerer's apprentice: Conversations with Carlos Castaneda. *Penthouse,* Dec **1972,** 4(4):83-86, 139-142.

Wallis, Roy, editor. *On the Margins of Science: The Social Construction of Rejected Knowledge,* Sociological Review Monograph 27. U. Keele **1979.**

Wasson, R[obert] **Gordon.** The divine mushroom: Primitive religion and hallucinatory agents. *Proceedings of the American Philosophical Society,* Jun **1958,** 102(3):221-223.

————. The hallucinogenic fungi of Mexico: An inquiry into the origins of the religious idea among primitive peoples. *Harvard University Botanical Museum Leaflets,* 17 Feb **1961,** 19(7):137-162. Revised versions in: Furst 1972:185-200; Ott & Bigwood 1978:63-84.

————. [Reviews C68.] *Economic Botany,* Apr-Jun **1969,** 23(2):197.

————. [Reviews C71.] *Economic Botany,* Jan-Mar **1972,** 26(1):98-99.

————. [Reviews C72.] *Economic Botany,* Jan-Mar **1973,** 27(1):151-152.

————. [Reviews C74.] *Economic Botany,* Jul-Sep **1974,** 28(3):245-246.

——, George & Florence **Cowan, &** Willard **Rhodes.** *María Sabina and her Mazatec Mushroom Velada.* Harcourt Brace Jovanovich **1974.**

——, Albert **Hofmann, &** Carl A. P. **Ruck.** *The Road to Eleusis: Unveiling the Secret of the Mysteries.* Harcourt Brace Jovanovich **1978.**

Wasson, Valentina Pavlovna & R. Gordon **Wasson.** *Mushrooms Russia and History,* 2 volumes. Pantheon **1957.** Edition limited to 512 copies.

Watkins, Mary M. *Waking Dreams.* Gordon & Breach (London) **1976.**

Weeks, Sheldon G. [Reviews C68, C71, C72, C74.] *Yagl-Ambu* (U. Papua New Guinea), May **1976,** 3(2):112-115.

Weil, Andrew T. The strange case of the Harvard drug scandal. *Look,* 5 Nov **1963,** 27(22):38, 43 44, 46, 48.

——. *The Natural Mind.* Houghton Mifflin **1972.**

——. Some notes on *Datura. Journal of Psychedelic Drugs,* Apr-Jun **1977,** 9(2):165 169.

Weiner, J. S. *The Piltdown Forgery.* Oxford **1955.**

——. Piltdown hoax: New light. *Nature,* 4 Jan **1979,** 277:10.

Weinstein, Deena. Fraud in science. *Social Science Quarterly,* Mar **1979,** 59(4):639-652.

Weitlaner, Roberto J. **&** Walter A. **Hoppe.** The Mazatec. *Handbook of Middle American Indians,* **1969,** 7:516-522.

Westfall, Richard S. Newton and the fudge factor. *Science,* 23 Feb **1973,** 179(4075):751-758.

Weyand, Clint. *Did Carlos Really Fly?* Author (19834 Gresham St, Northridge CA 91324) mimeograph **1976.**

Whan, Michael W. "Don Juan," Trickster, and hermeneutic understanding. *Spring,* **1978:**17 27.

White, Raymond C. The Luiseño theory of "knowledge." *American Anthropologist,* Feb **1957,** 59(1):1-19.

Whorf, Benjamin Lee. *Language, Thought, and Reality.* MIT **1956.**

Who's Who in America, 1976-1977, 39(1):532; 1978-1979, 40(1):556.

Wilber, Ken. *The Spectrum of Consciousness.* Theosophical Pub. Hse **1977.**

Wilk, Stan. [Reviews C71.] *American Anthropologist,* Aug **1972,** 74(4):921-922.

——. Castaneda: Coming of Age in Sonora. *American Anthropologist,* Mar **1977a,** 79(1):84-91.

——. Therapeutic anthropology and culture consciousness. *Anthropology & Humanism Quarterly,* Jun-Sep **1977b,** 2(3):12-18.

——. [Reviews CJ.] *American Anthropologist,* Dec **1977c,** 79(4):921.

——. On the experiential approach in anthropology: A reply to Maquet. *American Anthropologist,* Jun **1978,** 80(2):363-364.

Williams, Donald **&** W. Allen **Ashby.** City path: Following in the heart of don Juan. *Psychoanalytic Review,* Sum **1978,** 65(2):327-344.

Wilson, Colin. *Strange Powers.* Random House **1975.**

Wittgenstein, Ludwig. *Tractatus Logico-Philosophicus.* Humanities 1960.

Wolff, Geoffrey. *The Duke of Deception.* Random House **1979.**

Wolman, Benjamin B., editor. *Handbook of Parapsychology.* Van Nostrand, Reinhold **1977.**

Wongar, B[anumbir]. *The Track to Bralgu.* Little, Brown **1978.**

Wood, Nancy. [Letter.] *Time,* 26 Mar **1973,** 101(13):8.

World Almanac Book of the Strange. New American Library 1977.

Yablonsky, Lewis. [Reviews Noel 1976.] *Los Angeles Times Book Review,* 30 Nov **1975**:24.

Young, Dudley. [Reviews C68.] *New York Times Book Review,* 29 Sep **1968**:30.

Zentner, Joseph L. Pathways to the supernatural. *Journal of Interamerican Studies and World Affairs,* Aug **1976,** 18(3):379-388.

Zetetic Scholar (EMU Sociology, Ypsilanti MI 48197) [reviews CJ2], Apr **1979,** 1(3&4):130.

Zinker, Joseph. Chapter 10: Castanedian vision. In *Creative Process in Gestalt Therapy,* Brunner/Mazel **1977.**

Zuckerman, Harriet. Deviant behavior and social control in science. In Edward Sagarin, editor, *Deviance and Social Change,* Sage **1977**:87-138.

Index

"AG" indicates alphabetic entry in Appendix 44, Alleglossary.

After writing a term paper on D. H. Lawrence and the Andaman Islanders for Ralph Linton at Columbia in 1942, RICHARD de MILLE strayed from the ethnological path for 33 years, during which he: worked on Army Air Force training films; directed television programs at KTLA; got in on the ground floor of Scientology; got out; wrote a social-science-fiction story that was accepted by John W. Campbell Jr for Astounding (February 1953); earned a Ph.D. in clinical and measurement psychology at the University of Southern California (where he sat at the feet of J. P. Guilford); taught psychology at the University of California, Santa Barbara; wrote grant applications to HEW for a gang of desperate educational boondogglers; and learned to talk with computers at a DoD think tank. In 1970 he resumed his vocation as a writer. Besides numerous scholarly, scientific, and popular articles and several stories, he has published Put Your Mother on the Ceiling, an oft-quoted book of didactic imagination exercises for children, and, of course, Castaneda's Journey. While following the spoor of don Juan he acquired a most peculiar anthropological background, joined the American Anthropological Association, spoke at its 1978 meeting, and reviewed Second Ring of Power in the American Anthropologist. He is an associate of Current Anthropology, consulting editor to Zetetic Scholar and Skeptical Inquirer, and a member of the American Society for Psychical Research. He has edited diverse books by other writers. He is married and lives in Santa Barbara.

The Editor, equipped for Looking and Seeing.